TOYS

ANTIQUE AND COLLECTIBLE

DAVID LONGEST

COLLECTOR BOOKS

A Division of Schroeder Publishing Co., Inc.

The current values in this book should be used only as a guide. They are not intended to set prices, which vary from one section of the country to another. Auction prices as well as dealer prices vary greatly and are affected by condition as well as demand. Neither the Author nor the Publisher assumes responsibility for any losses that might be incurred as a result of consulting this guide.

Additional copies of this book may be ordered from:
Collector Books
P.O. Box 3009
Paducah, Ky. 42001

or

David K. Longest
P.O. Box 2183
Clarksville, IN 47131-2183

@ $14.95 Add $2.00 for postage and handling.

TABLE OF CONTENTS

ACKNOWLEDGMENTS

No book is ever the absolute, entire product of one person, for other persons and ideas constantly influence and contribute to an author's thinking. So it was with the making of this price guide, and there are many people to whom I will always be indebted for kindnesses and favors extended to me during the production of this book.

First, I thank the collectors who shared their very best with me. To Bill and Mary Furnish, life-long collectors from Kentucky, I thank them from the depths of my heart for their encouragement all the while I was lugging my photographic equipment all around their home and setting up individual shots of seemingly countless toys. Their contributions to this book are only the tip of the iceberg of their unbelievable collection. They are collectors extraordinaire in the truest since of the word and go far beyond simply purchasing items for their many now-filled shelves. They encourage, support, and constantly share their wealth with younger and newer collectors. But, Bill's not through collecting. He constantly vows that he's now at a state where "the toys have to collect him," that is, they have to jump right out at him before he buys them now. I know he's kidding. He still gets that same twinkle in his eyes when he personally describes a new antique toy discovery. And his card-catalogue, information filing system would be the envy of any collector, old or new. His research on his own toys made possible in one afternoon with me what could have taken weeks. For your kindness, support, friendship, and toy lover's fellowship, I thank you Bill and Mary.

Elmer and Viola Reynolds are the other couple who share a great amount of credit for this book. It was Elmer and Vi's energy for collecting that kindled my own interest in toys when I met them nine years ago at an auction where we were all bidding against one another. Had I known that auction house rivalry would turn into one of the warmest, best friendships of my life, I'm sure I would have dropped out early on in the bidding. As it worked out, a Minnie Mouse in the rocker Line Mar windup toy brought us all together that day (and neither Elmer nor I won the item!). When I arrived at their home for several days of photography work, Elmer and Vi turned their house completely over to me. With photo lighting sprawled out here and there and stacks of toys all over the place, I made their very organized, advanced toy collection look a wreck, and they graciously put it all back into order so that I could finish out my notes. Elmer and Viola love Kewpies, Mickey Mouse and all comic character collectibles. For their own kindnesses and favors to me, I wish them many fantastic toy bargains and discoveries in the years ahead. I owe them at least a huge trunkful of great windups. Elmer and Vi, I thank you. This couldn't have happened without you guys.

I also thank John Sharpe who offered me his toys in the original trunk he has always stored them in, even as a kid. He was patient and I am sure I must have kept the little treasures well over three months until I photograped them. For his patience and interest, I say thanks.

Also, a good measure of my toy knowledge and education has been gained from my contact with many fine dealers and collectors over the past fourteen years. To Joe and Juanita Reese, Doug Moore, Harry and Tom Hall, Joel Allen, Tom Tumbusch, Foster and Helene Pollack, Denver Sherry, Ted Hake, Garth's Auctions of Ohio, "Doc" and Julia Gernand, Bob Coup, Allan Kessler, Ken Schmitz, Donna Walker, Wes Johnson, Jim and Sue Miller, Dave Harris, Herb and Barb Smith of Smith House Toy Sales of Elliot Maine, and a host of others, whose names have escaped me at the present, I say THANKS. Thanks for being fine friends, fellow collectors and reputable dealers.

Finally, I dedicate this book to the two people who had to spend too much time without me while I was glued to the computer terminal. As I type these last words (this is the final section of the book I wrote) I am relieved to be able to return to my family. Imagine writing a dictionary and then taking all the photos to illustrate it...that's what this project seemed on bad nights. On good nights, it was a labor of love. For sticking with me during the good and the bad, I thank my wonderful wife, Ann, and my three- year-old daughter, Claire. You are the true reasons I got myself into all this. I love you both very much.

I'm now shutting down my Apple II E computer. Everything's done, everything's stored. You can take a long deserved rest until we update this edition, which will be at least a couple of years. It's a much deserved rest. Sleep well, new friend.

This book is lovingly dedicated to Ann and Claire.

INTRODUCTION

The price guide is intended to be both an informative tool for the novice and experienced collector alike, and an entertaining whirlwind trip through over one hundred years of toys and ten thousand entries.

The photographs placed throughout the layout are used as examples in the categories and as additional supplement to the chapter texts. All of the toys pictured in this book came from private collections. None are reprints from old toy catalo-ques. Two substantial private toy collections are the photographic basis for this book: The William and Mary Furnish collection of Kentucky and the Elmer and Viola Reynolds collection of Indiana. These collectors represent well over 100 years of enthusiastic and resourceful toy collecting, so the photographic sample here is an expansive one.

A few notes are needed here to best explain the use of this book. Whenever possible, the ACTUAL NAME of the toy as it appeared on the box or was referred to originally has been used. In some cases, generic terms have been used to proceed the brand name or actual toy name when it has been deemed to be more useful to the collector.

Toy chapters or sections in this price guide have been grouped by either type, function or age of the toy such as airplanes, cars, military toys, Disneyana, Golden Age Toys and Modern Toys. Obviously, with toys listed and organized by both type, age and function, there are examples of cross-listing where toys will appear listed in more than one chapter. This was a choice made by this author to facilitate easier use of this book by all collectors.

By the time this price guide makes it to the bookstores, there will already have been fluctua-tions in the toy collecting market. These short-term price fluctuations can certainly affect exact toy prices, but they are the least significant. Factors which greatly affect the interpretation and use of the prices in this book are regional differences in the toy collecting marketplace and the individual desire of the collector at the point of sale. The situation of the advanced collector at a toy auction who knowingly pays two or three times the book value of a toy because it completes a set or is one that is particularly desired cannot be taken into account in regard to the averages listed here.

Another factor which greatly influences the value and selling price of a toy is its condition. Different authors and toy guides treat condition and its relevance differently, but this author has chosen to list a low and a high price range for each toy. The user of the guide can assume that the lower range of the price field represents the toy to be in very fine or used condition, with no major flaws and worthy of being collected. The upper range of the toy price field represents the value of the toy to be in excellent to mint condition. If the MINT IN THE BOX value is listed, then the price reflects this accordingly.

Certainly, as with any book, there will be prices listed here that others may disagree with, but my standard for pricing is based upon auction reports, classified advertising asking prices, flea market, antique show, and toy show listing and selling prices. My purpose here is to give the new and experienced toy collector yet another "angle" on toy values based upon all resources available to me.

Use this new price guide to weave your way through the maze of thousands of antique and col-lectible toys and their prices always facing the general toy collector. Toy collecting is fun and it is a hobby, but it also requires homework, study, field work and a lot of self-educating for it to become satisfying and rewarding.

I hope this price guide will help every collector who reads it to become more knowledgable, and ultimately make his collecting more fun.

Happy collecting!

David K. Longest, author

BANKS

Bank collecting has long been a stalwart of the toy collecting field. One of the reasons this area of collecting has appealed to so many is its relatively abundant accessibility. Many early cast iron banks were virtually indestructible (except for rust) and consequently it seems that nearly every American family must have at least one old bank stored away somewhere.

Consider this author's own family. Growing up in a rural setting in Indiana, we had our own token representative of the Midwest, a barn. I played in the old barn frequently, hid in it, and thought I had successfully explored every nook and cranny by the time I was twelve. I was wrong. One afternoon, my older sister and her boyfriend explored the loft of the barn and rummaged through several old chests of drawers stored there. In the back corner of one of our family's long forgotten antiques was a cast iron Buster Brown and Tige bank in relatively good condition. It had been forgotten by someone decades ago, and when my sister brought it to my mother and father, they had no idea who the original owner was. It may have been secretly hidden in a drawer some 50 or 60 years earlier and then forgotten by an aunt, uncle or grandparent. But, the point here is that it survived. Forgotten for over half a century in a barn loft corner, it was in good condition.

Such frequent finds in countless families have certainly advanced bank collecting to what it is today, an integral facet of antique toy collecting. Because many banks are also associated with historical characters and figures, they are tangible links with America's past. Not only do banks represent history, in many cases, the banks themselves ARE history. This direct relationship to U.S. history and popular culture is a major attribute of bank collecting.

When studying banks, the novice soon recognizes that there are two main categories: still and mechanical. Still banks, as in an artist's still life painting, do not move. They have no active moving parts which function when the bank is utilized. Mechanical banks, on the other hand, have animated parts which often give the toys great action. Many collectors agree that the often fantastic action of mechanicals was designed as a reward for dropping in the daily coin. Dogs bark, cannons fire, wheels turn, and another penny is saved for a rainy day.

In regard to value and pricing, mechanical banks far outrun their still bank counterparts. Several factors apply here. As mentioned earlier, the still cast iron figural bank was relatively indestructible. Many of the banks were formed by foundry work where two simple halves of the figure were cast and then joined together by a connecting screw. Banks with the original connecting screw command higher prices than those with replacements, but this is not a significant defect. Mechanical banks are usually higher in asking price and value than still banks because of greater rarity, a more difficult chance of finding one complete with all moving parts, and stronger collector interest in this category of the field. New collectors to this area of collecting should seek out full knowledge of mechanical banks before paying hundreds or even thousands of dollars for mechanical banks that may be reproductions or incomplete.

Many of the price references used in this section reflect the prices realized at a unique bank auction held in Ohio, where a lifelong toy bank dealer and collector disposed of over 400 bank lots. The auction was held by Garth's Auction Service and liquidated items from the stock and collection of Andy and Susan Moore. Although prices realized from the sale were taken into account, the value estimates are this author's own. Susan and the late Andy Moore were the authors of an excellent reference book on bank collecting, *The Penny Bank Book*. Their book is a *must* reference work for anyone serious about bank collecting.

With many of the best old cast iron mechanical banks fetching hefty prices of five to ten thousand dollars in some instances, collectors should realize that the area of bank collecting is a volatile one. Pricing at point-of-sale can be just as impulsive. There are still bargains to be found out there in the collecting world among still banks. Use this listing to whet your appetite.

AIRPLANE, SPIRIT SAVING, aluminum still bank...$50.00-100.00

ALICE IN WONDERLAND BLOCK, brass bank 4"...$75.00-125.00

ALICE IN WONDERLAND, Disney, figural bank, Leeds China, 1950's $15.00-35.00

ALPHABET BANK, Octagonal shape, cast iron bank, 3⅓".....................................$700.00-1000.00

AMISH BOY HOLDING PIG, cast iron, still bank...$50.00-90.00

AMISH BOY, WHITE METAL BANK, some painted features, 4½".......................................$50.00-100.00

AMISH LADY CAST IRON BANK, 5" $75.00-125.00

ANDY GUMP BANK, painted, die-cast bank, 5½" tall $100.00-225.00

APPLE BANK, yellow cast iron, 5½" $600.00-850.00

ARMORED TRUCK BANK, BRINKS, steel, combination lock, 8" $150.00-225.00

ARMORED TRUCK BANK, Smith-Miller, "Bank of America"..$100.00-200.00

ARMOUR DELIVERY TRUCK, AD BANK, 8" $25.00-40.00

ARTILLERY BANK, MECHANICAL, SHOOTING ACTION, soldier and cannon, 6" $750.00-1,200.00

ASTRONAUT, Daily Dime Registering bank..$20.00-35.00

ATLAS HOLDING UP THE WORLD, pot metal, 5" bank $150.00-250.00

AUNT JEMIMA, modern bank, 12" $40.00-75.00

AUNT JEMIMA, smaller version cast iron bank, 8" tall, modern..$20.00-40.00

AUTO BANK, CHEVROLET, 1953 ....$50.00-75.00

AUTO, BANTHRICA CAR, 1924 ....$10.00-25.00

BABY IN EGG, lead figural bank, 7" tall, white finish $100.00-200.00

BABY, KEWPIE-LIKE TOT, recent, 6" cast iron $10.00-20.00

BAD ACCIDENT MECHANICAL BANK, mule and driver with cart, 10", cast iron...........$1,000.00-1,500.00

BANK BUILDING CAST IRON BANK "STATE BANK" 6", cupola on roof $100.00-150.00

BANK BUILDING CAST IRON BANK, bronze finish, 3½"...$100-150.00

BANK BUILDING DEPOSIT BANK, 4" in style of a Victorian bank building $60.00-100.00

BANK BUILDING WITH DOMED ROOF, silver/gold finish, cast iron, 5" still.........................$40.00-80.00

BANK BUILDING, small version with 2nd story cupola, 3" $40.00-90.00

BANK TOWER CAST IRON BANK, brown finish, cast iron 9"...$200.00-300.00

BANK, BUILDING FIGURAL "UNITED BANKING AND TRUST," 3".......................................$50.00-100.00

BARREL BANK, "SUNNY FUTURE - NY" $5.00-15.00

BASEBALL AND THREE BATS, cast iron still bank $300.00-500.00

BASEBALL PLAYER CAST IRON FIGURAL BANK, 1930's, 6"...$75.00-125.00

BASEBALL PLAYER, painted cast iron still bank, 6" $100.00-150.00

BATTLESHIP MAINE, still bank $200.00-275.00

BATTLESHIP OREGON, still bank.......$210.00-295.00

BEAKY, WARNER BROS. VULTURE, pot metal bank with tree trunk, 4" painted $75.00-125.00

BEAR CUB, 4", pot metal figural $75.00-120.00

BEAR CUB, SITTING, cast iron and painted, 2½"...$75.00-125.00

BEAR HOLDING A PIG, cast iron, 5"...$75.00-125.00

BEAR HOLDING STAFF, bank foundry pattern, 6" $75.00-110.00

BEAR STANDING ON BASE HOLDING ROD, 6" tall, cast iron $100.00-175.00

BEAR STEALING HONEY, figural cast iron bank, ornate foliage, 7" $150.00-200.00

BEAR, "TEDDY WANTS A PENNY", standing alum. bank, 6", begging $75.00-120.00

BEAR, cast iron still bank, standing, 5½" tall, plain $100.00-150.00

BEAR, CROUCHING, cast iron bank, 2½"...$50.00-100.00

BEAR, PANDA, die cast metal bank, painted, 4", sitting $100.00-160.00

BEAR, BANK, REALISTIC, HOLDING POT, 6" $75.00-125.00

BEAR, STANDING ALUMINUM FIGURAL STILL BANK, 6" $20.00-45.00

BEAR, STANDING cast iron bank, brown finish, 5½" $75.00-100.00

BEAR STANDING, 6½" cast iron bank,$175.00-300.00

BEAR, STANDING, aluminum still figural bank, 6" $120.00-200.00

BEEHIVE BANK AND STRING HOLDER, combination, 5½" cast iron $350.00-550.00

BEEHIVE BANK, with bear $100.00-200.00

BEGGAR BOY, CAST IRON BANK, seated 7" $100.00-200.00

BEGGAR, BLACK, "GIVE ME A PENNY," 5" tall, cast iron, still bank $40.00-70.00

BIBLE BANK with German inscription, cast iron, hinged cover, 3⅝" $250.00-400.00

ANDY PANDA TIN BOOK BANK with colorful lithography 5", c. Walter Lantz Prod., Reynolds collection, $20.00-55.00.

7

BANK BUILDING WITH FOUR TURRETS, cast iron, still bank, brown/gold finish, 6", Reynolds collection, $175.00-225.00.

BILLIKEN "Good Luck" BANK, gold/red, cast iron, 4" $75.00-110.00

BILLIKEN GOOD LUCK BANK, cast iron with spire-shaped window behind, 6" $60.00-85.00

BILLIKEN, STILL BANK, pot metal, white finish $30.00-55.00

BILLY BANK "GIVE BILLY A PENNY," painted cast iron small boy, 5" $35.00-70.00

BILLY CAN CLOWN BANK, cast iron still bank, 5" $100.00-200.00

BILLY POSSUM BANK, 3" tall cast iron $150.00-300.00

BIRD ON ROOF, japanned cast iron, mechanical bank $1,500.00-2,000.00

BIRD SITTING ON STUMP, cast iron, painted, 5" tall, delicate detail..............................$100.00-200.00

BISMARK MECHANICAL BANK, man sits inside pig, rare, 8", cast iron.....................$3,000.00-5,000.00

BLACK BOY BANK, two-faced, face on each side, 4" cast iron $75.00-125.00

BLACK BOY EATING WATERMELON, chalkware bank $20.00-50.00

BLACK BOY ON POT, chalkware $30.00-55.00

BLACK BOY STILL BANK, two-faced version, cast iron 4⅛" $120.00-165.00

BLACK MAMMY BANK, figural cast iron, 6" some paint..$90.00-140.00

BLACK MAN EATING COINS MECHANICAL BANK, 7" Shephard Hardware $200.00-350.00

BLACK MAN EATING COINS, MECHANICAL CAST IRON BANK, 6" $125.00-175.00

BLACK MAN SHARE CROPPER IN HAT BANK, cast iron, 5" some paint $25.00-50.00

BLACK MAN WITH HAT MECHANICAL BANK, eats coins, aluminum version, 6" $25.00-60.00

BLACKBIRD BANK, German, tin, lever action, 5" x 3", 1930's $20.00-40.00

BLACKPOOL TOWER, figural still cast iron bank, 7" brown finish $125.00-175.00

BONZO COMIC CHARACTER WITH SUITCASE, white metal, 5" $35.00-70.00

BOOK OF KNOWLEDGE, Dime registering bank $20.00

BOSTON BULL TERRIER, cast iron bank, half-seated pup, 4½" $125.00-175.00

BOY ROBBING BIRD'S NEST, MECHANICAL CAST IRON BANK, 8", painted $1,700.00-2,500.00

BOY SCOUT CAST IRON BANK, 8", version...$500.00-750.00

BOY SCOUT CAST IRON BANK, gold finish, 6" tall..$75.00-140.00

BOY WITH TOP HAT IRON BANK, German, white metal, 4" $75.00-125.00

BOY STEALING WATERMELON, cast iron mechanical bank...$800.00-1,250.00

BUCKET, cast iron, registering bank, Japan, 3", 1 cent register $50.00-100.00

BUFFALO BANK, AMHERST STOVES PIECE, 5" tall cast iron still bank.........................$125.00-225.00

BUFFALO BANK, cast iron, still bank, 3" tall, lots of fur $120.00-200.00

BUFFALO BANK, standing, cast iron, 3" $120.00-180.00

BUGS BUNNY WITH BARREL, pot metal bank, 5" $50.00-75.00

BUGS BUNNY WITH TREE TRUNK, 5", pot metal bank $50.00-75.00

BULL ON BASE, cast iron bank, 6" long $160.00-200.00

BULL, ABERDEEN ANGUS, aluminum still bank, black finish, 7" $40.00-85.00

BULL, ANGUS, aluminum still bank, black, 7½" long $30.00-65.00

BENJAMIN FRANKLIN, tin, registering thrift bank, 4" tall, lithographed design, Reynolds collection, $20.00-50.00.

BULLDOG, cast iron, 2", still figural bank, standing $50.00-100.00

BULLDOG, cast iron, seated, 3½" $50.00-100.00

BULLET BANK, ca. 1918, brass plate, 7" $10.00-15.00

BUNGALOW, House, 4"........................$100.00-150.00

BUS BANK, 6" sheet metal with wheels $40.00-80.00

BUSTER BROWN AND TIGE CAST IRON BANK, gold paint with red trim, 5" $80.00-185.00

BUSTER BROWN & TIGE CASHIER BANK, smaller version, cast iron, 5".....................$100.00-175.00

BUSTER BROWN AND TIGE CASHIER, 6½" version $70.00-120.00

BUSTER BROWN AND TIGE, comic character cast iron bank, gold/red trim, 5" $75.00-125.00

BUTTING BUFFALO MECHANICAL BANK, cast iron..$2,000.00-3,000.00

CAMEL, lying down with trunk on back, cast iron bank, 2"..$20.00-45.00

CAMEL, standing 5", cast iron bank with saddle...$30.00-70.00

CAMEL, standing, 7" tall with bronze-type finish, cast iron bank $35.00-75.00

CAMPELL KIDS, (soup promotion), cast iron, 3" tall, still bank $40.00-65.00

CAPITOL BUILDING, WASHINGTON, D.C.,lead still bank, bronze finish $10.00-20.00

CAPTAIN KIDD, STANDING BY A TREE WITH SHOVEL, cast iron, 5½", painted . $125.00-170.00

CASH REGISTER BANK, "Cash, Junior" Steel, 5" $150.00-200.00

CAST IRON MONEY POT, 5" tall, "N. and Co, Hardware" $100.00-150.00

CASTLE WITH TOWERS, 7" tall, cast iron, brown finish $300.00-500.00

CASTLE WITH TWO GIANT TOWERS CAST IRON BANK, brown finish, 7"...................$300.00-400.00

CAT AND BALL, figural, one piece, gold finish, 5½" long $250.00-350.00

CAT AND MOUSE MECHANICAL CAST IRON BANK 11" long $600.00-900.00

CAT BANK, "Lindy's Kat Bank" lead with silver, 5" $70.00-110.00

CAT HEAD "TY-UP" bank and string holder, recent, 6½" $20.00-50.00

CAT ON BASE, "Feed the Kitty," lead, 5" $50.00-100.00

CAT ON TUB, cast iron, still, 4"...........$50.00-100.00

CAT WITH BALL, LYING, 2", cast iron bank $150.00-200.00

CAT WITH BANDAGE AROUND HEAD, die cast metal, 4" $150.00-250.00

CAT WITH BOW, STANDING, cast iron, enameled finish, 4"..$20.00-50.00

CAT, FLUFFY WITH BOW AROUND NECK, 4", painted $40.00-70.00

CAT, PROUD POSE WITH BOW TIE, gold finish, 4½" tall, bow ribbon $150.00-275.00

CAT, SITTING, with bow, pot metal, 5", white finish..$20.00-50.00

CAT, SMALL, 4" seated, cast iron, still bank...$30.00-55.00

BILLIKEN, die cast, still bank 4" tall, natural finish, Reynolds collection, $30.00-60.00.

CAVALRY SOLDIER WITH RIFLE, painted cast iron still bank, 6" $20.00-45.00

CHARLIE CHAPLIN GLASS CANDY CONTAINER BANK, painted, 4" $75.00-150.00

CHARLIE McCARTHY COMPOSITION PAINTED BANK, 9" $75.00-125.00

CHIEF BIG MOON PAINTED MECHANICAL BANK, cast iron $750.00-1,250.00

CHURCH BANK, "OLD SOUTH CHURCH," cast iron bank, gold finish, 10".....................$500.00-800.00

CHURCHILL, WINSTON, bust bank, composition, 5" $175.00-250.00

CINCY STOVE, cast iron, light blue enamel, 3½" $30.00-55.00

CINDERELLA CERAMIC FIGURAL BANK, Walt Disney, 1950's, Leeds China $20.00-35.00

CLOCK BANK, "Money Saver" with molded clock hands, black/gold, 3½" $50.00-80.00

CLOCK BANK, ADVERTISING "ROCHESTER TRUST AND SAVE," cast iron 5" $80.00-130.00

CLOCK BANK, gilt rim, paper dial, 3½" tall, cast iron $25.00-50.00

CLOCK, ADVERTISING "WESTERN RESERVE AND TRUST CO." cast iron, 5" $80.00-130.00

CLOCK, CARRIAGE TYPE, sheet metal, 5½" tall figural bank $15.00-40.00

CLOWN BANK, brass foundry pattern, white paint, 6" $175.00-225.00

CLOWN CAST IRON BANK, tall curved hat, painted, 6" $110.00-195.00

CLOWN HEAD WITH CONE HAT, painted bank, pot metal, 4" $25.00-45.00

CLOWN HEAD WITH SMALL FUNNY HAT, pot metal bank $30.00-55.00

CLOWN HEAD, ANGRY FACE, HOOKED NOSE, pot metal, 3" $100.00-200.00

CLOWN MECHANICAL BANK "Humpty Dumpty Bank," clown eats coins, 7½" $200.00-400.00

BANKS

CLOWN, cast iron, with top hat, holding horn, still bank, 6" tall, Reynolds collection, $70.00-125.00.

CLOWN ON GLOBE, painted cast iron, mechanical bank, 9" $1,000.00-1,500.00

CLOWN, Daily Dime Registering bank, tin, ...$10.00-20.00

CLOWN, ROUND, tin lithographed, spherical bank, 2" $25.00-50.00

CLOWN, standing cast iron bank, siver/red finish, 6" $70.00-120.00

CLOWN, tin, semi-mechanical, "eats" coins, 5", colorful $100.00-200.00

COCKATOO BANK, white metal, paint finish, 5" $150.00-300.00

COCKATOO with ball, lead and tin $150.00-225.00

COIN BANK, in shape of coin "Save Your Pennies," cast iron, 3" gold finish $100.00-150.00

COLONIAL WOMAN BANK by Staffordshire, 2" tall..$40.00-80.00

COTTAGE, silver plated bank, frame, hinged lid with key and lock, 4".................................$25.00-50.00

COUNTY BANK, cast iron building-shaped bank, 4¼" $100.00-150.00

COW, DAIRY, walking, cast iron bank, painted, 3½" tall $10.00-20.00

COW, gold finish cast iron bank, 5½" .$100.00-150.00

CROWING ROOSTER MECHANICAL BANK, cast iron $200.00-400.00

CUTIE DOG ON CUSHION, cast iron bank, 6", ears perked up $75.00-120.00

CUTIE DOG ON CUSHION, ear down, cast iron, with bee, 6" painted $80.00-125.00

DAFFY DUCK LEANING AGAINST A TREE TRUNK, pot metal bank, 4" $50.00-100.00

DAVENPORT HOUSE, pewter bank, 4" .$75.00-125.00

DAVY CROCKETT, metal bank, 1950's ..$20.00-40.00

DEER CAST IRON BANK, large 9" size, antlers intact $25.00-60.00

DEER, smaller version, cast iron bank, 6" $35.00-70.00

DEVIL, TWO-FACED (one on each side) cast iron bank. 4" $60.00-90.00

DEWEY BANK, BUST, GOLD, FIGURAL, 3", cast iron bank $25.00-50.00

DINAH MECHANICAL BANK, black woman, puts coin in mouth, England, 6½" $300.00-600.00

DISNEY CASH REGISTER BANK, by Marx, tin lithographed, 1950's, various characters ..$40.00-85.00

DO YOU KNOW ME? CLOWN BANK, cast iron, 6" $125.00-250.00

DOC YAK, 4½", cast iron, still bank ...$150.00-275.00

DOCTOR'S BAG, cast iron, still bank, marked "M.D.," 5½" long $60.00-100.00

DOG BANK, RETRIEVER, pack on back, 3½" $20.00-40.00

DOG BANK, SPITZ BREED, 4" tall, cast iron $100.00-200.00

DOG ON TUB, cast iron, still bank, 4" $50.00-100.00

DOG ON TURNTABLE, MECHANICAL, electroplated cast iron bank $300.00-500.00

DOG SITTING NEXT TO CHEST, tin and lead, 2" $45.00-75.00

DOG WITH DRUM, tin and lead bank, 2" $35.00-70.00

DOG, ENGLISH BULLDOG, 4" tall, cast iron bank, seated $150.00-300.00

DOG, FLUFFY, 3½", cast iron $60.00-90.00

DOG, GOLDEN RETRIEVER, cast iron, still bank, 6" long $100.00-225.00

DOG, HOUND WITH NOSE TO FLOOR, cast iron, 3" $40.00-70.00

DOG, HOWLING WITH HEAD UPTURNED, on base, cast iron, 5" $70.00-140.00

DOG, SCOTTIE, cast iron, 3" $135.00-200.00

DOG, SCOTTIE, pot metal, figural still, 5" $40.00-75.00

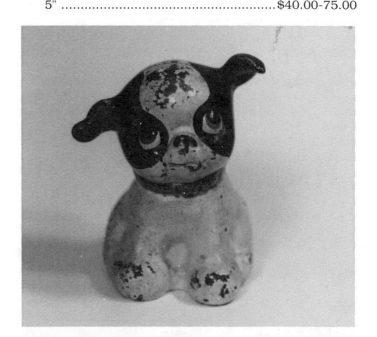

CUTIE DOG, painted cast iron bank, 4", Reynolds collection, $75.00-150.00.

DOG, SCOTTIE, seated, 5" tall, cast iron bank $200.00-300.00

DOG, SCOTTIE, seated, very large head, 3" cast iron bank $200.00-300.00

DOLPHIN BOAT BANK, SAILOR SITS INSIDE HOLDING ANCHOR, 4½", cast iron $150.00-225.00

DONALD DUCK CERAMIC CHARACTER BANK, 1940's, 8", Disney, by Leeds $12.00-28.00

DONALD DUCK COWBOY BANK, plastic, 1960's, ...$5.00-15.00

DONALD DUCK DIME REGISTER BANK, 1930's, W.D.E., tin...$40.00-95.00

DONALD DUCK DIME SAVINGS BANK, W.D.Ent., 1930's, metal, 3" $70.00-125.00

DONALD DUCK TELEPHONE BANK with Donald die-cut figure $75.00-100.00

DONALD DUCK, ceramic bank by Leeds China, 1940's $15.00-35.00

DONALD DUCK, painted pot metal bank, Walt Disney Enterprises $125.00-275.00

DONALD DUCK, wood composition standing by life preserver, Crown Toy, WDE $75.00-195.00

DONKEY BANK, Listerine Razor Blades premium ad piece, ...$15.00-30.00

DONKEY ON BASE, 7½", cast iron $300.00-500.00

DONKEY STILL BANK, silver lead, 5" $35.00-60.00

DONKEY WITH SADDLE, cast iron, still, 5" tall...$75.00-125.00

DONKEY, cast iron, still bank, 4" $20.00-40.00

DONKEY, still bank, pot metal, 4" $50.00-100.00

DOPEY COMPOSITION BANK, Crown Toy, Disney Ent., 1938, 7"...$50.00-95.00

DOPEY DIME REGISTER BANK, 1938, Walt Disney Enterprises, ...$35.00-70.00

DOT STOVE BANK, nickel finish, 4" $80.00-120.00

DUCK WITH TOP HAT ON TUB "Save for a rainy day," 5" cast iron....................................$200.00-300.00

DUCK, CAST IRON FIGURAL BANK, 5" painted features $100.00-135.00

DUCK, round, cast iron, paint, 4" $70.00-100.00

COW BANK, cast iron, black finish, 4½" long, Reynolds collection, $200.00-260.00.

DONKEY WITH SADDLE, cast iron, still bank, 7", Reynolds collection, $35.00-70.00.

DUCK, SQUATTY, cast iron, figural, yellow/red/black, 4" $200.00-300.00

DUCK CAST IRON BANK, painted, 5".$120.00-180.00

DUDE RANCH BANK, metal bank/lollipop candy container, 1950's......................................$15.00-30.00

DUMBO STILL BANK, ceramic, Walt Disney, by Leeds China, 1940's $15.00-30.00

DUTCH BOY CAST IRON BANK, smaller version, 6", sitting $200.00-400.00

DUTCH BOY CAST IRON STILL BANK 6½"...$75.00-120.00

DUTCH BOY CAST IRON STILL BANK, 8½", very large, painted $75.00-125.00

DUTCH BOY, 8" cast iron, still bank..$100.00-200.00

DUTCH CLEANSER, Ad bank $45.00-75.00

DUTCH GIRL CAST IRON, STILL BANK 6½" $90.00-180.00

DOG, BOXER, cast iron bank, 4" tall, seated, $175.00-350.00.

11

BANKS

DUTCH GIRL, SMALL, 5" cast iron, still bank $45.00-180.00

EAGLE AND EAGLETS WITH SNAKE, MECHANICAL, cast iron bank $500.00-850.00

EAGLE ON GLOBE BASE, recent, gold finish, 6" $10.00-35.00

EAGLE, cast iron bank, 4", sitting $75.00-125.00

EGG MAN cast iron still bank, 4".......$400.00-750.00

EGG SHAPED MAN WITH TOP HAT, 4" cast iron $120.00-180.00

EGYPTIAN TOMB STILL BANK, 6".......$75.00-150.00

EIFFEL TOWER BANK, cast iron, bronze/gold finish, 9" $400.00-600.00

ELEPHANT, WORCHESTER SALT AD PIECE, 4½", pot metal $125.00-250.00

ELEPHANT BANK, 7" long, cast iron, grey $80.00-120.00

ELEPHANT BANK, tin, seated on drum, bright lithographed, 5" $50.00-80.00

ELEPHANT CAST IRON BANK with swiveling trunk, black and gold, 2½" $150.00-200.00

ELEPHANT CAST IRON BANK, 3½", bronze finish $75.00-120.00

ELEPHANT CAST IRON BANK, with basket for rider (Howdah), green finish, 4" $20.00-40.00

ELEPHANT ON WHEELS, cast iron bank, 4" $200.00-250.00

ELEPHANT ON WHEELS, rolling cast iron bank, 4" $75.00-125.00

ELEPHANT SITTING ON BASE, white metal, salt ad piece, 4" $20.00-50.00

ELEPHANT WITH BASKET, cast iron bank, 6½" grey/gold/silver $50.00-100.00

ELEPHANT WITH DRUM, pot metal, seated, 4" $200.00-350.00

ELEPHANT WITH POP-UP MAN, MECHANICAL, cast iron bank $400.00-650.00

ELEPHANT WITH RIDER BASKET (howdah), gold finish cast iron, 6½"...........................$40.00-75.00

ELEPHANT WITH UPLIFTED TRUNK AND HINGED LID, lead $80.00-120.00

ELEPHANT ON CIRCUS TUB, still, cast iron, gold finish, 5½", Reynolds collection, $100.00-150.00

ELEPHANT WITH RIDING BASKET, cast iron, grey/gold/silver, 5", Reynolds collection, $75.00-100.00.

ELEPHANT, AFRICAN, LARGE EARS, 3½" cast iron, grey/gold/red $75.00-120.00

ELEPHANT, BABY CIRCUS WEARING PAINTED ON CLOTHES, 4" cast iron $50.00-90.00

ELEPHANT, G.O.P., 4", cast iron bank.$100.00-200.00

ELEPHANT, grey, G.O.P. label, modern ..$25.00-60.00

ELEPHANT, political inscription, 2", cast iron $100.00-200.00

ELF, cast iron figural, still, 10" $275.00-400.00

ELMER FUDD WITH TREE TRUNK, pot metal bank, 5" $50.00-100.00

FEED MY SHEEP, lead bank, 3" $50.00-95.00

FERDINAND THE BULL, wood compostion bank, Walt Disney Ent., Crown Toy $60.00-125.00

FIREMAN CAST IRON BANK, in dress uniform, 5½" tall, painted $50.00-100.00

FISHERMAN, ORIENTAL, CAST IRON STILL BANK, ...$65.00-90.00

FOOTBALL BANK marked "Official League Ball" nickel plate finish, 3" $150.00-200.00

FOOTBALL PLAYER HOLDING GIANT BALL OVERHEAD, cast iron, 5" $125.00-225.00

FOOTBALL PLAYER, 1920's, 6" cast iron, still bank $60.00-125.00

FOOTBALL PLAYER, cast iron, 6", gold paint $250.00-400.00

FOXY GRANDPA, comic character, still bank, painted, 5½" $75.00-125.00

FROG ON ROCK, MECHANICAL BANK, cast iron $200.00-400.00

FROG, cast iron by "Iron Art", 7" $95.00-150.00

FROG, DRESSED AS PROFESSOR, 3" cast iron still bank $75.00-110.00

GAS HEATER, "EUREKA" STILL TIN BANK, 5" $40.00-70.00

GAS PUMP STILL BANK, 5½", cast iron $150.00-225.00

GAS STOVE CAST IRON BANK, tin back, bronze finish, 5½" $60.00-100.00

GEM BANK, plated cast iron $300.00-600.00

GENERAL BUTLER AS A FROG, cast iron bank, 6½" $125.00-220.00

WALKING ELEPHANT CAST IRON BANK, 4", still bank curled trunk, Reynolds collection, $100.00-175.00.

GENERAL SHEPHERD BANK FOUNDRY PATTERN, 7" $175.00-250.00
GIRL SKIPPING ROPE, MECHANICAL, painted cast iron bank $10,000.00-15,000.00
GLOBE BANK WITH EAGLE ON TOP, cast iron, 5½" $100.00-200.00
GLOBE BANK, 5" bronze finish $100.00-150.00
GLOBE BANK, paper lithograph, on steel, wooden base, 4½", modern $15.00-25.00
GOLLIWOG FIGURAL ALUMINUM BANK, 6", troll-like creature...$75.00-125.00
GOLLIWOG, 6" TROLL-LIKE CREATURE STILL BANK, cast iron $50.00-100.00
GOOSE WITH BRONZE-LIKE FINISH, cast iron still bank, 5" tall $70.00-120.00
GRAF ZEPPELIN, 6½", cast iron $75.00-150.00
GRAF ZEPPELIN ON WHEELS, cast iron with nickel wheels, 8", silver finish $200.00-300.00
GRAF ZEPPELIN WITH WHEELS, cast iron, 8" $150.00-225.00
GRANDFATHER CLOCK FIGURAL CAST LEAD BANK, 7½" $20.00-45.00
GRIZZLY BEAR, lead, still, figural bank, 3" $25.00-50.00
GUN BOAT, cast iron figural bank, blue/white/brown, 8½" long $700.00-950.00
HAPPY DAYS BANK, tin barrel..............$10.00-20.00
HAPPY FATS CHARACTER GLASS CANDY CONTAINER/BANK, 4", painted $50.00-100.00
HEATER BANK "GEM HEATERS" Androth Brothers, N.Y., 4½" cast iron 150.00-200.00
HEATER STOVE BANK, marked "Cincy," brown/nickel $30.00-65.00
HEN SITTING ON NEST, cast iron, still bank, 3" tall $50.00-100.00
HIPPO CAST IRON BANK, 2½" tall $75.00-110.00
HOG BANK, marked "TAKE ALL I GET" cast iron, curled tail, 7" $90.00-140.00
HOLE IN ONE, BATTERY OPERATED BANK, Japan, 1950's, Golfer, plastic.........................$20.00-50.00
HOOP-LA MECHANICAL CAST IRON BANK, Clown holds hoop/dog jumps $900.00-1,400.00
HORSE AND HORSESHOE, "GOOD LUCK" BANK, cast iron, black and gold 4" $120.00-160.00
HORSE AND HORSESHOE "GOOD LUCK" CAST IRON

BANK 4", black $100.00-135.00
HORSE COVERED WITH BLANKET OR NET, 4" cast iron bank $40.00-80.00
HORSE IN BATHTUB, AC SPARK PLUG AD BANK, cast, rubber wheels $100.00-175.00
HORSE ON TUB, cast iron, still bank, front legs on tub, 5" $200.00-300.00
HORSE ON WHEELS, PRANCING, 5", cast iron, rolling bank...$200.00-400.00
HORSE RACE mechanical bank $800.00-2,000.00
HORSE, 4" cast iron bank, gold finish ...$30.00-50.00
HORSE, PRANCING POSE, 5", cast iron, gold finish $160.00-210.00
HORSE, PRANCING, cast iron bank, 4", black finish $20.00-45.00
HORSE REARING "BEAUTY" on round base 4½" tall, cast iron $25.00-50.00
HORSE, REARING, black on round base, 5" $50.00-100.00
HORSE, REARING UP ON ROCKY BASE, large 7" size, cast iron bank $100.00-200.00
HORSE, REARING UP, cast iron bank, smooth base, 7" $20.00-50.00
HORSE, REARING, cast iron bank, gold finish, 7½" $75.00-110.00
HORSE, SADDLE RIDING TYPE, cast iron bank, 4½" $10.00-35.00
HORSE, REARING, black finish, cast iron, 5" $30.00-50.00
HOUSE BANK, bronze finish, 4", single story with dormers..................................$125.00-175.00
HOUSE BANK, Bungalow style, 1920's, bronze finish, 4" $125.00-175.00
HOUSE BANK, cast iron, single story with dormers in roof, 4" $150.00-250.00
HUMPTY DUMPTY BANK, tin, 5½" tall, lithograph, egg-shaped...$100.00-200.00
HUMPTY DUMPTY PAINTED MECHANICAL BANK, cast iron $500.00-900.00
INDEPENDANCE HALL GLASS BANK, clear, 5" recent $10.00-20.00
INDEPENDENCE HALL, 9", cast iron, still bank...$150.00-225.00

ELEPHANT WITH HOWDAH CART CAST IRON BANKS, 6", $75.00-150.00; 4", $50.00-120.00, Reynolds Collection.

BANKS

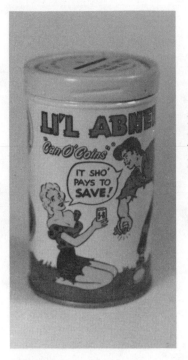

LI'L ABNER CAN O' COINS, tin can savings bank, 5", Reynolds collection, $20.00-40.00.

INDEPENDENCE HALL, cast iron, still bank, 11", gold finish.................................$650.00-900.00

INDIAN AND BEAR PAINTED CAST IRON mechanical bank $800.00-1,200.00

INDIAN BANK, crossed arms, metal, white finish, 4"...$50.00-90.00

INDIAN CHIEF HEAD, 4" pot metal bank...$80.00-135.00

INDIAN CHIEF WITH MULTI-COLORED FEATHERS, painted, pot metal, 3½".................$75.00-125.00

INDIAN CHIEF, 4", gold, cast iron......$100.00-225.00

INDIAN FAMILY, BUST OF FIGURES, 4"...$150.00-300.00

INDIAN HEAD METAL FIGURAL BANK, 3½"...$40.00-70.00

INDIAN MAIDEN WITH SINGLE FEATHER HEADBAND, pot metal bank, 3"..........................$70.00-110.00

INDIAN SHOOTING BEAR, MECHANICAL BANK, 7½" cast iron $300.00-500.00

INDIAN, FULL FIGURE, cast iron bank, 6" tall $100.00-200.00

JEWEL CHEST STILL BANK, cast iron with brass knob, 6½" long $150.00-250.00

JEWEL CHEST, cast iron bank, nickel finish, 6½"...$100.00-140.00

JIMINY CRICKET, wood composition bank, Crown Toy, Walt Disney Ent. $50.00-100.00

JONAH AND THE WHALE painted cast iron mechanical bank...$500.00-750.00

JUKE BOX, 1940's, version, plastic, colorful, 6"...$20.00-35.00

JUMBO SAVINGS BANK, tin lithograph, excellent, 5", made in England, Elephant $200.00-300.00

KEWPIE GLASS CANDY CONTAINER/BANK, tin lid, painted, 3" $75.00-125.00

KEWPIE KNOCK-OFF (unauthorized) COMPOSITION BANK, 5" $30.00-50.00

KEYSTONE COP BUST, "EVERY COPPER HELPS," 6" cast iron, still bank.....................$100.00-175.00

KEYSTONE COP WITH BILLY CLUB, figural cast iron bank 5" $110.00-165.00

KING MIDAS AND HIS GOLD, cast iron, still bank, 5" $60.00-95.00

KODAK advertising bank, camera shaped, c. 1900 ....$200.00-300.00

LEATHER OR DOCTOR'S CASE, cast iron bank, 6" bronze finish $150.00-200.00

LIBERTY BELL BANK, cast iron, 3½" bronze finish $10.00-20.00

LIBERTY BELL BANK, cast iron, figural, 2¾" long $120.00-170.00

LIBERTY BELL CAST IRON BANK, 2½", white finish $10.00-25.00

LIBERTY BELL ON WOODEN BASE, 7" cast iron except for base $90.00-135.00

LIBERTY BELL WITH CLOCK BANK, white metal with bronze finish, c. 1926 ....$100.00-150.00

LIBERTY BELL, 4" cast iron $50.00-110.00

LIFESAVERS TIN PACK-SHAPED BANK, candy premium....................................$25.00-50.00

LIGHT HOUSE BANK, "Light of the World," recent, 9½" tall $20.00-50.00

LIGHTHOUSE WITH DOG IN FRONT, German, 4" tin and lead....................................$100.00-150.00

LIGHTHOUSE, MECHANICAL painted cast iron bank $700.00-1,000.00

LINDBERG BUST, cast aluminum, still, 6½"...$100.00-225.00

LION AND MONKEYS MECHANICAL BANK, cast iron, lion trees monkeys, 9" $300.00-500.00

LION AND MONKEYS, MECHANICAL cast iron (painted) bank $800.00-1,200.00

LION BANK, cast iron, still bank $65.00-85.00

LION BANK, cast iron, gold finish, 5" $20.00-40.00

LION CAST IRON BANK, gold finish, low profile, stalking $30.00-70.00

LION CAST IRON BANK, gold finish, standard pose, 5" long.......................................$25.00-50.00

LION ON TUB, 4" cast iron, gold finish .$60.00-90.00

LION ON TUB, cast iron still bank, gold finish, 5" tall $75.00-125.00

LION ON TUB, cast iron, 4" $50.00-100.00

LION ON WHEELS, cast iron bank, rolls, silver finish, 5" $75.00-125.00

LION ON WHEELS, cast iron rolling bank, gold finish, 4½" $175.00-250.00

LION ON WHEELS, rolling cast iron bank, 5" $30.00-75.00

LION, cast iron bank, red/gold, 5" $20.00-65.00

LION, cast iron, 3" long, gold finish $40.00-75.00

LION, CHUNKY BODY BUILD, cast iron, gold finish, 5" $30.00-50.00

LION, WALKING, cast iron, still bank, 5⅛" gold finish $25.00-50.00

LITTLE BEAR, white metal, painted, 4" .$40.00-80.00

LITTLE DOG BANK "CUTIE" cast iron, still, 4" $50.00-85.00

LITTLE JOE, MECHANICAL, cast iron, (painted) bank $150.00-275.00

LITTLE RED RIDING HOOD, cast iron bank, girl with wolf, 5"..................................$125.00-225.00

LOG CABIN BANK, ceramic, Abe Lincoln birthplace, 4" $10.00-20.00

MAGIC DIME REGISTERING BANK, tin $20.00-40.00

MAILBOX BANK, cast iron, "U.S. AIR MAIL," marked Hubley, 5½" tall $100.00-150.00

MAILBOX BANK, U.S. MAIL, 4", low profile $100.00-150.00

MAMMY WITH SPOON, 6", cast iron, still bank $85.00-135.00

MAMMY, BLACK, WITH BASKET OF CLOTHES, 5½", pot metal, painted $100.00-150.00

MAN IN BARREL, BLACK CAST IRON, 3½" $200.00-400.00

MAN WITH GUN MECHANICAL BANK "Creedmore," 6½" tall, cast iron...........................$200.00-300.00

MANTLE CLOCK CAST IRON BANK, 5¼", ornate cabinet, made in U.S.A. $50.00-100.00

MANTLE CLOCK CAST IRON BANK, ornate finish, 7" long $25.00-45.00

MARY AND HER LITTLE LAMB, cast iron, still bank $100.00-250.00

MASON, MECHANICAL, painted cast iron, 7½" $1,600.00-2,000.00

MELLON FURNACE, 3½" cast iron, still bank...$85.00-120.00

MERMAID BOAT, BOY SITS IN BOAT WITH FISH, cast iron, 4" $75.00-100.00

MERRY-GO-ROUND BANK, cast iron, figural, 4" on base $150.00-225.00

MERRY-GO-ROUND, MECHANICAL cast iron bank, 6¼" $9,000.00-13,000.00

MEXICAN ON BURRO, still bank............$10.00-25.00

MICKEY MOUSE,MECHANICAL BANK (five fingers) tin lithograph $1,250.00-2,250.00

MICKEY MOUSE DRUM MAJOR BANK, 1950's, hard plastic, 8" tall $15.00-25.00

MICKEY MOUSE JAM JAR (GLASER-CRANDELL CO.) BANK, with label, 1930's $50.00-125.00

MICKEY MOUSE LEATHER COVERED BOOK BANK, 1933..$40.00-75.00

MICKEY MOUSE METAL DIME SAVINGS BANK, W.D. Ent.,1930's, 3" $65.00-110.00

MICKEY MOUSE PLAYING A BANJO, pot metal bank, 5" $150.00-300.00

MICKEY MOUSE POST OFFICE TIN LITHOGRAPH BANK, column, red/bl/white $45.00-95.00

MICKEY MOUSE STANDING BY TRUNK, composition, by Crown Toy, 6" $100.00-150.00

MICKEY MOUSE STANDING WITH HANDS ON HIPS, 9" tall, aluminum $100.00-200.00

MICKEY MOUSE TELEPHONE METAL BANK, with Mickey die-cut figure........................$75.00-100.00

MICKEY MOUSE TREASURE CHEST BANK, leather covered, 1930's $50.00-125.00

MICKEY MOUSE WITH MANDOLIN, white metal bank with polychrome, 4½" $125.00-225.00

MICKEY MOUSE, cast iron standing still bank (old version) hands on hips $750.00-2,000.00

MICKEY MOUSE, CERAMIC HEAD FIGURAL, Japan, 1930's $40.00-125.00

MICKEY MOUSE, STANDING, CERAMIC BANK, by Leeds, 1940's Walt Disney $15.00-30.00

MILK CAN STILL BANK, brass, 3½".....$25.00-50.00

MILKING COW, cast iron bank, 7" $150.00-200.00

MONKEY AND COCONUT MECHANICAL CAST IRON BANK, painted $1,700.00-2,400.00

MONKEY CAST IRON MECHANICAL BANK, painted by Hubley $300.00-450.00

MONKEY, 8½", figural, cast iron bank....$10.00-20.00

MOSQUE "JEWEL BANK," 4" cast iron, nickel finish $80.00-120.00

MUTT AND JEFF, cast iron bank, 5", gold finish, Reynolds collection, $100.00-175.00.

MONKEY, HAT-TIPPER, tin, semi-mechanical, 5" "THANK YOU" Reynolds collection, $40.00-80.00.

15

BANKS

PIG BANK, cast iron, seated, gold finish, Reynolds collection, $15.00-30.00.

MOSQUE BANK, green finish, cast iron, 4" $40.00-80.00

MOSQUE WITH GOLD DOME, silver, finish, 4", cast iron $40.00-80.00

MOURNER'S PURSE, lead, 1902, 5" $35.00-75.00

MULE ENTERING BARN, mechanical.$700.00-1,100.00

NEGRO PLAYING BANJO, still cast iron bank, 16" $300.00-650.00

NICKEL REGISTER CAST IRON KETTLE BANK, 3" $75.00-125.00

NORTH POLE BANK, ice cream maker design, brass foundry pattern, 4" $150.00-300.00

NORTH POLE ICE CREAM FREEZER, cast iron bank, 4" $250.00-400.00

OLD LIBERTY BELL BANK, 4", cast iron still $75.00-100.00

OLD MAN WITH HANDS IN POCKETS (the capitalist) 5", cast iron bank............................$75.00-145.00

ORGAN GRINDER AND DANCING BEAR, mechanical bank................................$1,600.00-2,200.00

ORIENTAL CHILD ON PILLOW, cast iron bank, 5" $150.00-200.00

ORNATE POST, 5" brass bank $50.00-100.00

ORNATE POST, brass bank, 7½" $50.00-100.00

ORNATE SPACE HEATER BANK, cast iron still bank, black finish, 6½" $70.00-100.00

OUR EMPIRE BANK, fancy cast iron pattern, brown finish, 7" $100.00-150.00

OWL BANK, cast iron, 4", painted $100.00-150.00

OWL BANK, MECHANICAL, painted cast iron, turns head, 4" $300.00-500.00

OWL ON STUMP BANK, "Be Wise Save Money," 5", cast iron bank $200.00-500.00

OWL, bronze finish, cast iron, 4" $25.00-50.00

PAGODA BANK, aluminum, 6" $75.00-125.00

PAGODA BANK, oriental house with steep roof, 5", cast iron silver/gold finish $200.00-300.00

PARLOR STOVE, figural cast iron bank, 7" $150.00-250.00

PEACH ON ORNATE STAND, recent, 6" cast iron bank..$40.00-85.00

PELICAN WITH ARAB, MECHANICAL, painted, cast iron bank $1,600-2,200.00

PENNY TRUST COMPANY SAFE BANK, glass, 3" $20.00-30.00

PERSHING BANK, CAST IRON FIGURAL BUST, bronze finish, 8" $100.00-140.00

PETER'S WEATHERBIRD figural cast iron bank, shoe premium, 4" $70.00-120.00

PETER'S WEATHERBIRD SHOES, Premium bank, tin and paper, 2" $10.00-25.00

PIANO SHAPED BANK, sheet metal, bronze, 5" $80.00-140.00

PIG "I MADE CHICAGO FAMOUS," 5½" long cast iron bank $35.00-65.00

PIG BANK "INVEST IN PORK," black cast iron, 7" $150.00-190.00

PIG BANK, bronze foundry pattern, gold paint, 7" long $20.00-40.00

PIG BANK, cast iron "Decker's Iowana," 4½" $60.00-105.00

PIG, "INVEST IN PORK," 7" cast iron bank $30.00-65.00

PIG, Murphy's Rotary Pig," 3", cast iron, still bank $40.00-80.00

PIG, CAST IRON STILL BANK, 8", bronze finish $75.00-110.00

PIG, CAST IRON WITH BRONZE FINISH, 7", coin slot under tail $100.00-145.00

PIG, CAST IRON, dark finish, 6½" $50.00-100.00

PIG, cast iron, white finish, still bank ..$35.00-65.00

PIG, chalkware, 7", still bank $20.00-40.00

PIG, SMILING SQUATTY, lead, bronze finish, 4" long $20.00-40.00

PINOCCHIO COMPOSITION BANK, by Crown Toy, 1930's, Disney, 6" tall $45.00-100.00

PINOCCHIO, Walt Disney's, wood composition, bank, 5" by Crown Toy $60.00-125.00

PIRATE CHEST, lead cast bank with bronze finish, 2½" tall $10.00-25.00

PIRATE LEANING ON TREASURE CHEST, pot metal bank, 6" $50.00-100.00

PIRATE SITTING ON TREASURE CHEST, pot metal, 6" $20.00-50.00

PIRATE, white metal, painted features, 6" $20.00-50.00

PLUTO, by Disney, ceramic still bank, Leeds China $15.00-30.00

MARX METAL, RADIO BANK, red with combination opening knob, Reynolds collection, $50.00-100.00.

16

POLICEMAN WITH BILLY CLUB, KEYSTONE COP, 5½" tall, cast iron $50.00-100.00

PONY, "MY PET," CAST IRON FIGURAL, 4" $45.00-75.00

PONY BANK, small, cast iron, 3" with bridle and saddle.................................$20.00-50.00

POOR TIRED TIM STILL BANK, tin lithograph, 5" tall.......................................$75.00-125.00

POPEYE METAL DIME REGISTER BANK, 3", c. 1930's, colorful lithograph $25.00-65.00

PORKY PIG WITH TREE TRUNK, pot metal bank, 4" $50.00-100.00

PORKY THE PIG BANK, cast iron, painted, 6", with "Porky" on front............................$100.00-200.00

POSSUM BANK, 2½" cast iron still $75.00-150.00

PRANCING HORSE, 7" cast iron with bright black finish $60.00-100.00

PRANCING HORSE, small with oval base, gold finish, 5" $15.00-40.00

PRANCING HORSE BANK, still cast iron, 7" $75.00-105.00

PRUDENTIAL REGISTERING BANK, patented 1890 ....$300.00-500.00

PUMP, lead bank, 4½"..........................$50.00-100.00

PUNCH AND JUDY PUPPET THEATRE BANK, tin, 4½" $50.00-100.00

RABBIT, LARGE STANDING, 6½" tall, cast iron, still bank $30.00-60.00

RABBIT CAST LEAD BANK, 4½", silver finish $120.00-180.00

RABBIT IN CABBAGE MECHANICAL BANK, 4½" tall $250.00-500.00

RABBIT, BEGGING, cast iron, still bank, 5½" tall $50.00-90.00

RABBIT CROUCHING, cast iron, still 3".$25.00-55.00

RABBIT, DRESSED UP IN TOP HAT, 5", tin bank, still $20.00-40.00

ARABIAN SAFE SAVINGS BANK, key opens front door, cast iron with ornate Arabian scenes, Reynolds collection, $125.00-250.00.

RABBIT, LYING DOWN WITH EARS PULLED BACK, 2½" tall, cast iron $50.00-100.00

RADIATION STOVE, tin, 5¼" tall $90.00-140.00

RADIO BANK, 1930's console model, cast iron, blue/gold, 6" tall..................................$100.00-150.00

RADIO BANK, cast iron, figural, red finish with nickel plate door, 4" $40.00-80.00

RADIO BANK, white metal, Zenith, gold finish, 3½" $30.00-55.00

RADIO, CAST IRON STILL BANK, blue and gold, 3¼" $80.00-110.00

RED GOOSE SHOES, cast iron bank, goose, 3¼" $40.00-80.00

RED GOOSE SHOES PREMIUM CAST IRON BANK, 4" $50.00-100.00

RHINO CAST IRON BANK, painted, 2½" $150.00-275.00

ROLY POLY MONKEY BANK, tin lithograph bank, 6" $250.00-400.00

ROOSEVELT NEW DEAL BANK, bronze finish, 5", still bank..................................$150.00-250.00

ROOSEVELT, FRANKLIN D., BUST BANK, die cast metal, 4½" tall $150.00-300.00

ROOSTER WITH MAN'S FACE, unusual, 5" cast iron, still bank $200.00-300.00

ROYAL THRONE BANK, cast iron, "E. R. 1953" bronze finish, 8" $50.00-75.00

RUMPELSTILTSKIN CAST IRON BANK 6" $200.00-400.00

SAFE BANK, "National Safe," some parts tin, nickel finish, 5" $40.00-80.00

SAFE BANK "Fidelity Safe," cast iron savings bank, brown/gold, 3" $75.00-110.00

SAFE BANK, "National Safe Deposit" black and gold, 6", cast iron $50.00-100.00

SAFE BANK "Treasure Safe," J. & E. Stevens Co., 1897, cast iron, nickel finish...........$50.00-100.00

ROOSTER CAST IRON BANK, brass-look finish, 5", Reynolds collection, $150.00-275.00.

BANKS

SAINT BERNARD WITH PACK, still bank, 5⅜" long, cast iron, Reynolds collection, $80.00-120.00.

SAFE BANK, "SECURITY SAFE DEPOSIT," black/gold trim, pat. 1888, 8" $350.00-500.00

SAFE BANK, "Security Safe Deposit," cast iron bank, black/gold, 4" $30.00-55.00

SAFE BANK, CAST IRON, safe behind bars version, 5½" nickel finish $80.00-135.00

SAFE SHAPED BANK, with combination lock, cast iron, black/gold trim, 4" $50.00-100.00

SAFE SHAPED FIGURAL BANK, 3", cast iron, still $20.00-40.00

SAFE, COMBINATION LOCK, cast iron, 4"... ....$50.00-85.00

SAFETY DEPOSIT BANK, KEYLESS, 6" nickel finish, safe shaped $150.00-225.00

SAILOR, SALUTING WITH RIFLE, 5½" size, still bank $40.00-70.00

SAILOR, SALUTING WITH RIFLE, 6", cast iron $60.00-90.00

SAINT BERNARD (DOG) WITH PACK ON BACK, cast iron bank, brown/gold, 5½" $50.00-90.00

SAINT BERNARD DOG cast iron bank, very large, 11" long, painted $150.00-240.00

SAN GABRIEL MISSION BANK, figural, cast iron, 5" $600.00-900.00

SANTA AND CHIMNEY, mechanical bank, cast iron, early, painted $700.00-1,000.00

SANTA CLAUS AT CHIMNEY, pot metal, figural, still bank, painted, 4" $175.00-300.00

SANTA CLAUS BANK, cast iron, pack over back, up-right, 5" $40.00-70.00

SANTA CLAUS CAST IRON BANK with arms folded in front, 5½", painted $125.00-170.00

SANTA CLAUS CAST IRON BANK, still bank, painted, 5½" with tree $150.00-250.00

SANTA CLAUS LEANING WITH PACK ON HIS BACK, cast iron bank, 4", painted $200.00-400.00

SANTA CLAUS, POT METAL, 4" tall, holding cane and bag of toys, still bank.......................$40.00-70.00

SANTA, ORIENTAL VERSION with lighter in cap, lead 4" $50.00-100.00

SAVE AND SMILE MONEY BOX, BLACK MAN HEAD, 4", cast iron bank $150.00-225.00

SAVE AND SMILE, ORNAMENTAL HANGING BANK, 7" cast iron $80.00-135.00

SAVING SAM, cast iron, 1920's $85.00-160.00

SAVINGS BANK, clear glass, modern, 4" $20.00-40.00

SCOTTIE DOG BANK, composition, black, 5" $10.00-25.00

SCOTTIE PUPPIES IN BASKET, pot metal still bank, 4½" $75.00-100.00

SCOTTIE, black, still, cast iron, 3" $40.00-85.00

SEAL BANK, cast iron, figural, still bank, 3" on rock $75.00-135.00

SEAL CAST IRON BANK, still, black/silver, 3½" $200.00-350.00

SECOND NATIONAL DUCK BANK, tin lithograph, mechanical bank, Disney, 1950's $50.00-100.00

SHEEP CAST IRON, FIGURAL BANK, gold finish, 5½" $40.00-70.00

SHEEP, "FEED MY SHEEP," pot metal bank, gold finish $35.00-65.00

SHEEP, WALKING, 3", cast iron $100.00-200.00

SHERIDAN ON HORSE WITH BASE, cast iron still bank, 6", gold finish $250.00-400.00

SHRINER'S HAT (FEZ) ALUMINUM BANK, red and black, 5½" $50.00-75.00

SLEEPING BEAUTY, WALT DISNEY'S, ceramic figural bank, Leeds China, 1950's $15.00-35.00

SNIFFLES THE MOUSE WITH TREE TRUNK, pot metal bank, 5"...................................$50.00-100.00

SNOOPY CERAMIC BANK, 1960's $15.00-25.00

SNOW WHITE AND THE SEVEN DWARFS DIME SAVINGS BANK, Disney, 1930's $40.00-100.00

SNOW WHITE CERAMIC CHARACTER BANK, 8" tall, 1938, c. W. Disney, by Leeds $15.00-40.00

SNOW WHITE CERAMIC FIGURAL BANK, by Leeds China, 1940's, glazed $20.00-35.00

SOLDIER BANK, cast iron, painted, 5". $45.00-100.00

SPEAKING DOG MECHANICAL BANK, c. 1885, cast iron, 7"..$500.00-800.00

SQUIRREL FIGURAL BANK, MECHANICAL, 6" cast iron $125.00-200.00

SQUIRREL HOLDING NUT, cast iron bank, 4" $100.00-200.00

STATE BANK, two-story, cast iron building bank, 4" $50.00-100.00

STATUE OF LIBERTY, registering bank .$10.00-25.00

STORK, HOLDING BABY, cast iron, still bank $600.00-950.00

STOVE BANK "ROPER," green finish, manufactured by Arcade, 4", battery operated $80.00-130.00

STOVE BANK, MANUFACTURED BY ARCADE, 4", white finish $60.00-90.00

STREET CAR "MAIN STREET" CAST IRON BANK, gold finish, 6½" long $300.00-475.00

STREET URCHIN, black cast iron, boy and vendor's cart, 3" $125.00-175.00

SUN BONNET SUE (recent version) cast iron, painted 7½" $40.00-95.00

TAMMANY MECHANICAL BANK, man in chair, 6" $200.00-350.00

TANK BANK, cast iron, 7" long, WWI-type bank with dark finish $200.00-300.00

TANK BANK, made in U.S.A., gold finish, 4½" $85.00-130.00

STUMP SPEAKER, CAST IRON MECHANICAL, BANK (reproduction), by Book of Knowledge, Reynolds collection, $50.00-135.00.

TANK SAVINGS BANK, natural version, no paint, nickel guns, 9" $150.00-250.00
TANK, CAST IRON BANK, WWI VERSION, 8" long, brown and gold $150.00-225.00
TEDDY AND THE BEAR, MECHANICAL, painted cast iron...................................$1,000.00-1,400.00
TEDDY BEAR BANK, CELLULOID, 5" $20.00-45.00
TEDDY ROOSEVELT BUST BANK, 5" bronze finish, cast iron still bank $75.00-175.00
TEEPEE, metal still bank, 4½" $40.00-60.00
THREE LITTLE PIGS LEATHER COVERED BOOK BANK, 1930's, Disney $25.00-60.00
THREE MONKEY'S, "See No Evil," etc., 3" cast iron bank $150.00-275.00
TOLL HOUSE BANK, 4", blue/silver $50.00-100.00
TOP HAT "PASS AROUND THE HAT," cast iron 2½" figural bank $50.00-100.00
TOP HAT BANK, tin, 3½" $40.00-75.00
TOP HAT BANK, tin, word "College," printed on brim, 4½" tall $50.00-90.00
TRANSVAAL MONEY BOX, cast iron squatty man in top hat, foundry pat./pipe $300.00-600.00
TREASURE CHEST STILL BANK, cast iron, gold finish, 3" $60.00-95.00
TRICK DOG MECHANICAL BANK, patented 1888, cast iron, clown/hoop/barrel, 9" $200.00-400.00
TRICK DOG MECHANICAL CAST IRON BANK by Hubley, Made in U.S.A., 9" $200.00-450.00
TRICK DOG, MECHANICAL BANK, painted cast iron, Hubley, 9½" $400.00-750.00

TRICK PONY MECHANICAL PAINTED CAST IRON BANK, pat. 1885 ....$900.00-1,300.00
TRUCK BANK, "Armored Truck," sheet metal construction, 6" $20.00-40.00
TURKEY CAST IRON BANK, 3½", black paint $30.00-60.00
TURKEY CAST IRON BANK, brown/red trim, 4" $60.00-90.00
TURKEY CAST IRON BANK, still, 4", brown/red $250.00-375.00
TWO BILLY GOATS BUTTING, 4" cast iron bank $20.00-45.00
TYPEWRITER BANK, premium of Peter Paul Typewriter Co. $60.00-100.00
U.S. MINT, cast iron, still bank, 3½"......$20.00-40.00
U.S. MAIL CAST IRON BANK, green/gold, 4½" $20.00-50.00
U.S. MAIL MAILBOX BANK, green/gold 3½" cast iron, older version $40.00-70.00
U.S. MAIL, cast iron bank, red/gold, 5", still bank..$20.00-50.00
U.S. MAIL, cast iron bank, siver & red, 3½", still bank..$20.00-50.00
U.S. MAIL, cast iron, still bank, red/gold, 5", still bank..$20.00-50.00
U.S.S. PIG, cast aluminum still bank, 6" $30.00-50.00
UNCLE SAM MECHANICAL, CAST IRON BANK, pat. 1886, 11" tall $750.00-1,200.00
UNCLE SAM PAINTED CAST IRON, mechanical bank $1,200.00-1,800.00
UNCLE SCROOGE (Disney character) PLASTIC BANK WITH MONEY BAG $10.00-20.00
UNCLE TOM, MECHANICAL BANK, painted cast iron $300.00-550.00
VAULT SAFE BANK, "Fidelity Trust Vaults," brown/white, 6½", cast iron $350.00-500.00
VICTORIAN COTTAGE CAST IRON BANK, 1½" story with bronze finish, 5"....................$100.00-150.00
VILLA FANCY HOUSE BANK marked "1882" brown/gold 5½" $150.00-200.00
VON HINDENBERG, BUST, figural bank, lead, 9" $275.00-400.00
WAGON, PRAIRIE, cast iron, recent 7" ..$10.00-20.00
WASHINGTON, GEORGE, CAST IRON BUST BANK, 8", still bank $20.00-40.00
WASHINGTON MONUMENT CAST IRON FIGURAL BANK, 6", gold finish $100.00-150.00
WESTMINSTER ABBEY CAST IRON FIGURAL BANK, gold finish, 6½"..............................$140.00-200.00
WHIPPET DOG ON BASE, cast iron, still bank, gold finish, 5" long $100.00-150.00
WILLIAM TELL, MECHANICAL, painted cast iron bank $800.00-1,250.00
WISE PIG, cast iron still figural, 7"........$30.00-60.00
WISE PIG, lead figural, still bank, white finish, 6½" $30.00-70.00
WOOLWORTH BUILDING, cast iron, still bank, 8" $75.00-120.00
WORLD WAR ONE SOLDIER, cast iron still bank, 7" $100.00-200.00
WOVEN BASKET CAST IRON BANK, 3" $50.00-75.00

BATTERY OPERATED TOYS

Battery operated toys are a definite brainchild of the baby boomer era of the 1950's and the 1960's. With the common marketing of long lasting standard C and D cell batteries in the 1950's and their relative inexpense, toy makers in the United States and abroad jumped on the "battery op." bandwagon as if they had just discovered nuclear fusion. And for what batteries did for the imaginations of inventive toy designers, battery operated power touched the daily lives of all American children.

Ask the layman on the street what was the greatest thing batteries did for toys and he would probably say action. But fine action toys had been around in the form of clockwork wound toys for at least a century, and battery operation simply turned the "wind key" into an on-off switch. Now, the new and revolutionary miracle that battery operation brought to toys was - light! Batteries allowed penlights to sparkle, blink, flash and flicker, adding novelty to action.

With the addition of battery power, the windup drinking bear could now have a hollow nose that glowed red from too much booze or a clown that could drop his drawers and his face could blush. The perfect marriage of time and place could not have been better in regard to our importation of fine Japanese battery operated toys in the 1950's and 1960's when toy designs from that country were at their best.

Most battery operated toys include a single figure performing several actions. The battery operated monkey may not only play the cymbals, in another cycle of action his eyes might light up or he might chatter his teeth. Battery operated toys very often feature several quite different actions all presented in a repeating cycle.

Although many battery operated toys are recent enough to be found as bargains, their popularity and prices are increasing proportionately. Here, at the start of the 1990's, thirty years removed from the "golden years" of production, the market is poised to take off. For the record, this author will commit to print that early battery operated toys may be *the most representative toys of the 1950's and 1960's;* the same as windups were to the 1920's and 1930's.

No single manufacturer stands out as the "flagship" producer of battery operated toys. Many small Japanese companies competed for this market and it would take a dictonary just to sort their trademarks. Many of these companies utilized plastics and vinyls in their designs to allow light bulbs placed within the translucent interiors to make the toy "glow." As opposed to the common rule of thumb in toy collecting that plastic use diminishes value, plastic in a battery operated toy does not significantly affect the value.

A sub-group of standard battery operated toys is remote controlled toys. Most battery operated designs usually position two or more D or C cell batteries in the base of the toy to give it weight and balance, and the animal or figure sits or stands on this base. There is usually an on/off switch attached directly to this base. On remote controlled battery operated toys, the power supply comes from the remote control box (about the size of two D-cell batteries placed end to end) where the batteries are stored and the on/off switches are located. This design allowed remote controlled battery operated toys to be "freed" from the heavy weight of batteries in their bases so puppies could jump, bears could walk, and cars could drive lightly along; all connected by power cords from the switchbox to the toy itself.

If a collector is really serious about collecting these toys, he should always keep two C and D batteries in his pocket when "shopping." Contrary to what might seem obvious, all dealers don't keep batteries in their battery operated toys. If a dealer claims he doesn't have batteries for the toy, but it DOES work, the collector should politely offer his battery, with the explanation that he doesn't doubt the dealer's word, but he would simply like to see the toy in action. People don't buy automobiles without driving them...toy collectors shouldn't buy windups or battery operated toys without seeing them in action!

If it doesn't work, pass it by. Home repair jobs on battery operated toys can often end up less repair work and more like an autopsy, where the toy is permanently dismantled and rendered worthless forever. Buy these toys in excellent condition ONLY and always check the battery storage compartment for corrosion problems from old batteries. Slight damage in this area can be sanded or filed away, but severe damage may have already eaten up internal wire connections and working parts.

These relatively modern collectibles are already hot properties among many general toy collectors. As we move from the age of metal toys and battery power, the collector interest will only intensify.

AMERICAN FOOTBALL PLAYER, 5½", Japan $45.00-70.00

ANSWER GAME MACHINE, Robot, Amico, Japan, 1950's, 15" $150.00-300.00

ATTACKING MARTIAN ROBOT, 9" $50.00-125.00

BALL PLAYING BEAR, 11", tin and celluloid, unusual combination action $125.00-225.00

BALLOON VENDOR, tin tray and bell $125.00-300.00

BARNEY BEAR DRUMMER, Japan, 11" remote control, tin and plastic $35.00-60.00

BARNEY BEAR, 11" in box $100.00-225.00

BENJALI TIGER, Marx, 12" plastic head..$40.00-85.00

BLACKSMITH BEAR, boxed, Japan, A1, 10" plush $100.00-165.00

BLUSHING WILLY, Japan, 11" tin and plastic, pours drink, eyes roll $40.00-85.00

BREWSTER THE ROOSTER, Marx, Japan, 10" plush, stop and go action $35.00-60.00

BROADWAY TROLLEY, Japan, battery operated, 12", all tin $25.00-50.00

BUBBLE BLOWING BUNNY, 8" $100.00-200.00

BUBBLE BLOWING MONKEY, Alps, Japan, 10½" $45.00-80.00

BUBBLE MONKEY, 11", in box $100.00-200.00

BUSY HOUSEKEEPER BEAR, Alps, 1950's, 9" plush, in box $80.00-135.00

CAPTAIN BLUSHWELL, Japan, 11", pours drink, blushes, eyes roll $30.00-60.00

CHARLIE THE DRUMMING CLOWN, Alps, Japan, 10" $65.00-135.00

CHARLIE WEAVER, by TN, Japan, 12", Furnish collection, $50.00-125.00.

CHEE CHEE CHIHUAHUA, Mego, Japan, remote controlled, 8", plush $20.00-40.00

CHIMP PORTER, Acro, Japan, plush and vinyl, in box $35.00-70.00

CHIPPY THE CHIPMUNK, Alps, Japan, 12", plush, remote controlled 30.00-60.00

COCKADOODLEDOO ROOSTER, Japan, 7", walks, crows..$45.00-75.00

CRAGSTAN CRAP SHOOTER, with box .$50.00-195.00

CRAGSTAN TEDDY BEAR peanut vendor $100.00-300.00

CRAWLING BABY, LineMar, in box, celluloid with fabric clothes, 10" $40.00-80.00

CYCLING DADDY, Japan, 10", peddles bike, in box $45.00-105.00

DENNIS THE MENACE, battery operated, xylophone player $200.00-300.00

DENNIS THE MENACE, in box $200.00-475.00

DOLLY DRESSMAKER, 8", Japan, vinyl head, celluloid hands, rubber $70.00-120.00

DREAMBOAT HOTROD, Japan, 1950's, 7" car, handsome boy driver $65.00-135.00

DRINKING CAPTAIN, Japan $75.00-150.00

DRINKING KITTY, Japan, 10" plush $40.00-65.00

ELEPHANT, walking, Japan, remote controlled, plush over metal, ball $30.00-40.00

FISHING POLAR BEAR, Alps, Japan $70.00-135.00

FRANKENSTEIN MONSTER, 13", vinyl face, blushes, pants fall down $75.00-145.00

FRANKIE THE ROLLER SKATING MONKEY, Alps, Japan, 12", remote controlled..............$45.00-100.00

GINO NEOPOLITAN BALLOON BLOWER, Japan, 11" tin with vinyl head, box $50.00-95.00

GOLDEN LOCOMOTIVE, Sunrise, Japan, tin, bump and go $25.00-40.00

GOOD TIME CHARLIE, Japan, blushes, pours drinks...$50.00-95.00

GORILLA, 1960's, remote controlled and powered $200.00-400.00

GREAT GARLOO, THE UNTAMED, remote controlled, Marx, 23" plush $100.00-200.00

GREEDY PUP, candy eating dog, Alps, Japan $45.00-95.00

GREYHOUND BEEP BEEP BUS, NGS, Japan, 20", in box $250.00-450.00

HAPPY FIDDLER CLOWN, Alps, tin, 10", fabric clothes, box $150.00-300.00

HAPPY SAD CLOWN, Japan, cloth and vinyl, changes his expression $60.00-120.00

HAPPY SANTA, Alps, Japan, 12" remote controlled, composition face $125.00-195.00

HAPPY SANTA, Alps, Japan, 9", plays trap drum set $70.00-150.00

HI-JINX CLOWN, 11", tin, cloth and celluloid, clown and monkey figures...........................$35.00-70.00

HI-QUE MONKEY, 1950's, 17" high, tin base, cloth, rubber body $140.00-200.00

HOBO PLAYING ACCORDIAN, 11", cloth, tin, plastic, clown with monkey...........................$85.00-165.00

HOOTY THE HAPPY OWL, Alps, Japan, 9", remote controlled, hoots and flaps $35.00-70.00

ICE CREAM CYCLE, Japan $200.00-650.00

JOLLY PIANIST, Japan, 8", plush dog in red vest, plays piano $35.00-65.00

BATTERY OPERATED TOYS

KING FLYING SAUCER, Japan, 8", plastic and metal, blue and silver $55.00-110.00

LUNAR BUG FLYING MOON CRAFT, remote controlled, 1965, plastic $15.00-30.00

MACK THE TURTLE, 9", fabric clothes, tin shell $85.00-165.00

MC GREGOR, Japan, 11", cloth clothes, tin Scotsman smokes cigar, boxed $60.00-120.00

MECHANIZED ROBOT, "Robbie," battery operated $1,3000.00-2,000.00

MERCURY COUGAR, 1967 model $65.00-95.00

MIGHTY KONG GORILLA, tin and plush, remote controlled, Marx, Japan $150.00-250.00

MISS FRIDAY, THE TYPIST, Japan, 8" .$75.00-125.00

MISTER HUSTLER ROBOT, 11", astronaut face in helmet and shield $250.00-750.00

MONKEY, CRAGSTAN CRAP SHOOTING, Alps, Japan, 9" $35.00-75.00

MOON HELICOPTER, Marx, Japan, remote controlled, 7", NASA $30.00-55.00

MOTHER BEAR, spanking baby bear .$100.00-200.00

MOUNTAIN SPECIAL EXPRESS LOCOMOTIVE, MT. Japan, bump and go $40.00-55.00

MUSICAL CHIMP, CK, Japan, cloth and plush, plays cymbals $35.00-70.00

NASA SPACECRAFT, DAIYA, Japan, 12", two sections $65.00-110.00

NUTTY MAD INDIAN, Marx $125.00-200.00

PAPA BEAR, 9", in original box $100.00-165.00

PEPPY PUPPY, Japan, remote controlled, plush, 9", boxed $35.00-60.00

PETER THE DRUMMING RABBIT, Japan, 13", remote controlled, plush, pink $50.00-100.00

PICNIC BEAR, 10" $140.00-220.00

PICNIC BUNNY, in box $80.00-120.00

PIGGY COOK, Japan, 10", cloth and vinyl, shakes pan and pepper $35.00-60.00

PINOCCHIO non-Disney version, w/box.$100.00-200.00

PLAYFUL PUP IN SHOE, Japan, plush, 10", bump and go......................................$15.00-30.00

POPEYE, BUBBLE BLOWING, LineMar, Japan, 12", all tin, except pipe.............................$400.00-700.00

POWER SHOVEL, Alps, Japan, steam shovel, boxed, remote control $40.00-70.00

PRINCESS FRENCH POODLE, Alps, plush, 11" $25.00-50.00

PUFFY MORRIS cigarette smoker $90.00-150.00

RABBIT, B-Z, Japan, 7", tin rabbit with bump and go action $20.00-40.00

RABBITS AND THE CARRIAGE, S & E, Japan, plush, tin $85.00-195.00

ROARING GORILLA, MT, Japan, 10", tin with rubber hands, boxed $90.00-165.00

ROCK 'N ROLL MONKEY, in box $75.00-200.00

ROCKY, (Fred Flinstone Knock-off) Japan,

boxed $70.00-150.00

SANTA BANK, NOEL, Japan, 10" $150.00-200.00

SANTA BANK, Trim a Tree Product......$75.00-150.00

SANTA ON SCOOTER, 10", orig. box .$125.00-225.00

SANTA ON SCOOTER, MT, JAPAN, 8", tin and vinyl..$65.00-100.00

SHAKING ANTIQUE CAR, TN, Japan, 9", man in hat drives $50.00-75.00

SHAKING OLD TIMER CAR, CRAGSTAN, 10", tin, rattle action $50.00-95.00

SILVER RAY SECRET WEAPON SCOUT, ROBOT SPACEMAN, Japan, 9" $150.00-275.00

SKY PATROL FLYING SAUCER, 1950's. $125.00-175.00

SLEEPING BABY BEAR, LineMar, Japan, 8" $80.00-140.00

SMOKING AND SHOE SHINING PANDA BEAR, Japan, 11", plush $35.00-65.00

SMOKING BULLDOZER, 9" x 7", tin and plastic, Japan, bump and go action.........................$40.00-95.00

SMOKING BUNNY, remote controlled, 10" pink coat, walks, smokes pipe $50.00-75.00

SMOKING GRANPA, Sans, Co., Japan..$85.00-150.00

SMOKING POP LOCOMOTIVE, SAN, Japan, 50's, 11, smokes, bump and go action $20.00-45.00

SOLAR X SPACE ROCKET, tin, 16".....$45.00-135.00

SPACE FRONTIER APOLLO 12 ROCKET, 18" rocket $75.00-150.00

SPACE ROCKET PISTOL, tin, 1950's, 9" long $35.00-95.00

SPACE TANK WITH ROBOT, 10" $60.00-140.00

SPACECRAFT APOLLO, Alps, 9", three astronauts $65.00-120.00

SPANKING BEAR, LineMar, Japan, 1950's, 9" mama spanks baby bear $120.00-225.00

SPARKY SEAL, Japan, 7" plush and tin, in box $35.00-60.00

STEAM ROLLER, Y, JAPAN, tin lithograph, 8" $40.00-80.00

SUPER ASTRONAUT, 12" mint, in box .$125.00-180.00

SUPER ASTRONAUT, tin and plastic, fires guns, 10" with pencil sharpener.......................$10.00-25.00

TEDDY BALLOON BLOWING BEAR, eyes/voice, in box, 11"......................................$150.00-275.00

TEDDY THE ARTIST, Japan, plush $75.00-100.00

TOM AND JERRY CAR, 12" $200.00-450.00

TRACTOR, CONSTRUCTION, LineMar, Japan, remote controlled, 7" $100.00-170.00

TRIX-A-BALL, Marx, ball balancing game ..$15.00-30.00

TWO GUN SHERIFF, CRAGSTAN, 11" tall with boots, hats, etc...$75.00-140.00

WAGON MASTER, covered wagon $200.00-400.00

WHISTLING SPOOKY TREE, Marx, 14", bump and go, great action..................................$200.00-400.00

YO-YO MONKEY, 11" plush, holds big banana $20.00-55.00

BOATS AND AIRPLANES

Wilbur and Orville Wright and Robert Fulton have permanently etched their names into the history books of American school children. One pair perfected the airplane while the latter is credited with inventing the steamboat. And nearly as instantaneously as their inventions became a part of our daily lives, toy representations of their innovations became popular among children.

Although boats and airplanes are not nearly as massive a collecting category as cars and trucks, they offer their own interesting uniqueness to the general toy collecting field. Many general-line toy collectors focus on all transportation type toys and so boats and airplanes help to "round out" their transportation toy collections.

Each of the two categories is impressive in its own right. Marklin boats (German) today sometimes command thousands of dollars in the collecting marketplace and are extremely rare in mint condition because they contain so many small detail parts. And pristine tin and metal airplane toy examples are hard to find because these usually took quite a beating. Imagine the boy of the 1930's with a new airplane in hand that could only roll along on the ground. The temptation must have certainly been too great. Countless

thousands of them must have been hand "launched" off the porch or table top. Consequently, airplanes are often found in the worst of shapes. A toy dump truck may have taken a good beating in regard to wear and tear, but it never had to fly. Thus, it is a lucky collector who can aquire mint condition airplanes of the 1920's through the 1940's. Collectors who find airplanes of collectible vintage at respectable asking prices which are also in excellent condition rarely pass them up.

Many of the boat examples in this listing are friction or momentum powered, and few were actually intended to float. This is a real blessing in disguise for the collector, for had these toys "hit the water" forty years ago, they probably would not have survived the rust. Since they were designed and intended as land toy versions of sea-going vessels, most have wheels on the bottom and holes in their hulls. Many fine examples of these survive today.

Although some collectors may specialize in the areas of boat or airplane collecting, these categories are particularly popular among general antique toy collectors who are interested in the entire realm of transportation toy collecting.

MARX WINDUP PLANE WITH PILOT, 6", 1930's, all tin, Furnish collection, $35.00-70.00.

SHEET METAL AIRPLANE, SUPER MAINLINER, three tail fins, 13" wingspan, Furnish collection, $30.00-50.00.

BOATS AND AIRPLANES

ALPS, Japan, tin friction plane, 7" wingspan, Furnish collection, $30.00-65.00.

AEROMAIL PLANE, Strauss................$150.00-300.00

AIR FRANCE SIX ENGINE "CROSS OF THE SOUTH," tin lithograph, airplane...................$250.00-600.00

AIRCRAFT CARRIER, ASC, Japan, all tin, friction, 14½"..$60.00-135.00

AIRCRAFT CARRIER, Japan, tin friction, 9½" with two 2" navy jets........................$60.00-95.00

AIRCRAFT CARRIER, KB, Japan, battery operated, 13"...$100.00-165.00

AIRCRAFT CARRIER, MY, Japan, 1950's 8" long, tin, friction, planes on deck..................$60.00-150.00

AIRPLANE BY A. C. WILLIAMS, 5½", single cockpit...$75.00-195.00

AIRPLANE BY SCHUCO, "LUFTHANSA" 16" battery operated, 727......................$150.00-395.00

AIRPLANE, A. C. WILLIAMS, double cockpit, eight cylinder engine..............................$150.00-225.00

AIRPLANE, BRITISH EMPIRE, penny toy, 3" long, tin...$50.00-100.00

AIRPLANE, FRANCE, penny toy, Japan, 3" long, tin...$50.00-100.00

AIRPLANE, ITALIA plane, penny toy, Japan, 3" long, tin...$50.00-100.00

AIRPLANE, penny toy, Japan, with rising sun on wings, 3" long, tin.......................................$50.00-100.00

AIRPLANE, Playtime Airlines, LineMar, Japan, tin friction, 7" with four props.....................$50.00-95.00

AIRPLANE, POP-UP, Gunthermann, Germany, 1925, tin windup, lever action................$125.00-250.00

AIRPLANE, square-winged, Chein, early, tin windup, 7" wingspan......................................$75.00-140.00

ALPS PASSENGER PLANE, 1950's, tin friction, 7" wingspan..$30.00-65.00

AMERICAN EAGLE CARRIER PLANE, by Hubley, 1971, cast metal, boxed..............................$30.00-60.00

AQUAPLANE, by Chein, 1930's, 8½" long, tin windup, floats..$100.00-200.00

ARNOLD OCEAN LINER,....................$200.00-400.00

ARNOLD VIKING BOAT, modern type boat, 1930's, two stacks, 8"...$200.00-400.00

ARROW V8 RACE BOAT, Japan, tin windup, 9" with driver...$35.00-60.00

B-17 WWII IDENTIFICATION PLANE, 1942, hard rubber..$50.00-125.00

B-24 BOMBER, Marx, 1940, tin windup, 18" wingspan...................................$100.00-250.00

B-29 BOMBER, Y, Japan, tin friction, 1950's 19"...$100.00-200.00

B-29 Tin lithograph, plane with metal props, 19" early version...$250.00-650.00

B-50 BOMBER, Bandai, Japan, 7½" wingspan, tin friction...$75.00-150.00

BATTLESHIP NEW YORK, by ARCADE, cast iron, 1912, 20" long.........................$1,000.00-1,600.00

BATTLESHIP USS WASHINGTON, Marx, 1950's, 14" friction, sparkling............................$35.00-75.00

BATTLESHIP, Yamato, Japan, tin, candle-powered, 7" long..$25.00-45.00

BLENHEIM Bomber................................$25.00-50.00

BOAT, ARNOLD, tin windup, 12" long, single stack...$60.00-100.00

BREMEN PLANE, cast iron..................$200.00-400.00

BRISTOL BULLDOG AIRPLANE, S. and E., Japan...$150.00-275.00

BUDDY L AIR CRUISER, pressed steel plane with large 27" wingspan..................................$200.00-400.00

BUDDY L TRANSPORT AIRPLANE, 27" long..$175.00-350.00

BUDDY L TUGBOAT, 28" long, red.....$200.00-600.00

CHINA CLIPPER, Chein, tin, 10"........$200.00-395.00

COAST GUARD SEA PLANE, Ohio Art, 1950's, tin windup, 10" boxed..............................$40.00-90.00

COMET JET LINER, DeHaviland, 19".$200.00-450.00

COMET JETLINER, Y, Japan, all tin friction, four engine, DeHaviland......................$100.00-200.00

CONVAIR 880 TWA plane with stand, friction..$250.00-550.00

CROSS OF THE SOUTH AIR FRANCE, six-engine airplane, tin lithograph......................$250.00-600.00

DC-7 by Cragstan, battery operated, 19", original box...$150.00-350.00

DC-8 JETLINER, tin friction with 16" wingspan, "National Airline of the Stars".................$40.00-95.00

DISNEY AIRPLANE, LineMar, Japan, all tin, friction, 7½" wingspan, four props..............$125.00-225.00

DOUGLAS DC-7C TWA AIRLINER, Cragstan, battery operated, tin...................................$125.00-300.00

DOUGLAS FIGHTER PLANE, 18", tin, lithograph...$100.00-250.00

EASTERN AIRLINES PLANE, Hadson, Japan, 1950's, tin friction, 12" wingspan...............$75.00-135.00

FIGHTER AIRPLANE, Marx, battery operated, 1950's, remote controlled..............................$35.00-75.00

BABY L SPEEDBOAT, made in USA, 10", floats, tin windup/tin pilot, Furnish collection $65.00-140.00.

FIGHTER JET, USAF, Marx, 7", BO $25.00-75.00

FIGHTER JET XF 160, 10" tin $70.00-125.00

FIGHTER PLANE, FS-059, TN, Japan, 1950's, 13" wingspan, BO $75.00-165.00

FIGHTER PLANE, PF256, Yone, Japan, tin, friction, plastic propeller spins $40.00-80.00

FIGHTER PLANE, XF 160, BO $125.00-195.00

FIRE PATROL BOAT, Japan, BO, 12" tin lithograph with box...$70.00-130.00

FLIP-OVER AIRPLANE, manufactured by Marx, tin wind-up $35.00-65.00

FLYING CAR by Bloomer and Schuler, West Germany, 1940's 7".......................................$150.00-450.00

GRUMANN NAVY PANTHER JET, FOLD-A-WING, all tin, 8½" wingspan $65.00-150.00

GUNTHERMANN AIRLINER, 1935, 25" wingspan $700.00-1,500.00

GERMAN-MADE BATTLESHIP, working propeller, 17", gun turrets, twin stacks, Furnish collection, $200.00-475.00.

CHINA CLIPPER by Wyandotte, blue/white, 1930's, 13" wingspan, Furnish collection, $65.00-135.00.

GYRO PLANE, 1930's, 5" tin windup, helicopter with four blades...$60.00-125.00

HAWK SPEEDBOAT, Sutcliffe, England, tin windup, 12" $45.00-95.00

HELICOPTER, ACME, 5", original box, 1950's $10.00-20.00

HELICOPTER, Irwin, boxed, 1950's.........$15.00-30.00

HELICOPTER, Mercury 107, 10" boxed ..$120.00-175.00

HESS SPEEDBOAT, 12", German, 1920's. $200.00-450.00

HOT JOB SEAPLANE, tin windup, Ohio Art, boxed $60.00-100.00

HUBLEY "AMERICA" AIRPLANE, grey with red trim, 14" long $400.00-750.00

HUBLEY AIRPLANE, 5¾" $50.00-125.00

HUBLEY FLYING CIRCUS, in box $75.00-150.00

HUBLEY MAN IN SPEEDBOAT "Baby". $200.00-400.00

HUBLEY P-38, airplane $40.00-65.00

HUBLEY P-38 FIGHTER PLANE, 1950's, 13" wingspan, cast metal plane $30.00-75.00

JET AIRPORT, by Sears, Japan, 1960's, BO, set with four planes......................................$100.00-300.00

JET PLANE BASE, 1950's, BO, tower, launch bases, jets, etc. $200.00-375.00

JET PLANE, Marx, 1950's, 6", friction....$15.00-40.00

KAYTEE BIWING GLIDER PLANE, Kakar toys, 10" long, tin friction $30.00-75.00

KILGORE AIRPLANE, 6" $50.00-150.00

LEHMANN BOMBER, boxed $700.00-1,400.00

LEHMANN PASSENGER, boxed $400.00-900.00

LINDSTROM FLEET, 1920's, boxed set of three 7" to 10" boats $150.00-300.00

LINDSTROM MISS AMERICA SPEED BOAT, tin windup, 7" $65.00-130.00

LINDSTROM ROW BOAT, WOODEN, 1920's, 10" $50.00-100.00

LINDSTROM SAILBOAT, wooden, cloth sails, 1920's $50.00-100.00

LINDSTROM SPEEDBOAT, USA, 1930's, large engine version, 12" tin windup..................$100.00-200.00

LIONEL #44, speedboat $450.00-800.00

LIONEL SPEED BOAT, with stand......$400.00-650.00

LOCKHEED JET, F-90, 1950's, Japan 4" long, tin lithograph $40.00-100.00

LOOPING PLANE, Marx, 1940, 7" wingspan, tin windup $50.00-75.00

LUFTHANSA AIRPLANE BY SCHUCO, 16" BO, 727 ....$150.00-395.00

CITY OF NEW YORK CAST IRON, SIDEWHEELER STEAMBOAT, 15", Furnish collection, $150.00-350.00.

BOATS AND AIRPLANES

DAYTON STEEL BOAT, 12" long, friction powered, Furnish collection, $75.00-150.00.

LUXURY CRUISER, Japan, wooden, BO, 1950's $85.00-165.00

LUXURY LINER, U.S. Zone Germany, Wolverine, boxed, double stacks.......................$45.00-95.00

MAGIC BOAT, KO, Japan, tin windup, lever action, 8" long, driver action $50.00-85.00

MARKLIN BATTLESHIP, 1900, 24".$1,000.00-3,000.00

MENGEL PLAYTHINGS SPEED BOAT, outboard motor...$200.00-350.00

MONOPLANE, Girard, 1930, tin windup plane, 12" boxed...$140.00-250.00

MOON PATROL HELICOPTER "MOON SCOUT", Marx, NASA logo, windup............................$30.00-85.00

MOTORBOAT, Chein, tin windup, 7" crank action, 1950's $10.00-20.00

MOTORBOAT, Chein, tin windup, 9" long, 1950's $15.00-25.00

MOTORBOAT, Japan, BO, wood with metal, 12" long, boxed $65.00-125.00

NAVY FIGHTER TRIGGER PLANE, 8" wingspan, Japan pistol action, 1960's $20.00-35.00

NEPTUNE TUG BOAT, BO, 15", Japan ..$35.00-75.00

OCEAN LINER, German, penny toy, three stacks, 5" long $110.00-200.00

ORKIN CRAFT MOTOR BOAT with winding crank...$400.00-700.00

PAN AM BOEING 727, tin friction, United Airlines, engine noise.......................................$25.00-60.00

PASSENGER AIRLINER, friction, all tin, DC-7...$125.00-300.00

PASSENGER AIRLINER, friction, all tin, DC-8...$100.00-250.00

PASSENGER SHIP, 6", friction, Japan, in box, 1950's $65.00-125.00

RESCUE HELICOPTER, Japan, BO, 9", boxed $25.00-40.00

ROYAL DUTCH AIRLINES ELECTRA JET, KLM, TN, Japan, BO, ... $100.00-200.00

S.S. AMERICA BOAT ON WHEELS, 12", Wyandotte $100.00-200.00

SAILBOAT, tin and wood, 11" x 10", Toytinkers, Evanston, Ill. $25.00-50.00

SCHUCO 13", tin lithograph, submarine, 1930's, German $100.00-195.00

SCHUCO MOTOR BOAT, 14", in box .$150.00-295.00

SCHUCO NEW YORK PARIS AIRPLANE, small tin toy, 4" with pilot.....................................$200.00-400.00

SCHUCO SPEED BOAT, 3003, U.S. Zone Germany, 7" plastic, windup, keywound $60.00-135.00

SEA BOARD WORLD AIRLINES 15" all metal airplane $150.00-295.00

SEA FURY BOAT WITH OUTBOARD ENGINE, Allyn, metal, 20" long raceboat $50.00-100.00

SEA PLANE, Chein, 1930's, tin windup, 8", silver/red/blue $65.00-100.00

SEAGULL PLANE, CAST IRON $400.00-700.00

SEASCAPE TUGBOAT, Marx, Japan, BO, remote controlled, 7" long.....................................$20.00-45.00

SHOOTING FIGHTER PLANE, TN, Japan, BO, 9", boxed, sound $75.00-130.00

SKYBIRD FLYERS, Marx, two planes, 7" tower, 1930's 100.00-200.00

SMOKING JET PLANE, TN, Japan, BO, 12" long, tin jet fighter $65.00-90.00

SPEEDBOAT, Haji, Japan, 1950's, 8" long, tin with plastic $40.00-75.00

SPIRIT OF ST. LOUIS by Metalcraft, #800 ....$200.00-400.00

STEELCRAFT Army Scout Airplane.....$125.00-350.00

STRATO CLIPPER, PAN AM, W. Germany, 1955, four engine, BO, propellers work $200.00-350.00

STRATO-CRUISER, LineMar, Capitol Airlines, four engine, 14" BO $150.00-225.00

SUBMARINE, SSN, friction, Japan, 1950's, lever action, 10" boxed...$60.00-120.00

THUNDER JET SPEED BOAT, Japan, 1950's, tin BO remote controlled, 10" $30.00-65.00

THUNDER JET SPEED BOAT, Japan, 1950's, all tin, BO, remote controlled $65.00-125.00

TIN BOAT WITH OUTBOARD MOTOR, 15", BO, boxed...$125.00-175.00

TOOTSIETOY BIPLANE, 1930's, 4" $20.00-45.00

TOOTSIETOY MONOPLANE, 1930's, 4" ..$20.00-45.00

TOOTSIE TOY SET OF SIX BATTLESHIPS, 5" $125.00-175.00

TRANSPORT AIRPLANE, 7" Wyandotte...$15.00-35.00

FLYING FORTRESS METAL AIRPLANE, four engines, four-blade propellers, 12" long, Furnish collection, $50.00-110.00.

MARX WINDUP PLANE with dual machine gun action, tin with metal, 7", Furnish collection, $40.00-80.00.

TRANSPORT PLANE AND FIGHTER PLANE on original card, 1950's $6.00-15.00
TRI-MOTOR FORD AIRPLANE, Tootsie-toy $65.00-125.00
TUGBOAT, SAN, Japan, BO, all tin, 12" $65.00-90.00
TUGBOAT, SAN, Japan, tin, BO, 13", original box $75.00-120.00
TURNOVER CIRCUS PLANE, Yone, Japan, clown pilot, tin windup $20.00-40.00
U.S. AIR FORCE MILITARY COMMAND JET, tin, BO, 14" wingspan $60.00-125.00
U.S. ARMY FIGHTER PLANE, Marx, 1940, tin windup, 8" wingspan, boxed $100.00-200.00
U.S. ARMY HELICOPTER, Japan, BO, 9" boxed $25.00-40.00
U.S. ARMY WHIZ SKY FIGHTER, Girard, 1925, 9" long, tin windup biplane $250.00-550.00
U.S. MARINE AIR SEA RESCUE PLANE, Ideal, 1960's plastic windup, 10" long $20.00-55.00
U.S. NAVY HELICOPTER, Japan, BO, 9", boxed $25.00-40.00
USAF F-80 FIGHTER PLANE, Japan, 7" wingspan, all tin, friction with noise $50.00-100.00
USAF HELICOPTER, tin, friction, 10" long, British, c. 1950's $25.00-45.00
USAF JET, 1950's tin friction jet with lithograph of pilots in cockpit $10.00-35.00
USAF STARFIRE JET, 9" wingspan, two pilots lithograph, tin, friction, ... $60.00-125.00
USAF TROOP CARRIER PLANE, Bandai. Japan, C124

STEAM POWERED TIN TOY BOAT, actually works when boiler is "fired," 15", Furnish collection, $75.00-175.00.

TIN BOAT WITH PAINT DETAILS "MAINE," 6", working rudder and propeller, Furnish collection, $50.00-135.00.

SCHUCO "ELECTRO SUBMARINO," 1950's, 12" long, Furnish collection, $50.00-95.00.

Globemaster, 17" tin $85.00-350.00
USS WASHINGTON , battleship $60.00-95.00
WEEDON, steam powered boat $400.00-700.00
WORLD WAR II TIN WINDUP PLANE with bomb rack and bombs $60.00-95.00
ZEPPELIN, by Metalcraft, 27" $175.00-250.00

BOOKS AND PAPER

Book and paper ephemera among toy enthusiasts is not usually a primary area of collecting, that is, most toy collectors do not seek these out first. Most toy collectors who collect children's books usually do so as a secondary sideline interest to supplement their particular collecting specialty, picking up the odd, unique or inexpensive items that relate to their own collections.

Doll collectors go for Victorian and early children's books. Military and soldier collectors look for books with a war, historical or battle theme. Disneyana collectors look for printed matter with Walt Disney copyrights. In all instances, toy collectors often use books as background material for displays. Books look excellent in display cases when behind toys of a similar subject.

Common sense should apply when purchasing old children's books. Insect damage, water staining, and natural aging are three severe threats to old books. Always leaf entirely through an old book when considering to buy it, looking for in-complete pages, loose spines, soiling, drawing or scribbling on pictures, or missing pages. All of these defects can seriously devalue a book. If a dealer insists that you do not remove a plastic covering wrapped around an old book and will not let you inspect it even if they undo the wrapper, pass it by. Don't buy a book with the insides sight unseen.

One of the very positive aspects of book collecting is the relative inexpense of printed items. Most books, even those over a hundred years old, are relatively affordable. For the patient and resourceful collector who is willing to trudge through miles of flea markets, rummage and garage sales, they can be downright cheap.

This listing also includes items of paper ephemera such as ad cards, trade cards, store signs, posters, and holiday related paper memorabilia. As with all paper items, age and condition are the most important factors influencing the pricing of these items.

SHIRLEY TEMPLE IN THE LITTLE PRINCESS MOVIE BOOK C. 1939, Saalfield Publishing, Reynolds collection, $20.00-40.00.

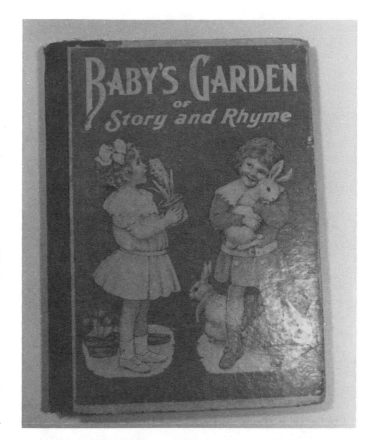

BABY'S GARDEN OF STORY AND RHYME, child's book, ca. 1917, $10.00-35.00.

A MICKEY MOUSE ALPHABET BOOK, 1930's, Whitman, hardcover $50.00-100.00
ABBOT AND COSTELLO IN JACK AND THE BEAN-STALK SHEET MUSIC, 1952 ....$10.00-30.00
ADVENTURES OF JACK AND BETTY, 1913 ....$10.00-20.00
AESOP'S FABLES, illustrated by Tenniel, 1848 ....$50.00-100.00
AESOP'S FABELS, Rackman, 1939 ....$20.00-40.00
ALADDIN, Cupples and Leon, 1915 ....$10.00-25.00
ALICE IN WONDERLAND PAINT BOOK, 1950, Disney. Whitman $10.00-15.00
ALICE IN WONDERLAND PAINT BOOK, Whitman, 1951 ....$5.00-10.00
ALICE IN WONDERLAND PUNCH-OUT BOOK, 1950's $20.00-45.00
ALICE IN WONDERLAND STATIONERY, 1950's Disney, boxed set $20.00-35.00
ALL THE FUNNY FOLKS, King Features, 1926 ....$50.00-80.00
ANDERSON'S FAIRY TALES $5.00-10.00
ANIMAL STORIES, Platt and Munk Publishers, 1942, Thornton, author $10.00-20.00
ANN SHERIDAN PAINT BOOK, large version $10.00-20.00
ANNETTE COLORING BOOK, 1950's Walt Disney Productions $10.00-20.00
ANOTHER MICKEY MOUSE COLORING BOOK, Mickey on Donkey, serenades Minnie, 1930's $50.00-120.00
APPLE PIE ABC BOOK, 1899 ....$10.00-25.00
AROUND THE ZOO, 1910 ....$10.00-22.00

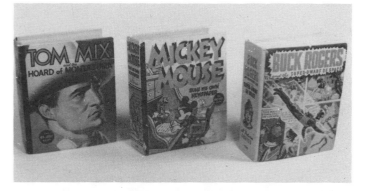

BIG LITTLE BOOKS, 1930's, Tom Mix, Mickey Mouse, Buck Rogers, by Whitman, $15.00-35.00 each.

AVA GARDNER CUT-OUT DOLLS, Whitman, 1949 ....$10.00-25.00
BABES IN TOYLAND PUNCHOUT BOOK, Disney, 1950's $10.00-35.00
BABY'S DOINGS, published by Saalfield, linen-like, 1904 ....$15.00-25.00
BAMBI BETTER LITTLE BOOK, c. Walt Disney Prod., 1940's $15.00-40.00
BAMBI CUT-OUT BOOK, 1940's, complete and uncut $50.00-125.00
BAMBI HANKY BOOK, 1940's $40.00-100.00
BAMBI PAINT BOOK, Walt Disney's "Bambi," 1940's, large format $20.00-50.00
BAMBI PICTURE BOOK, 1940's, paper cover $20.00-35.00
BAMBI STORYBOOK, Walt Disney, Grosset and Dunlap, 1947 ....$10.00-30.00
BAMBI'S CHILDREN, Better Little Books, 1940's $10.00-30.00
BARNEY GOOGLE BOOK, published by Saalfield, 1935 ....$35.00-75.00

BARNEY GOOGLE by Billy DeBeck, 1935, Saalfield, 4" x 6", Reynolds collection, $15.00-35.00.

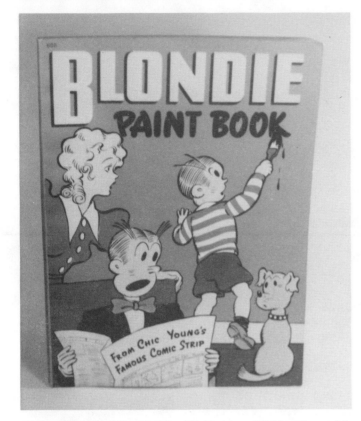

BLONDIE PAINT BOOK, Whitman, 1941, Reynolds collection, $15.00-30.00.

BARNEY GOOGLE FOX TROT SHEET MUSIC, 1923 ....$15.00-30.00

BEATLES', A HARD DAY'S NIGHT book, 1964 paperback $10.00-20.00

BEATLES', YELLOW SUBMARINE, paperback book, 1960's $5.00-10.00

BEDKNOBS AND BROOMSTICKS, Walt Disney, Little Golden Book $3.00-5.00

BEN AND ME, Walt Disney, Little Golden Book..$3.00-8.00

BETTE DAVIS PAPER DOLLS, Merrill, 1942...$20.00-40.00

BETTY BOOP AND BIMBO, BRIDGE SCORE PAD, 1930's $20.00-40.00

BETTY BOOP SHEET MUSIC, "Poor Cinderella," 1934...$35.00-70.00

BETTY GRABLE COLORING BOOK, dated 1951...$25.00-40.00

BIG ANIMALS, Saalfield, 1937 ....$10.00-20.00

BIG RED, Disney, Little Golden Book $2.00-5.00

BILLY WHISKER'S (GOAT), published by Saalfield, 1931...$10.00-20.00

BLONDIE CHARACTER, Die-Cut Valentine .$5.00-15.00

BLUE FAIRY FROM DISNEY'S PINOCCHIO VALENTINE, mechanical, 1939.....................$10.00-20.00

BOAT BUILDERS, Walt Disney, Grosset and Dunlap, 1938...$20.00-40.00

BOB HOPE COLORING BOOK, Saalfield, 1954...$15.00-30.00

BONGO THE BEAR, Disney storybook, 1940's, tall format..$10.00-20.00

BONZO PENCIL TABLET, "A Dog's Life," 1930's $25.00-60.00

BONZO POST CARD, British, 1930's $15.00-35.00

BONZO POST CARD, English, by Valentines, 1930's $15.00-25.00

BOY'S KING ARTHUR, Scribner, 1939 ...$20.00-35.00

BRER RABBIT RIDES THE FOX, Walt Disney, Grosset and Dunlap, 1947 ....$10.00-22.00

BRER RABBIT, WALT DISNEY'S BETTER LITTLE BOOK, 1950's $10.00-30.00

BRINGING UP FATHER BOOK, 1930's ...$30.00-50.00

BRINGING UP FATHER COLORING BOOK, Whitman, 1936...$20.00-35.00

BRINGING UP FATHER SONG FOLIO, 1924...$15.00-34.00

BRINGING UP FATHER, THE BIG BOOK, 1926, 10" x 10"...$25.00-55.00

BROWNIE CHARACTER DECAL BOOK, Vol. 1, 1896...$35.00-65.00

BROWNIE CHARACTER DECAL BOOK, Vol. 2, 1896...$35.00-65.00

BROWNIE'S ADVERTISING SIGN FOR SNAGPROOF BOOTS, 7" x 10"...............................$20.00-40.00

BUCK JONES IN ROCKY RHODES, hardcover book, 1935...$20.00-45.00

BUCK JONES AND THE NIGHT RIDERS, Big Big Book, 1937, colorful $25.00-50.00

BUCK JONES IN THE FIGHTING CODE, Big Little Book, 1934 ....$15.00-35.00

BUCK JONES RANGER CLUB, membership card..$8.00-15.00

BUGS BUNNY AND HIS PALS, Whitman Better Little Book, 1945 ....$15.00-30.00

BULLETMAN FLYING DETECTIVE, small booklet, Fawcett Publications, 1940's $15.00-30.00

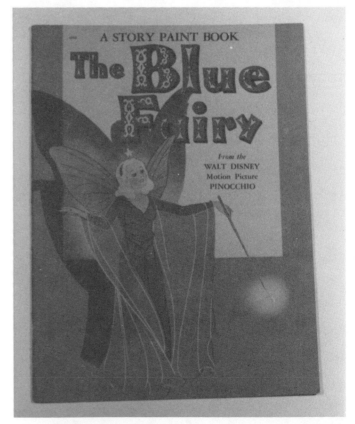

THE BLUE FAIRY STORY PAINT BOOK, 1939, from Walt Disney's Pinocchio, $15.00-30.00.

BUSTER BROWN POSTER, 1905...........$60.00-120.00
BUSTER BROWN AND MARY JANE'S PAINT BOOK, Outcault, 1907, 10" x 14" $100.00-200.00
BUSTER BROWN AND TIGE TRADE AD CARD, 1900.....................................$25.00-50.00
BUSTER BROWN CALENDAR, 1916 ....$20.00-45.00
BUSTER BROWN MARCH TWO STEP SHEET MUSIC, 1907..................................... $20.00-40.00
BUSTER BROWN POST CARD, 1905 .... $15.00-30.00
CAPTAIN KANGAROO SCHOOL TABLET, 1950's $5.00-10.00
CAPTAIN MARVEL, Small Booklet, Fawcett Publications, 1940's $15.00-30.00
CHARLIE CHAPLIN COLORING BOOK, 1917...$20.00-45.00
CHARLIE CHAPLIN IN EASY STREET, Storm-Greg., 1932...$20.00-45.00
CHARLIE CHAPLIN IN THE GREAT DICTATOR COLORING BOOK, Saalfield, 1941...........$25.00-55.00
CHARLIE CHAPLIN UP IN THE AIR, Book published by Donahue, 1917...........................$50.00-100.00
CHARLIE CHAPLIN WALK, sheet music, 1915...$40.00-80.00
CHARLIE MC CARTHY BOOK, A DAY WITH CHARLIE MC CARTHY, red cover $35.00-65.00
CHARLIE MC CARTHY GET WELL CARD, 1930's $10.00-25.00
CHARLIE MC CARTHY MAZUMA PLAY MONEY, original package $15.00-30.00

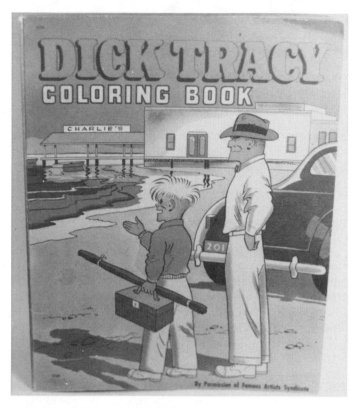

DICK TRACY COLORING BOOK, Saalfield, 1946, Reynolds collection, $10.00-20.00.

CHARLIE MC CARTHY MEETS SNOW WHITE, book, Whitman, 1930's.................................$20.00-45.00
CHARLIE MC CARTHY PAINT BOOK, 1930's $15.00-30.00
CHARLIE MC CARTHY PAINT BOOK, Whitman, 1938, 11" by 13" $35.00-60.00
CHARLIE MC CARTHY, SO HELP ME MR. BERGEN, book, 1930's $20.00-35.00
CHATTERBOX, 1916...............................$15.00-30.00
CHESTER GUMP FINDS HIDDEN TREASURE, Whitman, 1934 ....$20.00-40.00
CHILD'S GARDEN OF VERSES, Scribners, 1933...$30.00-45.00
CINDERELLA AND THE MAGIC WAND, New Better Little book, 1950 ....$5.00-15.00
CINDERELLA PAINT BOOK, 1950's, Whitman $10.00-20.00
CINDERELLA, Walt Disney's Better Little Book, tall version, 1950's $10.00-30.00
CINDERELLA, Whitman, picture book, 1950...$10.00-20.00
CISCO KID AND PANCHO COLORING BOOK, Saalfield Publishing Co. $10.00-20.00
CISCO KID BREAD LABELS from Tip Top Bread, set of three $3.00-8.00
CISCO KID COMIC ALBUM, 1953 ....$10.00-20.00
CLARABELLE THE COW, small Disney storybook, 1930's $10.00-25.00
CLAUDETTE COLBERT PAPER DOLL BOOK, Saalfield, 1943...$20.00-40.00
CLEO THE GOLDFISH FROM PINOCCHIO, mechanical valentine, 1939 ....$10.00-20.00
CLEO THE GOLDFISH PAPER MASK, 1939, Walt Disney, from Pinocchio.......................$10.00-20.00

BROWNIE BUNNY AND TEDDY BEAR BOOK, Whitman Publishing, 1916, $10.00-30.00.

COWBOYS AND INDIANS PUNCH-OUT BOOK by Gabriel, 1927 ....$50.00-85.00

DALE EVANS AND BUTTERMILK, Whitman book, 1956..$5.00-10.00

DAVID COPPERFIELD BIG LITTLE BOOK 1930's, Freddy Bartholomew on cover $15.00-35.00

DAVY CROCKETT COLORING BOOK, 1950's, Walt Disney Productions $10.00-20.00

DAVY CROCKETT'S KEELBOAT RACE, Little Golden Book, Walt Disney................................$3.00-6.00

DEBBIE REYNOLD'S COLORING BOOK, 1953... $15.00-30.00

DEBBIE REYNOLDS TWO PAPER DOLLS AND CLOTHES, Whitman, 1957 ....$15.00-30.00

DEBBIE REYNOLDS WITH MAGIC STAY ON CLOTHES, Whitman, 1958 ....$15.00-30.00

DICK TRACY AND THE INVISIBLE MAN PLAY SCRIPT, Quaker premium $15.00-30.00

DICK TRACY CHRISTMAS CARD, 1940's $5.00-10.00

DICK TRACY CRIME DETECTION FOLIO, 1940's $75.00-195.00

DICK TRACY PAINT BOOK, 1935, large size..$25.00-50.00

DICK TRACY POP-UP BOOK, *Capture of Boris Arson* $45.00-90.00

DICK TRACY, THE ADVENTURES OF DICK TRACY BIG BOOK, Whitman, 1934 ....$20.00-60.00

DISNEYLAND COLORING BOOK, Whitman, 1950's $10.00-20.00

DISNEYLAND, LET'S BUILD DISNEYLAND PUNCH-OUT BOOK, 1950's $10.00-30.00

DOC THE DWARF PAPER MASK, 1938, Walt Disney Enterprises $10.00-25.00

DONALD DUCK AND CLARA CLUCK CUT-OUT BOOK, 1930's, rare....................................$100.00-150.00

DONALD DUCK AND SANTA CLAUS, Walt Disney, Little Golden Book $3.00-6.00

DONALD DUCK AND THE CHRISTMAS CAROL, Little Golden Book $2.00-4.00

DONALD DUCK AND THE MOUSEKETEERS, Little Golden Book $2.00-4.00

DONALD DUCK ARMY PAINT BOOK, 1940's, large version $15.00-30.00

DONALD DUCK BIG LITTLE BOOK "DONALD DUCK SEES STARS," 1930's $20.00-35.00

DONALD DUCK BIG LITTLE BOOK, "HUNTING FOR TROUBLE," 1930's $20.00-35.00

DONALD DUCK BOOK, "Donald's Lucky Day," Whitman hardcover, 1940 ....$20.00-40.00

DONALD DUCK BREAD WRAPPER, 1950's, Purity Maid bread $10.00-30.00

DONALD DUCK CHARACTER VALENTINE, 1938, mechanical, Donald in sombrero $10.00-20.00

DONALD DUCK DRAW AND PAINT BOOK, Whitman, 1936, large format..............................$35.00-60.00

DONALD DUCK FORGETS TO DUCK, Better Little Books $15.00-35.00

DONALD DUCK GETS FED UP, Better Book, 1940..$10.00-25.00

DONALD DUCK HELP WANTED, Whitman picture book, 1950's $5.00-12.00

DONALD DUCK HUNTING FOR TROUBLE, Big Little

Book, 1938 ....$10.00-30.00

DONALD DUCK IN DISNEYLAND, Little Golden Book, 1950's $2.00-4.00

DONALD DUCK LOST DOG FOUND, Little Golden Book..$2.00-4.00

DONALD DUCK PRIZE DRIVER, Little Golden Book, Disney, 1950's $2.00-5.00

DONALD DUCK SEES SOUTH AMERICA, Disney, Heath Publishers, 1940's $8.00-22.00

DONALD DUCK STORYBOOK, 1930's, large format, Donald holds book on cover $30.00-75.00

DONALD DUCK SUNOCO INK BLOTTER, 1940's $10.00-20.00

DONALD DUCKS ADVENTURE, Little Golden Book, Disney $3.00-6.00

DONALD DUCK'S CHRISTMAS TREE, Little Golden Book..$3.00-6.00

DONALD DUCK'S SAFETY BOOK, Little Golden Book, 1950's $3.00-6.00

DONALD DUCK'S TOY SAILBOAT, Little Golden Book..$4.00-8.00

DONALD DUCK'S TOY TRAIN, Little Golden Book..$4.00-8.00

DONALD DUCK, THE LIFE OF DONALD DUCK, Walt Disney, 1930's $40.00-85.00

DOPEY, "HE DON'T TALK NONE," linen-like, 1930's, Walt Disney $20.00-50.00

WALT DISNEY'S DONALD DUCK, linen-like book, 1935, $75.00-150.00.

DOPEY CHARACTER PAPER MASK, Gillette premium, 1938...$10.00-25.00

DOPEY POST CARD, 1940's, W.D.P., "I'm Dopey"..$5.00-10.00

DORIS DAY COLORING BOOK, 1958.....$10.00-20.00

DOROTHY AND THE WIZARD OF OZ, L. Frank Baum, Reilly and Lee, 1908 ....$20.00-40.00

DR. KILDARE NOTEBOOK, 1962 ....$10.00-20.00

DRAGNET ADVENTURE BOOK, 1958.......$5.00-10.00

DRAW AND PAINT DONALD DUCK BOOK, c. Disney, Whitman, 1930's, large format...........$30.00-65.00

DUMBO BETTER LITTLE BOOK, Walt Disney Productions, 1940's $10.00-30.00

DUMBO, THE STORY OF THE FLYING ELEPHANT, 1940's, soft cover $20.00-35.00

ELIZABETH TAYLOR COLORING BOOK, Whitman, 1950...$15.00-30.00

ELIZABETH TAYLOR CUT-OUT DOLLS, Whitman, 1949...$20.00-40.00

ELLA CINDERS book, hardcover, by Whitman, 1934...$20.00-40.00

ELMER THE ELEPHANT, linen-like book, Walt Disney, 1930's $30.00-60.00

ELSIE THE COW FUNBOOK, 1950's $10.00-20.00

ESTHER WILLIAMS COLORING BOOK, 1950...$10.00-30.00

EVE ARDEN COLORING BOOK, dated 1953...$10.00-30.00

FAITHFUL FRIENDS SHAPE BOOK, 1915.$10.00-20.00

FANTASIA BOOK, "STORIES FROM FANTASIA," Walt Disney, 1940's $40.00-75.00

FANTASIA PAINT BOOK, 1941, large format, flowers and fairies on cover $100.00-150.00

FANTASIA PAINT BOOK, Walt Disney, 1940's $30.00-75.00

FANTASIA SOUVENIR PROGRAM, 1940's, colorful pastel color $15.00-35.00

FANTASIA, Walt Disney's Punch-out book, 1940, rare $100.00-225.00

FATHER TUCK'S COMIC NURSERY RHYMES, 1911...$10.00-20.00

FAVORITE FAIRY TALES, 1917 ....$5.00-15.00

FELIX ANNUAL BOOK, Comic Adventures of Felix, 1923...$50.00-110.00

FELIX THE CAT ENGLISH POST CARD, 1924...$20.00-35.00

FELIX THE CAT TRANSFER PICTURES ON CARD, 1930's $20.00-40.00

FERDINAND THE BULL CUT-OUT BOOK, 1930's, colorful, large format $50.00-100.00

FIGARO AND CLEO, Random House, Disney, 1940...$10.00-20.00

FIGARO THE CAT PAPER MASK, Gillete premium, 1938...$10.00-20.00

FIVE LITTLE PUSSY CATS, 1940 ....$5.00-15.00

FOREST FRIENDS FROM SNOW WHITE AND THE SEVEN DWARFS, 1930's, storybook..$25.00-50.00

FOXY GRANDPA BOOK, THE LATEST ADVENTURES, Donohue, 1905, ...$30.00-75.00

FREDDY BARTHOLMEW IN LITTLE LORD FAUNTLEROY, 1936, Saalfield $15.00-35.00

FROST KING, published by Whitman, 1939...$10.00-20.00

WALT DISNEY'S DANCE OF THE HOURS BOOK FROM FANTASIA, Harper and Brothers Publishers, 1941, $20.00-40.00.

FUNNY STORIES ABOUT DONALD AND MICKEY, Walt Disney, large paperback, 40's $10.00-22.00

GENE AUTRY, "LAW OF THE RANGE," Better Little Book, 1939 ....$10.00-20.00

GENE AUTRY "THE HAWK OF THE HILLS," Better Little Book, 1942..............................$10.00-30.00

GENE AUTRY AND THE LAND GRAB MYSTERY, Better Little Book, 1940's $10.00-20.00

GENE AUTRY AND THE MYSTERY OF PAINT ROCK CANYON, Better Little Book $10.00-20.00

GENE AUTRY AND THE RAIDERS OF THE RANGE, Better Little Book $10.00-20.00

GENE AUTRY BOOK "APACHE COUNTRY," 1952...$10.00-20.00

GENE AUTRY COLORING BOOK, 1950's, 8" x 11"...$10.00-25.00

GENE AUTRY COLORING BOOK, large format, 1949...$15.00-35.00

GENE AUTRY COMIC, by Dell, 1950's $5.00-12.00

GENE AUTRY COWBOY PAINT BOOK, Merrill Publishing, 1940 ....$35.00-65.00

GENE AUTRY IN PUBLIC COWBOY NUMBER ONE, Big Little Books, 1938 ....$12.00-25.00

GENE AUTRY SINGS, Song Folio, Western Music Publishing, 9" by 12" $10.00-20.00

GENE AUTRY WRITING TABLET, 1950's, unused $10.00-20.00

GEPETTO PAPER MASK, Gillette premium, 1939, Walt Disney $10.00-25.00

GLENDA OF OZ, 1920..........................$20.00-35.00

GLORIA JEAN PAPER DOLLS, Saalfield, 1940 ....$25.00-50.00

GOLDILOCKS POP-UP BOOK, Blue Ribbon Press, 1934 ....25.00-60.00

GONE WITH THE WIND PAINT BOOK, Merrill, 1940 ....$35.00-65.00

GONE WITH THE WIND PAPER DOLLS, Merrill, 1940 ....$75.00-150.00

GOOFY MOVIE STAR, Little Golden Books, Disney $2.00-5.00

GRACE KELLY COLORING BOOK, 1956 .$20.00-40.00

GREEN HORNET COLORING BOOK, 1960's $10.00-15.00

GRIMMS FAIRY TALES, 1914 ....$25.00-50.00

GUN JUSTICE, FEATURING KEN MAYNARD, Big Little Books, 1930's $12.00-25.00

GUNSMOKE, Television Book, 1966 ....$5.00-10.00

HANNA BARBERRA CHRISTMAS ALBUM, 1965 ....$3.00-5.00

HAROLD TEEN PAINT BOOK, 1932 ....$15.00-35.00

HIAWATHA, Disney, 1938, linen-like $10.00-35.00

HONEST JOHN AND GIDDY, Random House, Disney, 1940 ....$10.00-22.00

HOPALONG CASSIDY AD POSTER, framed, 1950's $20.00-45.00

HOPALONG CASSIDY AND LUCKY AT COPPER GULCH, animated book $20.00-45.00

HOPALONG CASSIDY AND THE STAMPEDE, 5" book, by Doubleday, 1950's $5.00-15.00

HOPALONG CASSIDY AND THE STOLEN TREASURE, 5" book by Doubleday, 1950 ....$5.00-15.00

HOPALONG CASSIDY ANNUAL, English .$15.00-40.00

HOPALONG CASSIDY BIRTHDAY CARD, "NOW YOU'RE 6," Buzza, 1950 ....$5.00-15.00

HOPALONG CASSIDY BIRTHDAY PARTY SET, paper, 1950's $30.00-60.00

HOPALONG CASSIDY CUT OUT COLORING BOOK, 1950 ....$10.00-25.00

HOPALONG CASSIDY COLORING OUTFIT, 1950, original box $50.00-75.00

HOPALONG CASSIDY COLORING BOOK, 1954 ....$20.00-45.00

HOPALONG CASSIDY FAN CLUB CARD, 1950'S, paper $5.00-10.00

HOPALONG CASSIDY GIFT ROUND UP, large ad poster, framed $10.00-25.00

HOPALONG CASSIDY ICE CREAM CONTAINER, paper, quart $10.00-20.00

HOPALONG CASSIDY PARTY INVITATION, 1950's, Buzza $6.00-12.00

HOPALONG CASSIDY PICTURE, glass, framed, Hoppy and Topper $35.00-50.00

HOPALONG CASSIDY QUICK MAGAZINE, (Hoppy on cover) May 1, 1950 ....$5.00-12.00

HOPALONG CASSIDY SCRAPBOOK, 1950's, simulated leather cover, 14" $40.00-65.00

HOPALONG CASSIDY SONG FOLIO, Consolidated Music Publishers $5.00-15.00

HOPALONG CASSIDY'S SUGAR CONES BOX, decorated, 1950's $10.00-25.00

HOWDY DOODY CHRISTMAS CARD, 1950's $5.00-10.00

HOWDY DOODY COLORING BOOK, Whitman, 1950's $5.00-15.00

HOWDY DOODY FOLLOW THE DOTS BOOK, 1950's, Whitman $5.00-15.00

HOWDY DOODY FUDGE BAR WRAPPER, 1950's $20.00-30.00

HOWDY DOODY FUN BOOK, Whitman, 1951 ....$10.00-20.00

HOWDY DOODY IN THE WILD WEST, Simon and Schuster, 1952 ....$10.00-20.00

HOWDY DOODY Mars Candy Premium Figure $10.00-20.00

HOWDY DOODY PUNCH-OUT PUPPET SHOW BOOK, Whitman, 1952 ....$20.00-40.00

HOWDY DOODY SURPRISE FOR HOWDY DOODY BOOK, Whitman Tell-a-Tale, 1950 ......$5.00-10.00

HUCKLEBERRY HOUND OFFICIAL CLUB PICTURE, 1960's $5.00-10.00

JACK AND THE BEANSTALK, 1911 ......$10.00-20.00

JACK WEBB'S SAFETY SQUAD COLORING BOOK, 1955 ....$10.00-20.00

JACKIE COOPER STAR OF SKIPPY, Big Little Book, 1933 ....$15.00-30.00

JACKIE GLEASON, coloring book, 1956 ....$5.00-15.00

JACKIE GLEASON FUNNY BOOK FOR BOYS AND GIRLS, Lowe, 1956 ....$10.00-20.00

JANE POWELL PAPER DOLLS BOOK, 1952 ....$15.00-30.00

JANE WITHERS BOOK, HER LIFE STORY, Whitman Publishing, 1936 ....$20.00-40.00

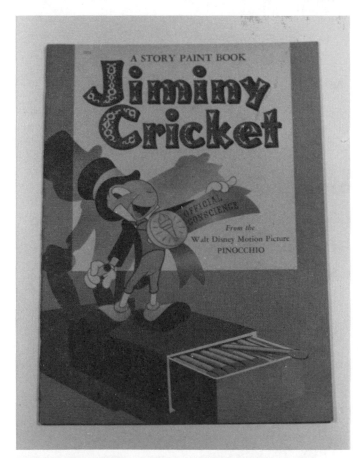

JIMINY CRICKET STORY PAINT BOOK, 1939, c. Walt Disney Productions, $15.00-30.00.

JANE WYMAN, pencil tablet $10.00-30.00

JIGGS AD CARD c. George McManus, 1930 .... $20.00-40.00

JIMINY CRICKET PAPER MASK, Walt Disney Productions, 1939 .... $10.00-25.00

JOAN CARROLL COLORING BOOK, Saalfield, 1942 .... $10.00-25.00

JOHNNY APPLESEED, Little Golden Book, Walt Disney $3.00-8.00

JUNE ALLYSON COLORING BOOK, 1952 . $20.00-35.00

JUNGLE BOOK, Kipling, Century, 1899.. $10.00-20.00

KATZENJAMMER KIDS STORYBOOK, Whitman, 1937 .... $20.00-55.00

KATZENJAMMER KIDS MAGIC DRAWING AND COLORING BOOK, 1930's $30.00-50.00

KELLOGG'S FUNNY JUNGLELAND, 1909 . $20.00-35.00

LANA TURNER PAINT BOOK, Whitman, 1947 .... $15.00-30.00

LAND OF OZ, 1939 .... $20.00-30.00

LASSIE COLORING BOOK SET, Whitman . $10.00-30.00

LEAVE IT TO BEAVER BOOK, Whitman, 1962 .... $5.00-10.00

LEAVE IT TO BEAVER, A COLORING BOOK, Saalfield, 1958 .... 10.00-20.00

LITTLE ENGINE THAT COULD, Platt and Munk, 1954 .... $3.00-7.00

LITTLE LULU AT THE SEASHORE, 1946.. $10.00-20.00

LITTLE LULU STORE DISPLAY FOR KLEENEX, 10" tall $20.00-45.00

LITTLE LULU VALENTINE, 1950's $10.00-25.00

LITTLE ORPHAN ANNIE, $1,000,000, Big Little Book, 1930's $15.00-30.00

LITTLE ORPHAN ANNIE AND CHIZZLER, Big Little Book, 1930's $15.00-30.00

LITTLE ORPHAN ANNIE AND DADDY WARBUCKS, Little Library, 1930's $10.00-20.00

LITTLE ORPHAN ANNIE AND HER DOG SANDY, Little Library, 1930's $10.00-20.00

LITTLE ORPHAN ANNIE AND JUMBO, Blue Ribbon Press Book, Pop-up, 1935 .... $125.00-220.00

LITTLE ORPHAN ANNIE AND THE GHOST GANG, Big Little Book, 1930's $15.00-30.00

LITTLE ORPHAN ANNIE AND THE GOONYVILLE MYSTERY, Better Little Book $12.00-25.00

LITTLE ORPHAN ANNIE AND THE HAUNTED HOUSE, book, Cupples and Leon, 1930's $20.00-45.00

LITTLE ORPHAN ANNIE AND THE MYSTERIOUS SPICEMAKER, Big Little Books $15.00-30.00

LITTLE ORPHAN ANNIE AND THE PINCH PENNYS, book, Little Library, 1930's $10.00-20.00

LITTLE ORPHAN ANNIE AND UNCLE DAN, Cupples and Leon book, 1930's $20.00-45.00

LITTLE ORPHAN ANNIE AT HAPPY HOME, book, Little Library, 1930's $10.00-20.00

LITTLE ORPHAN ANNIE BIG PAINT AND CRAYON BOOK, 1930's, Brunette Annie $20.00-40.00

LITTLE ORPHAN ANNIE BOOK, Cupples and Leon, early, 1925, Annie with doll $30.00-50.00

LITTLE ORPHAN ANNIE BUCKING THE WORLD, Cupples and Leon, 1929 .... $20.00-45.00

LITTLE ORPHAN ANNIE COLOR BOOK, 1930's, McLoughlin, Annie paints sign $20.00-45.00

LITTLE ORPHAN ANNIE CRAYON AND COLORING BOOK, McLoughlin, 1933 .... $30.00-60.00

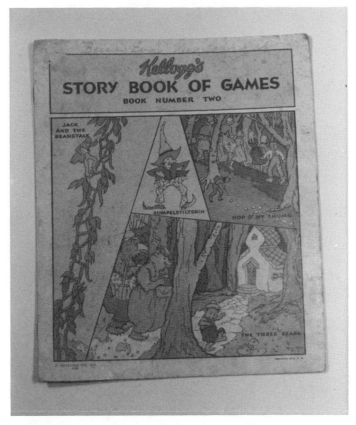

KELLOGGS STORY BOOK OF GAMES, ca. 1931, $10.00-35.00.

LITTLE ORPHAN ANNIE FINDS MICKEY, book, Little Library, 1930's $10.00-20.00

LITTLE ORPHAN ANNIE IN COSMIC CITY, Cupples and Leon, 1930's $20.00-45.00

LITTLE ORPHAN ANNIE IN THE CIRCUS, Cupples and Leon, 1930's $20.00-45.00

LITTLE ORPHAN ANNIE LITTLE LIBRARY, miniature books, set of six, boxed $65.00-125.00

LITTLE ORPHAN ANNIE NEVER SAY DIE, Cupples and Leon book, 1930's $20.00-45.00

LITTLE ORPHAN ANNIE PAPER COSTUME SET, television ad premium, 1940's $20.00-40.00

LITTLE ORPHAN ANNIE PAPER HINGEES SET, in envelope, 1944 .... $10.00-25.00

LITTLE ORPHAN ANNIE POP-UP BOOK, by Pleasure Books, 1935 .... $100.00-200.00

LITTLE ORPHAN ANNIE'S COLORING BOOK, 1943, Saalfield, 11" by 15" $30.00-60.00

LITTLE ORPHAN ANNIE, A WILLING HELPER, Cupples and Leon, 1932 .... $20.00-45.00

LITTLE ORPHAN ANNIE, THE STORY OF, Big Big Book, Whitman, 1934 .... $50.00-80.00

LITTLE PETS ABC, McLoughlin Brothers, 1906 .... $15.00-35.00

LITTLE PIG BIRTHDAY CARD, 1st Birthday, Disney, 1934, Hall Brothers $10.00-25.00

LITTLE PIGS PICNIC, Disney, 1930's-1940's, Heath $8.00-20.00

LITTLE RED RIDING HOOD AND THE BIG BAD WOLF, Disney, 1930's, paperback $20.00-45.00

LITTLE RED RIDING HOOD PENCIL BOX, Dixon, 1934, figural, die-cut $75.00-150.00

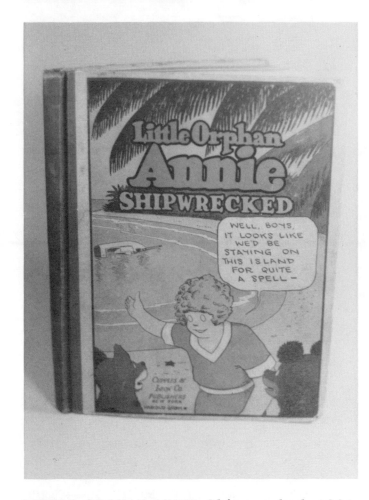

LITTLE ORPHAN ANNIE *Shipwrecked*, 1931,
Cupples and Leon, Reynolds collection, $20.00-45.00.

LITTLE RED RIDING HOOD POP-UP BOOK,
1934...$30.00-55.00
LITTLE WIDE AWAKE, Victorian vintage book,
1883,...$30.00-50.00
LITTLE WOMEN FEATURING KATHRYN HEPBURN,
Whitman Books, 1934.......................$20.00-40.00
LONE RANGER AND HIS HORSE SILVER, Big Little
Books, 1939...................................$12.00-25.00
LONE RANGER AND THE RENEGADES, Better Little
Books, 1939 ....$10.00-20.00
LONE RANGER AND THE SILVER BULLETS, Better
Little Books, 1946, ... $10.00-20.00
LONE RANGER AND THE TEXAS RENEGADES,
hardcover book, Grosset and Dunlap..$15.00-40.00
LONE RANGER BLOTTER, premium for Bond
Bread $10.00-20.00
LONE RANGER Collector's Album #1 .....$20.00-35.00
LONE RANGER FOLLOWS THROUGH, Better Little
Books, 1941....................................$10.00-20.00
LONE RANGER PAINT BOOK, Whitman,
1940...$20.00-45.00
LONE RANGER PAINT BOOK, Whitman,
1941...$10.00-25.00
LONE RANGER SCRAPBOOK, 1950's,
Whitman $25.00-45.00
LUCILLE BALL AND DESI ARNAZ COLORING BOOK,
1950's $15.00-30.00

LUCILLE BALL PAPER DOLLS, Saalfield,
1945...$20.00-40.00
LUDWIG VON DRAKE, Little Golden Books, Walt
Disney $2.00-6.00
MAD HATTER'S TEA PARTY, Walt Disney, Little Golden
Books, 1950's...................................$3.00-8.00
MAGIC DRAWING BOOK OF TRAINS AND SHIPS,
1916...$10.00-22.00
MARGARET O'BRIEN COLORING BOOK,
1943...$10.00-25.00
MARGARET O'BRIEN PAINT BOOK, Whitman,
1930's $15.00-35.00
MARY POPPINS PAPER DOLLS CUT-OUT BOOK,
1960's, Walt Disney $10.00-25.00
MARY POPPINS, WALT DISNEY'S COLORING BOOK,
1960's $5.00-10.00
MICKEY AND MINNIE MOUSE DOLL CUT-OUT BOOK,
Saalfield, 1933 ....$50.00-110.00
**MICKEY AND MINNIE MOUSE MECHANICAL VALEN-
TINE**, 1930's, W.D.Ent., ...$20.00-40.00
MICKEY AND THE BEANSTALK PAINT BOOK,
1948 ....$10.00-25.00
**MICKEY MOUSE "THE WEDDING PARTY" SHEET
MUSIC**, 1930's.................................$20.00-45.00
MICKEY MOUSE ABC BOOK, 1930's,
hardcover $45.00-75.00
MICKEY MOUSE ALPHABET ABC BOOK, hardcover,
Mickey with letter on cover, 1930's...$60.00-95.00

**MICKEY MOUSE CRUSOE BOOK, paperback,
Whitman, 1936, $35.00-60.00.**

MICKEY MOUSE AND BOBO THE ELEPHANT, Big Litte Book, 1935................................$10.00-30.00

MICKEY MOUSE AND DONALD DUCK GAG BOOK, paper, Whitman, 1938 ....$40.00-80.00

MICKEY MOUSE AND HIS HORSE TANGLEFOOT, McKay, 1936..$50.00-95.00

MICKEY MOUSE AND HIS SPACE SHIP, Little Golden Books, 1950's $2.00-6.00

MICKEY MOUSE AND PLUTO THE RACER, Big Little Book, 1936 ....$10.00-30.00

MICKEY MOUSE AND PLUTO THE RACER, Big Little Book, 1930's $15.00-30.00

MICKEY MOUSE AND THE BAT BANDIT, Big LIttle Book, 1935 ....$10.00-25.00

MICKEY MOUSE AND THE SACRED JEWEL, Big Little Book, 1936 ....$10.00-25.00

MICKEY MOUSE BEDTIME STORIES, Child's book, 1930's $35.00-60.00

MICKEY MOUSE BIRTHDAY CARD, 1930's, Hall Brothers, folds out to poster $40.00-75.00

MICKEY MOUSE BIRTHDAY CARD, 1935, Hall Brothers $15.00-35.00

MICKEY MOUSE BLOTTER, Sunoco, Premium, 1940's $10.00-20.00

MICKEY MOUSE BOOK #3, David McKay Publishers, 1933..$65.00-150.00

MICKEY MOUSE BOOK #4, David McKay Publishers, 1934..$50.00-125.00

MICKEY MOUSE BOOK FOR COLORING, 1930's, die-cut cover, Mickey ice-skating $25.00-50.00

MICKEY MOUSE BOOK, "WALT DISNEY'S WILD WEST," 1930's $75.00-125.00

MICKEY MOUSE BOXED STATIONERY SET, 1930's $45.00-60.00

MICKEY MOUSE CARDBOARD PLAYHOUSE, O. B. Andrews Company, 1934, paper envelope $100.00-250.00

MICKEY MOUSE CARDBOARD TOY CHEST, Odora Company, 1939 ....$50.00-125.00

MICKEY MOUSE MOUSE CHOCOLATE BAR AD CARD, 1930's, England $50.00-145.00

MICKEY MOUSE CLUB SCRAPBOOK, 1950's $10.00-20.00

MICKEY MOUSE COLORING BOOK, Saalfield, 1931, pictures Mickey with children $30.00-75.00

MICKEY MOUSE COOKIE PREMIUM HAT, 1930's, paper..$35.00-80.00

MICKEY MOUSE COOKIES BOX, 1930's rare if complete $100.00-200.00

MICKEY MOUSE COOKIES, National Biscuit Co., 1940's $10.00-30.00

MICKEY MOUSE CROWN PLAY TOGS AD CARD, 1930's $50.00-100.00

MICKEY MOUSE CUT-OUT DOLL BOOK, large version, 1930's $50.00-100.00

MICKEY MOUSE DRAWING TABLET, Walt Disney Ent., 1930's $20.00-40.00

MICKEY MOUSE FIRE BRIGADE, hardcover book with dust jacket, Disney, 1930's................$25.00-55.00

MICKEY MOUSE FOLD-OUT BIRTHDAY GREETING CARD, 1934, Hall Brothers $60.00-100.00

MICKEY MOUSE FOUNTAIN PEN AD CARD, 1930's, Inkograph Company $75.00-150.00

MICKEY MOUSE GOES CHRISTMAS SHOPPING, Little Golden Book..$4.00-8.00

MICKEY MOUSE GREETING CARD, EXTRY! EXTRY! by Hall Brothers, 1934 ....$20.00-40.00

MICKEY MOUSE HAPPY NEW YEAR CARD, Hall Brothers, 1930's $20.00-40.00

MICKEY MOUSE HAS A BUSY DAY, storybook, 1930's $20.00-40.00

MICKEY MOUSE HEALTH SHOES FOR BOYS AND GIRLS AD CARD, 1930's...................$35.00-70.00

MICKEY MOUSE HINGEES, 1940's, in envelope $10.00-20.00

MICKEY MOUSE IN BLAGGARD CASTLE, Big Little Book, 1934 ....$10.00-30.00

MICKEY MOUSE IN KING ARTHUR'S COURT, pop-up book, 1930's $100.00-200.00

MICKEY MOUSE IN NUMBERLAND, book, Whitman, 1938..$30.00-70.00

MICKEY MOUSE IN PIGMY LAND, paperback, 1930's, Disney $35.00-65.00

MICKEY MOUSE IN YE OLDEN DAYS, Pop-up Book 5", rare $75.00-150.00

MICKEY MOUSE LIBRARY AND TOY BOXED BOOK SET, 1930's, David McKay, rare,.. $125.00-275.00

MICKEY MOUSE MAGAZINE, Bryant and Chapman, 1930's $35.00-70.00

MICKEY MOUSE MOVIE STORIES, BOOK TWO, 1930's, hardcover, rare edition $100.00-200.00

POP-UP MICKEY MOUSE IN YE OLDEN DAYS BOOK, 5", 1930's, $75.00-150.00. CLARABELLE, THE COW, Whitman Storybook, 1930's, $10.00-25.00.

MICKEY MOUSE MOVIE STORIES, hardcover, 1930's, Mickey waving on front $50.00-125.00

MICKEY MOUSE NURSERY PICTURE, 1940's $10.00-20.00

MICKEY MOUSE PALETTE, premium giveaway, 1930's $25.00-50.00

MICKEY MOUSE PAPER MASK, 1930's, Einson-Freeman $25.00-55.00

MICKEY MOUSE PENCIL AND ERASER SET ON ORIGINAL CARD, 1930's $50.00-100.00

MICKEY MOUSE PENCIL BOX, figural cardboard, die-cut, Dixon, 1930's $70.00-145.00

MICKEY MOUSE PICTURE CARD ALBUM, 1930's, for bubble gum cards $25.00-65.00

MICKEY MOUSE POST CARD, English, "BIRTHDAY WISHES," 1930's $15.00-25.00

MICKEY MOUSE POST TOASTIES CEREAL BOX CUT-OUTS (each) $8.00-15.00

MICKEY MOUSE PRESENTS A WALT DISNEY SILLY SYMPHONY, 1934, Big Little Book ...$10.00-20.00

MICKEY MOUSE RUNS HIS OWN NEWSPAPER, Big Little Book, 1937 ....$15.00-40.00

MICKEY MOUSE SAILS FOR TREASURE ISLAND, Big Little Book, 1933 ....$10.00-30.00

MICKEY MOUSE SCHOOL TABLET, Powers Paper, 1930's $15.00-30.00

MICKEY MOUSE SCRAPBOOK, large, 1930's, Mickey and Minnie on cover $45.00-70.00

MICKEY MOUSE SERIES, NUMBER ONE, David McKay, 1931...............................$100.00-200.00

MICKEY MOUSE 7TH BIRTHDAY CARD, 1930's, W. D. Ent. $20.00-35.00

MICKEY MOUSE SHEET MUSIC "WHAT NO MICKEY MOUSE?", 1930's $20.00-45.00

MICKEY MOUSE SILLY SYMPHONIES BOOK, 1930's, "Babes in the Woods".....................$65.00-130.00

MICKEY MOUSE SOAP AD CARD, c. 1930's, Walt Disney $40.00-85.00

MICKEY MOUSE STANDOUT BOOK, Whitman, 1936...$35.00-70.00

MICKEY MOUSE SURPRISE STICKERS AND HEALTH CHART, 1930's $20.00-40.00

MICKEY MOUSE THE DETECTIVE, Big Little Book, 1934...$10.00-28.00

MICKEY MOUSE THE MAIL PILOT, Big Little Book, 1933...$20.00-40.00

MICKEY MOUSE TRANSFER-O'S ALBUM, Paas Dye Co., 1930's 20.00-35.00

MICKEY MOUSE VALENTINE "WHAT'S BETTER THAN A KISS?" Hall Brothers, 1935 ..$15.00-35.00

MICKEY MOUSE VALENTINE, "A Dear Little Boy," Hall Brothers, 1935...............................$15.00-35.00

MICKEY MOUSE WADDLE BOOK, 1930's, complete with waddle characters...................$150.00-375.00

MICKEY MOUSE WALT DISNEY ANNUAL, Whitman, 1937 ....$35.00-65.00

MICKEY MOUSE'S FRIENDS WAIT FOR THE COUNTY FAIR, 1930's, paperback $25.00-65.00

MICKEY MOUSE'S PICNIC, Little Golden Book, 1950's $5.00-9.00

MICKEY MOUSE, "THE WEDDING PARTY" 1930's sheet music, Robert Bagar $15.00-60.00

MICKEY MOUSE, THE POP-UP MICKEY MOUSE BOOK, Blue Ribbon Press, 1933 ....$100.00-225.00

MOON MULLINS CRAYON BOOK, Frank Willard, 1930's McLoughlin Brothers, Reynolds collection, $20.00-45.00.

MOTHER GOOSE IN MOTION PICTURES, Buzza, 1930's, $15.00-30.00.

MICKEY MOUSE, THE STORY OF MICKEY MOUSE, BIG, BIG BOOK, 1935 .... $50.00-85.00

MICKEY MOUSE, THE WALT DISNEY PAINT BOOK, 1930's, large $25.00-50.00

MICKEY ROONEY PAINT BOOK, 1940 .. $20.00-40.00

MICKEY SEES THE U.S.A., Heath, 1940's $10.00-20.00

MICKEY'S DOG PLUTO ALL PICTURE COMICS (tall book) 1940's $10.00-30.00

MIGHTY MOUSE COLORING BOOK, 1953 .... $10.00-20.00

MINNIE MOUSE "MERRY CHRISTMAS" CARD, Hall Brothers, 1935 .... $20.00-40.00

MINNIE MOUSE PENCIL BOX, Dixon, figural, die-cut, 1934 .... $50.00-125.00

MINNIE MOUSE, THE POP-UP MINNIE MOUSE BOOK, 1930's, Blue Ribbon Press $75.00-150.00

MONKEES BOOK, WHO'S GOT THE BUTTON, 1968 .... $5.00-8.00

MOON MULLIN'S DRAWING AND TRACING BOOK, McLoughlin Brothers, 1932 .... $20.00-40.00

MORRELL'S DISNEY CALENDAR, 12 beautiful pastel pictures, Disney, 1942, ... $100.00-250.00

MOTHER GOOSE POP-UP BOOK, Blue Ribbon Press, 1934 .... $35.00-75.00

MUNSTER'S PAPER DOLLS, Whitman, 1966 .... $5.00-15.00

MUTT AND JEFF, THE ADVENTURE OF, book by Cupples and Leon $20.00-35.00

MUTT SHELL GASOLINE STANDUP FIGURE, 23" tall, 1934 .... $45.00-75.00

MY ABC BOOK, cloth, Saalfield, 1909 .... $15.00-25.00

MY FAVORITE GAMES, Saalfield, 1921 . $15.00-25.00

NEW WIZARD OF OZ, Baum, Bobbs-Merrill, 1903 .... $30.00-60.00

NOAH'S ARK, Walt Disney version, 1950's, Little Golden Book 1906 .... $2.00-6.00

NURSERY PETS, published by Saalfield, 1906 .... $10.00-30.00

OLIVE OYL CEREAL BOX FACE MASK, 1950's $5.00-10.00

OLLIE BAKES A CAKE, Wonder Books, 1964 .... $5.00-10.00

ONE HUNDRED AND ONE DALMATIONS, Walt Disney, Little Golden Book .... , $3.00-5.00

ORPHAN ANNIE PAPER FACE MASK, premium of Ovaltine, 1930's $20.00-40.00

ORPHAN ANNIE SHEET MUSIC, "Little Orphan Annie," 1925 .... $20.00-65.00

ORPHAN ANNIE WEE LITTLE BOOKS, boxed set, Whitman $50.00-125.00

OUR GANG COLORING BOOK, published by Saalfield, 1938 .... $20.00-40.00

OUR GANG COLORING BOOK, Saalfield, 1938, color cover $25.00-45.00

OUR GANG INK BLOTTER, Majestic Radios, ca. 1930's $15.00-35.00

OUR GANG, A STORY OF, storybook by Whitman, 1929, hardcover $25.00-40.00

OZMAN OF OZ, J.R. Niel, illustrator, 1907, hardcover edition $15.00-22.00

PANCHO MASK (CISCO KID), paper, Tip Top Bread premium $10.00-15.00

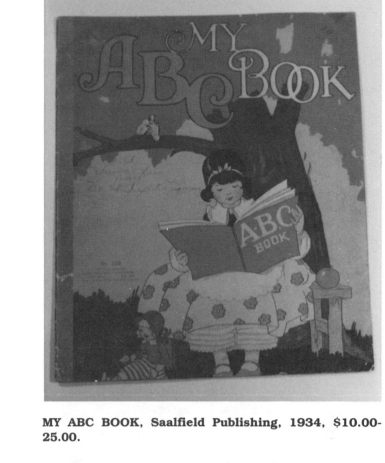

MY ABC BOOK, Saalfield Publishing, 1934, $10.00-25.00.

A STORY OF OUR GANG, Whitman, 1929, with movie still photos, Reynolds collection, $15.00-35.00.

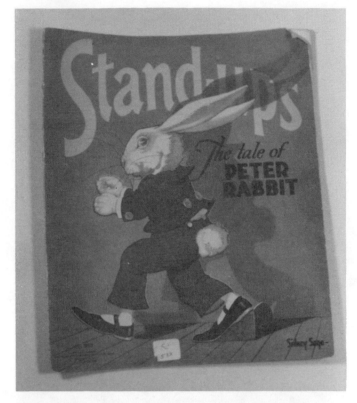

STAND-UPS, THE TALE OF PETER RABBIT, punch-out book, Saalfield, 1934, $20.00-65.00.

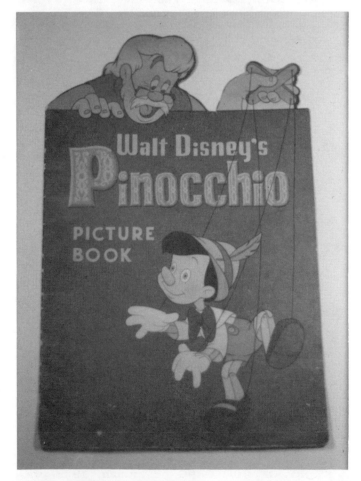

WALT DISNEY'S PINOCCHIO, picture book, 1939, die-cut top edge, $40.00-65.00.

PATRIOTIC PAINT BOOK, Goldsmith Publishing, 1919 ....$10.00-22.00

PECULIAR PENGUINS BOOK, David McKay Publisher, Walt Disney, 1935 ....$30.00-50.00

PERRI AND HER FRIENDS, Walt Disney, Little Golden Book..$1.00-4.00

PERRY WINKLE BOOKMARK, 1940's.......$5.00-15.00

PETER AND THE WOLF STATIONERY, Disney, 1940's, note paper for children $5.00-10.00

PETER AND THE WOLF, Little Golden Book, Walt Disney $5.00-10.00

PETER PAN AND WENDY, Little Golden Book, 1950's..$3.00-6.00

PETER PAN COLORING BOOK, Whitman, 1950's..$10.00-20.00

PETER PAN FUN BOOK, 1950's, Whitman, Walt Disney $10.00-20.00

PETER PAN PUNCH-OUT BOOK, 1950's, Walt Disney $20.00-40.00

PETER PAN, Grosset and Dunlap, 1942 ..$5.00-12.00

PETER PAN, Whitman novel, 1950's, Disney version $5.00-15.00

PIED PIPER OF HAMLIN, Kate Greenaway illustrations $35.00-70.00

PIED PIPER OF HAMLIN, Dunlap illustrations, 1910 ....$10.00-18.00

PINOCCHIO BETTER LITTLE BOOK, 1940, red cover, Whitman $15.00-40.00

PINOCCHIO BREAD WRAPPER, 1940's, complete $20.00-40.00

PINOCCHIO CAROUSEL VALENTINE, 1940, mechanical, extra large $15.00-30.00

PINOCCHIO CHARACTERS VALENTINE, coach and coachmen, 1940, very large $15.00-30.00

PINOCCHIO CIRCUS PUNCH-OUT SET, premium, 1940's, paper $40.00-85.00

PINOCCHIO CUT-OUT PAPER DOLLS BOOK, Whitman, 1939, large format.............................$25.00-60.00

PINOCCHIO FRAMED CHARACTER PRINTS, 11" x 14", 1939, set of four framed...............$100.00-250.00

PINOCCHIO GOOD TEETH CERTIFICATE, 1939, colorful $15.00-30.00

PINOCCHIO HARDCOVER BOOK, "PINOCCHIO," Walt Disney, 1940 ....$20.00-45.00

PINOCCHIO PAINT BOOK, Whitman, large version, 1939, paper cover $20.00-45.00

PINOCCHIO PAPER MASK, Gillete premium, 1939, Walt Disney $10.00-25.00

PINOCCHIO PICTURE BOOK, thick inside pages, 1939, Pinocchio with apple $25.00-45.00

PINOCCHIO POST TOASTIES PAPER CUT-OUT, from cereal boxes, each figure....................$5.00-10.00

PINOCCHIO SCHOOL TABLET, 1940, paper, Pinocchio with Stromboli on cover $15.00-35.00

PINOCCHIO SCHOOL TABLET, 1940, Pinocchio with Gepetto on cover $15.00-35.00

PINOCCHIO SCRAPBOOK, Whitman, 1939, exceptionally large $30.00-65.00

PINOCCHIO SERIES DECALOMANIA SET, 1940, eight figures $25.00-40.00

PINOCCHIO SHEET MUSIC, "Give a Little Whistle," 1940, Walt Disney $10.00-20.00

PINOCCHIO SHEET MUSIC, "When You Wish Upon a Star," 1940 ....$10.00-20.00

PINOCCHIO VALENTINE, Gepetto on raft, 1940, Disney $15.00-30.00

PINOCCHIO, Brundage illustrator, 1924..$15.00-25.00

PINOCCHIO, Walt Disney's cut-out book, complete $50.00-150.00

PINOCCHIO'S CHRISTMAS PARTY GIVEAWAY BOOK, toy store $10.00-25.00

PIPER LAURIE COLORING BOOK, 1953.$10.00-30.00

PLUTO COLORING BOOK, Whitman, 1960's $5.00-10.00

PLUTO SUNOCO INK BLOTTER, 1940's, paper $10.00-20.00

PLUTO THE PUP GOES TO SEA, Little Golden Book, Walt Disney $3.00-6.00

PLUTO THE PUP, Big Little Book, 1938.$10.00-25.00

POLLYANA paper doll book, 1960 ....$10.00-20.00

POPEYE BIG, BIG BOOK, Thimble Theatre, 1935 ....$45.00-95.00

POPEYE CARTOON BOOK, published by Saalfield, 1934 ....$40.00-80.00

POPEYE EGG TRANSFERS, 1936, in envelope $15.00-35.00

POPEYE ORBIT GUM FLIP BOOK PREMIUM, 1933 ....$20.00-45.00

POPEYE PAINT BOOK, McLoughlin Brothers, 1932 ....$25.00-55.00

POPEYE POP-UP BOOK, "In Among the White Savages," Blue Ribbon Press, 1934 .....$100.00-225.00

POPEYE SCRAPBOOK, 1929 ....$25.00-45.00

POPEYE SONG BOOK, Famous Music, 1936 ....$20.00-45.00

POPEYE THIMBLE THEATRE LUCKY BUCKS PLAY MONEY, 1930's $10.00-25.00

POPULAR COMICS BOXED SET OF CHRISTMAS CARDS, 1950's $35.00-65.00

RAGGEDY ANDY BOOKS, Gruelle, in gift box $15.00-30.00

RAGGEDY ANN AND ANDY WITH MOVABLE ILLUS-TRATIONS, 1940's $10.00-25.00

RAGGEDY ANN AND ANDY, NICE FAT POLICEMAN, Gruelle, 1942 ....$15.00-30.00

RED RYDER ACTING SHERIFF, Better Little Book, 1949 ....$10.00-20.00

RED RYDER AND CIRCUS LUCK, Better Little Book, 1940 ....$10.00-20.00

RED RIDER AND LITTLE BEAVER, Better Little Book, 1940's $10.00-20.00

RED RYDER AND THE SECRET CANYON, Better Little Book, 1940 ....$10.00-20.00

RED RYDER AND THE SECRET OF WOLF CANYON, hardcover, Whitman, 1941 ....$8.00-20.00

RED RYDER AND THE SQUAW TOOTH RUSTLERS, Better Little Book, 1940's $10.00-20.00

RED RYDER AND THE SQUAW TOOTH RUSTLERS, Big Little Book, 1946 ....$12.00-25.00

RED RYDER COMIC, Dell, 1950 ....$4.00-10.00

RED RYDER PLAYMATES CHILDREN'S GLOVES AD POSTER, 1949 ....$30.00-60.00

RED RYDER THE FIGHTING WESTERER, Better Little Book, 1940's $10.00-20.00

RED RYDER WAR ON THE RANGE, Better Little Book, 1940 ....$10.00-20.00

REG'LAR FELLERS BOOK, Cupples and Leon, 1928 ....$30.00-50.00

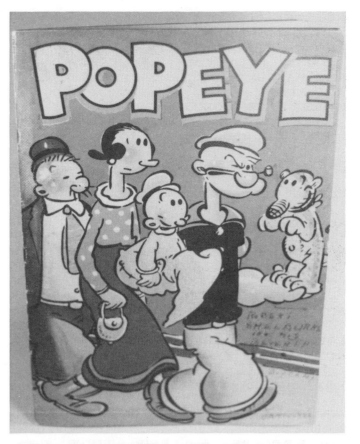

POPEYE, linen-like book, #892, King Features Syndicate, 1937, Reynolds collection, $20.00-50.00.

RAGGEDY ANN AND ANDY COLORING BOOK, #2498, Saalfield, c. 1944, $15.00-30.00.

BOOKS AND PAPER

REG'LAR FELLERS IN THE ARMY, hardcover, 1943 ....$25.00-50.00

RHONDA FLEMING PAPER DOLLS, Saalfield, 1954 ....$20.00-40.00

RITA HAYWORTH IN CARMEN, PAPER DOLLS, by Saalfield, 1948 ....$15.00-35.00

ROBBER KITTEN STORYBOOK, published by Whitman, 1938, Walt Disney $15.00-30.00

ROCK HUDSON CUT-OUTS, Whitman, 1957 ....$10.00-25.00

ROCKY THE FLYING SQUIRREL AND FRIENDS BOOK, 1960..$5.00-12.00

ROY ROGERS AND DALE EVANS COLORING BOOK, 1951 ....$15.00-25.00

ROY ROGERS AND DALE EVANS CUT-OUT PAPER DOLLS, Whitman, 1954 ....$25.00-50.00

ROY ROGERS AND DALE EVANS PAPER DOLL BOOK, Whitman, 1950's,.............................$15.00-35.00

ROY ROGERS AND TRIGGER POST CARD, from Roy and Dale fan club, 1955 ....$10.00-30.00

ROY ROGERS ARCADE PICTURE, card from arcade vendor, movie pose.............................$7.00-20.00

ROY ROGERS COLORING BOOK, 1951 .$15.00-25.00

ROY ROGERS MARCH OF COMICS, Sears ad premium...$15.00-30.00

ROY ROGERS PICTURE, autographed print, 1950's $10.00-25.00

ROY ROGERS RANCH CALENDAR, 1959, paper, color litho...$50.00-100.00

ROY ROGERS SOUVENIR BOOK, dated 1950 ....$20.00-40.00

SANTA'S TOY SHOP, Walt Disney, 1950's, Little Golden Book..$2.00-5.00

SAVAGE SAM, Little Golden Book, Disney ..$2.00-4.00

SCHOOL DAYS IN DISNEYVILLE, Heath, 1939..$12.00-25.00

SCRAPPY'S ANIMATED PUPPET THEATRE Pillsbury premium, 1936 ....$30.00-75.00

SEVEN DWARFS MECHANICAL VALENTINE, 1930's, Dwarfs look into cottage $15.00-30.00

RED RYDER HARDCOVER BOOKS WITH DUST JACK-
ETS: Red Ryder and the Adventure at Chimney
Rock, Whitman, $8.00-20.00, Red Ryder and the
Secret of the Lucky Mine, $8.00-10.00, Reynolds
collection.

SHIRLEY TEMPLE AT PLAY, Saalfield book, 1930's,
Reynolds collection, $20.00-35.00.

SEVEN DWARFS VALENTINE, Disney, 1940, mechanical, Dwarfs at foot of bed..................$10.00-30.00

SHADOW BOOKMARK, 1940's, 3" $5.00-15.00

SHAGGY DOG, THE, Walt Disney, Little Golden Book..$2.00-4.00

SHARI LEWIS AND HER PUPPETS COLORING BOOK by Saalfield, 1960's $5.00-10.00

SHIRLEY TEMPLE BOOK SET "FIVE BOOKS ABOUT ME," Saalfield, 1936 ....$100.00-200.00

SHIRLEY TEMPLE BOOK, HEIDI, Saalfield, 1937 ....$15.00-35.00

SHIRLEY TEMPLE BOOK, THE LITTLE COLONEL, original, dust jacket $20.00-45.00

SHIRLEY TEMPLE BOXED PAPER DOLL SET, 1930's $30.00-65.00

SHIRLEY TEMPLE BOXED STATIONERY, 1930's $30.00-65.00

SHIRLEY TEMPLE CHRISTMAS BOOK, Saalfield, 1937...$20.00-40.00

SHIRLEY TEMPLE CHRISTMAS CARD, Hallmark, 1935...$15.00-30.00

SHIRLEY TEMPLE COLORING BOOK, CROSSING THE COUNTRY..$15.00-25.00

SHIRLEY TEMPLE COLORING BOOK, Saalfield, 1936...$25.00-50.00

SHIRLEY TEMPLE COMPOSITION BOOK, 1930's $20.00-40.00

SHIRLEY TEMPLE DIMPLES BOOK, Saalfield, 1936...$20.00-30.00

SHIRLEY TEMPLE IN LITTLE MISS BROADWAY, Saalfield, 1938.....................................$20.00-45.00

SHIRLEY TEMPLE IN STOWAWAY, book, Saalfield, 1937...$20.00-40.00

SHIRLEY TEMPLE, NOW I AM EIGHT, book by Saalfield, 1937 ....$15.00-35.00

SHIRLEY TEMPLE ON THE MOVIE LOT, Saalfield, 1930's $20.00-40.00

SHIRLEY TEMPLE SCHOOL TABLET, 1930's $15.00-35.00

SHIRLEY TEMPLE SCRAPBOOK, 1935, Saalfield $40.00-85.00

SHIRLEY TEMPLE SONG ALBUM, 1930's $20.00-30.00

SHIRLEY TEMPLE STARRING ROLES, paperback book, Saalfield, 1930's $20.00-40.00

SHIRLEY TEMPLE, TWINKLETOES, book Saalfield, 1930's $20.00-40.00

SHIRLEY TEMPLE WRITING TABLET, 1935, Western Tablet $20.00-40.00

SHIRLEY TEMPLE'S FAVORITE POEMS BOOK, 1936 ....$15.00-30.00

SHIRLEY TEMPLE, THIS IS MY CRAYON BOOK, Saalfield, 1935 ....$20.00-40.00

SHOES AND SHIPS AND SEALING WAX, 1928 ....$10.00-20.00

SILLY SYMPHONIES POP-UP BOOK, Mickey Mouse, 1930's, rare $100.00-200.00

SILLY SYMPHONY BOOK TO COLOR, 1930's, paper book, large format, Disney $50.00-100.00

SILLY SYMPHONY PAPER FAN, Walt Disney, 1930's, three pigs, wolf, etc. $35.00-60.00

SILLY SYMPHONY PENCIL BOX, Joseph Dixon, 1930's $50.00-100.00

SKEEZIX STATIONERY boxed set of writing papers, 1926 ....$10.00-18.00

SKIPPY AND OTHER HUMOR, hardcover book, 1929, 64 pages, ...$35.00-60.00

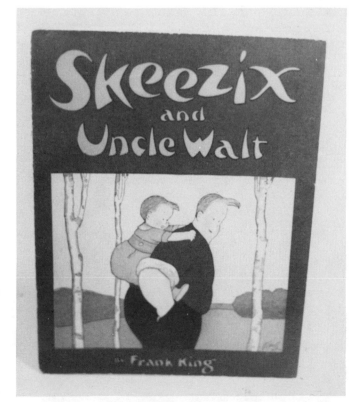

SKEEZIX AND UNCLE WALT, book by Frank King, c. 1924, paperback, Reynolds collection, $15.00-30.00.

SKIPPY RADIO CHARACTER SHEET MUSIC, 1930's $10.00-25.00

SKIPPY SHEET MUSIC, 1930's $10.00-25.00

SLEEPING BEAUTY AND THE GOOD FAIRIES, Little Golden Book, 1950's $2.00-7.00

SLEEPING BEAUTY PAPER DOLLS BOOK, Disney, Whitman, 1959 ....$10.00-25.00

SMILIN' JACK COLORING BOOK, by Saalfield, copyright 1946 ....$20.00-40.00

SMITTY BOOKMARK, 1940's, 3" $5.00-15.00

SMITTY CHARACTER STORYBOOK, Cupples and Leon, 1928 ....$15.00-30.00

SNOW WHITE JINGLE BOOK, 1930's, complete $30.00-60.00

SNOW WHITE AND THE PRINCE AT THE WISHING WELL, English post card, 1930's $10.00-30.00

SNOW WHITE AND THE PRINCE ON THE BALCONY, English post card, 1930's $15.00-35.00

SNOW WHITE AND THE SEVEN DWARFS, from the famous picture by Walt Disney, Grosset and Dunlap, 1938 ....$20.00-50.00

SNOW WHITE AND THE SEVEN DWARFS "ANIMALS" BOOK, 1930's, large format $20.00-40.00

SNOW WHITE AND THE SEVEN DWARFS ARMOUR PREMIUM STAMPS, Disney, 8, 1930's $20.00-65.00

SNOW WHITE AND THE SEVEN DWARFS BIG LITTLE BOOK, Whitman, 1938 ....$20.00-40.00

SNOW WHITE AND THE SEVEN DWARFS CUT-OUT BOOK, Whitman, 1938, rare $75.00-150.00

SNOW WHITE AND THE SEVEN DWARFS DRAWING TABLET, paper, 1937 ....$20.00-40.00

SNOW WHITE AND THE SEVEN DWARFS FRAMED PICTURE, 1930's, trough scene $30.00-65.00

SNOW WHITE AND THE SEVEN DWARFS LINEN-LIKE BOOK, yellow cover $20.00-45.00

SNOW WHITE AND THE SEVEN DWARFS MECHANICAL VALENTINE, 1939, heart-shaped $10.00-22.00

SNOW WHITE AND THE SEVEN DWARFS PAINT AND CRAYON SET, Whitman, 1938 ....$20.00-55.00

SNOW WHITE AND THE SEVEN DWARFS PAINT BOOK, 1938, giant format $30.00-70.00

SNOW WHITE AND THE SEVEN DWARFS PAPER DOLL SET, boxed version, 1938 ....$50.00-100.00

SNOW WHITE AND THE SEVEN DWARFS PAPER DOLLS, Whitman, book version, 1938 $30.00-75.00

SNOW WHITE AND THE SEVEN DWARFS POST TOASTIES CUT-OUT FIGURES, each .$5.00-10.00

SNOW WHITE AND THE SEVEN DWARFS SCRAPBOOK, large format, poster cover 1930's $50.00-125.00

SNOW WHITE AND THE SEVEN DWARFS SHEET MUSIC, "Heigh Ho," 1938, Disney $10.00-25.00

SNOW WHITE AND THE SEVEN DWARFS TREASURE CHEST, cardboard, 1939, Odora & Co. $50.00-125.00

SNOW WHITE AND THE SEVEN DWARFS VALENTINE, mechanical, dwarfs at door $10.00-25.00

SNOW WHITE FLOUR SACK, 1950's common $5.00-10.00

SNOW WHITE MECHANICAL VALENTINE, 1938, stands in front of cottage, large $15.00-30.00

SNOW WHITE AND THE SEVEN DWARFS PAINT BOOK, c. Walt Disney Ent., Whitman, 1938, $20.00-45.00.

SNOW WHITE PAPER MASK, by Gillette, premium, 1938 ....$10.00-25.00

SNOW WHITE VALENTINE, dancing with dwarfs, mechanical, 1938 ....$10.00-25.00

SNOW WHTE VALENTINE, mechanical, baking pies, 1938..$10.00-25.00

SONJA HENIE "ONE IN A MILLION," ink blotter...$10.00-20.00

SOUPY SALES BOOK by Wonder Books, 1965..$3.00-6.00

SPIN AND MARTY, Walt Disney, 1950's, Mickey Mouse Club $5.00-10.00

STEVE CANYON COLORING BOOK, 1952, large size...$10.00-20.00

STORY OF HAPPY HOOLIGAN, McLoughlin Brothers, 1932 ....$20.00-40.00

STORY OF PETER RABBIT, 1908 ....$20.00-40.00

SUCH A LIFE! DONALD DUCK, Better Little Book, 1939 ....$10.00-25.00

SUPERMAN BUBBLE GUM WRAPPER, 1930's, rare $75.00-195.00

SWISS FAMILY ROBINSON, Little Golden Book, Disney version $2.00-4.00

TERRY AND THE PIRATES BOOK by Random House, 1946..$20.00-40.00

TERRY AND THE PIRATES HINGEES SET, in original envelope $5.00-15.00

TERRY AND THE PIRATES POP-UP BOOK, Blue Ribbon Press, 1935 ....$100.00-200.00

THE ADVENTURES OF MICKEY MOUSE, BOOK NUMBER 2, 1930's $50.00-125.00

THE COUNTRY COUSIN, Walt Disney, hardcover, David McKay, 1938.......................................$20.00-40.00

THE GOLDEN TOUCH, MICKEY MOUSE PRESENTS, 1930's $35.00-65.00

THE GREMLINS FROM THE WALT DISNEY PRODUCTION, 1940's, Random House $20.00-35.00

THE HOUSE THAT JACK BUILT, McLoughlin Brothers, 1899 ....$30.00-55.00

THE MAN FROM U.N.C.L.E., soft cover book by Wonder Books, 1960's $3.00-7.00

THE SWORD IN THE STONE, Walt Disney, Little Golden Book, ...$1.00-3.00

THE TORTOISE AND THE HARE, hardcover, 1930's, Disney Studio Art $10.00-35.00

THE VICTORY MARCH, Disney, Random House storybook, 1942...$20.00-60.00

THE WISE LITTLE HEN, hardcover with dust jacket, 1930's, Disney $10.00-35.00

THE WONDERFUL TAR BABY, Walt Disney, hardcover, Grosset and Dunlap, 1947.................$10.00-25.00

THE THREE CABALLEROS, Walt Disney, hardcover, 1940's $20.00-60.00

THREE LITTLE KITTENS, Saalfield, 1940 .$5.00-10.00

THREE LITTLE PIGS PAPER COMPOSITION BOOK, 1930's, Walt Disney, Wolf cover $20.00-40.00

THREE LITTLE PIGS PAPER MASK, 1930's, single...$10.00-25.00

THREE LITTLE PIGS PENCIL TABLET, 1935, paper cover $20.00-35.00

THREE LITTLE PIGS SILLY SYMPHONY ILLUSTRATED BOOK, 1930's.....................................$40.00-80.00

THREE LITTLE PIGS SILLY SYMPHONY, 1930's, Walt Disney, hardcover with jacket $20.00-60.00

THREE LITTLE PIGS SILLY SYMPHONY CUT-OUT BOOK, 1935 ....$50.00-125.00

THREE ORPHAN KITTENS BOOK, David McKay, 1936...$15.00-35.00

THREE PIGS BIRTHDAY CARD, 6 YEARS, HALL BROTHERS, 1934 ....$10.00-20.00

THUMPER AND THE SEVEN DWARFS BIG LITTLE BOOK, 1940's $15.00-30.00

THUMPER STORYBOOK, Grosset and Dunlap, 1947, c. Walt Disney $10.00-30.00

THUMPER, WALT DISNEY'S, Grosset and Dunlap, 1942, with dust jacket.....................$15.00-30.00

TILLIE THE TOILER DRAWING BOOK, 1930's..$20.00-35.00

TIM McCOY AND THE SANDY GULCH STAMPEDE, Big Little Book, 1930's......................$12.00-25.00

TIM McCOY POLICE CAR ACTION STORY BOOK, Columbia Pictures, Whitman, 1930's .$20.00-40.00

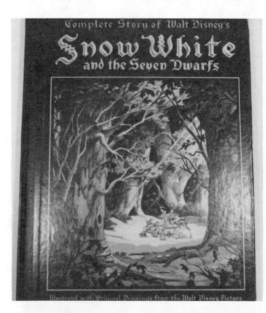

COMPLETE STORY OF WALT DISNEY'S SNOW WHITE AND THE SEVEN DWARFS, Grosset and Dunlap, 1937, $40.00-80.00.

TIM McCOY THE WESTERNER, Big Little Books, 1930's $12.00-25.00

TIN WOODSMAN OF OZ, Baum, Reilly and Lee, 1918..$20.00-40.00

TOBY TORTOISE AND THE HARE, storybook, Whitman, 1938..$10.00-30.00

TOBY TYLER, Walt Disney's, Little Golden Book..$3.00-6.00

TOM MIX AND THE HOARD OF MONTEZUMA, Big Little Book $12.00-25.00

TOM MIX COLORING BOOK FOR STRAIGHT SHOOTERS, 1950's $20.00-50.00

TOM MIX DRAW AND PAINT BOOK, Whitman, 1930's $25.00-40.00

TOM MIX RALSTON PREMIUM COMIC BOOK, NUMBER 2..$15.00-40.00

TOM MIX, "THE FABULOUS TOM MIX," book published by Prentice Hall, 1967 ....$10.00-25.00

TOM MIX, THE LIFE OF, Ralston Straight Shooter Premium Book $45.00-85.00

TORTOISE AND THE HARE BOOK, David McKay, 1936, Walt Disney..$20.00-40.00

TREASURE ISLAND, Walt Disney version, 1950's, Whitman novel..$5.00-10.00

UNCLE REMUS, STORIES, Big Golden Book, Simon and Schuster, 1947..$10.00-25.00

UNCLE WIGGILY'S WOODLAND GAMES, 1936..$10.00-20.00

WALT DISNEY'S BAMBI, Better Little Book, 1942..$10.00-35.00

WALT DISNEY'S BRER RABBIT, New Better Little Book, 1949 ....$5.00-15.00

WALT DISNEY'S CINDERELLA PAINT BOOK, Whitman, 1950..$10.00-22.00

WALT DISNEY'S DISNEYLAND ON THE AIR, Little Golden Book $3.00-8.00

WALT DISNEY'S DONALD DUCK GREAT KITE MAKER, 1949, Tiny Tales Book $5.00-15.00

WALT DISNEY'S DUMBO, Better Little Book, 1941..$10.00-30.00

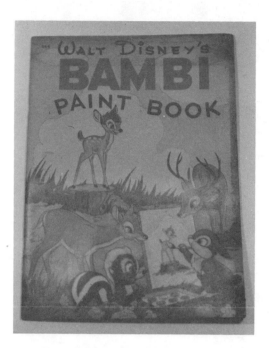

WALT DISNEY'S BAMBI PAINT BOOK, 1942, large size, $20.00-50.00.

THE ADVENTURES OF MICKEY MOUSE, BOOK 1, paperbound version, David McKay, 1931, $50.00-110.00.

WALT DISNEY'S FERDINAND, THE BULL, linen-like book, c. 1938, $20.00-40.00.

WALT DISNEY'S PINOCCHIO, illustrated storybook Whitman, 1939, $25.00-50.00.

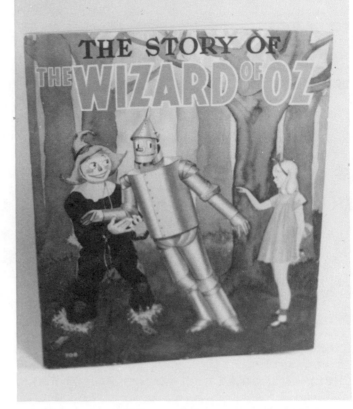

THE STORY OF THE WIZARD OF OZ, Whitman, 1939, Reynolds collection, $10.00-20.00.

WALT DISNEY'S DUMBO, Little Golden Book, first edition $10.00-20.00

WALT DISNEY'S FANTASIA, hardcover book, 1940's, Random House $20.00-50.00

WALT DISNEY'S GRANDPA BUNNY, Little Golden Book $2.00-5.00

WALT DISNEY'S JIMINY CRICKET FIRE FIGHTER, Little Golden Books $2.00-4.00

WALT DISNEY'S JIMINY CRICKET, Random House, 1940 ....$10.00-25.00

WALT DISNEY'S SILLY SYMPHONY, MICKEY'S MAGIC HAT, Whitman, 1937 ....$20.00-55.00

WALT DISNEY'S SILLY SYMPHONY STORIES, Big Little Book, 1936 ....$20.00-50.00

WALT DISNEY'S SURPRISE PACKAGE storybook, hardcover, 1940's $10.00-35.00

WALT DISNEY'S THE RELUCTANT DRAGON, 1940's, hardcover $10.00-30.00

WALT DISNEY'S, THE UGLY DUCKLING, hardcover $10.00-25.00

WATER BABIES, 1909 ....$35.00-60.00

WHO'S AFRAID OF THE BIG BAD WOLF? sheet music, 1930's, Walt Disney $10.00-25.00

WINKY DINK LITTLE GOLDEN BOOK, 1956 ....$10.00-15.00

WIZARD OF OZ, DOROTHY CHARACTER MASK, paper, Einson-Freeman, 1939 ....$15.00-30.00

WIZARD OF OZ SCARECROW MASK, paper, Einson-Freeman, 1939 ....$15.00-30.00

WIZARD OF OZ WIZARD'S MASK, paper, Einson-Freeman, 1939 ....$15.00-30.00

WIZARD OF OZ, THE STORY OF, Whitman, 1939 coloring book $15.00-35.00

WONDER BOOK FOR BOYS AND GIRLS, Nathaniel Hawthorne, 1887, cloth $30.00-65.00

WONDER WOMAN CHARACTER VALENTINE, 1940's $10.00-15.00

WYATT EARP COLORING BOOK, 1950's .$10.00-20.00

YELLOW KID AD CARD, postal card size, early $20.00-45.00

YELLOW KID COMPOSITION BOOK, c. 1896, Richard Outcault $75.00-120.00

YELLOW KID MOVIE FLIP BOOK, 1885 ....$10.00-175.00

ZAUBERLINDA, THE WISE WITCH, Smith, 1901 ....$10.00-30.00

ZORRO, by Whitman, 1958 ....$5.00-15.00

ZORRO, Walt Disney, Little Golden Book, 1950's $5.00-8.00

CARS AND TRUCKS

Transportation toys represent one of the largest areas of toy collecting today. The various types, sizes and periods of vehicle toys offer today's collector a great diversity of choices. Since Americans have long been known for their perpetual love affair with the automobile, it comes as no surprise that one of the wildly popular areas of toy collecting centers upon cars.

The listing in this section barely scratches the surface of the entire realm of toy automobile production over the past 80 years, but it is a representative sample of the various manufacturers, makes and periods of production of a host of vehicles. The production of toy cars is as broad and all-emcompassing of the 20th Century as is the manufacture of real autos. The craftsmanship which helped to produce many of the early 20th Century tinplate and clockwork type autos (Lehmann and Carette) makes one wonder whether the toys were produced with the child or the adult in mind.

While a collector holds an early Lehmann auto in his hand, he not only senses a unique link with his historical past, he also senses the beauty of the toy as art. The lithography, the attention to detail and scale, and certainly the action of the toy all contribute to the appeal that drives some early toy auto prices into the thousands of dollars range. (Enough to purchase a *real* car!)

One of the main appeals of toy vehicles to the collector is their unique diversity. Toys are available to collectors which trace the entire development of the automobile from its earliest days to the present. This allows advanced toy collectors to specialize in particular areas of interest such as Japanese windup autos, Japanese friction, friction in general, German windups or Marx autos to name only a few. The possibilities for specialization within the field of toy car collecting seems almost limitless. Nooks, niches and crannies of specialization are always there to be discovered.

Another appeal of toy automobile collecting seems paradoxical to the appeal of diversity just mentioned, for not only are the makes, models and shapes of toy autos seemingly astronomically diverse, but they also have a comfortable uniformity about them when displayed as an entire collection. To an unknowledgable visitor who walks into a toy car collector's den or in front of his showcase, a normal polite comment might be "Oh...you collect little cars! Lots of cars." And the outsider's observation might end with a comment about why there are so many. But, the collector knows the true signficance and importance of his own collection. Whether outside visitors recognize it or not, each individual toy auto collection is a miniature museum of antique and collectible automobiles, and the collector becomes the curator of the collection. The toy vehicle collection is a miniature museum of transportation, science, technology, craftsmanship and in many cases, design art.

Toy autos and trucks can be classified into many categories. The most obvious are form and function, such as cars and trucks. But each of the function classifications can be broken into specific subgroups in regard to basic mechanization, or simply - how they work: windup, lever action, friction, battery operated or momentum. Windup autos usually have an exterior key or button which allows the owner to wind tension upon the spring or drive mechanism. Friction autos utilize a simple law of physics which allows for the storage of inertia, or the delay of it. When a friction auto is rolled by hand on the floor (usually in the same direction it will travel when released), an internal flywheel is set into motion which continues to power the vehicle after it leaves the child's hand. Battery operated autos utilize electric motors. Finally, when autos are listed as "momentum" it is the fancy trade term for a car that won't roll unless the child gives it momentum, or simply pushes it along the ground or down a hill. In other words, momentum autos just "roll."

Major manufacturers of toy autos and trucks are Lehmann of Germany (tin windup early autos with drivers and superb lithography), Louis Marx (tin windups and momentum cars and trucks), Buddy L (large windups and momentum cars and trucks), Arcade (cast iron momentum vehicles), Hubley (cast iron and metal momentum cars and trucks) and a host of smaller U.S. and foreign manufacturers.

One of the most volatile areas of toy collecting today is in the realm of 1950's and 1960's tin scale model autos by foreign manufacturers. Japanese, U.S. Zone German and English tin cars are avidly sought by today's collectors, and these relatively "newer" collectibles are still out there at yard sales and flea markets to be found at reasonable prices.

As the "baby boomers," who played with these toy cars in the 1950's and 1960's when they were kids now scramble to find the ones they left behind, the demand for them is soaring. When many of these collectors return home to rummage through old toy boxes and closet shoe boxes looking for those great little metal cars, often they find that Mom threw them out or gave them away! If they want to fetch replacements for these great little cars, they know they must do it quickly. With the increasing popularity of such fine magazines as *Antique Toy World* which devotes much its space to toy cars, the popularity of collecting toy vehicles is certain to continue on the upswing.

CARS AND TRUCKS

ALPS PRESSMOBILE CAR, 6", tin windup, Japan $30.00-65.00

AMBULANCE CAR, Japan, Haji, 4" $20.00-40.00

AMBULANCE VAN #3043, BY Schuco, US Zone Germany, 4½" long...................................$30.00-55.00

AMBULANCE, Dinky Toys, Great Britain, 1930's, 4" $30.00-70.00

AMBULANCE, STURDITOY, 26", 1920's, painted steel..$200.00-375.00

AMBULANCE, Wyandotte, 1930's, steel, 11", wood tires $40.00-80.00

AMPHIBIAN AUTO, UHU, manufactured by Lehmann, 9½" tin lithograph, windup $700.00-1,000.00

ANDY GUMP IN HIS CAR, #348 Tootsietoy, 1930's, 3"...$65.00-125.00

ARCADE BUICK, 8" cast iron auto, c. late 1920's, metal wheels $500.00-800.00

ARCADE BUS, 8", cast iron.................$450.00-750.00

ARCADE BUS, Fageol, 13" cast iron ...$400.00-625.00

ARCADE BUS, 1930's, 8" long, cast iron $100.00-200.00

ARCADE BUS, double-decker, c. 1920's, 8" long $300.00-650.00

ARCADE cast iron ice truck $150.00-350.00

ARCADE cast iron intern'l truck $1,400.00-2,300.00

ARCADE CENTURY OF PROGRESS TRUCK, cast iron, 10", dated 1933...................................$35.00-80.00

ARCADE CHEVROLET CAB, 8" cast iron, 1920's, metal tires $500.00-750.00

ARCADE CHEVROLET, 1928, white tires, 8" long $80.00-200.00

ARCADE CHEVY COUPE, 1929, 8" long $400.00-750.00

ARCADE COUPE, (two-toned) 5", 1920's, metal wheels $75.00-145.00

ARCADE COUPE, 1928, 5" long, painted cast iron $100.00-165.00

ARCADE COUPE, 5" long, cast iron....$175.00-300.00

ARCADE COUPE, 6½" long, solid wheels, 1920's $100.00-180.00

ARCADE COUPE, 9", 1920's, cast iron ..$350.00-700.00

ARCADE COUPE, cast iron, solid wheels, (no spokes), 6¾" long, 1920's $100.00-200.00

ARCADE DUMP TRUCK, International Harvester, 10" $250.00-500.00

ARCADE DUMP TRUCK, International Harvester, 11" long $200.00-350.00

ARCADE DUMP TRUCK, cast iron, spoked wheels, 6", low bed truck $70.00-125.00

ARCADE FAGEOL BUS, 12" long $300.00-650.00

ARCADE FIRE TRUCK, 7½" long, cast iron $350.00-750.00

ARCADE FIRE TRUCK, cast iron, 15" long $100.00-300.00

ARCADE FORD SEDAN, 1920's, boxed..$900.00-1,700.00

ARCADE FORD WITH RUMBLE SEAT in back $30.00-65.00

ARCADE GASOLINE TRUCK, 13", cast iron, 1920's...$550.00-1,000.00

ARCADE GREYHOUND BUS, 1930's, 8" long, cast iron $75.00-225.00

ARCADE MACK WRECKER TRUCK, cast iron, 11" with white rubber tires, Furnish collection, $200.00-450.00.

ARCADE GREYHOUND PEOPLE MOVER, 1936 Great Lakes Exposition, cast iron...............$30.00-70.00

ARCADE HOOK AND LADDER FIRE TRUCK, 16", cast iron $200.00-500.00

ARCADE MACK DUMP TRUCK, cast iron, 13" long $400.00-700.00

ARCADE MACK GASOLINE TRUCK, 1920's, 13", cast iron $400.00-600.00

ARCADE MACK OIL TRUCK, 1920's, 10" long, cast iron $400.00-650.00

ARCADE Model A Coupe $500.00-800.00

ARCADE Model A Ford, cast iron, 1929, white rubber tires $200.00-400.00

ARCADE MODEL A WRECKER, 1920's, cast iron, winch works, 11" metal tires $350.00-500.00

ARCADE MODEL A, 8½" version $200.00-400.00

ARCADE MODEL T BANK, cast iron, 1920's $60.00-100.00

ARCADE MODEL T FORD COUPE, 1922, 6½" long, cast iron, spoked wheels $200.00-400.00

ARCADE MODEL T, 6", rubber tires $100.00-200.0

ARCADE SEDAN, 4¾" cast iron, metal wheels, 1930's $50.00-95.00

ARCADE SEDAN, 5", cast iron, 1920's ..$100.00-150.00

ARCADE SEDAN, late 1930's, 8" cast iron $100.00-200.00

ARCADE SEMI, cast iron truck, 1920's..$30.00-60.00

ARCADE STAKE TRUCK, cast iron, 7" long $75.00-180.00

ARCADE STAKEBODY TRUCK, 7½" long, 1920's, cast iron, metal wheels $100.00-250.00

ARCADE TOW TRUCK, 4", cast iron $40.00-80.00

ARCADE TRUCK, Chevrolet, ca. 1920's, 9" long $300.00-850.00

ARMY TOW TRUCK B-LINE, BUDDY L. 1950's, plastic mint in box with winch $10.00-20.00

ARMY TRUCK AND TRANSPORT, by Buddy L. 1940's, steel $75.00-155.00

ARMY TRUCK, Marx, 1950's, 14", tin with plastic cover $30.00-50.00

ASSORTED CAR SET, by Matushita, Japan, tin friction, twelve car set............................$35.00-60.00

ASTIN MARTIN, CORGI, 5", long $20.00-30.00
AUBURN RUBBER AIRPORT LIMOUSINE, rubber, 8" long $10.00-20.00
AUBURN RUBBER FIRE ENGINE, red, 8" long, rubber tires $10.00-20.00
AUBURN RUBBER FORD, 1930's $5.00-15.00
AUBURN RACER, rubber $15.00-30.00
AUBURN RUBBER RACE CAR, 10" long with goggled driver..$10.00-20.00
AUBURN RUBBER RACE CAR, 1930's, 6"..$10.00-20.00
AUSTIN CAST IRON WRECKER, 4", ca. 1920's, chain and hook $40.00-70.00
AUSTIN STAKEBODY CAST IRON FLATBED TRUCK, 4", 1920's, metal wheels $40.00-70.00
AUTO BY KENTON, 6", cast iron $70.00-135.00
AUTO CARRIER TRUCK, metal, boxed, 1950's with two Ford Fairlanes, 18"..................$200.00-350.00
AUTO CYCLE MOTORCYCLE, Harley Davidson, tin, friction, Japan, 9", 1958 ....$150.00-275.00
AUTO CYCLE, tin lithograph, friction motorcycle, 9" long $200.00-595.00
AUTO TRANSPORT TRUCK, Marx, 1940, pressed steel, 14" with two plastic cars..................$65.00-95.00
AUTO, ATC, Japan, 12½", 1960 ....$125.00-200.00
AUTOBUS, Lehmann, #590, German, 8", lithographed tin $750.00-1,000.00
BANDAI MG MIDGET in original box .$200.00-350.00
BANDAI MUSTANG FBI COMMANDER, tin friction, Japan, 11" long $40.00-75.00
BANDAI OF JAPAN VOLKSWAGEN BEETLE, 14", large version, battery operated $60.00-125.00
BANK OF AMERICA TRUCK, by Smith Miller, steel, 14"..$90.00-150.00
BARCLAY ARMORED CAR, 1937 ....$5.00-15.00
BARCLAY BEER TRUCK, 4", slush metal..$5.00-15.00
BARCLAY CAR CARRIER with two cars..$20.00-35.00
BARCLAY COUPE, 1930's $10.00-18.00
BARCLAY COUPE, 3" long, 1930's $8.00-15.00
BARCLAY DOUBLE-DECKER BUS, 4".....$10.00-20.00
BARCLAY MACK PICKUP TRUCK, 3½" ..$10.00-20.00
BARCLAY MILK TRUCK with milk cans, #377...$10.00-20.00
BARCLAY OPEN TRUCK, 3½" $5.00-10.00
BARCLAY RACE CAR, white tires, 4".....$12.00-20.00
BARCLAY STAKE TRUCK, slush metal, 5".$10.00-15.00
BATMOBILE, plastic, 1972 copyright, battery operated, 12", blue $45.00-95.00
BELL TELEPHONE TRUCK by Hubley 5½"..$200.00-400.00
BENTLY SPORTS COUPE, Dinky Toy, two seater, 1930's, 3½"..$35.00-70.00
BING FORD MODEL T, German, 4" ...$200.00-400.00
BING GARAGE WITH BLUE LIMOUSINE AND RED CAR, original box $400.00-650.00
BING MODEL T auto $400.00-600.00
BING MODEL T SEDAN, tin windup, 6½" long $250.00-400.00
BING OPEN DOOR SEDAN, 1930, tin windup, 6". black and blue, doors open $250.00-450.00
BING OPEN TOURER AUTO, 1928, tin, clockwork windup, 8½" $300.00-600.00
BING TIN LITHOGRAPHED BUS, 10" long $1,400.00-1,800.00

BING MODEL T tin $500.00-850.00
BING TOURING CAR, two seater, 12" long $750.00-950.00
BLUE RIBBON BUS, TN, Japan, tin, friction, BO, headlights, 10" $100.00-200.00
BOATTAIL RACER, #3, Marx, 1930's, 5" tin windup racer $30.00-60.00
BOATTAIL RACER, cast iron, probably Arcade, 5", nickel plated wheels $65.00-110.00
BRITAINS, BLUEBIRD DIE-CAST, with original box, 1930's $300.00-600.00
BUDDY L ARMY TRUCK AND TRANSPORT, 1940's, steel $75.00-155.00
BUDDY L BUS, 1930's $500.00-1,000.00

AUBURN RUBBER RACER, 6" long, rubber wheels, red, Reynolds collection, $15.00-30.00.

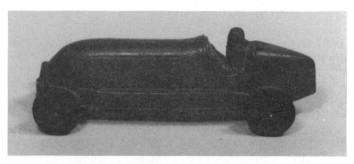

CAST IRON AND PRESSED METAL AUTO WITH DRIVER, 15", Furnish collection, $150.00-350.00.

EARLY AUTOMOBILE, sheet metal body, cast iron frame, painted cast iron tires, 15", Furnish collection, $100.00-300.00.

CARS AND TRUCKS

BEAR CAT RACER #8, tin windup, 7" long $50.00-135.00, STREAMLINED RACER by Billen Toy, #12 U.S. Zone Germany, 6", $40.00-80.00, Furnish collection.

BUDDY L coal truck, 1920's pressed steel $150.00-300.00

BUDDY L CURTISS CANDY TRUCK ad art $100.00-145.00

BUDDY L DUMP TRUCK, 1931 flat-bed type, 24", Firestone tires $450.00-700.00

BUDDY L FIRE TRUCK WITH LADDER, ca. 1930's $500.00-700.00

BUDDY L FLIVVER pickup truck $400.00-800.00

BUDDY L FORD DUMP TRUCK, 1920's, steel, enamel paint $300.00-500.00

BUDDY L FORD TRUCK, 12", 1920's .$200.00-400.00

BUDDY L FORD TRUCK, OPEN BED, pressed steel $150.00-300.00

BUDDY L ICE CREAM TRUCK, 1950's, 22" long $150.00-275.00

BUDDY L ICE TRUCK, 1920's, pressed steel $250.00-400.00

BUDDY L LADDER TRUCK $900.00-1,800.00

BUDDY L PUMPER FIRE TRUCK, 1920's, pressed steel $150.00-300.00

BUDDY L SAND AND GRAVEL TRUCK, 1940's, 14" pressed steel $35.00-60.00

BUDDY L SAND AND GRAVEL TRUCK, 1940's, pressed steel, 13", lever action $50.00-100.00

BUDDY L silver coupe $200.00-500.00

BUDDY L STAKE TRUCK, 1920's $200.00-400.00

BUDDY L STATION WAGON WITH TEEPEE CAMPER, 14" wagon, 10" camper $100.00-200.00

BUDDY L water tank sprinker truck ..$500.00-1,000.00

BUDDY L WOODEN MOVING VAN, 1940's, 26" long $150.00-225.00

BUICK CONVERTIBLE by Hubley, 6½" .$70.00-125.00

BUICK, ALUMINUM MODEL TOY, 1954, friction 8" $45.00-75.00

BUMP AND GO CAR, late 1950's, tin and metal construction, foreign $100-00-200.00

BUS, ARCADE, 8", cast iron $450.00-750.00

BUS, cast iron, Arcade, Fageol, 13" $400.00-625.00

BUS, CONTINENTAL TRAILWAYS, HS, Japan, 1950's, tin, friction, 10" $25.00-50.00

BUS, DOUBLE DECKER, by Kenton, ca. 1920's, 7" long $250.00-450.00

BUS, INTER-STATE, by Ferdinand Strauss, 1928, 10" windup, tin $200.00-400.00

CABLE REPAIR TRUCK, SY, Japan, all tin, friction, 12" marked, "BELL" $65.00-120.00

CADILLAC ELDORADO, by Dinky Toys, England, 4½", 1950's $20.00-45.00

CADILLAC POLICE CAR, Japan, 1950's, tin friction, 5" long $25.00-40.00

CADILLAC SEDAN, Bandai, Japan, tin, friction, 10" long $40.00-70.00

CADILLAC STATION WAGON, Woody, 1940's, 21", tin, by Wyandotte $60.00-125.00

CADILLAC, 1961, Japan, Y, 9", tin, friction $50.00-125.00

CADILLAC, 1962, Japan, 9", tin, friction $40.00-80.00

CADILLAC, Antique model, SSS Japan, tin friction, 6" $20.00-35.00

CADILLAC, GOLD MARUSAN $1,200.00-2,000.00

CADILLAC, Kingsize 13", BO $175.00-400.00

CADILLAC, TIN, TN COMPANY, Japan, 7", friction, green version, mint/boxed $35.00-70.00

CADILLAC, TIN, TN COMPANY, Japan, 7", friction, red version, mint/boxed $35.00-70.00

CADILLAC, TN, Japan, 1953, 13", tin, friction $200.00-350.00

CADILLAC, TN, Japan, 7", tin, friction, red with chrome trim $30.00-65.00

CAR AND TRAILER SET, Japan, 1950's, tin, friction, blue/silver, 16" $75.00-175.00

CAR AND TRAILER TIN FRICTION SET, 1950's, Japan, 8" long, both boxed $10.00-20.00

CAR AND TRAILER, Japan, 13" tin friction, Oldsmobile, 1950's $65.00-135.00

CAR AND TRAILER, Japan, tin, friction, 16" red car pulls silver trailer $65.00-100.00

CAR CARRIER WITH FOUR CARS, cast iron, by Hubley, 10" long $300.00-575.00

CAR CARRIER with two cars, Barclay ...$20.00-35.00

CAR SET (ASSORTED) MATUSHITA, Japan, tin, friction, twelve cars $35.00-60.00

CARETTE LIMOUSINE, 1911, 15" ..$5,000.00-7,000.00

CARETTE TOURING CAR, Germany (Nuremberg) 1915, 15", spring driven $1,500.00-2,700.00

CARGO HAULER TRUCK WITH TRAILER, Japan, 1950's, 9" $15.00-20.00

CAST IRON DOUBLE DECKER SIGHTSEEING BUS, with cast-in riders, 9", Furnish collection, $250.00-450.00.

CEMENT MIXER by Buddy L $200.00-500.00

CEMENT TRUCK BY STRUCTO, all metal, 22" long $200.00-400.00

CHAD VALLEY DELIVERY TRUCK, 1940's, carries lithograph games on top, 9¾" $100.00-250.00

CHAD VALLEY ENGLISH POLICE CAR, tin windup, 7" $150.00-295.00

CHAD VALLEY TIN TAXI, 9" $100.00-140.00

CHAMPION #27 RACING CYCLE, Japan, 10" long $50.00-95.00

CHAMPION #58 RACER, by Bentley, 6" tin, Indy style racer..$60.00-100.00

CHAMPION MACK DUMP TRUCK, 1930's, 7"..$100.00-150.00

CHAMPION MOTORCYCLE WITH RIDER, 4½", cast iron, police figure $50.00-75.00

CHAMPION WRECKER, cast iron, 7"......$30.00-65.00

CHEIN GREYHOUND BUS, tin windup, 6", wood tires $50.00-95.00

CHEIN JUNIOR BUS, 1920'S, 9" $40.00-95.00

CHEIN MACK "HERCULES" TRUCK, tin, 7½" long $100.00-175.00

CHEIN MACK TRUCK, tin lithograph, Motor Express, 20" long $75.00-125.00

CHEIN ROADSTER, 1920's, 8½", tin.......$40.00-80.00

CHEIN WOODY CAR, 1940's, 5", red, tin, windup $20.00-45.00

CHEIN YELLOW CAB, 7" $100.00-200.00

CHEIN YELLOW TAXI, early tin windup, 6", orange/black $25.00-50.00

CHEVROLET PICKUP, tin, friction, Japan, 8", 1960's $30.00-45.00

CHEVROLET TRUCK, Japan, 1950's, 7" long, friction, pickup $30.00-45.00

CHEVROLET, tin, friction, Occupied Japan...$50.00-80.00

CHEVY PICKUP TRUCK, Indian Head trademark, Japan, 8" friction...$20.00-50.00

CHITTY CHITTY BANG BANG MOVIE CAR, by Corgi, mint in box, 1960's.........................$60.00-100.00

CHRYSLER AIRFLOW SALOON by Dinky Toys, 1930's, 4" long $40.00-80.00

CHRYSLER AIRFLOW, cast iron car, 4½" 1930's $50.00-95.00

CHRYSLER RACING CAR by Hubley, ca. 1930's $35.00-70.00

CLARK, D. P. TOURING CAR, 10½", early friction car, 1906..$150.00-300.00

COCA COLA ROUTE TRUCK, S, Japan, 1950's BO, tin, 12" long $100.00-200.00

COCA COLA TRUCK, Marx, 1940's, tin, 18" $60.00-90.00

COCA COLA TRUCK, Marx, 1950's, metal..$125.00-200.00

COCA COLA TRUCK, sheet steel, 1920's with large bottles $200.00-450.00

COFFEE DUMP TRUCK, 11" long, tin, 1930's $40.00-80.00

COMMANDER CAR, West German, 1955, tin, friction, 16", lithograph $75.00-150.00

CONSTRUCTOR CAR BY MECCANO, car #1, with original box.................................$700.00-1,100.00

CONTINENTAL TRAILWAYS BUS, HS, Japan, 1950's, all tin friction, 10" $25.00-50.00

RED CONVERTIBLE, 1950's, 7" long, plastic windshield, Furnish collection, $40.00-100.00.

CONVERTIBLE SPORTS CAR, Distler, US Zone Germany, 10", tin windup $150.00-300.00

CONVERTIBLE WOODIE CAR, by Wyandotte, 1940's, metal, 12" long $70.00-150.00

CONVERTIBLE, electric, by Marx, 20" ...$70.00-125.00

CONVERTIBLE, tinplate, K, Japan, 4" $20.00-40.00

COR-COR, SEDAN, 20", Sheet Steel, Cor-Cor Toys, Washington, Indiana $200.00-300.00

CORGI CHIPPERFIELD CIRCUS giraffe transport $50.00-85.00

COUPE WITH RUMBLE SEAT OPEN, cast iron, 6", 1920's...$150.00-300.00

COUPE, GIRARD, USA 1935, pressed steel, orange windup car, 15" long $200.00-375.00

COUPE, Nickel Toy, pre-war Germany, tin 6", green..$50.00-75.00

COURTLAND FIRE CHIEF CAR with siren, tin windup, 7", original box $45.00-90.00

CRAGSTAN FRICTION DREAM CAR, boxed..$100.00-175.00

CRAGSTAN ICE CREAM TRUCK, tin..$150.00-250.00

CRASH CAR, Hubley, 1930's, cast iron 5", motorcycle with cart on back $40.00-95.00

DAYTON COUPE, pressed steel 1920's, 12" $50.00-100.00

DAYTON FIRE TRUCK including ladders, ca. 1915, 18" long $200.00-500.00

DESOTO SPORTSMAN, 1958 hard plastic dealer promotion $45.00-70.00

DELIVERY TRUCK, Nickel toy, 5", German, tin pre-war.......................................$40.00-65.00

DELUXE DELIVERY VAN, metal, 1940's, 11½" $35.00-60.00

SWISS CONVERTIBLE, 5½" metal windup with rubber tires, Furnish collection, $35.00-75.00.

CARS AND TRUCKS

DENT CAST IRON TANKER TRUCK, 10" white rubber tires $800.00-1,400.00

DENT FIRE TRUCK, 8" long, cast iron ..$50.00-85.00

DENT ICE CREAM TRUCK, 1930's, 8", cast iron truck $200.00-400.00

DENT MODEL T, ca. 1920's, cast iron.$70.00-150.00

DENT PATROL TRUCK, 1920's, 6½" long with driver $300.00-450.00

DENT SEDAN, 7½" long, 1930's $300.00-500.00

DENT TRUCK, 10", cast iron $150.00-300.00

DENT YELLOW CAB, 8" $200.00-400.00

DENT YELLOW CAB, 8", cast iron $300.00-550.00

DINKY TOYS armored car $10.00-20.00

DINKY TOYS CADILLAC ELDORADO, 4½", 1950's $20.00-45.00

DINKY TOYS CHRYSLER AIRFLOW SALOON, 4" long $40.00-80.00

DINKY TOYS FORD FAIRLANE, 1962, 4½" long $15.00-35.00

DINKY TOYS RACE CAR WITH AIRFLOW TYPE REAR FENDERS, 1930's $25.00-60.00

DINKY TOYS RACE CAR, 4", 1950's......$30.00-70.00

DINKY TOYS ROLLS ROYCE, 1930's, 4" long $50.00-100.00

DINKY TOYS STUDEBAKER, GOLDEN HAWK, 1950's, 4½" $25.00-50.00

DISTLER CONVERTIBLE SPORTS CAR, US Zone Germany, tin windup, 10" $150.00-300.00

DISTLER LILLIPUT MIDGET AUTO, US Zone Germany, 2½" long $30.00-60.00

DISTLER LIMOUSINE, tin lithograph, 12" long $600.00-800.00

DISTLER MOTORCYCLE, German, tin lithograph, ...$900.00-1,500.00

DISTLER PACKARD CONVERTIBLE, US Zone Germany, 1940's, 10", tin, windup, box $225.00-350.00

DODGE CHARGER, 1966, 426 Hemi', dealer promotion model $40.00-65.00

DODGE COUPE, Japan, 1950's, tin friction, 12" long $75.00-185.00

DODGE SALERNO ENGINEERING DEPT. TRUCK, (SAMPLE)...........................$600.00-1,100.00

DOEPKE FIRE TRUCK with ladder, 29" long $100.00-175.00

DOEPKE JAGUAR, 17" long sports model $100.00-275.00

DANDEE OIL TRUCK, tin, windup by J. Chein, 9" long, Furnish collection, $125.00-200.00.

DRAY FLATBED, by Hubley, cast iron 4½" long, Furnish collection, $35.00-75.00.

DOUBLE DECKER BUS by Kenton, 1920's, 8", cast iron $400.00-675.00

DUMP TRUCK by Smith Miller, 11", cast metal $80.00-150.00

DUMP TRUCK by Wyandotte, 11", pressed steel $25.00-50.00

DUMP TRUCK, Husky Construction $25.00-35.00

DUMP TRUCK, Marx, 1950's, tin, friction motor, boxed, 12" long $55.00-100.00

DUMP TRUCK, SSS, Japan, tin friction, 6" Mack truck with lever action $25.00-45.00

DUMP TRUCK, STRUCTO HI-LIFT, 12" long $50.00-100.00

DUMP TRUCK, Turner, original box, 26" long $300.00-650.00

DUMP TRUCK, Turner, red/blue, 20" .$150.00-295.00

DUMP TRUCK, windup, by Structo, 12" long $100.00-225.00

EDSEL (POLICE VERSION) 1950's, friction, Japan, in original box $75.00-195.00

EDSEL TAXI, tin, friction, by Haji, Japan, 7½" tall $100.00-175.00

EDSEL, 1958 promotional car used by dealers, in original box $75.00-125.00

ELECTRIC CONVERTIBLE by Marx, 20" $70.00-125.00

EMERGENCY CAR, Japan, Haji, 4" $20.00-40.00

ESSO TRUCK, 18", friction, tanker ...$200.00-350.00

EXAMICO 4001 CAR, SCHUCO, Germany, tin windup, 5" long $60.00-100.00

EXPRESS VAN, SSS, Japan, tin friction 6", Mack truck $25.00-45.00

FAGEOL BUS by Arcade, 12" $300.00-650.00

FARM TRUCK BY Structo, steel, 20" with seven plastic animals $50.00-100.00

FARM TRUCK, Alps, Japan, 11", BO, with mooing cow $75.00-120.00

FAST FREIGHT TRUCK, by Buddy L, pressed steel, 1940's, 20" long $75.00-125.00

FERRARI FORMULA I, BY CORGI metal scale model $45.00-75.00

FIRE CHIEF CAR with siren, Courtland, tin, windup, box, 7" $45.00-90.00

FIRE CHIEF CAR, Cohn, pull toy, 9", bell rings ....$$30.00-65.00

FIRE CHIEF CAR, Japan, 11½", BO, bump and go $25.00-45.00

FIN TRUCK AIRFLOW DESIGN, 4" long, Sun Rubber, USA, Furnish collection, $20.00-45.00.

HORSE DRAWN FIRE PUMPER, cast iron, 16", original paint, two horses, Furnish collection, $500.00-1,000.00.

FIRE CHIEF CAR, Lupor, USA, 1950's, 6½" long, tin windup, boxed $25.00-55.00

FIRE CHIEF CUSTOM CAR, Japan, 14", tin, ...$40.00-80.00

FIRE CHIEF RADAR CAR 1950's, BO, 12" long $40.00-85.00

FIRE ENGINE by Marx, sheet iron, 9" long $45.00-75.00

FIRE ENGINE by Sturditoy, 1920's 33" long, sheet steel, with ladder............................$500.00-700.00

FIRE ENGINE, Japan, Bunny trademark, 8", tin, friction...$40.00-60.00

FIRE ENGINE, Old Smokey, Japan, tin, friction, 7" with siren noise..................................$30.00-50.00

FIRE PATROL, FIRE WAGON, 16" $100.00-175.00

FIRE PUMPER by Kenton 11", cast iron $400.00-700.00

FIRE TRUCK BY GIRARD, 12" long, tin, 1920's $60.00-120.00

FIRE TRUCK, Girard, 14" long $200.00-400.00

FIRE TRUCK, HOOK AND LADDER, by Wyandotte $60.00-120.00

FIRE VEHICLE SET "ANTIQUE" 14 pieces, SSS Japan, 1950's, tin $100.00-200.00

FIRESTONE TRUCK, by Marx, 14" long, metal, 1950's $40.00-65.00

FIRE TRUCK by Hubley, 13" $200.00-425.00

FISHER LITHOGRAPH, TINPLATE TAXI, 1910 ....$800.00-1,400.00

FLIVVER PICK-UP TRUCK, Buddy L..$400.00-800.00

FORD COUPE by Hubley, 1930's $25.00-45.00

FORD FAIRLANE, DINKY TOYS, England, 1963, 4½" long..$15.00-35.00

FORD FIRE CHIEF CAR, friction motor, Japan, 6", red, in taxi box $10.00-25.00

FORD GALAXY PROMO, 1963, aqua, 8", plastic $20.00-40.00

FORD HIGHWAY PATROL, BO, 10", in original box $50.00-125.00

FORD MODEL T, Bing, Germany, 6" $200.00-400.00

FORD OLD TIMER, 1915, Bandai, Japan, tin friction, 7" long $20.00-35.00

FORD SEDAN, 1920's, Arcade, boxed..$900.00-1,700.00

FORD TAXI KORSKOLA, original box, BO, 9½" long...$75.00-150.00

FORD TRUCK, Buddy L, 1920's, 12" long $200.00-450.00

FORD, 1964, Ichiko, Japan, 13", tin, friction..$60.00-100.00

FRANKLIN CAST IRON AUTO, 8" long, ca. 1910..$300.00-500.00

FRICTION CAR, Alps, Japan, 1930's sedan, 5" long, blue version $25.00-50.00

FRICTION CAR, Alps, Japan, sedan, 5" long, red, boxed $25.00-50.00

G-MEN CAR, Electrotoy, Japan, 1950's, tin, BO, 8", in box $150.00-350.00

G-MEN CAR, Japan, tin, friction, 6" $50.00-75.00

GANG BUSTER CAR by Marx, 1930's, 14" long $200.00-400.00

GARAGE AND SERVICE CENTER, Wyandotte, 1935, two-car $75.00-175.00

GARAGE TRUCK, Japan, tin friction, 1950's, 5" lever-action $10.00-35.00

GAS TRUCK, tin, 11" long, ca. 1930's ...$40.00-65.00

GASOLINE TRAILER TRUCK, Japan, tin friction, 10" long $20.00-40.00

GASOLINE TRUCK, cast iron with metal wheels, 7", 1920's $100.00-150.00

GASOLINE TRUCK, Japan, 4" long, tin, friction..$10.00-20.00

GIRARD COUPE, USA, 1935, pressed steel, orange colored car, windup, 15" $200.00-375.00

GIRARD FIRE CHIEF SIREN COUPE, 14½" long $200.00-350.00

GIRARD FIRE TRUCK, 12", tin, 1920's .$60.00-120.00

CAST IRON FIRETRUCK, red, 6" long, Reynolds collection, $100.00-200.00.

CARS AND TRUCKS

GIRARD FIRE TRUCK, 14" long $200.00-400.00

GIRARD TOURING BUS, tin, 12" long, ca. 1920's $50.00-100.00

GIRARD TOURING BUS, tin, 1920's, 12" long $70.00-110.00

GIRARD WRECKER TRUCK, 1920's, tin windup, 10", with driver $70.00-135.00

GM COACH PASSENGER BUS, BO, Japan, 1950's, 16" $150.00-350.00

GOOD HUMOR ICE CREAM TRUCK, 1950's $40.00-60.00

GOOFY'S STOCK CAR, Linemar, 6" tin, friction $100.00-220.00

GRAHAM PAIGE #3 CAR, Kosugee, pre-war Japan, 6", tin windup, red, boxed $100.00-200.00

GREYHOUND BEEP BEEP BUS, N.G.S. Japan, 20", BO $200.00-450.00

GREYHOUND BUS by LineMar, Japan, remote controlled, 10", 1950's $65.00-120.00

GREYHOUND BUS, Chein, 6", tin windup, wood tires $50.00-95.00

GREYHOUND BUS, Daiya, Japan, 1950's, tin friction, 9" $20.00-35.00

GREYHOUND BUS, metal, 13", Japan, friction with large roof racks $20.00-45.00

GREYHOUND BUS, metal, friction, 1960's, 10" long $25.00-65.00

GTO, PONTIAC, 1967, dealer promotion, plastic model $40.00-65.00

GUNTHERMAN, GOLDEN ARROW RECORD CAR, clockwork, 21" long $700.00-1,200.00

GUNTHERMAN LITHOGRAPHED TINPLATE, "VIS-A-VIS," 12" clockwork drive $10,000.00-13,000.00

HARLEY DAVIDSON MOTOCYCLE with tin pistons "Auto Cycle" on box, 9" long $300.00-750.00

HESS MOBILE, early auto, friction, 1900's, lever on front, German $200.00-400.00

HI SPEED RACER, Japan, 1960's, 12", BO, Indy style bump and go $40.00-85.00

HI-WAY EXPRESS TRUCK, Marx, 1940's, 16", tin, tin tires $45.00-85.00

HIGHWAY PATROL CAR, TPS, Japan, 20" x 8" track, boxed seat $65.00-135.00

HIGHWAY PATROL JEEP, Daiya, Japan, ca. 1950's BO, 10" $70.00-130.00

HIGHWAY PATROL STATION WAGON, Japan, 9", tin $40.00-80.00

HIGHWAY PATROL CUSTOM CAR, Japan, 14", tin friction...$35.00-70.00

HOGE FIRE CHIEF CAR, 15" $750.00-1,100.00

HOOK AND LADDER FIRE TRUCK, by Wyandotte $60.00-120.00

HOOK AND LADDER TRUCK, Hubley, 8" boxed, cast metal $30.00-55.00

HORSELESS CARRIAGE BY HILLCLIMBER, cast iron, 7", woman driver $300.00-600.00

HOT ROD #23 by Marx, Japan, 1967 tin, friction motor, 8" long $15.00-30.00

HOT ROD, BANDAI, Japan tin lithograph, boxed $60.00-120.00

HOUSE TRAILER WITH PONTIAC AUTO, SSS, Japan, 1950's $40.00-85.00

HUBER STEAM ROLLER, cast iron, 15" long, construction vehicle $2,500.00-4,000.00

GIRARD FIRE CHIEF CAR, windup, metal with siren, 14", red, Reynolds collection, $200.00-350.00.

GREYHOUND BUS, 1930's, cast metal, 5¾", white rubber tires, Furnish collection, $20.00-55.00.

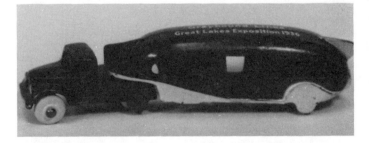

GREYHOUND LINES GREAT LAKES EXHIBITION, 1936, Arcade, 6½", truck and trailer, Furnish collection, $30.00-70.00.

HEINZ TRUCK with ad decals, sheet steel, white with rubber tires, Reynolds collection, $50.00-120.00.

HUBLEY AIRFLOW, 6" car $95.00-175.00
HUBLEY BELL TELEPHONE TRUCK, 1930's, cast iron, white tires, winch works $300.00-500.00
HUBLEY BELL TELEPHONE TRUCK, 5½" $200.00-400.00
HUBLEY CAR CARRIER, cast iron, four cars, 10" long $300.00-575.00
HUBLEY CAST IRON DUMP TRUCK, 7½" long $200.00-400.00
HUBLEY CAST IRON MOTORCYCLE COP with side car $300.00-400.00
HUBLEY CAST IRON MOTORCYCLE, three wheels $400.00-700.00
HUBLEY CAST IRON RACER, 7" long. $150.00-300.00
HUBLEY CAST IRON SEDAN, 1920's, 7" long $200.00-275.00
HUBLEY CHRYSLER RACING CAR, 1930's $35.00-70.00
HUBLEY CRASH CAR, 5", 1930's, cast iron motorcycle with cart on back $40.00-95.00
HUBLEY DUMP TRUCK, 4½", 1930's, white rubber tires..................$50.00-85.00
HUBLEY DUMP TRUCK, late 1930's, 7½", white rubber tires $90.00-150.00
HUBLEY FIRETRUCK WITH METAL LADDERS, 1938, 13" long $300.00-550.00
HUBLEY FIRETRUCK, 13" long..........$200.00-425.00
HUBLEY FIRETRUCK, 5", 1930's $50.00-75.00
HUBLEY FORD COUPE, ca. 1930's $25.00-45.00
HUBLEY HOOK AND LADDER TRUCK, cast metal, boxed, 8" long $30.00-55.00
HUBLEY LADDER TRUCK, ca. 1940's, 14" long $100.00-200.00
HUBLEY LIMOUSINE, 1920's, 7"..........$50.00-100.00
HUBLEY LINCOLN ZEPHYR, 1937 ......$100.00-225.00
HUBLEY MOTORCYCLE, cast iron, 9" $100.00-160.00
HUBLEY PARCEL POST MOTORCYCLE WITH SIDECAR, cast iron $2,000.00-4,000.00
HUBLEY RACE CAR, #22, cast iron, 7½" long $175.00-325.00
HUBLEY RACE CAR, #2241, 7", 1930's .$30.00-60.00
HUBLEY RACE CAR, #2241, ca. 1930's, 7½" long $30.00-60.00
HUBLEY RACER, #629, 7" long, 1936 ...$20.00-40.00
HUBLEY SERVICE CAR, 5" 1930's $40.00-75.00
HUBLEY SERVICE COACH, cast iron, 5" long $300.00-450.00
HUBLEY SHOVEL TRUCK, 10", metal.$200.00-450.00
HUBLEY STAKE BED TRUCK, 3" long, cast iron $20.00-40.00
HUBLEY STAKE TRUCK, cast metal, mint in box, 7" long $25.00-50.00
HUBLEY STAKE TRUCK, ca. 1930's, 7" long, white rubber tires..................$70.00-125.00
HUBLEY STEAM SHOVEL..................$30.00-65.00
HUBLEY STOCKYARD TRUCK, with three pigs, #851, with original box $65.00-95.00
HUBLEY STREAMLINED RACER, 5", cast iron $35.00-70.00
HUBLEY TOW TRUCK, 1950's, 7" cast metal $10.00-20.00
HUBLEY TOW TRUCK, 9" long $100.00-225.00
HUBLEY WRECKER, 5", cast iron $35.00-80.00

HUBLEY WRECKER, 6" long $60.00-95.00
HUBLEY YELLOW CAB with luggage rack, 8" long $200.00-400.00
HUKI MOTORCYCLE WITH SIDECAR, US ZONE GERMANY, tin windup, 6" $150.00-350.00
HUNTER TRUCK WITH LION AND HUNTER, Japan, tin friction, 9" Chevy truck $85.00-135.00
HURRICANE RACER #7, Occupied Japan, 5" long, Indy style, KSG $80.00-135.00
ICE CREAM TRUCK, "DELICIOUS" Japan, tin friction, 1960, ...$70.00-175.00
ICE CREAM TRUCK, Artic Ice Cream, by Kilgore..................$750.00-1,200.00
ICE TRUCK Kenton, cast iron, 7½".....$150.00-300.00
ICE TRUCK, 1940's, metal, stakebody version, 11"..................$25.00-55.00
INTERSTATE BUS, Strauss, 10", 1928, double decker tin wind-up bus $200.00-400.00
ISETTA, Bandai, Japan, tin, friction motor, 7", door on front $100.00-250.00
ITO SEDAN, Lehmann, 1920's, 7" tin wind-up $200.00-450.00
JAGUAR by Doepke, 17" $100.00-275.00
JAGUAR by Marx, BO, 13" $200.00-400.00
JALOPY by Tootsietoy, 2", 1950's $5.00-10.00
JAGUAR XK 120, Dinky toys, 4" $20.00-40.00
JEEP, Japanese, friction, 9", 1960's........$12.00-20.00
JEEP, TURN-O-MATIC with gun, Japan, 11", BO, driver, boxed $70.00-120.00
JEEP DELAGE, auto $1,200.00-1,800.00
JEEP RENAULT, auto $1,500.00-1,800.00
JUNIOR BUS by Chein, 1920's, tin lithograph, 9"..................$40.00-95.00
KENTON AUTOMOBILE, 6", cast iron...$70.00-135.00
KENTON CATTLE TRUCK, 1930's, white rubber tires, 8" long, metal $150.00-225.00
KENTON DOUBLE DECKER BUS, 1920's, 7" long $250.00-450.00
KENTON DOUBLE-DECKER BUS, cast iron, 6½", 1930's $200.00-400.00
KENTON FIRE PUMPER, 11" cast iron .$400.00-700.00
KENTON FIRE TRUCK, 15", cast iron .$250.00-500.00
KENTON FLATBED PICKUP TRUCK, 7½", cast iron, 1930's, white rubber tires..................$100.00-185.00

ICE TRUCK, J. Chein and Company, USA, 1930's, yellow/green, windup, Furnish collection $125.00-175.00.

CARS AND TRUCKS

JUNIOR OIL TANK, tin, windup truck, Strauss, 8",
Furnish collection, $125.00-200.00.

KENTON ICE TRUCK, cast iron, 7½"..$150.00-300.00
KENTON LADDER TRUCK, FIRE ENGINE, 16" long,
cast iron with metal ladders $75.00-185.00
KENTON PONTIAC, 4" cast iron $50.00-100.00
KENTON TOURING CAR, 12" long......$175.00-350.00
KEYSTONE MOVING VAN, 1927, steel (painted),
24" long $350.00-500.00
KEYSTONE, PACKARD MAIL TRUCK,
26" long $100.00-200.00
KILGORE ARCTIC ice cream truck .$750.00-1,2000.00
KILGORE DUMP TRUCK, cast iron, ca.
1930's $100.00-150.00
KILGORE DOUBLE RIDER MOTORCYCLE,
4" long $70.00-150.00
KILGORE DUMP TRUCK, 1930's, 7" $65.00-185.00
KILGORE LIVESTOCK Stake Truck .$750.00-1,200.00
KILGORE ROADSTER, 3½"......................$35.00-70.00
KING RACER, GIANT, by Marx, tin wind-up,
1930's $35.00-70.00
KINGSBURY BUS, 18".................$400.00-600.00
LADDER TRUCK, BUSY FIRE DEPARTMENT, tin wind-
up in original box, Japan $100.00-225.00
LADDER TRUCK, by Doepke $300.00-600.00
LEHMANN OHO AUTO, tin..................$250.00-400.00
LEHMANN TERRA AUTO, tin, driver, original flag,
1920's $1,200.00-1,900.00
LEHMANN AUTOBUS #590, red and white
1910 ....$1,500.00-2,100.00
LEHMANN AUTOBUS, 8" tin lithograph,
windup $700.00-1,100.00
LEHMANN AUTOBUS, 8', lithograph,
tinplate $750.00-1,000.00
LEHMANN ITO SEDAN, 7", 1920's, tin
windup $200.00-450.00
LEHMANN LIMOUSINE, 12", working
lights $900.00-1,200.00
LEHMANN MOTORCOACH, ca. 1900 ..$400.00-750.00
LEHMANN UHU AMPHIBIAN AUTO, 9½", tin litho-
graph, windup, German $700.00-1,000.00
LILLIPUT MIDGET AUTO, Distler, US Zone Germany,
2½" long, tin windup.....................$30.00-60.00
LIMOUSINE BY HUBLEY, 1920's,
cast iron $50.00-90.00
LIMOUSINE by Lehmann, 12" working
electric lights $900.00-1,200.00
LIMOUSINE, AIRPORT, by Auburn, Rubber,
8" long $10.00-20.00

LIMOUSINE, ca. 1920's, Tipp and Company, German,
Dunlop cord tires $500.00-900.00
LIMOUSINE, Penny Toy, German,
1920's $100.00-275.00
LINCOLN CONTINENTAL, COUPE, CONVERTIBLE,
Bandai, Japan, 1950's, 11"...........$110.00-200.00
LINCOLN, 1950's, HONK-ALONG, friction drive,
Japan $100.00-225.00
LINEMAR POWER SHOVEL TRUCK, Japan, 1950's, tin
friction, 11"...........................$40.00-95.00
LIVESTOCK STAKE TRUCK by
Kilgore $750.00-1,200.00
LIVESTOCK TRAILER TRUCK AND TRAILER, Japan,
1950's, 9" long $15.00-20.00
LIVESTOCK TRUCK, Japan, tin, friction, 9" with
pull-down ramp $25.00-40.00
LUCKY CAR, Occupied Japan, tin windup, red,
4½" long...........................$20.00-40.00
LUCKY RACER, Japan, tin, 1950's, friction, 5", litho-
graph, boxed $80.00-125.00
LUMBER HAULER TRUCK, by Carr-car,
Swan Hill...........................$20.00-30.00
LUPOR FIRE CHIEF CAR, 1950's, 6½" long,
tin windup $25.00-55.00
MAC 700 MOTORCYCLE, US Zone Germany, Arnold,
8", tin windup $300.00-500.00
MACK DUMP TRUCK, cast iron, 8", by Arcade,
1920's $75.00-125.00
MACK DUMP TRUCK, WYANDOTTE, 1930's,
13" orange $50.00-100.00
MACK LOG TRUCK, by Smitty, 1950's, 36",
two units $250.00-450.00
MACK TRUCK, TIMBER CARRIER, Japan, 1950's tin
friction, 6" long, with logs $10.00-35.00
MAIL TRUCK, PACKARD, 26", tin, 1920's, flatbed with
cage $200.00-400.00
MAIL TRUCK, US MAIL, Marx, 1950's,
14" $50.00-100.00
MANOIL CHEMICAL TRUCK, #104.........$30.00-60.00
MANOIL FIRE ENGINE, #709 ....$10.00-20.00
MANOIL HARDTOP CONVERTIBLE, #717,
rubber wheels $12.00-25.00
MANOIL Roadster $10.00-25.00
MANOIL Sedan, #707, 1930's...................$5.00-15.00
MANOIL Sedan, #703...........................$30.00-60.00

**LEHMANN EHE AND COMPANY, windup truck,
6½" long/driver, Furnish collection, $400.00-750.00.**

MARKLIN SPIRIT FIRED FIRE ENGINE, German, 1902, 20" long...............................$10,000.00-28,000.00

MARS RACER #8, 5", Indy-style racer with driver...$30.00-50.00

MARX "SAND" MECHANICAL DUMP TRUCK, 1940's, steel $30.00-65.00

MARX AUTO TRANSPORT TRUCK 1940, 14" long with two plastic cars, steel $65.00-95.00

MARX BOATTAIL RACER, #3, tin windup, 5" long, 1930's $30.00-60.00

MARX COCA COLA TRUCK, 20" long, 1950's $40.00-95.00

MARX COCA COLA TRUCK, 1940's, tin, 18" long $60.00-90.00

MARX DAIRY FARM PICKUP TRUCK, 22" long $50.00-80.00

MARX DELUXE DELIVERY TRUCK, 1950's, 11" metal, with six delivery boxes $50.00-95.00

MARX DELUXE TRAILER TRUCK, 14", original box, 1950's $35.00-50.00

MARX DODGE SALERNO ENGINEERING DEPART-MENT, truck sample $600.00-1100.00

MARX DUMP TRUCK, 1930's.................$40.00-80.00

MARX DUMP TRUCK, 1950's, tin, friction motor, boxed, 12" long $55.00-100.00

MARX ELECTRIC CONVERTIBLE, tin and plastic, 20" long $70.00-125.00

MARX FIRE ENGINE, sheet iron, 1920's, 9" long $45.00-75.00

MARX GANG BUSTER CAR, 1930's, 14" long $200.00-400.00

MARX GIANT KING RACER, tin windup, 1930's $35.00-70.00

MARX HI-WAY EXPRESS TRUCK, 1940's 16" tin truck with tin tires $45.00-85.00

MARX HOT ROD #23, Japan, 1967, tin friction, 8" long $15.00-30.00

MARX MACK RAILROAD EXPRESS TRUCK, tin #7, 1930's $75.00-125.00

MARX MOTORCYCLE COP WITH SIDECAR, 8½" long, tin windup $100.00-200.00

MARX MOTORCYCLE POLICEMAN, 1920's, tin windup, 8", orange and blue $125.00-250.00

MARX MOTORCYCLE TROOPER, tin lithograph, windup, 1930's, ...$100.00-140.00

MARX MYSTERY CAR, 1940's, 10" long, press down activation..$65.00-125.00

MARX MYSTERY POLICE CYCLE, 1930's, tin wind-up yellow motorcycle, 4½".......................$45.00-75.00

MARX MYSTERY TAXI, 1930's, press down activation $40.00-90.00

MARX MYSTIC MOTORCYCLE, tin windup, 4½" long...$30.00-65.00

MARX PICKUP TRUCK, ca. 1940's, 9" long, blue and yellow with wood tires.......................$25.00-45.00

MARX POLICE MOTORCYCLE, 8" long, tin windup, red uniform on cop $100.00-200.00

MARX POLICEMAN ON MOTORCYCLE WITH SIDE-CAR, tin windup, 8" $100.00-200.00

MARX RACE CAR #12, tin lithograph, windup, large 16" $100.00-160.00

MARX RACER #3, tin, 5", lithograph ..$100.00-200.00

MARX MILK AND CREAM WAGON, 10" long, balloon tires, "Toylands," Reynolds collection, $100.00-225.00.

MARX OLD JALOPY, tin windup car, 6" long, black, colorful writing, Reynolds collection, $65.00-140.00.

TIN WINDUP BOY ON MOTORCYCLE, 8", probably German, 1920's, Furnish collection, $200.00-400.00.

CARS AND TRUCKS

MARX ROLLS ROYCE, made in Hong Kong, 1955, plastic, 6", original box $15.00-25.00

MARX ROYAL COUPE, tin windup car .$200.00-300.00

MARX SPEEDWAY COUPE, 1920's, BO, headlights, 8" long $185.00-300.00

MARX STAKE BED TRUCK, 1940's $25.00-50.00

MARX SUPER STREAMLINED RACER, 1950's, 17" long, tin windup $140.00-250.00

MARX U.S. MAIL TRUCK, 14", metal .$200.00-400.00

MARX U.S. MAIL TRUCK, 1950's, 14" $50.00-100.00

MARX VAN TRUCK, 1950's, plastic, boxed, 10" long $10.00-25.00

MARX WESTERN AUTO TRUCK, steel, 24" long $50.00-100.00

MARX WOODY SEDAN, tin friction, 7½".$20.00-40.00

MARX WRECKER TRUCK, 1930's, #T-16 $20.00-40.00

MARY OPEN TV CAR, tin, friction, Japan, Ashitoy, 7", TV lithograph on dash $45.00-95.00

MECCANO CONSTRUCTOR, CAR #1, convertible, no box $450.00-700.00

MECCANO CONSTRUCTOR CAR #1, sedan, in original box $700.00-1,100.00

MERCEDES BENZ 300 SE, Dinky Toy ...$35.00-50.00

MERCEDES BENZ 600 PULLMAN, Corgi .$65.00-90.00

MERCEDES BENZ SSS, Japan, 1950's 7", tin lithograph, friction $50.00-90.00

MERCEDES BENZ, ICHIKO, Japan, tin friction, 24", mint in box $100.00-150.00

MERCURY COUGAR, by Bandai, Japan, late 1960's, 10" long $40.00-75.00

MERCURY COUPE, Haji, Japan, 1960's, 11" long $100.00-200.00

METAL MASTERS TOW TRUCK, 1940 ..$30.00-50.00

METALCRAFT, "Coffee Truck Wrecker".$200.00-500.00

METALCRAFT DELIVERY TRUCK, 11", pressed steel $65.00-170.00

METALCRAFT HEINZ FOOD TRUCK, tin, 12" long $300.00-450.00

METALCRAFT VAN, 11", 1930's $50.00-100.00

METALCRAFT VAN, steel, 11".............$100.00-200.00

MG CONVERTIBLE, Japan, 5", tin friction...$25.00-40.00

MGA 1600, coupe, metal, (boxed)......$100.00-225.00

MICRO RACER 1041 by Schuco, West Germany, Indy style racer #7, boxed $40.00-80.00

MIGHTY HALF TRUCK, K, Japan, 1950's, BO, box $75.00-120.00

MINIC POST OFFICE TELEPHONE VAN, England, plastic windup, 3½", box $25.00-50.00

MINIC ROADSTER, tin windup, 4" $35.00-70.00

MINIC TRANSPORT EXPRESS TRUCK, tin windup, 1950's, 3½" $25.00-40.00

MINIC WRECKER, tin windup, 5" $40.00-65.00

MISTER SOFTEE ICE CREAM TRUCK, Japan, 1950's, 4" friction, tin $20.00-40.00

MOBILE CARRIER, Ashitoy, Japan, friction, tin, 17", three cars, boxed $75.00-125.00

MOBILGAS GASOLINE CARRIER, Japan, 1950's, 9", Ford $50.00-85.00

MODEL A COUPE, BY ARCADE, cast iron, metal wheels $500.00-800.00

MODEL A COUPE, BY ARCADE, cast iron, metal wheels $500.00-800.00

MODEL A FORD, ARCADE, cast iron 6½" long, 1929 ....$200.00-400.00

MODEL T AUTO by Bing $400.00-600.00

MODEL T by Dent, ca. 1920's $70.00-150.00

MODEL T SEDAN, Bing, Germany, tin windup, 6½" long, 1929 ....$250.00-400.00

MODEL T TYPE SEDAN, cast iron, 1930's, 5" spoked metal wheels $100.00-150.00

MOTO START motorcycle, Spain, 1950's.$30.00-65.00

MOTOR COACH, Lehmann, Germany, tin windup $300.00-600.00

MOTOR EXPRESS, CAST IRON TRUCK, 1930's, 7", white rubber tires.........................$100.00-200.00

MOTORCYCLE "PATROL," cast iron, 1930's, single policeman rider $30.00-60.00

MOTORCYCLE, by Distler, German tin lithograph $900.00-1,500.00

MOTORCYCLE by Ingap, Italy, 1935, 8" tin windup, red, #174 ....$120.00-225.00

MOTORCYCLE CABLE RIDER, MT, Japan, tin windup, 5" long $75.00-120.00

MOTORCYCLE COP WITH SIDECAR, Marx, tin windup, 8½" long $100.00-200.00

MOTORCYCLE POLICE WITH SIDE CAR, cast iron 5¼", 1930's, two police figures $70.00-145.00

MOTORCYCLE, POLICEMAN, Marx, ca. 1920's, tin windup, orange and blue, 8" $125.00-250.00

MOTORCYCE TROOPER BY MARX, tin lithograph, windup, 1930's $100.00-140.00

MOTORCYCLE WITH POLICEMAN AND SIDECAR, Marx, 8", tin windup....................$100.00-200.00

MOTORCYCLE WITH SIDECAR, by Hubley, parcel post version $2,000.00-4,000.00

MOTORCYCYLE WITH SIDECAR, Champion Hardware, 1940, cast iron, 5" long $300.00-500.00

MOTORCYCLE WITH SIDECAR, Huki, U.S. Zone Germany, tin windup, 6" $150.00-350.00

MOTORCYCLE WITH SIDECAR, Tippco, U.S. Zone Germany, 7", tin, Dunlap tires............$200.00-450.00

MOTORCYCLE WITH SIDECAR, Tippco, U.S. Zone Germany, 8", tin windup, red $175.00-350.00

MOTORCYCLE, Arnold, Germany, 8" long, tin windup, red #A643 ....$140.00-220.00

MOTORCYCLE, AUTO RACER, San Ei, Japan, tin friction, 6" racing pose $75.00-125.00

MOTORCYCLE, CRASH CAR, Hubley, 1930's, 5" cast iron with cart on back.....................$40.00-95.00

MOTORCYCLE, GERMAN, CKO, 8" $500.00-950.00

MOTORCYCLE. Harley Davidson, with tin pistons, "Auto Cycle," on box, 9" $300.00-750.00

MOTORCYCLE, Linemar, 1950's, 3" friction motor, red $25.00-40.00

MOTORCYCLE, MOTO START, Spain, 1950's, tin friction...$30.00-65.00

MOTORCYCLE, Occupied Japan, tin windup, 5" long $90.00-185.00

MOTORCYCLE, P.D. Patrol, tin, Japan, 8" long, friction..$40.00-85.00

MOTORCYCLE, Police "Auto" 1950's, 8" long, friction motor $60.00-100.00

MOTORCYCLE, Police Sergeant, France, 1950's, tin friction, 6½" $35.00-65.00

MOTORCYCLE, POLICE, #3, Marx, tin windup, 8½" long $85.00-175.00

MOTORCYCLE, ROOKIE COP, Marx, tin windup, 8½" long, yellow with driver $185.00-300.00

MOTORCYCLE, tin windup, orange/yellow with blue/green driver, 8" long $40.00-85.00

MOTORCYCLE, West German, tin friction, 6½", Dunlop tires...$30.00-55.00

MOTORCYCLE, #15, RACING, ED, Japan, 9", friction...$30.00-60.00

MOTORCYCLE WITH POLICE RIDER, cast iron, Champion, 4½", 1930's $50.00-75.00

MOTORCYCLE, CHAMPION #27 RACING CYCLE, Japan, 10" friction $50.00-95.00

MOTORCYCLE, Hubley, 9" cast iron ...$100.00-160.00

MOTORCYCLE, MAC 700, Arnold, U.S. Zone Germany, 8", tin wind-up $300.00-500.00

MOVING VAN by Keystone, 1927, steel truck, 24" long $350.00-500.00

MOXIE CAR horse with rider riding in car, Moxie advertising piece $800.00-1,650.00

MR. MAGOO CAR, by Hubley, 1961, BO, 9" old timer car, box...$100.00-200.00

MUSTANG FBI COMMANDER, Bandai, Japan, tin friction, 11"..$40.00-75.00

MUSTANG FORD, 1966 Dealer Promo. car in original box $70.00-140.00

MYSTERY CAR, Marx, 1940's, press down to activate, 10" long $65.00-125.00

MYSTERY POLICE CYCLE by Marx, 1930's, tin windup, yellow motorcycle, 4½" $45.00-75.00

MYSTERY POLICE CYCLE, KO, Japan, 1950's, lever action, 6" $150.00-250.00

NICKEL TOY COUPE, pre-war German, tin, 6" green $50.00-75.00

NON-FALL CAR by Schuco, Germany, tin windup, 4", dark green $40.00-60.00

NORTH AMERICAN VAN LINES TRUCK, Japan, 13" long, friction motor.............................$30.00-70.00

OHIO ROADSTER, 18" long, steel with friction motor..$200.00-375.00

OHO AUTO by Lehmann, all tin $250.00-400.00

OLD FASHIONED CAR #9, MT, Japan, tin, friction, 6" long $20.00-35.00

OLD JALOPY by LineMar, 1950's, 5" long, friction..$35.00-60.00

OLD SMOKEY FIRE ENGINE, Japan, tin friction, 7" with siren noise..................................$30.00-50.00

OLD TIMER 1915 FORD, Bandai, Japan, 7" tin friction car $20.00-35.00

OLDSMOBILE CAR AND TRAILER, Japan, 13", 1950's, tin friction..$65.00-135.00

OPEN TOURER AUTO, by Brimtoy of England, 1920, 10½" $250.00-500.00

PACKARD CONVERTIBLE, by Distler, U.S. Zone Germany, tin windup, 1940's, box $225.00-350.00

PACKARD MAIL TRUCK by Keystone, 26" long, metal wheels $100.00-200.00

PACKARD MAIL TRUCK, 1920's, metal flatbed with cage, 26" long................................$200.00-400.00

PASSENGER BUS, "GM COACH," Daiya, Japan, 1950's, tin lithograph, 16", BO, ...$150.00-350.00

PATROL CYCLE, tin, police version, in box, P. D. 8" long $150.00-295.00

PATROL MOTORCYCLE WITH SINGLE POLICEMAN RIDER, 6", 1930's $30.00-60.00

MARX WINDUP MIDGET RACER "MIDGET SPECIAL," #2 5" long, $100.00-200.00, MARX MIDGET, RACER #7 windup, 5" long, $100.00-200.00, Furnish collection.

MARX WINDUP ROADSTER with racing car, 9", Furnish collection, $100.00-225.00.

CAST IRON AUTO WITH WHITE RUBBER TIRES, 4", $25.00-65.00, MARX TRICKY TAXI TIN WINDUP, 4" $20.00-40.00, Furnish collection.

MOTORCYCLE WITH SIDECAR, U.S. Zone Germany, tin windup/driver, Furnish collection, $150.00-375.00.

CARS AND TRUCKS

PENNSYLVANIA, RAILROAD TRUCK, Japan, 1950's, tin friction, 7" long $35.00-60.00

PICKUP TRUCK by Tonka, 1950's, 12", steel $15.00-30.00

PICKUP TRUCK, MARX, 1940's, 9", blue and yellow with wooden tires $25.00-45.00

PIERCE ARROW by A. C. Williams $65.00-150.00

POLICE CAR (EDSEL) 1950's metal friction car, Japan $75.00-195.00

POLICE CAR, Chad Valley, English version, 7" windup $150.00-295.00

POLICE CAR, Japan, 1950's, tin friction, 5", Cadillac $25.00-40.00

POLICE CAR, MT, Japan, tin friction, 6", press roof action $20.00-45.00

POLICE CYCLE, MYSTERY, KO, Japan, 1950's, tin, lever action, 6" $150.00-250.00

POLICE MOTORCYCLE, #3, Marx, tin windup, 8½" long $85.00-175.00

POLICE MOTORCYCLE WITH SIREN by Marx, 1930's $150.00-250.00

POLICE MOTORCYCLE, Marx, 1930's, 8" long, tin windup, officer in red $100.00-200.00

POLICE PATROL TRUCK by Structo, 17" long $100.00-225.00

POLICE PATROL, Japan, policeman on three-wheeled motor cart, BO, 10" $100.00-225.00

POLICE TRUCK, cast iron, by Dent $500.00-850.00

PONTIAC BY KENTON, cast iron, 7", rubber tires $40.00-80.00

PONTIAC, KENTON, cast iron, 4" $50.00-100.00

PORSCHE 1005 RACER, SCHUCO, German, windup, 5" $40.00-65.00

PORSCHE with visible engine, Bandai $70.00-140.00

PORSCHE, tin windup, 1940's, U.S. Zone Germany, 8" long $50.00-75.00

POST OFFICE TELEPHONE VAN, by Minic, English, 3½" plastic, windup $25.00-50.00

POWER SHOVEL ON TRUCK, Linemar, Japan, tin friction, 11", 1950's $40.00-95.00

PRESSMOBILE CAR, Alps, tin windup, 6", Japan $30.00-65.00

RACE CAR #12 by Marx, tin lithograph, windup, 16" long $100.00-160.00

RACE CAR #5, Japan, tin, friction, 5", silver color, with driver $20.00-40.00

RACE CAR #77, Japan, Indy-type racer, 5", friction motor $20.00-50.00

RACE CAR BY HUBLEY, #2241, 7" long, ca. 1930's $30.00-60.00

RACE CAR WITH TURNING HEAD DRIVER, Japan, 5", tin friction, blue/white $30.00-50.00

RACE CAR, AIRSTREAM DESIGN, Dinky Toys 1930's $25.00-60.00

RACE CAR, West German, 5" long, tin, friction, red #5 ....$10.00-20.00

RACE CAR, West German, 5" long, tin friction, red, #4 ....$10.00-20.00

RACEMASTER #8 Lupor USA, ca. 1950's, 11", tin lithograph, original box $60.00-115.00

RACER #3, early Chein car, 1920's, Indy type racer, 7" long tin windup $125.00-275.00

RACER #39, by Lupor USA, 1950's, 12" Indy style racer, windup $85.00-150.00

RACE CAR, TIN, MOMENTUM, 12" long, Reynolds collection, **$30.00-65.00.**

BENZINE RACER BY HESS, Germany, tin, #5, Reynolds collection, **$125.00-250.00.**

RACER #52, tin windup, wood wheels, Indy style $30.00-55.00

RACER #629 by Hubley, 1939, 7" long $20.00-40.00

RACER #7, tin, friction motor, 8" long, Japan $70.00-100.00

RACER #7, Wells, England, 12½", tin windup, 1920's $200.00-300.00

RACER, by Schuco, W. German, 4", red $30.00-60.00

RACER, Nickel Toy, #52, pre-war, German, 6½" long $65.00-90.00

RACER, PORSCHE 1005, SCHUCO, German, windup, see-through, 5" $40.00-65.00

RACER, SLUSH CAST, 1930's, 3" $15.00-30.00

RACING CAR, Dinky Toys, 4", 1950's $30.00-70.00

RAILROAD EXPRESS TRUCK by Marx, 1930's $75.00-125.00

RAILWAY EXPRESS TRUCK, cast iron, 1930's 5", balloon type metal tires $150.00-250.00

RED ARROW BOAT TAIL RACER #7, Japan, 1950's, 11", red, tin $100.00-200.00

RED CROSS CAR, Japan, Haji, 4" $20.00-40.00

ROADSTER Chein, tin lithograph, 1920's, 8½" 40.00-80.00

ROADSTER by Minic, tin windup, 4" $35.00-70.00

ROADSTER by Ohio, pressed steel, 18", friction motor $200.00-375.00

ROADSTER CONVERTIBLE, cast iron, painted, 4½", 1930's $30.00-65.00

ROADSTER manufactured by Chein, 1920's, 8" tin lithograph $50.00-125.00

TIN RACER #5, 4" long, tin wheels, $30.00-60.00, TIN MERCEDES RACER #15, 4", tin wheels, $35.00-75.00, Furnish collection.

INDY RACER #3, steel with tin lithograph driver, 1930's, 12" long, $40.00-85.00, Furnish collection.

MARX WINDUP MIDGET RACER #4, 5", $100.00-200.00, MARX WINDUP MIDGET RACER #5, 5", $100.00-200.00, Furnish collection.

ROADSTER manufactured by Hess $800.00-1,400.00
ROADSTER, 1930's, cast iron, 3½", metal balloon-type tires...$30.00-65.00
ROADSTER, CAST IRON BUGGY TYPE, MAN DRIVING, ca. 1910, 6"...$100.00-175.00
ROCKET RACER #5, Japan, tin, friction makes engine noise $30.00-65.00
ROLLS ROYCE by Marx, Hong Kong, 1955, plastic, friction, black, 6" long $15.00-25.00
ROLLS ROYCE, SILVER GHOST, Corgi, mint in box $75.00-135.00
ROLLS ROYCE, Dinky Toys, 1930's, 4"....$50.00-100.00
ROYAL COUPE, tin, windup car, Marx ...$200.00-300.00
SAND AND GRAVEL TRUCK, Buddy L, 1940's, 14" pressed steel $35.00-60.00
SAND AND GRAVEL TRUCK, Buddy L, 1940's, pressed steel, 13" lever action $50.00-100.00
SATURN RACE CAR, Japan, 1950's, mint in box, 5" long $25.00-50.00

SCHOOLBUS, STOP-GO, Daiya, Japan, 13" long, BO..$50.00-125.00
SCHUCO AMBULANCE VAN #3043, US Zone Germany, 4½" long $30.00-55.00
SCHUCO EXAMICO 4001 CAR, Germany, tin windup, 5" long $60.00-100.00
SCHUCO NON-FALL CAR, German, tin windup, dark green, 4" long $40.00-60.00
SCHUCO PORSCHE 1005 RACER, German, windup, 5" $40.00-65.00
SCHUCO RACER, 4", red $30.00-60.00
SCHUCO TRUCK SET three trucks with garage, #3010..$150.00-300.00
SCHUCO VARIANTO #3041 Limo, U.S. Zone Germany, 4" long $30.00-55.00
SCHUCO VARIANTO ELECTRO TRUCK, #3112, West German, 4½" long................................$30.00-55.00
SCHUCO VOLKSWAGEN windup $30.00-60.00
SEDAN by Dent, 7½" long, 1930's...........$300.00-500.00
SEDAN PULLING TRAILER, cast iron, 1930's, 6½" total length $80.00-140.00
SEDAN WITH HOUSETRAILER, Wyandotte, 25" long $150.00-250.00
SEDAN, Auburn Rubber, green, license plate #500R...$12.00-20.00
SEDAN, CAST IRON, 4⅜", 1930's $40.00-80.00
SEDAN, cast iron, 5", 1930's, white rubber tires...$50.00-95.00
SEDAN, cast iron, by Hubley, 7" long $200.00-275.00
SEDAN COR-COR, Washington, Indian, sheet steel, 20" long $200.00-300.00
SEDAN, tin friction, K, Japan, 4" long $20.00-40.00
SHELL GAS TRUCK WITH TRAILER, Japan, 1950's, 9" long $15.00-20.00
SIDE DUMP TRUCK WITH TRAILER, Japan, 1950's, 9" long $15.00-20.00
SILVER COUPE by Buddy L $200.00-500.00
SLUSH CAST RACER, 3", 1930's................$15.00-30.00
SMITH MILLER BANK OF AMERICA TRUCK, steel, 14" long $90.00-150.00
SMITH MILLER DUMP TRUCK, cast metal, 11" long $80.00-150.00
SMITH MILLER Tow Truck $400.00-650.00
SMITTY FIRETRUCK, steel and cast metal, 36", 1950's $300.00-500.00
SMITTY MACK LOG TRUCK, 36", two units, 1950's $250.00-450.00
SPEEDING CAR PULLING MOTORCYCLE POLICEMAN, "Action Toys." Japan $300.00-500.00
SPEEDWAY COUPE, Marx, 1920's, tin windup, BO, headlights, 8" long $185.00-300.00
SPORTS AUTO, two piece cast iron, 1930's, 3½" long, balloon tires...$30.00-75.00
SPORTS CAR, convertible, by Distler, U.S. Zone Germany, 9" tin windup $175.00-300.00
SPOTLIGHT TRUCK, U.S. AIRFORCE, Marx...$120.00-160.00
STAKE BED TRUCK by Hubley, 3" long, cast iron $20.00-40.00
STAKE TRUCK by Wyandotte, 6", blue $15.00-35.00
STAKE TRUCK by Wyandotte, 7", red $20.00-40.00
STAKE TRUCK, by Auburn Rubber $15.00-25.00
STAKEBODY FLATBED TRUCK tin, "Reeves Coffee," 12" ca. 1930's $30.00-75.00

STAR KIST TUNA DELIVERY TRUCK, 1950's, ad car \$40.00-60.00

STATION WAGON WITH TEEPEE CAMPER, BUDDY L. 14" wagon, 10" camper \$100.00-200.00

STATION WAGON, K, Japan, 4", friction .\$20.00-40.00

STATION WAGON, KKK, Japan, 1950's, 9", friction...\$40.00-70.00

STEELCRAFT INTER-CITY BUS, 24" Deluxe Edition..\$650.00-1,000.00

STRAUSS HAUL-AWAY TRUCK #22, tin windup, 1920's \$100.00-200.00

STRAUSS INTER-STATE BUS, 10", tin lithograph, double-decker bus, windup \$200.00-400.00

STRAUSS LUX-A-CAB, tin lithograph, windup, 8" long \$200.00-450.00

STRAUSS TAXI, tin, windup \$300.00-500.00

STREAMLINED RACER, Hubley, 5", cast iron \$35.00-70.00

STRUCTO CEMENT TRUCK, 22" \$200.00-400.00

STRUCTO DUMP TRUCK, 1950's, pressed steel, 19", red, dumps \$40.00-70.00

STRUCTO FARM TRUCK steel, 20" with plastic animals \$50.00-100.00

STRUCTO FIRE PUMPER, 1920's, 21" \$200.00-300.00

STRUCTO GRADER, 18" long, 1950's, all metal \$25.00-60.00

STRUCTO HI-LIFT DUMP TRUCK, 12" .\$50.00-100.00

STRUCTO POLICE PATROL TRUCK, 17" long \$100.00-225.00

STRUCTO STEAM SHOVEL, STRUCTO EXCAVATING COMPANY, #605, 1950's, 16" long ...\$35.00-75.00

STRUCTO STEEL CARGO TRUCK, #702 with box \$100.00-140.00

STRUCTO WINDUP DUMP TRUCK, 12" long \$100.00-225.00

STUDEBAKER GOLDEN HAWK by Dinky Toys, England, 4½" \$25.00-50.00

STUDEBAKER, by Bandai, Japan, 1925 model, produced in 1950's, 10", friction \$75.00-145.00

STUDEBAKER, Hubley, Take-apart, 5" .\$125.00-300.00

TANKER TRUCK, MINIC, England, 6", Furnish collection, \$40.00-60.00.

STUDEBAKER, Occupied Japan, tin, windup, 4½" long, red with stop and go switch \$25.00-40.00

STUDEBAKER, Occupied Japan, tin, windup, tin tires, blue, 4" long, mint in box \$50.00-85.00

STURDITOY AMBULANCE, 1920s, painted steel, 26" long \$200.00-375.00

STURDITOY FIRE ENGINE, sheet metal, 1920's, 33" long \$500.00-700.00

STURDITOY FIRE TRUCK PUMPER, 26", 1920's \$200.00-350.00

STURDITOY MOVING VAN, 1920's, 26" long \$200.00-350.00

STURDITOY WATER TRUCK, 1920's, 24" with tank on flatbed \$200.00-400.00

SUNOCO OIL TANKER TRUCK, BUDDY L, plastic and metal \$15.00-30.00

SUPER STREAMLINED RACER, Marx, 1950's tin, windup, 17", colorful box \$140.00-250.00

SUPERSONIC SPEEDSTER, MT, Japan, 1950's, tin, friction, 7" rocket/car \$80.00-175.00

TANKER TRUCK, cast iron, by Dent, 10" with white rubber tires \$800.00-1,400.00

TAXI by Chad Valley, England, tin, 9" long \$100.00-400.00

TAXI, EDSEL, Haji, Japan, 7½" \$100.00-175.00

TAXI, TINPLATE, by Fisher, lithographed tinplate, 1910 ....\$800.00-1,400.00

THUNDERBIRD SPEEDSTER, 1950's, metal, 10½" long \$400.00-650.00

THUNDERBIRD, RN, made in West Germany, 1950's, 13" long, tin, friction \$100.00-200.00

TIN WINDUP CAR AND DRIVER WITH "BALLOON CORP" TIRES, 1920's \$100.00-250.00

TONKA CARNATION MILK TRUCK, 1950's \$25.00-50.00

TONKA CEMENT MIXER CONSTRUCTION TRUCK, 1960's \$40.00-75.00

TONKA FARM PICKUP TRUCK, 1960's, metal \$30.00-65.00

TONKA PICKUP TRUCK #2360, original box \$25.00-45.00

TONKA PICKUP TRUCK, 12", steel, 1950's \$15.00-30.00

CAST IRON SEDAN, 3", with metal wheels, Reynolds collection, \$35.00-80.00.

TONKA SERVI-CAR (three wheel Cushman type) 1960's $70.00-95.00

TONKA TRANSPORT WITH CARS, 1950's-1960's $60.00-120.00

TOOTSIETOY Bluebird Racer $60.00-85.00

TOOTSIETOY Buick Sedan.....................$30.00-50.00

TOOTSIETOY BOATTAIL ROADSTER, 6".$20.00-45.00

TOOTSIETOY BUICK SPECIAL, 1947, 4".$25.00-55.00

TOOTSIETOY CADILLAC, 6", 1954.........$15.00-30.00

TOOTISIETOY CADILLAC TOURING CAR, 1926..$40.00-80.00

TOOTSIETOY CHEVROLET, 1926...........$40.00-80.00

TOOTSIETOY CHEVROLET BEL AIR, 3", 1955 version $5.00-10.00

TOOTSIETOY CHRYSLER NEW YORKER, 6", 1953......................................$10.00-20.00

TOOTSIETOY COUPE, 1921, metal.........$15.00-30.00

TOOTSIETOY FORD FAIRLANE, 3", convertible...$5.00-10.00

TOOTSIETOY GAS AND OIL TRUCK, early, 5" long..$45.00-95.00

TOOTSIETOY JALOPY, 1950's, 2" long.....$5.00-10.00

TOOTSIETOY LONG DISTANCE HAULING TRUCK, 1930's...........................$50.00-100.00

TOOTSIETOY MOON MULLINS POLICE CAR, 1930's $100.00-200.00

TOOTSIETOY PLAYTIME SET: six car, two trucks, two planes, boxed..................$200.00-400.00

TOOTSIETOY PLYMOUTH STATION WAGON, 1940's, 4" long $35.00-70.00

TOOTSIETOY SHELL OIL TRUCK $20.00-40.00

TOOTSIETOY UNCLE WALT, DRIVING A ROADSTER (from Skeezix) $150.00-275.00

TOURING AUTO, cast iron, 10", spoked wheels, 1920's $300.00-500.00

TOURING BUS by Girard, 1920's, 12"...$70.00-110.00

TOURING BUS by Girard, 1920's, tin, 12" long...$50.00-100.00

TOURING CAR by Bing, two seater, 12", clockwork drive...........................$750.00-950.00

TOURING CAR BY CARETTE of Nuremberg, Germany, 1915, 15" long...........$1,500.00-2,700.00

TOURING CAR, D. P. CLARK, friction car, 1906, 10½" long...................$150.00-300.00

TOW TRUCK, Arcade, cast iron, 4" $40.00-80.00

TOW TRUCK, HUBLEY, 1950's, 7", cast metal...$10.00-20.00

TOYLAND DAIRY TRUCK, Girard, 10½"...$150.00-350.00

TRACTOR-TRAILER VAN, tin, 11", complete, swivel frame, 1930's...................$60.00-135.00

TRANSPORT EXPRESS TRUCK, Minic, 1950's, tin windup, 3½" long...............$25.00-40.00

TRICKY TAXI TIN WINDUP, 4" $20.00-40.00

TRUCK AND TRAILER SET, SSS, Japan, tin friction, 11", "S.I.E." marked $30.00-65.00

TRUCK WITH TRAILER, Cargo Hauler, 9", Japan, 1950's $15.00-20.00

TRUCK WITH TRAILER, Japan, Shell Gas, 1950's, 9" long.............................$15.00-20.00

TRUCK BY HESS, tin, lithograph.....$900.00-1,400.00

TRUCK, COCA COLA ROUTE, S, Japan, 1950's, BO, tin, 12"...........................$100.00-200.00

TRUCK, deluxe trailer, Marx, 14", boxed, 1950's $35.00-50.00

TRUCK, Marx, pre-war, pressed steel, windup $20.00-40.00

TRUCK, METALCRAFT HEINZ FOOD TRUCK, tin, 12" $300.00-450.00

TRUCK, NORTH AMERICAN VAN LINES, JAPAN, 13" long, friction $30.00-70.00

TRUCK, SAND AND GRAVEL, Buddy L, 1940's, pressed steel, lever action $50.00-100.00

TRUCK, Sun Rubber, yellow and blue, 5" long, rubber $15.00-25.00

TURNER DUMP TRUCK, original box, 26" $300.00-650.00

UHU AMPHIBIAN AUTO, by Lehmann, tin lithograph, windup, German $700.00-1,000.00

U.S. ARMY MILITARY POLICE CAR, 1950's, 9", plastic, friction, green $15.00-30.00

U.S. MAIL CAR, Japan, HAJI, 4" $20.00-40.00

U.S. MAIL TRUCK, Marx, 14" metal...$200.00-400.00

VAN TRUCK, Marx, 1950's, boxed, 10" ..$10.00-25.00

VAN, by Metalcraft, 1930's, 11"............$50.00-100.00

VARIANTO 3041, Limo, Schuco, U.S. Zone Germany, 4" long $30.00-55.00

VARIANTO ELECTRIC TRUCK, by Schuco, #3112, West Germany, 4½" long...................$30.00-55.00

VERSION 1758 CAR, U.S. Zone Germany, 5½" long..$65.00-135.00

VINTAGE AUTO #2, TN, Japan, tin, friction, 6", boxed $20.00-35.00

TIN LITHOGRAPH, FRICTION TRACTOR AND WAGON, 1950's, with driver, Reynolds collection, $40.00-75.00.

GERMAN TRACTOR WITH PLOW, marked SG Corporation, 3"x10", tin windup, 1920's, Reynolds collection, $85.00-200.00.

VOLKSWAGEN BEETLE, Bandai, Japan, 14" large version, BO $60.00-125.00

VOLKSWAGEN BEETLE, W. German, 5", blue, tin, friction $15.00-30.00

VOLKSWAGEN, manufactured by Schuco, windup W. Germany $30.00-60.00

VOLKSWAGEN, all metal 1960's, BO, 15" $100.00-225.00

VOLKSWAGEN, marked "Herbie's" #53, tin, Japan, BO $20.00-50.00

VOLKSWAGEN, tin, 1950's, remote controlled, BO, boxed $45.00-95.00

WATER SPRINKLER TRUCK, 1920's, tin lithograph $80.00-150.00

WATER TANK SPRINKLER TRUCK by Buddy L $500.00-1,000.00

WESTERN AUTO TRUCK, Marx, 25", steel $50.00-100.00

WOODIE BY WYANDOTTE retractable hard top $75.00-160.00

WOODIE CAR, Chein, 1940's, tin windup, 5", red $20.00-45.00

WOODY SEDAN by Marx, tin, friction, 7½" $20.00-40.00

WRECKER by Minic, tin wind-up, 5" $40.00-65.00

WRECKER TRUCK, Girard, 1920's, tin windup, 10" with driver $70.00-135.00

WRECKER TRUCK, WYANDOTTE, pressed steel, AAA logo, 12", tin tires $40.00-65.00

WRECKER, cast iron, 1930's, hook winch $50.00-85.00

WYANDOTTE WRECKER, Emergency Auto Service, 1950's, 15" $75.00-120.00

WRECKER, HUBLEY, 5" long $35.00-80.00

WRECKER, Manoil, #703 .... $30.00-60.00

WRIGLEY'S SPEARMINT GUM TRUCK, BUDDY L. 1930's $125.00-180.00

WRIGLEY'S SPEARMINT GUM TRUCK, TOOTSIETOY, 4" long $30.00-65.00

WYANDOTTE AMBULANCE, 1930's, 11", steel, wood tires $40.00-80.00

WYANDOTTE AMBULANCE, 1950's, tin lithograph $100.00-150.00

WYANDOTTE BUS, 6", pressed steel, 1930's $30.00-50.00

WYANDOTTE CADILLAC STATION WAGON, 21", tin, Woody type $60.00-125.00

WYANDOTTE CAR, rumble seat, 8" ... $175.00-300.00

WYANDOTTE CIRCUS TRUCK, 11" #503 .... $75.00-150.00

WYANDOTTE CONVERTIBLE WOODIE CAR, 1940's, metal, 12" long $70.00-150.00

WYANDOTTE DUMP TRUCK, 11", steel .. $25.00-50.00

WYANDOTTE DUMP TRUCK 6", 1930's.. $20.00-35.00

WYANDOTTE EMERGENCY AUTO SERVICE WRECKER, 1950's, 15" long $75.00-120.00

WYANDOTTE Hook and Ladder Fire Truck $60.00-120.00

WYANDOTTE MACK DUMP TRUCK, 1930's, 13", orange truck $50.00-100.00

WYANDOTTE PICKUP TRUCK, 1930's,

AUTO EXPRESS 548, cast iron flatbed truck, possibly Arcade, 9", Furnish collection, $150.00-400.00.

SUNSHINE BISCUIT TRUCK, metal, red and yellow, $65.00-125.00. AUBURN RUBBER RACER, Reynolds collection, $15.00-30.00.

6" $15.00-30.00

WYANDOTTE SEDAN WITH HOUSETRAILER, steel, 25" long $150.00-250.00

WYANDOTTE SEDAN, 6", metal, 1940's . $15.00-30.00

WYANDOTTE STAKE TRUCK WITH TRAILER, all metal $100.00-200.00

WYANDOTTE STAKE TRUCK, 6", blue .. $15.00-35.00

WYANDOTTE STAKE TRUCK, 7", red $20.00-40.00

WYANDOTTE TWO CAR GARAGE AND SERVICE CENTER, 1935 .... $75.00-175.00

WYANDOTTE WOODIE with retractable hard top $75.00-160.00

WYANDOTTE WRECKER TRUCK, pressed steel, AAA logo, 12", tin tires $40.00-65.00

YELLOW CAB by Dent, 8" long $200.00-400.00

YELLOW CAB by Dent, 8" cast iron ... $300.00-550.00

YELLOW CAB by Arcade, 1920's, original box $1,500.00-2,700.00

YELLOW CAB by Chein, 7" long $100.00-200.00

YELLOW CAB by Hubley with original luggage rack, 8" version $200.00-400.00

YELLOW CAB, tin lithograph, 7", by Chein $150.00-250.00

YELLOW TAXI, Chein, early, tin windup, 6", orange and black $25.00-50.00

CAST IRON TOYS

Cast iron toys are considered by some to be the "Cadillac" area of toy collecting because of the high quality of the toys and the high prices they command at toy shows and auctions. Ten years ago most antique toy experts would all have agreed that cast iron toys were the most prestigious items to collect in the entire toy field. Consequently, during the 1970's and on into the 1980's, cast iron toy prices rose steadily to record heights so it was not unusual to find some cast iron pieces with asking prices in the $2,000.00 to 3,000.00 range. This author's observation of the current trend, however, is that the market is leveling off. Prices have stabilized at the present and the norm here seems to be an emphasis on quality and less on astronomical pricing. Cast iron toy collecting has moved from fad and fashion to rational fun.

Horse drawn toys are another specialty collecting area. They are grouped along with cast iron toys in this chapter because the majority of cast iron toys WERE horse drawn. However, additons to the price list in this section are wood and paper lithographed horse drawn pull toys by Gibbs and other toy manufacturers along with Victorian era paper mache and wood horse and wagon type toys.

Advice to new collectors in the cast iron field is to read, learn, listen, and be patient. Seek out all knowledge possible from experienced dealers and collectors. With many early and later reproductions of cast iron toys continually hitting the toy market today, the new collector of cast iron toys must beware. It's easy to get taken. Although tales of unscrupulous and deceptive sellers torching the paint of new reproductions and then burying toys in the sand to achieve a quick aged patina are rare, the tales exist, so buyers should be forewarned. The best defense against deception in the marketplace is knowledge. If a collector wants to collect in the field of cast iron, he must become self-educated. Avoid altogether toys with too much rust, unless the collector himself wants to go into the restoration business.

Horse drawn toys are examples of how we used to get around. Because of our continuing interest in horses and their place in American hearts, close to that of the family dog, the addition of horse drawn toys fills a void. The horse drawn toy vehicle is a definitive link to another age gone by. They are pure nostalgia, but even more, they are elegant objects that tie together the history of man, machine, and horse.

HORSE DRAWN CART, 5" driver and partially covered bed, $65.00-140.00, Furnish collection.

CAST IRON HORSE PULLING TIN MILK WAGON/cast iron wheels, 6", $65.00-140.00, Furnish collection.

TIN HORSE PULLING COACH-TYPE WAGON, 7" cast iron wheels, $70.00-165.00, Furnish collection.

CAST IRON TOYS

ALPHABET BANK, octagonal shape, cast iron, 3½" long $700.00-1,000.00

AMERICAN STOVE, cast iron, 1920's, 8½". $75.00-125.00

AMISH BOY HOLDING PIG, cast iron, still bank $50.00-90.00

AMISH LADY CAST IRON BANK, 5" $75.00-125.00

APPLE BANK, yellow painted cast iron, 5½" long $600.00-850.00

ARCADE BUICK, 8" cast iron car, 1920's $500.00-800.00

ARCADE BUS, 8", cast iron $450.00-750.00

ARCADE BUS, double-decker, ca. 1920's, 8" long $200.00-650.00

ARCADE BUS, Fageol, 13", cast iron .. $400.00-625.00

ARCADE cast iron ice truck $150.00-350.00

ARCADE CENTURY OF PROGRESS TRUCK, cast iron, 10", dated 1923 ....$35.00-80.00

ARCADE CHEVROLET CAB, 8" cast iron, 1920's, metal tires $500.00-750.00

ARCADE CHEVROLET COUPE, 1928, 8" long, cast iron $350.00-550.00

ARCADE CHEVY COUPE, 1929, 8" $400.00-750.00

ARCADE COUPE, 5" long, cast iron $175.00-300.00

ARCADE COUPE, 5" long, two-toned, metal wheels, 1920's $75.00-145.00

ARCADE COUPE, 6½" long, solid wheels, 1920's $100.00-800.00

ARCADE COUPE, 9", 1920's, cast iron . $350.00-700.00

ARCADE DUMPTRUCK, cast iron, 6", low bed truck $70.00-125.00

ARCADE SEDAN, late 1930's, cast iron, 8" long $100.00-200.00

ARTILLERY, cast iron, 34" long with four horses and one cannon $1,000.00-2,000.00

BAD ACCIDENT MECHANICAL BANK, mule and driver with cart, 10" cast iron.............. 1,000.00-1,500.00

BANK BUILDING CAST IRON BANK, bronze finish, 3½" long $100.00-150.00

BANK TOWER BANK, cast iron, 9" $200.00-300.00

BANK, Pavilion, cast iron, ornamental, 1886, 3½" tall $150.00-300.00

BAROUCHE COACH WITH DRIVER AND TWO HORSES, cast iron, 1889 ....$800.00-1,600.00

BASEBALL AND THREE BATS, cast iron bank...$300.00-500.00

BEAR HOLDING A PIG, cast iron bank, 5" long $75.00-125.00

BEAR ON BELL GONG TOY, cast iron, 1914 ....$600.00-1,000.00

BEAR STEALING HONEY, cast iron bank, 7" long $150.00-200.00

BEAR, cast iron still bank, 2½" tall $50.00-100.00

BEGGING RABBIT CAST IRON BANK, 5½" tall $50.00-90.00

BELL RINGER GIRL with doll on horse head sled, 1892, "Daisy," cast iron $1,500.00-3,000.00

BELL RINGER HORSE ON PEDESTAL TOY, Gong Bell, 1892, cast iron $700.00-1,500.00

BELL RINGER HORSE WITH MONKEY ON SULKEY, 1892, cast iron $700.00-1,500.00

BIBLE BANK, cast iron $250.00-400.00

BILLIKEN STILL BANK, cast iron, 4", natural finish $30.00-60.00

CAST IRON SINGLE HORSE DRAWN CARRIAGE, 7" long, Furnish collection, $65.00-135.00.

BILLIKEN BANK "GOOD LUCK," gold and red paint, cast iron, 4" long $75.00-110.00

BILLY BANK "GIVE BILLY A PENNY," painted, cast iron, small boy, 5" $35.00-70.00

BILLY CAN CLOWN BANK, 5"..........$100.00-200.00

BILLY POSSUM BANK, 3" tall, ...$150.00-300.00

BIRD ON ROOF, Japanned, cast iron, mechanical bank $1,500.00-2,000.00

BISMARK MECHANICAL BANK, man inside pig, 8", cast iron, *very rare*....................$3,000.00-5,000.00

BLACK BEGGAR, "GIVE ME A PENNY" BANK, cast iron, 5" $40.00-70.00

BLACK MAMMY BANK, cast iron, 6" 90.00-140.00

BLACK MAN EATING COINS BANK, mechanical, cast iron, 6"..$125.00-175.00

BLUE HAY WAGON, cast iron and wood, 1910, 16" $500.00-1,000.00

BOSTON BULL TERRIER 4½", cast iron bank $125.00-175.00

BOY SCOUT cast iron bank, 6" $75.00-125.00

BOY SCOUT CAST IRON BANK, 8"....$500.00-750.00

BOYS STEALING WATERMELON, cast iron, mechanical bank $800-00-1,250.00

BUCKET, cast iron, registering bank.....$50.00-100.00

BUFFALO BANK, still bank, 3"..........$120.00-200.00

BUGGY WITH DRIVER, 5½" $40.00-85.00

BULL ON BASE, cast iron, still bank, 6" long $160.00-200.00

BULLDOG, still bank, cast iron, 3½" tall .$50.00-100.00

BUS, ARCADE, 8", cast iron...............$450.00-750.00

BUSTER BROWN AND TIGE BANK, 5", cast iron, gold finish $80.00-185.00

BUTTING BUFFALO, cast iron, mechanical bank $2,000.00-3,000.00

CAMEL LYING DOWN, cast iron bank, 2" $20.00-45.00

CAMPBELL KIDS, cast iron, still bank, 3" tall...$40.00-65.00

CART PULLED BY BULLS, two-wheeled .$40.00-85.00

CART, HORSE DRAWN WITH DRIVER, cart partly covered, cast iron, 5" $65.00-140.00

CART PULLED BY ELEPHANT, 7", cast iron $40.00-75.00

CASTLE WITH TWO TOWERS, cast iron bank, 7" $300.00-500.00

CAST IRON, COAL WAGON DRAWN BY SINGLE HORSE WITH DRIVER, 9", Furnish collection, $100.00-225.00.

CAST IRON FARM WAGON PULLED BY COW WITH BLACK DRIVER, 7", cast iron wheels, Furnish collection, $75.00-165.00.

CAT AND MOUSE BANK, cast iron, mechanical, 11" $600.00-900.00

CAT ON TUB BANK, cast iron, still, 4".$50.00-100.00

CAT WITH BALL, LYING, cast iron, still bank $150.00-200.00

CAT WITH BOW, STANDING, cast iron, still bank, 4" $20.00-50.00

CAVALRY SOLDIER WITH RIFLE, cast iron bank, 6" $20.00-45.00

CHIME BELL, PULL TOY, 1886, cast iron and metal, 5½" long $300.00-600.00

CINDERELLA'S CHARIOT, CAST IRON BELL RINGER, Gong Bell, 1893.........................$2,000.00-4,000.00

CLOWN BANK, cast iron, holding horn, 6" tall...$70.00-125.00

CLOWN BELL TOY WITH TWO BELLS, cast iron, 1914, 7" $500.00-1,000.00

CLOWN CAST IRON BANK, 6"............$110.00-195.00

CLOWN ON GLOBE, CAST IRON BANK, mechanical, 9" $1,000.00-1,500.00

CLOWN, STANDING, still bank, 6" $70.00-120.00

COACH, TALLY-HO, ca. 1890's, Carpenter, seven riders, four horses $2,000.00-3,200.00

CONFECTIONARY BANK, cast iron, 1886, lady in shop $600.00-1,250.00

CONTRACTOR'S WAGON, cast iron toy, black horses, 1892, red wagon..........................$700.00-1,250.00

COUNTY BANK, cast iron building shaped bank, still, 4¼" $100.00-150.00

COW BANK, still bank, 4½" $200.00-260.00

CROUCHING RABBIT CAST IRON BANK, 3" $25.00-55.00

CROWING ROOSTER mechanical bank .$200.00-400.00

DAIRY COW WALKING, cast iron, still bank, 3½" tall $10.00-20.00

DENT ICE CREAM TRUCK, 1930's, 8", cast iron $200.00-400.00

DENT MODEL T, 1920's, cast iron $70.00-150.00

DENT PATROL TRUCK, 1920's, 6½" long, with driver...$300.00-450.00

DENT SEDAN, 7½", cast iron, 1930's .$150.00-300.00

DENT YELLOW CAB, 8", cast iron $300.00-550.00

DING DONG BELL, pull toy, cast iron, two figures on platform with well, 1902 ....$1,000.00-2,000.00

"DO YOU KNOW ME?" clown bank, 6".$125.00-250.00

DOCTOR'S BAG, cast iron still bank, "M.D." on bag $60.00-100.00

DOG BANK, HOWLING WITH UPTURNED NECK, cast iron, 5" $70.00-140.00

DOG CART, CAST IRON CART WITH DRIVER, 12" 1889 ....$750.00-1,500.00

DOG ON TUB CAST IRON STILL BANK, 4" $50.00-100.00

DOG, BOXER, 4" cast iron, still bank, seated $175.00-350.00

DOG, English Bulldog, still bank, 4" seated $150.00-300.00

DOLPHIN BOAT BANK, cast iron, sailor holds anchor, 4½" $150.00-225.00

DONKEY WITH SADDLE CAST IRON BANK, 5" tall...$75.00-125.00

DOUBLE TRUCK WITH DRIVER AND TWO HORSES, cast iron, 1889 ....$1,000.00-1,700.00

DRAY WITH DRIVER, cast iron, 19", 1889..$700.00-1,400.00

DRAY, with horse and standing driver, 11½" long, 1892 ....$600.00-1,200.00

DUCK, CAST IRON FIGURAL BANK, 5", painted $100.00-135.00

DUTCH BOY CAST IRON STILL BANK, 8" $100.00-200.00

DUTCH GIRL CAST IRON, STILL BANK, 5" $45.00-80.00

EGG SHAPED MAN WITH TOP HAT BANK, cast iron, 4" $120.00-180.00

ELEPHANT BANK, cast iron, 7" long....$80.00-120.00

ELEPHANT CAST IRON BANK, WITH SWIVELING TRUNK, 2½"...................................$150.00-200.00

ELEPHANT ON WHEELS, cast iron rolling bank, 4" $200.00-250.00

ELEPHANT STANDING ON CIRCUS TUB, cast iron, still bank, 5½" $100.00-150.00

ELEPHANT WITH RIDER BASKET (HOWDAH), cast iron, 6½" $40.00-75.00

ELF BANK, cast iron, still, 10" $275.00-400.00

ENGINE HOUSE FIVE, cast iron with canvas cover, 26", 1892 ....$700.00-1,000.00

ENGINE NUMBER 125, cast iron, 1892 fire engine, 19"...$1,000.00-2,000.00

EXPRESS WAGON, 1890's, 17½" long with two horses, cast iron $700.00-1,400.00

CAST IRON TOYS

FARM WAGON, cast iron with farmer and horse, 16", 1892 ....$500.00-1,000.00

FIRE CAPTAIN'S WAGON, cast iron toy, 1892, 12½" long $700.00-1,250.00

FIRE CHIEF'S WAGON, cast iron, 1892 ....$750.00-1,200.00

FIRE COMPANY HOOK AND LADDER TRUCK, 1889, cast iron, 24" long $1,000.00-2,000.00

FIRE ENGINE HOSE CART, cast iron, 1889, with driver, rider and two horses $800.00-1,600.00

FIRE ENGINE HOSE WAGON, #155, 1892, 10" long $800.00-1,500.00

FIRE ENGINE PUMPER with driver and two horses, cast iron, 1889 ....$600.00-1,300.00

FIRE ENGINE PUMPER, 16", 1892 ..$800.00-1,700.00

FIRE PATROL WAGON with driver, two horses and three firemen, 18" $1,200.00-2,200.00

FIRE PUMPER, Kenton, cast iron, 11". $400.00-700.00

FIRE PUMPER, cast iron, ca. 1930's $40.00-85.00

FIRE PUMPER WAGON with two horses and two firemen, 8", probably German $100.00-225.00

FIRE TRUCK, ARCADE, cast iron, 7½". $350.00-750.00

FIRE TRUCK by Dent, cast iron, 8" $50.00-85.00

FLYING ARTILLERY WAGON, cast iron, 1892, 24" long, two horses, seven soldiers with cannon $1,000.00-1,800.00

FORD SEDAN, ARCADE, 1920's, in original box $900.00-1,700.00

FORD SEDAN, ARCADE, cast iron, 1920's, boxed $900.00-1,700.00

FOXY GRANDPA COMIC CHARACTER, STILL BANK, 5½" $75.00-125.00

FROG ON ROCK, MECHANICAL BANK, cast iron $200.00-400.00

FROG PROFESSOR CAST IRON BANK, 3" long $75.00-110.00

GAS STOVE CAST IRON BANK, 5½" ...$60.00-100.00

GASOLINE TRUCK, ARCADE, 13", cast iron, 1920's $550.00-1,000.00

GENERAL BUTLER AS A FROG CAST IRON BANK, 6½" $125.00-220.00

GIBBS ENGLISH PONY CART, 1914, 13" long $200.00-500.00

GIBBS GREY BEAUTY RACERS, double horses pull wagon, 1912 ....$300.00-700.00

GIBBS HORSE PULLING CART THAT PUMPS, 1912, wood and paper lithograph $450.00-1,000.00

GIBBS PACING BOB, single horse pulling two-wheeled cart, 1912 ....$175.00-350.00

GIBBS PONY CIRCUS WAGON, 14" long with double horses, bright lithograph $1,000.00-2,000.00

GIBBS PONY PACER PULLING CART, 7" long, 1912, cast metal, wood, paper lithograph. $200.00-400.00

GIBBS SINGLE HORSE GYPSY WAGON, 1912, 14" long $200.00-500.00

GIBBS TWO HORSE COVERED GYPSY WAGON, ca. 1912, two horses and wagon $500.00-1,000.00

GIBBS U.S. MAIL WAGON WITH HORSE, 1914, 12" long $150.00-375.00

GLOBE BANK WITH EAGLE ON TOP, cast iron bank, 5½" $100.00-200.00

GOLLIWOG CAST IRON BANK, troll-like creature, 6" tall $50.00-100.00

GOOSE CAST IRON BANK, 4" $100.00-500.00

GERMAN, WESTERN-STYLED STAGE COACH, tin windup, with two horses, Furnish collection, $100.00-225.00.

CAST IRON FIRE PUMPER WITH TWO HORSES, 16" long, Furnish collection, $600.00-1,200.00.

FIRE WAGON PUMPER, single horse, 7", swivel joint attachment, Furnish collection, $70-160.00.

WINDUP FIRE PUMPER WAGON WITH TWO HORSES AND TWO FIREMEN, tin lithograph, 8", probably German, Furnish collection, $100.00-225.00.

TIN HORSE DRAWING TALL TIN CARRIAGE, folk-type, Furnish collection, $70.00-150.00.

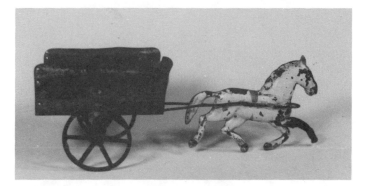

PAINTED TIN HORSE PULLING HAY CART, 8", Furnish collection, $75.00-175.00.

LION BANK, 6", $60.00-120.00, PRANCING HORSE, 6", black, $50.00-95.00, Furnish collection.

PONY DRAWING CART, 3½", $35.00-85.00. MAN ON WAGON WITH PACING HORSE, $50.00-100.00, Furnish collection.

GRAF ZEPPELIN, bank with wheels, cast iron, 8" long $150.00-225.00

GREYHOUND BUS, Arcade, cast iron, 1930's...$75.00-225.00

GUN BOAT cast iron bank, 8½" long ..$700.00-950.00

HEN SITTING ON NEST, cast iron, still bank, 3"...$50.00-100.00

HIPPO CAST IRON BANK, 2½" tall $75.00-110.00

HOG BANK "TAKE ALL I GET," cast iron, curled tail, 7"...$90.00-140.00

HOOK AND LADDER FIRE TRUCK, cast iron, 16" long $200.00-500.00

HOOP-LA MECHANICAL CAST IRON BANK, clown holds hoop, dog jumps...............$900.00-1,400.00

HORSE COVERED WITH BLANKET, cast iron bank $40.00-80.00

HORSE ON TUB, cast iron bank, 5" ..$200.00-300.00

HORSE ON WHEELS, PRANCING, 5" cast iron rolling bank $200.00-400.00

HORSE DRAWN CART WITH DRIVER, partly covered cast iron, 5" $65.00-140.00

HORSE, 4", gold finish, bank $30.00-50.00

HORSE PULLING COACH-TYPE WAGON, tin, 7", cast iron wheels $70.00-165.00

HORSE, REARING UP, black finished cast iron, smooth base, 7" tall $20.00-50.00

HORSE WAGON WITH SINGLE DRIVER AND HORSE, cast iron, Ives, 1890's $800.00-1,750.00

HUBLEY BELL TELEPHONE TRUCK, 1930's, cast iron, winch works, white tires $300.00-500.00

HUBLEY CAR CARRIER, cast iron, four cars, 10" long $300.00-575.00

HUBLEY CAST IRON "NODDER," 1910 ....$750.00-1,800.00

HUBLEY cast iron motorcycle cop with side car...$300.00-400.00

HUBLEY, CAST IRON MOTORCYCLE, three wheels $400.00-700.00

HUBLEY, CAST IRON RACER, 7".......$150.00-325.00

HUBLEY SEDAN, 1920's, 7" $200.00-275.00

HUBLEY CRASH CAR, 5", 1930's, cast iron motorcycle with cart on back $40.00-95.00

HUBLEY PARCEL POST MOTORCYCLE WITH SIDE-CAR, cast iron $2,000.00-4,000.00

HUBLEY RACE CAR #22, cast iron, 7½" long $175.00-325.00

HUBLEY SERVICE COACH, cast iron, 5" long $300.00-450.00

HUBLEY STAKE BED TRUCK, 3", cast iron $20.00-40.00

INDEPENDENCE HALL, cast iron bank, 9" long $150.00-225.00

INDIAN AND BEAR PAINTED BANK, cast iron, mechanical $800.00-1,200.00

INDIAN CHIEF BANK, gold finish, cast iron, 4" $100.00-225.00

INDIAN SHOOTING BEAR, mechanical bank, 7½", cast iron $300.00-500.00

INDIAN, FULL FIGURE CAST IRON BANK, 6" tall...$100.00-200.00

INTERNATIONAL HARVESTER DUMP TRUCK, Arcade, cast iron, 10" long $250.00-500.00

CAST IRON TOYS

INTERNATIONAL TRUCK, ARCADE, cast iron $1,400.00-2,300.00

JEWEL CHEST BANK, cast iron with brass knob, 6½" long $150.00-250.00

JEWEL TOY RANGE WITH ORNATE STACK AND SHELF, #15 .... $100.00-250.00

JEWEL TOY RANGE, #10, cast iron, toy stove, 1892 .... $100.00-200.00

JOCKEY ON HORSE, CAST IRON PLATFORM TOY, Gong Bell, 1914, 7" $700.00-1,200.00

JONAH AND THE WHALE, painted, cast iron, mechanical bank $500.00-750.00

KENTON DOUBLE DECKER BUS, 1920's, 8", cast iron $400.00-675.00

KEWPIE-LIKE CAST IRON BANK, 6", recent $10.00-20.00

KEYSTONE COP BUST "EVERY COPPER HELPS," cast iron, still bank $100.00-175.00

KEYSTONE COP WITH BILLY CLUB, cast iron bank $110.00-165.00

LIBERTY BELL cast iron bank, 3½" $10.00-20.00

LIBERTY BELL cast iron bank, 4" $50.00-110.00

LIBERTY CHIME PULL TOY, cast iron, 7½" long, 1886, Liberty with flag $1,000.00-1,650.00

LIGHTHOUSE PAINTED MECHANICAL cast iron bank $700.00-1,000.00

LION AND MONKEYS MECHANICAL CAST IRON BANK, lion, trees, monkeys, 9".... $800.00-1,200.00

LION BANK, cast iron, still $65.00-85.00

LION CAST IRON BANK, low profile, stalking $30.00-70.00

LION ON TUB, CAST IRON BANK, 4" gold finish $60.00-90.00

LION ON WHEELS BANK, 5" $30.00-75.00

LITTLE JOE MECHANICAL CAST IRON BANK, painted $150.00-275.00

LITTLE RED RIDING HOOD, CAST IRON BANK, girl with wolf, 5" $125.00-225.00

MACK DUMP TRUCK by Arcade, cast iron bank, 13" $400.00-700.00

MACK OIL TRUCK, cast iron, 1920's, 10", cast iron $400.00-650.00

MAMMY WITH SPOON, CAST IRON BANK 6" tall $85.00-135.00

MAN IN BARREL, CAST IRON BANK, black, 3½" $200.00-400.00

MECHANICAL, CAST IRON FIRE ENGINE with driver, rider. two horses, 1892, 19" $1,200.00-2,400.00

MECHANICAL FIRE ENGINE HOUSE WITH FIRE ENGINE, 1892, cast iron $700.00-1,600.00

MERMAID BOAT CAST IRON BANK, boy sits in boat with fish, 4" $75.00-100.00

MERRY GO ROUND, EXTREMELY RARE, mechanical, cast iron, 6¼" $9,000.00-13,000.00

MILKING COW BANK, cast iron, 7"....$150.00-200.00

MODEL A WRECKER, 1920's, cast iron, winch works, 11", metal tires $250.00-500.00

MODEL CART WITH LARGE WHEEL ON HORSE'S FOOT, cast iron, 13", 1892 .... $400.00-800.00

MODEL T BANK, ARCADE, cast iron, 1920's $600.00-1,000.00

MONKEY CHIME CHARIOT TOY, cast iron and metal, 1886, 6" long $500.00-1,000.00

TOYLAND'S FARM PRODUCTS MILK AND CREAM WAGON, windup, 12", tin lithograph, Furnish collection, $65.00-150.00.

CAST IRON MILK WAGON PULLED BY BLACK HORSE, 12" long, 7" tall, Furnish collection, $100.00-275.00.

MONKEY ON ORGAN, CAST IRON, MECHANICAL BANK, 1889 .... $800.00-1,300.00

MONKEY, 8½", cast iron bank $100.00-200.00

MONKEYMOBILE BELL TOY, 1903, cast iron $500.00-950.00

MOTORCYCLE BY HUBLEY, cast iron, 9" $100.00-160.00

MOTORCYCLE PATROL, 1930's $30.00-60.00

MOTORCYCLE POLICE WITH SIDE CAR, two police figures, cast iron, 1930's, 5".......... $70.00-145.00

NEGRO PLAYING BANJO, still, cast iron bank, 16" $300.00-650.00

OLD LIBERTY BELL, still, cast iron bank, 4" $75.00-100.00

OLIVER FARM TRACTOR WITH PLANTER, cast iron, Arcade $110.00-150.00

ORIENTAL FISHERMAN, cast iron bank.$65.00-90.00

OWL BANK, seated on rectanglar base, 4", painted $100.00-150.00

PAGODA BANK, oriental house, cast iron, 5", silver/ gold finish $200.00-300.00

PANAMA DIRT CART, cast iron wagon with driver and horses, 20", 1914 .... $1,000.00-1,600.00

PELICAN WITH ARAB, mechanical, cast iron, bank, painted $1,600.00-2,200.00

PERSHING BANK, bust figural, bronze, 8" $100.00-140.00

PIG BANK, "INVEST IN PORK," black, cast iron bank, 7" $150.00-190.00

PIG BANK, seated pose, cast iron, gold finish $15.00-30.00

POLICE TRUCK, cast iron by Dent $500.00-850.00

PONTIAC BY KENTON, cast iron, 4" $50.00-100.00

PONY "MY PET," FIGURAL CAST IRON BANK, 4" $45.00-75.00

PONY CART, cast iron, 4" long $100.00-250.00

PONY EXPRESS WAGON, cast iron, 14", 1892, one horse and driver $600.00-1,100.00

PONY PHAETON CAST IRON RIG, 1892, with one lady driver $1,000.00-1,800.00

PONY BANK, small, 3", cast iron, still, with bridle and saddle...$20.00-40.00

PRANCING HORSE, 7", cast iron bank $75.00-105.00

RADIO BANK, 1930's, console model, cast iron $100.00-150.00

RAILWAY EXPRESS TRUCK, cast iron, 1930's, 5", balloon type, metal tires $150.00-250.00

RED GOOSE SHOES PREMIUM CAST IRON BANK, 4" $50.00-100.00

REVOLVING BELL CHIME TOY, rolls, 1889, cast iron, and metal $250.00-500.00

ROADSTER, CAST IRON, 3½" version, metal balloon-type tires $30.00-65.00

ROADSTER, cast iron, late 1930's, white rubber tires.......................................$35.00-75.00

ROOSTER CAST IRON, STILL BANK, brass-look finish, 5" $150.00 275.00

RUMPELSTILTSKIN CAST IRON BANK, 6" $200.00-400.00

SAD IRON AND STAND, 1886, cast iron, child's toy $20.00-40.00

SAINT BERNARD DOG, cast iron bank, 11", very large bank $150.00-240.00

SANTA AND CHIMNEY MECHANICAL BANK, cast iron $700.00-1,000.00

SANTA AND HIS SLEIGH, cast iron, 1880's, 17", rare....................................$1,000.00-2,000.00

SANTA CLAUS BANK, cast iron, pack over back, up-right, 5" $40.00-70.00

SANTA CLAUS CAST IRON BANK, by tree, painted, 5½" $150.00-250.00

SANTA CLAUS CAST IRON BANK, 1889, mechanical $600.00-1,300.00

SAVING SAM CAST IRON BANK, 1920's . $85.00-160.00

SCOTTIE CAST IRON BANK, 3 ....$40.00-85.00

SEATED BEGGAR BOY CAST IRON BANK, 7" $100.00-200.00

SHEEP FIGURAL BANK, cast iron, 5½" .$40.00-70.00

SHEEP, WALKING POSE, 3", cast iron bank $100.00-200.00

SINGLE TRUCK, CAST IRON PULL TOY WITH DRIVER AND MERCHANDISE, 1889 ....$800.00-1,700.00

SINGLE TRUCK, CAST IRON TOY WITH GALLOPING HORSE FIGURE, 15", 1889 ....$400.00-1,000.00

SMALL CAT, cast iron bank, 4", seated .$30.00-55.00

SOLDIER cast iron bank, painted, 5" ...$45.00-100.00

SQUIRREL BANK, cast iron, still, 6" ..$125.00-200.00

SQUIRREL HOLDING NUT CAST IRON BANK, 4" $100.00-200.00

STAKE TRUCK, cast iron, Arcade, 7" ...$75.00-180.00

STOVE, cast iron, 4", 1886 ....$100.00-250.00

STOVE BANK, ARCADE, 4" cast iron $60.00-90.00

STOVE, CAST IRON, ORNATE BASE BURNER STOVE, 1892, 12½" tall $50.00-130.00

STREAMLINED RACER, Hubley, cast iron, 5" $35.00-70.00

STUMP SPEAKER, mechanical bank . $900.00-1,400.00

SULKY WITH JOCKEY CAST IRON TOY, 1889 ....$750.00-1,500.00

SURREY WITH LADY DRIVER, cast iron toy, 1914, 13" long $600.00-1,300.00

SURREY, CAST IRON, with driver in tall top hat and single horse, 15", 1892 ....$1,000.00-1,700.00

TANK BANK, cast iron, 7" long WWI-type $200.00-300.00

TEDDY AND THE BEAR, mechanical, cast iron bank, painted $1,000.00-1,400.00

THREE MONKEYS "SEE NO EVIL" BANK, cast iron $150.00-275.00

TOP HAT "PASS AROUND THE HAT," cast iron bank, 2½" $50.00-100.00

TOW TRUCK, ARCADE, cast iron, 4" $40.00-80.00

TRANSFER WAGON, cast iron, 18" with driver and double horses $700.00-1,500.00

TRICK DOG, MECHANICAL CAST IRON BANK by Hubley, 9" $200.00-450.00

TRUCK, CHEVROLET, 1920's, 9" long Arcade $300.00-850.00

TURKEY CAST IRON BANK, 4" $250.00-375.00

TWO BILLY GOATS BUTTING, CAST IRON BANK, 4" $20.00-45.00

TWO FACED BLACK BOY BANK, 4" $75.00-125.00

UNCLE SAM MECHANICAL CAST IRON BANK, 1886, 11" $750.00-1,200.00

UNCLE TOM, MECHANICAL, CAST IRON BANK, painted $300.00-550.00

WALKING LION CAST IRON BANK, still, 5⅛", gold finish $25.00-50.00

WASHINGTON MONUMENT, CAST IRON BANK, still, 6" $100.00-150.00

WILLIAM TELL PAINTED, MECHANICAL, CAST IRON BANK $800.00-1,250.00

WISE PIG, cast iron, still bank, 7" $30.00-60.00

WOVEN BASKET BANK, 3" $50.00-75.00

WOVEN BASKET CAST IRON BANK, 7" $100.00-200.00

GIBBS TOY U.S. MAIL, PULLTOY, #27, 1910's metal and lithograph paper on wood, $150.00-300.00, Furnish Collection.

CIRCUS AND CARNIVAL RELATED TOYS

Circus and carnival related items have been grouped together in this listing. This small section includes toys that relate to the circus in either design or function and toys that owe their design to carnival type rides.

When discussing toys of this category, the outstanding toy in this area is the Schoenhut Humpty Dumpty Circus. Although several versions of this toy were manufactured over the years, all are extremely collectible. Single Schoenhut animals and human performers from the original sets command hundreds of dollars today. Found complete, boxed, and in mint condition, the Schoenhut Humpty Dumpty Circus can sell for thousands of dollars.

The Schoenhut clowns, animals and circus acts are most desirable items today because of their unique wood and wood composition jointed design. Found in the complete set with the realistic cloth circus tent, it is a true museum piece.

In the heyday of the local amusement park when nearly every medium sized city had its own local version of Coney Island, complete with a roller coaster, toy manufacturers began to imitate the rides and attractions that made the parks so popular to young visitors. Windup rocket rides, ferris wheels, carousels, auto parks, round swings, and roller coasters by Marx, Unique Art and other manufacturers are permanent reminders of the importance neighborhood amusement parks once enjoyed in American family life.

CHEIN FERRIS WHEEL, windup toy, all metal, Reynolds collection, $100.00-200.00.

WOLVERINE DRUM MAJOR WINDUP, 15" tall, #27, all tin, Reynolds collection, $60.00-135.00.

A PEEP AT THE CIRCUS PICTURE PUZZLE, 1887 McLoughlin Brothers, boxed $100.00-250.00

ACROBATIC CLOWN, lever action, wood, 1940, 6" $15.00-30.00

ACROBATIC MARVEL, rocking monkey windup, 1930's, Marx..$60.00-90.00

ACROBATIC MONKEY, all celluloid, Japan, 5" red tux, circles on hands $35.00-65.00

ACROBATIC MONKEY, Marx, 1930's tin windup, balances on two chairs $60.00-95.00

ACROBATIC MONKEY by Wolverine $90.00-150.00

ACTION CLOWNS, Expert Toys, 7" tin momentum, clowns turn and spin.........................$35.00-60.00

BALANCING CLOWN, Chein, windup, 1930's, 5" $25.00-65.00

BALANCING CLOWN, U.S. Zone Germany, clown balances on hands, 5" tin $50.00-100.00

BIG TOP CIRCUS, G. E. PREMIUM, 60 punch-outs, 1950...$20.00-50.00

BRADLEY'S CIRCUS, Milton Bradley, 1882 boxed game.....................................$100.00-200.00

BRUNO THE SPECTACLE BEAR, Japan, windup, 7" tin and plush $35.00-65.00

BUMPER CAR WINDUP, 6½" tin lithograph...$50.00-100.00

BUSTER BROWN AT THE CIRCUS, 1900's, boxed card game $75.00-135.00

CHAMPION WEIGHT LIFTER MONKEY, BO, 10", lifts weights over head...............................$35.00-60.00

CHARLIE THE DRUMMING CLOWN, Alps, Japan, 10", celluloid face, tin base $65.00-135.00

CHARLIE THE DRUMMING CLOWN, BO, Japan, 10" $65.00-135.00

CHEIN MERRY GO ROUND WITH SWAN CHAIRS, tin wind-up, 11" $200.00-400.00

CHEIN ROLLER COASTER, tin $125.00-195.00

CHEIN SPACE RIDE, lever action with music, tin lithograph, boxed $100.00-300.00

CHICK MERRY GO ROUND, Japan, celluloid windup, 7" boxed...$15.00-35.00

CIRCUS BAND WAGON, Courtland, tin momentum, plastic wheels, 12" $20.00-40.00

CIRCUS BOXED CARDBOARD GAME, 1914...$125.00-250.00

CIRCUS CYCLIST, Hi-Wheel, TPS, Japan, tin windup, 7" $90.00-150.00

CIRCUS DRUMMER, celluloid and tin, pre-war windup $400.00-950.00

CIRCUS ELEPHANT, KA, Japan, windup, 7" tin elephant pushes ball, umbrella spins $45.00-90.00

CIRCUS GAME, 1947 ....$25.00-40.00

CIRCUS MONKEY ON HORSEBACK, tin windup, 1950's, Haji, Japan $35.00-55.00

CIRCUS PARADE, tin wind-up, 11" elephant with hinged ears, three clowns, TPS....................$60.00-135.00

CIRCUS PERFORMERS LUNCH PAIL, 1930's $10.00-25.00

CIRCUS SEAL, MT, Japan, tin windup, 5" walks on flippers, ball spins.............................$30.00-65.00

CIRCUS, REVELL, C-31, with bareback rider, horses, ladders, etc., 1940's $85.00-110.00

CLOWN AT MUSIC STAND, tin lithograph, toy, 7" $50.00-135.00

CLOWN BANK, brass foundry pattern, white paint, 6" $175.00-225.00

CLOWN BELL TOY WITH TWO BELLS, cast iron, 1914 bell toy, 7" long $500.00-1,000.00

CLOWN CAST IRON BANK, tall curved hat, painted, 6" $110.00-195.00

CLOWN DRUMMER BY SCHUCO, manufactured in Germany, 4½" windup $50.00-110.00

CLOWN FIDDLER, manufactured by Schuco, 4½", windup $50.00110.00

CLOWN HEAD WITH SMALL FUNNY HAT, pot metal bank..$30.00-55.00

CLOWN IN BARREL, Chein, 1930's, 8" tin windup, waddles $125.00-250.00

CLOWN MAKING THE LION JUMP THROUGH THE HOOP, TPS, Japan, 50's $100.00-175.00

CLOWN MECHANICAL BANK, "Humpty Dumpty Bank," clown eats coins, 7½" $200.00-400.00

CLOWN MOTOR CYCLE, friction, 1950's, boxed...$125.00-250.00

CLOWN ON DONKEY, windup, pre-war, 6" clown on donkey $50.00-125.00

CLOWN ON DONKEY, U.S. Zone Germany, Bloomer and Schuler tin windup, 6" $100.00-150.00

CLOWN ON GLOBE, painted, cast iron, mechanical bank, 9" tall $1000.00-1500.00

CLOWN ON STICK ANIMATED TOY, lever action on single stick, 1890 ....$100.00-300.00

CLOWN PLAYING FLUTE AND DRUM, tin wind-up, 9" $80.00-160.00

CLOWN ROLY POLY, 4", all celluloid, sits on ball, Japan, 1930's $100.00-200.00

CLOWN TENPINS GAME, 1912 boxed with ball...$100.00-165.00

CLOWN WITH CONE HAT, painted bank, pot metal, 4" tall..$25.00-45.00

CLOWN WITH PARASOL, Chein, 1920's, 8" spins parasol on nose $100.00-175.00

CLOWN, HAPPY FIDDLER, BO, Alps, Japan, 10" $150.00-300.00

CLOWN, cast iron, still bank, 6" holding horn $70.00-125.00

CLOWN, Daily Dime Registering Bank, tin $10.00-20.00

CLOWN, round, tin lithograph, 2" $25.00-50.00

CLOWN, tin, semi-mechanical, "eats" coins, 5", colorful $100.00-200.00

COUNTY FAIR GAME, Parker Brothers, boxed, board game $75.00-100.00

CRAZY CLOWN, Yone, Japan, tin windup, plastic wheels, 4½" long..$20.00-40.00

DISNEYLAND EXPRESS, CASEY JR. CIRCUS TRAIN, tin windup, Marx, 12", boxed $65.00-95.00

DISNEYLAND FERRIS WHEEL, Chein, 1940's $100.00-250.00

DOG DRESSED IN PARADE OUTFIT PULL TOY, Fisher Price, 1934 pull toy $50.00-95.00

DOG ON ICE CREAM WAGON pull toy, Fisher Price, 1940 ....$50.00-100.00

DUMBO, Marx windup, 1949, tin, Walt Disney Productions $100.00-240.00

ELEPHANT STANDING ON CIRCUS TUB, still cast, iron bank, gold finish, 5½" $100.00-150.00

CIRCUS AND CARNIVAL TOYS

ELEPHANT WITH DRUM, seated, pot metal, 4" $200.00-350.00

FERRIS WHEEL TRUCK, tin, BO, 11" double Ferris wheel $145.00-285.00

FERRIS WHEEL, pre-war German, tin windup, four men in four gondolas $145.00-300.00

FLYING CIRCUS by Unique Art, boxed, elephant, plane and clown $195.00-325.00

GIBBS PONY CIRCUS WAGON, 14", two horses pulling paper/wood lithograph wagon ..$1,000.00-2,000.00

GONDOLA RIDE, 10", lithograph, four gondolas with children, riders and music.............$100.00-200.00

HAPPY SAD CLOWN, Japan, BO, cloth and vinyl, changes expression $60.00-120.00

HAPPY THE TROMBONE PLAYER, tin windup, TPS, Japan, 10", tin and cloth $90.00-150.00

HIPPODROME CIRCUS GAME, Milton Bradley, 1895, 16" x 11", circus lid $95.00-200.00

HOKEY POKEY ICE CREAM PUSH CART VENDOR, 1910, German $1,500.00-2,500.00

HOPPO THE MONKEY, tin windup, Marx, 1925, 8", plays cymbals $65.00-120.00

ICE CREAM CART by Courtland, tin lithograph with large ball, 1940's $60.00-95.00

JET ROLLER COASTER, Wolverine, tin windup, ramp toy, 12" boxed $55.00-120.00

JOLLY JOCKO, pre-war, Japan, 5" plush monkey combs his hair, windup................................$30.00-60.00

JUMBO ELEPHANT XYLOPHONE PLAYER, Fisher Price, 1937 ....$100.00-145.00

LEHMANN CLOWN ON DONKEY, tin windup, 1911 ....$250.00-500.00

LONG NECKED clown car $900.00-1,500.00

MERRY BALL BLOWER CIRCUS TRUCK, Japan, 5", tin windup $50.00-95.00

MERRY GO ROUND, boxed card game, 1914...$25.00-60.00

MERRY GO ROUND WITH CLOWN, tin lithograph, platform pull toy, 1929 ....$250.00-500.00

MERRY GO ROUND, Wolverine, tin with airplanes and horses $85.00-165.00

MERRY GO ROUND CAROUSEL CIRCUS WAGON, pull toy by Toy Kraft, 1930's $50.00-125.00

MICKEY MOUSE CIRCUS GAME, Marks Brother, 1930's boxed, marble action $300.00-600.00

MICKEY MOUSE PARADE DRUMMER with bass drum and cymbals, 1938 Fisher-Price $100.00-250.00

MICKEY MOUSE TUMBLING CIRCUS PULL TOY, Nifty, early 1930's, Disney, wood $500.00-950.00

MISTER DAN THE HOTDOG EATING MAN, TN, Japan, windup, 7", box $25.00-55.00

MONKEY MOTOR CYCLE, Japan, friction, 1950's, boxed...$150.00-300.00

MONKEY RIDING A CANDY CART, 1950's, tin lithograph $40.00-70.00

MUSICAL ELEPHANT, Japan, tin windup, 6", plays drum and cymbals $35.00-65.00

MUSICAL KIDDY GO ROUND CAROUSEL, Unique Art, boxed...$150.00-300.00

ROCKET RIDE, W. German, tin lever action, rockets swing out, 7½" $45.00-75.00

ROCKET RIDE, W. German, 1955, tin lever action, 8" with four rockets $45.00-100.00

ROLLER SKATING HOBO CLOWN, TPS, Japan, 6", tin

ACROBATIC MARVEL, Marx windup toy, 12", base 8" wide, Reynolds collection, $60.00-90.00.

windup $85.00-195.00

SCHOENHUT CAMEL with glass eyes, 9" tall...$100.00-250.00

SCHOENHUT CIRCUS CAGE WAGON, painted wood with leopard inside $800.00-1,500.00

SCHOENHUT HIPPO WITH PAINTED EYES, from circus $100.00-250.00

SCHOENHUT HUMPTY DUMPTY CIRCUS, figures, tent, animals, accessories.................$3,000.00-7,000.00

SCHOENHUT HUMPTY DUMPTY CIRCUS TENT, (tent only) $300.00-650.00

SCHOENHUT LADY circus rider $100.00-200.00

SCHOENHUT LEOPARD, wood with jointed limbs $100.00-300.00

SCHOENHUT lion tamer $100.00-250.00

SCHOENHUT white circus horse $100.00-200.00

SEE SAW MONKEYS, Distler, German, 1920's, 10" long $175.00-400.00

SEE SAW MONKEYS, Distler, German, 1920, tin windup, 10" $175.00-400.00

SHOOTING GALLERY, Wyandotte $75.00-155.00

SMILING SAM THE CARNIVAL MAN, clown windup, Alps, Japan, 9" $100.00-175.00

TIN CARNIVAL SET, WYANDOTTE, Merry Go Round, Ferris wheel, airplanes $260.00-380.00

TOTO THE CLOWN, George S. Scott Manufacturing $150.00-200.00

TOYLAND SEE SAW, tin lithograph of carnival rides, windup, 7" $110.00-195.00

TUMBLING CLOWN CELLULOID WIND-UP, Japan, 1930's $100.00-200.00

WOLVERINE acrobatic monkeys $90.00-150.00

WOLVERINE CAROUSEL, in original box $400.00-600.00

CLOWN WITH MOUSE BY SCHUCO, windup, Germany, 4½" tall, Reynolds collection, $50.00-110.00.

ACROBATIC GIRLS, celluloid windup, 12", jointed celluloid figures with canopy top, whirls when wound, Japan, Reynolds collection, $150.00-300.00.

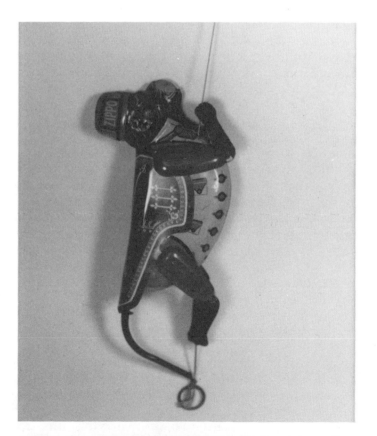

ZIPPO, TIN CLIMBING MONKEY, climbs string when ring is pulled, Reynolds collection, $70.00-140.00.

COMIC CHARACTER TOYS

When Richard Outcault first penned his Yellow Kid comic strip at the beginning of this century it is doubtful that he realized the potential impact his little character would have upon the world. From the Yellow Kid, early Foxy Grandpa and Buster Brown pages, Americans learned to love the comic strips in their newspapers. As it is with all popular characters today, the next step after the public acceptance and popularity of a strip in the newspapers was mass marketing. Nearly as soon as the Yellow Kid hit the first pages of newsprint, toy producers were interested in capitalizing on his success.

It is because the comics contributed in such a fun way to the humor and leisure of Americans that they became such popular subjects for toys during the first two decades of this century.

Then the 1920's hit and the toy market must have become absolute madness. By the early 1920's, American and German toy makers were utilizing unique lithographic processes and tin fabrication presses to churn out literally thousands of remarkable comic character toys. Because comic characters were typically very strong graphic figures with clear outlining and bright colors, their likenesses transformed quite well into tin lithographed toys.

In the past 10 years, tin windup comic character toys have led in the forefront as a volatile, extremely competitive area of collecting. Comic character toys are pleasing to look at and display, in addition to maintaining a strong element of humorous action. Because they are designed in the likenesses of famous, recognizable characters, it is getting close to impossible to acquire such toys at bargain prices. Most dealers and collectors today are very knowledgeable about current toy values. The fact that the toys have a clearly recognizable comic character as their subject makes them doubly difficult to acquire at a low price since the character itself often dates the toy exactly and helps to authenticate the item.

Generally, as in the case of certain windup comic character toys by Louis Marx, the generic non-character equivalent of an identical toy may sell for less than 50% the value of its comic character counterpart. Popeye carrying the twin parrot cages as a windup would bring nearly twice as much as the Marx Red Cap Porter under most conditions, and these are identical toys except for the color lithograph! It is clear to see the value built into a good comic character toy.

The 1930's comic character windups by Louis Marx and Unique Art are some of the best toy designs of this century. The Popeye The Champ windup toy by Louis Marx featuring celluloid boxer figures of Bluto and Popeye with loose jointed swinging arms not only sports a unique and attractive exterior design, the windup mechanism inside is also out of the ordinary. The mechanism allows the toy boxing to be acted out in "rounds" so that at the end of each furious fighting sequence (about 30 seconds or so) one of the two fighters gets knocked into the ropes with the sounding of a bell. This toy is not only a fine addition to any toy collection; it's also great fun to watch!

The host of comic characters presented in this list represents the comics from the 1960's through the 1980's. Metal, wood, tin, plastic and composition toys are all presented in this listing.

Novice collectors who start anew in this field of collecting should realize that it is both expansive and expensive, especially the latter, if the collector wants to focus on early comic characters. Specializing is probably the best goal here. By concentrating on early comic characters, tin windups of comic characters, or later comic characters, the inexperienced collector can soon discover his own particular tastes and what his budget will allow within the field. Trying to collect 80 years of toys for all comic characters can be draining and frustrating, so specializing within this category seems to be a reasonable solution.

The "funny papers" have been a part of American daily life for almost a century. The comic character toys inspired by these strips are not only objects of attractive popular art, they are also historical objects reminding us of the significance that newspapers have had upon our society. These toys are lasting reminders and among the realm of toy collecting, they are here to stay!

CHESTER AND ANDY GUMP, jointed metal/composition dolls, c. 1920's, Reynolds collection, $200.00-475.00 each.

BARNEY GOOGLE AND SPARK PLUG WINDUP, Nifty, German, 7", Furnish collection, $900.00-1,350.00.

ALEXANDER (Dagwood's son), wood composition figure, 3" c. 1944, K.F.S. $15.00-25.00

ALPHONSE AND GASTON COMIC CHARACTER BANDANA, 12" square $50.00-90.00

ALPHONSE AND GASTON AUTOMOBILE, by Kenton, animated movement $875.00-1,470.00

ALPHONSE AND GASTON HANKY, ca. 1900's, Fred Opper characters $20.00-40.00

ALPHONSE IN CART CAST IRON NODDER, ca. 1900's $650.00-1,100.00

ANDY GUMP 348 AUTOMOBILE, cast iron, manufactured by Arcade, 7" long.............$725.00-1,100.00

ANDY GUMP 348 CAR manufactured by Tootsietoy, pot metal, 3" long $155.00-285.00

ANDY GUMP ASH TRAY, floor standing model, folk art, 28" $35.00-65.00

ANDY GUMP BISQUE NODDER FIGURE, 4", German $35.00-70.00

ANDY GUMP cast iron bank, 5", Arcade .$195.00-300.00

ANDY GUMP FACE MASK, Listerine premium, 1930's $20.00-35.00

ANDY GUMP GERMAN NODDER BISQUE FIGURE, 4" tall..$45.00-85.00

ANDY PANDA BANK, COMPOSITION, 6".$20.00-45.00

ANDY PANDA CERAMIC PLANTER, 1958, Walter Lantz, 5" $15.00-30.00

ANDY PANDA GLAZED CHINA FIGURE, 1940, Walter Lantz $40.00-80.00

ANNIE ROONEY WOOD COMPOSITION FIGURE, 1940's, 5" tall...................................$20.00-40.00

AUNT EPPIE HOGG (TOONERVILLE CHARACTER), RIDING A TRUCK, tin windup...$875.00-1,400.00

BABY SPARKLE PLENTY COLORING BOOK, Saalfield, 1949, 11" x 14"..................................$15.00-30.00

BABY SPARKLE PLENTY DOLL, by Ideal, in original, 14" box $125.00-225.00

BABY, FROM THE FAMILY, bisque spring head nodder..$35.00-60.00

BARNEY GOOGLE AND SPARK PLUG BISQUE FIGURINE, German, 3" x 3"....................$95.00-145.00

BARNEY GOOGLE AND SPARK PLUG, tin windup, 7" tall, German, by Nifty $900.00-1,350.00

BARNEY GOOGLE BOOK, published by Saalfield, 1935...$20.00-40.00

BARNEY GOOGLE CHINA FIGURE, 4", 1920's, German $35.00-75.00

BARNEY GOOGLE FOX TROT SHEET MUSIC, ca. 1923 ....$15.00-30.00

BARNEY GOOGLE MUG, German, 1920's .$25.00-50.00

BARNEY GOOGLE PLASTER FIGURE, ca. 1920's, 9" tall...$50.00-85.00

BARNEY GOOGLE RIDING SPARK PLUG, PLASTER FIGURE, 9" tall, colorful, 1930's $50.00-110.00

BARNEY GOOGLE SALT AND PEPPER SHAKERS, 1940's, 3" tall ....,............$20.00-40.00

BARNEY GOOGLE STUFFED DOLL, 12", ca. 1920's or 1930's $65.00-140.00

BARNEY GOOGLE WOODEN DOLL FIGURE, ca. 1922, by Schoenhut, jointed $350.00-525.00

BARNEY RUBBLE CHARACTER VINYL FIGURE, 10" tall, 1960's......................................$10.00-20.00

BARNEY RUBBLE RIDING DINO, tin windup by Louis Marx, ca. 1960's, 8" long..................$45.00-85.00

COMIC CHARACTER TOYS

BATMAN AND ROBIN BOOKENDS, 1960, plaster, c. National Periodical Public $40.00-75.00

BATMAN CHARACTER BELT on original card, c. 1966, Morris Belt Company $20.00-50.00

BATMAN COFFEE MUG, ceramic, 1950's .$10.00-15.00

BATMAN GLASS TUMBLER, 1960's $5.00-10.00

BATMAN KNIFE, shaped like a Bat plane, German $15.00-30.00

BATMAN RING, picture changes, 1960's .$10.00-15.00

BEETLE BAILEY COMPOSITION NODDER, 7", 1950's $30.00-60.00

BETTY BOOP AND BIMBO bridge cards $10.00-20.00

BETTY BOOP AND BIMBO FIGURAL CHINA ASTRAY, 1930's $60.00-125.00

BETTY BOOP AND BIMBO SCORE PAD, 1930's, 4" $20.00-40.00

BETTY BOOP AND KOKO GLAZED CHINA SAUCER, 3", 1930's $20.00-35.00

BETTY BOOP AND MICKEY MOUSE CEREAL BOWL, 6" in diameter, glazed ceramic $65.00-95.00

BETTY BOOP BISQUE CHARACTER FIGURE, Drummer $35.00-65.00

BETTY BOOP BISQUE FIGURE PLAYING FRENCH HORN, 4" tall, ca. 1930's $30.00-50.00

BETTY BOOP BISQUE FIGURE, 3" tall ..$20.00-45.00

BETTY BOOP CELLULOID BUCKLE, 1930's $20.00-45.00

BETTY BOOP CELLULOID FIGURE PLAYS VIOLIN, 1930's $45.00-95.00

BETTY BOOP CELLULOID WINDUP TOY, Japan, 7" tall $135.00-275.00

BETTY BOOP CHALK STRING HOLDER, 10" across, string comes out of mouth $65.00-135.00

BETTY BOOP DOLL BLANKET, 1930's Max Fleisher Studio Copyright $45.00-80.00

BETTY BOOP HANKY, 9" square, 1930's .$15.00-35.00

BETTY BOOP LUSTERWARE ASHTRAY, 1930's, glazed ceramic $75.00-135.00

BETTY BOOP POCKET WATCH, 1920's-1930's, character face $175.00-300.00

BETTY BOOP SHEET MUSIC "Poor Cinderella," 1934 .... $35.00-70.00

BETTY BOOP TAMBOURINE, unmarked knock-off item $20.00-45.00

BETTY BOOP WALL POCKET, glazed ceramic, picture on front, 6" tall $65.00-100.00

BIMBO BISQUE FIGURE, 2" tall $15.00-40.00

BIMBO MUSICIANS BISQUE FIGURES SET, three different figures, each 4" $95.00-165.00

BIMBO PLAYING A VIOLIN, 3" bisque figure, 1930's $15.00-35.00

BIMBO, BETTY BOOP'S DOG, jointed wood and composition, 1930's, 7" with label $300.00-500.00

BLONDIE AND DAGWOOD BLOCKS, King Features Syndicate, 1951, 11" x 7" box $25.00-55.00

BLONDIE AND DAGWOOD DOLL STROLLER, 1950's, metal lithograph $35.00-65.00

BLONDIE CHARACTER DIE-CUT VALENTINE, Dagwood comic strip $5.00-15.00

BLONDIE GOES TO LEISURELAND, Westinghouse Premium game $20.00-45.00

BLONDIE MINIATURE LEAD FIGURE, ca. 1940's, 2½" $15.00-22.00

BLONDIE PAINT SET, tin box, 1952 ...... $10.00-20.00

BLONDIE PAINTS, paint set in metal box, 1946 American Crayon Company $6.00-14.00

BLONDIE WOOD COMPOSITION FIGURE, 1944, K.F.S., 5" $18.00-30.00

BLONDIE'S JALOPY WIND-UP CAR, Louis Marx, 1935 K.F.S., tin lithograph $675.00-1,250.00

BLONDIE'S PEG SET, boxed peg board set, colorful box, 1934 .... $25.00-50.00

BLUTO DIPPY DUMPER TIN WINDUP CHARACTER TOY, Marx, 1930's, celluloid figure $275.00-600.00

BONZO BISQUE FIGURE, 3", 1930's $20.00-50.00

BONZO BISQUE FIGURE, 4", painted $20.00-45.00

BONZO CELLULOID JOINTED FIGURE, 1930's, 4" $150.00-300.00

BONZO CHINA DISH, 7", 1930's. $20.00-45.00

BONZO CIGARETTE HOLDER, (unauthorized) 1930's $20.00-30.00

BONZO GERMAN PORCELAIN FIGURE, 1930's, 2½" tall $50.00-85.00

BONZO PENCIL TABLET, "A DOG'S LIFE," ca. 1930's $25.00-60.00

BONZO POST CARD, British, 1930's $15.00-35.00

BONZO POST CARD, English, by Valentines, 1930's $15.00-25.00

BONZO THE DOG SCOOTER TOY WINDUP, 7" long, made in Germany $275.00-425.00

BOOB MCNUTT TIN WINDUP, 9½", tin lithograph, manufactured by Strauss $425.00-895.00

BOOB MCNUTT, manufactured by Schoenhut, 1920's, 9" tall, wood and composition $275.00-385.00

BOOB MCNUTT TIN WINDUP, by Strauss, c. 1925, 9" $300.00-650.00

BOZO THE CLOWN TIN YOYO, 1950's, Japan $5.00-10.00

BRINGING UP FATHER BIG BIG BOOK, 1930's $30.00-50.00

BRINGING UP FATHER BISQUE FIGURES, boxed set of three, each 4" $135.00-195.00

BRINGING UP FATHER BOOK, Whitman, 1936, ... $25.00-50.00

BRINGING UP FATHER COLORING BOOK, 1930's $20.00-35.00

BRINGING UP FATHER SONG FOLIO, 1924 .... $15.00-35.00

BRINGING UP FATHER, The Big Book, 1926, 10" x 10" $25.00-55.00

BROWNIE CAST IRON FIGURE, 3" tall, no paint, date uncertain $30.00-65.00

BROWNIE CHARACTER CAMERA by Eastman Kodak, based upon Palmer Cox character ...$65.00-125.00

BROWNIE CHARACTER CHINA PLATE, 6", ca. 1890's $20.00-40.00

BROWNIE CHARACTER CLOTH DOLLS, set of six, 1892 by Palmer Cox $300.00-500.00

BROWNIE CHARACTER DECAL BOOK, c. 1896, Volume 1 .... $35.00-65.00

BROWNIE CHARACTER PLATE, ca. 1900's, 7" in diameter, glazed china $20.00-65.00

BROWNIE PLANTER BY PALMER COX, 1890's, 4", rare item $100.00-250.00

BROWNIE PLATE, glazed china, 9" with Brownie characters around rim $35.00-70.00

BROWNIE WOODEN BAND FIGURES by Palmer Cox, ca. 1900's, 8" tall, five pieces $80.00-180.00

BROWNIES ADVERTISING SIGN for Snagproof Boots, 7" x 10" $20.00-40.00

BROWNIES BY PALMER COX BOWLING SET, ca. 1892, figure 12" $125.00-225.00

BROWNIES HAND MIRROR, ca. 1900, 9" tall..$50.00-125.00

BROWNIES SPOON, silverplate, figural $30.00-64.00

BROWNIES WOOD PUZZLE by Palmer Cox, ca. 1891, 12" x 10", wood and paper $75.00-145.00

BUCK ROGERS TOOTSIETOY BATTLE CRUISER, #1031 ....$70.00-125.00

BUCK ROGERS TOOTSIETOY BATTLE CRUISER, #1032 ....$70.00-125.00

BUDDY TUCKER GLAZED CHINA PLATE, ca. 1900's, Outcault character, 7" $45.00-95.00

BUGS BUNNY AND HIS PALS, Whitman Better Little Book, 1945 ....$15.00-30.00

BUGS BUNNY BANK, chalkware, early and rare $75.00-135.00

BUGS BUNNY BANK, pot metal, Bugs stands by barrel $35.00-95.00

BUGS BUNNY CERAMIC FIGURE, Evan K. Shaw Company, 1950's, 4" $20.00-45.00

BUGS BUNNY CERAMIC PLANTER, ca. 1950's $15.00-30.00

BUGS BUNNY CERAMIC PLANTER, marked Warner Brothers, glazed, 7" $10.00-25.00

BUGS BUNNY DOLL, 20", 1940's, all felt with linen face $100.00-200.00

BUGS BUNNY PLASTER STATUE, 9", probably 1930's $30.00-75.00

BUGS BUNNY RUBBER SQUEEZE TOY, 1930's, 8" $30.00-70.00

BUGS BUNNY SOAP, Warner Brothers, 1930's, boxed $20.00-45.00

BUGS BUNNY TRICYCLE, wood and paper lithograph, pull toy, Brice Toy, 11"......................$25.00-75.00

BUGS BUNNY WRISTWATCH, 1930's....$75.00-145.00

BULLETMAN FLYING DETECTIVE, small booklet, Fawcett, 1940's..................................$15.00-30.00

BUSTER BROWN AD POSTER, 1900's .$60.00-120.00

BUSTER BROWN AND MARY JANE'S PAINT BOOK, R. Outcault, 1907, 10" x 14" $100.00-200.00

BUSTER BROWN AND TIGE CAST IRON PULL TOY, 7½" long, Tige pulls cart $425.00-725.00

BUSTER BROWN AND TIGE CHINA BOWL, 8" diameter, ca. 1900's $35.00-60.00

BUSTER BROWN AND TIGE TRADE AD CARD, ca. 1900 ....$25.00-50.00

BUSTER BROWN BRASS RING.............$20.00-40.00

BUSTER BROWN CALENDAR, 1916, 8" x 13"...$20.00-45.00

BUSTER BROWN CIGAR, 5", in original colorful wrapper $20.00-40.00

BUSTER BROWN HANKY,1900's, ...$25.00-55.00

BUSTER BROWN MARCH TWO STEP SHEET MUSIC, copyright 1907....................................$20.00-40.00

BUSTER BROWN PAINT BOOK, die-cut, 1916..$35.00-70.00

BUSTER BROWN, "Pin the Tail on Tige" game, paper, ca. 1900's $100.00-150.00

BUSTER BROWN PLAYING CARDS, early,

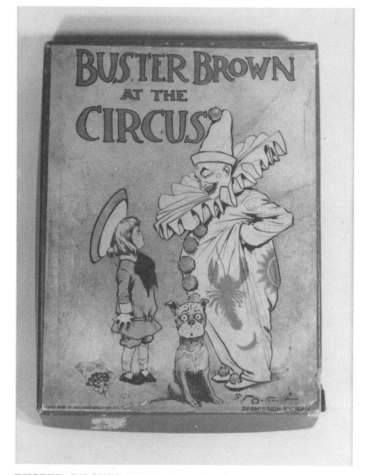

BUSTER BROWN AT THE CIRCUS, ca. 1900's, boxed card game, Selchow and Righter, NY, Reynolds collection, $75.00-135.00.

boxed $35.00-70.00

BUSTER BROWN POST CARD, 1905 .....$15.00-30.00

BUSTER BROWN ROLY POLY, early, composition $125.00-250.00

BUSTER BROWN RUBBER SQUEAK TOY, ca. 1900's, rare $75.00-150.00

BUSTER BROWN RUBBER STAMPS, 5", box with lithograph illustration, 1900's $55.00-130.00

BUSTER BROWN SPOON, silverplate, embossed handle $15.00-35.00

BUSTER BROWN TEA SET, Germany, three pieces, cup, saucer and plate $85.00-135.00

BUSTER BROWN tin whistle $15.00-30.00

BUTTERCUP (BABY) TIN WINDUP, 8" long, tin lithograph, German..............................$425.00-795.00

BUTTERCUP BABY CHARACTER, composition figure, wood composition, spring action $85.00-145.00

CAPTAIN AND THE KIDS BELL RINGER TOY, ca. 1900's, cast iron.........................$775.00-1,250.00

CAPTAIN MARVEL tie clip, 1946, Fawcett Publication, on original card $12.00-25.00

CAPTAIN MARVEL, Fawcett Publication, small booklet, 1940's $15.00-30.00

CAPTAIN MARVEL, JR., small booklet, Fawcett Publication, 1940's $15.00-30.00

CASPER THE FRIENDLY GHOST DOLL, 1960's, pull-string voice, Mattel $15.00-30.00

COMIC CHARACTER TOYS

BUTTER CUP AND SPARERIBS, pull toy, Nifty, German, 1920's, Reynolds collection, $200.00-500.00.

CHARLIE McCARTHY AND MORTIMER SNERD PRiVATE CAR, tin windup, 1930's, Reynolds collection, $350.00-700.00.

CASPER THE FRIENDLY GHOST, magic color paint set, 1960 ....$15.00-30.00

CASPER THE FRIENDLY GHOST RECORD, 1962, 78 RPM $5.00-10.00

CATNIP CLOTH CHARACTER PUPPET by Gund, 1960's $5.00-15.00

CHARLIE CHAPLIN BELL RINGER TOY, cast iron/metal $685.00-825.00

CHARLIE CHAPLIN BOXER CHAMPION, windup toy by Schuco, German $500.000-795.00

CHARLIE McCARTHY BASS DRUMMER WINDUP TOY, Marx, tin lithograph, ca. 1939 ....$450.00-865.00

CHARLIE McCARTHY CHILD'S VENTRILOQUIST PUPPET, Effanbee, 1930's, 17" $225.00-450.00

CHARLIE McCARTHY DANCER TOY, wood puppet, boxed, by Marks Brothers................$85.00-125.00

CHARLIE McCARTHY FLYING HATS GAME, Whitman, 1938...$20.00-35.00

CHARLIE McCARTHY GAME OF TOPPER, Whitman, 1938 ....$35.00-65.00

CHARLIE McCARTHY MAZUMA PLAY MONEY, original package $15.00-30.00

CHARLIE McCARTHY PICTURE PUZZLES, 1938, boxed, set of two $40.00-90.00

CHARLEY McCARTHY PUT AND TAKE BINGO GAME,

Whitman, 1938 ....$45.00-75.00

CHARLIE McCARTHY QUESTION AND ANSWER GAME, boxed, ca. 1930 ....$20.00-40.00

CHESTER GUMP BISQUE CHARACTER NODDER, German, 3" tall $45.00-85.00

CHESTER GUMP bisque, German, 2" $20.00-40.00

CHESTER GUMP FINDS HIDDEN TREASURE, Whitman publication, 1934 ....$20.00-40.00

CHESTER GUMP FINDS THE HIDDEN TREASURE BOOK, Whitman, 1934 ....$20.00-35.00

CHESTER GUMP IN CART PULLED BY HORSE, cast iron, ca. 1905 ....$400.00-750.00

CHING CHOW BISQUE NODDER FIGURE, German $45.00-85.00

CLARABELLE, THE CLOWN WOODEN PUSH PUPPET, manufactured by Kohner, c. Kagran .$25.00-50.00

CLARABELLE THE CLOWN (HOWDY DOODY CHARACTER, MARIONETTE) boxed toy ..$75.00-150.00

COOKIE (Dagwood and Blondie's daughter) wood compostion figure, 2" tall $15.00-25.00

COOKIE, FROM BLONDIE, wood composition figure, 1944, 3" tall $15.00-35.00

DADDY WARBUCKS BISQUE NODDER, 3", German $35.00-70.00

DADDY WARBUCKS BISQUE NODDER, German, 3½" tall $60.00-95.00

DADDY WARBUCKS PLASTER FIGURE, 6", 1940's, Professional Art Products $15.00-30.00

DAFFY DUCK PULL TOY, manufactured by Brice Toy and Novelty, 1950's $35.00-70.00

DAGWOOD BUMSTEAD PLANTER, head figural, 5", K.F.S. $15.00-35.00

DAGWOOD MINIATURE, LEAD FIGURE, ca. 1940's, 3" tall...$15.00-22.00

DAGWOOD WOOD COMPOSITION FIGURE, 5" tall, marked "1944 K.F.S." $18.00-30.00

DAGWOOD'S SOLO FLIGHT AIRPLANE, manufactured by Marx, 9" long, ca. 1935 ....$200.00-425.00

DAISY MAE MINIATURE LEAD FIGURE, 3", ca. 1940's $15.00-22.00

DENNIS THE MENACE XYLOPHONE PLAYER, BO, toy $100.00-225.00

DENNIS THE MENACE HAND PUPPET, 1950's, cloth and vinyl head $5.00-15.00

DENNIS THE MENACE CREAM PITCHER, 1960's $10.00-15.00

DENNIS THE MENACE FIGURAL WATER PISTOL, 1950's, boxed...................................$20.00-40.00

DENNIS THE MENACE GLOVES, western-type fringe, 1960's $15.00-30.00

DENNY DIMWIT COMPOSTION FIGURE, 11" tall, 1948, often mistaken as Dopey $35.00-60.00

DENNY DIMWIT COMPOSITION FIGURE, 1930's, 4" $20.00-40.00

DICK TRACY AND B.O. PLENTY POCKET KNIVE, 1950's $15.00-35.00

DICK TRACY AND JUNIOR SALT AND PEPPER SET, plaster, 1940's $15.00-30.00

DICK TRACY AND THE INVISIBLE MAN PLAY SCRIPT, Quaker premium $15.00-30.00

DICK TRACY AUTOMATIC POLICE STATION, Marx, original box, station and car $75.00-150.00

DICK TRACY BADGE, Secret Service Patrol Sargeant $15.00-30.00

DICK TRACY CARDBOARD DECODER, Post cereal premium....................................$15.00-30.00

DICK TRACY CHRISTMAS CARD, 1940's.$5.00-10.00

DICK TRACY CRIME DETECTION FOLIO, circa 1940.................................$75.00-195.00

DICK TRACY CRIME STOPPER WALLET red, no box..$10.00-20.00

DICK TRACY DETECTIVE BUTTON, 1", circa 1930..$10.00-25.00

DICK TRACY FLASHLIGHT, ca. 1950's..$15.00-35.00

DICK TRACY HAND PUPPET, dated 1961..$10.00-20.00

DICK TRACY HANDCUFFS with the original card...$10.00-20.00

DICK TRACY HINGEES PAPER SET, 1945, in paper envelope.....................................$15.00-30.00

DICK TRACY HINGEES SET, in paper envelope...$5.00-20.00

DICK TRACY INVISIBLE MAN PLAY SCRIPT, Quaker cereal premium, 1939.......................$25.00-40.00

DICK TRACY JIGSAW PUZZLE, boxed, from 1940's, Jaymar..$15.00-30.00

DICK TRACY JUNIOR CRIME DETECTION FOLIO, in original envelope.................................$35.00-75.00

DICK TRACY Junior Official Detective Secret Symbol Decoder...$40.00-80.00

DICK TRACY MASTER DETECTIVE GAME, 1961, boxed..$20.00-40.00

DICK TRACY PAINT BOOK, circa 1935, large size..$25.00-50.00

DICK TRACY PLASTIC WRIST RADIO, circa 1950..$20.00-45.00

DICK TRACY PLAYING CARD GAME, ca. 1937, Whitman..$20.00-40.00

DICK TRACY POLICE CAR BY MARX, 9" long (no box)...$45.00-90.00

DICK TRACY POP-UP, BOOK "Capture of Boris Arson"..$45.00-90.00

DICK TRACY RUBBER STAMP PRINTING SET, 1930's..$20.00-40.00

DICK TRACY SECRET CODE BOOK, published in 1939..$25.00-45.00

DICK TRACY SECRET CODE MAKER, circa 1930..$30.00-55.00

DICK TRACY SECRET DETECTIVE MAGIC TRICKS, 1939 Quaker premium.......................$20.00-45.00

DICK TRACY SIREN PISTOL, with red metal housing..$25.00-50.00

DICK TRACY SPARKLING RIOT CAR, Louis Marx, original box.......................................$75.00-125.00

DICK TRACY SUPER DETECTIVE MYSTERY CARD GAME, Whitman, 1937.......................$20.00-40.00

DICK TRACY TARGET, 17" diameter, ca. 1930's, extremely colorful.................................$25.00-60.00

DICK TRACY TIN BADGE, New York Police Department, logo, detective.........................$10.00-25.00

DICK TRACY WALLET, Crimestoppers.....$10.00-20.00

DICK TRACY WATCH, 1930's, watch in original box...$150.00-300.00

DICK TRACY WRIST RADIO 1940's...$125.00-200.00

DICK TRACY, THE ADVENTURES OF DICK TRACY BIG, BIG BOOK, Whitman, 1934......$20.00-60.00

DICK TRACY HAND PUPPET, 1960's, vinyl head...$10.00-20.00

DINO (Flintstones) ceramic bank, 1960's.$10.00-20.00

DINO THE DINOSAUR CHARACTER FIGURE, vinyl, 1960, Hanna Barberra Productions ...$10.00-20.00

ELLA CINDERS GAME BY MILTON BRADLEY, 1944, 9" x 14"...$20.00-40.00

ELLA CINDERS HARDCOVER BOOK, by Whitman, 1934..$20.00-40.00

ELMER FUDD AMERICAN POTTERY FIGURE, 1940's, 6½" tall...$40.00-85.00

ELMER FUDD FIRE CHIEF, 1950's wood pull toy..$20.00-45.00

CHARLIE McCARTHY BENZINE BUGGY, tin windup, 1930's, Reynolds, collection, $350.00-800.00.

CHARLIE McCARTHY AND MORTIMER SNERD, tin windup walkers, 1930's, Reynolds collection.

81

COMIC CHARACTER TOYS

ELMER FUDD FIRE CHIEF BELL RINGER PULL TOY, #7, wood with paper lithograph, 1950's, Reynolds collection, $20.00-45.00.

FELIX THE CAT WINDUP, tin, 1924, Nifty, German, Reynolds collection, $385.00-600.00.

FAVORITE FUNNIES JIGSAW PUZZLE, 1, Gasoline Alley and others, ca. 1940 .... $10.00-20.00
FELIX THE CAT ANNUAL BOOK, COMIC ADVENTURES OF FELIX, 1923 .... $50.00-110.00
FELIX THE CAT CELLULOID PLACE CARD HOLDER, die-cut, 1930's $50.00-125.00
FELIX THE CAT CERAMIC ASHTRAY, 1930's, 4", no markings $35.00-70.00
FELIX THE CAT CREAM TOFFEE, rare, tin can, Pat Sullivan $100.00-225.00
FELIX THE CAT SCHOOL COMPANION PENCIL BOX, 1939 .... $50.00-70.00
FELIX THE CAT BEAD GAME UNDER GLASS, 3" $20.00-50.00

FELIX THE CAT CAST IRON FIGURE, circa 1920's, 3" $175.00-300.00
FELIX THE CAT CELLULOID FIGURE, 2" tall, walking Felix, ca. 1920's $25.00-55.00
FELIX THE CAT CELLULOID FIGURE, ca. 1920, 6" tall with violin $35.00-85.00
FELIX THE CAT CHILD'S TEA SET, three pieces, china with Felix decals $70.00-125.00
FELIX THE CAT CREAM TOFFEE TIN, 4" x 6", c. Pat Sullivan, rare $200.00-400.00
FELIX THE CAT DANDY CANDY GAME, c. 1957, 7" x 14" box $15.00-35.00
FELIX THE CAT DOLL, Chad Valley, with button on ear $150.00-225.00
FELIX THE CAT DOLL, dressed in cowboy suit, ca. 1920's, 14" $300.00-500.00
FELIX THE CAT POST CARD FROM ENGLAND, 1924 .... $20.00-35.00
FELIX THE CAT FIGURE, small, celluloid, 2" $35.00-60.00
FELIX THE CAT GLAZED CHINA SALT SHAKER, 1930's, 2" $25.00-50.00
FELIX THE CAT JOINTED DOLL, manufactured by Chad Valley, 12" tall $75.00-145.00
FELIX THE CAT JOINTED WOOD DOLL, 8", ca. 1922, probably by Schoenhut $95.00-145.00
FELIX THE CAT JOINTED WOOD FIGURE, 4" tall, Schoenhut, ca. 1922-1924 .... $55.00-95.00
FELIX THE CAT JOINTED-ARM CHALK FIGURE, 14" tall, ca. 1920's $45.00-95.00
FELIX THE CAT LEAD FIGURE, 2", 1920's, enameled finish $50.00-80.00
FELIX THE CAT ON A SCOOTER, ca. 1924, Nifty, German, tin lithograph toy $385.00-600.00
FELIX THE CAT PENCIL CASE, 1930's, dark green, 8" long $30.00-50.00
FELIX THE CAT PENCIL CASE, ca. 1950's with paper label on top $22.00-35.00
FELIX THE CAT PLACE HOLDER, 1930's. $40.00-65.00
FELIX THE CAT TIN DART TARGET, circa 1950 .... $10.00-20.00
FELIX THE CAT TIN LITHOGRAPH PULL TOY, 8" long, Nifty, Germany $345.00-495.00
FELIX THE CAT TIN WINDUP, 7" tall, no markings, possibly Nifty, Germany $350.00-625.00
FELIX THE CAT TRANSFER PICTURES ON ORIGINAL 1930's SHEET, 4" x 9", German $20.00-40.00
FELIX THE CAT WOOD COMPOSITION JOINTED DOLL, 13" tall, with Felix decal $265.00-400.00
FELIX THE CAT WOODEN WALKING TOY, 11" tall, 1930's $65.00-145.00
FELIX THE CAT yarn holder $15.00-30.00
FELIX THE CAT CAST IRON HOLDING UMBRELLA, approximately 3", ca. 1920's $95.00-195.00
FELIX THE CAT CLOTH WINDUP, Pat Sullivan, 1922, 11" $600.00-950.00
FELIX THE CAT, MINIATURE, WOOD JOINTED FIGURE, 1930's, 2½" tall $50.00-80.00
FLASH GORDON PENCIL BOX, 1951, Eagle Pencil Company $15.00-40.00
FLINTSTONES CAMERA, 1960's $10.00-15.00
FLINTSTONES WINDUP FLIP OVER TANK, by LineMar, 1961, tin lithograph $100.00-200.00

FLINTSTONES FRED AND BARNEY BASEBALL GLASS, 4", 1964 ....$5.00-10.00

FLINTSTONES TURNOVER TANK, LineMar, circa 1960......................................$75.00-125.00

FLUB-A-DUB MARIONETTE, boxed, Kagran (Howdy Doody character) $125.00-225.00

FLUB-A-DUB PLASTIC CHARACTER TOY, original box, 3" tall $15.00-40.00

FLUB-A-DUB SCOPE DOODLE CHARACTER PUPPET, Peter Puppet Playthings, boxed.........$20.00-45.00

FOXY GRANDPA BELL RINGER TOY, cast iron, ca. 1900's $375.00-700.00

FOXY GRANDPA bisque figure (large) ...$50.00-100.00

FOXY GRANDPA BOOK, THE LATEST ADVENTURES, Donohoe, 1905 ....$30.00-75.00

FOXY GRANDPA CLOTH DOLL, ca. 1900's, 12" tall...$100.00-225.00

FOXY GRANDPA COMPOSITION NODDER, 7" tall $40.00-85.00

FOXY GRANDPA GAME, pin-the-hat-on-type, ca. 1910, paper party game $110.00-165.00

FOXY GRANDPA FIGURE, bisque, 8" $75.00-125.00

FOXY GRANDPA NODDER ASHTRAY, made in Austria, 3" wide $75.00-190.00

FOXY GRANDPA RUBBER STAMPS SET, ca. 1905, Selchow and Righter, 7" box $50.00-100.00

FOXY GRANDPA WOOD COMPOSITION DOLL, 12" tall with movable mouth $125.00-255.00

FRED FLINTSTONE AND DINO, by LineMar, 1960's, 22", battery operated.........................$85.00-200.00

FRED FLINTSTONE RIDING DINO, ca. 1962, tin lithograph and plastic, Line Mar $55.00-85.00

FRED FLINTSTONE VINYL CHARACTER FIGURE, 1960, 12" tall $10.00-20.00

FRED FLINTSTONE GAME, made by Transogram, 1961 ....$10.00-30.00

GASOLINE ALLEY, WALT AND SKEEZIX CARD GAME, boxed, Milton Bradley, 1927 ....$35.00-55.00

GLOOMY GUS IN A CART, cast iron toy with movable wheels, Harris Toy, ca. 1900 ....$375.00-575.00

GLOOMY GUS MAJOLICA CANDLE HOLDER, 1930's $35.00-80.00

GLOOMY GUS MAJOLICA FIGURE, 6" tall, 1920's $35.00-75.00

GREEN HORNET COLORING BOOK, 1960's $10.00-15.00

GREEN HORNET JIGSAW PUZZLES, set of four $20.00-40.00

GUMPS GINGER ALE BOTTLE, Bon-Ton Beverages, amber, paper label $35.00-65.00

HAPPY HOOLIGAN "SEEING NEW YORK-899" BUS, cast iron with five riders $875.00-1,400.00

HAPPY HOOLIGAN "SIGHT SEEING AUTO-899," cast iron, five riders............................$875.00-1,400.00

HAPPY HOOLIGAN 7" JOINTED FIGURE, manufactured in Italy $100.00-250.00

HAPPY HOOLIGAN AUTOMOBILE, manufactured by N. N. Hill Brass, cast iron..........$900.00-1,400.00

HAPPY HOOLIGAN BISQUE FIGURE, 9", ca. 1910, German $75.00-135.00

HAPPY HOOLIGAN BISQUE, German, 5" tall, painted..$30.00-65.00

HAPPY HOOLIGAN bisque pencil holder, 8½", painted...$75.00-150.00

HAPPY HOOLIGAN CHARACTER ASH TRAY, 1930's, bisque $45.00-80.00

HAPPY HOOLIGAN CHARACTER DOLL, wood composition by Schoenhut $250.00-475.00

HAPPY HOOLIGAN CHARACTER PLANTER, Majolica, 5" tall glazed ceramic $65.00-95.00

HAPPY HOOLIGAN IN A CART WITH NODDER HEAD, cast iron, one horse $875.00-1,300.00

HAPPY HOOLIGAN MAJOLICA COOKIE JAR, 10", rare...$125.00-250.00

HAPPY HOOLIGAN NESTING TOYS, 4" tall largest piece, by Anri of Italy $45.00-60.00

HAPPY HOOLIGAN POLICE PATROL, cast iron, two horses, 19" long.........................$750.00-1,125.00

HAPPY HOOLIGAN ROLY-POLY, composition, 4" $75.00-120.00

HAPPY HOOLIGAN WINDUP TOY, tin lithograph by J. Chein, ca. 1932, 6" tall.............$175.00-250.00

FOXY GRANDPA WITH BUNNY BISQUE FIGURE, 5" tall, colorful, Reynolds collection, $75.00-130.00.

HAPPY HOOLIGAN BOWLING TYPE GAME, c. 1925, boxed, Furnish collection, $100.00-225.00.

COMIC CHARACTER TOYS

HAPPYFATS GIRL BISQUE DOLL, made in Germany, 4" tall $65.00-95.00

HAPPYFATS GIRL BISQUE FIGURE with jointed arms, Japan, 4" tall $35.00-65.00

HAROLD TEEN BISQUE FIGURE, 3¼" tall, circa 1930 ....$20.00-40.00

HAROLD TEEN BISQUE FIGURE, 4", circa 1930 ....$15.00-30.00

HAROLD TEEN PAINT BOOK, 1932 ....$15.00-35.00

HAROLD TEEN PAINT BOOK, McLoughlin Brothers, 1932, 10" x 13" $25.00-45.00

HECKLE AND JECKLE RUBBER SQUEEZE TOYS, pair, 7", 1958 ....$20.00-45.00

HENRY AND HENRIETTA RUNNING AWAY, celluloid windup, 1930's $1,100.00-1,650.00

HENRY AND HIS BROTHER, celluloid windup toy, ca. 1934 ....$1,200.00-2,300.00

HENRY AND THE SWAN CELLULOID WINDUP, 4" x 9", Japan $275.00-595.00

HENRY BISQUE FIGURE PLAYING AN ACCORDIAN, 4" $40.00-75.00

HENRY COMIC CHARACTER VINYL FIGURE, 8" tall, manufactured by Irwin, painted.........$20.00-65.00

HENRY RIDING ON AN ELEPHANT'S TRUNK, celluloid windup, 1930's $975.00-2,400.00

HENRY TRAPEZE, celluloid figure and metal wind-up, distributed by Borgfeldt $325.00-475.00

HERBIE BISQUE FIGURE, 2", 1930's $20.00-40.00

HERBIE BOOKMARK, 1930's, 3" $5.00-15.00

HI-WAY HENRY WINDUP CAR, ca. 1920's, tin lithograph $2,500.00-3,900.00

HOMER PIGEON PLANTER, CERAMIC, Walter Lantz, 1958 ....$15.00-25.00

HOWDY DOODY BOXED NITE LITE, 1950's, Leco Electric Manufacturing Company $20.00-40.00

HOWDY DOODY CERAMIC CHARACTER BANK, c. Bob Smith, 7" tall, glazed $15.00-35.00

HOWDY DOODY CHILD'S CERAMIC BREAKFAST SET (three pieces), 1950's, Taylor $30.00-65.00

HOWDY DOODY CHARACTER BUBBLE PIPES, boxed set, Lido Toy Company, 1950's.........$15.00-35.00

HOWDY DOODY CHARACTER MARIONETTE, Kagran, boxed, 16" tall $75.00-150.00

HOWDY DOODY CHARACTER UMBRELLA, 18" long, plastic, 1950's.....................................$25.00-45.00

HOWDY DOODY MAGIC PUZZLE BALL, made by Kagran $15.00-35.00

HOWDY DOODY RUBBER BALL, 5" diameter, 1950's $10.00-25.00

HOWDY DOODY SAND SET, plastic, on original card, ca. 1954, Kagran Corporation............$25.00-50.00

HOWDY DOODY TRAPEZE TOY, W. Germany, imported by Toy Novelty Associates.....$60.00-125.00

HOWDY DOODY UKE MUSICAL GUITAR, c. 1950, Kagran Corporation, 17" long $45.00-85.00

HOWDY DOODY VINYL WATER RING, Ideal Toy and Novelty $15.00-30.00

HOWDY DOODY WOODEN PUSH PUPPET, manufactured by Kohner, c. Kagran, 1950's ..$25.00-50.00

HOWDY DOODY'S ELECTRIC CARNIVAL GAME, Harriet Gilmar, Inc., 1950's $35.00-55.00

HOWDY DOODY'S OWN GAME, Parker Brothers, cards, balls and targets $35.00-75.00

HUCKLBERRY HOUND AND FRIENDS LUNCH BOX, 1961 by Alladin $5.00-15.00

HUCKLBERRY HOUND CAMERA, Sun Pix, boxed, 1964 ....$10.00-25.00

HUCKLEBERRY HOUND CHARM BRACELET, 1959, child's, various figures $5.00-10.00

HUCKLEBERRY HOUND PLASTIC FIGURAL BANK, 10", 1960's, rubber $5.00-15.00

HUCKLEBERRY HOUND SQUEEZE TOY by Dell, 1960's $5.00-10.00

HUCKLEBERRRY HOUND T.V. PLAYSET, Marx, 1960's $15.00-30.00

HUMPHREY CHARACTER DOLL, (Joe Palooka's pal) Ideal Toy, 1940, cloth $85.00-125.00

HUMPHREY MOBILE (Joe Palooka series) Wyandotte Toy Company, lithograph metal $125.00-250.00

IGNATZ MOUSE, early wood figure, jointed arms and legs $75.00-125.00

IGNATZ MOUSE ON A TRICYCLE, by Chein, 1932, wood and tin, 7" $200.00-400.00

IGNATZ MOUSE WOOD FIGURE, 6" tall, wire limb joints, 1920's $35.00-80.00

J. FRED MUGGS TRICYCLE TOY, N. N. Hill Brass Company, 1950's, 9" tall..................$65.00-135.00

JEEP, POPEYE STRIP FIGURE, animal doll, 13" composition, 1935 ....$200.00-400.00

JEFF WOOD COMPOSITION AND JOINTED METAL DOLL, 6", ca. 1920's $225.00-425.00

JETSONS WINDUP FIGURE BY MARX, 4" tall, 1960's $50.00-90.00

JIGGS BISQUE FIGURE, 3", 1930's........$20.00-50.00

JIGGS CHARACTER CHALK FIGURE, 8" tall, excellent detail $50.00-85.00

JIGGS CHARACTER DOLL, manufactured by Schoenhut, wood composition, 8" tall $175.00-300.00

JIGGS IN THE JAZZ CAR, tin lithograph, ca. 1924, tin windup by Nifty $1,200.00-1,875.00

JIGGS LUNCH BOX, tin, 6", 1930's $55.00-110.00

JIGGS FIGURE, made of wood composition, 4" tall...$20.00-40.00

JOE PALOOKA BICYCLE PUMP, Dodgers Sporting Goods Company, 9" long $25.00-45.00

JOE PALOOKA BOXING GLOVES, Medalist Manufacturing Company, plain box $45.00-90.00

JOE PALOOKA LUNCH KIT, tin lithograph with scenes on all sides......................................$25.00-45.00

JOE PALOOKA WOOD JOINTED FIGURE, 1940's, 4" tall...$40.00-80.00

JOE PALOOKA wrist watch, 1940's $75.00-165.00

KATZENJAMMER KIDS PUZZLE SET, 1920's, four in colorful box......................................$65.00-85.00

KATZENJAMMER KIDS STORY BOOK, Whitman, 1937, 8½" x 11"...$20.00-55.00

KATZENJAMMER (MAMA) CAST IRON BANK, ca. 1900's $275.00-450.00

KATZENJAMMER KIDS "MAMA'S DARLINGS" GAME, 1920's $40.00-80.00

KATZENJAMMER KIDS BOXED SET OF FOUR PUZZLES, Saalfield, 1933 ....$55.00-95.00

KATZENJAMMER KIDS CAST IRON PULL TOY, 1906, manufactured by Dent Co..........$725.00-1,100.00

KATZENJAMMER KIDS HOCKEY GAME, K.F.S., 1950, 7" x 10", boxed $25.00-45.00

KATZENJAMMER KIDS MAGIC DRAWING AND COL-
ORING BOOK, 1930's $30.00-50.00
KATZENJAMMER MAMA COMPOSITION DOLL, 1920's,
9" $200.00-400.00
KAYO COMPOSITION CHARACTER WITH MOVABLE
MOUTH, 13", ca. 1930's $110.00-225.00
KAYO GERMAN bisque nodder, 1930's $30.00-75.00
KAYO WOOD JOINTED DOLL, all wood construction,
4" tall $18.00-45.00
KAYO'S, ICE TRUCK, manufactured by Tootsietoy,
ca. 1930's $95.00-155.00
KIKO KANGEROO BOXING DOLL, 17", copyright by
Paul Terry, 1930's $125.00-175.00
KOKO THE CLOWN (BETTY BOOP CHARACTER),
BISQUE FIGURE, 3" tall $20.00-45.00
KOKO THE CLOWN BISQUE FIGURE, 4", circa
1930 ....$30.00-65.00
KOMIC KAMERA FILM VIEWER with films of Lone
Ranger, Orphan Annie, etc. $55.00-80.00
KRAZY KAT DOOR KNOCKER, made of solid brass,
early $100.00-225.00
KRAZY KAT ON A SCOOTER TIN WINDUP TOY, c.
1930's, by Nifty $275.00-425.00
KRAZY KAT PLANTER, ceramic, 1930's.$35.00-75.00
LAMB CHOPS (Shari Lewis character) Lamp Puppet,
1960's $20.00-45.00
LI'L ABNER AND DAISY MAE BOOKENDS, painted
plaster, 9" and 6" tall $50.00-95.00
LI'L ABNER CAN O' COINS METAL LITHOGRAPH
BANK, 1953, U.F.S. $15.00-30.00
LI'L ABNER CHINA PLATE, 1968 Capp
Enterprises $10.00-20.00
LI'L ABNER MINIATURE LEAD FIGURE, 1940's,
3" $15.00-22.00
LI'L ABNER SNACK VENDING MACHINE, metal con-
struction, 2' tall $200.00-425.00
LI'L ABNER BANK, tin lithograph, 1953.$20.00-40.00
LI'L ABNER SCHMOO SOAP, 1950's $15.00-30.00
LITTLE KING MARX PLASTIC WALKING TOY,
1963, 3"...$5.00-20.00
LITTLE KING WOOD COMPOSITION FIGURE,
3" tall, 1944 ....$30.00-65.00
LITTLE LULU BANK, plastic, 1900's $5.00-15.00
LITTLE LULU BEAN BAG DOLL, 10",
ca. 1940's $50.00-85.00
LITTLE LULU CLOTHESLINE SET, 1950's. $15.00-35.00
LITTLE LULU FELT DOLL, 1940's, 10" .$65.00-125.00
LITTLE LULU GLAZED CHINA TEA POT, 5" tall,
1950's $35.00-60.00
LITTLE LULU JIGSAW PUZZLE, Whitman,
1950's $15.00-35.00
LITTLE LULU RAG DOLL by Marge, copyright,
1944, 15"..$65.00-130.00
LITTLE LULU STORE DISPLAY FOR KLEENEX,
10" tall...$20.00-45.00
LITTLE LULU STUFFED CHARACTER DOLL, 1950's,
string hair...$50.00-110.00
LITTLE LULU VALENTINE, 1950's..........$10.00-25.00
LITTLE ORPHAN ANNIE AND JUMBO, Blue Ribbon
Press Book, Pop-Up, 1935 ....$125.00-220.00
LITTLE ORPHAN ANNIE BEAD GAME, tin and glass,
1930's, 5" tall $35.00-65.00
LITTLE ORPHAN ANNIE BOXED BISQUE CHARACTER
SET, four pieces, Japan.................$135.00-250.00

HENRY riding elephant's trunk, celluloid, windup, 1930's, Furnish collection, $975.00-2,400.00.

HENRY ON TRAPEZE, windup toy, 1930's, George Borgfeldt, distributor, celluloid, Reynolds collection, $465.00-675.00.

KATZENJAMMER KIDS CART WITH MAMA SPANK-ING, cast iron, 1906, Dent Manufacturing Company, Furnish collection, $725.00-1,100.00.

COMIC CHARACTER TOYS

MOON MULLINS AND KAYO, glazed china ashtray with lusterware base, bisque figures, Reynolds collection, $75.00-125.00.

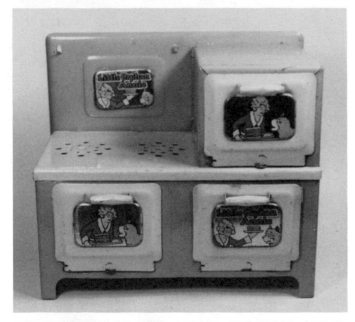

LITTLE ORPHAN ANNIE METAL ELECTRIC STOVE, 1930's, three doors open, Reynolds collection, $35.00-70.00.

LITTLE ORPAN ANNIE BUBBLE SET, 1930's, J. Pressman #025, 8" x 11" $55.00-90.00

LITTLE ORPHAN ANNIE CELLULOID DOLL with jointed arms, 1930's, 7" tall $125.00-300.00

LITTLE ORPHAN ANNIE CHARACTER ELECTRIC STOVE, aqua color, 1930's $45.00-95.00

LITTLE ORPHAN ANNIE circus embroidery set, 1930's, J. Pressman, 18" box $85.00-195.00

LITTLE ORPHAN ANNIE CRAYONS SET, Milton Bradley, #8442, 4" x 8", 1930's $45.00-85.00

LITTLE ORPHAN ANNIE CRAYONS, by Milton Bradley, 1930's $25.00-50.00

LITTLE ORPHAN ANNIE EMBROIDERY SPOOL, 1930's, 4" long, from set $10.00-20.00

LITTLE ORPHAN ANNIE HANKIE HOLDER in original box, 1930's $45.00-75.00

LITTLE ORPHAN ANNIE JACK SET on original card, 5" x 7", 1930's $25.00-45.00

LITTLE ORPHAN ANNIE KNITTING OUTFIT, #6830, J. Pressman, 1930, 8" x 5" $45.00-85.00

LITTLE ORPHAN ANNIE KNITTING OUTFIT by J. Pressman Company, 1930's $50.00-125.00

LITTLE ORPHAN ANNIE NAPKIN RING, 1933, World's Fair, metal $25.00-65.00

LITTLE ORPHAN ANNIE TEA SET, Germany, ceramic, teapot, 4" tall, twelve pieces $95.00-150.00

LITTLE ORPHAN ANNIE TRAVEL GAME, manufactured by Milton Bradley, #4523 ....$45.00-80.00

LORD PLUSHBOTTOM CHARACTER BISQUE NODDER, 4" tall, German........................$45.00-85.00

LUCY MILK GLASS CUP, 1960's $5.00-10.00

MAGGIE AND JIGGS BISQUE FIGURES, 1930's, German, 3½", pair..................................$70.00-130.00

MAGGIE AND JIGGS MINIATURE LEAD FIGURES, 3" and 2", ca. 1940's, pair $35.00-50.00

MAGGIE AND JIGGS SALT AND PEPPERS SET, brightly colored, glazed china, three pieces $55.00-95.00

MAGGIE AND JIGGS WINDUP, ca. George McManus, 7" x 5" tall, tin toy $650.00-1,100.00

MAGGIE CHALK FIGURE, 12" from "Bringing Up Father" comic strip $35.00-60.00

MAGGIE CHARACTER DOLL, Schoenhut, wood composition, 10" $175.00-300.00

MAMMY YOKUM DRINKING GLASS, 5"...$5.00-15.00

MANDRAKE THE MAGICIAN magic fan club pin $15.00-30.00

MANDRAKE THE MAGICIAN MAGIC KIT, K.F.S., by Transogram, 1949..............................$30.00-50.00

MARY MARVEL wrist watch....................$35.00-75.00

MERRY MAKERS MINSTREL BANK, Marx, tin wind-up, four mice and piano, 1930's ...$450.00-700.00

MICKEY McGUIRE SALT AND PEPPER SHAKERS, ceramic, Japan, Toonerville $20.00-40.00

MICKY CHARACTER MOUSE WOODEN TOY (not Disney), 5" tall..................................$35.00-75.00

MIGHTY MOUSE COLORING BOOK, early 1950's $10.00-25.00

MIGHTY MOUSE DOLL BY RUSHTON, circa 1950, 16" $75.00-135.00

MIGHTY MOUSE SKILL ROLL puzzle game, Terrytoons characters $30.00-75.00

MISTER BLUSTER, (HOWDY DOODY CHARACTER), MARIONETTE, boxed, Kagran $60.00-125.00

MISTER MAGOO ADVERTISING DOLL, 12", 1960's G.E. promotion $30.00-65.00

MISTER MAGOO CAR, manufactured by Hubley and dated 1961, 8" tall, metal..................$45.00-75.00

MOON MULLINS 2" BISQUE FIGURE, circa 1930 ....$15.00-35.00

MOON MULLINS AND KAYO BISQUE FLOWER PLANTER, 5" tall, 1920's..................$45.00-90.00

MOON MULLINS AND KAYO BOXED SOAP FIGURES, 4" and 2" tall, detailed paint $75.00-110.00

MOON MULLINS AND KAYO TOOTHBRUSH HOLDER, bisque, 4" tall $45.00-75.00

MOON MULLINS AND KAYO WINDUP HANDCAR, 6" long, tin lithograph $375.00-525.00

MOON MULLINS BISQUE COMIC FIGURE, 4" tall $20.00-45.00

MOON MULLINS BOXED BISQUE FIGURES SET, 2" to 4", four different characters $145.00-210.00

MOON MULLINS DRAWING AND TRACING BOOK, McLoughlin Brothers, 1932 ....$20.00-40.00

MOON MULLINS GLAZED TOOTHBRUSH HOLDER, 1930's, 5" $50.00-75.00

MOON MULLINS POLICE PATROL CAR by Tootsitoy, ca. 1930's $125.00-295.00

MORTIMER SNERD CRAZY CAR, windup, Louis Marx Company, 1930's $200.00-425.00

MORTIMER SNERD JACK-IN-THE-BOX, composition and wood, 1930's $100.00-200.00

MORTIMER SNERD PUPPET, rubber and cloth, original box, Hollywood Magic Company ..$35.00-60.00

MORTIMER SNERD TEETH, 1940, on original card..$20.00-40.00

MOVIE COMICS CHARACTER VIEWER, 1940, pictures, Skeezix, Orphan Annie $55.00-80.00

MR. BAILEY THE BOSS BISQUE NODDER FIGURE, 4", German $45.00-85.00

MR. MAGOO CHILDREN'S DRINKING GLASS, circa 1960..$5.00-10.00

MR. MAGOO DOLL, jointed legs, circa 1960, 16" $75.00-160.00

MUTT AND JEFF MECHANICAL FIGURE, tin lithograph, windup, ca. 1920's...........$575.00-1,200.00

MUTT AND JEFF MUSICAL ALBUM, ca. 1920, colorful cover $25.00-65.00

MUTT AND JEFF WOOD CIGAR BOX, 1920's, paper lithograph illustrations $35.00-80.00

MUTT AND JEFF, THE ADVENTURES OF MUTT AND JEFF BOOK, Cupples and Leon $20.00-35.00

MUTT FIGURE, celluloid 6", 1930's $45.00-110.00

MUTT SHELL GASOLINE STANDUP CARDBOARD FIGURE, 23" tall, ca. 1934 ....$45.00-75.00

MUTT WOOD COMPOSITION AND JOINTED METAL DOLL, 8" tall, ca. 1920's $225.00-425.00

NEBBS BOXED CARD GAME from Milton Bradley, 1930's $20.00-40.00

OLIVE OYL CEREAL BOX FACE MASK, 1950's $5.00-10.00

OLIVE OYL PONYTAIL HOLDER, 1950's .$5.00-15.00

OLIVE OYL WALKING TOY, composition, 5" tall, 1930's, ramp walker $50.00-90.00

OLIVE OYL WOOD JOINTED FIGURE, 1930's, 4" $45.00-90.00

ORPHAN ANNIE AND SANDY PLASTER SALT AND PEPPER SHAKERS, 3", 1930's..........$15.00-30.00

ORPHAN ANNIE BANDANA, 1930's Ovaltine premium...$35.00-60.00

ORPHAN ANNIE BEETLEWARE MUG, 1930's with mint decal $15.00-30.00

ORPHAN ANNIE FIGURE, bisque 3" $28.00-45.00

ORPHAN ANNIE NODDER, bisque German, 3½"...$60.00-95.00

A SELECTION OF LITTLE ORPHAN ANNIE TOYS, 1930's, doll value $150.00-350.00.

ORPHAN ANNIE AND SANDY BISQUE TOOTHBRUSH HOLDER, 1930's, 5", $60.00-125.00.

ORPHAN ANNIE BOXED SET OF WEE LITTLE BOOKS, 1930's, Whitman, set of six $125.00 200.00

ORPHAN ANNIE CELLULOID FIGURE, 7" tall, Japan, 1930's, jointed $125.00-250.00

PAL NAPKIN RING, Skeezix on box, wooden, colorful box, Reynolds collection, $35.00-75.00.

JOE PENNER AND HIS DUCK GOO-GOO, tin wind-up, 1930's, Reynolds collection, $200.00-425.00.

ORPHAN ANNIE CHARACTER WOOD JOINTED DOLL, 5" tall, 1930's $50.00-95.00

ORPHAN ANNIE CHILD'S WATCH, BOXED, 1930's, graphics on box lid $225.00-325.00

ORPHAN ANNIE CIRCUS in 10" x 14" envelope, 1930's...$100.00-175.00

ORPHAN ANNIE CIRCUS, original envelope, 1935, 10" tall, original box, 1930 ....$75.00-155.00

ORPHAN ANNIE COMPOSITION DOLL, jointed arms, 10" tall, original box, 1930 ....$160.00-325.00

ORPHAN ANNIE DIME REGISTER BANK, 1936, tin, 3" tall..$45.00-95.00

ORPHAN ANNIE FAMOUS COMICS JIGSAW PUZZLE, 7" square, boxed $20.00-55.00

ORPHAN ANNIE GOOFY CIRCUS, complete set $100.00-200.00

ORPHAN ANNIE IRONING BOARD SET, by Goshen Manufacturing, 1930's $75.00-125.00

ORPHAN ANNIE LUSTERWARE CERAMIC TEA SET, (five pieces) 1930's $65.00-110.00

ORPHAN ANNIE MINIATURE BISQUE FIGURE, 1½" tall $25.00-45.00

ORPHAN ANNIE MINIATURE LEAD FIGURE, ca. 1940's, 2" $18.00-25.00

ORPHAN ANNIE OILCLOTH DOLL, 10" tall, red dress, orange hair, 1930's $80.00-150.00

ORPHAN ANNIE OILCLOTH DOLL, ca. 1926, 15" tall, blue polka-dot dress........................$75.00-140.00

ORPHAN ANNIE OVALTINE PREMIUM PAPER FACE MASK, 1930's....................................$20.00-40.00

ORPHAN ANNIE PAINT BOX, Milton Bradley, large version, c. F.A.S. $60.00-95.00

ORPHAN ANNIE RUMMY CARDS, made by Whitman, 1930's $20.00-40.00

ORPHAN ANNIE SHEET MUSIC "Little Orphan Annie," 1925, published by Wyrick Music $20.00-65.00

ORPHAN ANNIE SHOOTING GAME by Milton Bradley, 1930's $50.00-110.00

ORPHAN ANNIE sport watch, 1930's $125.00-220.00

ORPHAN ANNIE STOVE, 8" with opening doors, electric cord, lithograph plates $35.00-75.00

ORPHAN ANNIE STOVE, metal construction with lithograph, plate, 4" tall $20.00-30.00

ORPHAN ANNIE STUFFED OILCLOTH DOLL, 13" tall, 1930's, red dress.............................$85.00-110.00

ORPHAN ANNIE WALL POCKET, Famous Artists Syndicate, china, 6" tall, Japan.......$75.00-110.00

ORPHAN ANNIE WHIRLOMATIC RADIO DECODER, 1942, premium $40.00-85.00

ORPHAN ANNIE WOODEN PULL TOY by Trixitoy, 13" long, painted highlights $60.00-95.00

ORPHAN ANNIE WOODEN PULL TOY by Trixitoy, 1930's, 8" long $75.00-135.00

ORPHAN ANNIE-NEVER SAY DIE BOOK, Cupples and Leon, 1930..$20.00-45.00

OSWALD RABBIT CERAMIC FIGURE, 5", by Walter Lantz, 1950's $20.00-35.00

OSWALD THE RABBIT GLAZED CERAMIC PLATE, 7", 1930's or 1940's...............................$20.00-40.00

OUR GANG COLORING BOOK, Saalfield, 1938, large format $25.00-45.00

OUR GANG PENCIL BOX, probably by Dixon, 1930's $25.00-50.00

PAL THE DOG, OILCLOTH DOLL (Skeezix character). 7" tall...$35.00-65.00

PAPPY YOKUM CHARACTER DOLL, vinyl, by Barry Toys $45.00-85.00

PAPPY YOKUM DRINKING GLASS, 5" $5.00-15.00

PAPPY YOKUM DRINKING GLASS 5", dated 1949...$10.00-20.00

PEANUTS CHARACTERS LUNCHBOX SET, 1959...$20.00-35.00

PEANUTS MAGNETIC BULLETIN BOARD, circa 1950 ....$20.00-40.00

PEANUTS METAL LUNCHBOX, 1950's ...$10.00-20.00

PEANUTS, CHARLIE BROWN PENCIL CASE AND SHARPENER, 1960's $5.00-10.00

PEANUTS CHARACTERS WRITING CASE, original, 1950's $20.00-45.00

PERRY WINKLE BISQUE NODDER, 2" tall, German, 1930's $40.00-65.00

PERRY WINKLE BOOKMARK, 1940's $5.00-15.00

PETER RABBIT LIONEL HANDCAR, 9" long, metal and wood composition $325.00-490.00

POGO CHARACTER VINYL FIGURES (set of six) ca. 1960's $40.00-100.00

POGO DRINKING CUP, 1950's, 4" $10.00-18.00

POGO POSSUM DRINKING CUP, 1960's ..$5.00-10.00

POGO'S POGOMOBILE, 1950's in original envelope $75.00-150.00

POPEYE "ADVENTURES OF POPEYE GAME" Transogram, 1957, 9" x 17" $15.00-35.00

POPEYE AND BLUTO WINDUP BOXING TOY, LineMar, 4" tall, tin and celluloid $125.00-350.00

POPEYE ASH TRAY, ca. 1935, Schavoior Rubber Company, 3" tall $100.00-225.00

POPEYE ASH TRAY, plaster, 6" $50.00-75.00

POPEYE BAGATELLE GAME, circa 1930, King Features $150.00-300.00

POPEYE BIFBAT, wooden paddle, 1929, 11" long...$30.00-50.00

POPEYE BIG BIG BOOK, Thimble Theater, 1935 ....$45.00-95.00

POPEYE BUBBLE BLOWING BATTERY OPERATED TOY, LineMar, 12" tall...................$400.00-700.00

POPEYE CARTOON BOOK by Saalfield, ca. 1934, 8" x 13"...$40.00-80.00

POPEYE CELLULOID FIGURE, circa 1930, 3" $20.00-45.00

POPEYE CELLULOID FIGURE, 5" tall, 1930's, smoking action $40.00-95.00

POPEYE CELLULOID FIGURE, ca. 1930's, 6" tall, jointed arms and legs $125.00-275.00

POPEYE CELLULOID WINDUP, 1930's, 8" marked "Foreign" $125.00-250.00

POPEYE CHALK CARNIVAL FIGURE with pipe, 1930's $50.00-100.00

POPEYE CHARACTER BAKELITE NAPKIN RING, yellow bakelite with decal $25.00-50.00

POPEYE CHARACTER CERAMIC COOKIE JAR, ca. 1940's, very large...............................$30.00-70.00

POPEYE CHARACTER LAMP, manufactured by Idealite, 11" tall $125.00-200.00

POPEYE CHARACTER TIN SPARKLER TOY, 1930's, Chein $55.00-80.00

POPEYE CHARM BRACELET, 1930's, enameled $50.00-85.00

POPEYE CHRITMAS LIGHT COVERS, in original box, 1930's $45.00-85.00

POPEYE COOKIE JAR, ceramic, 1950's, 10" tall $50.00-75.00

POPEYE DIPPY DUMPER TIN WINDUP TRUCK, Marx, Popeye figure is celluloid $275.00-600.00

POPEYE DRUMMER PULL TOY, 1929, wood with paper lithograph, labels $55.00-100.00

POPEYE EAGLE PENCIL BOX, 1929 .....$20.00-40.00

POPEYE EGG TRANSFERS, 1936, 5" square in original envelope $15.00-35.00

POPEYE EXPRESS PLATFORM TOY w/CIRCLING AIRPLANE, Marx, tin lithograph $375.00-600.00

POPEYE FOUTAIN PEN, 1930's, Penco ..$35.00-75.00

POPEYE GIANT COMPOSITION FIGURE, 15" with wooden pipe, 1930's $50.00-125.00

POPEYE GUITAR in original box $20.00-45.00

POPEYE GUITAR music box $35.00-70.00

POPEYE HANKY, 1930's $10.00-20.00

POPEYE INFLATABLE PUNCHING BAG, in box, 1950's $20.00-35.00

POPEYE IRON BOAT NIGHT LIGHT, 1935, rare $350.00-600.00

POPEYE JOINTED CELLULOID FIGURE, Japan, 1940's, 6"..$40.00-85.00

POPEYE LUNCH BOX manufactured by Thermos, dated 1964 ....$5.00-15.00

POPEYE MODELING CLAY, American Crayon Company, 1936 ....$25.00-65.00

POPEYE NAPKIN HOLDER, celluloid/Bakelite, amber, with decal, 1930's $20.00-40.00

POPEYE OFFICIAL TELESCOPE, United Products Company, 9", original box $50.00-125.00

POPEYE OIL PAINTING BY NUMBERS, late 1950's edition..$10.00-20.00

POPEYE oilcloth doll, 11", 1930's $125.00-170.00

POPEYE ON ROLLER SKATES, tin lithograph, Line Mar $375.00-625.00

POPEYE ON THE TRAPEZE, wooden hand toy, 8"..$30.00-50.00

POPEYE ON TRICYCLE TIN WINDUP, tin and cloth, Line Mar $700.00-1,200.00

POPEYE ORBIT GUM FLIP BOOK PREMIUM, 1933 ....$20.00-45.00

POPEYE PADDLE WAGON, wood and paper lithograph, 1930's $75.00-165.00

POPEYE PAINT BOOK, by McLoughlin Brothers, 1932, 10" x 13"...$20.00-35.00

POPEYE PAINT SET, Presto, 1961, boxed .$15.00-25.00

POPEYE PAINTS in tin box, 1933..........$10.00-30.00

POPEYE PARTY GAME, Whitman, 1937. $35.00-75.00

POPEYE PATROL CAST IRON MOTORCYCLE, 9", Hubley $500.00-800.00

POPEYE POP-UP BOOK, In Among the Savages, Blue Ribbon Press, 1934 ....$100.00-225.00

POPEYE PUNCHING BAG TIN WINDUP (overhead bag) Chein, 10" tall $375.00-675.00

POPEYE PUZZLE, size of puzzle 7" x 10", Jaymar, 1950's $10.00-20.00

POPEYE RAMP WALKER, composition figure, ca. 1930's $60.00-150.00

POPEYE ROLY POLY AND CORK GUN SET, dated 1958 by Knickerbocker $45.00-70.00

POPEYE ROW BOAT, manufactured by LineMar, all tin, Japan, rare $1,400.00-2,500.00

POPEYE RUBBER FIGURE, 8", 1930's $40.00-85.00

POPEYE SCRAP BOOK, 1929, 11" x 15" .$25.00-45.00

POPEYE SHIPWRECK GAME, 1933 by Einson Freeman $55.00-110.00

POPEYE SKILL GAME with beads, tin and glass, 1930's $40.00-65.00

COMIC CHARACTER TOYS

POPEYE SONG BOOK Famous Music, circa 1936 ....$20.00-45.00

POPEYE SPINACH DELIVERY, 5½", cast iron, manufactured by Hubley $375.00-550.00

POPEYE SPINNING SPARKLER TOY, J. Chein, round, 1959 ....$25.00-65.00

POPEYE SPINNING SPARKLER TOY, tin lithograph, die-cut head, German, 1930's $95.00-225.00

POPEYE STATUE, SEATED AS "THE THINKER," 1930's, plaster $40.00-85.00

POPEYE TANK TOY TIN WINDUP by Line Mar Toys, c. King Features Syndicate $75.00-225.00

POPEYE TARGET, masonite back, dated 1958, S.S. Spinacher design $20.00-35.00

POPEYE THE FLYER AIRPLANE AND TIN LITHOGRAPH TOWER, windup, Marx $375.00-545.00

POPEYE THE HEAVY HITTER, bell and mallet type, Chein $875.00-1300.00

POPEYE THE SAILOR CEREAL BOWL, 6", white china $20.00-40.00

POPEYE THE SAILOR CHILD'S CHARACTER HAT, cloth and vinyl, 1940 ....$35.00-65.00

POPEYE THE SAILOR IN A ROWBOAT, tin windup, by Hoge, 15" long $875.00-1,400.00

POPEYE THIMBLE THEATER LUCKY BUCKS PLAY MONEY, 1930's $10.00-25.00

POPEYE THIMBLE THEATER PLAY SET, walkers, Popeye, Olive and Wimpy $250.00-400.00

POPEYE TIN LITHOGRAPH PAIL, 1930's .$40.00-75.00

POPEYE TUMBLING WINDUP FIGURE by Line Mar, 5" $700.00-1,200.00

POPEYE WHERE'S ME PIPE GAME, 1937, in original box.........................$35.00-70.00

POPEYE WHISTLE FLASHLIGHT with original card $20.00-40.00

POPEYE WHITE CHALK IN BOX, 1936, American Crayon Company $10.00-25.00

POPEYE WOOD ASH TRAY DIE-CUT, possibly 1930's folk art..............................$65.00-125.00

POPEYE WOOD COMPOSITION FIGURE 5" tall 1930's $30.00-60.00

POPEYE WOOD COMPOSITION FIGURE, 5" tall, 1940's $20.00-40.00

POPEYE WOOD JOINTED AND COMPOSITION DOLL, by J. Chein, 1930's, 8" tall $100.00-200.00

POPEYE WOOD STEPPING STOOL, 1957 .$15.00-40.00

POPEYE WRIST WATCH by Kreisler ...$250.00-450.00

POPEYE WRITING TABLET, 1929, color cover $10.00-25.00

POPEYE'S BINGO FIVE IN A ROW-EH! game, copyright 1929 ....$30.00-60.00

POPEYE'S COMIC DEPARTMENT RUBBER STAMP SET by Stamper Kraft, 1935 ....$35.00-70.00

POPEYE MECHANICAL PENCIL, 1930's .$20.00-45.00

POPULAR COMICS CHRISTMAS CARD BOXED SET, Henry, Nancy and others, 1950's $35.00-65.00

PORKY PIG AND PETUNIA PIG PULL TOY by Fisher Price, c. 1940's $65.00-130.00

PORKY PIG BANK, cast iron, painted ..$45.00-105.00

PORKY PIG BISQUE BANK, circa 1930, 5" tall $65.00-125.00

PORKY PIG ceramic planter, 1940's $10.00-22.00

PORKY PIG CHINA BANK, 8" tall, probably ca. 1950's $20.00-40.00

PORKY PIG DOLL, with linen face, probably 1940's $30.00-65.00

PORKY PIG FIGURE, Evan K. Shaw, circa 1950 ....$30.00-65.00

PORKY PIG GLAZED CHINA FIGURE, 1940's, 5" probably Evan K. Shaw $25.00-60.00

PORKY PIG GLAZED CHINA PLANTER, 1940's, 4" $15.00-35.00

PORKY PIG, TIN WINDUP, 9" tall, dated 1939 ....$65.00-90.00

PORKY PIG WINDUPS (two versions) 9" tall, ca. 1939, tin, Reynolds collection, $65.00-90.00 each.

POWERFUL KATRINKA AND JIMMY WINDUP, 1920's, Nifty, Furnish collection, $525.00-925.00.

PORKY PIG, tin, windup walker, Marx...$45.00-80.00

PORKY PIG WRIST WATCH, 1949, Warner Brothers $100.00-200.00

PRINCE VALIANT BOARD GAME, boxed.$15.00-30.00

PRINCESS SUMMER FALL WINTER SPRING, (Howdy Doody character) marionette, boxed.$65.00-125.00

RACHEL BISQUE COMIC CHARACTER NODDER, German, 4" $45.00-85.00

RACHEL COMIC CHARACTER PAINTED SOAP FIGURE, 3" tall, 1930's $15.00-40.00

REG'LAR FELLERS BOOK, Cupples and Leon ca. 1928 ....$30.00-50.00

REG'LAR FELLERS IN THE ARMY, Hardcover book, 1943...$25.00-50.00

REG'LAR FELLERS PENCIL BOX, 6" x 11", Eagle Pencil Company $20.00-30.00

ROAD RUNNER CHARACTER PUZZLES, set of two, 1969...$5.00-10.00

ROCKY AND HIS FRIENDS GLAZED CERAMIC BANK, 1960's $15.00-35.00

ROCKY THE FLYING SQUIRREL AND FRIENDS BOOK, 1960..$5.00-12.00

RUDY THE OSTRICH (BARNEY GOOGLE CHARACTER) 9" tin lithograph windup by Nifty.$875.00-1,300.00

SANDY (ORPHAN ANNIE'S DOG) OILCLOTH DOLL, 8" tall, ca. 1930 ....$60.00-85.00

SANDY THE DOG CHARACTER wood jointed figure, 4", 1930's $45.00-85.00

SANDY TIN TOY, 8" long, 1930's, push tail down and he rolls, Sandy on collar $95.00-175.00

SANDY WOOD JOINTED CHARACTER TOY, 3½" tall, 1930's $35.00-65.00

SANDY, ORPHAN ANNIE'S DOG, MINIATURE LEAD FIGURE, 1" tall, ca. 1940's $18.00-25.00

SCHMOO BANK, LADY, ceramic $35.00-70.00

SCHMOO BANK, red plastic, 7" tall, dated 1948...$20.00-50.00

SCHMOO CERAMIC SALT AND PEPPER SHAKERS, ca. 1950's $20.00-40.00

SCHMOO LADY BANK, 7" tall, bottle made of glass..$30.00-65.00

SCHMOO WALL CLOCK, manufactured by Lux, 6" tall..$40.00-110.00

SCHMOO-FLY paddle ball game $10.00-15.00

SCHMOOS SALT AND PEPPER SHAKERS, Japan, glazed ceramic, 4" tall.......................$35.00-55.00

SCRAPPY AT THE SEASHORE, 3" pail, 1930's $40.00-80.00

SCRAPPY BANK, leather and metal Scrappy on front $35.00-75.00

SCRAPPY CHARACTER DRINKING GLASS, 1935, 5" $10.00-25.00

SCRAPPY CHRISTMAS TREE LIGHT SET, original box, Mazda $65.00-95.00

SCRAPPY DRINKING GLASS, 1935 ....$15.00-30.00

SCRAPPY'S ANIMATED PUPPET THEATER, Pillsbury premium, ca. 1936...........................$30.00-75.00

SHADOW BOOKMARK, 1940's, 3" $5.00-15.00

SKEEZIX AND UNCLE WALT BISQUE PENCIL HOLDER, c. F.A.S., Japan, 5" tall $40.00-70.00

SKEEZIX CHARACTER OILCLOTH DOLL, 12" tall...$50.00-85.00

SKEEZIX CHARACTERS BOXED BISQUE SET, with

Herbie, Uncle Walt, and Smitty $200.00-350.00

SKEEZIX STATIONERY boxed set of writing papers, 6" x 8", c. 1926 ....$10.00-18.00

SKIPPY AND OTHER HUMOR, HARDCOVER BOOK, 1929, 64 pages $35.00-60.00

SKIPPY CELLULOID FIGURE, jointed arms, 6" tall, extremely rare, 1930's $150.00-300.00

SKIPPPY FIGURAL TOOTHBRUSH HOLDER, 6", 1930's, bisque $50.00-100.00

SKIPPY HANKY, 1930's $10.00-25.00

SKIPPY SHEET MUSIC, 1930's $10.00-25.00

SCRAPPY CHARACTER PULL TOY, c. Columbia Pictures, 1930's, wood and metal, Reynolds collection, $60.00-125.00.

SCRAPPY AND HIS GIRLFRIEND BISQUE FIGURES, 3½", Japan, 1930's, Reynolds collection, each $25.00-60.00.

THREE LITLE PIGS CLOTH AND TIN WIND-UP TOYS, manufactured by Schuco, Germany, Furnish collection, $85.00-200.00.

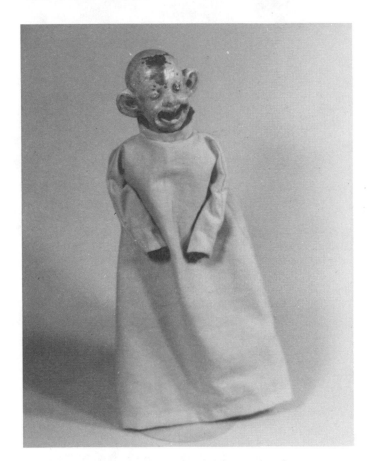

YELLOW KID METAL AND CLOTH DOLL 10", c. 1906, Furnish collection, $125.00-300.00.

SMILING JACK COLORING BOOK, By Saalfield, copyright 1946 ....$20.00-40.00

SMITTY AND HERBY 3-WHEEL MOTORCYCLE, Tootsietoy, 1930's $125.00-285.00

SMITTY BOOKMARK, 1940's, 3" $5.00-15.00

SMITTY CHARACTER STORYBOOK, Cupples and Leon, 1928 ....$15.00-30.00

SMITTY RIDING A SCOOTER, WINDUP, Marx, 8" tall, ca. 1930's $550.00-875.00

SMITTY TARGET GAME BY MILTON BRADLEY, 1930's $65.00-125.00

SMITTY TEA SET, German, six pieces, 1930's $85.00-140.00

SMITTY TOOTSIETOY FIGURE WITH HERBIE IN SIDECAR, 1930's $65.00-140.00

SNIFFLES CHARACTER BANK, painted pot metal $25.00-65.00

SNOOKUMS ASHTRAY, by Nippon $85.00-150.00

SNOOKUMS BABY CLOTH DOLL, 5" tall, from Newly-weds comic strip $40.00-85.00

SNOOPY AIRPLANE, metal, 1960's............$5.00-10.00

SNOOPY CHARACTER MUG, dated 1958.$15.00-30.00

SNOOPY MILK GLASS CUP, 1960's $5.00-10.00

SNOOPY SQUEEZE TOY, rubber, 1958...$10.00-20.00

SNOOPY WALLET, vinyl, 1960's $5.00-10.00

SNOWFLAKES AND SWIPES, tin lithograph, pull toy, ca. 1929 ....$450.00-1,050.00

SNUFFY SMITH AND HIS BROTHER SALT AND PEPPER SET, glazed ceramic, 4" $25.00-55.00

SPARE RIBS (DOG) JOINTED WOOD FIGURE, 3" tall, with decal...$50.00-125.00

SPARK PLUG flat wooden figure on wheels, ca. 1920's, yellow $45.00-95.00

SPARK PLUG GLASS CANDY CONTAINER, 4" long, 1930's...$40.00-80.00

SPARK PLUG GLASS CANDY CONTAINER, ca. 1920's, 3" tall $50.00-95.00

SPARK PLUG RUBBER SQUEAK TOY, c. 1923, 5" long $25.00-45.00

SPARK PLUG THE HORSE PULL TOY, 10" long, jointed wood on wheels, 1920's..................$150.00-225.00

SPARKLE PLENTY CHRISTMAS TREE LIGHTS, Mutual Equipment and Supply $60.00-130.00

STEVE CANYON COLORING BOOK, ca. 1952, large size $10.00-20.00

STEVE CANYON SPACE GOGGLES, 1940's, plastic and rubber $15.00-35.00

STEVE CANYON space helmet, 1960's $10.00-25.00

SUPERMAN ALARM CLOCK, 1930's animated, 1940 ....$300.00-650.00

SUPERMAN BUBBLE GUM WRAPPER, 1930's, rare..$75.00-195.00

SUPERMAN KIDDIE PADDLERS SWIM FINS, 1950's, packaged $50.00-85.00

SUPERMAN SPEED GAME manufactured by Milton Bradley $50.00-95.00

SUPERMAN OFFICIAL COSTUME, manufactured by Ben Cooper, 1950's $35.00-70.00

SUPERMAN SILVERPLATE CHARACTER SPOON, 1930's...$8.00-15.00

SUPERMAN SOCKS IN ORIGINAL BOX, 1949, eight pairs $100.00-200.00

SUPERMAN WINDUP TANK, TOY, Marx, Superman lifts tank, 4" tall $150.00-350.00

SUPERMAN WRIST WATCH, original, circa 1940 ....$150.00-275.00

SUPERMAN, Kellog's Pep Pin $8.00-20.00

SYLVESTER THE CAT HAND PUPPET, circa 1950 ....$10.00-20.00

TERRY AND THE PIRATES BOOK BY RANDOM HOUSE, 1946....................................$20.00-40.00

TERRY AND THE PIRATES HINGEES SET, in original envelope...$5.00-15.00

TERRY AND THE PIRATES JIGSAW PUZZLE, Jaymar, 7" x 10", 1946......................$20.00-40.00

TERRY AND THE PIRATES PICTURE RECORD, ca. 1948 ....$15.00-30.00

TERRY AND THE PIRATES POP-UP BOOK, Blue Ribbon Press, 1935......................$100.00-200.00

TILLIE THE TOILER DRAWING BOOK, circa 1930......................$20.00-35.00

TOM AND JERRY CAR, BO, circa 1950, 12", metal and plastic $100.00-225.00

TOM AND JERRY HAND PUPPET, 1952, cloth and vinyl $15.00-30.00

TOM AND JERRY ON HAT CERAMIC FIGURE, holds cigarettes, 1940's $60.00-100.00

TOM AND JERRY PLASTER FIGURES, circa 1940 ....$15.00-35.00 (for pair)

TOONERVILE TROLLEY TIN WINDUP CAR, circa 1922......................$450.00-800.00

TOONERVILLE TROLLEY GAME, boxed 9" x 17" game, 1927, Milton Bradley......................$50.00-85.00

TOONERVILLE TROLLEY POT METAL FIGURE, 3", painted green, metal wheels......................$135.00-210.00

TOONERVILLE TROLLEY TINY TIN LITHO. TOY, 2", German, Nifty $180.00-425.00

TWEETIE PIE HAND PUPPET, 1950's $10.00-20.00

UNCLE BIM bisque figure, 3", 1930's $20.00-40.00

UNCLE WALT AND SKEEZIX BOXED BISQUE FIGURES, 4, 2" to 4", colorful box $140.00-225.00

UNCLE WALT AND SKEEZIX BISQUE TOOTHBRUSH HOLDER, 1930's $65.00-100.00

UNCLE WALT BOOKMARK, 1940's, 3" $5.00-15.00

UNCLE WALT CHARACTER OILCLOTH DOLL, 25" tall......................$65.00-95.00

UNCLE WALT IN A ROADSTER, Tootsietoy, ca. 1932......................$75.00-175.00

UNCLE WIGGILY CHINA TEA CUP, dated 1924......................$15.00-25.00

UNCLE WIGGILY CRAZY CAR (later version) 7" long, rabbit in orange hat......................$225.00-425.00

UNCLE WIGGILY OVALTINE MUG, 1924, glazed ceramic, 3" $20.00-35.00

UNCLE WIGGILY TIN WINDUP CAR, 8½", rabbit in black top hat $450.00-950.00

UNCLE WILLIE AND EMMIE TOOTHBRUSH HOLDER, bisque, 1930's, Japan $50.00-95.00

UNCLE WILLY BISQUE COMIC CHARACTER FIGURE, 4" $20.00-45.00

WALLY WALRUS CERAMIC PLANTER, 7", 1958, 4", Walter Lantz $15.00-25.00

WIMPY CAST IRON FIGURE, 3", 1930's .$50.00-75.00

WIMPY CEREAL BOX FACE MASK, circa 1950......................$5.00-10.00

WIMPY CHARACTER PLASTER FIGURE, 9" tall, 1930's $30.00-60.00

WIMPY HAMBERGER, hamburger-shaped musical toy, dated 1936 ....$45.00-70.00

WIMPY WALKER, composition, from Thimble Theater set......................$40.00-65.00

WINNIE WINKLE CIGAR BOX, 1930's $25.00-50.00

WINNIE WINKLE GASOLINE ALLEY BAKING SET, copyright 1937......................$20.00-45.00

WONDER WOMAN CHARACTER VALENTINE, 1940's $10.00-15.00

WOODIE WOODPECKER ACTION WALL CLOCK, dated

1959, in original box......................$100.00-200.00

WOODY WOODPECKER CHINA PLANTER, 1960's, Walter Lantz $15.00-30.00

WOODY WOODPECKER SHEET MUSIC, dated 1947......................$10.00-20.00

YELLOW KID pin-back button $15.00-30.00

YELLOW KID AD CARD, postal card size, early $20.00-45.00

YELLOW KID CAP BOMB, cast iron, manufactured by Ives......................$100.00-225.00

YELLOW KID CAP BOMB, ca. 1900, cast iron (head only) $125.00-275.00

YELLOW KID CARD SET, ca.1896, R. Outcault, set of 25......................$150.00-325.00

YELLOW KID CAST IRON PAPERWEIGHT, early comic character item......................$100.00-225.00

YELLOW KID COMPOSITION BOOK, copyright 1896 by Richard Outcault $75.00-120.00

YELLOW KID COMPOSITION DOLL WITH ORIGINAL BUTTON, jointed, 7" $200.00-450.00

YELLOW KID GOAT CART, cast iron toy with Yellow Kid in back of cart $650.00-975.00

YELLOW KID GOAT CART, cast iron, 7", 1900's $350.00-700.00

YELLOW KID MC LOUGHLIN BROTHERS PUZZLE, McFadden's Row of Flats $200.00-350.00

YELLOW KID MOVIE FLIP BOOK, circa 1895......................$100.00-175.00

YELLOW KID PIN CUSHION, made of metal, early $150.00-350.00

YELLOW KID ROCKING CHAIR with imprint on backrest, 30" tall, rare $500.00-800.00

YOGI BEAR CAMERA, 1960's $15.00-30.00

YOGI BEAR RUBBER SQUEEZE TOY by Dell, 1960's $5.00-10.00

UNCLE WIGGILY TIN WINDUP CAR, 8½" long, c. 1936, $450.00-950.00.

COWBOY AND WESTERN COLLECTIBLES

Americans love their cowboys. They always have, they always will. Collecting of toy memorabilia associated with the American cowpoke scene is as popular as when the dime novel and Saturday afternoon matinee were in their "heyday." Why are they still so popular as collectibles? In part, because the western hero, like his prairie competitor, the Indian, is a vanishing breed. Since new western toys do not exist in today's toy stores, the old ones are even more collectible.

In this author's work as a theatre director, I was forced, several years ago to search for some large toy indians to use as props for our production of Agatha Christie's *Ten Little Indians.* It took a weekend-long search of six major toy stores in our metropolitan area before I finally located a dozen large plastic Indians; had I been searching for cowboys, they would have been equally as scarce. I thought the hunt would be an easy one. The point here is that western toys just aren't popular among today's children. Is that any surprise? The western hero comic books, television shows and movies that were so prevalent in the 1940's, 1950's, and even the 1960's have all but vanished from today's popular entertainment scene. There is no reason for the little child of today to know the cowboys or want to buy toys in their likeness in the toy store. This fact has made cowboy items of the 1970's and 1980's virtually extinct.

So with no new merchandise appearing about the western scene, collectors are confined to items from the 1930's through the 1960's as the area of concentration for their collecting. Novice western toy collectors have little new merchandise to collect today, so anyone entering the field as a newcomer must also concentrate on older merchandise. This scarcity of recent merchandise is a phenomenon peculiar to western collectibles. Disneyana collectors have toys produced from the 1950's through the present to accent their beginning collections. Space toy collectors of the 1930's through the 1950's can also assemble reasonably priced new collections of Star Wars and Star Trek memorabilia and car and truck collectors can still collect toys of the 1970's and 1980's, as vehicular toys are still being produced.

But the lack of new western toys and memorabilia on the current scene reinforces and often inflates pricing. The true "Baby Boomers" of the 1940's and 1950's love their favorite childhood cowboy heroes and they are now in the economically advantageous position of adulthood that enables them to pay dearly for their favorite Hoppy guns or that spectacular Red Ryder target set they wanted as a kid.

Western collectibles generally fall into one of two categories: guns and costumes or figures and memorabilia. Because young cowboys of the 1940's and 1950's wanted to look like their heroes, a vast array of gun and holster sets were available from the Lone Ranger and Gene Autry to Marshall Matt Dillon and Bat Masterson. Once toy producers realized the vast appeal of the cowboy to young Americans and their toy-buying parents, the toy factories must have worked around the clock turning out playthings in cowpoke likenesses. For every major western hero there were at least several different gun and holster sets available and no outfit was complete without a hat. Vintage cowboy character hats from the 1940's and 1950's are as rare today as many of the most desirable western gun sets.

In the other category of cowboy toys are the figures and memorabilia. These include character games, books, paper items, Marx playsets, radio and television western toys and related merchandise. Particularly popular today are Lone Ranger and Tom Mix items because of their tie-in to radio and highly collectible radio premiums. Also increasing rapidly in value are items associated with westerns on television since this genre of network entertainment is now extinct.

Buckle on your Lone Ranger six-shooters holster, put on your Hoppy hat, fasten your Zorro spurs, tie your Roy Rogers bandana and ride on into the sunset as you clippity-clop your way through the cowboy toy listing. You might even hear a distant cowboy crooning to the jagged hills..."Happy trails........"

ANNIE OAKLEY HARTLAND FIGURE on horseback, complete with accessories $50.00-100.00

BAT MASTERSON GUN AND HOLSTER SET with cane, 1950's, based on television series $40.00-80.00

BUCK JONES AND THE NIGHT RIDERS, large book, Big Big Book, 1937, colorful..............$25.00-50.00

BUCK JONES IN ROCKEY RHODES, hardcover book, 1935....................................$20.00-45.00

BUCK JONES IN THE FIGHTING CODE, Big Little Book, 1934 ....$15.00-35.00

BUCK JONES RANGER CLUB, membership card......................................$8.00-15.00

BUCK JONES RIFLE with compass, manufactured by Daisy $80.00-150.00

BUCKING BRONCO COWBOY ON HORSE, Lehmann, 1900's $400.00-800.00

BUCKING BRONCO, MT, Japan, 4", all celluloid wind-up horse and cowboy.........................$35.00-60.00

BUFFALO BILL JR. LEATHER WATCH, aluminum case..................................$12.00-25.00

BUFFALO BILL JUNIOR PREMIUM RING, boy's..$10.00-20.00

BUTTERMILK (Dale Evan's horse) tin piece, 2" tin lithograph........................$10.00-20.00

CISCO KID AND PANCHO COLORING BOOK, Saalfield Publishing Company $10.00-20.00

CISCO KID AND PANCHO MILK GLASS CEREAL BOWL, 1950's, black lettering $15.00-25.00

CISCO KID BREAD LABELS from Tip Top bread, three color $3.00-8.00

CISCO KID COMIC ALBUM, 1953 ....$10.00-20.00

CISCO KID MASK, premium from Tip Top Bread $15.00-20.00

COWBOY FIGURE, celluloid with jointed arms, Japan, 1930's $40.00-80.00

COWBOY KING PISTOL, by Stevens, 9" .$20.00-40.00

COWBOY ON HORSE TIN WINDUP, 6", ca. 1925, Marx.....................................$85.00-140.00

COWBOY RIDER WINDUP, Marx, tin, black horse version, 7", 1930's $140.00-250.00

COWBOY RIDING A HORSE, with lasso, windup, Marx, 1940's $65.00-105.00

COWBOY, CELLULOID, 7" figure, jointed arms, Japan, 1930's $45.00-100.00

COWBOYS AND INDIANS PUNCHOUT BOOK by Gabriel, 1927, 10" x 14".....................$50.00-85.00

DALE EVANS AND BUTTERMILK, Whitman book, 1956..$5.00-10.00

DALE EVANS BOXED HAT AND OUTFIT, ca. 1950's, set $45.00-90.00

DALE EVANS CHARACTER FIGURE, manufactured by Hartland, plastic $60.00-100.00

DALE EVANS CHARACTER NECKLACE, on card, lucky horseshoe, 1950's $10.00-22.00

DALE EVANS WRISTWATCH, by U.S. Time, ca. 1940's $75.00-135.00

DANIEL BOONE COONSKIN CAP, television, circa 1950....................................$15.00-25.00

DANIEL BOONE RIFLE, cap-shooting, flintlock type $20.00-45.00

DAVY CROCKETT HOLSTER SET, 1950's, leather, mint in box $30.00-55.00

DAVY CROCKETT POWDER HORN in original box $25.00-40.00

DAVY CROCKETT BADGE, Alamo type, or original, card, 1950's $10.00-20.00

DAVY CROCKETT barlow knife...............$10.00-20.00

DAVY CROCKETT belt and buckle $10.00-20.00

DAVY CROCKETT BOOK BAG, 1950's...$10.00-25.00

DAVY CROCKETT CANTEEN, 1950's $20.00-40.00

DAVY CROCKETT CARD GAME, boxed, circa 1950....................................$5.00-15.00

DAVY CROCKETT CERAMIC BABY DAVY, circa 1950....................................$10.00-20.00

DAVY CROCKETT CERAMIC LAMP AND SHADE, 1950's $35.00-75.00

DAVY CROCKETT DOLL, boxed, 1950's.$50.00-125.00

DAVY CROCKETT DRUM, 1950's $15.00-30.00

DAVY CROCKETT FLINTLOCK PISTOL, model kit, boxed $20.00-30.00

DAVY CROCKETT FRONTIER KNIFE, 1950's by Imperial Knife Company $20.00-40.00

DAVY CROCKETT GUITAR by Peter Puppet Playthings, 1950's $50.00-85.00

DAVY CROCKETT HUNTING GLASS, 1950's, telescope toy $20.00-35.00

DAVY CROCKETT JAIL KEYS & HANDCUFFS on original card $25.00-50.00

DAVY CROCKETT LAMP with original lampshade, plaster-composition $65.00-110.00

DAVY CROCKETT LEATHER PRINTED JACKET AND PANTS, 1950's..................................$50.00-95.00

DAVY CROCKETT LEATHER WALLET, circa 1950....................................$5.00-10.00

DAVY CROCKETT LUNCHBOX AND THERMOS SET, by Liberty National Corporation, circa 1950....................................$10.00-30.00

DAVY CROCKETT METAL BANK, circa 1950, 5¼" $10.00-20.00

DAVY CROCKETT MILK GLASS MUG, circa 1950....................................$10.00-20.00

DAVY CROCKETT OFFICIAL INDIAN FIGHTER CAP, coonskin type, original box $50.00-100.00

DAVY CROCKETT OFFICIAL INDIAN FIGHTER HAT, coonskin type cap $30.00-65.00

DAVY CROCKETT PEACE PIPE, 1950's.$15.00-30.00

DAVY CROCKETT PLASTER WALL PLAQUE, dated 1955 ....$20.00-40.00

DAVY CROCKETT POCKET KNIFE, Walt Disney Productions copyright $12.00-20.00

DAVY CROCKETT POP ACTION HAND GUN, tin lithograph, 1950's $25.00-45.00

DAVY CROCKETT POWDER HORN, 1950's, TV show tie-in $10.00-20.00

DAVY CROCKETT POWDER POUCH, 1950's, TV show tie-in $5.00-15.00

DAVY CROCKETT SIGNAL LIGHT, 1950's, TV show tie-in $10.00-20.00

DAVY CROCKETT SUITCASE, 1950's.....$15.00-25.00

DAVY CROCKETT SUSPENDERS, on original packaging card, 1950's $15.00-25.00

DAVY CROCKETT TENT, 1950's, for use over card table $25.00-55.00

DAVY CROCKETT WALLET, vinyl, 1950's ..$5.00-15.00

DAVY CROCKETT WAGON, tin, marked Walt Disney Productions, 1950's $45.00-65.00

DAVY CROCKETT WESTERN PLAY SET, plastic figures, ca. 1950's...............................$20.00-40.00

COWBOY AND WESTERN COLLECTIBLES

CELLULOID WESTERN FIGURES, Japan, 5" to 7" tall, Furnish collection, value of each, $40.00-80.00.

COWBOYS ON HORSEBACK, tin windups, U.S. Zone Germany, 5" and 6" tall, Furnish collection, value of each, $35.00-80.00.

DAVY CROCKETT WESTERN PRAIRIE WAGON, Child's wagon, 1950's $65.00-140.00
DAVY CROCKETT WOODEN HOBBY HORSE, ca. 1950's $75.00-125.00
FLINTLOCK JUNIOR PISTOL by Hubley, 7" long $10.00-30.00
FORT APACHE MARX PLAYSET, boxed, 1960's $35.00-80.00
FRONTIERLAND, Walt Disney's Official Game, Parker Brothers, 1950's, 16" x 8" $20.00-45.00
GALLOPING COWBOY, Daiya, Japan, 1950's, tin and celluloid windup in box........................$40.00-95.00
GENE AUTRY "THE HAWK OF THE HILLS," Better Little book, 1942 ....$10.00-30.00
GENE AUTRY AND RAIDERS OF THE RANGE, Better Little Book $10.00-20.00
GENE AUTRY AND THE LAND GRAB MYSTERY, Better Little Book, 1940's $10.00-20.00
GENE AUTRY AND THE MYSTERY OF PAINT ROCK CANYON, Better Little Book.................$10.00-20.00
GENE AUTRY BICYCLE HORN, circa 1950, mint $25.00-50.00

GENE AUTRY BOOK "APACHE COUNTRY," 1952...$10.00-20.00
GENE AUTRY BOOK "ROBIN HOOD OF TEXAS," 1947..$10.00-25.00
GENE AUTRY CAP PISTOL, pearl handles, Kenton $45.00-80.00
GENE AUTRY CHARACTER FILM, Carmel Hollywood Films, 3" 8 mm...................................$10.00-20.00
GENE AUTRY CHILD'S RAIN BOOTS, Autry logo, 8" tall, red and black $20.00-40.00
GENE AUTRY COLORING BOOK, 1949, large format $15.00-35.00
GENE AUTRY COLORING BOOK, circa 1950, 8" x 11"...$10.00-25.00
GENE AUTRY COMIC published by Dell Publishing, 1950's $5.00-12.00
GENE AUTRY COWBOY PAINT BOOK, Merrill Publishing Company, 1940, size 10" x 15" ..$35.00-65.00
GENE AUTRY GUITAR, by Silvertone, circa 1950...$50.00-110.00
GENE AUTRY GUITAR, standard size, circa 1950..$45.00-75.00
GENE AUTRY HORSESHOE NAIL RING, circa 1950...$35.00-60.00
GENE AUTRY IN PUBLIC COWBOY #1, Big Little Book, 1938 ....$12.00-25.00
GENE AUTRY LAW OF THE RANGE, Better Little Book, 1939 ....$10.00-20.00
GENE AUTRY PIN-BACK BUTTON, Sunbeam Bread premium...$10.00-20.00
GENE AUTRY PLASTIC RING, Dell Comics premium...$25.00-40.00
GENE AUTRY SINGS, Song Folio, Western Music Publishing Company, 9" x 12".................$10.00-20.00
GENE AUTRY SIX-SHOOTER CAP GUNS, pair, ivory-type handles, 9" long $45.00-90.00
GENE AUTRY TIN TRAY, with decal of Gene on Champion, 15" long..................................$65.00-110.00
GENE AUTRY TOY DRUM AND TRAP SET, 24" bass drum with Gene on horse $75.00-150.00
GENE AUTRY TOY PISTOL with flame red handle grips, signed Gene Autry $20.00-40.00
GENE AUTRY WRITING TABLET, 1950's, unused $10.00-20.00
GUN JUSTICE FEATURING KEN MAYNARD, Big Little Book, 1930's $12.00-25.00
GUNSMOKE MARSHALL MATT DILLON HOLSTER SET, 1950's $20.00-50.00
GUNSMOKE, television book, dated 1966 .$5.00-10.00
HOPALONG CASSIDY BINOCULARS, Hoppy logo, 1950's $15.00-35.00
HOPALONG CASSIDY 1950 COLORING BOOK, 10" x 14"..$10.00-25.00
HOPALONG CASSIDY AD POSTER, framed, 1950's $20.00-45.00
HOPALONG CASSIDY ALARM CLOCK, ca. 1950's metal $75.00-125.00
HOPALONG CASSIDY AND LUCKY AT COPPER GULCH, animated book $20.00-45.00
HOPALONG CASSIDY AND THE STAGECOACH, book, 5" square, Doubleday, 1950's $5.00-15.00
HOPALONG CASSIDY AND THE STAMPEDE, 5" book by Doubleday, dated 1950 ....$5.00-15.00

HOPALONG CASSIDY AND THE STOLEN TREASURE, book 5" Doubleday, 1950.....................$5.00-15.00

HOPALONG CASSIDY AND TOPPER pin-back button, 1½", red, white, black $15.00-25.00

HOPALONG CASSIDY ANNUAL, book, English, hardcover $15.00-40.00

HOPALONG CASSIDY AUTOMATIC TELEVISION SET, by Automatic Toy Company, boxed .$65.00-110.00

HOPALONG CASSIDY BATH RUG, ca. 1950's $10.00-30.00

HOPALONG CASSIDY BEAN BAG TOSS GAME, 1950's, boxed $20.00-35.00

HOPALONG CASSIDY BICYCLE HORN, 1950's, original box $65.00-95.00

HOPALONG CASSIDY BIRTHDAY CARD, "Now You're 6," Buzza, 1950...................................$5.00-15.00

HOPALONG CASSIDY BIRTHDAY PARTY SET, 1950's, paper $30.00-60.00

HOPALONG CASSIDY CANASTA GAME, card game set, original box.......................................$20.00-45.00

HOPALONG CASSIDY CERAMIC COOKIE JAR BARREL, Hoppy decal, 11" tall $65.00-135.00

HOPALONG CASSIDY CERAMIC PLATE, 9"D, Hoppy pictured on Topper $15.00-35.00

HOPALONG CASSIDY CEREAL BOWL, marked, W. S. George $10.00-20.00

HOPALONG CASSIDY CHARACTER MILK GLASS, 6" tall with Hoppy logo $5.00-10.00

HOPALONG CASSIDY CHILD'S ROCKING HORSE, ca. 1950's $110.00-175.00

HOPALONG CASSIDY CHINESE CHECKERS GAME, 1950's, boxed.......................................$25.00-55.00

HOPALONG CASSIDY CHUCK WAGON SET, plate, bowl and cup in display box $50.00-125.00

HOPALONG CASSIDY COASTER SET (four) from the 1950's $15.00-25.00

HOPALONG CASSIDY COLORING OUTFIT, 1950, in original box.......................................$50.00-75.00

HOPALONG CASSSIDY COLORING OUTFIT, paints and crayons $25.00-50.00

HOPALONG CASSIDY COWBOY OUTFIT AND COSTUME, boxed, 1950's $50.00-85.00

HOPALONG CASSIDY COWGIRL SUIT, boxed set $55.00-95.00

HOPALONG CASSIDY CUT-OUT COLORING BOOK, 1954...$20.00-45.00

HOPALONG CASSIDY DART BOARD IN ORIGINAL BOX, 1950's $45.00-90.00

HOPALONG CASSIDY DART BOARD with metal board, gun and darts, boxed......................$70.00-115.00

HOPALONG CASSIDY display plate, 1950's .$20.00-40.00

HOPALONG CASSIDY DOMINOES, boxed, game by Milton Bradley, 1950's $60.00-95.00

HOPALONG CASSIDY EARMUFFS, 1950's $10.00-30.00

HOPALONG CASSIDY FAN CLUB CARD, 1950's, paper..$5.00-10.00

HOPALONG CASSIDY FIELD GLASSES in original box, 1950's $35.00-75.00

HOPALONG CASSIDY FLASHLIGHT PISTOL, 1950's $35.00-65.00

HOPALONG CASSIDY GAME, boxed board game, Milton Bradley, 1950 ....$20.00-35.00

HOPALONG CASSIDY GIFT ROUND-UP large ad poster, framed..$10.00-25.00

HOPALONG CASSIDY GLASS PICTURE (framed) Hoppy riding Topper, wood frame $35.00-50.00

HOPALONG CASSIDY GOLD PLATED CAP PISTOL original box $65.00-110.00

HOPALONG CASSIDY GOOD LUCK HORSESHOE, 1950, c. William Boyd.......................$10.00-25.00

HOPALONG CASSIDY HAIR TRAINER in bottle, Rubicon, 1950...$10.00-20.00

HOPALONG CASSIDY HOLSTER SET, orange box, double holster, two guns $45.00-95.00

HOPALONG CASSIDY ICE CREAM CONTAINER, paper, quart size, black and yellow $10.00-20.00

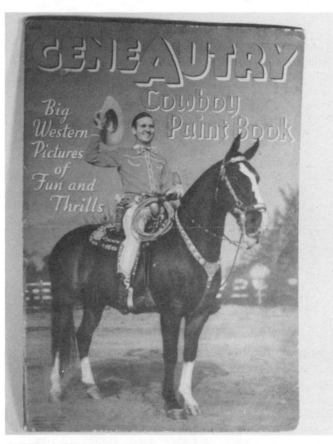

GENE AUTRY COWBOY PAINT BOOK, large size, Reynolds Collection, $15.00-35.00.

HOPALONG CASSIDY BLUE METAL LUNCHBOX, 1950's, $10.00-25.00. HOPALONG CASSIDY THERMOS $5.00-15.00, Reynolds collection.

HOPALONG CASSIDY AUTOMATIC TELEVISION SET, Automatic Toy Co., boxed, Reynolds collection, $65.00-10.00.

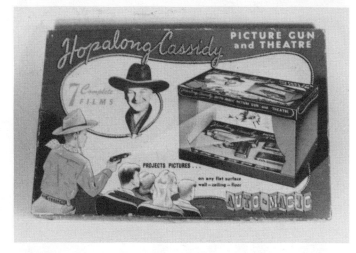

HOPALONG CASSIDY PICTURE GUN AND THEATRE, ca. 1950, Automagic, boxed set, Reynolds collection, $75.00-135.00.

HOPALONG CASSIDY JIGSAW PUZZLE, 1950's, Milton Bradley, boxed $10.00-25.00

HOPALONG CASSIDY LAMP AND NIGHT LIGHT, gun and holster shape..........................$80.00-130.00

HOPALONG CASSIDY LITHOGRAPH TARGET tin $35.00-65.00

HOPALONG CASSIDY MILK BOTTLE, 1 quart size, 1950's $10.00-30.00

HOPALONG CASSIDY MILK CUP, 5" tall, Hoppy logo, black on white $5.00-8.00

HOPALONG CASSIDY MILK GLASS CEREAL BOWL, 1950's, Hoppy logo $15.00-30.00

HOPALONG CASSIDY MILK GLASS CUP, 3" tall, red logo $12.00-20.00

HOPALONG CASSIDY MILK GLASS, circa 1950..$10.00-20.00

HOPALONG CASSIDY MUG, marked W. S. George $5.00-15.00

HOPALONG CASSIDY MUSICAL ROUND-UP, Songbook, collected tunes $10.00-20.00

HOPALONG CASSIDY NECKERCHIEF, 1950's, black satin $15.00-25.00

HOPALONG CASSIDY OFFICIAL HAT, 1950's, felt construction $20.00-45.00

HOPALONG CASSIDY on cover of Time Magazine, Nov. 27, 1950 ....$10.00-20.00

HOPALONG CASSIDY ON HIS HORSE, by Marx, 1950's $25.00-65.00

HOPALONG CASSIDY ON HORSE, Ideal, circa 1950 ....$20.00-45.00

HOPALONG CASSIDY PARTY INVITATION, 1950's, Buzza $6.00-12.00

HOPALONG CASSIDY PEN, ca. 1950's, manufactured by Parker $10.00-25.00

HOPALONG CASSIDY PENCIL CASE, circa 1950..$10.00-20.00

HOPALONG CASSIDY PICTURE GUN AND THEATRE, 1950, Automagic, boxed set $75.00-135.00

HOPALONG CASSIDY pocket knife $20.00-35.00

HOPALONG CASSIDY POGO STICK, 1950's, metal $45.00-85.00

HOPALONG CASSIDY QUICK MAGAZINE, (Hoppy on cover) May 1, 1950 ....$5.00-12.00

HOPALONG CASSIDY RADIO by Arvin, red hard plastic case, #441T $50.00-125.00

HOPALONG CASSIDY SCRAPBOOK, 1950's, simulated leather cover, 14" $40.00-65.00

HOPALONG CASSIDY SONG FOLIO, Consolidated Music Publishers $5.00-15.00

HOPALONG CASSIDY TELEVISION PUZZLES, Miltion Bradley, 12" square $20.00-40.00

HOPALONG CASSIDY TIN SHOOTING GAME, 1950's $65.00-100.00

HOPALONG CASSIDY TIN WINDUP TOY, by Marx, 9" tall rocking action..........................$95.00-145.00

HOPALONG CASSIDY TOY TIN RING, circa 1950..$5.00-15.00

HOPALONG CASSIDY TROUBLE SHOOTER, Doubleday, 5", book, c. 1950 ....$5.00-15.00

HOPALONG CASSIDY TELEVISION CHAIR, folding wooden chair, 1950's........................$45.00-125.00

HOPALONG CASSIDY TWIN GUNS, ebony type handle, ivory Hoppy figure $45.00-80.00

HOPALONG CASSIDY WALLET, leather, ca. 1950's $10.00-18.00

HOPALONG CASSIDY WASTEBASKET, 1950's, metal $15.00-30.00

HOPALONG CASSIDY WESTERN RAIN OUTFIT for a child, 1950's $40.00-85.00

HOPALONG CASSIDY SHOOTING GALLERY, windup $75.00-140.00

HOPALONG CASSIDY WOODBURNING SET, Bar 20, 1950's, boxed..................................$20.00-45.00

HOPALONG CASSIDY ZOOMERANG GUN, 1950's, in box $80.00-120.00

HOPALONG CASSIDY SUGAR CONES 1950's box, decorated $10.00-25.00

HORSE AND INDIAN WINDUP, marked U.S. Zone Germany, tin, 4" $50.00-100.00

INDIAN CHIEF AND HORSE, Elastolin composition figures $20.00-40.00

INJUN CHIEF WINDUP, Ohio Art, 8" long, crawls $50.00-100.00

LONE RANGER AND HIS HORSE SILVER, Big Little Book 1939 ....$12.00-25.00

LONE RANGER AND SILVER, TIN WINDUP TOY by Marx, 8" tall $110.00-195.00

LONE RANGER AND THE RED RENEGADES, Better Little Book, 1939 .... $10.00-20.00

LONE RANGER AND THE SILVER BULLETS, Better Little Book, 1946 .... $10.00-20.00

LONE RANGER AND THE TEXAS RENEGADES, hardcover book, Grosset and Dunlap. $15.00-40.00

LONE RANGER ATOM BOMB RING, Kix cereal premium $25.00-45.00

LONE RANGER BADGE, premium from Bond Bread $20.00-35.00

LONE RANGER BOARD GAME, 1938 copyright date, boxed $30.00-55.00

LONE RANGER BOARD GAME, 1939 ..... $25.00-40.00

LONE RANGER CARDBOARD DART TARGET by Marx, 1946 .... $25.00-60.00

LONE RANGER CHALK STATUE, 12", Ranger on horse $15.00-40.00

LONE RANGER CHALK STATUE, 16" carnival type novelty $15.00-45.00

LONE RANGER CINE-VUE FILM WITH VIEWER, 1930's, plastic $35.00-60.00

LONE RANGER COMPASS with bullet shape $35.00-70.00

LONE RANGER DART TARGET, circa 1940, 17" $20.00-40.00

LONE RANGER DEPUTY BADGE, tin mounted on card $10.00-20.00

LONE RANGER DOLL, composition, 20", cloth costume, 1938 .... $180.00-300.00

LONE RANGER DOUBLE TARGET SET by Marx, 1939, in original box $100.00-200.00

LONE RANGER FIGURE WITH SILVER, made by Hartland Plastics $65.00-125.00

LONE RANGER FILMSTRIP VIEWER ON CARD, 1955 .... $20.00-45.00

LONE RANGER FOLLOWS THROUGH, Better Little Book, 1941 .... $10.00-20.00

LONE RANGER GAME, 1938, boxed $20.00-45.00

LONE RANGER GAME, "HI-YO SILVER!," Parker Brothers, 1938 .... $35.00-70.00

LONE RANGER HAIR BRUSH, 1939, wooden handle $18.00-30.00

LONE RANGER LAPEL WATCH IN ORIGINAL BOX, rare $200.00-400.00

LONE RANGER MARIONETTE PUPPET with strings, in original box $50.00-80.00

LONE RANGER MOLDED PLASTER FIGURE, 1938, 4" tall, Ranger on Silver $20.00-35.00

LONE RANGER OFFICIAL GLOVES in original box, dated 1947 .... $50.00-100.00

LONE RANGER ON SILVER TIN WINDUP (Silver horse version) 8" tall $120.00-225.00

LONE RANGER OUTFIT, mask, badge and watch on display card $35.00-50.00

LONE RANGER OUTFIT, vest with matching chaps, hat, boxed $135.00-220.00

LONE RANGER PAINT BOOK, published by Whitman, 1940 .... $20.00-45.00

LONE RANGER PAINT BOOK, published by Whitman, 1941 .... $10.00-25.00

LONE RANGER PEDOMETER, made of metal, toy works $25.00-45.00

LONE RANGER PENCIL SHARPENER, silver bullet type $20.00-45.00

LONE RANGER PICTURE PRINTING SET, Stamp Kraft, 1939, 6" box $25.00-55.00

LONE RANGER POCKET WATCH, by New Haven, 1939 .... $125.00-250.00

LONE RANGER PONY BOY CAP PISTOLS, 1938, set of two with fancy holster $60.00-100.00

LONE RANGER RIDES AGAIN MOVIE VIEWER BOXED SET, Acme Plastics, 1940 .... $50.00-95.00

LONE RANGER RING TOSS SET, original box, 1950's $15.00-35.00

LONE RANGER safety scout badge $15.00-25.00

LONE RANGER SCRAPBOOK, circa 1950, by Whitman $25.00-45.00

LONE RANGER SHERIFF KEYS TO JAIL, on original packing card $10.00-35.00

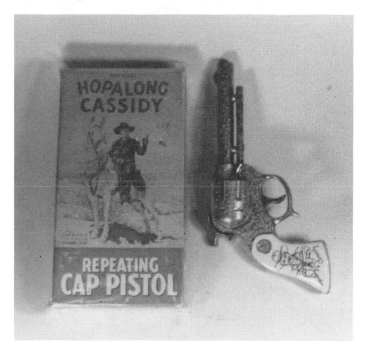

HOPALONG CASSIDY REPEATING CAP PISTOL, All Metal Products Company, boxed, Reynolds collection, $50.00-75.00.

LONE RANGER RIDES AGAIN MOVIE VIEWER, Acme Plastics, 1940, Reynolds collection, $50.00-95.00.

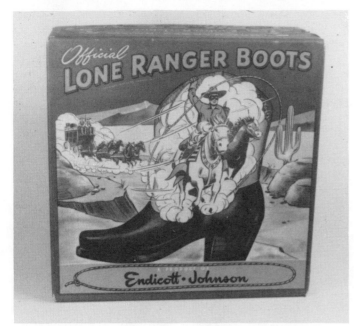

LONE RANGER BOOTS BY ENDICOTT-JOHNSON, boxed, Reynolds collection, $50.00-110.00.

LONE RANGER signal siren flashlight, in original box $40.00-75.00
LONE RANGER SILVERPLATE SPOON, circa 1930's $15.00-30.00
LONE RANGER SMALL BLOTTER, premium for Bond Bread $10.00-20.00
LONE RANGER SMALL CAP PISTOL, tin .$35.00-70.00
LONE RANGER sparkler pistol, boxed.. ...$45.00-75.00
LONE RANGER STEREO VIEWER REEL, (viewmaster) 1950's, original package $5.00-15.00
LONE RANGER TARGET GAME, manufactured by Marx, 1930's, boxed.................................$65.00-95.00
LONE RANGER TARGET GAME, Louis Marx, tin lithograph, dated 1938, boxed $25.00-75.00
LONE RANGER TARGET PRACTICE HAND-HELD BEAD GAME under glass $15.00-35.00
LONE RANGER TIN LITHOGRAPH PAINT BOX, unused, 1950's $10.00-20.00
LONE RANGER'S Collectors Album #1 .....$20.00-35.00
LONG TOM GUN manufactured by Kilgore, 10" long with original box $40.00-95.00
PALADIN WESTERN TELEVISION CHARACTER GUN AND HOLSTER SET, 9" guns $20.00-45.00
PANCHO MASK, (CISCO KID) paper, Tip Top Bread Premium..$10.00-15.00
PECOS BILL, Walt Disney character windup, plastic, Marx, 10", twirls rope $75.00-150.00
PIONEER CAP PISTOL manufactured by Stevens, 7½" long, 1950's $10.00-20.00
RANCHER CELLULOID WINDUP, 6", Occupied Japan, boxed $50.00-95.00
RED RANGER RID'EM COWBOY, by Wyandotte, tin windup $75.00-145.00
RED RYDER ACTING SHERIFF, Better Little Book, 1949...$10.00-20.00
RED RYDER AND CIRCUS LUCK, Better Little Book, 1940...$10.00-20.00

RED RYDER AND LITTLE BEAVER, Better Little Book, ca. 1940's $10.00-20.00
RED RYDER AND THE SECRET CANYON, Better Little Book, 1940 ....$10.00-20.00
RED RYDER AND THE SECRET OF WOLF CANYON, hardcover, Whitman, 1941 ....$8.00-20.00
RED RYDER AND THE SQUAW-TOOTH RUSTLERS, Better Little Book, 1940's $10.00-20.00
RED RYDER AND THE SQUAW-TOOTH RUSTLERS, Big Little Book, 1946 ....$12.00-25.00
RED RYDER COMIC, Dell, 1950 ....$4.00-10.00
RED RYDER GUN AND HOLSTER SET, by Daisy, colorful boxed set $50.00-125.00
RED RYDER HOLSTER, leather, no gun .$10.00-20.00
RED RYDER LUCKY COIN, 1940's...........$8.00-12.00
RED RYDER PICTURE RECORD, 1948 .$15.00-25.00
RED RYDER PLAYMATES CHILDREN'S GLOVES AD POSTER, ca. 1949 ....$30.00-60.00
RED RYDER PICTURE FRAME TRAY PUZZLE, 1950's $5.00-15.00
RED RYDER TARGET GAME, Whitman, 1939, colorful box and target $65.00-95.00
RED RYDER THE FIGHTING WESTERNER, Better Little Book, ca. 1940's $10.00-20.00
RED RYDER WAR ON THE RANGE, Better Little Book, 1940...$10.00-20.00
RIFLEMAN BOARD GAME, 1959, based on the television series $10.00-25.00
RIN TIN TIN COMPASS, from television series, 1950's $35.00-60.00
RIN TIN TIN PLASTER LAMP, 14" tall, extremely rare item $200.00-400.00
RIN TIN TIN RIFLE PEN, in mailer $35.00-60.00
RODEO PISTOL by Hubley, 1950's, 7" ...$10.00-22.00
ROUND UP TEX THE WHIRLING COWBOY, windup toy, Irwin, 1950's, plastic, box $15.00-45.00
ROY ROGERS AND DALE EVANS COLORING BOOK, 1951 ....$15.00-25.00
ROY ROGERS AND DALE EVANS CUT-OUT PAPER DOLLS, Whitman, 1954, unused $25.00-50.00
ROY ROGERS AND DALE EVANS PAPER DOLL BOOK, Whitman, 1950's...............................$15.00-35.00
ROY ROGERS AND DALE EVANS RECORD, 78 r.p.m., in original box, sleeve, 1950's $5.00-10.00
ROY ROGERS AND DALE EVANS THERMOS AND LUNCHBOX SET, 1960's....................$15.00-35.00
ROY ROGERS AND TRIGGER 620 SNAPSHOT CAMERA, Herbert George Company, 4" tall..$20.00-45.00
ROY ROGERS AND TRIGGER CAMERA, circa 1950's $20.00-50.00
ROY ROGERS AND TRIGGER GUITAR, bright logo on guitar, with strap $65.00-125.00
ROY ROGERS AND TRIGGER METAL CATTLE TRUCK, tin lithograph by Marx, 15" long.....$65.00-125.00
ROY ROGERS AND TRIGGER POST CARD, from Roy and Dale fan club, 1955 ....$10.00-30.00
ROY ROGERS AND TRIGGER RED BANDANA, figures on bandana $10.00-20.00
ROY ROGERS ARCADE CARD, close up facial pose of Roy Rogers..$7.00-20.00
ROY ROGERS ARCADE PICTURE, Roy on Trigger, movie pose...$7.00-20.00

ROY ROGERS BELT for a child, 1950's $15.00-40.00

ROY ROGERS BELT, 1950's $12.00-18.00

ROY ROGERS BELT BUCKLE WITH TRIGGER, ca. 1950's $35.00-60.00

ROY ROGERS BOLO TIE, original card .$10.00-15.00

ROY ROGERS BANK, boot shaped. $25.00-40.00

ROY ROGERS BOXED PAINT SET, ca. 1950's, 10" x 14" $25.00-55.00

ROY ROGERS CAP GUN, 9" long, marble and pearl type handles $25.00-60.00

ROY ROGERS CERAMIC PLATE AND MUG SET, 1950's $20.00-40.00

ROY ROGERS CHUCK WAGON, 1950's .$75.00-105.00

ROY ROGERS CLOCK, manufactured by Ingram, Roy moves $50.00-100.00

ROY ROGERS COLORING BOOK, 1951 .$15.00-25.00

ROY ROGERS COWBOY OUTFIT with spurs, gloves, original box $80.00-140.00

ROY ROGERS DEPUTY BADGE, on original card, tin, 1950's $10.00-22.00

ROY ROGERS DISPLAY PLATE, 1950's .$20.00-45.00

ROY ROGERS FIGURAL PLASTIC MUG, bust of Roy in hat, 4" tall $10.00-25.00

ROY ROGERS FIX-IT STAGECOACH, still in original box $35.00-65.00

ROY ROGERS GUN AND HOLSTER, Red holster, gun 5" long, small size.............................$20.00-50.00

ROY ROGERS "HAPPY TRAILS" pin-back type button $5.00-10.00

ROY ROGERS HARMONICA with the original display card...$35.00-55.00

ROY ROGERS HORSESHOE SET by Ohio Art, 1950's, in original package $40.00-80.00

ROY ROGERS HORSESHOE GAME manufactured by Ohio Art...$18.00-40.00

ROY ROGERS LAMP, plaster cast, bright paint, original shade, 2' tall $75.00-125.00

ROY ROGERS LARIAT FLASHLIGHT on the original card, 1950's $40.00-70.00

ROY ROGERS MARCH OF COMICS, Sears premium $15.00-30.00

ROY ROGERS MINI-GUN with the original card, 1950's $10.00-30.00

ROY ROGERS NECKERCHIEF SLIDE (gun-shaped slide) ca. 1950's $20.00-30.00

ROY ROGERS PAINT BY NUMBER SET, manufactured ca. 1954 ....$25.00-60.00

ROY ROGERS PICTURE AUTOGRAPHED PRINT, 1950's $10.00-25.00

ROY ROGERS PLASTIC FIGURE, Roy on Trigger, horse is rearing up $80.00-135.00

ROY ROGERS PLAYING CARDS, in mint condition, 1950's $15.00-25.00

ROY ROGERS RANCH CALENDAR, dated 1959, complete $50.00-100.00

ROY ROGERS RANCH LANTERN, by Ohio Art Company, #9, original box $50.00-95.00

ROY ROGERS RECORD 78 r.p.m. "Lord's Prayer" Little Golden Record, 1950's $5.00-15.00

ROY ROGERS RIFLE manufactured by Marx, ca. 1950's, 26" long $25.00-65.00

ROY ROGERS RIFLE, plastic, manufactured by Marx, 1950's $20.00-35.00

ROY ROGERS RODEO, 1950's, boxed $35.00-75.00

ROY ROGERS RODEO PLATE, manufactured by Rodeo, 6" in diameter $15.00-25.00

ROY ROGERS RODEO, boxed toy play set by Marx, ca. 1960's $25.00-75.00

ROY ROGERS SOUVENIR BOOK, book is dated 1950...$20.00-40.00

ROY ROGERS SPURS, pair with jewels .$10.00-25.00

ROY ROGERS STAGECOACH, play set in original box, 1950's $40.00-80.00

ROY ROGERS STRAIGHT SHOOTER GUN PUZZLE, 1950's, plastic on card $25.00-50.00

ROY ROGERS TENT (IN ORIGINAL BOX), ca. 1950's $60.00-95.00

ROY ROGERS TIN BANK, with Roy and horseshoe, 1950's $25.00-45.00

ROY ROGERS TOY WAGON, 1950's, 16" x 27", child's wagon...$50.00-125.00

ROY ROGERS TUCK-AWAY CAP GUN, on original card..$15.00-25.00

ROY ROGERS VINYL WALLET, 1950's $5.00-10.00

SKY KING BRASS DETECTO WRITER, circa 1960...$35.00-60.00

SKY KING, secret signal scope, 1960's ...$20.00-40.00

SMOKING TEX CAP PISTOL, by Hubley, 1960's, 7½" long $10.00-25.00

SURE SHOT WESTERN PISTOL manufactured by Hubley, 7" long..................................$10.00-20.00

TIM McCOY AND THE SANDY GULCH STAMPEDE, Big Little Book, 1930's $12.00-25.00

TIM McCOY THE WESTERNER, by Big Little Book, 1930's $12.00-25.00

TOM MIX AND THE HOARD OF MONTEZUMA, Big Little Book $12.00-25.00

TOM MIX AND TONY PIN-BACK BRASS BUTTON, 2" diameter $10.00-35.00

TOM MIX Arrowhead Compass, plastic $20.00-40.00

TOM MIX BIG LITTLE BOOK PICTURE PUZZLES, Whitman, 1938, two puzzles in box ..$45.00-75.00

TOM MIX BOOTS in original box $120.00-225.00

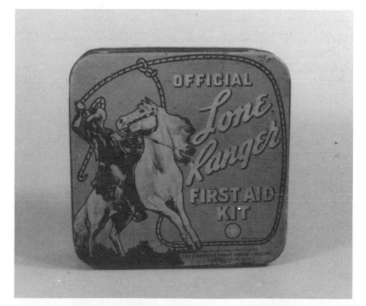

LONE RANGER OFFICIAL FIRST AID KIT, tin, American White Cross Labs, Inc., 1930's, 4" square, Reynolds collection, $25.00-45.00.

TOM MIX COLORING BOOK FOR STRAIGHT SHOOT-ERS, 1950's, 8½" x 11" $20.00-50.00

TOM MIX COMPASS MAGNIFIER, circa 1940....................$20.00-35.00

TOM MIX DECODER BUTTON, made of tin, circa 1930....................$35.00-75.00

TOM MIX DRAW AND PAINT BOOK, Whitman, 1930's $25.00-40.00

TOM MIX GLOW IN THE DARK BELT, radio premium....................$40.00-90.00

TOM MIX BIRD CALL, musical $12.00-22.00

TOM MIX IDENTIFICATION BRACELET, Straight Shooters $30.00-65.00

TOM MIX PARACHUTE, 1940's $60.00-100.00

TOM MIX PEN AND PENCIL SET, 1930's .$25.00-45.00

TOM MIX PERISCOPE, Ralston Straight Shooters premium....................$35.00-55.00

TOM MIX PLAY WATCH, 2" metal and plastic, pocket watch type $10.00-25.00

TOM MIX PUZZLE, Rexall Drugs premium give-away, 1930's in envelope $35.00-50.00

TOM MIX RALSTON PREMIUM COMIC BOOK number 2....................$15.00-40.00

TOM MIX RALSTON STRAIGHT SHOOTERS TELE-GRAPH (Entire Set) $50.00-100.00

TOM MIX RODEO ROPE, ca. 1930's by Mordt Company of Chicago....................$70.00-125.00

TOM MIX SHERIFF BADGE with siren..$20.00-35.00

TOM MIX SHERIFF BADGE WITH SIREN, 1930's or 1940's $20.00-40.00

TOM MIX SPURS, glow-in-the-dark $25.00-45.00

TOM MIX STRAIGHT SHOOTER BADGE, Ralston premium ad piece $20.00-45.00

TOM MIX TELESCOPE, 1930's $35.00-70.00

TOM MIX WOOD PISTOL, 1939 ....$40.00-85.00

TOM MIX, THE FABULOUS TOM MIX book, published by Prentice Hall, 1967 ....$10.00-25.00

TOM MIX, THE LIFE OF, Ralston Straight Shooter Premium Book $45.00-85.00

TONTO DOLL from Lone Ranger, 18" tall, composition head, hands $125.00-250.00

TROOPER CAP PISTOL by Hubley, 6" ...$10.00-15.00

TWO GUN SHERIFF, BO, remote control, 11", Cragstan, box....................$75.00-140.00

WAGON TRAIN WESTERN SIX GUN "ZING" cap gun, 11" copper color $40.00-65.00

WILD WEST COWBOY SET by Britains, English, #179, 1930's or 1940's, four cowboys $110.00-250.00

WYATT EARP BOARD GAME, dated 1958, boxed $15.00-30.00

WYATT EARP COLORING BOOK, 1950's .$10.00-20.00

WYATT EARP GUN AND HOLSTER SET without the box $25.00-65.00

WYATT EARP Lawman's Badge, 1950's ..$10.00-15.00

WYATT EARP MARSHALL'S BADGE, 1950's, on original card $12.00-18.00

WYATT EARP MILK GLASS MUG, 1950's.$5.00-10.00

LONE RANGER SIGNAL SIREN FLASHLIGHT in original box, Reynolds collection $40.00-75.00.

WYATT EARP TWO GUN AND HOLSTER SET, box pictures Hugh O'Brian, Hubley $45.00-90.00

ZORRO CHARM BRACELET, ca. 1960's, child's size $20.00-35.00

ZORRO CHILD'S COSTUME, play costume, not a Halloween costume $20.00-35.00

ZORRO HAND PUPPET, made of cloth and vinyl, ca. 1960's $8.00-15.00

ZORRO HAT WITH MASK ATTACHED, Bailey Company, Walt Disney's, 1950's $35.00-70.00

ZORRO OFFICIAL SHOOTING OUTFIT, Daisy, gun, rifle, cuffs, belt, boxed $65.00-125.00

ZORRO PENCIL HOLDER AND PENCIL SHARPENER, ceramic, 1950's, 6" Disney copy $35.00-65.00

ZORRO PUMP RIFLE, 1950's $15.00-25.00

ZORRO SECRET SCARF MASK, 1950's, with the original display card $25.00-55.00

ZORRO SECRET SIGHT MASK with the original card, 1950's $10.00-20.00

ZORRO TARGET GAME, 1950's with dart gun, Knickerbocker Plastic Company $30.00-95.00

ZORRO WATER PISTOL by Knickerbocker Plastic Company $20.00-40.00

ZORRO WHIP SET by M. Shimmel Sons, 1950's, whip and mask on display card $30.00-70.00

DISNEYANA

The collecting of Disneyana, the common term for merchandise related to any characters created by the Walt Disney Studios from 1928 to the present, is one of the fastest growing areas of toy collecting. Mickey Mouse is by far the most recognizable of all the Disney characters, but the scope of this area of collecting goes far beyond the famous mouse and his antagonistic friend, Donald Duck. The expansive list of Disney characters and merchandise is proof that Walt Disney knew how to market his creations successfully or he knew who to hire to do it for him. A man by the name of Kay Kamen is generally credited with being the driving force behind marketing Disney toys and getting retailers to expand their lines during the 1930's.

Although Disneyana sounds as if it is a major specialty of toy collecting itself, there are actually many smaller specialty areas of collecting within this category. To begin, the purest and earliest form of Disney collector is the fellow who collects only Mickey Mouse items from the 1930's. Hopefully this hypothetical "fellow" has a bankroll behind him because this area of collecting is the most expensive. Mickey Mouse items from this decade are recognizably marked either "Walt E. Disney," "Walt Disney" or "Walt Disney Enterprises." By the time the Disney studio reached 1940, the name was changed to "Walt Disney Productions."

Donald Duck toys from the 1930's run a close second to the great popularity of early Mickey Mouse items. Early Mickey is most easily recognized because he always wore red pants with large buttons on them, large yellow shoes and his two black eyes are referred to as "pie-eyed" because they look like little black pies with one piece cut out. Early Donald items are recognizable with the Disney markings listed above and the peculiar looking very long bill that early Donald figures and toys have. He's often referred to by collectors as "Long-billed Donald."

From the success of Disney's "Three Little Pigs" as a featurette film of the 1930's, billed as a "Silly Symphony," Walt Disney started to corner the market on animated feature films. "Snow White and the Seven Dwarfs" was Hollywood's first full-length animated film (1937) and after its success, the Disney studio was never the same. Toy collectors are treated to a vast wealth of 1930's Snow White and the Seven Dwarfs items because of the massive promotional and marketing campaign car-

ried out by Disney associates. There are dolls, storybooks, pull toys, banks, buckets, puzzles. games, figurines, tea sets and an almost countless array of Snow White items from the 1930's that are within the reach and price range of nearly every collector.

Disney's second significant feature film success was "Pinocchio" and so the steamroller effect of character marketing once again went to work. The list of items available for Snow White toys can be "dittoed" for Pinocchio items. In fact, many of the same Snow White toy manufacturer licensees simply produced a Pinocchio equivalent of a similar Snow White character toy. It is with Pinocchio that many early Disney collecting purists stop. If collectors specialize in only Disney items from the 1930's, then Pinocchio is the last of that decade's film characters, since the film was released in 1939.

Moving beyond the 1930's, many present Disney memorabilia fanatics are "discovering" the value of 1940's and 1950's Disney items. These would include such characters and films as Dumbo, Bambi, Alice in Wonderland, Peter Pan, Lady and the Tramp and others.

Particular manufacturers that are popular among today's Disneyana collectors are Marx windups, Ohio Art tea sets and sand pails, Fisher Price pull toys, Whitman 1930's books, Salem China ceramic plates and cups, Crown Toy and Novelty banks and dolls of the 1930's, Knickerbocker Toy Company dolls, Ideal Toy and Novelty dolls, and more recently, LineMar toys (Japanese Marx line) have moved into the forefront. Also popular, especially on the West Coast, are Disney ceramic figures by Evan Shaw and American Pottery and Louis Marx boxed Disneykin figures of the 1950's and 1960's.

With the great popularity of the Walt Disney Company's vacation kingdoms and the continual success of re-releases of old Disney classics plus The Disney Channel on cable television, it is clear that this is one group of characters that is here to stay. Since Mickey Mouse is now a senior citizen (he's sixty-two by this book's press time), he's moving into being a third and fourth generation character. As his age increases, his stature as an American popular symbol increases. For every early Disney toy that appears at antique shows and flea markets, there are several anxious collectors trying to get to it first.

DISNEYANA

ALICE IN WONDERLAND CERAMIC BANK, 1950's, Leeds $20.00-35.00

ALICE IN WONDERLAND CERAMIC PLANTER by Leeds, 1950's, pastel colors $15.00-40.00

ALICE IN WONDERLAND CERAMIC SALT AND PEPPER SHAKERS, 1950's, glazed $20.00-50.00

ALICE IN WONDERLAND FIGURAL WATCH STAND WITH ORIGINAL WATCH,1950's $25.00-50.00

ALICE IN WONDERLAND FIGURE, Evan K. Shaw Company, 1950's, 6" $50.00-95.00

ALICE IN WONDERLAND PAINT BOOK, 1950, Whitman $10.00-15.00

ALICE IN WONDERLAND PHONOGRAPH, 1950's, white with colorful decals $30.00-75.00

ALICE IN WONDERLAND PUNCH-OUT BOOK, 1950's $20.00-45.00

ANNETTE COLORING BOOK, 1950's Walt Disney Productions $10.00-20.00

BAMBI AMERICAN POTTERY FIGURE, 1940's, with butterfly on tail, 8" size $50.00-125.00

BAMBI BETTER LITTLE BOOK, Walt Disney's, 1940's $15.00-40.00

BAMBI CEREAL BOWL, 1946 by Evan K. Shaw $20.00-40.00

BAMBI CUP, Evan K. Shaw Company, 1947, 3", glazed white ceramic $15.00-30.00

BAMBI CUT-OUT BOOK, circa 1940s, if complete $50.00-125.00

BAMBI DOLL BY STEIFF with button in ear, 12" largest version $75.00-100.00

BAMBI DOLL BY STEIFF, 1940's, original tag and button in ear, 5" $25.00-50.00

BAMBI DOLL BY STEIFF, original tag and button in ear, 7", 1940's $50.00-75.00

BAMBI FIGURAL PLANTER made by Leeds, circa 1940 ....$15.00-35.00

BAMBI HANKY BOOK, 1940's, complete with hankies $40.00-100.00

BAMBI MILK PITCHER by American Pottery, 1940's, multi-color scene on front $50.00-100.00

BAMBI MODELCRAFT PAINTING AND MODELING SET, 1940's, boxed set $30.00-60.00

BAMBI PAINT BOOK, "WALT DISNEY'S BAMBI," ca. 1940's, large version $20.00-50.00

BAMBI PICTURE BOOK, circa 1940, paper cover $20.00-35.00

BAMBI PLATE, Evan K. Shaw Company, 1947, glazed white ceramic $20.00-35.00

BAMBI STORYBOOK, Walt Disney, Grosset and Dunlap, 1947 ....$10.00-30.00

BAMBI'S CHILDREN, Better Little Book, 1940's $10.00-30.00

BASHFUL CERAMIC TOOTHPICK HOLDER, English, S. Maw and Sons, 1930's $100.00-200.00

BASHFUL RUBBER TOY, Seiberling Latex, Akron, Ohio, 1937, 5" $20.00-50.00

BASHFUL THE DWARF MARIONETTE, Alexander Doll Company, 1930's $50.00-125.00

BASHFUL THE DWARF RUBBER FIGURE, Seiberling Latex, 1930's, 5" $20.00-50.00

BIG BAD WOLF ALARM CLOCK, 1930's, animated, red case $400.00-800.00

BIG BAD WOLF BELT on original card, 1930's, colorful lithograph ad card $40.00-95.00

BIG BAD WOLF BOXED RUBBER FIGURE, Seiberling Latex, 1930's, rare $150.00-250.00

BIG BAD WOLF GAME, by Parker Brothers, 1930's $35.00-75.00

BIG BAD WOLF INFLATABLE RUBBER DOLL, 1930's, Seiberling Latex $100.00-200.00

BIG BAD WOLF PLUSH DOLL, by Knickerbocker, 1930's $75.00-150.00

BLUE FAIRY DRINKING GLASS by Libbey, 1940 ....$10.00-20.00

BLUE FAIRY FROM PINOCCHIO VALENTINE, mechanical, 1939 ....$10.00-20.00

BONGO THE BEAR, manufactured by Gund, 1947, Fun and Fancy Free characters $25.00-60.00

BRER RABBIT, Walt Disney's Better Little Book (tall version) 1950's $10.00-30.00

CINDERELLA AND THE PRINCE WINDUP, boxed, plastic action toy, 1950's $50.00-100.00

CINDERELLA APRON, 1950's J. C. Penney premium, in original envelope $20.00-35.00

CINDERELLA CERAMIC PLANTER by Leeds, 1950's, pastel colors $15.00-40.00

CINDERELLA PAINT BOOK, ca. 1950's, Whitman, Cinderella in old dress $10.00-20.00

CINDERELLA PICTURE PUZZLE by Jaymar, boxed, 1950's $5.00-10.00

CINDERELLA SWEEPER, tin and brush construction, 1950's $20.00-40.00

CINDERELLA, Walt Disney's Better Little Book (taller version) 1950's $10.00-30.00

CLARABELLE THE COW BISQUE FIGURE, 3", 1930's $30.00-65.00

CLARABELLE THE COW DRINKING GLASS by Libbey, 1938 ....$10.00-25.00

CLARABELLE THE COW, small storybook, Whitman, 1930's $10.00-25.00

CLEO THE GOLDFISH (PINOCCHIO) PAPER MASK, Gillette premium, 1939 ....$10.00-20.00

CLEO THE GOLDFISH FROM PINOCCHIO rubber squeeze toy by Seiberling, 1940 ....$35.00-75.00

CLEO THE GOLDFISH FROM PINOCCHIO, 1939 mechanical valentine $10.00-20.00

CLEO THE GOLDFISH FROM PINOCCHIO, boxed soap, Lightfoot Schultz, 1940 ....$25.00-50.00

DAVY CROCKETT COLORING BOOK, 1950's, Walt Disney Productions $10.00-20.00

DISNEY CHARACTER GLOBE by Rand McNally and Company, 1940's $30.00-75.00

DISNEY PARADE ROADSTER by Marx, boxed windup car, large, 1950's $100.00-225.00

DISNEYLAND COLORING BOOK, published by Whitman, 1950's $10.00-20.00

DISNEYLAND FERRIS WHEEL by J. Chein, 1940's $100.00-250.00

DISNEYLAND MELODY PLAYER, crank operated music box, all metal, 1950's $40.00-85.00

DISNEYLAND MONORAIL BOXED SET by Schuco, 1950's, Alweg-Monorail $100.00-250.00

DOC AND DOPEY PULL TOY by Fisher Price, 1938, Walt Disney Enterprises, 12" long .$100.00-200.00

DOC CERAMIC FIGURE by American Pottery Company, 1940's, 6" version $100.00-175.00

DOC CERAMIC TOOTHPICK HOLDER, English, S. Maw and Sons, 1930's $100.00-200.00

DOC CHARACTER LAMP by LaMode Studios, 1930's, plaster/composition $75.00-150.00
DOC HANKY, 1930's $10.00-20.00
DOC RUBBER TOY, Seiberling Latex, Akron, Ohio, 5", 1938 ....$20.00-50.00
DOC THE DWARF DOLL by Knickerbocker, 1930's, large 15" size, cloth.......................$100.00-175.00
DOC THE DWARF DRINKING GLASS by Libbey, 1938 ....$10.00-20.00
DOC THE DWARF MARIONETTE, Alexander Doll Company, 1930's $50.00-125.00
DOC THE DWARF PAPER MASK, premium, 1938 ....$10.00-25.00
DOC THE DWARF TELEPHONE, 1930's, N. N. Hill Brass...$50.00-125.00
DONALD DUCK "DOUBLE DONALD" BISQUE TOOTHBRUSH HOLDER, ca. 1930's, long-billed...$150.00-275.00
DONALD DUCK "MUSCLEMAN" ON BEACH SAND PAIL, Ohio Art, 1930's, 3" $30.00-65.00
DONALD DUCK ADMIRAL BISQUE, 1930's. $30.00-65.00
DONALD DUCK ALARM CLOCK by Bayard, French, 1960's $100.00-200.00
DONALD DUCK AMERICAN POTTERY FIGURE, angry Donald, 1940's, 6" $100.00-200.00
DONALD DUCK AND CLARA CLUCK CUT-OUT BOOK, 1930's, rare.....................................$100.00-150.00
DONALD DUCK AND CLARA CLUCK TEA SET by Ohio Art, boxed, 1936..............................$75.00-125.00
DONALD DUCK AND MICKEY MOUSE DRUM, lithograph paper head, manufactured 1930's, 6½" diameter.....................................$70.00-125.00
DONALD DUCK AND PLUTO HANDCAR, windup train car with box by Lionel, 1930's ...$600.00-1,150.00
DONALD DUCK AND PLUTO RUBBER CAR, Sun Rubber, 1940's, 6½" long...................$35.00-70.00
DONALD DUCK ARMY PAINT BOOK, ca. 1940's, large size...$15.00-30.00
DONALD DUCK ART STAMP PICTURE SET, 1930's, angry Donald on lid, boxed $35.00-75.00
DONALD DUCK BAKELITE PENCIL SHARPENER, cross-shaped, Donald decal, 1930's $25.00-50.00
DONALD DUCK BALLOON, in original packaging, 1930's with paper feet $25.00-60.00
DONALD DUCK BANK, relish jar with colorful lid, 1940's, 5" $20.00-45.00
DONALD DUCK BIG LITTLE BOOK, "Hunting for Trouble," 1930's...............................$20.00-35.00
DONALD DUCK BIG LITTLE BOOK, "Donald Duck Sees Stars," 1930's...........................$20.00-35.00
DONALD DUCK BISQUE FIGURE, 1930's, turned up nose, strutting $35.00-70.00
DONALD DUCK BISQUE FIGURE, 1930's, 5", long-billed...$125.00-225.00
DONALD DUCK BISQUE FIGURE, 1930's, miniature 1" version $20.00-40.00
DONALD DUCK BISQUE FIGURE, Donald playing a violin, large 5" version $125.00-200.00
DONALD DUCK BISQUE FIGURE, Japan, 1930's large 6" figure, jointed arms $200.00-500.00
DONALD DUCK BISQUE FIGURE, long-billed, 1930's, 4½" tall $200.00-375.00
DONALD DUCK BISQUE, Donald playing a concertina, 5", long-billed..............................$130.00-250.00

DONALD DUCK BOOK "DONALD'S LUCKY DAY," Whitman, 1940, hardcover $20.00-40.00
DONALD DUCK BOXED SOAP SET, three figures of Donald, Lightfoot Schultz, 1930's ..$100.00-175.00
DONALD DUCK BREAD WRAPPER, 1950's, "Purity Maid" bread $10.00-30.00
DONALD DUCK BREAD WRAPPER, 1950's, bright colors $10.00-25.00
DONALD DUCK BROOM SWEEPER, Ohio Art, ca. 1940, Walt Disney Productions $35.00-80.00
DONALD DUCK CAMERA by Herbert George Company, boxed $45.00-80.00
DONALD DUCK CAMERA with the original box, 1940's $30.00-65.00
DONALD DUCK CARD GAME, Whitman, 1930's Angry Donald on lid $20.00-45.00
DONALD DUCK CARD GAME, Whitman, copyright 1941, W.D.P., complete...............................$30.00-55.00
DONALD DUCK CELLULOID FIGURE, 1930's, 3½" jointed toy, long-bill $85.00-200.00
DONALD DUCK CELLULOID WIND-UP NODDER, 6" tall, long-billed Donald, Japan $200.00-425.00
DONALD DUCK CERAMIC BANK BY LEEDS CHINA, ca. 1940's, 7" glazed $15.00-35.00
DONALD DUCK CERAMIC BANK, manufactured by Leeds, 1940's $20.00-40.00
DONALD CERAMIC BOOKENDS, 1950's, bright colors, Donald paints wall $25.00-50.00
DONALD DUCK CERAMIC CREAM PITCHER shaped like Donald, 7", 1930's......................$20.00-50.00
DONALD DUCK CERAMIC FIGURE, 1940's, Brayton's, Donald waves fist in air.................$100.00-200.00
DONALD DUCK CERAMIC LAMP manufactured by Leeds, 1940's $30.00-65.00
DONALD DUCK CHARACTER LAMP, Railley Corporation, ceramic with original shade ..$100.00-225.00
DONALD DUCK CHARACTER VALENTINE, 1938, mechanical, Donald in sombrero $10.00-20.00
DONALD DUCK CHOO-CHOO PULL TOY BY FISHER PRICE, 1940......................................$45.00-75.00
DONALD DUCK CLOTH DOLL by Knickerbocker, 1930's 12", long-bill $200.00-350.00
DONALD DUCK COMPOSITION BANK, Crown Toy, jointed head, 1930's $75.00-125.00
DONALD DUCK COMPOSITON DOLL BY KNICKERBOCKER, 1930's, in parade dress. $200.00-450.00
DONALD DUCK COMPOSITION HEAD UMBRELLA, long-bill, 1930's $50.00-100.00
DONALD DUCK COOKIE JAR, 14", by Leeds, 1940's, glazed ceramic $50.00-80.00
DONALD DUCK COWBOY BANK, 1960's, hard plastic, Donald on treasure trunk.................$10.00-25.00
DONALD DUCK COWBOY DOLL by Knickerbocker, 1930's, long-billed Donald $125.00-300.00
DONALD DUCK DIPSY CAR, Marx, windup, tin, plastic Donald, 6" $200.00-400.00
DONALD DUCK DOCTOR SET, 1940's, boxed set with hinged case, colorful $20.00-45.00
DONALD DUCK DOLL BY LARS of Italy, ca. 1960's, 26" tall $300.00-500.00
DONALD DUCK DOLL DRESSED AS SANTA CLAUS by Lars of Italy, recent but rare $125.00-225.00
DONALD DUCK DRAW AND PAINT BOOK, Whitman, 1936, large format.............................$35.00-60.00

105

DONALD DUCK DRINKING GLASS manufactured by Libbey, 1940 ....$10.00-20.00

DONALD DUCK DRUM MAJOR DOLL, Knickerbocker, 1930's, tall hat, cloth $125.00-250.00

DONALD DUCK DRUMMER WINDUP, LineMar, 1950's, 6" version..$125.00-275.00

DONALD DUCK DRUMMER, 6" windup by LineMar in original box $200.00-450.00

DONALD DUCK DUET, Donald and Goofy dancing windup by Marx, 1946, 10" $350.00-600.00

DONALD DUCK DUET, Donald plays drums while Goofy dances, 1940's, Marx $200.00-450.00

DONALD DUCK ELECTRIC SCISSORS by Royal American Corporation, boxed $35.00-60.00

DONALD DUCK ENGINEER PULL TOY, 1940's, Fisher Price, Donald on train $30.00-65.00

DONALD DUCK FIGURAL BAKELITE PENCIL SHARPENER, 1930's, red with decal.........$15.00-35.00

DONALD DUCK FIGURAL PENCIL SHARPENER, CELLULOID, long-billed, 3", painted $65.00-150.00

DONALD DUCK FIGURAL SOAP, boxed, Lightfoot Schultz Company, 1930's $25.00-70.00

DONALD DUCK FIGURAL TOOTHBRUSH HOLDER, bisque, 1930's, Donald by post $200.00-400.00

DONALD DUCK FIGURE, Seiberling Latex, 1930's, movable head, white body, 5" $65.00-110.00

DONALD DUCK FIGURINE, ceramic, Angry Donald, Evan K. Shaw Company, 1940's......$75.00-125.00

DONALD DUCK FIREMAN ON DISNEY FIRE TRUCK, 1950's, LineMar, rare $300.00-650.00

DONALD DUCK FISHER PRICE PUSH TOY, Donald figure on end of long stick, 1939 ...$65.00-135.00

DONALD DUCK FLASHLIGHT, 1936, Electric Manufacturing Corporation, boxed $50.00-125.00

DONALD DUCK FORGETS TO DUCK, Better Little Book $15.00-35.00

DONALD DUCK HAPPY EASTER TALKING GREETING CARD, 1930's $20.00-40.00

DONALD DUCK HAS HIS UPS AND DOWNS, a Walt Disney Storybook, 1930's $20.00-40.00

DONALD DUCK HOLDING A FLAG, a 3" bisque figure, 1930's $25.00-60.00

DONALD DUCK HOLDING A HORN BISQUE FIGURE, 1930's $20.00-60.00

DONALD DUCK HOLDING A RIFLE, a 3" bisque figure, 1930's $20.00-60.00

DONALD DUCK IN WALT DISNEY'S ROCKING CHAIR, rare tin windup, LineMar $275.00-500.00

DONALD DUCK INFLATABLE DOLL, 1936, Seiberling Latex, rare $100.00-175.00

DONALD DUCK JOINTED CELLULOID DOLL, 1930's, long-billed, 8" $200.00-400.00

DONALD DUCK JOINTED CELLULOID FIGURE, 1930's, 3" $50.00-100.00

DONALD DUCK LAMP, 1940's, American Pottery with original shade $100.00-225.00

DONALD DUCK LAMP, Donald stands by lamp-post, long-billed, Soreng-Manegold $1,000.00-2,000.00

DONALD DUCK LARGE XYLOPHONE PLAYER PULL TOY, manufactured ca. 1930's, version F.P. W.D. Enterprises $70.00-140.00

DONALD DUCK LARGE XYLOPHONE PLAYER PULL TOY, 1940's later version, W.D.P. ...$50.00-100.00

DONALD DUCK LONG-BILLED CERAMIC PLANTER 1930's, 7" tall $150.00-375.00

DONALD DUCK MARIONETTE, 1950's, Peter Puppet Playthings, boxed $35.00-80.00

DONALD DUCK MILK BOTTLE, manufactured by Libbey Glass, 1938 ....$40.00-80.00

DONALD DUCK MODELCRAFT CHARACTER MOLDING SET, 1940's, complete $25.00-50.00

DONALD DUCK MODELED IN SOAP, 1930's, Lightfoot Schultz, colorful box $50.00-100.00

DONALD DUCK NAPKIN RING, Bakelite, 1930's with decal $15.00-30.00

DONALD DUCK NAPKIN RING, Bakelite, 1930's, amber with decal, 3" $20.00-40.00

DONALD DUCK NATIONAL DUCK BANK, 1950's, J. Chein, semi-mechanical, 7" $65.00-125.00

DONALD DUCK NITE-LIGHT, 1930's, tin and cardboard, pen-light battery...................$65.00-110.00

DONALD DUCK ORANGE DRINK IN ORIGINAL CAN WITH LABEL, 1950's $10.00-20.00

DONALD DUCK PAIL, Ohio Art, 1930's, Donald on bicycle with nephews, 5", 1938 ....$45.00-90.00

DONALD DUCK PAINT AND CRAYON SET, 1930's, boxed in cardboard box $25.00-65.00

DONALD DUCK PAINT BOX, 1938, by Transogram, Walt Disney Enterprises $20.00-30.00

DONALD DUCK PAINT BOX, 1940's, probably English, 4" x 10" $15.00-30.00

DONALD DUCK PAINT BOX, by Transogram, ca. 1950's, 6" $10.00-20.00

DONALD DUCK PAINT SET, with tin box, ca. 1950's $10.00-20.00

DONALD DUCK PARTY GAME, manufactured by Parker Brothers, 1938............................$35.00-50.00

DONALD DUCK PENCILS, on original card, set of three, 1940's $10.00-25.00

DONALD DUCK PEN-LIGHT NITE-LIGHT, 1930's, tin with metal cylinder...........................$70.00-140.00

DONALD DUCK PILLOW CASE, tapestry-look, manufactured in 1939 ....$50.00-80.00

DONALD DUCK PLASTIC WINDUP TOY, 1950's, Marx, 7", tail spins $50.00-95.00

DONALD DUCK PLASTIC WINDUP TOY, Donald in sombrero with maracas, 1950's $50.00-85.00

DONALD DUCK PLUSH DOLL, manufactured ca. 1930's, long-bill, 12" $200.00-300.00

DONALD DUCK PLUSH PILLOW CASE, ca. 1930's $20.00-50.00

DONALD DUCK POP CORN CAN, 1950's, bright label $10.00-20.00

DONALD DUCK POP-UP PUPPET by Fisher Price, 1930's, wings move, squawks $50.00-125.00

DONALD DUCK PROJECTOR, manufactured ca. 1960's, gift boxed $25.00-50.00

DONALD DUCK PULL TOY by Fisher Price, 1930's, Donald with baton............................$50.00-110.00

DONALD DUCK PULL TOY by Fisher Price, 1930's, long-billed, wings flap....................$125.00-200.00

DONALD DUCK PULL TOY by Fisher Price, Donald pulls red cart, 1940's $30.00-70.00

DONALD DUCK PULL TOY, 1940's, Donald with baton pulls wagon, Fisher-Price $65.00-110.00

DONALD DUCK PULL TOY, Fisher Price, 1930's long-bill, cylinder wheels.........................$75.00-125.00

DONALD DUCK PULL TOY, Fisher Price, 1940's, Donald twirls baton, red base $35.00-75.00

DONALD DUCK PULL TOY, LONG-BILLED, Fisher Price, 1930's, hanging wings $75.00-195.00

DONALD DUCK PULL TOY, wooden by N. N. Hill Brass, 1930's, bell-ringer $50.00-125.00

DONALD DUCK PULL TOY, xylophone player, Fisher Price, 1938, 13" tall $100.00-200.00

DONALD DUCK PULLED BY PLUTO WINDUP, CELLU-LOID TOY, 1930's, Japan, rare ...$450.00-900.00

DONALD DUCK RAIL CAR, Lionel, 1930's, Donald and Pluto, windup, composition $400.00-900.00

DONALD DUCK ROLLING TOY, 4", Fisher Price, on ball-like wheels, 1930's $75.00-150.00

DONALD DUCK RUBBER FIGURE, hollow, Seiberling Latex, 1930's, long-bill $85.00-145.00

DONALD DUCK SAILOR SAND PAIL, 1930's, Ohio Art, 5", Donald as Admiral......................$55.00-110.00

DONALD DUCK SAND PAIL, Donald with nephews on beach, 5" Ohio Art $35.00-70.00

DONALD DUCK SEIBERLING LATEX FIGURE, 1930's, 6", movable head $75.00-110.00

DONALD DUCK SERVING TRAY, 1930's, Ohio Art, Donald as waiter $10.00-30.00

DONALD DUCK SHOVEL, 1939, tin, beach scene, Ohio Art, 6" x 7".......................................$75.00-135.00

DONALD DUCK SNOW SHOVEL, 1930's, Ohio Art, large version $100.00-200.00

DONALD DUCK SQUEAK TOY, Sun Rubber Company, 1949...$10.00-20.00

DONALD DUCK STORYBOOK, 1930's, large format, Donald holds book on cover $30.00-75.00

DONALD DUCK STUFFED DOLL, 13" by Knicker-bocker, 1930's, cloth $150.00-350.00

DONALD DUCK SUNOCO INK BLOTTER, manufactured ca. 1940's $10.00-20.00

DONALD DUCK SWEEPER, Donald dressed with hair in scarf as housewife, 1930's $40.00-70.00

DONALD DUCK TABLE LAMP, 1947, Railley Corporation, with original shade $100.00-200.00

DONALD DUCK TELEPHONE, upright type, figural Donald on base, 1930's $60.00-125.00

DONALD DUCK THE DRUM MAJOR, Knickerbocker Toy doll, 1930's $400.00-800.00

DONALD DUCK THE SKIER, large plastic windup by Marx, 1950's $100.00-175.00

DONALD DUCK TIDDLEY WINKS GAME, with box, 1950's $10.00-20.00

DONALD DUCK TIN TEA SET, complete set, boxed, Ohio Art, 1930's $75.00-135.00

DONALD DUCK TOOTHBRUSH HOLDER with Mickey and Minnie, bisque, 1930's.............$75.00-185.00

DONALD DUCK TOOTHBRUSH HOLDER, 5" bisque, 1930's, upturned long bill.............$100.00-225.00

DONALD DUCK TOY TELEPHONE AND COIN BANK, 1930's, metal, red with Donald $60.00-100.00

DONALD DUCK TRAPEZE TOY, windup, 1940's, manufactured by LineMar $100.00-250.00

DONALD DUCK WATERING CAN, 1930's, Enterprises, Ohio Art, 6" $30.00-75.00

DONALD DUCK WATERING CAN, long-spout, Donald and Donkey, Ohio Art, 1938 ....$40.00-80.00

DONALD DUCK WINDUP by Schuco, 1930's, original box, long bill $500.00-1000.00

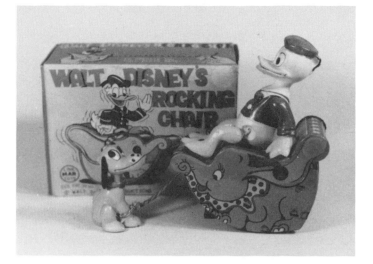

WALT DISNEY'S DONALD DUCK ON DUMBO ROCK-ING CHAIR, by LineMar, boxed, Reynolds collection, $400.00-850.00.

DONALD DUCK WINDUP CAR, 1950's, Marx, tin $65.00-110.00

DONALD DUCK WINDUP FIGURE by SchuCo, 1960's version, original box $75.00-135.00

DONALD DUCK WINDUP, 1950's, LineMar, 5", tail spins, holds umbrella $125.00-250.00

DONALD DUCK WITH MICKEY AND MINNIE TOOTH-BRUSH HOLDER, 1930's, bisque $75.00-150.00

DONALD DUCK WOOD COMPOSITION MARIONETTE, 1930's, Alexander Doll Company ...$125.00-250.00

DONALD DUCK'S OWN GAME, Walt Disney, 1930's party game $40.00-100.00

DONALD DUCK'S PARTY GAME, Parker Brothers, 1950's version $20.00-40.00

DONALD DUCK, THE LIFE OF, book by Walt Disney, 1930's $40.00-85.00

DONALD DUCK, WALT DISNEY'S 1935 linen-like early Donald Book, 9" x 13"....................$100.00-165.00

DOPEY AND THE DRUM NITE-LITE by La Mode Studios, 1930's $75.00-125.00

DOPEY BAKELITE PENCIL SHARPENER, 1930's Walt Disney Enterprises $15.00-40.00

DOPEY BOOK, Walt Disney Enterprises, "He Don't Talk None" linen-like $20.00-50.00

DOPEY CERAMIC BANK by Leeds China, 1940's, pastel colors $15.00-30.00

DOPEY CERAMIC FIGURE by American Pottery, 1940's, 6", highly glazed $100.00-175.00

DOPEY CERAMIC TOOTHPICK HOLDER, English, S. Maw and Sons, 1930's $100.00-200.00

DOPEY CHARACTER DRINKING GLASS manufactured by Libbey, 1938.................................$10.00-20.00

DOPEY CHARACTER KITE, made of paper and wood, 1930's $40.00-80.00

DOPEY CHARACTER LAMP by La Mode Studios, 1930's, bright colors $75.00-150.00

DOPEY CLOTH AND COMPOSITION DOLL, 1938, Chad Valley of England, 6" $100.00-170.00

DOPEY DIME REGISTER BANK, 1930's, all metal register bank $25.00-65.00

DOPEY HANKY, 1930's $10.00-20.00

DOPEY MUSICAL SWEEPER 1940's, Fisher Price Toys, all metal $40.00-70.00

DOPEY PAPER CHARACTER MASK, Gillette premium, 1938 ....$10.00-25.00

DOPEY PEN-LITE NITE-LITE, 1938, tin with metal cylinder $65.00-125.00

DOPEY RUBBER TOY, Seiberling Latex, Akron, Ohio, 1930's, 5" $20.00-50.00

DOPEY SOAKY TOY, a Colgate soap container, ca. 1960's $5.00-10.00

DOPEY THE DWARF COMPOSITION HEAD HANDLE UMBRELLA, 1930's $50.00-100.00

DOPEY THE DWARF MARIONETTE, Alexander Doll Company, 1930's $50.00-125.00

DOPEY THE DWARF MECHANICAL VALENTINE, 1938, holding candle $10.00-20.00

DOPEY THE DWARF ROLY POLY COMPOSITION TOY, by Crown Toy, 1938, unusual $45.00-90.00

DOPEY THE DWARF TABLE LAMP, 1947, Railley Corporation $50.00-135.00

DOPEY THE DWARF TIN WINDUP, by Chad Valley of England, 1930's $100.00-200.00

DOPEY WINDUP WALKER TOY, 1930's by Marx, 10" tin wind-up $125.00-200.00

DUMBO AMERICAN POTTERY FIGURE, 1940's with original label, 6" $25.00-70.00

DUMBO BABY FIGURINE, Evan K. Shaw, manufactured c. 1940's, 5" $45.00-90.00

DUMBO, BETTER LITTLE BOOK, a Walt Disney book, 1940's $110.00-300.00

DUMBO CERAMIC BANK manufactured by Leeds, 1940's $20.00-40.00

DUMBO CERAMIC BANK manufactured by Leeds, a small version $20.00-40.00

DUMBO COOKIE JAR by Leeds, 1940's .$30.00-55.00

DUMBO MECHANICAL WINDUP BY MARX, 1940's, 5", roll over action $100.00-200.00

DUMBO MILK PITCHER by Leeds, ceramic, 1940's $20.00-40.00

DUMBO SQUEEZE TOY by Dell, 1950's ...$5.00-15.00

DUMBO THE ELEPHANT BISQUE TOOTHBRUSH HOLDER, Japan, 1940's, rare $100.00-250.00

DUMBO, THE STORY OF THE FLYING ELEPHANT, 1940's, storybook, paper cover $20.00-35.00

ELMER ELEPHANT DRINKING GLASS by Libbey Glass, 1938 ....$10.00-25.00

ELMER ELEPHANT LINEN-LIKE BOOK, Walt Disney, 1930's $30.00-60.00

ELMER THE ELEPHANT MUSICAL WINDUP PLUSH DOLL, 1930's ....no price available

ELMER THE ELEPHANT PULL TOY by N. N. Hill Brass, 1930's $45.00-125.00

ELMER THE ELEPHANT PULL TOY, 1930's, Fisher Price, cylinder wheels $40.00-85.00

ELMER THE ELEPHANT RUBBER FIGURE by Seiberling Latex, 1930's $40.00-100.00

FANTASIA BOOK, "Stories from Fantasia," Walt Disney Productions, 1940's $40.00-75.00

FANTASIA CENTAUR HOLDING GRAPES, ceramic figure by Vernon Kilns, 1940 ....$500.00-950.00

FANTASIA ELEPHANT CERAMIC FIGURE by Vernon Kilns, 1940 ....$100.00-200.00

FANTASIA HIPPO DANCING FIGURE, ceramic by Vernon Kilns, 1940 ....$100.00-250.00

FANTASIA PAINT BOOK, a Walt Disney book, printed 1940's $30.00-75.00

FANTASIA SOUVENIR PROGRAM, 1940's, colorful pastels, paper item $15.00-35.00

FANTASIA UNICORN CERAMIC FIGURE by Vernon Kilns, 1940 ....$75.00-150.00

FANTASIA, PUNCH-OUT BOOK, a Walt Disney book, 1940, rare $100.00-225.00

FERDINAND AND THE MATADOR PULL TOY, 1930's, N. N. Hill Brass $100.00-200.00

FERDINAND THE BULL CHINESE CHECKERS, 1930's game $35.00-100.00

FERDINAND THE BULL COMPOSITION BANK, 1938, Walt Disney Ent., Crown Toy $40.00-100.00

FERDINAND THE BULL COMPOSITION DOLL, 1930's, by Knickerbocker Toy $50.00-100.00

FERDINAND THE BULL COMPOSITION DOLL, jointed by Ideal, 1930's $50.00-100.00

FERDINAND THE BULL COMPOSITION HEAD HANDLE UMBRELLA, 1930's $50.00-100.00

FERDINAND THE BULL CUT-OUT BOOK, 1930's, large format, colorful $50.00-100.00

FERDINAND THE BULL GAME, ca. 1930's, game with box, ...$40.00-80.00

FERDINAND THE BULL IN THE ARENA, checkers and marbles game, 1930's $45.00-100.00

FERDINAND THE BULL PENCIL SHARPENER, 1938, Bakelite with decal $15.00-35.00

FERDINAND THE BULL RUBBER FIGURE, Seiberling, 1930's, 5" $35.00-70.00

FERDINAND THE BULL TIN WINDUP manufactured by Marx, 1938 ....$65.00-125.00

FIGARO DRINKING FROM A DISH, ceramic figure, 1940's, Brayton's Laguna $100.00-200.00

FIGARO THE CAT (PINOCCHIO) PAPER MASK, Gillette premium, 1939 ....$10.00-20.00

FIGARO THE CAT, an American Pottery figure, ca. 1940's, 4" $25.00-70.00

FLOWER THE SKUNK, an American Pottery figure, ca. 1940's $20.00-40.00

FLOWER THE SKUNK PLANTER by Leeds, 4" version, 1940's $20.00-40.00

GEPETTO CERAMIC FIGURE, Brayton's Laguna Pottery, 1940's, standing $50.00-100.00

GEPETTO COMPOSITON FIGURE, 4" seated version, Multi Products, 1940 ....$35.00-70.00

GEPETTO COMPOSITION FIGURE, 5" standing, Multi Products, 1940 ....$20.00-40.00

GEPETTO PAPER MASK, Gillette premium, manufactured in 1939 ....$10.00-25.00

GIDDY THE CAT COMPOSITION FIGURE, 4", Multi Products of Chicago, 1940 ....$35.00-70.00

GOOFY BISQUE FIGURE, by Walt Disney Enterprises 3½", Japan, ca. 1930's $35.00-60.00

GOOFY CHARACTER BISQUE FIGURE, 4" tall, 1930's $25.00-60.00

GOOFY CHARACTER CLOTH DOLL, manufactured by Lars of Italy, recent $100.00-300.00

GOOFY PLASTIC WINDUP TOY, 1950's, 9", tail spins, Marx $50.00-75.00

GOOFY WINDUP TOY tin version by LineMar, 1950's $100.00-220.00

GRUMPY DWARF DRINKING GLASS manufactured by Libbey, 1938 ....$10.00-20.00

GRUMPY THE DWARF BOOKENDS, pair, by La Mode Studios, plaster compositon $100.00-200.00

GRUMPY THE DWARF MARIONETTE, 1930's, Alexander Doll Company $50.00-125.00

GRUMPY THE DWARF RUBBER FIGURE, Seiberling Latex, 1930's, 5" $20.00-50.00

HAPPY THE DWARF MARIONETTE, Alexander Doll Company, 1930's $50.00-125.00

HAPPY THE DWARF DRINKING GLASS by Libbey, 1938...$10.00-20.00

HIAWATHA, a Walt Disney book by David McKay, 1938...$15.00-35.00

HORACE HORSECOLLAR, BISQUE FIGURE, ca. 1930's, 4"......................................$35.00.70.00

HORACE HORSECOLLAR BISQUE ca. 1930's, 3" $30.00-65.00

HORACE HORSECOLLAR PULLING MICKEY MOUSE, celluloid figures, 1930's, rare ...$3,000.00-6,000.00

HORACE HORSECOLLAR PULLING MICKEY MOUSE, wooden, N. N. Hill Brass, 1936.....$100.00-200.00

JIMINY CRICKET an American Pottery figure, 1940's, 6"..$75.00-125.00

JIMINY CRICKET CERAMIC FIGURE, 2", Brayton's Laguna Pottery, 1940's.....................$50.00-125.00

JIMINY CRICKET COMPOSITION FIGURE, 3", Multi Products, 1940 ....$20.00-45.00

JIMINY CRICKET COMPOSITION FIGURE, 4", Multi Products, 1940 ....$30.00-65.00

JIMINY CRICKET COMPOSITION FIGURE, outstretched hand, Multi Products, rare...............$50.00-120.00

JIMINY CRICKET DOLL manufactured by Knickerbocker Toys, 1939 ....$150.00-300.00

JIMINY CRICKET DRINKING GLASS by Libbey, 1940...$10.00-20.00

JIMINY CRICKET HOLLOW RUBBER SQUEAK TOY, Seiberling Latex, 1930's $20.00-40.00

JIMINY CRICKET PAPER MASK, Gillette premium, 1939...$10.00-25.00

JIMINY CRICKET PENCIL SHARPENER, Bakelite, 1930's with decal $20.00-35.00

JIMINY CRICKET SNAP CLICKER, 1940.$10.00-20.00

JIMINY CRICKET THERMOMETER, by Bakelite, 1939...$40.00-65.00

JOE CARIOCA CHARACTER LAMP, ceramic figure-like American Pottery, 1940's................$100.00-200.00

JOE CARIOCA PARROT CLOTH DOLL by Lars of Italy, recent, but rare $100.00-200.00

JOE CARIOCA PARROT COOKIE JAR, 1940's by Leeds $25.00-50.00

LADY AND THE TRAMP COLORING BOOK, Whitman, 1954...$10.00-20.00

LADY AND THE TRAMP FRAME TRAY PUZZLE, 1954, Whitman......................................$5.00-10.00

LAMPWICK, (PINOCCHIO) COMPOSITION FIGURE, 5" Multi Products, 1940 ....$15.00-35.00

LITTLE RED RIDING HOOD PENCIL BOX, Dixon, 1930's, paper $40.00-80.00

LITTLE RED RIDING HOOD AND THE BIG BAD WOLF BOOK, David McKay, 1934.................$45.00-70.00

LITTLE RED RIDING HOOD DOLL, 1930's, George Borgfeldt...$100.00-175.00

LITTLE RED RIDING HOOD DOLL, Walt Disney, cloth/linen face, hood and cape.............$100.00-200.00

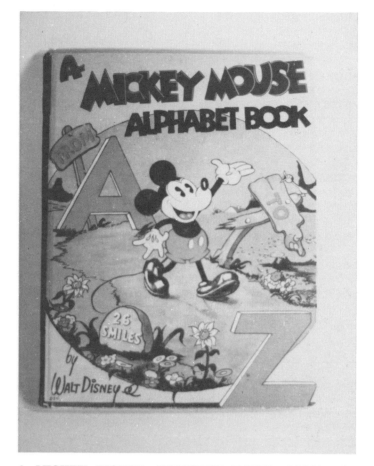

A MICKEY MOUSE ALPHABET BOOK, 1930's, by Walt Disney, hardcover, $40.00-80.00.

LUDWIG VON DRAKE BALL TOSS GAME, ca. 1960's $10.00-25.00

LUDWIG VON DRAKE FIGURAL BANK, ceramic, 1960's $10.00-30.00

LUDWIG VON DRAKE PLUSH DOLL, 1960's, Walt Disney Productions $35.00-60.00

LUDWIG VON DRAKE SQUEAK TOY, by Dell, ca. 1960's $5.00-10.00

LUDWIG VON DRAKE TALKING DOLL, 1960's, original box $40.00-85.00

LULUBELLE THE BEAR, (Bongo's girlfriend) Gund, 1947, Fun and Fancy Free................$25.00-50.00

MARY POPPINS CAROUSEL GAME, 1960's, by Parker Brothers $5.00-15.00

MARY POPPINS CLUTCH PURSE, by Aristocratic Leather Products, 1960's......................$5.00-15.00

MARY POPPINS COLORING BOOK by Walt Disney 1960's $5.00-10.00

MARY POPPINS PAPER DOLLS CUT-OUT BOOK, 1960's $10.00-25.00

MARY POPPINS WALLET, 1960's by Aristocratic Leather Products $10.00-20.00

MICKEY AND MINNIE MOUSE BAND BISQUE SET, boxed, four figures, 4".....................$145.00-285.00

MICKEY AND MINNIE MOUSE, CHILD'S DRAWING TABLET, 1930's, ...$50.00-90.00

MICKEY AND MINNIE MOUSE ALL STAR PARADE GLASS, 1930's $10.00-20.00

MICKEY AND MINNIE MOUSE DOLL CUT-OUT BOOK, Saalfield, 1933 ....$50.00-110.00

MICKEY AND MINNIE MOUSE LUSTERWARE CHINA TEA SET, 1930's complete, box $100.00-200.00

MICKEY AND MINNIE MOUSE MECHANICAL VALENTINE, 1930's, W. D. Enterprises $20.00-40.00

MICKEY MOUSE AND MINNIE MOUSE METAL MATCHBOX, engraved and painted, 1930's...$50.00-110.00

MICKEY AND MINNIE MOUSE ON A MOTORCYCLE, German, by Tipp, tin lithograph, 1928 ....$1,500.00-3,000.00

MICKEY AND MINNIE MOUSE ON ICE SKATES, 1930's tapestry rug with fringe $50.00-100.00

MICKEY AND MINNIE MOUSE PAIL, 8", 1930's Ohio Art, Mickey in gondola $50.00-95.00

MICKEY AND MINNIE MOUSE PARTY HORN, Marks Brothers, 1930's $35.00-65.00

MICKEY AND MINNIE MOUSE PARTY NOISEMAKER on stick, 1930's, Marks Brothers $30.00-65.00

MICKEY AND MINNIE MOUSE PILLOW COVER, 1930's, Mickey and Minnie/piano...................$25.00-60.00

MICKEY AND MINNIE MOUSE PORCELAIN POTTIE, 1930's, at Grand Piano $50.00-100.00

MICKEY AND MINNIE MOUSE PRINT SHOP, Fulton Specialty, 3" x 9" box $50.00-95.00

MICKEY AND MINNIE MOUSE SAND PAIL, Mickey pulls rabbit from hat, 1930's, 3".......$40.00-80.00

MICKEY AND MINNIE MOUSE SHOVEL, tin lithograph, 12", beach scene, Ohio Art $40.00-65.00

MICKEY AND MINNIE MOUSE SWINGING TRAPEZE FIGURES, windup, 1930's.............$300.00-700.00

MICKEY AND MINNIE MOUSE TAMBOURINE, Noble and Cooley, 1936 ....$200.00-300.00

MICKEY AND MINNIE MOUSE TRAP DRUM SET, Noble and Cooley, 1936, rare $200.00-300.00

MICKEY AND MINNIE MOUSE WALL POCKET, lusterware, blue rim, ceramic $65.00-130.00

MICKEY AND MINNIE MOUSE WASHING MACHINE, 1930's, Ohio Art $65.00-150.00

MICKEY AND MINNIE MOUSE WASTEBASKET, tan/red/black, large, 1930's $60.00-135.00

MICKEY AND PLUTO LUSTERWARE ASHTRAY, Mickey with quitar, 3" tall $65.00-95.00

MICKEY AND PLUTO PULL TOY, Mickey Mouse plays cymbals on Pluto's tail, 1930's $150.00-300.00

MICKEY FIRE DEPARTMENT, rubber fire truck by Sun Rubber Company $35.00-65.00

MICKEY MOUSE ICE SKATERS PULL TOY, N. N. Hill Brass, 1930's, rare $175.00-375.00

MICKEY MOUSE "DOUBLE MICKEY'S" PULL TOY, N. N. Hill Brass, rare..........................$200.00-400.00

MICKEY MOUSE "ON THE WARPATH" target shooting game, Nifty, 1930's, 13" $200.00-400.00

MICKEY MOUSE "THE FIRST STEP" savings bank, 1930's, rare...................................$100.00-200.00

MICKEY MOUSE SHEET MUSIC, "The Wedding Party," 1930's $20.00-45.00

MICKEY MOUSE AND DONALD DUCK CRAYONS SET, Transogram, c. 1940, metal box........$18.00-35.00

MICKEY MOUSE AND MINNIE MOUSE LIONEL HANDCAR, 1930's, boxed set...............$650.00-1,100.00

MICKEY MOUSE AND MINNIE MOUSE TOOTHBRUSH HOLDER, 1930's, 3", on couch $110.00-175.00

MICKEY MOUSE AND MINNIE MOUSE TOOTHBRUSH HOLDER, 5", manufactured in 1930's, figures standing....................................$85.00-150.00

MICKEY MOUSE (DOUBLE) COMIC COOKIE HAT, c. 1933 ....$50.00-85.00

MICKEY MOUSE (DOUBLE) TUMBLING CIRCUS TOY, Nifty, 1930's, wood, 11", rare $500.00-950.00

MICKEY MOUSE KITE, 1930's, Marks Brothers, rare $100.00-250.00

MICKEY MOUSE BISQUE FIGURE holding a song book, 3", 1930's $40.00-85.00

MICKEY MOUSE BISQUE FIGURE playing banjo, 3", bulbous nose, 1930's $40.00-80.00

MICKEY MOUSE BISQUE FIGURE playing drum, 3", 1930's, bulbous nose $40.00-80.00

MICKEY MOUSE BISQUE FIGURE, 3", 1930's, playing accordian $40.00-85.00

MICKEY MOUSE BISQUE FIGURE playing French horn, 3", bulbous nose, 1930's $40.00-80.00

MICKEY MOUSE BLACK RUBBER FIGURE, 3", by Seiberling, 1930's $50.00-95.00

MICKEY MOUSE BISQUE TOOTHBRUSH HOLDER, 5", stationary, hole in side $125.00-255.00

MICKEY MOUSE 7TH BIRTHDAY CARD, 1930's, W. D. Enterprises, shaped like "7" $20.00-35.00

MICKEY MOUSE ABC BOOK, hardcover, ca. 1930's, black and white illustrations $45.00-75.00

MICKEY MOUSE ACROBATIC CIRCUS, Marks Brothers, 1930's, rare $300.00-600.00

MICKEY MOUSE ACTION POP GUN, 1950's, Lido Toy, boxed $20.00-35.00

MICKEY MOUSE ALARM CLOCK, 1930's, Ingersoll, pie-eyed Mickey $120.00-200.00

MICKEY MOUSE ALARM CLOCK, 1960's, Bayard, French, red case, 1930's $50.00-100.00

MICKEY MOUSE ALARM CLOCK, by Ingersoll, ca. 1940's, boxed...................................$65.00-125.00

MICKEY MOUSE ALPHABET ABC BOOK, hardcover, 1930's, Mickey on cover....................$60.00-95.00

MICKEY MOUSE ALPHABET BOWL, 9" diameter, Bavarian China, 1930's.........................$50.00-125.00

MICKEY MOUSE ALPHABET BOWL, china, Bavarian, Walt E. Disney, 8", early $100.00-200.00

MICKEY MOUSE ALUMINUM PLAY SET, DISHES, three piece, 1930's $25.00-50.00

MICKEY MOUSE ALUMINUM BAKING SET, 1930's, Aluminum Specialty Company $75.00-100.00

MICKEY MOUSE AND DISNEY CHARACTERS, wind-up carousel, LineMar, 1950's.........$350.00-700.00

MICKEY MOUSE AND DONALD DUCK CHINA TEA SET, 1930's with Elmer Elephant ...$75.00-150.00

MICKEY MOUSE AND DONALD DUCK CRAYONS, GOLD MEDAL, 1950's......................$10.00-20.00

MICKEY MOUSE AND DONALD DUCK HANDCAR SET, MARX, 1950's, on tin flat $100.00-200.00

MICKEY MOUSE AND DONALD DUCK HANDCAR by Louis Marx, 1950's, boxed $75.00-150.00

MICKEY MOUSE AND DONALD DUCK with Christmas tree, Patriot China cup, 4" $35.00-75.00

MICKEY MOUSE AND FRIENDS, character globe, Rand McNally, 1940's $25.00-50.00

MICKEY MOUSE AND FRIENDS DISNEY SKI JUMP, 1930's, boxed target game $85.00-125.00

MICKEY MOUSE AND FRIENDS TIN LITHOGRAPH, Ohio Art, 1930's $60.00-125.00

MICKEY MOUSE AND MINNIE MOUSE SAND SHOVEL, large, Ohio Art, beach scene $75.00-125.00

MICKEY MOUSE AND MINNIE MOUSE TRAY, 8" x 10", entering restaurant, 1930's $50.00-100.00

MICKEY MOUSE AND PLUTO CERAMIC ASHTRAY, 1930's, Lusterware, 3".....................$85.00-135.00

MICKEY MOUSE AND PLUTO MODELED IN SOAP, boxed set, 1930's $65.00-125.00

MICKEY MOUSE AND PLUTO STANDING WITH CANE, large bisque figure, rare.................$400.00-800.00

MICKEY MOUSE AND PLUTO THE RACER, Big Little Book, 1930's.....................................$15.00-30.00

MICKEY MOUSE ART DECO CREAMER, French, 1930's, ceramic, Minnie on reverse $100.00-145.00

MICKEY MOUSE ART SET, by Dixon, 1930's, Mickey on plane on box lid $50.00-100.00

MICKEY MOUSE ASHTRAY, composition figure, 3", early, slate base $100.00-175.00

MICKEY MOUSE ASHTRAY, 5", bisque, Mickey has spring legs, 1930's $75.00-125.00

MICKEY MOUSE ASSEMBLY SET, in tube, 1950's, play set $20.00-30.00

MICKEY MOUSE BABY GRAND PIANO, 1930's, with Mickey decal on top $100.00-275.00

MICKEY MOUSE BAND DRUM, 1930's, 11", tin and paper drum......................................$75.00-125.00

MICKEY MOUSE BANJO, 1936, paper head, Noble and Cooley, very graphic $100.00-175.00

MICKEY MOUSE BARRETTES, 1930's, on original card..$20.00-45.00

MICKEY MOUSE BASEBALL BAT, 1930's, Draper-Maynard Company, wooden........................$25.00-45.00

MICKEY MOUSE BAVARIAN CHINA PLATE, 7", 1930's, Walter E. Disney $75.00-125.00

MICKEY MOUSE BEDTIME STORIES, child's book, 1930's $35.00-60.00

MICKEY MOUSE BEETLEWARE BOWL, plastic, 1930's $10.00-18.00

MICKEY MOUSE BEETLEWARE CUP, white with Mickey stencil, late 1930's $5.00-10.00

MICKEY MOUSE BEETLEWARE MUG, 1930's, Mickey stencil on side $10.00-20.00

MICKEY MOUSE BEETLEWARE PLASTIC BOWL, 1930's $10.00-20.00

MICKEY MOUSE BEING PULLED BY TANGLEFOOT (HORSE) N. N. Hill Brass, 1930's .$250.00-500.00

MICKEY MOUSE BELT, 1930's, by Hickok, leather and metal $20.00-55.00

MICKEY MOUSE BIG BIG BOX OF GAMES AND THINGS TO COLOR, 1930's..............$25.00-75.00

MICKEY MOUSE BIRTHDAY CANDLE HOLDERS, 1930's, Cypress Novelties $45.00-70.00

MICKEY MOUSE BIRTHDAY CARD, 1930's, Hall Brothers, folds out to poster $40.00-75.00

MICKEY MOUSE BISQUE FIGURES with hands on hips, 3" tall, 1930's.........................$25.00-40.00

MICKEY MOUSE BISQUE FIGURE nodding head, 1930's, 3¾", rare $100.00-200.00

MICKEY MOUSE BISQUE FIGURE wearing tuxedo and top hat, 4", 1930's $25.00-75.00

MICKEY MOUSE BISQUE FIGURE playing banjo, 1930's, 5".......................................$75.00-150.00

MICKEY MOUSE BISQUE FIGURE with catcher's mitt and equipment, 2½", 1930's..............$35.00-65.00

MICKEY MOUSE BISQUE FIGURE holding

ALARM CLOCKS BY BAYARD, French, 1960's, Reynolds collection, $50.00-100.00.

MICKEY MOUSE BOXED GAME TOKENS, 1930's, c. Walt E. Disney, Marks Brothers, $25.00-50.00.

rifle, 3"...$35.00-60.00

MICKEY MOUSE BISQUE FIGURE holding baseball bat, 3", 1930's...................................$25.00-70.00

MICKEY MOUSE BISQUE FIGURE with walking cane, 4½" 1930's $35.00-75.00

MICKEY MOUSE BISQUE FIGURE wearing night gown, 4", 1930's, ...$30.00-65.00

MICKEY MOUSE BISQUE FIGURE playing drum, 4"...$35.00-60.00

MICKEY MOUSE BISQUE FIGURE playing a drum, 5", 1930's $75.00-175.00

MICKEY MOUSE BISQUE FIGURE playing accordion, 1930's, 5"...$75.00-150.00

MICKEY MOUSE BISQUE FIGURE playing French horn, 1930's, 5"...$75.00-150.00

MICKEY MOUSE BISQUE FIGURE, 6", two movable arms, 1930's, jointed $65.00-155.00

MICKEY MOUSE BISQUE FIGURE playing sax, 3½", 1930's $35.00-65.00

MICKEY MOUSE BISQUE FIGURE on green base, two movable arms, 7½", 1930's $300.00-750.00

MICKEY MOUSE BISQUE FIGURE, standing on platform, 5", hands on hips $65.00-125.00

MICKEY MOUSE BISQUE TOOTHBRUSH HOLDER, 3", Mickey with Pluto $95.00-155.00

MICKEY MOUSE BISQUE TOOTHBRUSH HOLDER, standing pose with jointed arm, 5".$125.00-225.00

MICKEY MOUSE BISQUE FIGURE 1" tall, hand held up, waving, smallest one known $25.00-60.00

MICKEY MOUSE BISQUE FIGURE, 2½" tall, with baseball glove $35.00-60.00

MICKEY MOUSE BISQUE FIGURE, 3", movable arms with conductor's baton, 1930's, ... $45.00-120.00

MICKEY MOUSE BISQUE FIGURE standing by a garbage can, 4½" tall, 1930's $50.00-95.00

MICKEY MOUSE BISQUE FIGURE, 5" tall, two movable arms, 1930's $150.00-300.00

MICKEY MOUSE BISQUE FIGURE, Mickey holding a flag, 3¾" tall $30.00-65.00

MICKEY MOUSE BISQUE FIGURE, Mickey holding a sword, 3¼" tall, 1930's $25.00-55.00

MICKEY MOUSE BLACKBOARD, by Strathmore Company, 1940's, boxed $35.00-60.00

MICKEY MOUSE BLACKBOARD, easel type, stand-up, Richmond School Furn., 1930's $100.00-175.00

MICKEY MOUSE BLOCKS BY HALSAM, 1930's, eighteen block set, boxed $45.00-95.00

MICKEY MOUSE BLOTTER, SUNOCO PREMIUM, 1940's $10.00-20.00

MICKEY MOUSE BOOK FOR COLORING, 1930's, die-cut Mickey skating on cover $35.00-75.00

MICKEY MOUSE BOOK TO COLOR, Saalfield, 1937, die-cut top edge $25.00-50.00

MICKEY MOUSE BOOK, "WALT DISNEY'S WILD WEST," 1930's, hardcover, rare.......$75.00-125.00

MICKEY MOUSE BOOK, THE STORY OF MICKEY MOUSE, Big Big Book, 1935 ....$50.00-85.00

MICKEY MOUSE BOOKEND, 1930's, Mickey as scout, La Mode Studios $75.00-135.00

MICKEY MOUSE BOW AND ARROW SET on the original card, 1930's, ...$100.00-200.00

MICKEY MOUSE BOXED CRAYON SET, 1946, by Transogram, W.D.P. $15.00-35.00

MICKEY MOUSE BOXED HANKIES SET, lithograph lid, seven hankies, 1930's $125.00-225.00

MICKEY MOUSE BOXED PENCILS, manufactured ca. 1930's, Dixon $25.00-50.00

MICKEY MOUSE BOXED STATIONERY SET, 1930's $45.00-60.00

MICKEY MOUSE BRACELET, silverplate band with one figural Mickey in center $35.00-90.00

MICKEY MOUSE BRIDGE CARD GAME, boxed, Whitman, 1935, two decks $40.00-85.00

MICKEY MOUSE BUBBLE BUSTER GUN, 1930's, Kilgore Manufacturing Company, boxed $75.00-125.00

MICKEY MOUSE BY LAMPPOST CAST METAL ASHTRAY, 1930's, rare $200.00-400.00

MICKEY MOUSE CANDY MACHINE, 1930's, gumball-type, Hamilton Enterprises $200.00-450.00

MICKEY MOUSE CANE, 1930's, ceramic head, pie-eyed Mickey $40.00-85.00

MICKEY MOUSE CAR by Marx, tin windup with Disney characters, lithographed, 1950's $65.00-110.00

MICKEY MOUSE CAR, all tin, windup, by LineMar, Mickey drives $70.00-135.00

MICKEY MOUSE CARD "HAPPY NEW YEAR," by Hall Brothers, 1930's $20.00-40.00

MICKEY MOUSE CARD GAME, British, 1938, boxed $45.00-75.00

MICKEY MOUSE CARDBOARD PENCIL BOX, by Dixon, 1934, Mickey waving $65.00-145.00

MICKEY MOUSE CAST LEAD FIGURE, 4", Mickey holds umbrella, painted..................$100.00-250.00

MICKEY MOUSE CELLULOID AND METAL WINDUP DOLL, 1930's, five-fingered, rare $900.00-1,700.00

MICKEY MOUSE CELLULOID FIGURAL PENCIL SHARPENER, hollow, 1930's with base....$75.00-150.00

MICKEY MOUSE CELLULOID FIGURE WITH NODDING HEAD AND JOINTED ARMS, 1930's $200.00-450.00

MICKEY MOUSE CELLULOID HAND PUZZLE, "Ring the Nose," 1930's...........................$100.00-200.00

MICKEY MOUSE CELLULOID NAPKIN RING, Mickey's face, red, Bakelite, 1930's $25.00-50.00

MICKEY MOUSE CELLULOID PENCIL SHARPENER, 1", 1930's, decal.............................$20.00-45.00

MICKEY MOUSE CELLULOID PENCIL SHARPENER, Bakelite with brass ring, 1930's $20.00-40.00

MICKEY MOUSE CELLULOID RATTLE with handle, 1930's $100.00-200.00

MICKEY MOUSE CELLULOID WINDUP FIGURE, 1930's, rare $900.00-1,800.00

MICKEY MOUSE CELLULOID WINDUP NODDER, Japan, 1930's, flat version $100.00-275.00

MICKEY MOUSE CELLULOID WINDUP TOY, Mickey in wagon pulled by Pluto, 1930's.......$400.00-950.00

MICKEY MOUSE CERAMIC ASHTRAY, 1930's, Mickey plays drum on edge, 3" $45.00-100.00

MICKEY MOUSE CERAMIC BANK, manufactured by Leeds China, 1940's $15.00-30.00

MICKEY MOUSE CERAMIC WATCH STAND AND WATCH, 1950's version....................$65.00-100.00

MICKEY MOUSE CEREAL SPOON, premium, boxed, 1930's $25.00-50.00

MICKEY MOUSE CHALK CARNIVAL FIGURE, 1930's, 15", bright colors...............................$35.00-75.00

MICKEY MOUSE CHARACTER PUPPET BY GUND, 1960's, boxed.............................$10.00-35.00

MICKEY MOUSE CHILD'S BRACELET, 1930's, brass and celluloid $35.00-60.00

MICKEY MOUSE CHILD'S DIVIDED CERAMIC DISH, Patriot China, three figures...............$35.00-70.00

MICKEY MOUSE CHILD'S PURSE, 1930's, by King Innovations...$15.00-45.00

MICKEY MOUSE CHILD'S WAGON by Dayton Toy and Specialty, 1930's $75.00-195.00

MICKEY MOUSE CHINA ASHTRAY, glazed, 3", Mickey seated, 1930's $40.00-95.00

MICKEY MOUSE CHOCOLATE BAR, original wrapper, 1930's $25.00-50.00

MICKEY MOUSE CHRISTMAS PACKAGE TAG, 1930's, 3" square $20.00-30.00

MICKEY MOUSE CINE ART FILM in the original box, 1930's $15.00-35.00

MICKEY MOUSE CINE ART FILM, manufactured ca. 1930's, boxed....................................$15.00-25.00

MICKEY MOUSE CLOTHES BRUSH SET, with box, pie-eyed, 1930's $100.00-200.00

MICKEY MOUSE CLUB AUTO-MAGIC PICTURE GUN, in box, set, 1950's $25.00-45.00

MICKEY MOUSE CLUB BAND LEADER OUTFIT, boxed, L. M. Eddy Manufacturing, 1950's $55.00-95.00

MICKEY MOUSE CLUB DINNER SET, Molded Plastics, 1950's, three piece boxed $15.00-30.00

MICKEY MOUSE CLUB MAGIC ADDER, ca. 1950's, electronic quiz game $10.00-30.00

MICKEY MOUSE CLUB MAGIC ERASABLE PICTURES, 1950's, M. M. Club logo $10.00-25.00

MICKEY MOUSE CLUB MEMBERSHIP CARD, original 1930's $10.00-25.00

MICKEY MOUSE CLUB MOUSEGETAR-JR, by Mattel Incorporated, 1950's, boxed $25.00-50.00

MICKEY MOUSE CLUB MOUSEKETEER EARS, on display card, Empire Plastics, 1950's. $10.00-20.00

MICKEY MOUSE CLUB OFFICIAL CHILD'S COASTER WAGON, Radio Steel, 1950's $35.00-65.00

MICKEY MOUSE CLUB PIN-BACK BUTTON, 1930, Walt. E. Disney $30.00-60.00

MICKEY MOUSE CLUB SCRAP BOOK, manufactured ca. 1950's $10.00-20.00

MICKEY MOUSE CLUB TOOL CHEST, American Toy and Furniture, 1950's $20.00-40.00

MICKEY MOUSE CLUBHOUSE TREASURY BANK, 1950's or 1960's, boxed $25.00-60.00

MICKEY MOUSE COLORED PENCILS SET by Dixon, 1930's $20.00-45.00

MICKEY MOUSE COMB, 1930's, American Hard Rubber Company $50.00-75.00

MICKEY MOUSE COMING HOME GAME, Marks Brothers, boxed pieces and board $90.00-165.00

MICKEY MOUSE COMPOSITON DOLL, 1930, Knickerbocker Toy $100.00-200.00

MICKEY MOUSE COMPOSITION BANK, manufactured by Crown Toy, 1930's, 7" tall $50.00-95.00

MICKEY MOUSE COMPOSITION DOLL, Knickerbocker, 1939, hat and cape $250.00-550.00

MICKEY MOUSE COMPOSITION FIGURE, 6", Lionel from circus train set $95.00-225.00

MICKEY MOUSE COOKIE CUTTERS, 1930's Mickey box $50.00-75.00

MICKEY MOUSE COOKIE JAR, large, reverses to Minnie Mouse, Leeds, 1940's $40.0-95.00

MICKEY MOUSE COOKIES, 1930's version, complete box $50.00-125.00

MICKEY MOUSE COOKIES, in box, cookies by Nabisco, 1950's $5.00-15.00

MICKEY MOUSE CRAYON SET, tin, Transogram, 1930's, Mickey and Donald on lid $15.00-35.00

MICKEY MOUSE CREAMER, 1930's, foreign, 4" version, ceramic $50.00-100.00

MICKEY MOUSE CREAMER, Bavarian, China, 1930's, Mickey on toy train $75.00-145.00

MICKEY MOUSE CREAMER, open mouthed, foreign, tall 6" version, ceramic $70.00-125.00

MICKEY MOUSE CRICKET NOISE MAKER, 1930's, tin lithograph of Mickey $35.00-70.00

MICKEY MOUSE CRUSOE BOOK, large paperback, 1930's $35.00-60.00

MICKEY MOUSE CUP, Bavarian China, 1930's, Mickey sings a song $35.00-75.00

MICKEY MOUSE CUT-OUT DOLL BOOK, 1930's tall version $50.00-100.00

MICKEY MOUSE DART GUN TARGET, by Marks Brothers, 1930's, 10" diameter $35.00-75.00

MICKEY MOUSE DIE-CUT FIGURAL CELLULOID PENCIL SHARPENER, 1930's $25.00-55.00

MICKEY MOUSE DIME REGISTER BANK, 1938, W. D. Enterprises, 2" x 2" tin lithograph $55.00-95.00

MICKEY MOUSE LIONEL CIRCUS TRAIN CAR, 1934, tin lithograph, $100.00-200.00. MICKEY MOUSE WOOD COMPOSITION FIGURE, from Lionel Circus Train Set, 1930's, $125.00-250.00.

MICKEY MOUSE DOLL by Knickerbocker, cloth, 1930's, orange wood composition shoes, $200.00-450.00.

MICKEY MOUSE DIPSY CAR, manufactured ca. 1950's, Marx, boxed $125.00-225.00

MICKEY MOUSE DISNEYLAND FERRIS WHEEL, 1950's, Chein, windup $150.00-300.00

MICKEY MOUSE JOINTED WOOD COMPOSITION DOLL, ca, 1930's, doll features a movable head and jointed arms, doll by Knickerbocker, $400.00-800.00.

MICKEY MOUSE DISNEYLAND MELODY PLAYER, music box with crank, scrolls $50.00-85.00

MICKEY MOUSE DOLL BY DEAN'S RAG BOOK COMPANY of England, 12", 1930's $150.00-300.00

MICKEY MOUSE DOLL BY GUND, 1940's, cloth face $50.00-100.00

MICKEY MOUSE DOLL BY LARS of Italy, ca. 1970's, 15" tall $200.00-400.00

MICKEY MOUSE DOLL, 12" STUFFED, Knickerbocker, 1930's, felt shoes $200.00-400.00

MICKEY MOUSE DOLL, JOINTED WOOD COMPOSITION, Knickerbocker, 1930's, 12" .. $350.00-600.00

MICKEY MOUSE DOLL, stuffed, 14" Knickerbocker Toys, 1930's, composition shoes $175.00-400.00

MICKEY MOUSE DOLL, wood composition, 1930's, Knickerbocker, cape and hat $250.00-500.00

MICKEY MOUSE DRAWING TABLET, Walt Disney Enterprises, 1930's $20.00-40.00

MICKEY MOUSE DRUM MAJOR, DRUM SHAPED LAMP, ca. 1960's $20.00-35.00

MICKEY MOUSE DRUM, 10" diameter, 1930's, Enterprises, Ohio Art $95.00-135.00

MICKEY MOUSE DRUMMER BISQUE FIGURE, 1930's, Japan, 3" $30.00-75.00

MICKEY MOUSE DRUMMER, BO, by LineMar, 11" $125.00-250.00

MICKEY MOUSE DRUMMER, tin, lever action, by Nifty Toys, 1930's, rare $750.00-1,500.00

MICKEY MOUSE ELECTRIC STOVE, beige in color, with cord, actually heats $35.00-80.00

MICKEY MOUSE EMERSON PHONOGRAPH, 1934, Mickey decals in and out $250.00-500.00

MICKEY MOUSE ENGLISH HAPPYNAK TEA SET, tin lithograph $45.00-90.00

MICKEY MOUSE ENGLISH POST CARD, Mickey and Pluto, 1930's $10.00-30.00

MICKEY MOUSE EXPRESS, PLANE AND TRAIN WIND-UP, 1940's, Marx, boxed $200.00-375.00

MICKEY MOUSE FERRIS WHEEL, by J. Chein, 1950's, windup, tin $75.00-175.00

MICKEY MOUSE FIGURAL ASH TRAY, Mickey sits on edge, china, early, Japan $100.00-200.00

MICKEY MOUSE FIGURAL PENCIL CASE, 1930's, composition, Dixon.................... $75.00-150.00

MICKEY MOUSE FIGURAL SOAP, early 1930's, D. H. & Company, boxed $35.00-70.00

MICKEY MOUSE FIREMAN DOLL BY GUND, 1950's, 12" tall, with hat and boots $50.00-110.00

MICKEY MOUSE FISHER PRICE LOCOMOTIVE, 1930's, #432 .... $65.00-120.00

MICKEY MOUSE FISHING KIT, ca. 1930's, by Hamilton Metal Products $45.00-85.00

MICKEY MOUSE FLASHLIGHT BY USA LIGHT, 1930's, original box $50.00-125.00

MICKEY MOUSE FLASHLIGHT, 1936, by U. S. Electric Manufacturing $50.00-125.00

MICKEY MOUSE FLAT LEAD FIGURE, painted, 1930's, from foundry set $10.00-20.00

MICKEY MOUSE FRAMED PICTURE, manufactured ca. 1930's $15.00-30.00

MICKEY MOUSE FUN-E-FLEX-FIGURE, 4", 1930's, wood jointed doll $50.00-125.00

MICKEY MOUSE FUNNY FACTS, ELECTRIC GAME, Einson-Freeman Publishing Co. $60.00-125.00

MICKEY MOUSE GIANT SAND PAIL, Mickey and Minnie in fishing boat, Ohio Art $75.00-150.00

MICKEY MOUSE GLOBE-TYPE LAMP, Mickey decal, original shape, 1935 .... $40.00-125.00

MICKEY MOUSE GLOBETROTTER'S, U.S. MAP, premium, no stickers, original envelope . $75.00-125.00

MICKEY MOUSE GLOBETROTTER'S, U.S. MAP, complete with all stickers, 1930's $150.00-250.00

MICKEY MOUSE HAIRBRUSH AND COMB SET, boxed, 1930's, Henry Hughes Company $75.00-150.00

MICKEY MOUSE HAIRBRUSH SET, Mickey on box and handles, 1930's, two brushes $100.00-200.00

MICKEY MOUSE HALLMARK BIRTHDAY CARD, Hall Brothers, 1935 .... $15.00-35.00

MICKEY MOUSE HAND PUPPET, by Steiff, 1930's, velvet, button in ear $100.00-150.00

MICKEY MOUSE HAND PUPPET, manufactured by Gund, boxed, 1950's $10.00-25.00

MICKEY MOUSE HANDKERCHIEFS, boxed, by Hermann Handkerchief Co., set of 4 .... $85.00-125.00

MICKEY MOUSE HANKIE, manufactured in 1930's, fireman Mickey $10.00-25.00

MICKEY MOUSE HANKIE, manufactured in 1930's, Mickey flying kite $10.00-25.00

MICKEY MOUSE HANKIE, manufactured in 1930's, Mickey on scooter $10.00-25.00

MICKEY MOUSE HANKIE, manufactured in 1930's, Mickey on sled $10.00-25.00

MICKEY MOUSE HANKIES, boxed set of four, ca. 1930's, colorful box $75.00-125.00

MICKEY MOUSE HANKY, 1930's, green with lots of little Mickeys......................................$10.00-25.00

MICKEY MOUSE HAS A BUSY DAY STORYBOOK printed ca. 1930's $20.00-40.00

MICKEY MOUSE HINGEES, packaged in the envelope, 1940's $10.00-20.00

MICKEY MOUSE HOME FOUNDRY SET, complete set with box, 1930's $125.00-250.00

MICKEY MOUSE HURDY GURDY, tin lithograph, wind-up, 1930's with dancing Minnie $2,200.00-5,600.00

MICKEY MOUSE ICE CREAM LID from Southern Dairies, 1930's, 3" diameter...............$20.00-40.00

MICKEY MOUSE IN KING ARTHUR'S COURT, POP-UP BOOK, 1930's $100.00-200.00

MICKEY MOUSE IN NIGHTSHIRT BISQUE FIGURE, 4", 1930's $45.00-85.00

MICKEY MOUSE IN NUMBERLAND BOOK, printed ca. 1930's $45.00-105.00

MICKEY MOUSE IN YE OLDEN DAYS BOOK, small pop-up book, rare, 5".......................$75.00-150.00

MICKEY MOUSE INGERSOLL ALARM CLOCK, 1930's, green, 5" $200.00-350.00

MICKEY MOUSE IRON-ON TRANSFERS, manufactured by McCall's, 1934..............................$50.00-80.00

MICKEY MOUSE JOINTED HARD RUBBER FIGURE, Seiberling, 1930's, 7".......................$50.00-125.00

MICKEY MOUSE KEYSTONE MOVIE PROJECTOR, 1934, boxed $100.00-250.00

MICKEY MOUSE KIDDY NITE LIGHT, die-cut Mickey and tin cylinder, 1938 ....$50.00-125.00

MICKEY MOUSE DOLL, Knickerbocker, dressed as circus clown, 1930's.......................$300.00-600.00

MICKEY MOUSE LAMP WITH METAL GLOBE BASE, 1930's, with original shade $95.00-195.00

MICKEY MOUSE LAMP, Mickey sits in chair, Soreng-Manegold, 1936, rare $750.00-1,500.00

MICKEY MOUSE LARGE TIN LITHOGRAPH SAND SHOVEL, ca. 1930's, manufactured by Ohio Art, beach scene $75.00-150.00

MICKEY MOUSE LARGE WOOD JOINTED DOLL, as early 1930's, black/white/yellow $150.00-325.00

MICKEY MOUSE LATEXEEN RUBBER PANTS, baby's, 1930's, decorated box.........................$35.00-90.00

MICKEY MOUSE LEAD FIGURE, 2½", c. 1930's, rare $75.00-150.00

MICKEY MOUSE LEATHERETTE BOOK BANK, manufactured 1930's $35.00-70.00

MICKEY MOUSE LIBRARY OF GAMES, miniature card game library, 1940's..........................$15.00-35.00

MICKEY MOUSE LIONEL CIRCUS TRAIN, 1930's, boxed set $2,500.00-5,800.00

MICKEY MOUSE LOTTO GAME, 1950's, manufactured by Jaymar...$15.00-30.00

MICKEY MOUSE LUNCH KIT, 1930's, Geuder, Paeschke and Frey Co., rare..........$200.00-400.00

MICKEY MOUSE LUNCH KIT, oval shape, tin, 1930's, Gueder, Paeschke and Frey $100.00-200.00

MICKEY MOUSE LUSTERWARE CHINA TEAPOT, 1930's, blue rim, 3½" $25.00-50.00

MICKEY MOUSE LUSTERWARE TEAPOT, ca. 1930's, Mickey and Minnie in boat, brown ...$20.00-40.00

MICKEY MOUSE DRUM, 8", 1930's, Ohio Art, Walt Disney Enterprises, $65.00-110.00.

MICKEY MOUSE HOME FOUNDRY SET, complete in box, 1930's, $125.00-250.00.

MICKEY MOUSE LUSTERWARE TEA SET, 1930's, George Borgfeldt, boxed, china $100.00-225.00

MICKEY MOUSE LUSTERWARE TEA SET, gold, Japan, 1930's, twenty-two pieces $75.00-185.00

MICKEY MOUSE MAGAZINE, Santa Mickey is on cover, December, 1937 ....$50.00-125.00

MICKEY MOUSE MAGIC LANTERN SLIDES, 1930's boxed set, two slide strips.................$20.00-45.00

MAGIC MOUSE MAGIC SLATE, 1930's, small item with wooden pencil...........................$20.00-45.00

MICKEY MOUSE MAP OF THE UNITED STATES, Dixon, 1930's, Walt Disney Ent.....$100.00-200.00

MICKEY MOUSE MARIONETTE, 1930's, Madame Alexander, boxed $100.00-250.00

MICKEY MOUSE MARKS BROTHERS JIGSAW PUZZLE, 1930's, 7" x 9" $35.00-65.00

MICKEY MOUSE MARKS BROTHERS TARGET SET, W.D. Ent., 1930's, gun and darts ...$95.00-165.00

MICKEY MOUSE MASK, starched cotton, pie-eyed, toothy grin, 1930's $50.00-75.00

MICKEY MOUSE METAL DRUMMER, lever action, 1930's, Borgfeldt Dist., rare $650.00-1,250.00

MICKEY MOUSE METAL SPARKLER, by Nifty, 1930's, tin and metal, 5"...............................$75.00-150.00

MICKEY MOUSE METAL STAMP PAD, 1930's, from Fulton Specialty....................................$20.00-45.00

MICKEY MOUSE METAL STOVE, Metal Ware Corporation, 1936, electric...........................$50.00-85.00

MICKEY MOUSE METAL TELEVISION TRAY, "Wonderful World of Color," 1960's.............$5.00-10.00

MICKEY MOUSE METEOR TRAIN by Marx, windup, 1950's, four cars/engine.................$150.00-275.00

MICKEY MOUSE MILK BOTTLE, 1930's, black figures on clear glass.....................................$25.00-65.00

MICKEY MOUSE MILK BOTTLE, manufactured by Libbey Glass, 1930's..........................$25.00-50.00

MICKEY MOUSE MINIATURE PINBALL GAME, handheld, 1930's, Marks Brothers.............$35.00-75.00

MICKEY MOUSE MIRROR, 1930's.........$25.00-35.00

MICKEY MOUSE MOLDED CHEESECLOTH MASK, 1930's, toothy grin............................$25.00-60.00

MICKEY MOUSE MOUSEGETAR, full size, boxed Mattel, 1950's..$50.00-100.00

MICKEY MOUSE MOUSEKETEER TELEVISION, tin with record player, electric, 1950's....$40.00-80.00

MICKEY MOUSE MOUSEKETEERS WESTERN OUTFIT (costume) boxed, 1950's.....................$25.00-55.00

MICKEY MOUSE MOVIE STUDIO, by Standard Toykraft, 1940's boxed.....................................$50.00-125.00

MICKEY MOUSE MOVIE VIEWER, Craftsman Guild, 1940's with six films in box............$50.00-125.00

MICKEY MOUSE MOVIE VIEWER, plastic, by Craftsmen's Guild, 1940's, boxed.................$35.00-50.00

MICKEY MOUSE NECKTIE, manufactured by Nuemann Company, 1930's...............................$20.00-40.00

MICKEY MOUSE NEEDLEPOINT pillow cover, 1930's, Mickey and Minnie under umbrella...$25.00-60.00

MICKEY MOUSE NITE LIGHT, 1930's, 4" wood and tin, pen-light...................................$75.00-130.00

MICKEY MOUSE NITE LIGHT, CERAMIC, La Mode Studios, 1930's.....................................$65.00-130.00

MICKEY MOUSE NOMA CHRISTMAS LIGHTS SET, 1930's, boxed, eight lamp covers.....$75.00-175.00

MICKEY MOUSE NURSERY PICTURE, manufactured ca. 1940's...$10.00-20.00

MICKEY MOUSE OHIO ART SAND SET: 1930's pail, can, sifter, shovel, in box.............$100.00-225.00

MICKEY MOUSE OHIO ART TEA SET IN ORIGINAL BOX, 1934, two place settings........$75.00-135.00

MICKEY MOUSE OLD MAID CARD GAME, 1930's, Whitman..$25.00-50.00

MICKEY MOUSE ON A SCOOTER CELLULOID AND WOOD PULL TOY, 1930's, rare....$200.00-400.00

MICKEY MOUSE ON TRICYCLE WITH UMBRELLA, 1930's, celluloid and tin................$250.00-550.00

MICKEY MOUSE ON WOODEN ROCKING HORSE CELLULOID WINDUP, 1930s.............$500.00-1,000.00

MICKEY MOUSE ON WOODEN TRICYCLE by Steiff, (four wheels) pull toy, 1930's.....$500.00-1,250.00

MICKEY MOUSE PAINT AND CRAYON SET, ca. 1930's, Marks Brothers of Boston................$75.00-150.00

MICKEY MOUSE PAINT AND CRAYON SET, by Marks Brothers, 1930's, large set.............$125.00-200.00

MICKEY MOUSE PAINT BOX, metal, by Transogram, 1950's..$10.00-20.00

MICKEY MOUSE PAINT SET, 1950's, Spaceman Mickey and Rocket.....................................$10.00-20.00

MICKEY MOUSE PAINT SET, boxed, small version, Marks Brothers, 1930's...................$75.00-165.00

MICKEY MOUSE PAINTED BISQUE FIGURE, giant 9" size, 1930's, rare.........................$750.00-1,600.00

MICKEY MOUSE PAINTED WOOD DOLL, flex arms, 1930 George Borgfeldt, 8".............$250.00-550.00

MICKEY MOUSE PALETTE, a premium give-a-way toy, 1930's..$25.00-50.00

MICKEY MOUSE PANTOGRAPH by Marks Brothers, 1930, drawing set, boxed...............$100.00-200.00

MICKEY MOUSE PAPER MASK, 1930's .$20.00-35.00

MICKEY MOUSE PAPER MASK, manufactured by Einson Freeman, 1930's.........................$25.00-55.00

MICKEY MOUSE PAPER PARTY HAT, manufactured ca. 1950's..$5.00-10.00

MICKEY MOUSE PARTY GAME, Marks Brothers, pintail game, 1930's, boxed.................$65.00-150.00

MICKEY MOUSE PATRIOT CEREAL BOWL, Salem China, 1930's, Mickey and Pluto.......$25.00-65.00

MICKEY MOUSE PATRIOT CHINA BOXED SET, three pieces with display, rare...............$300.00-500.00

MICKEY MOUSE PATRIOT CHINA CUP, small, 2" with Mickey on front, 1930's...................$25.00-50.00

MICKEY MOUSE PENCIL BOX by Dixon, 1936, with Donald on cover...............................$20.00-40.00

MICKEY MOUSE PENCIL BOX by Dixon, 1936, with Minnie on cover.................................$25.00-50.00

MICKEY MOUSE PENCIL HOLDER, cardboard, by Dixon, die-cut, 1930's....................$100.00-200.00

MICKEY MOUSE PENCIL SHARPENER, Plastic Novelties, Mickey standing, 1930's.............$15.00-35.00

MICKEY MOUSE PENCIL TABLET, manufactured by Powers Paper, 1930's.........................$15.00-30.00

MICKEY MOUSE PIANO, 1930's, wood, with dancing figures, 10", Marks Brothers.......$900.00-1,700.00

MICKEY MOUSE PICTURE CARD ALBUM, 1930's, for bubble gum cards...........................$25.00-65.00

MICKEY MOUSE PICTURE PRINTING SET, Fulton, large set, red box...........................$100.00-150.00

MICKEY MOUSE PICTURE PUZZLES by Einson Freeman, 1930's, boxed set...................$100.00-200.00

MICKEY MOUSE PILLOW COVER NEEDLEPOINT, Mickey and Minnie in boat, 1930's...$25.00-60.00

MICKEY MOUSE PLANTER, Cowboy Mickey, manufactured ca. 1940's...............................$15.00-30.00

MICKEY MOUSE PLATE, Bavarian China, 1930's, gold rim, Mickey with tambourine.............$45.00-90.00

MICKEY MOUSE PLAYHOUSE, in envelope, 1934, cardboard, O. B. Andrews...................$100.00-200.00

MICKEY MOUSE POCKET COMB with sleeve, 1930's, American Hard Rubber......................$20.00-40.00

MICKEY MOUSE POCKET KNIFE, manufactured by Imperial Knife Company, 1930's........$20.00-40.00

MICKEY MOUSE POCKET WATCH BY INGERSOLL, in original box, 1930's.....................$250.00-550.00

MICKEY MOUSE POPCORN POPPER, 1930's, Empire Products, 1936.................................$50.00-95.00

MICKEY MOUSE POST TOASTIES BOX AD POSTER, large store display, rare.................$100.00-200.00

MICKEY MOUSE POST TOASTIES CEREAL BOX CUT-OUTS, 1930's, price each...................$8.00-15.00

MICKEY MOUSE POST TOASTIES CEREAL BOX, back sheet, uncut, price each $25.00-50.00

MICKEY MOUSE POST TOASTIES CEREAL BOX, complete and uncut.................................$50.00-85.00

MICKEY MOUSE PULL TOY, by N. N. Hill Brass, Double Mickeys pulled by Pluto $100.00-200.00

MICKEY MOUSE PULL TOY, upright figure, manufactured by N. N. Hill Brass, 1930's ...$75.00-125.00

MICKEY MOUSE PULLED BY HORACE HORSECOLLAR celluloid windup, 1930's $3,000.00-6,000.00

MICKEY MOUSE PULLED BY PLUTO, CELLULOID WINDUP, Japan, 1930's, rare $400.00-950.00

MICKEY MOUSE PUPPET, by Pelham, late 1960's, boxed $35.00-70.00

MICKEY MOUSE PUSH TOY, by Fisher Price, 1930's, 7" running Mickey $50.00-135.00

MICKEY MOUSE PUSH TOY, Fisher Price, Mickey running, 1930's, 6" long $50.00-85.00

MICKEY MOUSE QUOIT RING TOSS GAME by Spear, 1930's, Borgfeldt distributor $100.00-250.00

MICKEY MOUSE RACE CAR IN ORIGINAL BOX, 1930's, 4" long tin windup $100.00-225.00

MICKEY MOUSE RACING CAR, by Joseph Schneider, tin, windup in original box $75.00-150.00

MICKEY MOUSE RADIO BY EMERSON, white Bakelite version, 1930's $650.00-1,200.00

MICKEY MOUSE RECTANGULAR WRIST WATCH, 1930's, in original box $150.00-400.00

MICKEY MOUSE RID'EM STICK WITH WHEELS, George Borgfeldt, 1930's, rare $200.00-400.00

MICKEY MOUSE RIDING IN A CANOE, bisque figure, rare, 1930's......................................$100.00-300.00

MICKEY MOUSE RIDING TRICYCLE PULLING WAGON, celluloid and tin, 1930's $400.00-850.00

MICKEY MOUSE ROLATOY CELLULOID RATTLE, ca. 1930's, 3", W. D. $50.00-150.00

MICKY MOUSE ROLL'EM GAME, manufactured by Marks Brothers, 1930's, rare $150.00-350.00

MICKEY MOUSE ROLLER COASTER by J. Chein, 1950's, tin lithograph, windup $150.00-240.00

MICKEY MOUSE AND PLUTO PLATE BY PATRIOT CHINA, 1930's, 7", Walt Disney Enterprises, $40.00-80.00.

MICKEY MOUSE PARTY HORN by Marks Brothers, 1930's, $35.00-75.00. MICKEY MOUSE FISHER PRICE TOY, 1930's, $50.00-135.00.

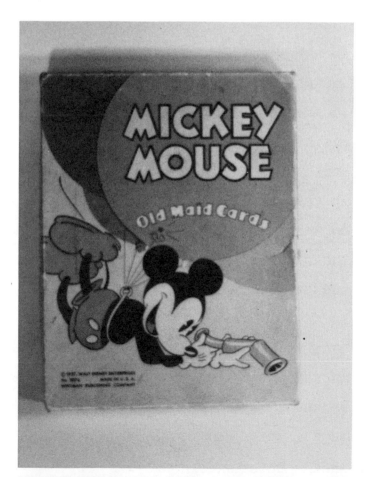

MICKEY MOUSE OLD MAID CARD GAME, c. Walt Disney Enterprises, 1937, by Whitman Publishing, $30.00-60.00.

MICKEY MOUSE PULL TOY BY N. N. HILL BRASS,
1930's, toy moves with bell-ring action in wheels,
$100.00-200.00.

MICKEY MOUSE RUBBER BALL, 1930's, Seiberling Latex Products $50.00-100.00

MICKEY MOUSE RUBBER FIGURE, 1930's, jointed, Seiberling, no box, 6" $65.00-125.00

MICKEY MOUSE RUBBER FIGURE, jointed, Seiberling Latex, original box $125.00-275.00

MICKEY MOUSE RUG, 1930's, early Mickey on roller skates pulled by Pluto $50.00-125.00

MICKEY MOUSE RUG, Pluto pulling Mickey, Alexander Smith and Sons, 1930's $50.00-100.00

MICKEY MOUSE RUNNING PULL TOY, N. N. Hill Brass, 1930's $75.00-150.00

MICKEY MOUSE SAFETY BLOCKS by Halsam, large set, thirty blocks, 1930's $50.00-100.00

MICKEY MOUSE SAFETY BLOCKS by Halsam, small set of fifteen blocks, 1935 ....$25.00-60.00

MICKEY MOUSE SAFETY FILM, 16 mm, 1930's Mickey on box $25.00-50.00

MICKEY MOUSE SALT, PEPPER AND SUGAR BOWL, early Disney, German, china, 3" $100.00-250.00

MICKEY MOUSE SAND PAIL, 1930's, 8", Mickey's Parade, Ohio Art $90.00-145.00

MICKEY MOUSE SAND PAIL, 3" Ohio Art, Mickey at a lemonade stand $45.00-95.00

MICKEY MOUSE SAND PAIL, 5", Ohio Art Enterprises Mickey on island, 1930's $50.00-85.00

MICKEY MOUSE SAND PAIL, 5", by Happynak of England, 1930's $45.00-95.00

MICKEY MOUSE AND SAND PAIL, 6", Ohio Art, 1930's, Mickey and Donald in boat $45.00-75.00

MICKEY MOUSE SAND PAIL, Golfing Mickey, 8", Ohio Art, W. D. Enterprises $65.00-105.00

MICKEY MOUSE SAND PAIL, manufactured by Ohio Art, 1930's, 6", "Mickey's Garden" ...$65.00-130.00

MICKEY MOUSE SAND SIFTER, manufactured by Ohio Art, 1930's, tin lithograph $55.00-90.00

MICKEY MOUSE SANTA PLANTER, manufactured by Leeds, 1940's $20.00-35.00

MICKEY MOUSE SAXOPHONE, made in Czechoslavakia, 16", 1930's, Mickey decal $100.00-200.00

MICKEY MOUSE SCHOOL TABLET, manufactured by Powers Paper, 1930's $15.00-30.00

MICKEY MOUSE SCISSORS, 1930's, with little Mickey on handle, metal $50.00-95.00

MICKEY MOUSE SCOOTER JOCKEY, 1949, MAVCO Inc., hard plastic windup, box...........$45.00-95.00

MICKEY MOUSE SCRAPBOOK, large, 1930's, Mickey and Minnie on cover $45.00-70.00

MICKEY MOUSE SEASIDE TIN PAIL, 4" under beach umbrella, Ohio Art, 1930's $45.00-75.00

MICKEY MOUSE SHEET MUSIC, "What! No Mickey Mouse?," 1930's $20.00-45.00

MICKEY MOUSE SHOOTING GAME, Marks Brothers, 1930's, rifle and targets $200.00-400.00

MICKEY MOUSE SILLY SYMPHONIES BOOK, 1930's, large, "Babes in the Woods" $65.00-130.00

MICKEY MOUSE SILLY SYMPHONY SOAP SET, 1930's, boxed, five characters, rare $100.00-250.00

MICKEY MOUSE SILVERPLATE BOWL in character box by International Silver, 1930's ..$75.00-150.00

MICKEY MOUSE SILVERPLATE CHILD'S DISH, 1930's, Mickey on horse $35.00-75.00

MICKEY MOUSE SILVERPLATE CUP, boxed, International Silver, 1934 ....$60.00-120.00

MICKEY MOUSE SILVERPLATE SET, child's, in original box, spoon and fork $120.00-200.00

MICKEY MOUSE SILVER SPOON, Mickey on handle, 1930's $10.00-25.00

MICKEY MOUSE SITTING, 2¾", manufactured ca. 1930's, bisque figure...................$65.00-125.00

MICKEY MOUSE SKI JUMP TARGET GAME, American Toy Works, boxed, 1930's $50.00-125.00

MICKEY MOUSE SKITTLE BALL GAME, boxed, 1930's, Marks Brothers $100.00-200.00

MICKEY MOUSE SLATE DANCER, by Distler, German, 1929, exceptionally rare $1,200.00-2,000.00

MICKEY MOUSE SMALL BASS DRUM, Mickey picture on paper head, 1930's $100.00-200.00

MICKEY MOUSE SMALL COMPOSITION FIGURE, 1930's, painted $50.00-85.00

MICKEY MOUSE SOAKY TOY, ca. 1960's, Colgate bubble bath container $5.00-15.00

MICKEY MOUSE SOAP FIGURES in original box 1930's, Lightfoot Schultz, 1935, rare $100.00-200.00

MICKEY MOUSE SOAP SET, 1930's, Mickey and World Globe, Lightfoot Schultz $75.00-125.00

MICKEY MOUSE SOAP, 10", 1930's, display card, full figure Mickey $75.00-125.00

MICKEY MOUSE SOLDIER TARGET SET, by Marks Brothers, 1930's, boxed..................$100.00-300.00

MICKEY MOUSE SPARKLER, tin, lever action, 1932, black and white, rare $65.00-125.00

MICKEY MOUSE SPEEDWAY CARS RACING SET, (boxed) 1936, 10 cars, rare $300.00-500.00

MICKEY MOUSE SPORT BINIOCULARS, 1940's, boxed, plastic $20.00-40.00

MICKEY MOUSE SQUEAK DOLL, manufactured by Sun Rubber Company $10.00-20.00

MICKEY MOUSE STEIFF VELVET DOLL, 7" tall, 1930's $300.00-500.00

MICKEY MOUSE STEIFF VELVET DOLL, 5" tall, manufactured ca. 1930's.....................$200.00-400.00

MICKEY MOUSE STEIFF VELVET DOLL, larger version 9" tall.....................$500.00-900.00

MICKEY MOUSE STENCIL SET, 1930's, manufactured by Spear, distributed by Borgfeldt.$150.00-225.00

MICKEY MOUSE STUFFED DOLL by Gund, 1950's, vinyl face.....................$20.00-40.00

MICKEY MOUSE STUFFED DOLL by Gund, ca. 1947, large size.....................$50.00-75.00

MICKEY MOUSE STUFFED DOLL, Knickerbocker 1935, dressed as cowboy.....................$200.00-500.00

MICKEY MOUSE SUGAR BOWL, 1930's, Patriot china, 3" tall.....................$25.00-60.00

MICKEY MOUSE SURPRISE STICKERS AND HEALTH CHART, 1930's.....................$20.00-40.00

MICKEY MOUSE SWEEPER, 1930's, Ohio Art, Mickey and Minnie at piano.....................$75.00-125.00

MICKEY MOUSE TALKIE JECTOR, by Movie Jector Company, 1935, with record.....................$125.00-275.00

MICKEY MOUSE TEA TRAY, 1930's, Ohio Art, 8" x 11", Mickey in cafe.....................$40.00-75.00

MICKEY MOUSE TV bank, ceramic, 1961.$10.00-15.00

MICKEY MOUSE TELEVISION CAR, 1950's, by Marx, in original box.....................$65.00-135.00

MICKEY MOUSE THE MUSICIAN, plastic and tin windup, Marx, 1950's.....................$65.00-150.00

MICKEY MOUSE TIE RACK, 1930's.....................$25.00-60.00

MICKEY MOUSE TIN CHARACTER TOP 10", George Borgfeldt, 1930's, orange.....................$45.00-110.00

MICKEY MOUSE TIN CHARACTER TOP, spins, 7", many 1930's Disney characters.....................$65.00-110.00

MICKEY MOUSE TIN CLARINET, 1930's, Mickey Mouse decal.....................$75.00-150.00

MICKEY MOUSE TIN CORNET, 1930's, Mickey decal, George Borgfeldt.....................$100.00-200.00

MICKEY MOUSE TIN PAIL, 6", buried treasure version, 1930's, Ohio Art.....................$50.00-95.00

MICKEY MOUSE TIN TOP, small 8" version, ca. 1930's, Disney characters.....................$50.00-80.00

MICKEY MOUSE TIN TROMBONE, Mickey Mouse decal, manufactured ca. 1930's,.....................$150.00-250.00

MICKEY MOUSE TIN WASH TUB, 6" x 2", Mickey and Minnie, by Ohio Art, 1930's.....................$45.00-75.00

MICKEY MOUSE TOFFEE TIN, manufactured by Sharp's, English tin.....................$200.00-400.00

MICKEY MOUSE TOOL CHEST, by Hamilton Metal Products, 1935.....................$35.00-75.00

MICKEY MOUSE TOOTHBRUSH ON ORIGINAL CARD, 1930's with Mickey decal.....................$20.00-50.00

MICKEY MOUSE TOOTHBRUSH HOLDER, 5", movable arm, pointed nose, 1930's, bisque.$125.00-250.00

MICKEY MOUSE TOOTHBRUSH, 1930's, on original card.....................$50.00-95.00

MICKEY MOUSE TOOTHPASTE, original tube and box, 1930's, Kent Dental Laboratory.$50.00-95.00

MICKEY MOUSE TOP, 10" version, many 1930's Disney characters.....................$50.00-75.00

MICKEY MOUSE TOY CHEST, ca. 1930's, cardboard lithograph.....................$75.00-150.00

MICKEY MOUSE TOY CHEST, 1939, by Odora Company, cardboard construction.....................$75.00-150.00

MICKEY MOUSE TOY LANTERN OUTFIT, Ensign Ltd., English, 1930's, boxed.....................$150.00-350.00

MICKEY MOUSE TRACTOR manufactured by Sun Rubber Company.....................$35.00-65.00

MICKEY MOUSE TRANSFER-O'S ALBUM, by Paas Dye Company, 1930's.....................$20.00-35.00

MICKEY MOUSE TRAP DRUM SET, Noble and Cooley, 1930's, three drums.....................$200.00-400.00

MICKEY MOUSE TRAPEZE CELLULOID WINDUP TOY, 1930's, boxed.....................$300.00-600.00

MICKEY MOUSE MECHANICAL RACING CAR in original box, 1930's, 4" long, Reynolds collection, $100.00-225.00.

MICKEY MOUSE AND PLUTO HARDCOVER BOOK, 1930's, $60.00-125.00. MICKEY MOUSE CREAMER, French, 1930's, Art Deco design, $100.00-200.00.

MICKEY MOUSE OHIO ART PAIL, 1930's, 3" tall, tin value, $50.00-100.00. MICKEY MOUSE OHIO ART PAIL, 1930's, 6" tall, tin, value 65.00-150.00.

MICKEY MOUSE TIN SAND PAIL by Ohio Art, 6", 1930's $75.00-200.00.

MICKEY MOUSE TREASURE CHEST LEATHERETTE BANK, 1930's $75.00-125.00

MICKEY MOUSE TRICYCLE (VELOCIPEDE), Colson Company, 1934 rare $200.00-500.00

MICKEY MOUSE TRIKETOY, Dean's Ragbook England, 1930's, very rare $600.00-1,400.00

MICKEY MOUSE TUMBLING TOY ACROBAT, squeeze wooden sticks, Marks, 1940's $10.00-20.00

MICKEY MOUSE TURNABOUT FIGURAL COOKIE JAR, Minnie on reverse, Leeds, 1947 .... $50.00-95.00

MICKEY MOUSE UMBRELLA, 1930's, Mickey on cloth, probably Japan $50.00-125.00

MICKEY MOUSE UMBRELLA, 1940's, Mickey head on handle, Louis Weiss $20.00-45.00

MICKEY MOUSE VELVET DOLL, 1930's, Charlotte Clark design, Borgfeldt, 6" $250.00-500.00

MICKEY MOUSE VELVET DOLL, Charlotte Clark design, 1930's, 11" $400.00-800.00

MICKEY MOUSE VELVET DOLL, early 1930's, Charlotte Clark design, 15" $850.00-1,200.00

MICKEY MOUSE WADDLE BOOK, 1930's, complete with waddle figures $300.00-500.00

MICKEY MOUSE WALKING CELLULOID FIGURE, fragile, 1930's, 3", arms at side $125.00-200.00

MICKEY MOUSE WALT DISNEY ANNUAL, Whitman, 1937 .... $35.00-65.00

MICKEY MOUSE WALT DISNEY'S TIDDLEY WINKS GAME, 1950's $10.00-20.00

MICKEY MOUSE WASH TUB, 1950's, large yellow, metal tub with various characters $10.00-25.00

MICKEY MOUSE WASTEBASKET, 1930's, large with various characters, tin $50.00-125.00

MICKEY MOUSE WATCH BOX (only) dated 1938, Mickey in top hat and cane $35.00-70.00

MICKEY MOUSE WATCH FOB, manufactured by Ingersoll, ca. 1930's $25.00-50.00

MICKEY MOUSE WATERING CAN by Ohio Art, Mickey plays saxophone, large $50.00-125.00

MICKEY MOUSE WATERING CAN, 3", tin, blue/black/white, early Mickey $45.00-95.00

MICKEY MOUSE WATERING CAN, Mickey with rooster, long spout, Ohio Art, 1930's $45.00-95.00

MICKEY MOUSE WATERING CAN, Ohio Art, 1930's, 6", Mickey plays a saxophone $50.00-100.00

MICKEY MOUSE WATERING CAN, Ohio Art, 1930's, Mickey in garden $35.00-75.00

MICKEY MOUSE WEATHER FORECASTER, 1940's, plastic, boxed $25.00-60.00

MICKEY MOUSE WEATHERHOUSE, 1940's, plastic child's barometer $25.00-45.00

MICKEY MOUSE WEEKLY MAGAZINE, single issue, English, 1930's $25.00-40.00

MICKEY MOUSE WHEELBARROW by Toy Kraft, 1930's, four wheels $35.00-80.00

MICKEY MOUSE WHITE SLATE DRAWING SET, Platt and Munk Company, 1930's $50.00-95.00

MICKEY MOUSE WINDUP TOY manufactured by Schuco, 1930's, 4" $200.00-400.00

MICKEY MOUSE WINDUP TRAPESE TOY BY GYM-TOYS, 1940's $60.00-125.00

MICKEY MOUSE WINDUP WALKER, ca. 1929, by Distler, German, rare $1,000.00-2,000.00

MICKEY MOUSE WOOD AND COMPOSITION DOLL, early 1930's, "lollipop" hands, 9" ... $400.00-650.00

MICKEY MOUSE WOOD COMPOSITION DOLL, early 1930's, "lollipop" hands, 7" $300.00-550.00

MICKEY MOUSE WOOD RADIO BY EMERSON, 1930's, wood-tone version $550.00-900.00

MICKEY MOUSE WOOD SLED, manufactured by Flexible Flyer, ca. 1930's $65.00-125.00

MICKEY MOUSE WOODEN CAR with wooden Mickey driver, Borgfeldt, 1930's, green $75.00-175.00

MICKEY MOUSE WOODEN PULL WAGON, Toy Kraft, 1935 ....$75.00-125.00

MICKEY MOUSE WOODEN WAGON by Toy Kraft, 1930's $100.00-200.00

MICKEY MOUSE XYLOPHONE PLAYER, Fisher Price, 12" tall, 1930's $50.00-125.00

MICKEY MOUSE YARN SEWING SET, by Marks Brothers, extremely colorful, 1930's $100.00-200.00

MICKEY MOUSE, AN ABC BOOK, 1930's, large color illustrations $50.00-85.00

MICKEY MOUSE, MINNIE MOUSE AND DONALD DUCK TOOTHBRUSH HOLDER, BISQUE FIGURES 1930's $75.00-195.00

MICKEY MOUSE, THE POP-UP BOOK, manufactured ca. 1930's $95.00-195.00

MICKEY MOUSE, THE POP-UP BOOK, Blue Ribbon Books, 1933 ....$100.00-225.00

MICKEY MOUSE, THE WALT DISNEY PAINT BOOK, large, 1930's, Mickey on cover $25.00-50.00

MICKEY'S AIR PILOT, Rubber plane by Sun Rubber Company $35.00-65.00

MINNIE MOUSE BISQUE FIGURE, 4½", Minnie with umbrella $35.00-75.00

MINNIE MOUSE BISQUE FIGURE, 1930's, 3" tall, hands on hips $25.00-40.00

MINNIE MOUSE BISQUE FIGURE, 1930's, Minnie sitting, 3" $30.00-60.00

MINNIE MOUSE BISQUE FIGURE, 3", with hands hips, 1930's $25.00-50.00

MINNIE MOUSE BISQUE FIGURE, 4", 1930's, wearing nightgown...$30.00-60.00

MINNIE MOUSE BISQUE FIGURE, 5", 1930's, two movable arms $75.00-150.00

MINNIE MOUSE BISQUE FIGURE, 5", 1930's, hands on hips $65.00-145.00

MINNIE MOUSE BISQUE FIGURE, 5", standing next to a garbage can $75.00-150.00

MICKEY MOUSE BISQUE FIGURE, Minnie dressed as nurse, 3", 1930's, rare $100.00-200.00

MINNIE MOUSE BISQUE PIN CUSHION, 1930's, Minnie pushes wheelbarrow, rare $150.00-300.00

MINNIE MOUSE CERAMIC FIGURE HOLDING A BROOM, American Pottery, 1947 ...$100.00-200.00

MINNIE MOUSE CERAMIC FIGURE, American Pottery with broom, 1940's...........................$75.00-145.00

MINNIE MOUSE CHARACTER PUPPET by Gund, 1960's boxed $10.00-35.00

MINNIE MOUSE COMB, 1930's, with sleeve, American Hard Rubber $20.00-40.00

MINNIE MOUSE CUP, 3", Patriot China, 1930's, Minnie with a mirror.....................................$20.00-45.00

MINNIE MOUSE CUP, china by Patriot China, 1930's, 2" Minnie on front $20.00-40.00

MINNIE MOUSE DOLL manufactured by Gund, 1940's, cloth face $50.00-100.00

MINNIE MOUSE DOLL BY LARS of Italy, ca. 1970's, 15" tall $150.00-300.00

MINNIE MOUSE DOLL manufactured by Knickerbocker, 1930's, cowgirl $300.00-600.00

MINNIE MOUSE DOORSTOP, ca. 1930's, 12" tall, wood, folk art...$25.00-45.00

MINNIE MOUSE FIGURAL ASH TRAY, china, Minnie sits on edge, 1930's, Japan $100.00-200.00

MICKEY MOUSE OHIO ART TEA SET in original box, 1930's, lithographed tin, $100.00-200.00.

MICKEY MOUSE BISQUE FIGURE, 6" tall, Japan, 1930's, $125.00-300.00. MICKEY MOUSE WOOD COMPOSITON AND SLATE ASH TRAY, 1930's, $75.00-150.00.

121

MICKEY AND MINNIE MOUSE TAMBOURINE, c. Walt Disney Enterprises, 1930's, $100.00-200.00.

MINNIE MOUSE FIGURAL SOAP, 1930's, D. H. & Company, boxed $35.00-70.00

MINNIE MOUSE FLAT LEAD FIGURE, 1930's, painted, from foundry set $10.00-25.00

MINNIE MOUSE FOLK ART FIGURE DOORSTOP, wood, 19330's, 14"..$45.00-75.00

MINNIE MOUSE FUN-E-FLEX FIGURE, 4", 1930's, wood jointed doll $50.00-125.00

MINNIE MOUSE HAND PUPPET manufactured by Gund, boxed, 1950's....................................$10.00-25.00

MINNIE MOUSE HULA DANCER VALENTINE, 1930's, W. D. Enterprises, mechanical...........$10.00-25.00

MINNIE MOUSE IN NIGHTSHIRT, bisque figure, 4" tall, 1930's...$45.00-85.00

MINNIE MOUSE MARIONETTE, 1930's, Madame Alexander, wood composition $100.00-250.00

MINNIE MOUSE MECHANICAL ROCKER, windup, in rocking chair, LineMar, box $300.00-600.00

MINNIE MOUSE NURSERY PICTURE, manufactured ca. 1940's $10.00-20.00

MINNIE MOUSE PAPER MASK, 1930's ..$20.00-35.00

MINNIE MOUSE PAPER MASK, manufactured ca. 1930's, Einson Freeman $25.00-55.00

MINNIE MOUSE PAPER PARTY HAT, manufactured ca. 1950's $5.00-10.00

MINNIE MOUSE PATRIOT CHINA CUP, small, 2" tall with Minnie, 1930's...........................$25.00-50.00

MINNIE MOUSE PUSHING FELIX THE CAT, tin windup, Spanish, 1929, rare $1,800.00-3,200.00

MINNIE MOUSE RUBBER BALL, Seiberling Latex Products, 1930's $50.00-100.00

MINNIE MOUSE SAUCER, Patriot China, 1930's, 5" diameter $20.00-40.00

MINNIE MOUSE SITTING, BISQUE, manufactured ca. 1930's, 2¾" tall $60.00-120.00

MINNIE MOUSE SMALL FRAMED PICTURE, manufactured c. 1930's $15.00-30.00

MINNIE MOUSE SQUEAK DOLL, Sun Rubber Company, 1950's $10.00-20.00

MINNIE MOUSE STUFFED DOLL, vinyl face, by Gund, 1950's $20.00-40.00

MINNIE MOUSE TOOTHBRUSH HOLDER, 5", movable arm, pointed nose, 1930's, bisque .$125.00-250.00

MINNIE MOUSE WASHING MACHINE, metal and plastic, windup, 1940's $35.00-65.00

MINNIE MOUSE WASHING MACHINE, Precision Specialties, 1950's, boxed $50.00-75.00

MINNIE MOUSE, THE POP-UP BOOK, printed ca. 1930's $75.00-150.00

PANCHITO THE ROOSTER, CLOTH DOLL by Lars of Italy, recent, but rare $200.00-400.00

PANCHITO THE ROOSTER, CERAMIC, 1940's, Evan K. Shaw $65.00-135.00

PANCHITO THE ROOSTER, TABLE LAMP, 1947, Railley Corporation, with shade $75.00-125.00

PECOS BILL, PLASTIC WINDUP COWBOY BY MARX, 1950's $25.00-60.00

PECULIAR PENGUINS BOOK, David McKay, c. Walt Disney, 1935 ....$30.00-50.00

PEGLEG PETE, CLOTH DOLL by Lars of Italy, recent but rare $100.00-300.00

PETER PAN COLORING BOOK, Whitman, 1950's, Peter as Indian chief on cover $10.00-20.00

PETER PAN FUN BOOK, 1950's, published by Whitman $10.00-20.00

PETER PAN PLANTER by Leeds, ca. 1950's, pastel colors, Peter by treasure $20.00-40.00

PETER PAN PUNCH-OUT BOOK, 1950's $20.00-40.00

PETER PIG SOAP, boxed set, Lightfoot Schultz Company, 1935 ....$30.00-65.00

PINOCCHIO ALARM CLOCK, metal case, by Bayard, French, 1960's $100.00-200.00

PINOCCHIO ALPINE HAT, 1940's, with feather and Pinocchio logo $20.00-40.00

PINOCCHIO AND CLEO THE GOLDFISH PULL TOY, N. N. Hill Brass, 1940 ....$75.00-150.00

PINOCCHIO AND FIGARO THE CAT PULL TOY, 1940, N. N. Hill Brass..............................$75.00-150.00

PINOCCHIO ART STAMP PICTURE SET, boxed rubber stamp set, 1939 ....$40.00-85.00

PINOCCHIO ASSORTED POST TOASTIES BOX CUTOUTS, price for each figure $5.00-10.00

PINOCCHIO BETTER LITTLE BOOK, 1940, Whitman, red cover $15.00-40.00

PINOCCHIO BISQUE FIGURE, 1939, 4" ...$25.0-50.00

PINOCCHIO BISQUE FIGURE, 1939, 6" .$50.00-100.00

PINOCCHIO BOOKENDS, Multi Products of Chicago, 1940, pair $100.00-200.00

PINOCCHIO BOXED PICTURE PUZZLES, 1939, set of two, attractive box $40.00-75.00

PINOCCHIO BREAD WRAPPER, ca. 1940's, complete wrapper $20.00-40.00

PINOCCHIO CELLULOID BABY RATTLE, manufactured 1940, by Amloid $50.00-85.00

PINOCCHIO CERAMIC FIGURE, manufactured by American Pottery, 1940's $70.00-125.00

PINOCCHIO CHARACTERS VALENTINE, mechanical, Pinocchio rides in coach $15.00-25.00

PINOCCHIO CIRCUS PUNCH-OUT PREMIUM SET, 1940's, paper $40.00-85.00

PINOCCHIO COMPOSITON BANK, Pinocchio rides a turtle, Crown Toy, 1939 ....$100.00-200.00

PINOCCHIO COMPOSITION FIGURE, 4", Multi Products, 1940 ....$20.00-40.00

PINOCCHIO COMPOSITION FIGURE, 5", Multi Products, 1940 ....$25.00-50.00

PINOCCHIO CUT-OUT PAPER DOLLS BOOK, Whitman, 1939, large format...............................$25.00-60.00

PINOCCHIO DRINKING GLASS, manufactured by Libbey, 1940...$10.00-20.00

PINOCCHIO FIGURAL BOXED SOAP, 1940, Lightfoot Schultz Company....................................$35.00-75.00

PINOCCHIO FIGURAL COMPOSITION BANK, Crown Toy, 5", colorful 1930's $40.00-100.00

PINOCCHIO FIGURAL PEN HOLDER, 7", wood composition, Multi Products, 1940 ....$50.00-125.00

PINOCCHIO FRAMED CHARACTER PRINTS, set of four, 1939, framed in wood $100.00-250.00

PINOCCHIO GOOD TEETH CERTIFICATE, 1939, colorful sheet $15.00-30.00

PINOCCHIO HAND PUPPET, Crown Toy, composition head, 1939, cloth body $20.00-45.00

PINOCCHIO HANKIES, boxed set, 1940 .$30.00-75.00

PINOCCHIO HARDCOVER BOOK, Random House, 1940, wood-like cover $20.00-45.00

PINOCCHIO JOINTED WOOD DOLL, by Ideal, 12" version with original label $100.00-200.00

PINOCCHIO LUNCH PAIL, 1940's, red and black, cylinder shape...$20.00-40.00

PINOCCHIO LUNCH PAIL, rectangular, 1940, red and black, tin $20.00-45.00

PINOCCHIO MEAL TIME BEETLEWARE PLASTIC DINNERWARE SET, 1940, original box ..$40.00-80.00

PINOCCHIO ON UNICYCLE PULLING A CART, pull toy by Fisher Price, 1930's $100.00-200.00

PINOCCHIO PAINT BOOK, Whitman, large version, 1939, paper cover $20.00-45.00

PINOCCHIO PAINT BOX, 1940's, Walt Disney Productions, tin paint set $10.00-25.00

PINOCCHIO PAPER MASK, Gillette premium, 1939...$10.00-25.00

PINOCCHIO PICTURE BOOK, 1939, GEPETTO ON COVER, die-cut top edge $40.00-65.00

PINOCCHIO PICTURE BOOK, stiff inside pages, 1939, Pinocchio with apple on cover $25.00-45.00

PINOCCHIO PITFALLS MARBLE GAME, 1940, boxed game $50.00-85.00

PINOCCHIO PLAYING CARD GAME, 1939, Whitman, Jiminy Cricket on box lid $25.00-50.00

PINOCCHIO RING THE NOSE GAME, hand-held, 1940, wood and paper lithograph $30.00-60.00

PINOCCHIO RUBBER BALL, inflated, Seiberling Latex, Akron, 1940.......................................$20.00-45.00

PINOCCHIO RUBBER FIGURE, Seiberling Latex, 1940, 5", squeaks $30.00-75.00

PINOCCHIO SCHOOL TABLET, 1940, paper, Pinocchio with Stromboli $15.00-35.00

PINOCCHIO SCHOOL TABLET, 1940, pictures Pinocchio with Gepetto $15.00-35.00

PINOCCHIO SCRAP BOOK, manufactured by Whitman, 1939, very large size $30.00-65.00

PINOCCHIO SERIES DECALOMANIA SET, eight figures, 1940 ....$25.00-40.00

PINOCCHIO SNAP CLICKER, 1940, tin ..$10.00-20.00

PINOCCHIO SNAP TOGETHER SET, by Knapp of Indianapolis, 1940 ....$25.00-60.00

PINOCCHIO THE ACROBAT tin windup rocking toy by Marx, 1939 ....$200.00-375.00

PINOCCHIO THE MERRY PUPPET GAME, by Milton Bradley, 1939, boxed $40.00-90.00

PINOCCHIO THERMOMETER, by Bakelite, ca. 1940 ....$50.00-75.00

PINOCCHIO TIN WINDUP WALKER TOY, 1939, by Louis Marx, 10" $125.00-200.00

PINOCCHIO WOOD COMPOSITION AND JOINTED DOLL by Ideal, giant version $300.00-750.00

MICKEY AND MINNIE MOUSE BISQUE TOOTHBRUSH HOLDER FIGURES WITH A JOINTED ARM, 1930's, 5", $125.00-325.00.

MICKEY MOUSE WATERING CAN, Ohio Art Walt Disney Ent., 1930's, tin, lithograph, $35.00-70.00.

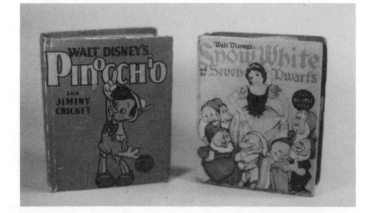

PINOCCHIO BETTER LITTLE BOOK, colorful cover, 1940, Whitman, $15.00-40.00. **SNOW WHITE AND THE SEVEN DWARFS BIG LITTLE BOOK**, Whitman, 1938, $20.00-40.00.

PINOCCHIO WOOD COMPOSITION BANK by Crown Toy and Novelty, 1939, $70.00-120.00. **PINOCCHIO PAPERBACK BOOK**, 1939, $20.00-40.00.

PINNOCHIO WOOD COMPOSITION DOLL BY CROWN TOY, 1939, 10" version $60.00-140.00

PINOCCHIO WOOD COMPOSITION DOLL, original box, Ideal Toy, 1940, 12" $150.00-300.00

PINOCCHIO WOOD COMPOSITION DOLL by Knickerbocker, 14", 1939 .... $100.00-250.00

PINOCCHIO WOOD COMPOSITION WINDUP WALKER, large, 1939, version $200.00-400.00

PINOCCHIO WOOD JOINTED AND CLOTH DOLL by Krueger, 1940 .... $100.00-250.00

PINOCCHIO WOOD JOINTED DOLL by Ideal Toy, 1939, 8" version $75.00-125.00

PINOCCHIO'S CHRISTMAS PARTY, Christmas toy store premium give-away $10.00-25.00

PINOCCHIO, HARDCOVER BOOK, Walt Disney's "Pinocchio," 1940 .... $20.00-45.00

PINOCCHIO, PIN THE NOSE ON PINOCCHIO GAME, 1939, Parker Brothers $50.00-125.00

PINOCCHIO CUT-OUT BOOK, Walt Disney, (if complete) $50.00-150.00

PLUTO ACROBAT TOY, LineMar, 1950's, metal and celluloid, boxed $125.00-250.00

PLUTO ALARM CLOCK by Bayard, French, 1960's $100.00-200.00

PLUTO AMERICAN POTTERY FIGURE, 1940's, ceramic, 6", original label $100.00-200.00

PLUTO BANK, ceramic figural by Leeds, 1940's, yellow/black $20.00-40.00

PLUTO CERAMIC CREAMER, small 2" version, Patriot China $20.00-40.00

PLUTO CERAMIC CUP, made by Patriot, China, 1930's $25.00-55.00

PLUTO CLOTH DOLL by Lars of Italy, recent but rare $100.00-200.00

PLUTO COLORING BOOK, Walt Disney's, Whitman, 1960's $5.00-10.00

PLUTO COMICS TALL COMIC BOOK, hardcover, 1930's, "Mickey's Dog" $20.00-40.00

PLUTO FIGURINE, American Pottery, 1940's, 6" seated $50.00-110.00

PLUTO HAND PUPPET by Gund, 1960's, boxed $10.00-30.00

PLUTO HARD RUBBER FIGURE, 1930's Seiberling, 6", red $40.00-90.00

PLUTO LANTERN by LineMar, 1950's, c. Walt Disney Productions $50.00-120.00

PLUTO MECHANICAL VALENTINE, W. D. Enterprises, 1930's $10.00-30.00

PLUTO MECHANICAL WINDUP TOY, plastic, by Marx, large version, Pluto in hat $100.00-175.00

PLUTO MODELED IN SOAP, 1930's, Lightfoot Schultz, colorful box $45.00-80.00

PLUTO PLASTIC FRICTION TOY by Marx, 1950's, Pluto's nose to ground, 6" $35.00-90.00

PLUTO PLUSH TOY by Gund, 1940's wears studded collar, yellow plush $50.00-120.00

PLUTO PULL TOY by Fisher Price, 1930's, 6" long, cylinder wheels $50.00-125.00

PLUTO PULLING A CART CERAMIC PLANTER by Leeds, 1940's $20.00-40.00

PLUTO PULLING CART TIN FRICTION TOY, by Line Mar, 9" long $100.00-225.00

PLUTO ROLLING LEVER ACTION TOY, Marx, 1930's, push tail action, tin $50.00-125.00

PLUTO RUBBER FIGURE, large 7" version, 1930's, Seiberling Latex Products $50.00-95.00

PLUTO SALT AND PEPPER SHAKERS, 1940's, by Leeds, ceramic $10.00-30.00

PLUTO SNIFFING GROUND, ceramic figure by Brayton's Laguna Pottery, 1940's $50.00-125.00

PLUTO SOAP BOXED SET, 1930's, three Plutos, Lightfoot Schultz Company $50.00-125.00

PLUTO SQUEAK TOY, Sun Rubber Company, 1949 .... $15.00-25.00

PLUTO STRING PUPPET, boxed, 1950's . $20.00-40.00

PLUTO SUNOCO INK BLOTTER, 1940's . $10.00-20.00

PLUTO THE PUP BISQUE FIGURE, 1930's, Japan, orange, Walt E. Disney, 3" $25.00-50.00

PLUTO THE PUP DRINKING GLASS manufactured by Libbey, 1938 .... $10.00-25.00

PLUTO THE PUP FUN-E-FLEX FIGURE, 1930's, wood and wire jointed, 4" $45.00-100.00

PLUTO THE PUP INFLATABLE DOLL, 1936, Seiberling Latex, 1936 .... $75.00-150.00

PLUTO THE PUP PUPPET manufactured by Fisher Price, 1930's $10.00-25.00

PLUTO THE PUP STUFFED DOLL, 1930's, large 12" with collar, plush $100.00-200.00

PLUTO WATCH ME ROLLOVER WINDUP BY MARX dated 1939 W.D. Enterprises $50.00-125.00

PLUTO WINDUP TOY, 6" tall, manufactured by Line-Mar, 1950's $100.00-275.00

PLUTO, CROUCHING FRICTION TOY, 4", manufactured by LineMar $65.00-130.00

PLUTO, ROLLOVER, windup toy by Marx, tin lithograph with original box $125.00-230.00

PLUTO, WALT DISNEY'S MAGIC SLATE, 5", cardboard $20.00-35.00

POLLYANA PAPER DOLL, 1960's $10.00-20.00

PONGO THE PUP CERAMIC FIGURE, 1961, from "101 Dalmations" $5.00-15.00

PRINCE (FROM SNOW WHITE) MARIONETTE, 1930's, Alexander Doll Company $100.00-200.00

RED RIDING HOOD, Walt Disney's Own Game, 1930's, boxed game set $35.00 60.00

ROBBER KITTEN STORYBOOK, Walt Disney, 1938, published by Whitman $15.00-30.00

SILLY SYMPHONY LIGHTS BY NOMA, boxed Christmas light set with globes $100.00-200.00

SILLY SYMPHONIES POP-UP BOOK, Mickey Mouse, 1930's, rare $100.00-200.00

SLEEPING BEAUTY FRAME TRAY PUZZLE, 1959, published by Whitman $5.00-10.00

SLEEPING BEAUTY PAPER DOLLS BOOK, Whitman, 1959 .... $10.00-25.00

SLEEPY THE DWARF by Knickerbocker, 1930's, large 15" size, all cloth $100.00-175.00

SLEEPY THE DWARF DOLL by Knickerbocker, 1930's, large 15" size, with tag $100.00-175.00

SLEEPY THE DWARF DRINKING GLASS, by Libbey, 1938 .... $10.00-20.00

SLEEPY THE DWARF MARIONETTE, by Alexander Doll Company, 1930's $50.00-125.00

SLEEPY THE DWARF MARIONETTE, wood composition, Alexander Doll Co., 1930's $50.00-125.00

SLEEPY THE DWARF RUBBER TOY, c. 1930's, Seiberling Latex, 5" $20.00-50.00

SNEEZY THE DWARF DRINKING GLASS manufactured by Libbey, 1938 .... $10.00-20.00

SNEEZY THE DWARF RUBBER FIGURE, Seiberling Latex, 1930's, Akron, Ohio, 5" $20.00-50.00

SNOW WHITE AND THE SEVEN DWARFS, neckties, boxed, 1937, set of four $40.00-120.00

SNOW WHITE AND DOPEY TELEPHONE, 1930's, N. N. Hill Brass $75.00-145.00

SNOW WHITE AND THE PRINCE AT THE WISHING WELL, English post card, 1930's $10.00-30.00

SNOW WHITE AND THE PRINCE, English post card, 1930's $15.00-35.00

SNOW WHITE AND THE PRINCE PULL TOY, N. N. Hill Brass, 1930's, very rare $125.00-250.00

SNOW WHITE AND THE SEVEN DWARFS ALARM CLOCK by Bayard, French, 1960's $100.00-200.00

PINOCCHIO WOOD JOINTED DOLL BY IDEAL TOY AND NOVELTY, 1940, 8", $75.00-150.00.

PINOCCHIO RIDING DONKEY PULL TOY BY FISHER PRICE, 1939, bell ringing action, $50.00-135.00.

PINOCCHIO WOOD COMPOSITION FIGURE by Multi Products of Chicago, 1940, 7" tall, $50.00-120.00. JIMINY CRICKET WOOD COMPOSITION FIGURE by Multi Products, 4", $25.00-60.00.

PINOCCHIO WOOD FIGURES, c. 1940 by Multi Products of Chicago, $20.00-65.00.

SNOW WHITE AND THE SEVEN DWARFS ALUMINUM TEA SET, original 1930's box, set $100.00-200.00
SNOW WHITE AND THE SEVEN DWARFS ART STAMP RUBBER STAMP SET, 1937, boxed . $45.00-90.00
SNOW WHITE AND THE SEVEN DWARFS baby rattle on stick with celluloid top $100.00-200.00
SNOW WHITE AND THE SEVEN DWARFS BABY RATTLE, ring handle with celluloid $50.00-125.00

SNOW WHITE AND THE SEVEN DWARFS BAKELITE NAPKIN RING, 1938 .... $20.00-50.00
SNOW WHITE AND THE SEVEN DWARFS BIG LITTLE BOOK, Whitman, 1938 .... $20.00-40.00
SNOW WHITE AND THE SEVEN DWARFS BOOK, "Animals," large format, 1930's $20.00-40.00
SNOW WHITE AND THE SEVEN DWARFS BOXED CHINA TEA SET, 9 pieces, 1937 .... $75.00-175.00
SNOW WHITE AND THE SEVEN DWARFS RUBBER FIGURES, Seiberling, all 8 boxed ... $200.00-500.00
SNOW WHITE AND THE SEVEN DWARFS SAFETY BLOCKS, Halsam, 1930's, 32 pieces, boxed $50.00-125.00
SNOW WHITE AND THE SEVEN DWARFS CAST IRON FIGURES by Lincoln Logs, 1930's, (set) $125.00-250.00
SNOW WHITE AND THE SEVEN DWARFS COMPLETE BISQUE SET, dwarfs, 5", Snow White, 7" $300.00-750.00
SNOW WHITE AND THE SEVEN DWARFS CUT-OUT DOLLS AND DRESSES, book, 1937 . $40.00-80.00
SNOW WHITE AND THE SEVEN DWARFS CUT-OUT BOOK, Whitman, 1938, rare $75.00-150.00
SNOW WHITE AND THE SEVEN DWARFS DRAWING TABLET, paper, 1937 .... $20.00-40.00
SNOW WHITE AND THE SEVEN DWARFS EMERSON RADIO, 1938, wood case, colorful . $500.00-1000.00
SNOW WHITE AND THE SEVEN DWARFS FIGURES by Goebel, complete 1950's set $300.00-500.00
SNOW WHITE AND THE SEVEN DWARFS, flat rubber die-cut figures, boxed,1930's $100.00-200.00
SNOW WHITE AND THE SEVEN DWARFS GAME, Milton Bradley, 1938 boxed game $30.00-75.00
SNOW WHITE AND THE SEVEN DWARFS GAME, Parker Brothers, 1938 .... $50.00-125.00
SNOW WHITE AND THE SEVEN DWARFS GAME, Tek Toothpaste premium, 1930's $50.00-100.00
SNOW WHITE AND THE SEVEN DWARFS HANDKER-CHIEFS, boxed set of 8, 1930's $100.00-200.00
SNOW WHITE AND THE SEVEN DWARFS LINEN-LIKE BOOK, yellow cover $20.00-45.00
SNOW WHITE AND THE SEVEN DWARFS LUNCH-BOX, 1930's, red/black/white $20.00-40.00
SNOW WHITE AND THE SEVEN DWARFS Magic Lantern Slides, boxed, set complete $50.00-100.00
SNOW WHITE AND THE SEVEN DWARFS MECHANICAL VALENTINE, 1939, heart shaped $10.00-22.00
SNOW WHITE AND THE SEVEN DWARFS MIRROR, for vanity set, logo on reverse $35.00-60.00
SNOW WHITE AND THE SEVEN DWARFS PAINT BOOK, 1938, giant format $30.00-70.00
SNOW WHITE AND THE SEVEN DWARFS PAINT BOOK, 1938, Whitman, horizontal $20.00-45.00
SNOW WHITE AND THE SEVEN DWARFS PAPER DOLL SET, boxed version, 1938 ..... $50.00-100.00
SNOW WHITE AND THE SEVEN DWARFS PAPER DOLLS, Whitman, book, 1938 .... $30.00-75.00
SNOW WHITE AND THE SEVEN DWARFS PIANO, Marks Brothers, 1938, rare $400.00-1,200.00
SNOW WHITE AND THE SEVEN DWARFS PICTURE PUZZLES, two in box, Whitman, 1938 .... $50.00-125.00

SNOW WHITE AND THE SEVEN DWARFS PICTURE, wash trough scene, 1938, framed $30.00-65.00

SNOW WHITE AND THE SEVEN DWARFS PLASTER CASTER SET, original box, 1930's .$50.00-125.00

SNOW WHITE AND THE SEVEN DWARFS POST TOASTIE CEREAL BOX CUT-OUTS, each $5.00-10.00

SNOW WHITE AND THE SEVEN DWARFS SAFETY BLOCKS by Halsam, 1930's, set of nine $25.00-60.00

SNOW WHITE AND THE SEVEN DWARFS SAND PAIL, 9" version, Ohio Art $35.00-90.00

SNOW WHITE AND THE SEVEN DWARFS SCRAPBOOK, large format, poster-type cover $50.00-125.00

SNOW WHITE AND THE SEVEN DWARFS SOAPS, book version, eight pieces, 1938 .....$50.00-125.00

SNOW WHITE AND THE SEVEN DWARFS SPOON AND FORK SET, manufactured by International Silver $50.00-100.00

SNOW WHITE AND THE SEVEN DWARFS TAP-AWAY SET, craft set, 1930's $50.00-85.00

SNOW WHITE AND THE SEVEN DWARFS TARGET GAME, boxed, 1930's, targets slide .$75.00-150.00

SNOW WHITE AND THE SEVEN DWARFS TIN SAND PAIL, Ohio Art, 5" tall $35.00-70.00

SNOW WHITE AND THE SEVEN DWARFS TOY BOX ON WHEELS, 1960's version $20.00-35.00

SNOW WHITE AND THE SEVEN DWARFS TREASURE CHEST TOY BOX, 1930's, cardboard $65.00-140.00

SNOW WHITE AND THE SEVEN DWARFS WASHING MACHINE, 1940's, plastic windup $25.00-75.00

SNOW WHITE AND THE SEVEN DWARFS WATERING CAN, 5", Ohio Art, 1930's $50.00-95.00

SNOW WHITE AT THE WISHING WELL NITE LIGHT, La Mode Studios, 1930's $100.00-200.00

SNOW WHITE BABY PANTS, rubber, boxed in bright lithograph, box, 1930's $50.00-85.00

SNOW WHITE BABY RATTLE, celluloid, cylinder on stick, Lodi, 1938 ....$100.00 200.00

SNOW WHITE BOOKENDS, (pair) 1930's, La Mode Studios $100.00-200.00

SNOW WHITE CERAMIC TOOTHPICK HOLDER, English, S. Maw and Sons, 1930's $125.00-250.00

SNOW WHITE CHARACTER COMB, 1938 with original decals $10.00-30.00

SNOW WHITE CHARACTER LAMP, 1930's, by La Mode Studios, with original shade.$100.00-200.00

SNOW WHITE COMPOSITON DOLL by Knickerbocker, 1937, jointed arms, 12" $100.00-250.00

SNOW WHITE DAIRY RECIPES BOOK, premium, 1940's, American Dairy Association ...$10.00-15.00

SNOW WHITE DOLL, cloth and linen with character decorated dress, 1930's $100.00-225.00

SNOW WHITE DRINKING GLASS, by Libbey, 1938 ....$10.00-25.00

SNOW WHITE FIGURAL WATCH STAND with 1960's watch $20.00-45.00

SNOW WHITE FLOUR SACK, circa 1950, common $5.00-10.00

SNOW WHITE HAIR BARRETTE, 1938, with decal $20.00-35.00

SNOW WHITE HANKY, 1930's, pink $10.00-20.00

SNOW WHITE JINGLE BOOK, circa 1930, complete $30.00-60.00

SNOW WHITE MARIONETTE, 1930's, wood composition, by Alexander Doll Company ..$125.00-200.00

SNOW WHITE MEALTIME BEETLEWARE SET, original box, 1938, three pieces $50.00-100.00

SNOW WHITE METAL FIGURAL CHILD'S PIN, Brier Manufacturing, 1938 ....$10.00-35.00

SNOW WHITE METAL SERVING TRAY, 1930's, red/black/white $20.00-65.00

SNOW WHITE MOVING PICTURE MACHINE, premium paper piece, 1930's $35.00-100.00

SNOW WHITE NITE LITE by La Mode Studios, 1930's $50.00-125.00

SNOW WHITE PAPER MASK, Gillette premium, 1939 ....$10.00-25.00

SNOW WHITE PENCIL SHARPENER, rectangular, Bakelite, 1938 with decal.......................$15.00-35.00

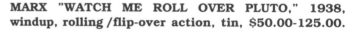

MARX "WATCH ME ROLL OVER PLUTO," 1938, windup, rolling /flip-over action, tin, $50.00-125.00.

PINOCCHIO WINDUP by Marx, 1939, $150.00-275.00.
DOPEY WINDUP by Marx, 1938, $150.00-275.00.

PINOCCHIO WOOD COMPOSITION DOLL by Crown Toy and Novelty, 1930's with jointed arms, $50.00-125.00. JIMINY CRICKET wood composition bank, 1930's, by Crown Toy, $50.00-100.00.

SNOW WHITE PULLED BY DOC AND DOPEY PULL TOY, 1938, N. N. Hill Brass $75.00-195.00

SNOW WHITE REFRIGERATOR by Wolverine, 1960's $10.00-20.00

SNOW WHITE RUBBER TOY, jointed arms and head, Seiberling, 1930's..........................$100.00-250.00

SNOW WHITE SERIES TINKERSAND PICTURES, boxed, 1938, W. D. Enterprises.........$60.00-95.00

SNOW WHITE SILVER CUP, 1938, Cartier fine jewelers, extremely rare $200.00-450.00

SNOW WHITE SINK manufactured by Wolverine, 1960's $10.00-20.00

SNOW WHITE SOAKY TOY, Colgate Soap container, 1960's $5.00-10.00

SNOW WHITE STOVE manufactured by Wolverine, 1960's $10.00-20.00

SNOW WHITE SUNSHINE BEVERAGE BOTTLE, 1938, rare $35.00-75.00

SNOW WHITE TELEPHONE, 1930's, N. N. Hill Brass..$65.00-125.00

SNOW WHITE WISHING WELL CERAMIC BANK, 1960's, Enesco....................................$10.00-20.00

THREE LITTLE PIGS ART STAMP PICTURE SET, 1930's, Who's Afraid.....Wolf? $35.00-80.00

THREE LITTLE PIGS BISQUE TOOTHBRUSH HOLDER, 1930's, Pigs building a wall.............$50.00-100.00

THREE LITTLE PIGS BISQUE TOOTHBRUSH HOLDER, 1930's, Pigs standing $40.00-80.00

THREE LITTLE PIGS BOWL, Patriot China, 1930's $20.00-50.00

THREE LITTLE PIGS RUBBER FIGURES, Seiberling Latex, 1930's, set of three, boxed ..$200.00-400.00

THREE LITTLE PIGS CELLULOID WINDUP TRAPEZE TOY, 1930's, three figures $100.00-250.00

THREE LITTLE PIGS COMPOSITION BOOK, 1930's, paper, Big Bad Wolf on cover $20.00-40.00

THREE LITTLE PIGS FLASHLIGHT, 1936, Electric Manufacturing Corporation $50.00-100.00

THREE LITTLE PIGS FRAMED PRINT, 1930's, color, 11" x 14"...$20.00-45.00

THREE LITTLE PIGS JIGSAW PICTURE PUZZLES, Jaymar, 1940's $10.00-20.00

THREE LITTLE PIGS PAPER MASK, 1930's, premium..$10.00-25.00

THREE LITTLE PIGS PENCIL TABLET, 1935, paper cover $20.00-35.00

THREE LITTLE PIGS PLATE, Patriot China, 1930's $15.00-40.00

THREE LITTLE PIGS PLAYING CARD SET, boxed, 1930's $15.00-35.00

THREE LITTLE PIGS PLUSH DOLLS, set of three, 1930's, Knickerbocker Toy.............$150.00-300.00

THREE LITTLE PIGS SILLY SYMPHONY CUT-OUT BOOK, 1930's $50.00-125.00

THREE LITTLE PIGS SILLY SYMPHONY ILLUSTRATED BOOK, 1930's..................................$40.00-80.00

THREE LITTLE PIGS SPOON AND FORK SET, International Silver, 1934 ....$35.00-70.00

THREE LITTLE PIGS WASH TUB by Ohio Art, tin lithograph, with miniature washboard.$30.00-65.00

THREE LITTLE PIGS, DRUMMER PIG WINDUP. Schuco, German, 1930's $100.00-200.00

THREE LITTLE PIGS, FIDDLER PIG WINDUP by Schuco, German, 1930's $100.00-200.00

THREE LITTLE PIGS, FIFER PIG WINDUP by Schuco, 1930's 4"...$100.00-200.00

THREE LITTLE PIGS, WHO'S AFRAID OF THE BIG BAD WOLF GAME, 1930's, Disney .$50.00-100.00

THREE LITTLE PIGS, FIFER PIG CUP, Patriot China, 1935 ....$20.00-35.00

THREE ORPHAN KITTENS BOOK, David McKay, 1936 ....$15.00-30.00

THUMPER AND THE SEVEN DWARFS, Big Little Book, 1940's $15.00-30.00

THUMPER STORYBOOK, Grosset and Dunlap, 1947, c. Walt Disney $10.00-30.00

THUMPER THE RABBIT, SQUEAK TOY, (Bambi), Sun Rubber Company, 1949 ....$5.00-15.00

THUMPER THE RABBIT, American Pottery Figure, 4", 1940's $20.00-60.00

THUMPER THE RABBIT PULL TOY by Fisher Price, 1930's $70.00-125.00

THUMPER'S GIRLFRIEND American Pottery Figure, 1940's, 4" $15.00-50.00

TINKER BELLS, Walt Disney Productions, figural xylophone set, 1950's $100.00-200.00

TOBY TORTOISE AND THE HARE, storybook, Whitman, 1938..$10.00-30.00

TORTOISE AND THE HARE BOOK, David McKay, 1936..$20.00-40.00

UNCLE REMUS ZIP GAME, boxed bagatelle type game, 1940's $20.00-45.00

UNCLE SCROOGE BANK, ceramic, 1961, Scrooge in bed reclining $10.00-20.00

UNCLE SCROOGE DOLL manufactured by Lars of
Italy, recent but rare......................$150.00-300.00
WALT DISNEY CHARACTERS EMBROIDERY SET,
1930's, boxed, very colorful $50.00-100.00
WALT DISNEY SKI JUMP TARGET GAME, 1930's,
boxed, American Toy Works.............$60.00-140.00
WALT DISNEY'S GAME PARADE, boxed game set,
American Toy Works, 1930's..............$50.00-95.00
WICKED QUEEN MARIONETTE (FROM SNOW WHITE),
1930's Alexander Doll Company $100.00-200.00
WICKED WITCH (FROM SNOW WHITE) MARIONETTE,
Alexander Doll Company, 1930's ...$125.00-250.00

DOPEY, AMERICAN POTTERY, glazed ceramic figure,
6", $100.00-175.00.

WALT DISNEY'S STORY OF CLARABELLE COW, small
format, hardcover book, 1930's, $15.00-30.00.

SNOW WHITE CERAMIC BANK by Leeds China,
1940's, $15.00-40.00. PETER PAN CERAMIC
PLANTER by Leeds, 1940's, $10.00-30.00.

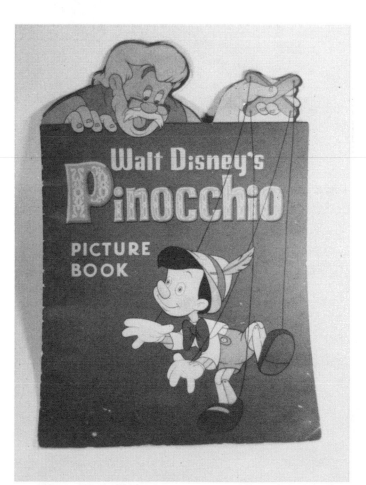

PINOCCHIO PICTURE BOOK, c. Walt Disney 1939 by
Whitman with die-cut top edge, color illustrations
inside, $35.00-80.00.

WALT DISNEY ENTERPRISES, MICKEY AND MINNIE MOUSE SERVING TRAY from a 1930's Ohio Art set, $25.00-60.00.

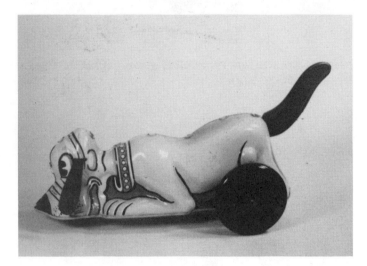

MARX TIN PLUTO TOY, 1938, push down tail action drives dog forward, $50.00-125.00.

BISQUE SNOW WHITE AND DWARF FIGURES, 1930's, Japan, dwarfs are all 5", $40.00-85.00.

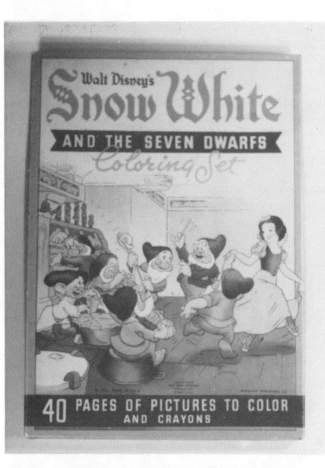

SNOW WHITE AND THE SEVEN DWARFS, boxed coloring set, Walt Disney Enterprises, 1930's, Whitman, $30.00-65.00.

SNOW WHITE SAND PAIL, OHIO ART, 1938, pictures Snow White and seven dwarfs, 5", $25.00-60.00.

GAMES AND PUZZLES

Toys presented in this section are all related by function; parlor games, board and table games and puzzles. They cover the range of paper and cardboard game production from the 1870's to the recent modern collectible games of the 1960's, ninety years of simple home entertainment.

By far the most frequently listed type of game is the board game. These games utilized a fold-out or jointed board which was usually twice the size of the game box when fully extended. Inside were usually packed the instructions (either a booklet or printed on the inside of the cover lid), some means of advancing the game (dice or spinners) and the playing tokens. Some games also utilized card sets as a part of the action of the game.

Antique game collecting is highly popular among today's collectors. The lithography of the old Parker Brothers and McLoughlin Brothers games from the turn of the century and beyond is often superb. Original game boxes are often as beautiful or even more spectacular than the contents inside. One collector who contributed items for the photos in this book takes great pride in his game displays and rightly so. For every game he purchases, he has the game box, playing board and all playing pieces mounted in a rich looking shadow box frame display. As visitors walk into the game hall in his home, they are treated to a true feast for the eyes. Antique games *are* beautiful old toys!

Collectors should take inventory of a game before purchasing it. The first place to look for all contents of the game is the instructions printed inside the box lid or the enclosed instruction booklet. You should find a brief inventory of all the items needed to play the game. Match that list with what's in the box and it is easy to see if the game is complete. Tokens and playing pieces are important and complete games with all pieces are certainly more valuable than incomplete versions, but the most important elements of an antique game are the box and the game board. Both should be structurally sound, relatively clean, and free of water damage.

Puzzles are included in this category because they were generally treated as a game by the original owners and many game collectors of today also collect antique puzzles. Puzzle boxes are often as beautiful (or more so) than the puzzle contained inside because the box lid is not dissected like the picture inside on the puzzle. But collecting puzzles as a specialty or investment is something near to a mathematician's nightmare, since the nitty gritty process of counting all the pieces in the box is usually inevitable. Certainly the *best* way to purchase an antique puzzle is with the item fully assembled in front of you. The empty box is then placed alongside the assembled puzzle. This display arrangement allows the collector to see the whole thing, not only how beautiful it looks but also that it is complete. If a puzzle is unassembled in the box, even counting the pieces doesn't insure that all the *correct* pieces are there. A collector may find that he has four hundred pieces that are supposed to be in the box, after he has spent twenty minutes counting them, only to be horrified when he gets home that ten or twenty of the pieces are from some other puzzle.

This problem is not a reflection of the toy dealer. Usually it stems from the fact that puzzle boxes were often stored in other boxes and in the shuffle, lids fall open and pieces get mixed. If the collector can be patient and buy puzzles which are assembled, his collection will be better off in the long run.

The items presented in this list cause us to reflect back upon a time when evening life was tranquil. With no television, VCR's, video games, or home computers, the exiting way to spend an evening with the children or a loved one was to gather in the drawing room and play a parlour game until bedtime. Those quiet days are gone, but the games and puzzles remain behind as reminders of the days when family members actually paid attention to one another at night.

BUSTER BROWN AT THE CIRCUS BOXED CARD GAME, 1900's, Reynolds collection, $75.00-135.00.

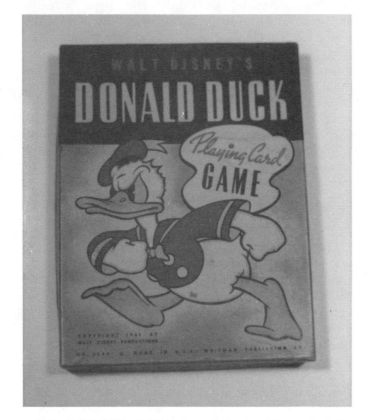

WALT DISNEY'S DONALD DUCK PLAYING CARDS, 1941, Whitman, $30.00-55.00.

A PEEP AT THE CIRCUS PICTURE PUZZLE, 1887, boxed, McLoughlin Brothers $100.00-250.00

ACROSS THE CONTINENT, A GAME OF TRAVELS, Parker Brothers, 1892 ....$100.00-300.00

ACROSS THE SEA BOXED BOARD GAME, 1914, 15" x 16" box $100.00-250.00

ALFRED HITCHCOCK PRESENTS GAME, Milton Bradley, 1958 ....$15.00-30.00

ALFRED HITCHCOCK'S WHY MYSTERY GAME, 1967 ....$10.00-20.00

ALL STAR BASEBALL GAME #183 made by Cadaco, ...$10.00-15.00

AMUSING GAME OF INNOCENTS ABROAD, boxed board game, 1892 ....$150.00-325.00

AMUSING GAME OF THE CORNER GROCERY, 1890's, boxed board game $100.00-200.00

ANDY GUMP HIS GAME, 1920's.............$50.00-85.00

AROUND THE WORLD WITH NELLIE BLY, McLoughlin, ca. 1890 ....$100.00-200.00

ARTISTIC CUBES PUZZLE, 1892 ....$100.00-225.00

AUTHOR'S CARD GAME, 1890's, early boxed card game $100.00-200.00

AUTO RACING GAME, manufactured in 1929, boxed board game $50.00-85.00

AUTOMATIC BOWLING GAME, manufactured in 1929, 24" long $50.00-125.00

BAGATELLE BOARD, ca. 1889, 16" long, paper, wood with spring action $50.00-125.00

BARBIE QUEEN OF THE PROM GAME, circa 1960...$20.00-40.00

BASEBALL GAME, metal box with drum, 1921 ....$35.00-70.00

BASKETBALL GAME by McLoughlin Brothers, 1890's, very rare $50.00-900.00

BATMAN AND ROBIN GAME, 1965 ....$20.00-30.00

BATMAN BOARD GAME, 1966 ....$15.00-25.00

BATTLE GAME, THE, Parker Brothers, 1890's with soldiers $200.00-400.00

BATTLE OF MANILLA BAY PUZZLE, McLoughlin Brothers, 1898.........................$75.00-150.00

BAZOOKA BAGATELLE GAME, ARMY THEME, Marx, 1950's $20.00-45.00

BEATLES GAME, FLIP YOUR WIG, 1960's $35.00-75.00

BEETLE BAILEY OLD ARMY GAME, Milton Bradley, 1960's $10.00-30.00

BETTY BOOP BOXED BRIDGE DECK AND SCORE PADS, 1930's $100.00-225.00

BEVERLY HILLBILLIES CARD GAME, 1960's, Milton Bradley..$5.00-10.00

BEVERLY HILLBILLIES JIGSAW PUZZLE, boxed, 1960's $5.00-10.00

BICYCLE RACE CARDBOARD GAME, 1910, boxed...$100.00-200.00

BIG BAD WOLF GAME, by Parker Brothers, circa 1930...$35.00-75.00

BIG BUSINESS GAME, manufactured by Transogram, 1936...$20.00-55.00

BILLY BUMPS VISIT TO BOSTON GAME, 1890's reading game $100.00-200.00

BILLY WHISKERS BOARD GAME, boxed .$30.00-75.00

BIZZY ANDY MARBLE GAME, boxed marble game $20.00-40.00

BLACK CAT FORTUNE TELLING GAME, Parker Brothers $35.00-60.00

BLINKEY BLINX TIDDLEY WINKS GAME, 1929...$30.00-65.00

BLONDIE GOES TO LEISURELAND, Westinghouse premium game $20.00-45.00

BLOW FOOTBALL GAME, ca. 1912 table top game, boxed $50.00-100.00

BOY SCOUT PROGRESS GAME, Parker Brothers, 1926...$45.00-95.00

BRADLEY'S CIRCUS, Milton Bradley, 1882, boxed game $100.00-200.00

BRADLEY'S CROQUET SET, 1875 ......$100.00-175.00

BROWNIE AUTO RACE GAME, 1930's ...$35.00-70.00

BROWNIE CHARACTER TENPINS GAME, circa 1890 ....$200.00-450.00

BROWNIES WOOD PUZZLE by Palmer Cox, 1891, 12" x 10" wood and paper $75.00-145.00

BUFFALO HUNT BOXED CARDBOARD GAME, 1914 ....$100.00-250.00

BULL IN CHINA SHOP, Milton Bradley ..$20.00-40.00

BURROWES POOL TABLE, 1934, 71" long, child's version..$200.00-400.00

BUSTER BROWN PIN THE TAIL ON TIGE GAME, paper, 1900's $100.00-150.00

BUSTER BROWN PLAYING CARDS, early, boxed $35.00-70.00

BUYING AND SELLING GAME, 1903 ......$35.00-70.00

CABIN BOY BOXED BOARD GAME, cardboard, ca. 1910, 11" square $100.00-225.00

CALLING ALL CARS GAME, Parker Brothers, ca . 1930's $20.00-40.00

CAPTAIN GALLANT ADVENTURE GAME, Transgram, 1955..$15.00-30.00

CAPTAIN GALLANT DESERT FORT GAME, 1956, pictures Buster Crabbe $20.00-45.00

CAPTAIN KIDD TREASURE GAME, Parker Brothers, ca. 1890's $100.00-200.00

CASPER THE GHOST GAME, Milton Bradley, 1959..$10.00-15.00

CATS AND MICE AND TOUSEL, McLoughlin Brothers Game, 1890's $100.00-225.00

CHARLIE CHAN CARD GAME, 1939 ......$20.00-45.00

CHARLIE CHAN, THE GREAT CHARLIE CHAN DE-TECTIVE GAME, made by Milton Bradley Company, 1937 .... $50.00-100.00

CHARLIE CHAPLIN, Chasing Charlie Game, by Spears Games of England $60.00-125.00

CHARLIE McCARTHY FLYING HATS GAME, Whitman, 1938..$20.00-35.00

CHARLIE McCARTHY GAME OF TOPPER, Whitman, 1938..$35.00-65.00

CHARLIE McCARTHY PICTURE PUZZLES, 1938, boxed, two in set $40.00-90.00

CHARLIE McCARTHY PUT AND TAKE BINGO GAME, Whitman, 1938 ....$45.00-75.00

CHARLIE McCARTHY QUESTION AND ANSWER GAME, boxed, ca. 1930 ....$20.00-40.00

CHESTER GUMP IN THE CITY OF GOLD, Milton Bradley..$40.00-80.00

CHIVALRY LAWN GAME, made in 1875, similar to croquet $100.00-200.00

CHRISTMAS GOOSE GAME, McLoughlin Brothers, 1890 ....$150.00-300.00

CHUTES AND LADDERS, 1943 ....$15.00-30.00

CINDERELLA BOXED CARD GAME, 1914. $25.00-50.00

CINDERELLA PICTURE PUZZLE by Jaymar, 1950's, Disney $5.00-10.00

CIRCUS BOXED CARDBOARD GAME, made in 1914 ....$125.00-250.00

CIRCUS GAME, 1947 ....$25.00-40.00

CITADEL GAME, Parker Brothers, 1940 .$20.00-40.00

CLOWN TENPINS GAME, 1912, boxed with ball $100.00-165.00

COCK-A-DOODLE-DOO BOXED CARDBOARD GAME, 1914 ....$100.00-200.00

COLLEGE BOAT RACE, McLoughlin Brothers, 1900 ....$100.00-200.00

COMBINATION BOARD GAME ASSORTMENT, boxed, 1925..$35.00-70.00

COOTIE GAME, 1921, no similarity to modern "Cootie" game $50.00-100.00

COUNTY FAIR GAME, PARKER BROTHERS, boxed board game $75.00-100.00

COURTSHIP AND MARRIAGE GAME, dated 1864 ....$100.00-225.00

CRAZY TRAVELER GAME, ca. 1892 board game $100.00-200.00

CRISS CROSS SPELLING SLIPS, CAT AND DUCK, McLoughlin Brothers, 1890 ....$75.00-150.00

CROKINOLE BOXED CARD GAME, 1914, 15" x 16" box $100.00-150.00

CROOKED MAN GAME, 1914, boxed cardboard game, 8" x 14" $75.00-160.00

CROQUET SET, Bradley's Patent, made in 1875...$100.00-175.00

CURLY LOCKS CARDBOARD GAME, circa 1910 ....$100.00-200.00

DARK SHADOWS GAME, 1960's, based upon television series...$10.00-25.00

DAVY CROCKETT CARD GAME, circa 1950, boxed $5.00-15.00

DECK RING TOSS GAME, made in 1912, boxed set $50.00-120.00

CLOWN RING TOSS GAME, 1907, 14" tall, Furnish collection, $40.00-75.00.

FAMILIAR OBJECTS GAME, by Spears, England, Furnish Collection, $50.00-100.00.

FISH POND GAME by Milton Bradley of Springfield, Mass. Furnish collection, $75.00-150.00.

DEFENDERS OF THE FLAG, 1920's $20.00-40.00

DELMAR DERBY HORSE RACING GAME, 1949..$20.00-30.00

DENNIS THE MENACE BASEBALL GAME, tin lithograph, 1960 ....$10.00-30.00

DENNIS THE MENACE FRAME TRAY PUZZLE, 1960, Whitman $5.00-10.00

DEPARTMENT STORE, McLoughlin Brothers, 1898 ....$125.00-200.00

DICEX BASEBALL GAME......................$25.00-55.00

DICK TRACY JIGSAW PUZZLE, boxed, from 1940's, Jaymar $15.00-30.00

DICK TRACY MASTER DETECTIVE GAME, 1961, boxed $20.00-40.00

DICK TRACY PLAYING CARD GAME, made by Whitman $20.00-40.00

DICK TRACY SUPER DETECTIVE MYSTERY CARD GAME, Whitman, 1937 ....$20.00-40.00

DIG, A GOLD MINING GAME, Parker Brothers, 1940 ....$20.00-40.00

DISNEYLAND MONORAIL GAME, made by Parker Brothers $15.00-30.00

DISSECTED MAP OF THE UNITED STATES, 1892, boxed...$100.00-225.00

DOCTOR BUSBY BOXED CARD GAME, circa 1910..$25.00-60.00

DONALD DUCK card game, Whitman, 1941.$30.00-55.00

DONALD DUCK COMIC PICTURE PUZZLE, Parker Brothers, 1950's $15.00-25.00

DONALD DUCK PARTY GAME, Parker Brothers, 1938 ....$35.00-50.00

DONALD DUCK TIDDLEY WINKS GAME, boxed, 1950's $10.00-20.00

DONALD DUCK'S OWN PARTY GAME, 1950's version, Parker Brothers $20.00-40.00

DONKEY TAIL PARTY GAME, Whitman, boxed, 1941 ....$10.00-35.00

DOWN ON THE FARM PICTURE PUZZLE BLOCKS, 1903, boxed $100.00-200.00

DOWN THE PIKE GAME, Milton Bradley, 1904 ....$50.00-125.00

DR. KILDARE GAME, 1967 ....$15.00-30.00

DR. KILDARE MEDICAL GAME FOR THE YOUNG, 1962 board game by Ideal $10.00-20.00

DRAGNET GAME, 1967 ....$15.00-30.00

DREAMLAND, Parker Brothers, 14" x 21" boxed board game $70.00-125.00

DREAMLAND WONDER RESORT GAME, 1914, box 14" x 23"...$150.00-300.00

DRUMMER BOY BOXED CARDBOARD GAME, 1914, 10" x 20" box $100.00-225.00

ED WYNN FIRE CHIEF GAME, 1934 ...$75.00-135.00

EDDIE CANTOR JIGSAW PUZZLE, Einson Freeman, 1933 ....$20.00-40.00

EDDIE CANTOR TELL IT TO THE JUDGE game $20.00-40.00

ELLA CINDERS GAME, by Milton Bradley, 1944, 9" x 14"..$20.00-40.00

FAST MAIL CARDBOARD GAME, 1919, 10" x 20" box $100.00-175.00

FAVORITE FUNNIES JIGSAW PUZZLE, Gasoline Alley and others, 1940 ....$10.00-20.00

FELIX THE CAT DANDY CANDY GAME, 1957, 7" x 14" box $15.00-35.00

FERDINAND THE BULL CHINESE CHECKERS GAME, 1938..$35.00-100.00

FERDINAND THE BULL GAME, boxed, 1930's, full size $40.00-80.00

FERDINAND THE BULL IN THE ARENA checkers and marbles game, 1930's.....................$45.00-100.00

FIBBER McGEE, Milton Bradley, 1930's .$20.00-50.00

FIDDLE TENNIS GAME, manufactured by Schoenhut, 1938..$25.00-50.00

FIRE FIGHTERS BOXED CARDBOARD GAME, 1914, 7" x 16" box $200.00-350.00

FIVE IN A ROW BOXED GAME, (cats on lid), 1900's $75.00-150.00

FLIGHT TO PARIS GAME, made by Milton Bradley, 1920's $50.00-125.00

FLINTSTONES STONE AGE TIDDLEY WINKS GAME, 1961..$15.00-30.00

FLIVVER GAME, 1929, boxed board game .$70.00-130.00

FLOOR CROQUET, 1912, boxed $100.00-225.00
FLYING ACES boxed board game $35.00-80.00
FLYING NUN GAME, Milton Bradley, 1968 .$5.00-10.00
FOOT RACE BOXED CARDBOARD GAME, 1914 ....$100.00-150.00
FORTUNE TELLER GAME, boxed cardboard game, ca. 1910, 14" x 21"................................$100.00-200.00
FORTUNE TELLER GAME, Milton Bradley, ca. 1905..$50.00-125.00
FORTY NINERS GOLD MINING GAME, circa 1930..$20.00-40.00
FOX AND HOUNDS BOXED BOARD GAME, ca. 1912..$100.00-200.00
FOXY GRANDPA CARD GAME, 1903, boxed $50.00-125.00
FRED FLINTSTONE GAME, STONE AGE, Transogram, 1960's $10.00-25.00
FRED FLINTSTONE TARGET GAME, manufactured 1960's $10.00-20.00
FROG SCHOOL BOXED CARDBOARD GAME, 1914, 11" x 11" box $75.00-150.00
FROG WHO WOULD A WOOING GO boxed cardboard game, 10" x 18", 1914 ....$100.00-250.00
FRONTIERLAND, Walt Disney's Official Game, Parker Brothers, 1950's $20.00-45.00
FUN AT THE CIRCUS, McLoughlin Brothers, 1897, 17" square game $100.00-230.00
GAME OF ABC BOXED GAME, 1914 .$100.00-200.00
GAME OF AMERICAN HISTORY, Parker Brothers, 1892 board game $100.00-200.00
GAME OF BASEBALL, McLoughlin Brothers, 1886..$300.00-500.00
GAME OF BEAUTY AND THE BEAST, boxed cardboard game, 1914, 9" square box $125.00-250.00
GAME OF FISHPOND, 1889, made by Westcott, boxed..$100.00-200.00
GAME OF FOOTBALL, Parker Brothers, 1890's boxed game $100.00-250.00
GAME OF LETTERS, Parker, 1890's $50.00-90.00
GAME OF LOUISA, 1890's, boxed......$125.00-225.00
GAME OF LUCK, Parker Brothers, 1892 boxed game $100.00-200.00
GAME OF MERRY CHRISTMAS, Parker Brothers, 1898..$200.00-450.00
GAME OF MODERN AUTHORS, card game, 1921..$10.00-25.00
GAME OF MONETA "Money Makes Money Game," 1889, F. A. Wright, publishers $150.00-275.00
GAME OF MOTHER GOOSE, ca. 1914, cardboard game, box 10" x 20" $125.00-275.00
GAME OF NORTH POLE BY AIRSHIP, McLoughlin Brothers, 1897 ....$200.00-400.00
GAME OF PITCH, 1914, boxed skill game, 11" x 11" box $100.00-200.00
GAME OF ROBIN HOOD, boxed board game, 1895..$100.00-275.00
GAME OF SHUFFLEBUG, 1921 ....$30.00-70.00
GAME OF STEEPLE CHASE BOXED CARDBOARD GAME, 1914, 7" x 16" $100.00-200.00
GAME OF TOM SAWYER, Milton Bradley, 1930's $30.00-65.00
GAME OF TRAVEL, board game, 1890's .$100.00-200.00

GASOLINE ALLEY WALT AND SKEEZIX CARD GAME, boxed, Milton Bradley, 1927 ....$35.00-55.00
GEOGRAPHICAL LOTTO GAME, 1921 ...$30.00-65.00
GET THE BALLS BASEBALL GAME, circa 1930 ....$20.00-30.00
GILBERT METAL PUZZLES, 1920 ....$40.00-65.00
GOING TO THE FIRE, BOXED CARDBOARD GAME, 1914 ....$150.00-300.00
GOOD OLD GAME OF PROVERBS, Parker Brothers, 1890's boxed game $75.00-150.00
GRANDMA'S MINCE PIE GAME, McLoughlin Brothers, 1890 ....$100.00-200.00
GREAT BATTLEFIELD'S GAME, ca.1890's, board game $100.00-200.00
GREEN HORNET JIGSAW PUZZLES, set of four $20.00-40.00
GROUCHO TELEVISION QUIZ GAME, Pressman, 1950's $10.00-30.00
HAND OF FATE GAME, McLoughlin Brothers, 1901, 15" square box $70.00-140.00

HAPPY HOOLIGAN GUN AND TARGET GAME early Milton Bradley, 1925, (see color photos for box lid), Furnish collection, $100.00-250.00.

HAPPY HOOLIGAN GAME, Milton Bradley, 1925, target set, Furnish collection, $100.00-250.00.

GAMES AND PUZZLES

HARDWOOD TENPINS BOXED GAME, made in 1889 ....$100.00-200.00

HICKETY PICKETY puzzle $20.00-40.00

HIPPODROME GAME, Milton Bradley, 1895, Circus scene on lid $100.00-250.00

HOOP GUN GAME, 1921, hoops reverse direction into targets $100.00-200.00

HOPALONG CASSIDY BEAN BAG TOSS GAME, 1950's boxed $20.00-35.00

HOPALONG CASSIDY CANASTA GAME, card set, original box..$20.00-45.00

HOPALONG CASSIDY CHINESE CHECKERS GAME, 1950's, boxed...............................$25.00-55.00

HOPALONG CASSIDY GAME, Milton Bradley, 1950...$20.00-35.00

HOPALONG CASSIDY JIGSAW PUZZLE, boxed, Milton Bradley, 1950's $10.00-25.00

HORSE PUZZLE, McLoughlin Brothers, 1898 ....$75.00-125.00

HORSELESS CARRIAGE GAME, McLoughlin Brothers, 1900 ....$100.00-200.00

HOWDY DOODY ELECTRIC CARNIVAL GAME, Harriet-Gilmar, Incorporated, 1950's $35.00-55.00

HOWDY DOODY'S OWN GAME, Parker Brothers, cards, balls and targets $35.00-75.00

HUMPTY DUMPTY GAME, Lowell Games$10.00-15.00

I DREAM OF JEANNIE BOARD GAME, 1965, Milton Bradley..$10.00-25.00

IMPROVED GAME OF FISHPOND, 1890's, long box version......................................$100.00-250.00

IMPROVED GEOGRAPHICAL CARDS, 1890's, boxed...$100.00-150.00

IMPROVED GEOGRAPHICAL GAME, Parker Brothers, 1890's $100.00-200.00

INDIAN CHIEF PUZZLE, 1930's, wood....$20.00-45.00

IVANHOE, CARD GAME by Parker Brothers, 1890's, boxed game.......................................$30.00-65.00

JACK AND JILL boxed card game, 1924.$25.00-50.00

JACK AND JILL GAME, boxed cardboard game, 1914, 7" x 16" $100.00-225.00

JACK AND THE BEANSTALK, made by Transogram, 1957...$5.00-15.00

JACK SPRATT BOXED CARDBOARD GAME, 1914, 8" x 14" $75.00-150.00

JACKIE GLEASON AND AWAY WE GO GAME, Transogram, 1956, 10" x 19" $25.00-55.00

JAN MURRAY'S TREASURE HUNT board game $10.00-20.00

JOHNNY'S HISTORICAL GAME, Parker, 1890's boxed game $100.00-225.00

JUMPERS BOXED GAME, McLoughlin Brothers, 1900 ....$100.00-200.00

JUMPY TINKER GAME, TOY TINKERS, made in 1915 ....$25.00-50.00

JUNIOR AUTORACE GAME, 1925 ....$50.00-100.00

KATZENJAMMER KIDS HOCKEY GAME, 1950, 7" x 10" boxed $25.00-45.00

KATZENJAMMER KIDS MAMA'S DARLINGS GAME, 1920's, boxed..................................$40.00-80.00

KATZENJAMMER KIDS PUZZLE SET, 1920's, boxed, four in set $65.00-85.00

KENTUCKY DERBY RACING GAME, spinner type, boxed, 1960's $10.00-20.00

KENTUCKY DERBY RACING GAME, Whitman, 1930's $20.00-40.00

KING PIN BOWLING ALLEY, made by Baldwin, tin lithograph...$40.00-70.00

KITTY KAT CUP BALL boxed game $20.00-55.00

KNUCKLE BILLIARD, 1892, Parker Brothers boxed game $100.00-250.00

KRESKIN ESP GAME, 1967, made by Milton Bradley..$10.00-20.00

KUKLA AND OLLIE GAME, 1962, made by Parker Brothers $10.00-25.00

LASSO THE JUMPING RING A NOVEL GAME, 1912, boxed ring game, clown on box.....$100.00-250.00

LEAVE IT TO BEAVER MONEY MAKER BOARD GAME, Gomalco Productions, 1950's $15.00-35.00

LEAVE IT TO BEAVER ROCKET TO THE MOON SPACE GAME, 1959 ....$15.00-30.00

LIMITED MAIL AND EXPRESS GAME, Parker Brothers, 1895 ....$100.00-225.00

LINDY FLYING GAME, made by Parker Brothers, 1927 ....$40.00-80.00

LITERARY GAME OF QUOTATIONS, Parker Brothers, 1892 ....$100.00-200.00

LITTLE BLACK SAMBO DART GAME, made by Wyandotte $50.00-95.00

LITTLE BO-PEEP BOXED CARDBOARD GAME, 1914, 8" x 14" $100.00-200.00

LITTLE DAISY'S PICTURE PUZZLES, McLoughlin Brothers, 1890, 2 8" puzzles $80.00-150.00

LITTLE GOLDENLOCKS AND THE THREE BEARS McLoughlin Brothers Game, 1892 .$250.00-500.00

LITTLE JACK HORNER BOXED CARDBOARD GAME, 1914, 7" x 16"................................$75.00-175.00

LITTLE LULU JIGSAW PUZZLE, Whitman, 1950's $15.00-35.00

LITTLE NEMO GAME, boxed, 9" square, 1914 ....$100.00-200.00

LITTLE ORPHAN ANNIE BEAD GAME, tin and glass, 1930's, 5" tall $35.00-65.00

LITTLE ORPHAN ANNIE JACK SET, 1930's, on original card $24.00-45.00

LITTLE ORPHAN ANNIE JIGSAW PUZZLE, Jaymar, 1940's $15.00-30.00

LITTLE ORPHAN ANNIE TO THE RESCUE GAME, 1930's $30.00-60.00

LITTLE ORPHAN ANNIE TRAVEL GAME, Milton Bradley...$45.00-80.00

LITTLE RED RIDING HOOD BOXED CARDBOARD GAME, 1914, 10" X 20" box $150.00-300.00

LITTLE SOLDIER BOXED CARDBOARD GAME, 1914 ....$100.00-225.00

LITTLE TOTS SCROLL PUZZLE, Milton Bradley, 1900's $65.00-125.00

LOCOMOTIVE PICTURE PUZZLE, 1892, 18" x 24" boxed..$100.00-300.00

LOGOMACHY OR WAR OF WORDS GAME, made in 1903 ....$40.00-80.00

LONE RANGER BOARD GAME, 1938, full size $30.00-85.00

LONE RANGER GAME, HI-YO SILVER! Parker Brothers, 1938 ....$35.00-70.00

LONE RANGER TARGET PRACTICE, hand-held bead game under glass $15.00-35.00

LOST DIAMOND GAME, McLoughlin Brothers, 1898, boxed $100.00-200.00

LOST IN SPACE GAME, made by Milton Bradley, 1965 ....$15.00-35.00

LUCILLE BALL GAME, 1950's $20.00-40.00

LUDWIG VON DRAKE TIDDLEY WINKS, Disney, 1960's, Whitman $10.00-20.00

MAGIC SPELLING WITH BEWITCHED LETTERS GAME, McLoughlin Brothers, 1900 .$75.00-140.00

MAGNETIC FISH POND GAME, four pole set, 1925 ....$50.00-85.00

MAN FROM UNCLE PLAYING CARDS, made in 1965 ....$5.00-10.00

MARY POPPINS GAME, 1960's, with magic whirl merry-go-round, boxed $20.00-35.00

MENAGERIE GAME, 1895, board game, in original box $200.00-400.00

MERRY GAME OF THE COUNTRY AUCTION, 1890's, boxed $100.00-200.00

MERRY GO ROUND BOXED CARD GAME, made in 1914 ....$25.00-60.00

MESSENGER BOY GAME, cardboard, 10" x 20" box, 1910 ....$75.00-145.00

MICKEY MOUSE CIRCUS GAME, Marks Brothers, 1930's, boxed, marble action $300.00-600.00

MICKEY MOUSE COMING HOME GAME, Marks Brothers, 1930's, Disney Ent. $90.00-160.00

MICKEY MOUSE DOMINOES, 1930's $30.00-70.00

MICKEY MOUSE GAME OF FUNNY FACTS HOT OFF THE GRIDDLE, 1930's $200.00-400.00

MICKEY MOUSE HOOPLA GAME, Marks Brothers, 1930's, large stand-up target $200.00-400.00

MICKEY MOUSE OLD MAID CARD GAME, 1930's, Whitman $25.00-50.00

MICKEY MOUSE QUOIT RING TOSS GAME by Spears Games, England, 1930's $100.00-250.00

MICKEY MOUSE ROLL-EM GAME, Marks Brothers, 1930's, rare....................................$150.00-350.00

MICKEY MOUSE SHOOTING GAME, Marks Brothers, 1930's, five character targets $200.00-400.00

MICKEY MOUSE SKI JUMP TARGET GAME, American Toy Works, boxed, 1930's $50.00-125.00

MICKEY MOUSE SOLDIER TARGET SET, Marks Brothers, 1930's, boxed $100.00-300.00

MISS MUFFET BOXED BOARD GAME, 1914, 7" x 16" $100.00-200.00

MISTRESS MARY BOXED CARDBOARD GAME, 1914 ....$100.00-225.00

MONKEES GAME, 1967 ....$20.00-30.00

MOON SHOT GAME, 1967, Cadaco $5.00-10.00

MOTHER GOOSE GAME, boxed cardboard game, 7" square box, 1914 ....$100.00-170.00

MOTHER GOOSE GAME, Selchow and Righter, ca. 1915 ....$100.00-150.00

MOTHER GOOSE SCROLL PUZZLE, McLoughlin Brothers, 1894 ....$100.00-200.00

MOTHER HUBBARD BOXED BOARD GAME, 1914 ....$100.00-225.00

MOTOR RACE, Wolverine, metal spinner game, 1925 ....$30.00-60.00

MOVIELAND KEENO GAME, Wilder Manufacturing Company, 1929 ....$50.00-95.00

MOVING PICTURE GAME, Milton Bradley, 1920's $30.00-70.00

MR. ED BOARD GAME, Parker Brothers, 1962, based on TV show $10.00-20.00

MR. NOVAK BOARD GAME, Transogram, 1963, based on TV show $10.00-20.00

MICKEY MOUSE PIN-TAIL PARTY GAME by Marks Brothers, 1935, Walt Disney Enterprises, $65.00-150.00.

MICKEY MOUSE BAGATELLE GAME by Chad Valley of England, $200.00-400.00.

GAMES AND PUZZLES

MUNSTERS CARD GAME, made by Milton Bradley, 1966 ....$10.00-15.00

MY FAVORITE MARTIAN GAME, 1963 ..$10.00-25.00

MY MOTHER SENT ME TO THE STORE GAME, 1915 ....$30.00-60.00

NAPOLEON SOLO MAN FROM UNCLE GAME, Ideal, 1965 ....$10.00-20.00

NAVAL WAR, McLoughlin Brothers, publishers, 1898 ....$100.00-200.00

NEBBS BOXED CARD GAME, Milton Bradley 1930's $20.00-40.00

NEW AND IMPROVED FISH POND GAME, McLoughlin Brothers, 1890's $125.0-250.00

NEW DISSECTED MAP OF THE WORLD, McLoughlin Brothers, 1892, boxed $100.00-250.00

NOAH'S ARK TOSS GAME, 1925, ring action or marbles $100.00-150.00

NORTH POLE GAME, 1914, boxed cardboard game $75.00-175.00

NUMERICA GAME, Parker Bros., 1894 .$50.00-100.00

O'GRADY'S GOAT, Milton Bradley, 1906 .$30.00-70.00

OFFICE BOY BOARD GAME, 1892 ......$50.00-150.00

OH! MIN! ANDY GUMP GAME, 1920 ...$40.00-100.00

OLD GLORY, Parker Brothers, 1899 ...$100.00-250.00

OLD MAID CARD GAME, ca. 1889 ....$30.00-65.00

OLD WOMAN AND PIG PUZZLE, McLoughlin, 1900's $100.00-200.00

ON THE WARPATH, THE MICKEY MOUSE SHOOTING GAME, 1930's $150.00-300.00

ORPHAN ANNIE FAMOUS COMICS JIGSAW PUZZLE, 7" square $20.00-55.00

ORPHAN ANNIE RUMMY CARDS, Whitman, 1930's $20.00-40.00

OUR GANG TIPPLE TOPPLE GAME, 1930, Hal Roach Studios $40.00-85.00

PARIS GAME, McLoughlin Bros., 1900 .$100.00-200.00

PARTRIDGE FAMILY GAME, television show based, 1960's $5.00-15.00

PATTY DUKE GAME, 1963 ....$5.00-10.00

PEANUTS GAME, Selchow and Richter Company, 1959 ....$10.00-30.00

PEANUTS THE GAME OF CHARLIE BROWN AND HIS PALS, 1959 board game $10.00-20.00

PECULIAR GAME OF MY WIFE AND I, "GOING TO TOWN," 1890's, boxed $125.00-200.00

PEG BASEBALL GAME, Parker Bros $30.00-60.00

PERRY MASON THE MISSING SUSPECT GAME, 1950's $15.00-25.00

PETER CODDLE BOXED CARD GAME, made in 1914 ....$25.00-50.00

PETER CODDLE BOXED CARD GAME, story game, 1889 ....$70.00-150.00

PETER GUNN DETECTIVE GAME, 1960 .$15.00-30.00

PETER PAN A GAME OF ADVENTURE, 1950's, Walt Disney $20.00-40.00

PETER PETER PUMPKIN EATER BOXED CARDBOARD GAME, 1914, 8" x 14" $100.00-200.00

PETER RABBIT GAME, Milton Bradley, ca. 1910, boxed board game $50.00-125.00

PHIL SILVER'S SERGEANT BILKO "YOU'LL NEVER GET RICH," 1950's $15.00-40.00

PIED PIPER OF HAMELIN GAME, Walt Disney Silly Symphony, Parker Brothers $30.00-60.00

PINOCCHIO PIN THE NOSE ON PINOCCHIO GAME, 1939, Parker Brothers $50.00-125.00

PINOCCHIO PLAYING CARDS GAME, 1939, Jiminy Cricket on lid $25.00-50.00

PINOCCHIO RING THE NOSE HAND HELD GAME, wood and paper, 1940 ....$30.00-60.00

PITFALLS OF PINOCCHIO BOXED MARBLE BOARD GAME, 1940 ....$50.00-85.00

POLLYANA, board game, made by Parker Brothers, 1914 ....$20.00-45.00

POPEYE ADVENTURES OF POPEYE GAME, Transogram, 1957, 9" x 17" $15.00-35.00

POPEYE BAGATELLE GAME, 1930'S, King Features $150.00-300.00

POPEYE PARTY GAME, made by Whitman, 1937, 15" x 26" $30.00-60.00

POPEYE PICTURE PUZZLES, four in box, 1932 ....$30.00-65.00

POPEYE SHIPWRECK GAME, 1933 by Einson Freeman $55.00-110.00

POPEYE SKILL GAME WITH BEADS, tin and glass, 1930's $40.00-65.00

POPEYE'S BINGO, FIVE IN A ROW, EH!, game, copyright 1929 ....$30.00-60.00

PRESIDENTIAL ELECTION GAME, 1892, boxed board game $200.00-400.00

PROGRESSIVE QUERIES GAME, circa 1900, boxed $35.00-70.00

PRICE IS RIGHT GAME, based on television game show 1960's $5.00-15.00

PRINCE VALIANT BOARD GAME boxed ..$15.00-30.00

PRINCESS IN THE TOWER, boxed board game by Parker Brothers, 1890's $150.00-300.00

PUSS-IN-BOOTS TARGET GAME with ball, 1890's $100.00-250.00

QUIZ KIDS OWN GAME, Parker Brothers, 1940 ....$20.00-50.00

RACE FOR THE CUP CARDBOARD GAME, 1914 ....$100.00-200.00

RACE FOR THE NORTH POLE, Milton Bradley, 1900's $40.00-80.00

RALPH EDWARDS THIS IS YOUR LIFE GAME, 1950's $10.00-20.00

RAT PATROL BOARD GAME, Transogram, 1966 ....$10.00-20.00

RED RYDER TARGET GAME, Whitman 1939, colorful box and target $65.00-95.00

REX AND THE KILKENNY CATS, Parker Brothers board game, 1892 ....$75.00-150.00

RIFLEMAN, THE BOARD GAME, 1959, television version $10.00-25.00

RING MY NOSE GAME, ca. 1912, boxed ring game $100.00-150.00

ROAD RUNNER CHARACTER PUZZLES, 1969, set of four $5.00-10.00

ROBINSON CRUSOE GAME, ca. 1914, 7" x 16" box $200.00-400.00

ROUND THE WORLD BOXED CARDBOARD GAME, 7" square, ca. 1914 ....$100.00-200.00

ROY ROGERS HORSESHOE GAME by Ohio Art $18.00-40.00

ROY ROGERS PLAYING CARDS, boxed, manufactured in 1950's $15.00-25.00

ROY ROGERS RODEO GAME, manufactured in 1950's, boxed $35.00-75.00

SAILOR BOY BOXED CARDBOARD GAME, 1914 ....$100.00-200.00

SANTA CLAUS CUBE PUZZLES, 1892, in original box $100.00-250.00

SANTA CLAUS PICTURE PUZZLE, 1892, Victorian scroll puzzle, boxed $300.00-500.00

SCRABBLE GAME, 1953 ....$5.00-15.00

SCRIPTURE CARDS, IMPROVED, 1888 McLoughlin cards set, each 6" x 9" $75.00-145.00

SEVENTY-SEVEN SUNSET STRIP GAME, 1960, Warner Brothers $15.00-35.00

SHIRLEY TEMPLE PLAYING CARDS WITH ORIGINAL BOX, 1930's $30.00-65.00

SHOOT THE CHUTES SKILL BALL GAME, Marx, 1950's $25.00-50.00

SHOOT THE CROWS IN THE CORN TARGET SET, 1925 ....$75.00-125.00

SKATING RACE GAME, Chafee and Selchow, 1898 ....$100.00-300.00

SKILLBALL GAME, floor platform with target holes, 1929 ....$20.00-50.00

SLEEPING BEAUTY FRAME TRAY PUZZLE, 1959, Whitman $5.00-10.00

SLEEPING BEAUTY GAME, Walt Disney, manufactured in 1959 ....$10.00-25.00

SLICED ANIMALS DISSECTED PICTURE PUZZLES, 1903 ....$65.00-140.00

SMITTY GAME, Milton Bradley, 1930's ..$30.00-65.00

SNAKE EYES GAME, Junior Edition $20.00-65.00

SNAKE GAME, McLouglin Brothers, manufactured in 1890's $75.00-125.00

SNOW WHITE AND THE SEVEN DWARFS GAME, Milton Bradley, 1938 boxed game $30.00-75.00

SNOW WHITE AND THE SEVEN DWARFS GAME, Parker Brothers, 1938 ....$50.00-125.00

SNOW WHITE AND THE SEVEN DWARFS TARGET GAME, boxed, 1930's, target slide...$75.00-150.00

SNOW WHITE AND THE SEVEN DWARFS TEK TOOTHPASTE PREMIUM GAME, 1930's $50.00 100.00

SPELLING BOARD, 14" long, 1889 learning game $50.00-125.00

SPOOF THE CHEER UP GAME, 1921 boxed card game $10.00-30.00

STEEPLE CHASE, THE IMPROVED GAME, McLoughlin Brothers, 1892 ....$200.00-400.00

STRANGE GAME OF FORBIDDEN FRUIT, 1890's, boxed $50.00-125.00

STREET CAR GAME, Parker Brothers ..$50.00-100.00

STREET CAR GAME, made by Parker Brothers, 1890's $100.00-200.00

SUPERMAN PICTURE PUZZLE, 1940's ...$25.00-75.00

SWORD IN THE STONE, Disney, Parker Brothers, 1960's $10.00-20.00

TABLE CROQUET GAME, 1912 ....$100.00-200.00

TABLE CROQUET SET, 1889 ....$50.00-100.00

TABLE TENNIS GAME, McLoughlin Brothers boxed set, 1910 ....$100.00-150.00

TABBY CAT BOXED GAME, ...$15.00-30.00

TALE OF WELLS FARGO, 1959 boxed board game $15.00-30.00

PUNCH AND JUDY GAME, by Clover, German, Furnish collection, $50.00-135.00.

THE GAMES OF RAGGEDY ANN, 1941, Milton Bradley, c. Johnny Gruelle Company, Furnish collection, $20.00-40.00.

TEDDY BEARS SCROLL PUZZLES, 1918, colorful litho box $45.00-100.00

TEK-NO-CRAZY ROBOT GAME $10.00-20.00

TERRY AND THE PIRATES JIGSAW PUZZLE, Jaymar, 7" x 10", 1946 ....$20.00-40.00

THE PRICE IS RIGHT BOARD GAME, original 1958 version $10.00-30.00

THREE BLIND MICE, GAME OF, Milton Bradley, 1930's $20.00-40.00

THREE LITTLE KITTENS BOXED CARDBOARD GAME, ca. 1910.......................................$100.00-225.00

THREE LITTLE PIGS JIGSAW PUZZLES, Jaymar, 1940's $10.00-20.00

THREE LITTLE PIGS PLAYING CARDS SET, boxed, Disney, 1930's $15.00-35.00

THREE LITTLE PIGS WHO'S AFRAID OF THE BIG

BAD WOLF GAME, 1930's, Disney .$50.00-100.00

THUNDERBALL, JAMES BOND GAME, 1965 by Gilrose...$10.00-20.00

TIP THE BELL BOY GAME, 1925 ....$35.00-95.00

TIVOLI GAME OF MARBLES, 1886, cup with target...$100.00-150.00

TOM MIX PUZZLE, REXALL DRUGS, premium giveaway, 1930's $35.00-50.00

TOMMY KELLY PECK'S BAD BOY WITH THE CIRCUS 1939, Milton Bradley Game $20.00-45.00

TOMORROWLAND, ROCKET TO THE MOON GAME, Walt Disney's, 1950's $20.00-40.00

TOONERVILLE TROLLEY GAME, boxed 9" x 17" game, 1927, Milton Bradley $50.00-85.00

TOONIN RADIO GAME, 1925, unusual.$65.00-150.00

TOURING, Parker Brothers, 1937 ....$15.00-30.00

TRAIN PUZZLE, made by Milton Bradley, 1882, in box $100.00-200.00

TRAVEL GAME WITH LOWELL THOMAS, 1947..$25.00-60.00

TROLLEY CAME OFF BOXED BOARD GAME by Parker Brothers, 1914................................$100.00-175.00

TRUNK BOX LOTTO GAME, 1890's, McLoughlin Brothers $40.00-85.00

TUG OF WAR, 1898, made by Chaffee and Selchow $150.00-300.00

TURN OVER GAME, made by Milton Bradley, 1915...$30.00-65.00

UNITED STATES POSTMAN GAME, ca. 1914, in box 10" x 20" $100.00-200.00

UNCLE REMUS ZIP GAME, Bagatelle, 1940's $20.00-45.00

UNCLE SAM'S MAIL GAME, 1914, 15" x 16" cardboard game $200.00-500.00

UNCLE WIGGILY GAME by Milton Bradley, 1918...$20.00-45.00

UNCLE WIGGILY GAME, 1954 ....$20.00-30.00

UNITED STATES AIR MAIL GAME, Parker Brothers, 1930's $35.00-70.00

THUNDERBALL, JAMES BOND GAME, 1965 by Gilrose...$10.00-20.00

UNITED STATES SPELLING PUZZLE, boxed, 1889..$50.00-130.00

VICTOR, THE BOXED CARDBOARD GAME, 1914..$75.00-150.00

WALT DISNEY'S ADVENTURELAND GAME, Parker Brothers $10.00-30.00

WALT DISNEY'S CHARACTER SCRAMBLE ALPHABET PLAY SET AND GAME, 1940's $50.00-100.00

WALT DISNEY'S DISNEYLAND GAME, circa 1950...$15.00-35.00

WALT DISNEY'S GAME PARADE, boxed set of games, 1939...$75.00-130.00

WALT DISNEY'S MY FIRST GAME, made in 1955...$20.00-40.00

WALT DISNEY'S OWN GAME OF LITTLE RED RIDING HOOD, 1930's boxed $50.00-100.00

WAR AT SEA GAME, McLoughlin Brothers, 1898...$200.00-300.00

WATERLOO, A BATTLE GAME, 1895, boxed board game $100.00-300.00

WHITE SQUADRON PICTURE PUZZLES, ships, McLoughlin Brothers, 1892 ....$100.00-200.00

WILD WEST BOXED CARDBOARD GAME, 1914, 9"

square box $150.00-275.00

WINGS, THE AIR MAIL GAME, Parker Brothers, 1928 ....$50.00-100.00

WINNIE THE POOH GAME, ca. 1930's original $50.00-75.00

WINNIE THE POOH GAME, Disney version, 1960's $10.00-20.00

WIZARD GAME, Fulton Specialty Company, 1921...$30.00-75.00

WONDERFUL GAME OF OZ, Parker Broters, boxed board game, 1920's $100.00-200.00

WONDERFUL JOE GAME, McLoughlin Brothers $40.00-65.00

WORLD'S COLUMBIAN EXPOSITION PICTURE PUZZLE BLOCKS, 32 in set, 1892 ....$200.00-400.00

WORLD'S COLUMBIAN EXPOSITION PICTURE PUZZLES, McLoughlin, 1892, six puzzles $200.00-475.00

WORLD'S EDUCATOR GAME, 1889......$75.00-150.00

WORLD'S FAIR GAME, 1939 ....$50.00-125.00

WORLD'S FAIR GAME, Parker Brothers, 1890's, boxed board game $200.00-400.00

WYATT EARP TELEVISION BOARD GAME, dated, 1958, boxed $15.00-30.00

YACHT RACE AT SANDY HOOK GAME, McLoughlin Brothers, 1890 ....$150.00-300.00

YANKEE DOODLE A GAME OF AMERICA, 1895 boxed board game $250.00-500.00

YANKEE TRADER BOARD GAME, Corey Games, 1941 ....$20.00-45.00

YELLOW KID McLoughlin Brothers Puzzle, McFadden's Row of Flats $200.00-350.00

YELLOW KID PUZZLE, MCFADDEN'S ROW OF FLATS, 1898 by Richard Outcault $150.00-350.00

YOUNG PEOPLE'S GEOGRAPHICAL GAME, 1890's, Parker Brothers $100.00-250.00

ZOO PUZZLES, ca. 1922, eight puzzle picture set, boxed $50.00-100.00

TOY TOWN PARCEL POST GAME, by J. W. Spears Games, England, boxed set, Furnish collection, $200.00-350.00.

SOLDIERS ON GUARD TARGET AND GUN SET, McLoughlin Brothers, New York, Furnish collection, $100.00-250.00.

TOYTOWN TELEGRAPH BOXED PLAY SET, Parker Brothers, Salem, Mass. 1911, Furnish collection, $100.00-275.00.

SNOW WHITE AND THE SEVEN DWARFS COLORING SET, Whitman, 1938, boxed set, $30.00-65.00.

GOLDEN AGE TOYS: THE TOYS OF THE 1920's AND 1930's

Two significant decades in the course of American history were the 1920's and the 1930's. During this 20 year time period, America rebounded from a World War with the zaniness of the "roaring twenties," only to be harshly initiated into the realm of economic austerity with the Great Depression and the difficult years to follow. It often seems odd that some of the greatest and most imaginative toys ever produced were manufactured during these decades.

If the collector understands that fun, imaginative and colorful toys have always been a great escape for both American children and their parents who purchase them, it seems a little less peculiar that one of our toughest times would produce some of the most wonderful toys.

The big word for the toy industry of these two decades is a short one; *tin*. It seems that toymakers during this period were able to sculpt within that medium almost as ingeniously as an artist with clay. Regardless of the contention by cast iron specialists that *their* medium is the best reflection of early toy Americana, all toy lovers agree that there is just something inexplicably fantastic about an old tin toy in pristine condition. Tin lithographed toys of the 1920's and 1930's are sculptural, durable, and brightly colored. Except for the number one enemy, rust, tin toys have aged well.

If the reader were to simply scan through the descriptions of the toys listed in this section, the word "tin" will appear several hundred times. This metal was the significant toy material during these two decades.

Many collectors agree that these decades were truly a "golden age" for toy production both in America and abroad. With the Lehmann and Schuco companies of Germany turning out high quality windup toys, and Unique Art and the Louis Marx Company mass producing wonderful toys here at home, collectors have come to recognize these decades as two of the greatest ever in toy history. In addition to the tin toys and windups manufactured by these companies, Arcade, Hubley, Wyandotte and of course, Buddy L, produced excellent toy car replicas in sheet metal, steel, tin and cast iron.

If this author could take one hundred dollars with him and step into a time machine to take him back to a toy store anywhere in time, even though greater fortune could be made by stepping into earlier toy decades, I would choose the twenties or the thirties. These decades are much earlier than my own childhood, but I simply like these toys. Granted, it would be a subjective decision, but there's just "something about these toys..."

A CHILD'S GARDEN OF VERSES, Scribner's book, 1933 ....$30.00-45.00

A MICKEY MOUSE ALPHABET BOOK, 1930's, Whitman, hardcover $50.00-100.00

AIRPLANE, Pop-up, Gunthermann, Germany, 1925 tin windup, lever action $125.00-250.00

ALL THE FUNNY FOLKS BOOK, King Features book, 1926...$50.00-80.00

AMERICAN stove, cast iron, 1920's, 8½".$75.00-125.00

ANDY "ANDREW BROWN" TIN WINDUP" of Amos 'n Andy, by Marx, 1930 ....$250.00-550.00

ANDY GUMP FACE MASK, 1930's, Listerine premium..$20.00-35.00

ANDY GUMP IN HIS CAR by Tootsietoy, 1930's, 3" $65.00-125.00

AQUAPLANE by Chein, 1930's, 8½" long, tin windup plane, floats $100.00-200.00

ARCADE BUICK, 8" cast iron auto, 1920's, metal wheels $500.00-800.00

ARCADE BUS, 1930's, 8", cast iron $100.00-200.00

ARCADE CENTURY OF PROGRESS TRUCK, 10" cast iron, 1933 ....$35.00-80.00

ARCADE CHEVROLET CAB, 8", cast iron, 1920's, metal tires.....................................$500.00-750.00

ARCADE CHEVY COUPE, 1929, 8" $400.00-750.00

ARCADE COUPE, 1920's, cast iron, 9" $350.00-700.00

ARCADE FORD SEDAN, 1920's, cast iron, boxed...$900.00-1,700.00

ARCADE GREYHOUND PEOPLE MOVER, 1936 Great Lakes Exposition, cast iron $30.00-70.00

ARCADE MACK GASOLINE TRUCK, 1920's, 13", cast iron $400.00-600.00

ARCADE MACK OIL TRUCK, 1920's, 10" cast iron $400.00-650.00

ARCADE MODEL A WRECKER, 1920's, cast iron, 11" $350.00-500.00

ARCADE MODEL T BANK, made of cast iron, 1920's...$600.00-1,000.00

ARCADE SEMI, cast iron truck, 1920's ..$30.00-60.00

ARMORED CAR WITH GUN TURRET, 1930's, Britains $50.00-80.00

ARNOLD VIKING BOAT, modern style, 1930's, two stacks, 8" $200.00-400.00

AUBURN RUBBER INFANTRY SET, 1939, fifteen figures, boxed $70.00-120.00

AUSTIN STAKEBODY CAST IRON FLATBED TRUCK, 4", 1920's $40.00-70.00

AUTO BANK, Banthrica car, 1924 ....$10.00-25.00

AUTOMATIC BOWLING ALLEY GAME, 1929, 24" long $50.00-125.00

BABY PLATE AND MUG, Swedish enamel, 1930...$10.00-30.00

BALANCING CLOWN WINDUP, Chein, 1930's, 5" $25.00-65.00

BALLERINA WINDUP, Marx, 1930's tin with toothed rod windup $50.00-95.00

BARCLAY ARMORED CAR, 1937 ....$5.00-15.00

BARCLAY COUPE, 3" long, 1930's............$8.00-15.00

BARKY PUPPY, DOG PULL TOY, by Fisher Price, 1931...$50.00-80.00

BARNACLE BILL WINDUP, Chein, 1940, salty sailor, Popeye look-alike $80.00-195.00

BARNEY GOOGLE AND SPARK PLUG CHINA FIGURE, 1920's, 4", German $35.00-75.00

BARNEY GOOGLE AND SPARK PLUG TIN WINDUP, Nifty, Germany, 1920's, 7", boxed .$900.00-1,350.00

BARNEY GOOGLE BOOK, published by Saalfield, 1935...$35.00-75.00

BARNEY GOOGLE PLASTER FIGURE, 1920's, 9" tall..$50.00-85.00

BASEBALL GAME, metal box with drum, 1921...$35.00-70.00

BASEBALL PLAYER CAST IRON FIGURAL BANK, 1930's, 6"..$75.00-125.00

BENTWOOD ARM CHAIR, child's, 1930's.$20.00-45.00

BETTY BOOP ALL CELLULOID WINDUP NODDER, 1930's, Japan, 7" $650.00-1,300.00

BETTY BOOP AND BIMBO FIGURAL ASH TRAY, 1930's $60.00-125.00

BETTY BOOP AND KOKO GLAZED CHINA SAUCER, 1930's $20.00-35.00

BETTY BOOP CELLULOID BUCKLE, circa 1930...$20.00-45.00

BETTY BOOP CELLULOID FIGURE, plays violin, 1930's $45.00-95.00

BETTY BOOP DOLL BLANKET, 1930's, Max Fleischer Studio copyright $45.00-80.00

BETTY BOOP POCKET WATCH, 1920's and 1930's $175.00-300.00

BIG BUSINESS GAME, by Transogram, made in 1936...$20.00-55.00

BIG WOODEN GOOSE PULL TOY, circa 1920, 10" tall..$100.00-200.00

BILLY WHISKERS BOOK Saalfield 1931..$10.00-20.00

BING OPEN DOOR SEDAN, 1930, tin windup, 6" $250.00-450.00

BING OPEN TOURER AUTO, 1928, tin clockwork windup, 8½" $300.00-600.00

BINGOLA RECORD PLAYER with two records, 1920's $100.00-200.00

BISSEL'S LITTLE HELPER CLEANING SET, 1920's $25.00-75.00

BLACKBIRD BANK, German, tin lever action, 1930's, 5" $20.00-40.00

BLACKIE THE DRUMMER BEAR PULL TOY, Fisher Price, 1939 ....$55.00-110.00

BLONDIE'S JALOPY WINDUP CAR, Louis Marx, 1935, K.F.S. tin lithograph $675.00-1,250.00

BLUE FAIRY PINOCCHIO VALENTINE, 1939, mechanical $10.00-20.00

BLUE WILLOW DOLL DISH SET, 1930's, in original box with twelve pieces $50.00-75.00

BLUTO DIPPY DUMPER DUMP TRUCK, celluloid and tin, Marx, 1930's $275.00-600.00

BOAT BUILDERS BOOK, Disney, Grosset and Dunlap, 1938 ....no price available

BOATTAIL RACER #3 Marx, 1930's, tin windup racer, 5" $30.00-60.00

BONZO, THE DOG SCOOTER TOY, WINDUP, 7" long, made in Germany........................$275.00-425.00

BOOB McNUTT, Strauss, 1920's tin windup, 9" $350.00-700.00

BOY SCOUT PROGRESS GAME, Parker Brothers, 1926...$45.00-95.00

BOY'S KING ARTHUR BOOK, Scribner and Sons, 1939...$20.00-35.00

BRINGING UP FATHER BISQUE FIGURES, boxed set of three, each 4" tall $135.00-195.00

GOLDEN AGE TOYS

BRINGING UP FATHER BOOK, 1930's ...$30.00-50.00

BRINGING UP FATHER SONG FOLIO, made in 1924 ....$15.00-34.00

BROWNIE AUTO RACE GAME, 1930's ...$35.00-70.00

BUCK JONES AND THE NIGHT RIDERS, Big Big Book, 1937 ....$25.00-50.00

BUDDY L COAL TRUCK, circa 1920, pressed steel $150.00-300.00

BUDDY L FORD DUMP TRUCK, 1920's ..$300.00-500.00

BUDDY L ICE TRUCK, circa 1920, pressed steel $250.00-400.00

BUDDY L STAKE TRUCK, 1920's $200.00-400.00

BUGS BUNNY SOAP, 1930's, Warner Brothers, boxed $20.00-45.00

BUGS BUNNY WRISTWATCH, 1930's $75.00-145.00

BUNNIES PULLING EGG CART PULL TOY, Fisher Price, 1937 ....$50.00-125.00

BURROWES POOL TABLE, 1934, 71" long, child's version $200.00-400.00

BUS, INTER-STATE, Strauss, 1928 tin windup, 10" $200.00-400.00

CALLING ALL CARS GAME, by Parker Brothers, 1930's $20.00-40.00

CASH REGISTER, Play Store brand, 1930's, 5" x 5", metal $20.00-45.00

CAT PUSHING BALL WINDUP made by Marx, 1930's $45.00-85.00

CHAMPION MACK DUMP TRUCK, circa 1930, 7" $100.00-150.00

CHARLIE CHAN CARD GAME, 1939 ......$20.00-45.00

CHARLIE CHAPLIN IN EASY STREET BOOK, Storm-Greg., 1932 ....$20.00-45.00

CHARLIE McCARTHY GET WELL CARD, circa 1930 ....$10.00-25.00

CHARLIE McCARTHY MEETS SNOW WHITE, book, Whitman, 1930 ....$20.00-45.00

CHARLIE McCARTHY PUT AND TAKE BINGO GAME, 1930's $20.00-40.00

CHARLIE McCARTHY WOOD DANCER TOY, boxed, Marx Brothers $85.00-125.00

CHARLIE McCARTHY BASS DRUMMER WINDUP TOY, Mars, 1939 ....$450.00-865.00

CHEIN JUNIOR BUS, 1920's, 9" $40.00-95.00

CHEIN MACK TRUCK, tin lithograph, Motor Express, 20" $75.00-125.00

CHEIN ROADSTER, 1920's, 8½", tin $40.00-80.00

CHESTER GUMP FINDS HIDDEN TREASURE, Whitman, 1934 ....$20.00-40.00

CHICKEN WINDUP, German, 1920's, tin, 7", tin lithograph $90.00-225.00

CHILD'S TABLE, 1920's, red enameled with black stripe trim, 23" tall $20.00-45.00

CHRYSLER AIRFLOW CAST IRON CAR, 4½", 1930's, ...$50.00-95.00

CLARABELLE THE COW BISQUE FIGURE, Disney, 1930's, 3" $30.00-65.00

CLARABELLE THE COW, Disney storybook, 1930's $10.00-25.00

CLOWN IN BARREL, Chein, 1920's, 8" tin windup $125.00-250.00

CLOWN WITH PARASOL TIN WINDUP, Chein, 1920's, 8" $100.00-175.00

COFFEE DUMP TRUCK, 11", tin, 1930's.$40.00-80.00

COUPE, GIRARD, 1935, pressed steel, orange windup car, 15" $200.00-375.00

COWBOY ON HORSE, Marx, 1925, 6" windup $80.00-140.00

COWBOY RIDER, Marx, 1930's, black horse version, windup, tin, 7" $140.00-250.00

COWBOYS AND INDIANS PUNCH-OUT BOOK by Gabriel, 1927 ....$50.00-85.00

CRASH CAR, Hubley, 1930's, cast iron, 5" motorcycle with cart on back $40.00-95.00

CRYSTEEL child's ABC table, 1920's... $50.00-100.00

DAGWOOD'S SOLO FLIGHT WINDUP AIRPLANE, Marx, 1935, 9" $200.00-425.00

DANCING LASSIE, Lindstrom, USA, 1930's, tin windup $65.00-135.00

DAPPER DAN, made by Marx, USA, 1920 Jigger Bank $600.00-900.00

DAYTON COUPE, pressed steel, 1920's, 12" $50.00-100.00

DEFENDERS OF THE FLAG GAME, 1920's, boxed $20.00-40.00

DELUXE ELECTRIC RANGE FOR LITTLE GIRLS, 1920's $45.00-110.00

DENNY DIMWIT COMPOSITION FIGURE, 1930's, 4" $20.00-40.00

DENT ICE CREAM TRUCK, 1930's, 8" cast iron truck $200.00-400.00

DENT MODEL T ca. 1920's, cast iron..$70.00-150.00

DENT PATROL TRUCK, 1920's, 6½" long with driver $300.00-450.00

DICK TRACY CODE MAKER, 1930's $30.00-55.00

DICK TRACY DETECTIVE BUTTON, 1", 1930's $10.00-25.00

DICK TRACY PAINT BOOK, 1935 ....$25.00-50.00

DICK TRACY RUBBER STAMP PRINTING SET, 1930's $20.00-40.00

DICK TRACY SECRET DETECTIVE MAGIC TRICKS, 1939 Quaker Oats premium $20.00-45.00

DICK TRACY SUPER DETECTIVE MYSTERY CARD GAME, Whitman, 1937 ....$20.00-40.00

DICK TRACY WATCH, 1930's, boxed ..$150.00-300.00

DINKY TOYS RACE CAR WITH AIRFLOW REAR FENDERS, 1930's $25.00-60.00

DOBBIN THE PONY PULL TOY, Fisher Price, 1938 ....$50.00-120.00

DOC AND DOPEY PULL TOY, Fisher Price, 1938 ....$100.00-200.00

DOC CHARACTER LAMP, Disney, LaMode Studios, 1930's $75.00-150.00

DOC THE DWARF PAPER MASK, 1938 Walt Disney Enterprises $10.00-25.00

DOLL TRUNK WITH LINED INSERT, 1930's, 18" long $30.00-90.00

DOLLY STROLLER single handle on back, open, wood and tin, 1920's $40.00-85.00

DONALD DUCK AND CLARA CLUCK CUT-OUT BOOK, 1930's, rare......................................$100.00-150.00

DONALD DUCK AND PLUTO HANDCAR, windup train car with box, Lionel, 1930's $600.00-1,150.00

DONALD DUCK ART STAMP PICTURE SET, 1930's, angry Donald on lid $35.00-75.00

DONALD DUCK BISQUE FIGURE, 1930's, 5" long-billed version $125.00-225.00

DONALD DUCK CELLULOID WINDUP NODDER, 1930', long-billed Donald $200.00-425.00

DONALD DUCK CHARACTER VALENTINE, 1938, mechanical, Donald in sombrero $10.00-20.00

DONALD DUCK DIME REGISTER BANK, 1930's, metal, 3" square $40.00-95.00

DONALD DUCK FIGURAL BAKELITE PENCIL SHARPENER WITH DECAL, 1930's ..$15.00-35.00

DONALD DUCK FIGURAL TOOTHBRUSH HOLDER, bisque, 1930's, Donald by post $200.00-400.00

DONALD DUCK HUNTING FOR TROUBLE, Big Little Book, 1938 ....$10.00-30.00

DONALD DUCK NITE LITE, 1930's, tin and cardboard, pen-light battery $65.00-110.00

DONALD DUCK PAINT AND CRAYON SET, 1930's, boxed in cardboard box $25.00-65.00

DONALD DUCK PARTY GAME by Parker Brothers, 1938 ....$35.00-50.00

DONALD DUCK RUBBER FIGURE, jointed neck, 5", long-billed, 1930's $65.00-110.00

DONALD DUCK SERVING TRAY, Ohio Art, Donald as waiter, red, 1930's $10.00-30.00

DONALD DUCK SNOW SHOVEL, 1930's, Ohio Art, large version, Disney scene $100.00-200.00

DONALD DUCK SOAP FIGURES, boxed, three figures, Lightfoot-Schultz, 1930's................$100.00-175.00

DONALD DUCK TELEPHONE AND COIN BANK with Donald, 1930's, metal, red..............$60.00-100.00

DONALD DUCK THE DRUM MAJOR KNICKERBOCKER DOLL, 1930's $400.00-800.00

DONALD DUCK TIN TEA SET, boxed, complete, Ohio Art, 1930's $75.00-135.00

DONALD DUCK WATERING CAN, 1930's, Walt Disney enterprises, 6"......................................$30.00-75.00

DONALD DUCK WINDUP by Schuco, Germany, 1930's, long-billed, boxed $500.00-1,000.00

DOPEY CLOTH AND COMPOSITION DOLL, 1938, Chad Valley, 6" $100.00-170.00

DOPEY COMPOSITION BANK, Crown Toy and Novelty, 1938, 7" $50.00-95.00

DOPEY DIME REGISTER BANK, 1938, tin, square, Walt Disney $35.00-70.00

DOPEY THE DWARF MECHANICAL VALENTINE, 1938, holding candle $10.00-20.00

DOPEY THE DWARF WINDUP, Disney, Chad Valley of England, tin, 1930's $100.00-200.00

DOPEY TIN WINDUP by Marx, 1930's, Walt Disney, Enterprises, 10" $125.00-200.00

DRUM MAJOR with red jacket, Wolverine 1930's, 14" $60.00-120.00

DUCK WINDUP, 1930's, tin, 9" long, zig-zag action $20.00-45.00

EASTER BUNNY PULL TOY, Fisher Price, 1936 ....$40.00-80.00

ED WYNN FIRE CHIEF GAME, 1934 ...$75.00-135.00

ELECTRIC MAGIC LANTERN, circa 1920 with slides $50.00-120.00

ELECTRIC RANGE FOR LITTLE GIRLS, circa 1930 ....$20.00-45.00

ELEPHANT ON PLATFORM WITH WHEELS PULL TOY, tin, 9", 1920's.....................$150.00-300.00

ELMER THE ELEPHANT LINEN-LIKE BOOK, Walt Disney, 1930's $30.00-60.00

LEHMANN COACH, 5" long, tin windup with driver, Furnish collection, $300.00-650.00.

FELIX ANNUAL BOOK, Comic Adventures of Felix, 1923 ....$50.00-110.00

FELIX SCHOOL COMPANION PENCIL BOX, 1939...$50.00-70.00

FELIX THE CAT BEAD GAME UNDER GLASS, 3" $20.00-50.00

FELIX THE CAT CELLULOID PLACE CARD HOLDER, 1930's, die-cut $50.00-125.00

FELIX THE CAT CHILD'S TEA SET, three pieces, china, with Felix decals $70.00-125.00

FELIX THE CAT CREAM TOFFEE, rare tin can, c. Pat Sullivan $100.00-225.00

FELIX THE CAT ON A SCOOTER, Nifty, German, 1924, tin lithograph, toy $385.00-600.00

FELIX THE CAT WOODEN WALKING TOY, 11" tall, 1930's $65.00-145.00

FERDINAND THE BULL CHINESE CHECKERS GAME, 1930's $35.00-100.00

FERDINAND THE BULL CUT-OUT BOOK, 1930's, colorful $50.00-100.00

FERDINAND THE BULL WINDUP TOY by Marx, 1938, tall spins, tin lithograph $65.00-125.00

FERDINAND THE BULL WOOD COMPOSITION BANK, Crown Toy, Disney, 1939.................$60.00-125.00

FIBBER McGEE GAME, Milton Bradley, 1930's $20.00-50.00

FIBER REED STROLLER, push or pull type, 1930 ....$100.00-150.00

FIDDLE tennis game, Schoenhut, 1938 ..$25.00-50.00

FIGARO THE CAT PAPER MASK, Gillette premium, 1938...$10.00-20.00

FIGHTING COCKS WINDUP, Nifty, Germany, 1920 ....$200.00-500.00

FIRE TRUCK, Girard 12", tin, 1920's ..$60.00-120.00

FLIGHT TO PARIS GAME, Milton Bradley, 1920's $50.00-125.00

FLIVVER GAME, made in 1929, boxed board game $70.00-130.00

FOOTBALL PLAYER, circa 1920, 6", cast iron bank $60.00-125.00

FORD COUPE made by Hubley, 1930's, cast iron $25.00-45.00

FORTY NINERS GOLD MINING GAME, boxed board game, 1930's................................$20.00-40.00

FREDDY BARTHOLOMEW IN LITTLE LORD FAUNTLEROY, 1936 book, Saalfield .$15.00-35.00

GAME OF MODERN AUTHORS, card game, 1921 ....$10.00-25.00

GAME OF SHUFFLEBUG, 1921 ....$30.00-70.00

GAME OF THREE BLIND MICE, Milton Bradley, 1930's $20.00-40.00

GANG BUSTER CAR by Marx, circa 1930, 14" $200.00-400.00

GARAGE AND SERVICE CENTER, Wyandotte, two-car, 1935 ....$75.00-175.00

GASOLINE ALLEY, Walt and Skeezix Card Game, boxed, Milton Bradley, 1927 ....$35.00-55.00

GEOGRAPHICAL LOTTO GAME, 1921 ...$30.00-65.00

GEPETTO PAPER MASK, Gillette premium, 1939, Walt Disney $10.00-25.00

GET THE BALLS BASEBALL GAME, circa 1930 ....$20.00-30.00

GIANT KING RACER, by Marx, tin windup, 1930's $35.00-70.00

GILBERT METAL PUZZLES, 1920 ....$40.00-65.00

GIRARD HANDCAR, 1930's, tin lithograph, two men pump hand car, 6" long $80.00-175.00

GOLDILOCKS POP-UP BOOK, Blue Ribbon Press, 1934 ....$25.00-60.00

GOOSE, by Unique Art, 1930's, tin lithograph, neck bobbing action $40.00-70.00

GRANNY DOODLE PULL TOY, Fisher Price, 1930's $40.00-100.00

GUN JUSTICE, FEATURING KEN MAYNARD, Big Little Books, 1930's $12.00-25.00

HAM AND SAM MINSTRELS, Strauss, tin lithograph, windup, 1920's $250.00-475.00

HAPPY HOOLIGAN CHARACTER ASH TRAY, 1930's, bisque $45.00-80.00

HAPPY HOOLIGAN WINDUP TOY, tin lithograph, Chein, 1932, 6"....................................$175.00-250.00

HAROLD LLOYD TIN WINDUP WALKER, Marx, 1930's, 11" $175.00-400.00

HAROLD TEEN BISQUE FIGURE, 3¾" tall, circa 1930 ....$20.00-40.00

HAROLD TEEN PAINT BOOK, 1932.......$15.00-35.00

HENRY AND HIS BROTHER CELLULOID WINDUP TOY, 1934 ....$1,200.00-2,300.00

HENRY RIDING ON THE ELEPHANT, celluloid wind-up toy, 1930's $975.00-2,400.00

HENRY THE ACROBAT TRAPEZE WINDUP TOY, metal and celluloid, 1930's $465.00-675.00

HERBIE BISQUE FIGURE, 2", 1930's $20.00-40.00

HEY HEY THE CHICKEN SNATCHER, tin windup, Marx, 1920's $600.00-1,200.00

HI-WAY HENRY WINDUP CAR, ca. 1920's, tin lithograph, comic character car $2,500.00-3,900.00

HOPPO THE MONKEY tin windup, Marx, 1925, 8" plays cymbals $65.00-120.00

HOUSE BANK, Bungalow style, 1920's, bronze finish, 4" $125.00-175.00

HUBLEY CHRYLSER RACING CAR, circa 1930 ....$35.00-70.00

HUBLEY DUMP TRUCK, 4½", 1930's, with white rubber tires $90.00-150.00

HUBLEY FIRETRUCK WITH METAL LADDERS, 1938, 13" long $300.00-550.00

HUBLEY LINCOLN ZEPHER, 1937 ......$100.00-225.00

HUBLEY SERVICE CAR, 5" version, 1930's $40.00-75.00

HUBLEY LIMOUSINE, 1920's, 7"............$50.00-90.00

IGNATZ MOUSE ON A TRICYCLE by Chein, 1932, wood and tin, 7" $200.00-400.00

IGNATZ MOUSE WOOD FIGURE, 6" tall, wire limb joints, 1920's $35.00-80.00

ITO SEDAN, Lehmann, circa 1920, 7" tin windup $200.00-450.00

JANE WITHERS, HER LIFE STORY, book published by Whitman, 1936......................$20.00-40.00

JAZZBO JIM, Marx windup, 1920's, roof dancer, 9" $300.00-500.00

JEFF WOOD COMPOSITION AND JOINTED METAL DOLL, 6", 1920's $225.00-425.00

JENNY THE BALANCING MULE, Strauss, 1920's tin windup, 9" $250.00-535.00

JIGGER, made by Lindstrom 8", circa 1930, a dancer..$150.00-275.00

JIGGS BISQUE FIGURE, 3", 1930's........$20.00-50.00

JIGGS LUNCHBOX, tin, 6", 1930's.........$55.00-110.00

JIMINY CRICKET PAPER MASK, Disney, 1939, Gillette premium.......................................$10.00-25.00

JIMINY CRICKET WOOD COMPOSITION BANK, Crown Toy, Walt Disney Enterprises $50.00-100.00

JOHNNY JUMBO THE ELEPHANT PULL TOY, Fisher Price, 1933 ....$45.00-120.00

JOY RIDERS by Marx, crazy car, 1925, 7", tin lithograph $150.00-375.00

JUNIOR AUTO RACE GAME, 1925 ......$50.00-100.00

KATZENJAMMER KIDS STORYBOOK, Whitman, 1937 ....$20.00-55.00

KATZENJAMMER KIDS MAGIC DRAWING AND COLORING BOOK, 1930's $30.00-50.00

KATZENJAMMER KIDS PUZZLE SET, 1920's, four in box $65.00-85.00

KATZENJAMMER MAMA COMPOSITION, DOLL, 1920's, 9"....................................$200.00-400.00

KAY GERMAN bisque nodder, 1930's $30.00-75.00

KAYO COMPOSITION FIGURE WITH MOVABLE MOUTH, 13" 1930' $110.00-225.00

KAYO'S ICE TRUCK, manufactured by Tootsietoy, 1930's $95.00-155.00

KENTON CATTLE TRUCK, 1930's, white rubber tires, 8" long, metal $150.00-225.00

KENTON DOUBLE DECKER BUS, 1920's, 7" long, cast iron $250.00-450.00

KENTON FLATBED PICK-UP TRUCK, 7½", cast iron, 1930's, white rubber tires..............$100.00-185.00

KENTUCKY DERBY GAME, Whitman, 1930's $20.00-40.00

KILGORE CAST IRON DUMP TRUCK, 1930's $100.00-150.00

KITCHEN CABINET FOR LITTLE GIRLS, 1930, 26", enameled $40.00-125.00

KNOCKOUT CHAMPS BOXING WINDUP TOY, 1930's, tin lithograph, Marx $200.00-400.00

KRAZY KAT PLANTER, 1930's $35.00-75.00

LEHMANN TERRA AUTO, driver and original flag, 1920's $1,200.00-1,900.00

LET THE DRUMMER BOY PLAY, Marx, 1930's, tin windup walking drummer, bass $80.00-150.00

LIBERTY BELL WITH CLOCK BANK, white metal with bronze finish, 1926 .... $100.00-150.00

LIMOUSINE, TIPP AND COMPANY, German, Dunlop Cord tires 1920's, ... $500.00-900.00

LINDSTROM FLEET, 1920's, boxed set of three, 7" to 10" boats $150.00-300.00

LINDSTROM SPEED BOAT, USA, 1930's, large engine version, 12" tin windup $100.00-200.00

LINDY FLYING GAME, Parker Brothers, 1927 .... $40.00-80.00

LITTLE COWBOY ON HORSE PULL TOY, 1938, Fisher Price $50.00-120.00

LITTLE LADY KITCHEN MINIATURE PLAY KITCHEN, metal and carboard, 1930 .... $50.00-135.00

LITTLE ORPHAN ANNIE AND JUMBO, Blue Ribbon Press Pop-up Book, 1935 .... $125.00-220.00

LITTLE ORPHAN ANNIE BUCKING THE WORLD, Cupples and Leon Book, 1929 .... $20.00-45.00

LITTLE ORPHAN ANNIE COLORING BOOK, Annie paints sign, McLoughlin, 1930's $20.00-45.00

LITTLE ORPHAN ANNIE CRAYONS SET, Milton Bradley, 1930's, 4" x 8" box $45.00-85.00

LITTLE ORPHAN ANNIE JACK SET, 1930's on original card $24.00-45.00

LITTLE ORPHAN ANNIE JIGSAW PUZZLE, boxed, 1930's $30.00-70.00

LITTLE ORPHAN ANNIE NAPKIN RING, 1933 World's enameled tin $25.00-65.00

LITTLE ORPHAN ANNIE TEA SET, German, ceramic, teapot 4" tall, twelve pieces $95.00-150.00

LITTLE ORPHAN ANNIE TRAVEL GAME, Milton Bradley, #4523 .... $45.00-80.00

LITTLE RED RIDING HOOD AND THE BIG BAD WOLF, David McKay, 1934, Disney ... $45.00-70.00

LONE RANGER TARGET GAME, 1930's, metal target, Reynolds collection, $30.00-65.00.

MARX CRAZY CAR TIN WINDUP, 1930's, 6", Furnish collection, $100.00-225.00.

LITTLE RED RIDING HOOD PENCIL BOX, Disney, by Dixon, 1930's $40.00-80.00

LITTLE RED RIDING HOOD POP-UP BOOK, 1934 .... $30.00-55.00

LITTLE WOMEN FEATURING KATHRYN HEPBURN, Whitman Book, 1934 .... $20.00-40.00

LONE RANGER BOARD GAME, 1938, full

LEHMANN RUCK-RUCK TIN WINDUP AUTO, three-wheeled with driver, Furnish collection, $300.00-600.00.

size $30.00-55.00

MAGGIE AND JIGGS BISQUE FIGURES, 3½" tall, pair $70.00-130.00

MAGGIE AND JIGGS WINDUP, George McManus, 7" tin lithograph $650.00-1,100.00

MAGGIE CHARACTER DOLL manufactured by Schoenhut, 10" tall.............$175.00-300.00

MAGNETIC FISHPOND GAME, four pole set, 1925 ....$50.00-85.00

MAIL TRUCK, Packard, 26", tin, circa 1920, flatbed cage $200.00-400.00

MARGARET O'BRIEN PAINT BOOK, Whitman, circa 1930 ....$10.00-25.00

MARX FIRE ENGINE, sheet iron, circa 1920, 9" $45.00-75.00

MARX MACK RAILROAD EXPRESS TRUCK, tin #7, 1930's $75.00-125.00

MARX MERRY MAKERS BAND, 1920's, tin lithograph, windup mouse band $300.00-650.00

MARX MOTORCYCLE POLICEMAN, 1920's, tin windup, 8", orange and blue.............$100.00-140.00

MARX MOTORCYCLE TOPPER, tin lithograph, windup, 1930's $100.00-140.00

MARX MYSTERY POLICE CYCLE, 1930's, windup, 4½", tin $40.00-90.00

MARX MYSTERY TAXI, 1930's, press-down activation, tin $40.00-90.00

MARX SPEEDWAY COUPE, 1920's, BO, headlights, 8" $185.00-300.00

MECHANICAL DRUMMER, Chein, 1930's, 9" $75.00-125.00

METALCRAFT VAN, 11", 1930's $50.00-100.00

MICKEY AND MINNIE MOUSE SHOVEL, tin, 12" long, beach scene lithograph.............$40.00-65.00

MICKEY AND MINNIE MOUSE TAMBOURINE, Noble and Cooley, 1936 ....$100.00-200.00

MICKEY AND MINNIE MOUSE WALL POCKET, blue and tan lusterware, 1930's $65.00-130.00

MICKEY AND MINNIE MOUSE WASHING MACHINE, 1930's, Ohio Art $65.00-150.00

MICKEY AND MINNIE MOUSE WASTEBASKET, all characters, 1930's $60.00-135.00

MICKEY MOUSE ACROBATIC CIRCUS, 1930's, Marks Brothers $300.00-600.00

MICKEY MOUSE ALPHABET BOWL, Bavarian China, 1930's $50.00-125.00

MICKEY MOUSE ALUMINUM BAKING SET, 1930's $75.00-100.00

MICKEY MOUSE AND THE SACRED JEWEL, Big Little Book 1936 ....$10.00-25.00

MICKEY MOUSE ART SET by Dixon, Mickey in plane on box lid, 1930's, rare $50.00-100.00

MICKEY MOUSE BABY GRAND PIANO, 1930's, with Mickey decal on toy $100.00-275.00

MICKEY MOUSE BANJO, Noble and Cooley, 1930's $100.00-225.00

MICKEY MOUSE BEDTIME STORIES, Child's book, 1930's $35.00-60.00

MICKEY MOUSE BIG BIG BOX OF GAMES AND

THINGS TO COLOR, 1930's $25.00-75.00

MICKEY MOUSE BIRTHDAY CARD, 1930's, Hall Brothers, folds out to poster $40.00-75.00

MICKEY MOUSE BISQUE FIGURE, 1930's, 5", playing French horn $75.00-150.00

MICKEY MOUSE BISQUE FIGURE, giant, 9" size, 1930's on pedestal $750.00-1,600.00

MICKEY MOUSE BLACKBOARD, easel type, 1930's $100.00-175.00

MICKEY MOUSE BOXED HANKIES SET, 1930's, colorful lid on box $125.00-225.00

MICKEY MOUSE BOXED STATIONERY SET, 1930's $45.00-60.00

MICKEY MOUSE BUBBLE BUSTER GUN, 1930's Kilgore Manufacturing Company, boxed.......$75.00-125.00

MICKEY MOUSE CARDBOARD TOY CHEST, 1930's $75.00-150.00

MICKEY MOUSE CELLULOID RATTLE WITH HANDLE, 1930's $100.00-200.00

MICKEY MOUSE CHILD'S CERAMIC DIVIDED DISH, 1930's, Patriot China $35.00-70.00

MICKEY MOUSE CINE ART FILM IN ORIGINAL BOX, 1930's $15.00-35.00

MICKEY MOUSE CLOTHES BRUSH SET, boxed, 1930's $100.00-200.00

MICKEY MOUSE COMING HOME GAME, Marks Brothers, board and little box $90.00-165.00

MICKEY MOUSE COMPOSITION FIGURE, 1930's, 6" from Lionel train set, waving...........$95.00-225.00

MICKEY MOUSE CREAMER, Bavarian china, 1930's Mickey on toy train $75.00-145.00

MICKEY MOUSE DART GUN TARGET SET, 1930's, Marks Brothers, with box, gun..........$35.00-75.00

MICKEY MOUSE DOLL, stuffed, 12", Knickerbocker, 1930's felt shoes $200.00-400.00

MICKEY MOUSE DOMINOES, 1930's $30.00-70.00

MICKEY MOUSE DRAWING TABLET, Walt Disney Enterprises, 1930's $20.00-40.00

MICKEY MOUSE DRUM, 8" diameter, Ohio Art, 1930's $65.00-110.00

MICKEY MOUSE FLASHLIGHT BY USA LIGHT, 1930's, original box $50.00-125.00

MICKEY MOUSE FUN-E-FLEX FIGURE, 4", 1930's, wood stick-type figure $50.00-125.00

MICKEY MOUSE HANKIE, 1930's, Mickey flying kite $10.00-25.00

MICKEY MOUSE FOUNDRY SET, complete in box, 1930's $125.00-250.00

MICKEY MOUSE IN NUMBERLAND BOOK, Whitman, 1938................................$30.00-70.00

MICKEY MOUSE INGERSOLL ALARM CLOCK, 1930's $120.00-200.00

MICKEY MOUSE LIONEL CIRCUS TRAIN, 1930's complete boxed set $2,500.00-5,800.00

MICKEY MOUSE LUNCH KIT, 1930's $200.00-400.00

MICKEY MOUSE MAGIC SLATE, 1930's, small item $20.00-45.00

MICKEY MOUSE MARIONETTE, 1930's, Alexander Doll Company $100.00-250.00

MICKEY MOUSE METAL DIME SAVINGS BANK, W. D. Enterprises, 1930's, 3" square $65.00-110.00

MICKEY MOUSE NOMA CHRISTMAS LIGHTS, 1930's, boxed with eight lamp covers $75.00-175.00

MICKEY MOUSE PAINT AND CRAYON SET, Marks Brothers of Boston $75.00-150.00

MICKEY MOUSE PANTOGRAPH, Marks Brothers, 1930 drawing set, boxed $100.00-200.00

MICKEY MOUSE PAPER MASK, 1930's . $20.00-35.00

MICKEY MOUSE PARTY NOISEMAKER ON STICK, 1930's, Marks Brothers $30.00-65.00

MICKEY MOUSE POCKET KNIFE by Imperial Knife Company, 1930's $20.00-40.00

MICKEY MOUSE PRINT SHOP, Fulton Specialty, 3" x 9" box, 1930's $50.00-95.00

MICKEY MOUSE PUSH TOY, Fisher Price, Mickey running, 1930's, 6" long $50.00-85.00

MICKEY MOUSE RADIO by Emerson, white Bakelite version, 1930's $650.00-1,200.00

MICKEY MOUSE SAND PAIL, 5" tin, by Happynak of England, 1930's $45.00-85.00

MICKEY MOUSE SAND PAIL, buried treasure version, 1930's, Ohio Art $50.00-95.00

MICKEY MOUSE SILLY SYMPHONY SOAP SET, 1930's, five characters, rare $100.00-250.00

MICKEY MOUSE SKITTLE BALL GAME, boxed 1930's, Marks Brothers $100.00-200.00

MICKEY MOUSE SOLDIER TARGET SET, Marks Brothers, 1930's, boxed $100.00-300.00

MICKEY MOUSE STANDING BY A TRUNK, wood composition bank, made by Crown Toy, 1930's $100.00-150.00

MICKEY MOUSE SUGAR BOWL, Patriot China, 1930's, 3" tall $25.00-60.00

MICKEY MOUSE TALKIE JECKTOR WITH BOX, 1935 .... $125.00-275.00

MICKEY MOUSE TIN TOP, 8" version, 1930's Disney characters $50.00-85.00

MICKEY MOUSE TREASURE CHEST BANK, leather covered, 1930's $50.00-125.00

MICKEY MOUSE WATERING CAN, Ohio Art, 1930's, Mickey in garden $35.00-75.00

MICKEY MOUSE WOOD SLED, Flexible Flyer, 1930's with Mickey and Minnie decal $65.00-125.00

MICKEY MOUSE WOODEN PULL WAGON, by Toycraft, 1930's $100.00-200.00

MICKEY MOUSE, THE WALT DISNEY PAINT BOOK, large format, 1930's $25.00-50.00

MINNIE MOUSE CUP, Patriot China, 1930's, Minnie with mirror $20.00-45.00

MINNIE MOUSE, THE POP-UP MINNIE MOUSE BOOK, 1930's Blue Ribbon Press $75.00-150.00

MODEL T by DENT, cast iron, 1920's . $70.00-150.00

MOON MULLINS AND KAYO BISQUE FLOWER PLANTER, 1920's, 5" tall $45.00-90.00

MOON MULLINS AND KAYO BOXED SOAP FIGURES, 4" and 2" tall, detailed paint $75.00-110.00

MOON MULLINS AND KAYO WINDUP HANDCAR, 6" long, tin lithograph $375.00-525.00

MOON MULLINS BISQUE FIGURE, 2", circa 1930 .... $15.00-35.00

MOON MULLINS DRAWING AND TRACING BOOK, McLoughlin Brothers, 1932 .... $20.00-40.00

MOON MULLINS GLAZED TOOTHBRUSH HOLDER, 1930's, 5" $50.00-75.00

MOON MULLINS POLICE CAR BY TOOTSIETOY, 1930's $125.00-295.00

MORTIMER SNERD BASS DRUMMER TIN WINDUP TOY, Marx, 1939 .... $450.00-865.00

MORTIMER SNERD CRAZY CAR, Marx, 1930's, windup, tin lithograph $200.00-425.00

MORTIMER SNERD JACK IN THE BOX, composition and wood, 1930's $100.00-200.00

MOTHER GOOSE POP-UP BOOK, Blue Ribbon Press, 1934 .... $35.00-75.00

MOTORCYCLE BY INCAP, Italy, 1935, 8" tin windup, red, #174 .... $120.00-225.00

MOTORCYCLE POLICE WITH SIDE CAR, cast iron, 5½", 1930's, two policeman $70.00-145.00

MUTT AND JEFF MUSICAL ALBUM, 1920, colorful cover $25.00-65.00

MUTT CELLULOID FIGURE, 6", 1930's . $45.00-110.00

MUTT WOOD JOINTED COMPOSITION AND METAL DOLL, 8" tall, 1920's $225.00-425.00

MYSTERY POLICE CYCLE, 1930's, Marx, tin windup, 4½" $45.00-75.00

NEBBS BOXED CARD GAME from Milton Bradley, 1930's $20.00-40.00

ORPHAN ANNIE BISQUE NODDER FIGURE, German, 3½" tall $60.00-95.00

ORPHAN ANNIE CIRCUS IN ORIGINAL ENVELOPE, 1935, 10" X 14" $75.00-155.00

ORPHAN ANNIE IRONING BOARD SET, Goshen Manufacturing, 1930's $75.00-125.00

ORPHAN ANNIE LUSTERWARE TEA SET, 1930's, five pieces $65.00-110.00

ORPHAN ANNIE OILCLOTH DOLL, 1926, 15" tall with blue polka-dot dress $75.00-140.00

ORPHAN ANNIE PAPER FACE MASK, premium of Ovaltine, 1930's $20.00-40.00

MARX MILTON BERLE CRAZY CAR, 1930's, tin windup 6", Reynolds collection, $150.00-275.00.

ORPHAN ANNIE RUMMY CARDS, Whitman, circa 1930 ....$20.00-40.00

ORPHAN ANNIE SHOOTING GAME, Milton Bradley, 1930's $50.00-110.00

ORPHAN ANNIE WALL POCKET, Famous Artist's Syndicate, china, 6" tall, Japan.......$75.00-110.00

OUR GANG COLORING BOOK, made by Saalfield, 1938...$25.00-45.00

OUR GANG PENCIL BOX, Dixon, 1930's $25.00-50.00

PASTRY COOK UTENSILS, 1930 ....$20.00-45.00

PERRY WINKLE BISQUE NODDER, 2" tall, German, 1930's $40.00-65.00

PHONOGRAPH, Tiny Tot, 1930 ....$40.00-80.00

PINOCCHIO ART STAMP PICTURE SET, 1939, boxed rubber stamps $40.00-85.00

PINOCCHIO BISQUE FIGURE, 1939, 4" .$25.00-50.00

PINOCCHIO BOXED PICTURE PUZZLES, 1939, set of two, attractive box.............................$40.00-75.00

PINOCCHIO COMPOSITION BANK, 1939, Crown Toy, Walt Disney, 5" $45.00-100.00

PINOCCHIO SCRAP BOOK, made by Whitman, 1939,...$30.00-65.00

PINOCCHIO THE ACROBAT, Marx, 1939 Walt Disney Productions, rocking windup $150.00-300.00

PINOCCHIO THE MERRY PUPPET GAME, Milton Bradley, 1939, boxed $40.00-90.00

PINOCCHIO TIN WINDUP WALKER TOY, 1939, Marx, Disney $125.00-200.00

PINOCCHIO WOOD COMPOSITION AND JOINTED DOLL, Ideal, giant version $300.00-750.00

PINOCCHIO WOOD COMPOSITION DOLL BY CROWN TOY, 1939, 10" version $60.00-140.00

PLAY GOLF, Strauss, 1920's, Golfer on green windup, 5" $300.00-575.00

PLUTO HARD RUBBER FIGURE, Seiberling Latex, 1930's, 6" long, red...........................$40.00-90.00

PLUTO MECHANICAL VALENTINE, circa 1930...$10.00-30.00

PLUTO MODELED IN SOAP, boxed, colorful graphics, Lightfoot Schultz, 1930's $45.00-80.00

PLUTO THE PUP BISQUE FIGURE, 1930's, Japan, orange color, 3" Disney.....................$25.00-50.00

PLUTO WATCH ME ROLL OVER WINDUP TOY, Marx, 1930s, Walt Disney Enterprises $50.00-125.00

PLUTO MOTORCYCLE WITH SIREN, by Marx, 1930's $150.00-250.00

POPEYE AND OLIVE OYL ON THE ROOF tin windup roof dancers, 1930's $400.00-950.00

POPEYE CARTOON BOOK, made by Saalfield, 1934...$40.00-80.00

POPEYE CAST IRON BOAT NIGHT LIGHT, 1935...$350.00-600.00

POPEYE DRUMMER PULL TOY, 1929, wood with paper lithograph labels.....................$55.00-100.00

POPEYE EGG TRANSFERS, 1936, 5" square envelope $15.00-35.00

POPEYE FOUNTAIN PEN, 1930's, Penco.$35.00-75.00

POPEYE METAL DIME REGISTER BANK, 3", 1930's, colorful lithograph $25.00-65.00

POPEYE MODELING CLAY, American Crayon Company, 1936..$25.00-65.00

POPEYE OILCLOTH DOLL, 1930's, 11" $125.00-170.00

POPEYE PADDLE WAGON, wood and paper lithograph, 1930's $75.00-165.00

POPEYE PARTY GAME Whitman, 1937, 15" x 26"...$30.00-60.00

POPEYE PENCIL BOX, 1929, Eagle........$20.00-40.00

POPEYE PICTURE PUZZLES, 1932, four in box $30.00-65.00

POPEYE PLASTER FIGURE, 8", circa 1922, K.F.S. $35.00-80.00

POPEYE POP-UP BOOK, Blue Ribbon Press, 1934 ....$100.00-225.00

POPEYE SCRAP BOOK, 1929 ....$25.00-45.00

POPEYE SPINACH DELIVERY by Hubley, cast iron, 5½" $375.00-550.00

POPEYE THE CHAMP BIG FIGHT BOXING TOY, Marx windup, 1930's $1,000.00-2,000.00

POPEYE THIMBLE THEATRE PLAY SET, Walkers, Popeye, Olive and Wimpy...............$250.00-400.00

POPEYE WHERE'S ME PIPE GAME, 1937, boxed $35.00-70.00

PORKY PIG BISQUE BANK, 1930's, 5".$65.00-125.00

PORKY PIG, Marx, 1939 tin, wind-up.$125.00-225.00

POWERFUL KATRINKA AND JIMMY WIND-UP, 1920's, tin $525.00-925.00

RACE CAR #2241, Hubley, 1930's, 7"......$30.00-60.00

RACE CAR, AIRSTREAM DESIGN, Dinky Toys, 1930's $25.00-60.00

RACER #3, Chein, 1920's Indy-type racer, 7" long tin windup $125.00-275.00

RACER #629 by Hubley, 1939, 7" long .$20.00-40.00

RACER #7, Wells, England, 12½" tin windup, 1920's $200.00-300.00

RADIO BANK, 1930's console model, cast iron, blue and gold, 6"...$40.00-80.00

RAP AND TAP IN A FAMILY SCRAP TIN WINDUP, 1925, Unique Art...........................$250.00-550.00

REAL ELECTRIC TOY IRON, circa 1930, metal $10.00-20.00

RED DINING SET FOR CHILDREN, wood, enameled 17", five pieces $30.00-60.00

RED RANGER RID'EM COWBOY, Wyandotte windup, 1930's, 6"..$125.00-300.00

ROADSTER BY CHEIN, tin lithograph, 1920's, 8½" $40.00-80.00

ROADSTER, CAST IRON, late 1930's, 5", white rubber tires $35.00-75.00

ROCKING CHAIR, white enameled, 1923, blue bird stencil on back, 10" seat $25.00-65.00

ROCKING MONKEY ACROBATIC MARVEL windup, Marx, 1930's.......................................$60.00-90.00

ROLLOVER AIRPLANE by Marx, 1920's tin windup $90.00-140.00

ROLLOVER CAT, Marx, 1930's, black cat pushed tin lithograph ball $35.00-95.00

ROLL TOP DESK, child's, 1923, all wood construction $100.00-200.00

RUDY VALEE VALENTINE, 1920's..........$15.00-30.00

SAVING SAM CAST IRON BANK, circa 1920 ....$85.00-160.00

SCHOENHUT TOY UPRIGHT PIANO, 1930, twenty-two keys...$50.00-110.00

SCHUCO SUBMARINE, 13" tin lithograph, 1930's, German $100.00-195.00

SEA PLANE, Chein, 1930's, tin windup, 8" silver/red/blue...$65.00-100.00

SEDAN, CAST IRON, 4⅜", 1930's $40.00-80.00

SEDAN, CAST IRON, 5", 1930's, white rubber tires $50.00-95.00

SEDAN PULLING TRAILER, cast iron, 1930's, 6½" total length $80.00-140.00

SEE SAW MONKEYS, Distler, German, 1920, tin wind-up, 10" $175.00-400.00

SEWING BASKET FOR LITTLE GIRLS, 1920's, wicker $10.00-35.00

SEWING BASKET FOR LITTLE GIRLS, small size, 1920's, stand-up legs, wood $10.00-35.00

SEWING MACHINE, child's, with original carrying case, 1930 ....$50.00-75.00

SEWING SET, Princess Elizabeth, 1937 ..$30.00-60.00

SHIP AHOY tin windup, 1925, lighthouse, similar to Honeymoon Express $600.00-1,200.00

SHIRLEY TEMPLE AT PLAY BOOK, Saalfield, 1930's $20.00-35.00

SHIRLEY TEMPLE CHRISTMAS CARD, Hallmark, 1935..$15.00-30.00

SHIRLEY TEMPLE PAPER DOLLS SET, circa 1930 ....$30.00-65.00

SHIRLEY TEMPLE THIS IS MY CRAYON BOOK, Saalfield, 1935.....................................$20.00-40.00

SHIRLEY TEMPLE WRITING TABLET, 1935 Western Tablet $20.00-40.00

SINGER SEWING MACHINE #20, 1926 .$50.00-70.00

SKI BOY, Chein, 1930's, 6" boxed $100.00-200.00

SKIPPY AND OTHER HARDCOVER HUMOR BOOK, 1929, sixty-four pages $35.00-60.00

SKYBIRD FLYER TIN WINDUP PLANE AND ZEPPELIN CIRCLE TOWER, 1930's $200.00-350.00

SKYBIRD FLYERS, Marx, two planes on tower, 7" tower, 1930's $100.00-200.00

SMITTY CHARACTER STORYBOOK, Cupples and Leon, 1928...$15.00-30.00

SMITTY TEA SET, German, six pieces, manufactured in 1930's...$85.00-140.00

SNOW WHITE AND DOPEY TELEPHONE, 1930's, N. N. Hill Brass...............................$75.00-145.00

SNOW WHITE AND THE PRINCE ENGLISH POST CARD, 1930's $15.00-35.00

SNOW WHITE AND THE PRINCE PULL TOY, N. N. Hill Brass, 1930's, Disney.............$125.00-250.00

SNOW WHITE AND THE SEVEN DWARFS BAKELITE NAPKIN RING, 1938 ....$20.00-50.00

SNOW WHITE AND THE SEVEN DWARFS DIME SAVINGS BANK, 1938, Disney $40.00-100.00

SNOW WHITE AND THE SEVEN DWARFS MECHANICAL HEART-SHAPED VALENTINE, 1938...$10.00-22.00

SNOW WHITE AND THE SEVEN DWARFS OHIO ART TIN PAIL, colorful, 9" version $35.00-90.00

SNOW WHITE AND THE SEVEN DWARFS PLASTER CASTER SET, 1930's, original box .$50.00-125.00

SNOW WHITE AND THE SEVEN DWARFS TAP-AWAY ART SET, 1930's, boxed....................$50.00-85.00

SNOW WHITE AND THE SEVEN DWARFS TEA SET, tin, Ohio Art, 1930's, boxed $100.00-200.00

SNOW WHITE AND THE SEVEN DWARFS TIN SAND PAIL Ohio Art, 5" tall $35.00-70.00

SNOW WHITE AT THE WELL, NITE LITE, LaMode Studios, 1930's $100.00-200.00

SNOW WHITE DRINKING GLASS, made by Libbey, 1938...$10.00-25.00

SNOW WHITE HAIR BARRETTE, circa 1930, decal $20.00-35.00

SNOW WHITE JINGLE BOOK 1930's, ...$30.00-60.00

SNOW WHITE PULLED BY DOC AND DOPEY PULL TOY, 1938, N. N. Hill Brass $75.00-195.00

SNOW WHITE SERIES TINKERSAND PICTURES BOXED SET, 1938 Walt Disney Enterprises......................................$60.00-95.00

SNOW WHITE TELEPHONE, manufactured by N. N. Hill Brass, 1930's $65.00-125.00

SNOWFLAKES AND SWIPES tin lithograph, pull toy, 1929 ....$450.00-1,050.00

SODA FOUNTAIN BENT IRON CHAIR AND TABLE SET, 1920's, child size $75.00-150.00

SPARK PLUG COMIC CHARACTER HORSE GLASS CANDY CONTAINER, 1920's, 3" tall .$50.00-95.00

SPARK PLUG rubber squeak toy,1923, 5"$25.00-45.00

SPARKLING TANK, Marx, 1930's tin windup, 10" $50.00-90.00

STEEL BABY BUGGY, 1930's $35.00-70.00

STORY OF THE WIZARD OF OZ COLORING BOOK, Whitman, 1939 ....$15.00-35.00

STRAUSS HAUL-AWAY TRUCK #22, tin windup, 1920's $100.00-200.00

STRUCTO STEEL FIRE PUMPER TRUCK, 1920's, 21" $200.00-300.00

STURDITOY FIRE ENGINE, sheet steel, 1920's, 33" long $500.00-700.00

SUNNY SUZY WASHING MACHINE WITH WRINGER, metal and tin, 1934 ....$35.00-85.00

TEA SET, Turquoise blue colored enamel set, fifteen pieces, boxed $40.00-80.00

TEAPOT, Doc and Snow White, Disney, 1937...$20.00-50.00

TERRY AND THE PIRATES POP-UP BOOK, Blue Ribbon Press, 1935 ....$100.00-200.00

THE GOLDEN TOUCH, Mickey Mouse Presents, 1930's book $35.00-65.00

THREE LITTLE PIGS ART STAMP PICTURE SET, 1930's $35.00-80.00

THREE LITTLE PIGS FLASHLIGHT, 1930's, Electric Manufacturing Company.................$50.00-100.00

TIN WINDUP MOTORCYCLE, 1930's, with tin tires and side car, Furnish collection, $200.00-400.00.

THREE LITTLE PIGS LEATHER COVERED BOOK BANK, 1930's, Disney $25.00-60.00

THREE LITTLE PIGS PAPER COMPOSITION BOOK, 1930's, Big Bad Wolf cover $20.00-40.00

THREE LITTLE PIGS PLATE, Patriot China, 1930's $15.00-40.00

THREE LITTLE PIGS PLAYING CARD SET, boxed, 1930's, Disney $15.00-35.00

THREE LITTLE PIGS TOOTHBRUSH HOLDER, 1930's, Disney, bisque $50.00-100.00

TILLIE THE TOILER DRAWING BOOK, 1930's $25.00-40.00

TIN TEA SET, Ohio Art, 1930's, boxed with little girls on top $50.00-95.00

TOM MIX DRAW AND PAINT BOOK, Whitman, 1930's $50.00-95.00

TOM MIX PUZZLE, Rexall Drugs premium, 1930's $35.00-50.00

TOMMY KELLY PECK'S BAD BOY WITH THE CIRCUS GAME, Milton Bradley, 1939 .... $20.00-45.00

TOONERVILLE TROLLEY GAME, boxed 9" x 17", Milton Bradley, 1927 .... $50.00-85.00

TOONERVILLE TROLLEY tin lithograph, windup, 1920's, all original $450.00-800.00

TOOTSIETOY BI-PLANE, 1930's, 4" $20.00-45.00

TOOTSIETOY CADILLAC TOURING CAR, 1926 .... $40.00-80.00

TOOTSIETOY DOLL FURNITURE miniature kitchen sink $15.00-30.00

TOOTSIETOY DOLL FURNITURE, 1920's, miniature candelabra $10.00-20.00

TOOTSIETOY DOLL FURNITURE, 1925, dining room set $30.00-55.00

TOOTSIETOY DOLLHOUSE IN ORIGINAL CARTON, 1925 .... $150.00-300.00

TOOTSIETOY DOLLHOUSE FURNITURE, 1925 floor lamp $5.00-15.00

TOOTSIETOY DOLLHOUSE FURNITURE, console radio, brown, 1920's $20.00-35.00

TOOTSIETOY DOLLHOUSE GRAND PIANO with bench $20.00-45.00

TOOTSIETOY DOLLHOUSE LIBRARY TABLE, miniature, 1925 .... $10.00-20.00

TOOTSIETOY DOLLHOUSE ROCKING CHAIR, miniature, 1925 .... $10.00-25.00

TOOTSIETOY DOLLHOUSE VICTROLA, made in 1925 .... $20.00-40.00

TOOTSIETOY FURNISHED MANSION, circa 1930 .... $200.00-400.00

TOOTSIETOY LONG DISTANCE HAULING TRUCK, 1930's $50.00-100.00

TOOTSIETOY MINIATURE TEA CART, dollhouse furniture, 1920's $15.00-30.0

TOOTSIETOY MONOPLANE, 1930's, 4" .. $20.00-45.00

TOOTSIETOY MOON MULLINS POLICE CAR, 1930's $100.00-200.00

TORTOISE AND THE HARE, 1930's Walt Disney Studio hardcover book $10.00-35.00

TOY LUNCHEON LINEN SET, 1920's, rabbit and animal motif, cloth and napkins $10.00-25.00

TRICKY TAXI WINDUP, Marx, circa 1930, 4½" $20.00-40.00

UNCLE WALT IN A ROADSTER, Tootsietoy, 1932 .... $75.00-175.00

POPEYE CHARACTER CHRISTMAS LIGHT COVERS, 1930's, boxed, Reynolds collection, $75.00-125.00.

UNCLE WIGGILY CRAZY CAR, rabbit driving, Marx, 1935, tin wind-up, 7" $300.00-650.00

UNCLE WIGGILY'S WOODLAND GAMES, 1936 .... $10.00-20.00

UNITED STATES AIRMAIL GAME, Parker Brothers, 1930's $35.00-70.00

U.S. ARMY WHIZ SKY FIGHTER, Girard, 1925, 9" long tin windup bi-plane $250.00-550.00

VALORA CHILD'S PHONOGRAPH, 1930, crank phonograph $50.00-90.00

VANITY SET, Ivory colored, mirror, brush, comb, 1920's $10.00-34.00

WAFFLE IRON for little girls, 1922 .... $10.00-25.00

WALT DISNEY SKI JUMP TARGET GAME, 1930's, American Toy Works $60.00-140.00

WALT DISNEY'S GAME PARADE, boxed game set, 1930's, American Toy Works $50.00-95.00

WALT DISNEY'S SILLY SYMPHONY STORIES, Big Little Book, 1936 .... $20.00-50.00

WHISTLING TEA KETTLE, child's version, 1930's, aluminum $10.00-35.00

WIMPY CAST IRON FIGURE, 1930's, 3".$50.00-75.00

WIMPY HUMBERGER, Kazoo type hamburger shaped toy, dated 1936 .... $45.00-70.00

WINNIE THE POOH GAME, 1930's, non-Disney original $50.00-75.00

WORLD'S FAIR GAME, 1939 .... $50.00-125.00

WRECKER TRUCK, Girard, 1920's tin windup, 10" with driver $70.00-135.00

WRIGLEY'S SPEARMINT GUM TRUCK, Buddy L, 1930's $125.00-180.00

WRISTWATCH FOR LITTLE GIRLS, tin and leather, 1920's toy watch $10.00-30.00

WYANDOTTE AMBULANCE, 1930's, 11" steel, wood tires $40.00-80.00

YELLOW CAB MANUFACTURED BY ARCADE, 1920's, original box $1,500.00-2700.00

ZOO PUZZLES, 1922, eight puzzle picture set, boxed $50.00-100.00

MILITARY TOYS AND SOLDIERS

It was once said that in the history of mankind there has never been a weapon made that has not been used. In regard to toys, this statement is probably more true, there has never been a military weapon made that was not in some way assimilated into a toy. Barring only designs not available to the public on grounds of national security, from the Civil War to Vietnam, our wars have inspired our toys.

This seems a horrible reflection of our society that war toys should even exist for the entertainment of children. But with so much of our family and national history tied into our involvement in one or more or the many wars that we have fought in the past two centuries, the fact that military toys remain popular today is simply a reflection of our own tempestuous past.

Military toys in this listing include both vehicles and soldiers, guns and playsets. The Louis Marx Company was one of the chief producers of tin windup toys of the 1920's, 1930's and 1940's, so many of the company's fine examples are listed here.

Collectors of military toys may occasionally focus upon toys related to only one war, but generally they are likely to be military toy generalists who collect soldiers, tanks, toy guns and related items.

Since our own military assaults and defenses of the past century have been made with the help of all armed forces, our military toys reflect the total involvement of boats, airplanes, land vehicles and the individual soldier.

Military toys often exhibit fine action and were built sturdily to survive the countless dirt pile and sand box battles where their wars were waged. These toys range from sophisticated remote controlled battery operated tanks to the simplest figural lead cast foot soldier. When displayed together, a host of military toys can radiate an impressive display of prowess. Prices today range from the very modest for recent toys to extremely expensive for unusual military windup toys or rare complete and boxed soldier sets.

It should also be noted here that even general-line toy collectors have an interest in military toys, both from their transportation link and their historical background. These military toys are a clear reflection of our own history, long after the real wars have been fought and the last wastes of war removed, the toys will remain as a reminder of our past and what we risked for our freedom.

MILITARY TOYS AND SOLDIERS

BRITAINS SOLDIERS, cast lead, each 2" tall, $5.00-10.00.

BRITAINS MOUNTED SOLDIERS, 1940's-1950's, each $5.00-15.00.

AIR DEFENSE MISSLE LAUNCHER, 1950's, Japan, BO, instrument panel launches $100.00-225.00

AIR SEARCHLIGHT RESCUE TRUCK, Japan, tin friction, 7" long, boxed $45.00-95.00

AIRBORNE COMMAND BURP GUN, sparkling, 1950's, 14" blue plastic MIB $25.00-40.00

AIRCRAFT CARRIER, ASC, Japan, all tin friction, 14½" long $60.00-135.00

AIRCRAFT CARRIER, KB, Japan, BO, 13" long $100.00-65.00

AIRCRAFT CARRIER, Mars, West Germany, plastic windup, 8" $15.00-30.00

AIRCRAFT DEFENDER, Auburn Rubber ..$5.00-10.00

AIRCRAFT GUNNER, Auburn Rubber $4.00-7.00

AMMO CARRIER SOLDIER, Barclay.........$7.00-12.00

ARMORED ATTACK SET, Marx, Japan, BO, 6" Jeep, 5" tank, fourteen army men, etc. $60.00-95.00

ARMORED CAR WITH ACK ACK, TWO CANNONS, 1950's, 7" in box..............................$45.00-85.00

ARMORED CAR WITH GUN TURRET, 1930's, Britains $50.00-80.00

ARMORED CAR, eight wheeled, French, 1920's tin

windup, 9" $100.00-250.00

ARMORED VEHICLE, early tank, 1930's, Kellerman, tin windup, 4" $60.00-90.00

ARMY AMBULANCE, Auburn Rubber $5.00-10.00

ARMY AND AIR FORCE TRAINING CENTER with box...$35.00-65.00

ARMY AND NAVY SHOOTING GALLERY manufactured by Marx $65.00-110.00

ARMY CANNON BY MANOIL $5.00-15.00

ARMY CANNON, Auburn Rubber $10.00-20.00

ARMY COMBAT TANK, tin, 1940's, BO .$25.00-50.00

ARMY COVERED WAGON. 1950's, Dinky Toys, 4", detachable canopy $10.00-30.00

ARMY TOW TRUCK, BUDDY L, 9" with plastic winch $10.00-20.00

ARMY TRUCK AND TRANSPORT, Buddy L, 1940's, 31" long $75.00-155.00

ARMY TRUCK, Marx, 1950's, 14" plastic tires, tin, canvas cover $30.00-50.00

ARMY TURNOVER TANK, Marx, 1940, tin windup, 8" $50.00-80.00

ARMY WATER TANK TRUCK, 1950's, 3", Dinky Toys $15.00-30.00

ATOMIC TANK, by Beets Inc. $250.00-425.00

AUBURN RUBBER INFANTRY SET, 1939, fifteen figures, boxed $70.00-120.00

AUBURN RUBBER SOLDIER charging with machine gun $5.00-12.00

AUBURN RUBBER SOLDIER, figure holding binoculars $5.00-15.00

BARCLAY AA gun $15.00-25.00

BARCLAY bench with two soldiers..........$15.00-25.00

BARCLAY blue sailor, lead figure, pod-foot soldier $4.00-8.00

BARCLAY bomb thrower $5.00-10.00

BARCLAY cannon, 3½" $5.00-15.00

BARCLAY cannon, 7" $10.00-20.00

BARCLAY civilians, moulded lead figures, ten assorted $30.00-65.00

BARCLAY cycle officer $5.00-10.00

BARCLAY field kitchen vehicle, olive drab.$10.00-15.00

BARCLAY field phone $5.00-15.00

BARCLAY flag bearer, pod foot moulded lead soldier $4.00-8.00

BARCLAY girl ice skater $5.00-10.00

BARCLAY gunner $8.00-12.00

BARCLAY lead bazooka soldier, pod-foot $4.00-8.00

BARCLAY lead pot foot soldier, pilot $4.00-8.00

BARCLAY machine gunner, pod foot moulded lead soldier $4.00-8.00

BARCLAY marine soldier, pod-foot $4.00-8.00

BARCLAY negro porter with wisk broom ..$5.00-10.00

BARCLAY newsboy $5.00-10.00

BARCLAY pilot with parachute...................$5.00-10.00

BARCLAY policeman with right arm raised.$5.00-10.00

BARCLAY radio operator with antenna ...$40.00-65.00

BARCLAY rifleman, pod foot lead soldier $4.00-8.00

BARCLAY schoolboy $5.00-10.00

BARCLAY armored vehicles set of 8 ....$80.00-125.00

BARCLAY set of 14 soldiers $80.00-125.00

BARCLAY, set of 15 pod-footed lead soldiers, selection $40.00-80.00

BARCLAY single man AA truck, olive drab

paint $8.00-12.00
BARCLAY ski trooper $25.00-50.00
BARCLAY SOLDIER peeling potatoes $10.00-20.00
BARCLAY SOLDIER shooting from wall ..$10.00-25.00
BARCLAY SOLDIER with gas mask $5.00-10.00
BARCLAY SOLDIER with searchlight $5.00-10.00
BARCLAY SOLDIER Officer with pistol $5.00-10.00
BARCLAY SOLDIER standing and firing ...$5.00-10.00
BARCLAY SOLDIERS on raft $30.00-60.00
BARCLAY SOLDIERS set of twelve all with tin helmets $75.00-125.00
BARCLAY SOLDIERS, TWO MEN with mobile cannon $10.00-20.00
BARCLAY SOLDIER, figure carrying sound detector equipment $5.00-10.00
BARCLAY TORPEDO cannon truck $8.00-12.00
BARCLAY TWO-MAN cannon $8.00-12.00
BARCLAY TYPIST, figure $5.00-10.00
BARCLAY WOUNDED SOLDIER lead figure on crutches $5.00-10.00
BATTLE OF THE BLUE AND GRAY PLAY SET, Marx $100.00-250.00
BREN GUN CARRIER AND CREW, Britains, 1940's-1950's $50.00-125.00
BRITAINS AMBULANCE SET #1512, circa 1940 ....$125.00-225.00
BRITAINS ARMY AMBULANCE WITH DRIVER, 1930's $125.00-300.00
BRITAINS BUCK ROGERS FIGURES, six pieces, extremely rare set $1,200.00-2,000.00
BRITAINS CANADA FORT HENRY GUARDS, boxed $75.00-125.00
BRITAINS DISPLAY SET, sixty seven pieces, 1950's..$1,500.00-3,800.00
BRITAINS HOWITZER CANNON, 4½" $30.00-60.00
BRITAINS RED ARMY INFANTRY lead figures with helmets $50.00-100.00
BRITAINS UNION CAVALRY figures in original box $50.00-85.00
BRITAINS WEST POINT CADETS in original box $65.00-100.00
BRITAINS, CONFEDERATE INFANTRY $75.00-125.00
BRITAINS, EGYPTIAN camel corps $100.00-200.00
BRITAINS, MARCHING BRITISH SAILORS in box $75.00-125.00
CANNON TRUCK, with one man on rear, by Barclay $10.00-20.00
CANNON, by Barclay, 7" $10.00-20.00
CANNON, Britain, metal, boxed, 4", royal artillery...$10.00-25.00
CANNON HOWITZER, 25 pounder, 8", box $10.00-25.00
CANNON, MARBLE SHOOTING, cast iron, 1887, 15" $75.00-150.00
CANNON, PREMIER, cast metal, 1940's, black rubber tires, 5" $10.00-25.00
CANNON, tin, Marx, 1930's $80.00-175.00
CAST IRON ARTILLERY CARRIAGE, IVES, 1890's, two horses, two riders $700.00-1,500.00
CLIMBING FIGHTING SPARKLING TANK, Marx, 1930's, tin windup, 10" $50.00-90.00
COMBAT MOTORCYCLE, tin windup, Bunny trademark, Japan, friction, 8" $125.00-250.00

COMMAND POST, measurements 12" x 16", marked Germany $1,200.00-1,500.00
COMMANDO JOE, Ohio Art, tin windup, soldier crawls with rifle $65.00-140.00
COVERED ARMY TENDER with caterpillar wheels, Britains, 1950's-1960's $100.00-200.00
COWBOYS AND INDIANS, GS, four 3" cowboys, four Indians with four horses $175.00-375.00
DIVE BOMBER, DOUGLASS DAUNTLESS KIT, monogram, model, 1967, 14" $10.00-20.00
DOCTOR FIGURE, by Barclay $15.00-25.00
DOUGHBOY TANK Marx, 1930's, boxed tin windup, 10" long with pop-up soldier $85.00-145.00
DOUGHBOY, Chein, ca. 1920's, tin windup figure, WWI soldier waddles $120.00-225.00
ELASTOLIN BRITISH ARTILLERY MAN .$15.00-25.00
ELASTOLIN DOUGHBOY OFFICER WITH SWORD, 3½" $15.00-25.00

BRITAINS LEAD SOLDIERS, assorted styles, each $5.00-15.00.

STEEL CANNON, MORSER HOWITZER, 10½" long, Furnish collection, $40.00-85.00.

COWBOY FIGURES, 5" to 8" tall, by Trico, Japan, Furnish collection, each $10.00-25.00.

INDIAN FIGURES BY ELASTOLIN, 3" to 7" tall, composition type, Furnish collection, each $10.00-25.00.

ELASTOLIN FLAG BEARER, pre-war Japan, 6½" $10.00-20.00

ELASTOLIN GERMAN REGIMENT WITH HITLER AND FOURTEEN OTHER FIGURES, men and horses $200.00-400.00

ELASTOLIN HORSES AND RIDERS, pair soldiers with swords, 5½" $30.00-70.00

ELASTOLIN LANCER, mounted figure carrying lance $20.00-45.00

ELASTOLIN RIFLEMEN, pre-war Germany, 3¾", seventeen in lot............................$150.00-200.00

ELASTOLIN RIFLEMEN, pre-war Germany, five in set, 5½" $40.00-75.00

ELASTOLIN SALUTING GERMAN GENERAL figure...$50.00-85.00

ELASTOLIN SCOTTISH GUARDS SET, fifteen pieces $140.00-225.00

ELASTOLIN SOLDIERS SET, twenty pieces, foot soldiers, mortar, machine gunners $100.00-225.00

ELASTOLIN SOLDIERS SET, 3" pre-war figures, set of five $30.00-65.00

ELASTOLIN SWORDSMEN, pre-war Germany, three in lot, 4"....................................$30.00-55.00

ELASTOLIN WWI SOLDIER BAND SET, five figures $80.00-140.00

FIELD KITCHEN VEHICLE, by Barclay, olive drab $10.00-15.00

FLAG BEARER, #701, Barclay.................$5.00-15.00

FORT APACHE PLAYSET, Marx, boxed..$40.00-75.00

GENERAL MACARTHUR, J. H. Miller plaster figure, 1950......................................$20.00-30.00

GERMAN SOLDIERS, ELASTOLIN, band figures, 3", seven figure set $50.00-85.00

GREY IRON marine $10.00-20.00

GREY IRON Royal Canadian Police.........$10.00-20.00

GREY IRON U.S. Naval Officer................$10.00-15.00

HEAVY HOWITZER ON TRACTOR WHEELS, cannon, Britains $50.00-125.00

HEIGHTFINDER SOLDIER WITH APPARATUS, 1940's, Britains $35.00-75.00

HELMETED OFFICER, grey iron soldier ...$8.00-15.00

HONEST JOHN MISSLE LAUNCHER, 1964, Dinky Toys $20.00-35.00

HORSE DRAWN FIELD KITCHEN, German, 1930's, 7", tinplate $100.00-200.00

JEEP, heavy gauge tinplate, 1950, 7" $40.00-80.00

JEEP, #1 Minic, boxed, tin windup, 3" ..$15.00-35.00

KNEELING GERMAN SOLDIER, Barclay...$7.00-12.00

LEAD SOLDIER TRENCH AND FENCE LANDSCAPE, 12" x 11" plus fences $70.00-105.00

LEAD SOLDIERS TENT ASSORTMENT, boxed, six tents $30.00-50.00

LEAD SOLDIERS, BRITAINS, #1791 Signal Corp Dispatch motorcycle riders $110.00-200.00

LEGION BUGLAR grey iron cast soldier ...$8.00-15.00

LIDO REVOLUTIONARY WAR SET, eight pieces, 1950's set $20.00-40.00

LINEOL CHARGING Flag Bearer $50.00-110.00

LINEOL NAZI SOLDIER marching..........$20.00-45.00

LINEOL SOLDIERS SET, fifty pieces, composition soldiers $400.00-575.00

MACHINE GUNNER, pre-war, Japan celluloid soldier windup action, 7" $125.00-225.00

MANOIL aviator holding missile...............$15.00-30.00

MANOIL crawling scout..........................$30.00-50.00

MANOIL deep sea diver $10.00-25.00

MANOIL gasoline wagon...........................$8.00-15.00

MANOIL gasoline trailor $20.00-35.00

MANOIL grenade thrower $15.00-25.00

MANOIL lead soldier, advancing wearing gas mask $8.00-12.00

MANOIL lead soldier, kneeling and firing weapon...$8.00-12.00

MANOIL lead soldier, seated with phone.$10.00-15.00

MANOIL lead soldier stretcher bearer $8.00-12.00

MANOIL lead soldier #65, diver $8.00-12.00

MANOIL military vehicles set, seven pieces $60.00

MANOIL tank $8.00-15.00

MANOIL torpedo wagon $8.00-15.00

MANOIL NURSE FIGURE, cast soldier....$10.00-20.00

MANOIL OBSERVER with binoculars......$10.00-20.00

MANOIL SHELL CARRIER figure $10.00-30.00

MANOIL SNIPER, soldier $5.00-15.00

MANOIL SOLDIER with barbed wire.......$15.00-25.00

MANOIL SOLDIERS, set of five, stretcher bearer, tractor, bicyclist, etc. $20.00-40.00

MANOIL WATCHMAN with lantern $10.00-25.00

MANOIL WATER WAGON, vehicle $8.00-15.00

MARCHING SOLDIER with rifle, J. H. MIller, 1950, 4½" $10.00-15.00

MARKLIN TANK, German, early, tin windup, 8½" $250.00-450.00

MARX ANTI-TANK SET with metal figures, boxed...$250.00-395.00

MARX ARCTIC EXPLORERS SET, twenty pieces, ca. 1950's, boxed $75.00-150.00

MARX FORT APACHE PLAYSET with original box $40.00-75.00

MARX TANK, 10", large size, 1950's $25.00-55.00

MARX TOY ARMY AND NAVY SHOOTING GALLERY, boxed $65.00-110.00

MARX TURNOVER TANK, 1940's, tin windup, 4" long with engine noise $20.00-55.00

McLOUGHLIN BROTHERS, fifty soldiers on parade, boxed...$100.00-325.00

MIGNOT FRENCH ARTILLERY WAGON, in original box $50.00-100.00

MILITARY AMBULANCE, 1930's, metal truck with red cross, 11" long...............................$175.00-350.00

MILITARY AMBULANCE, Dinky Toys, 1956, 4" $25.00-40.00

MILITARY TRUCK VEB EAST GERMANY, 1940's, 4", tinplate, towing wagons $100.00-250.00

MILITARY VEHICLES LOT by Manoil, wagons, guns, cannons, seven pieces $60.00-90.00

MISSLE LAUNCHER, Japan, battery operated, all tin, 7" ICBM launcher, box $65.00-100.00

MISSLE LAUNCHING TANK, battery operated, remote controlled, 10" with tin targets $150.00-265.00

MISSLE VEHICLE WITH ERECTOR MECHANISM, 1960's, Dinky Toys $20.00-45.00

MOTOR MACHINE GUN CORPS, motocycle with side car, 1920's, two riders $50.00-120.00

MOTOR UNIT, Barclay, olive drab $10.00-15.00

MOTORCYCLE RIDER, by Manoil $20.00-30.00

NAZI ON HORSEBACK, tin windup, Bloomer-Schuler, 1936, 5" $275.00-520.00

PILOT IN FLIGHT GARB, lead soldier, by Moulded Miniatures $20.00-40.00

PRINCE VALIANT PLAY SET, 1950's .$125.00-225.00

PRONE MACHINE GUNNER, grey iron $8.00-15.00

PRONE RIFLEMAN SOLDIER, Barclay $7.00-12.00

RED CROSS NURSE, grey iron $10.00-15.00

RENAULT TANK, Barclay $10.00-18.00

RIFLE SOLDIER, Barclay $7.00-12.00

SEARCHLIGHT TRUCK, Dinky Toys, 3", WWII $100.00-200.00

SEARCHLIGHT, Auburn Rubber $10.00-20.00

SEARCHLIGHT, by Barclay $10.00-20.00

SKYBIRD FLYER TIN WINDUP AND ZEPPELIN CIRCLE TOWER, 1930's $200.00-350.00

SOLDIER BANJO PLAYER, black face, manufactured

by Manoil...$40.00-60.00

SOLDIER BANJO PLAYER, white face, manufactured by Manoil...$20.00-35.00

SOLDIER WITH RIFLE, WWI, Barclay $5.00-15.00

ELASTOLIN U.S. LANCERS, 4" to 6" high, composition, Furnish collection, $20.00-40.00.

G. I. JOE AND K-9 PUPS TIN WINDUP WALKER TOY, Reynolds collection, $75.00-150.00.

**MANOIL SOLDIERS, with metal helmets, 2" to 4",
Reynolds collection, each $5.00-12.00.**

**MARX JUMPIN' JEEP 22 C, tin windup with crazy
car, action, 6", Furnish collection, $50.00-95.00.**

SOLDIER WWI, prone firing rifle, tin windup,
7" $80.00-125.00
SOLDIERS OF FORTUNE, eight flat tin lithograph sol-
diers $30.00-65.00
SOLDIERS, grey iron, lot of twelve $80.00-120.00
SOLDIERS, KROO SAILORS, ZULU WAR, #343, Sha-
mus Wade..$50.00-75.00
**SOLDIERS, LEAD, PRINCE ALFRED'S OWN CAPE
TOWN CAVALRY**, #319, 1869 ....$50.00-75.00
SOLDIERS, LEAD, TRINIDAD LIGHT HORSE, 1897,
Shamus Wade.....................................$50.00-75.00
SOLDIERS, MOUNTED COSSACK RIFLEMEN, three
on horseback $30.00-50.00
SOLDIERS, ROYAL INDIAN NAVY, #325 1897, Sha-
mus Wade, ca. 1965 ....$50.00-75.00
SOLDIERS, TWENTY PIECE SET BY ELASTOLIN with
mortar and machine gunners $100.00-225.00
SOLDIERS, WOODS IRREGULARS, ZULU WAR, #331,
two, 2½" $50.00-75.00

SPARKLING TANK, 4", 1930's, Marx $45.00-95.00
SPARKLING TANK, friction, 1960's, M-4, all tin, boxed,
8" $35.00-70.00
SPARKLING TANK, GAMA, U.S. ZONE GERMANY, 4"
with pop-up soldier, tin $45.00-90.00
SPARKLING TANK, GAMA, U.S. ZONE GERMANY,
large version $55.00-100.00
SPARKLING TANK, Marx, 1962, tin and plastic, wind-
up $10.00-30.00
STANDING RIFLEMAN, by Barclay $7.00-12.00
STRETCHER BEARER SOLDIER, J. H. Miller,
1950...$10.00-15.00
TANK ON A BATTLEFIELD tin windup, 9" x 6" terrain,
2" tank, boxed $35.00-95.00
TANK, 1933, Dinky Toys, 3½", ...$20.00-40.00
TANK, Dinky Toys, 3½", 1937 ....$30.00-45.00
TANK, light, 1930's, Dinky toys, 2½" ...$20.00-40.00
TANK, MARX, 10", large size, 1950's, tin windup,
action $25.00-55.00
TANK, MARX, 1930's, tin windup, 10" with bright
track hubs, side guns $60.00-120.00
TANK, MOBILE, PELLET SHOOTING, battery oper-
ated, Tomy, recent, 8" long $25.00-35.00
TANK, ONE MAN, by Barclay $8.00-12.00
TANK, SPARKLING, with box, 1930's ...$75.00-225.00
TEDDY ROOSEVELT ROUGH RIDERS, cardboard sol-
diers set, 1900's $100.00-250.00
TENTS AND STRETCHERS SET, six pieces, lead sol-
dier scale $25.00-45.00
TOMMY GUNNER SOLDIER, by Barclay ..$7.00-12.00
TRENCH AND SOLDIER SET, by Built-Rite,
in box $25.00-55.00
TRENCH SECTION, original box, 6" x 12".$200.00-400.00
TRENCH SETS FOR LEAD SOLDIERS, two composi-
tion trenches, by Elastolin $30.00-50.00
TROOP CARRIER, Dinky $5.00-10.00
TRUCK ARMY TRANSPORT, six-wheeled pulling water
tank, trailer, 1930's $50.00-110.00
TURNOVER TANK, Marx, tin windup, 4"
long $20.00-55.00
U.S. ARMY FIGHTER PLANE, Marx, boxed, 8" wing-
span, tin windup $100.00-200.00
U.S. CAVALRY MOUNTED OFFICER, figure on
horse $15.00-25.00
U.S. MILITARY POLICE CAR, 1950's, 9" plastic fric-
tion, green with siren.........................$15.00-30.00
WOODEN SOLDIERS SET, 12" with wooden gun, 16",
target set, 1921 ....$100.00-225.00
WOUNDED SOLDIER, Auburn Rubber $5.00-10.00
WWI TANK, Marx, tin windup, 5" $30.00-60.00

**MANOIL MACHINE GUNNERS WITH METAL HEL-
METS, 2" tall, value of each: $5.00-13.00.**

MISCELLANEOUS TOYS

This chapter includes toys which were difficult to classify in any of the other chapters or last minute prices which were added to the data base. The main categories which are represented in this file are advertising, farm items, guns, locomotive and train toys, penny toys and premiums.

Advertising toys are toys which were produced to advertise or popularize a product. Premiums are also given away free or with some bonus offer as a sort of public service to valued customers. Both advertising toys and premium toy collecting are active fields where the "hottest" area of premium collecting is the RADIO PREMIUM field.

Penny toys were produced mainly in Germany and Japan but the German tin lithographed miniatures usually command higher prices in the antique toy market than do their Japanese counterparts. Penny toys can range from the very simple wheeled toy to ornate miniature mechanical mechanisms. By far, the most common examples, yet still highly valuable are transportation toys such as cars, horse drawn wagons and vehicles, along with trains.

The listing of guns in this section is rather generic and collectors will want to look more closely for gun listings in the SPACE TOYS and COWBOY sections.

GEORGE WASHINGTON AS A BOY CANDY CONTAINER, RARE, 9" tall, 1920's, Furnish collection, $200.00-400.00.

PLANTERS PEANUT plastic windup "Mr. Peanut", 9" tall, Reynolds collection, $35.00-70.00.

159

ROI-TAN ADVERTISING CAR WITH SIGN ON TOP, red car with yellow sign, 1930's or 1940's, Furnish collection, $45.00-80.00.

CAST LEAD DOGS AND DEER, each 1" to 3½" tall, Reynolds collection, value each $20.00-45.00.

ACTION TOY, MERRY MASONS, Wolverine, 1950's, hand powered toy $25.00-50.00

ADVERTISING, ERTL, Bell Telephone bank truck, all plastic $10.00-20.00

ADVERTISING, Beulah the Cow pitcher, Elsie-like Borden item, 4½" $10.00-25.00

ADVERTISING, BUSTER BROWN WITH TIGE SHOE STORE DISPLAY, 28" $200.00-350.00

ADVERTISING, CHEVROLET VEGA DEALER PROMO, plastic car $10.00-15.00

ADVERTSING, COCA-COLA ROUTE TRUCK, Japan, 1950's, battery operated, tin 12" long ad box $100.00-200.00

ADVERTISING, COCA-COLA TRUCK, Marx, 1940's, tin, 18" long, Coke logo $60.00-90.00

ADVERTISING, Coke dispenser, 1960's, Chilton, 10" plastic with four glasses $30.00-60.00

ADVERTISING, Crackerjacks mask, marked 1930's $8.00-12.00

ADVERTISING, Dixie, Buster Crabbe/Flash Gordon, premium lid $15.00-30.00

ADVERTISING, Little Debi doll, Horseman, 1972..$10.0-30.00

ADVERTISING, MOBILGAS GASOLINE CARRIER TRUCK, Japan, 1950's, 9" Ford $50.00-85.00

ADVERTISING, MOXIE CAR, driver on horse in car, toy $800.00-1,600.00

ADVERTISING, NAUGA, Uniroyal ad item for Naugahide, 14" creatue $12.00-20.00

ADVERTISING, NIPPER, RCA dog, plastic salt and pepper shakers, 3½" $10.00-20.00

ADVERTISING, NORTH AMERICAN VAN LINE TRUCK, Japan, friction, 13" long $30.00-70.00

ADVERTISING, PILLSBURY DOUGHBOY DOLL, 1970's $5.00-8.00

ADVERTISING, REDI-KILOWATT brass pin on original card, 1955 ....$12.00-18.00

ADVERTISING, REDI-KILOWATT EAR CLIPS, 1950's $5.00-10.00

ADVERTISING, ROLY POLY FIGURE, Satisfied Customer.......................................$200.00-425.00

ADVERTISING, SKEEZIX SHOE AD CARD on mirror $30.00-60.00

ADVERTISING, TIGER BANK, Humble oil, 9" vinyl, 1960's $10.00-15.00

ADVERTISING, TONY THE TIGER, windup, by Marx..$50.00-155.00

ADVERTISING, U.S. ROYAL GIANT TIRE TOY, 1961, World's Fair souvenir, 9"................$60.00-125.00

ADVERTISING, Uncle Ludwig Von Drake and Donald Duck cups, 1960's, RCA $10.00-25.00

ADVERTISING, WESTERN AUTO TRUCK, Marx, steel, 24" $50.00-100.00

AIRPLANE RIDE, VACATION, LAND, Yone, Japan, tin windup $50.00-110.00

AUTO RACE SET, GRAND PRIX, Technofix, West German, all tin $50.00-110.00

BASKETBALL PLAYER, ATC, Japan, 1950's, all tin, plunger action, 7"...........................$90.00-145.00

BLOCKS SET, picture cubes, children in auto, 1910 ....$200.00-300.00

BULLDOZER, Marvelous Mike robot-driven bulldozer, boxed...$150.00-300.00

BULLDOZER, windup, Structo, steel, circa 1920 ....$100.00-200.00

CABLE CARS SET, Japan, tin, battery operated, 8" long $35.00-65.00

CANDY CONTAINER, Brownie character, composition, figural................................$500.00-900.00

CATERPILLAR EARTHMOVER, manufactured by Marx, 11" long $100.00-300.00

CONSTRUCTION SET, manufactured by Marklin, boxed, 1950's $85.00-165.00

CONSTRUCTION VEHICLE, by SLIK TOYS, Oliver OC-6 crawler, in box...........................$250.00-400.00

CONTROL TOWER, air control tower, Japan, 5", lever action, 2" planes $35.00-75.00

DRIVE-IN THEATRE PLAYSET, manufactured by Remco, 9" x 14" $50.00-125.00

ERECTOR SET, by Gilbert, 10" box $75.00-200.00

FARM ANIMALS, Farmyard Series lead set of figures, pig, rooster, and others $15.00-30.00

FARM SET, AUBURN RUBBER TRACTOR AND FARM SET, two pieces................................$15.00-45.00

FARM SET, barn with nine cows, "Golden Guernsey Milk" $35.00-55.00

FARM SET, BARN TOY CARDBOARD with 14 wooden animals, original box, 1950's $35.00-50.00

FARM SET, Marx, tin 1950's, barn box, double team horses, dray wagon, and more $60.00-125.00

FARM TOY, WINDMILL PUMP, tin cyclone, 1917, 16½" tall...$125.00-325.00

FARM TRUCK, STRUCTO, steel, 20" with seven plastic animals, boxed $50.00-100.00

FLYING HELICOPTER SKYPORT, Marx, 1950's, 5" terminal on 12" base, boxed $40.00-95.00

FOOTBALL KICKER with cardboard stand-up background...$125.00-275.00

FORDSON TRACTOR by Arcade............$45.00-105.00

FRICTION TOY, INSECT PROCESSION, Japan, all tin, 8" long, beetles $10.00-20.00

GAME, Chiromagica $200.00-500.00

GAME, Little Orphan Annie, running with ball $30.00-75.00

GAME, Mail Express and Accomodations, by McLoughlin Brothers...................................$500.00-900.00

GAME, Mansion of Happiness, W. & S. B. Ives, 1843 ....$500.00-900.00

GAME, The Magestic Game of Asiatic Ostrich, 1812 ....$300.00-700.00

GAME, The Skating Race Game, 1900, boxed lithograph $75.00-175.00

GAME, The Susceptibles, A Parlor Amusement Game, McLoughlin Brothers...................$200.00-600.00

GAME, Tobogganning at Christmas, McLoughlin Brothers $250.00-600.00

GAME, Visit of Santa Claus, manufactured by McLoughlin Brothers..........................$450.00-1,300.00

GAME, REWARD OF VIRTUE, handpainted game...$900.00-1,700.00

GARAGE, Techno-Lift, German $75.00-150.00

GAS PUMPS, Arcade, cast iron, 5" tall, three in set $100.00-200.00

GAS STATION, Mobile, 2" tall, miniature car, "Jet" $50.00-100.00

GUN BOOK, Hubley Cap Pistol Factory Book, 1949 ....$15.00-25.00

GUN BOOK, Hubley Cap Pistol Factory Book, 1957 ....$15.00-25.00

GUN BOOK, Hubley Cap Pistol Factory Book, 1958 ....$10.00-20.00

GUN GAME, Sambo Dart Game, with gun, made of tin, ...$50.00-125.00

GUN SET, Zorro Set Gun, mask, whip and lariat $20.00-40.00

GUN, Airborne Commando Burp Gun, Marx, 1950's, 14" long, plastic $25.00-40.00

GUN, Buck Rogers 25th Century Pop Gun, Daisy, 1930's, 10" long $60.00-120.00

GUN, Buffalo Bill Cap Gun $10.00-20.00

GUN, cast iron cap gun, "King" $10.00-35.00

GUN, G-Man Mechanical Gun, tin, LineMar, boxed, 4" long $35.00-65.00

GUN, Hubley cap gun, original sticker $15.00-30.00

GUN, Hubley Pirate Pistol in the original box $75.00-125.00

GUN, Johnny Ringo Guns and Holsters Set, complete $30.00-60.00

GUN, Junior Cap Pistol #25, repeating, by Stevens, 1930, 4" long with box $40.00-80.00

GUN, Red Ranger Gun with Holster Set, 1950's $8.00-20.00

GUN, Roy Rogers Cap Pistol $10.00-20.00

GUN, Roy Rogers Tuckaway Gun on card $15.00-30.00

GUN, Space Gun, Daiya, Japan, 7½", 1950's tin wind-up, sparking $15.00-30.00

GUN, Texan Fifty Shot Pistol, Hubley, 1950's, 9" in box $25.00-60.00

GERMAN PENNY TOY CARRIAGE WITH SINGLE HORSE, 2" long, all tin lithograph, Furnish collection, $100.00-225.00.

PENNY TOY BOAT WITH TWO TEAM RACERS, tin, German, 4", Furnish collection, $150.00-300.00.

GERMAN TIN LITHOGRAPH, PENNY TOY GOOSE, $85.00-190.00. GERMAN TIN LITHOGRAPH, PENNY TOY CATS ON LOG, $100.00-225.00, Furnish collection.

MISCELLANEOUS TOYS

PENNY TOYS; GERMAN, MOTHER WITH CHILD IN WHEELED HIGH CHAIR AND BABY CARRIAGE, 2" long, Furnish collection, $125.00-240.00.

TIN WINDUP "PENNY TOY" FIRE ENGINE WTIH LADDER, Furnish collection, $200.00-400.00.

GUN, Wagon Train Western Zing Cap Gun, 11", copper color $40.00-65.00

GUN, Wild Bill Hickock Cap Pistol $10.00-25.00

GUN, Wyatt Earp Cap Gun, single $10.00-35.00

GUN, Zooka Pop Pistol, manufactured by Daisy, 1930's, steel $10.00-25.00

GUN, Zorro Pump Rifle $15.00-25.00

GUNS, Popeye Pistols, by Halso, K. R. S., 1961, two 6" guns on character card......................$25.00-45.00

GUNS, Wells Fargo Holster Set $30.00-60.00

LOCOMOTIVE WITH TENDER, Pennsylvania Railroad #369, Mohawk Railroad $35.00-75.00

LOCOMOTIVE WRECKING CAR #1020, manufactured by Buddy L.....................................$350.00-750.00

LOCOMOTIVE, battery operated Mountain Express, Japan, 16" long $40.00-55.00

LOCOMOTIVE, Fisher, pre-war Germany, tin windup, 6½" $40.00-85.00

LOCOMOTIVE #3CGB, German, momentum, tin 6" long $40.00-60.00

LONDON BRIDGE, Technofix, U.S. Zone Germany, 44" long, 4" windup cars $40.00-95.00

MINIATURE TOWN, Boxville Toy Town, Superior Paper Company, 1930's $40.00-70.00

MODEL CAR, Chevy Bel-aire, customized, stock car, 1957, ca. 1969 ....$10.00-22.00

MODEL CAR, dealer promo, Ford Galaxy, 1963, aqua, 8" plastic $20.00-40.00

MODEL CAR, Rambler, 1962, taxi model, dealer promo...$15.00-25.00

MODEL CAR, Rolls Royce, 1931, ca. 1960's, monogram $5.00-12.00

MODEL CAR, Skid-doo, 1932, manufactured by Aurora, ca. 1963 ....$4.00-8.00

MODEL CAR, Studebaker Lark, 1962 .....$15.00-25.00

MODEL CAR, Thunderbird, Darryl Starbird, 1958 Revell, 1966..$10.00-25.00

MODEL KIT, tank, manufactured by Aurora, 1960's, Japanese $5.00-15.00

MONORAIL, battery operated, tin $50.00-100.00

MONORAIL, Schuco, Disneyland, 1950's, set, rare $300.00-600.00

MUSICAL TOP, clown, Chein, clown head handle, 1950's, 7" $40.00-90.00

MUSICAL TOY, cathedral, by Chein, 1930's tin windup crank music box........................$70.00-125.00

MUSICAL TOY, Trinity Chimes, by Schoenhut wood and paper, lithograph $700.00-1,500.00

NESTING BLOCKS, Jenny Wren and Cock Robin, 1900's $85.00-175.00

PARACHUTE, USA, toy, 1915, 10" x 3" .$10.00-20.00

PENNY TOY OCEAN LINER, German, tin lithograph, 5" long $115.00-200.00

PENNY TOY ALLIGATOR, early German tin lithograph, 5" long $50.00-125.00

PENNY TOY BEAR #3 RACER, pre-war Japan, tin, tin wheels $25.00-45.00

PENNY TOY BOAT, German, 4" two stacks, tin lithograph with tin wheels $95.00-225.00

PENNY TOY DONKEY PULLING CART, German, tin lithograph, 4½" yellow cart..............$80.00-150.00

PENNY TOY, FIGHTING ROOSTERS, made in Germany $65.00-140.00

PENNY TOY, GAS STATION AND CAR, limousine, Distler, German $200.00-400.00

PENNY TOY, HORSE WITH JOCKEY RIDER, pre-war Germany, 3½" tin $120.00-225.00

PENNY TOY, HORSE, pre-war Germany, tin, 3½" long...$70.00-135.00

PENNY TOY, LIMOUSINE, Fisher Phaeton, early, Germany, 4" with driver, tin $95.00-175.00

PENNY TOY, LIMOUSINE, made in Germany, G.F. logo $75.00-150.00

PENNY TOY, TAXI, Distler, German, 1915, 3" long red and blue, open $95.00-225.00

PENNY TOY, TRAIN SET, Japan, locomotive and three cars, 6½", box....................................$25.00-75.00

PENNY TOY, ZEPPELIN, pre-war Japan, 6" long, tin, silver paint..$35.00-70.00

PIANO, Marx Play-away, original box $40.00-100.00

PISTOL, ROCKET DART PISTOL, by Daisy, 1930's, 7" steel $10.00-25.00

PISTOLS, DIA, Japan, box of twelve 3" tin water pistols, cowboy print on handle $30.00-65.00

POOL PLAYERS, Ranger, steel game ..$85.00-160.00

PREMIUM, Captain Midnight, 1945 Code-O-Graph magnifier/decoder $45.00-70.00

PREMIUM, Captain Midnight Whistle Decoder, 1940's $35.00-60.00

PREMIUM, G. E. BIG TOP CIRCUS, 1950, sixty punch-outs $20.00-50.00

PREMIUM, Jack Armstrong Pedometer $35.0050.00

PREMIUM, Kellogg's "Wheel of Knowledge" . $8.00-12.00

PREMIUM, Kellogg's Pep Pin, featuring Barney Google, ...$5.00-12.00

PREMIUM, Kellogg's Pep Pin, features Chester Gump $5.00-15.00

PREMIUM, Kellogg's Pep Pin, Elmer $5.00-10.00

PREMIUM, Kellogg's Pep Pin, Felix $15.00-35.00

PREMIUM, Kellogg's Pep Pin, Gordon. $10.00-25.00

PREMIUM, Kellogg's Pep Pin, Fritz...........$5.00-10.00

PREMIUM, Kellogg's Pep Pin, Jiggs $5.00-15.00

PREMIUM, Kellogg's Pep Pin, Kayo $5.00-15.00

PREMIUM, Kellogg's Pep Pin, Maggie $5.00-15.00

PREMIUM, Kellogg's Pep Pin, Nina $5.00-10.00

PREMIUM, Kellogg's Pep Pin, Olive Oil $10.00-20.00

PREMIUM, Kellogg's Pep Pin featuring Little Orphan Annie, ...$5.00-15.00

PREMIUM, Kellogg's Pep Pin, featuring Perry Winkle $5.00-15.00

PREMIUM, Kellogg's Pep Pin, Phantom ...$15.00-30.00

PREMIUM, Kellogg's Pep Pin, Pop-links $5.00-15.00

PREMIUM, Kellogg's Pep Pin, Skeezix $5.00-15.00

PREMIUM, Kellogg's Pep Pin, Smilin' Jack . $5.00-15.00

PREMIUM, Kellogg's Pep Pin, Stover $5.00-15.00

PREMIUM, Kellogg's Pep Pin, Superman ...$5.00-12.00

PREMIUM, Kellogg's Pep Pin, The Shadow . $5.00-15.00

PREMIUM, Kellogg's Pep Pin, Tiny Tim ..$10.00-20.00

PREMIUM, Kellogg's Pep Pin, Twins $10.00-20.00

PREMIUM, Little Orphan Annie's Ovaltine Shake-up game with plastic cup $50.00-75.00

PREMIUM, Lone Ranger Pedometer $40.00-60.00

PREMIUM, LITTLE ORPHAN ANNIE DECODER PIN, 1937 ....$20.00-40.00

PREMIUM, LITTLE ORPHAN ANNIE OVALTINE BEE-TLEWARE CUP, 1930's $10.00-25.00

PREMIUM, LITTLE ORPHAN ANNIE'S SAFETY GUARD DECODER, whirlomatic, 1942............$30.00-60.00

PREMIUM, PENNY'S MICKEY MOUSE BACK TO SCHOOL BUTTON, celluloid, 1930's . $40.00-75.00

PREMIUM, ROY ROGERS MARCH OF DIMES, Sears premium book $15.00-30.00

PREMIUM, SUPERMAN, blue plastic flying figure, 5" Pep Premium $40.00-80.00

PREMIUM, TOM MIX GLOW IN THE DARK BELT, Radio Show Premium $45.00-95.00

PREMIUM, TOM MIX MAGNET RING, circa 1930 ....$25.00-45.00

PULL TOY, MONKEY ON WHEELS, by Steiff, felt, clown hat and ruffle, 8", jointed ...$150.00-300.00

SAND TOY SET, by Chein, duck mold, sifter, frog on card $10.00-30.00

SCARF, RANGER KERCHIEF, Buck Jones $30.00-60.00

SKI JUMPER, Wolverine windup in original box $125.00-200.00

SPACE PISTOL, Space Rocket pistol, tin Japan, 1950's, battery operated, 9" $35.00-95.00

SPARKLER TOY, Bee and Flower, 1930's tin lithograph, 4"...$20.00-35.00

SPARKLER TOY, Cat's Meow, boxed, Ranger Toys, 1950's, tin, 6"....................................$15.00-35.00

SPARKLER TOY, by Chein, 5", on the original card...$10.00-20.00

TOOTSIE TOY FIRE DEPARTMENT BOXED PLAY SET, four vehicles, Furnish collection, $100.00-200.00.

SPEEDWAY, Mars Streamline Speedway, 1920's, two 4" cars, boxed $80.00-175.00

STEAM ENGINE, Markline, 15" $575.00-875.00

STEAM ENGINE, Weeden $60.00-125.00

STEAM SHOVEL, by Structo, green, steel, wood wheels $35.00-60.00

STREET CAR, Sunny Andy, by Wolverine, 1920's, tin pull toy $150.00-300.00

STUFFED ANIMAL, LAMB, "Lamby," manufactured by Steiff...$45.00-60.00

TARGET SET, PRACTICE TARGET RANGE, by Marx, 1950's, Arcade game, 11" $20.00-35.00

TEETER TOTTER by Gibbs, 1915, 14" long with boy and girl $115.00-195.00

TOY BOOK, Toy a Day Book, by LineMar, Japan, 1950's, twenty-nine little toys $25.00-45.00

TRACTOR AND FLATBED TRAILER, GAMA, U.S. Zone Germany, tin windup 3" $40.00-85.00

TRACTOR AND TRAILER, manufactured by Structo, cattle box $20.00-55.00

TRACTOR, American Tractor, Marx, 1920's, tin wind-up, 8", with accessories $95.00-175.00

TRACTOR, by Bing, Germany, 1910, tin windup, 10" $250.00-500.00

TRACTOR, CONSTRUCTION, GIANT REVERSING, by Marx, 1950's, tin windup, 14" $80.00-150.00

TRACTOR, COURTLAND, tin, boxed, 1950's,

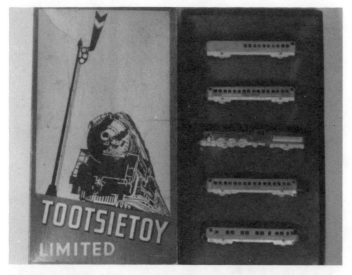

TOOTSIETOY BOXED TRAIN SET "LIMITED," Furnish collection, $100.00-250.00.

TIN WINDUP CAT WITH BALL, 4", Marx, Reynolds collection, $45.00-95.00.

ZILOTONE TIN WINDUP MUSICAL TOY by Wolverine, Reynolds collection, $100.00-225.00.

6" long $50.00-80.00

TRACTOR, CRANE-TYPE, boxed, Japan, battery operated, remote controlled, 8", all tin $45.00-85.00

TRACTOR, ELECTRIC, K55, Japan, battery operated, 7", in box $45.00-95.00

TRACTOR, FARM TRACTOR, #273R AREAD with cast iron man..$40.00-80.00

TRACTOR, SELECTO-O-SPEED, manufactured by Hubley $200.00-450.00

TRACTOR, Marx windup with rubber tracks, tin lithograph, 1930's $100.00-165.00

TRACTOR, #165, Massey Ferguson $25.00-45.00

TRACTOR, midget, climbing, by Marx, tin windup, 5" $30.00-55.00

TRACTOR, Oliver Farm Tractor with planter, cast iron, by Arcade..$75.00-135.00

TRACTOR, STEAM, TN, Japan, tin friction, 7" $60.00-105.00

TRAIN AND TRACK SET, Ranger mechanical, 1950's, tin windup $35.00-75.00

TRAIN SET, IVES, cast iron, windup engine #1, 1924, set $300.00-450.00

TRAIN SET, by Marx, 1950's, windup plastic locomotive, tin cars, 6" long $35.00-65.00

TRAIN SET, O GAUGE, U.S. Zone Germany, with box $200.00-350.00

TRAIN STATION, #3, O GAUGE, by Hornby, 14", tin lithograph $40.00-75.00

TRAIN STATION, Union Station, Automatic Toy Company, 1950's $35.00-70.00

TRAIN, Cor-Cor locomotive and pullman car, 1948 ....$450.00-700.00

TRAIN, Cragstan electric shuttle, engine and five cars, boxed $75.00-150.00

TRAIN, Halloween, U.S. Zone Germany, two 4" cars, 10" tunnel set $90.00-180.00

TRAIN, shuttling train and freight yard, Alps, battery operated, 7" locomotive, 1950's $85.00-140.00

TRAIN, tin windup pre-war Japan, 6" long, 11 pieces of track in box..$60.00-120.00

TROLLEY, mountain climber, Sparkling..$100.00-225.00

TROLLEY, tin toy, Broadway 270, Chein .$35.00-75.00

TRUCK, Farm truck, Alps, Japan, battery operated, 11" with rubber mooing cow $75.00-100.00

TRUCK, Open Livestock, Japan, 9", tin, 1950's, boxed $15.00-25.00

WATER PISTOL, red tin, by Wyandotte, 1930's, boxed $25.00-50.00

WINDUP RACE GAME, Sunny and Rabbit Chase Wolverine, three 2" greyhounds race ...$120.00-195.00

WINDUP TRACK TOY, boy on cart, celluloid, with O gauge track..$250.00-650.00

WINDUP, Main Street, Marx, orig. box ...$200.00-300.00

ZILOTONE, musical windup, clown plays, Wolverine, with six records............................$150.00-375.00

MODERN TOYS

Toys presented in the listing of this classification represent general line items manufactured from 1940 to the present. The period of toy production from 1940 through the 1950's is often referred to as "post-war" toys with earlier items of the 1940's and the 1930's referred to as "pre-war." However, since these definitions do not fall at exact decade beginning and ending dates, this classification, Modern Toys, will take the reader through nearly three full decades of toy production, 1940's through 1960's.

In keeping with the other chronological chapters of this book (Victorian Toys and Golden Age Toys) this listing will present a sample of toys produced during this period regardless of their particular type or function. Some cross-listing has been done here, with listed toys also listed in other categories, but there are also many toys included in this Modern Toys classification that are not included in any other chapter in this book.

Particular areas to watch in regard to present dealer interest are 1950's and 1960's tinplate autos, LineMar windup toys, Fisher Price pull toys, television-related items and collectibles associated with the movies.

Modern toys are generally the most reasonably priced of all collectibles because of their relative newness and abundant supply, but as every collector knows, today's modern toys will be tomorrow's antiques. So it never hurts to collect or store away that favorite toy of only twenty years ago in safe keeping. Today's bargains are sure to be tomorrow's treasures.

**HUBLEY HOOK AND LADDER TRUCK, boxed, 8",
Reynolds collection, $35.00-65.00.**

**GREYHOUND SCENIC CRUISER FRICTION BUS, 7",
Japan, 1960's, Furnish collection, $25.00-60.00.**

COURTLAND TRUCK, 12" long sheet metal construction, Reynolds collection, $25.00-60.00.

NBC TELEVISION VAN, battery operated, RCA promotion ads, 1960's, metal, Reynolds collection, $75.00-135.00.

77 SUNSET STRIP BOARD GAME, based on television series 1960, Warner $15.00-35.00

ADAM 12 LUNCHBOX, 1972.....................$5.00-10.00

ADDAMS FAMILY, "THE THING," battery operated bank, 1960's......................$20.00-45.00

ADDAM'S FAMILY LUNCHBOX, 1960's $5.00-10.00

ADVENTURES OF POPEYE GAME, by Transogram, 1957.............................$15.00-35.00

ALFRED HITCHCOCK PRESENTS MYSTERY GAME, by Milton Bradley, 1958 ....$15.00-30.00

ALICE IN WONDERLAND DISNEY PLANTER, Leeds China, 1950.............................$20.00-35.00

ALICE IN WONDERLAND PUNCH-OUT BOOK, 1950's, Disney $20.00-45.00

ALLIE GATOR PULL TOY, by Fisher Price, 1960.............................$10.00-20.00

AMERICAN FLAGSHIP AIRPLANE PULL TOY, 1940, by Fisher Price $50.00-150.00

AMERICAN LOGS set by Halsam, 1950's, boxed $10.00-25.00

AMSCO DOLL-E-DISH TIME, kitchen cleaning set, on card, 1955 ....$5.00-10.00

AMSCO KIDDIE SHU-SHINE BANK, red plastic kit, 1950's.............................$5.00-10.00

ANDY PANDA CERAMIC PLANTER, 1958, Walter Lantz, 5".............................$15.00-30.00

ANDY PANDA CERAMIC CHINA FIGURE, 1940's, Walter Lantz $40.00-80.00

ANIMAKERS TOY ANIMAL MAKING BLOCKS, boxed, 1940's $20.00-30.00

ARTHUR GODFREY UKELELE includes song book $20.00-45.00

BABA LOOEY THE DONKEY, 5½" ceramic figure, 1960's, Hanna Barbera $5.00-10.00

BAMBI CUT-OUT BOOK, circa 1940, uncut, Disney $50.00-125.00

BAMBI DOLL by Steiff, large 12" long version, 1942 ....$75.00-100.00

BAMBI STORY BOOK, 1947, Disney, Grosset and Dunlap $10.00-30.00

BARNEY RUBBLE RIDING DINO TIN WINDUP, Marx, 1960's, 8".............................$70.00-140.00

BARNEY RUBBLE VINYL SQUEAK TOY, circa 1960.............................$5.00-10.00

BAT MASTERSON HOLSTER, CANE AND VEST SET, by Carnell $20.00-45.00

BATMAN AND ROBIN GAME, 1965 ....$20.00-30.00

BATMAN AND ROBIN TALKING CLOCK, circa 1960.............................$20.00-40.00

BATMAN BATBRUSH ON ORIGINAL CARD, 1960's $12.00-18.00

BATMAN BOARD GAME, 1966 ....$15.00-25.00

BATMAN MILK GLASS, 1966...................$5.00-10.00

BATMAN TELEVISION VERSION LUNCHBOX, 1960's $5.00-10.00

BEATLES CAR NODDERS, set of four, early 1960's $300.00-600.00

BEATLES DOLL, Paul, Remco, 1960's $40.00-60.00

BEATLES INFLATABLE CARTOON DOLLS, set of four $50.00-100.00

BEN CASEY NOTEBOOK, 1962..............$10.00-20.00

BEN CASEY OVERNIGHT CASE, vinyl, circa 1960.............................$20.00-30.00

BEN CASEY, M. D. GAME, made by Transogram, 1961.............................$10.00-20.00

BEVERLY HILLBILLIES CARD GAME, 1960's, Milton Bradley.............................$5.00-10.00

BEVERLY HILLBILLIES FRAME TRAY PUZZLE, Jaymar, 1963 ....$5.00-10.00

BEVERLY HILLBILLIES LUNCHBOX, from television series, 1960's $5.00-10.00

BIG BILL PELICAN, wood and plastic, Fisher Price pull toy, 1961 ....$10.00-20.00

BLOCK WAGON WITH PAPER LITHOGRAPH, 15" long, 1950's, Gong Bell Toys $10.00-20.00

BLONDIE AND DAGWOOD BLOCKS, boxed, 1950's $25.00-40.00

BLONDIE AND DAGWOOD DOLL STROLLER, 1950's, metal $35.00-65.00

BLONDIE PAINTS, paint set in metal box, 1946 American Crayon $6.00-14.00

BONANZA LUNCH KIT WITH THERMOS, circa 1960.............................$5.00-15.00

BONANZA LUNCHBOX SET, from television series, complete, 1960's $10.0-20.00

BONANZA TIN MUG, 1960's $10.00-20.00

BOUNCY RACE CAR, large plastic tires, 1960, Fisher Price.............................$5.00-15.00

BOZO THE CLOWN NODDER manufactured by Bayard, 1950's $40.00-85.00

BOZO THE CLOWN RADIO, packaged in original box, 1960's $20.00-35.00

BOZO THE CLOWN TIN YO-YO, 1950's...$5.00-10.00

BUCKY BURRO PULL TOY, made by Fisher Price, 1955 ....$30.00-65.00

BUDDY BULLFROG, Fisher Price pull toy, circa 1960.............................$5.00-15.00

BUGS BUNNY ALARM CLOCK, 1940's, manufactured by Ingraham $200.00-400.00

BUGS BUNNY CAST METAL PLANTER, 6", 1940's $50.00-100.00

BUGS BUNNY CERAMIC PLANTER, circa 1950.............................$15.00-30.00

BUGS BUNNY DOLL, 20", 1940's, all felt with linen face $100.00-200.00

BUGS BUNNY TALKING HAND PUPPET, by Mattel, 1960's, pull-string voice $5.00-15.00

BUNNIES PULLING EGG CART, by Fisher Price, 1940 ....$50.00-125.00

BUNNY RACER PULL TOY, Bunny in race car, 1942 ....$35.00-65.00

CACKLING HEN PULL TOY, Fisher Price, 1958.............................$10.00-30.00

CAPTAIN KANGEROO'S, FINGERPAINTS SET, 1956.............................$15.00-30.00

CARPET SWEEPER, 1950's, by Ideal Toy, brittle plastic $10.00-20.00

CASPER THE FRIENDLY GHOST DOLL, 1960's, talking, Mattel $15.00-35.00

CASPER THE FRIENDLY GHOST GUITAR, crank type, by Mattel, 1959 ....$10.00-20.00

CASPER THE FRIENDLY GHOST JACK IN THE BOX, 1960's, Mattel, metal and plastic $10.00-20.00

CASPER THE GHOST LITTLE GOLDEN RECORD, 1962.............................$3.00-6.00

CASPER THE GHOST RECORD, 1962 .....$5.00-10.00

CATNIP CLOTH CHARACTER PUPPET by Gund, 1960's $5.00-15.00

CHARLIE THE TUNA LAMP, 1960's $25.00-45.00

CHARLIE THE TUNA WRIST WATCH, circa 1960.................................$20.00-45.00

CHATTER MONKEY PULL TOY, by Fisher Price, 1957.................................$10.00-35.00

CINDERELLA AND THE PRINCE WINDUP, boxed, action toy, 1950's $50.00-100.00

CINDERELLA CERAMIC PLANTER, Disney, by Leeds, 1950's $15.00-40.00

CINDERELLA PICTURE PUZZLE, Jaymar, 1950's, boxed $5.00-10.00

CINDERELLA SWEEPER, 1950's, tin $20.00-40.00

CONCENTRATION GAME, based on television game show 1959 ....$5.00-10.00

COWBOY AND INDIAN SAND PAIL AND SHOVEL, 1950's, 6" pail, 8" shovel, metal........$10.00-35.00

CRANK MUSIC BOX, Ohio Art, 1940's, tin lithograph of little German children...................$10.00-25.00

CRICKET PULL TOY, Fisher Price, 1955.$10.00-30.00

CURLEY, THREE STOOGES HAND PUPPET, 1950's $10.00-20.00

DALE EVANS AND BUTTERMILK, by Whitman Book, 1956.................................$5.00-10.00

DALE EVANS BOXED HAT AND OUTFIT, 1950's, set $45.00-90.00

DALE EVANS HAT, 1950's, felt.............$10.00-20.00

DALE EVANS WRIST WATCH, made by U.S. Time $75.00-135.00

DANIEL BOONE COONSKIN CAP, 1950's, television version $15.00-25.00

DARK SHADOWS GAME, 1960's boxed game, based on television show $10.00-25.00

DEBBY REYNOLD'S DOLL WITH MAGIC STAY ON CLOTHES, by Whitman, 1958 ....$15.00-30.00

DELIVERY VAN by Ideal, plastic, green, red, yellow, 5" long.................................$5.00-15.00

DENNIS THE MENACE BASEBALL GAME, 1960, tin lithograph.................................$10.00-30.00

DENNIS THE MENACE FIGURAL WATER PISTOL, 1950's, boxed.................................$20.00-40.00

DENNIS THE MENACE FRAME TRAY PUZZLE, 1960, by Whitman $5.00-10.00

DENNIS THE MENACE HAND PUPPET, 1950's, cloth and vinyl $5.00-15.00

DICK TRACY CRIME DETECTION FOLIO, circa 1940.................................$75.00-195.00

DICK TRACY FLASHLIGHT, 1950's $15.00-35.00

DICK TRACY HAND PUPPET, 1961 ....$10.00-20.00

DICK TRACY HINGEES SET, in envelope.$5.00-20.00

DICK TRACY JIGSAW PUZZLE, boxed, 1940's, by Jaymar $15.00-30.00

DICK TRACY MASTER DETECTIVE GAME, 1961, boxed $20.00-40.00

DICK TRACY PLASTIC CAMERA, 1940's.$20.00-40.00

DICK TRACY PLASTIC WRIST RADIO, 1950's $20.00-45.00

DING DONG DUCKY PULL TOY, by Fisher Price, 1949.................................$20.00-55.00

DING DONG SCHOOL SHAKE-UP MUG, Ovaltine, 1950's $15.00-30.00

DINO THE DINOSAUR CERAMIC BANK, circa 1960.................................$15.00-35.00

DINO THE DINOSAUR Flintstones character vinyl figure, 1960's $10.00-20.00

DINO THE DINOSAUR VINYL SQUEAK TOY, 1960, 12".................................$5.00-10.00

DISNEY CHARACTER GLOBE by Rand McNally, 1940's $30.00-75.00

DISNEYLAND COLORING BOOK, by Whitman, 1950's $10.00-20.00

DISNEYLAND FERRIS WHEEL, made by J. Chein, 1940's $100.00-250.00

DISNEYLAND MELODY PLAYER, crank operated, 1950's, music box, all metal $40.00-85.00

DISNEYLAND MONORAIL BOXED SET, Schuco, 1950's $100.00-250.00

DOCTOR KILDARE GAME, 1967 ....$15.00-30.00

DOG CLOWN PULL TOY by Gong Bell Manufacturing, 1949.................................$10.00-20.00

DOG ON ICE CREAM WAGON PULL TOY, by Fisher Price, 1940 ....$50.00-100.00

DOGGIE HAND CAR, pull toy by Gong Bell, 1950's $10.00-20.00

DOLL STROLLER WITH WOODEN HANDLE, tin lithograph, Ohio Art, 1950's, bears $20.00-45.00

DONALD DUCK ALARM CLOCK by Bayard, French, 1960's $100.00-200.00

DONALD DUCK AND PLUTO RUBBER CAR, Sun Rubber, 1940's.................................$35.00-70.00

DONALD DUCK CERAMIC FIGURE, ANGRY DONALD, Evan K. Shaw Company, 1940's......$75.00-125.00

DONALD DUCK CHOO-CHOO TRAIN PULL TOY, 1940, Walt Disney $45.00-75.00

DONALD DUCK DOCTOR'S SET, 1940's, case boxed $20.00-45.00

DONALD DUCK DRUMMER WINDUP, LineMar, 6" version, boxed.................................$200.00-450.00

DONALD DUCK DUET, Marx windup, 1946, 10".................................$350.00-600.00

DONALD DUCK ENGINEER PULL TOY, 1940's, by Fisher Price.................................$30.00-65.00

DONALD DUCK PAINT SET, 1950's, tin box $10.00-20.00

DONALD DUCK PULL TOY WITH MECHANICAL PLASTIC FEET, 1955, by Fisher Price $30.00-65.00

DONALD DUCK PULL TOY, Donald pulls red car, 1940's, by Fisher Price $30.00-70.00

DONALD DUCK SQUEAK TOY, Sun Rubber Company, 1940's $10.00-20.00

DONALD DUCK SUNOCO INK BLOTTER, 1940's $10.00-20.00

DONALD DUCK TABLE LAMP, 1947, Railley Corporation, with original shade $100.00-200.00

DONALD DUCK THE SKIER, large plastic windup by Marx, 1950's $100.00-175.00

DONALD DUCK TIDDLEY WINKS GAME, 1950's $10.00-20.00

DONALD DUCK WEARING CHECKERED COAT WITH STRAW HAT PULL TOY, 1940, F.P. $100.00-200.00

DONALD DUCK WINDUP CAR, 1950's, manufactured by Marx $65.00-110.00

DORIS DAY COLORING BOOK, 1958.....$10.00-20.00

DOROTHY HAMIL DOLL by Ideal, 1977.$20.00-40.00

DR. KILDARE MEDICAL GAME FOR THE YOUNG, 1962, Ideal.................................$10.00-20.00

DRAGNET ADVENTURE BOOK, 1958.......$5.00-10.00

MODERN TOYS

DRAGNET CRIME LAB, 1950's $20.00-45.00
DRAGNET GAME, 1967 ....$15.00-30.00
DRAGNET PLASTIC DART GUN, 1955...$10.00-20.00
DRAGNET POLICE HOLSTER SET, 1955, Jack Webb on the box..$20.00-60.00
DRAGNET TALKING POLICE CAR, circa 1950..$40.00-75.00
DRAGNET TRIPLE FIRE TARGET GAME, circa 1955...$25.00-60.00
DRUM, OHIO ART, 6" metal, marching children around sides...$10.00-20.00
DUMBO AMERICAN POTTERY CERAMIC FIGURE WITH LABEL, 1940's $25.00-70.00
DUMBO MECHANICAL WINDUP by Marx, 1940's, 5" roll over action $100.00-200.00
DUTCHIE DOG pull toy by Gong Bell, 1950, wood, paper, metal wheels $10.00-20.00
EGG TRUCK DRIVEN BY FARMER DUCK, by Fisher Price, 1947 pull toy $35.00-60.00
ELEPHANT RIDING TRICYCLE WITH ROLLER WHEELS, by Fisher Price, 1950 ....$20.00-45.00
ELIZABETH TAYLOR COLORING BOOK, by Whitman, 1950..$15.00-30.00
ELLA CINDERS GAME manufactured by Milton Bradley, 1944 ....$20.00-40.00
ELMER FUDD AMERICAN POTTERY FIGURE, 1940's, 6½" tall $40.00-85.00
ELMER FUDD FIRE CHIEF, 1950's, pull toy...$20.00-45.00
ELSIE THE COW FUNBOOK, 1950's $10.00-20.00
ELSIE'S DAIRY TRUCK, manufactured by Fisher Price, 1948...$65.00-135.00
ELVIS PRESLEY, King of Rock Game.......$5.00-15.00
EMENEE MUSICAL ACCORDION IN CARRYING CASE, 1957..$15.00-30.00
EMERGENCY LUNCHBOX, tv series $5.00-10.00
FARM TRUCK WITH THE CAMPBELL'S SOUP KIDS, 1954, by Fisher Price......................$50.00-130.00
FAT ALBERT LUNCHBOX, 1970's $3.00-8.00
FAT ALBERT VINYL DOLL, 1970's $4.00-10.00
FELIX THE CAT DANDY CANDY GAME, ca. 1957, boxed $15.00-35.00
FELIX THE CAT PENCIL CASE, 1950's.$22.00-35.00
FERDINAND THE BULL AND THE MATODOR PULL TOY, N. N. Hill Brass, 1940 ....$100.00-250.00
FIREBALL XL5 LUNCHBOX, 1960's $10.00-20.00
FISHER PRICE BAND WAGON pulled by two horses, 1940..$40.00-80.00
FISHER PRICE CASH REGISTER, 1960 ..$5.00-15.00
FISHER PRICE CIRCUS, 1962, circus wagon, trapeze acts, figures, and more $25.00-70.00
FISHER PRICE GABBY GOOFY DUCKS, mother and three babies, 1959 ....$15.00-30.00
FISHER PRICE GENERAL HAULING HORSE AND WAGON PULL TOY, 1940 ....$40.00-80.00
FISHER PRICE HUCKLEBERRY HOUND XYLOHONE PLAYER, 1961 ....$15.00-40.00
FISHER PRICE RUNNING BUNNY CART, 1958 wooden pull toy $10.00-20.00
FISHER PRICE SCHOOL BUS WITH LITTLE PEOPLE, 1959 wood and plastic $10.00-30.00
FIX-IT TRUCK, Ideal Toy, hard plastics, truck with accessories, 8" $10.00-20.00

FLINTSTONES STONE AGE TIDDLEY WINKS GAME, 1961...$15.00-30.00
FLINTSTONES WINDUP FLIP OVER TANK, LineMar, 1961, tin lithograph $100.00-200.00
FLINTSTONES CAMERA, 1960's $10.00-15.00
FLIP WILSON GERALDINE DOLL, 1970's..$15.00-30.00
FLIPPER LUNCH BOX KIT, 1960's $5.00-10.00
FLOWER THE SKUNK AMERICAN POTTERY FIGURE, Bambi, 1940's....................................$20.00-40.00
FOX PUSH ALONG TOY manufactured by Gong Bell, 1940's $20.00-40.00
FRED FLINTSONE PULL TOY, by Fisher Price, 1960's $20.00-65.00
FRED FLINTSTONE AND DINO BATTERY OPERATED TOY, LineMar, 22" long $100.00-275.00
FRED FLINTSTONE GAME, STONE AGE, by Transogram, 1960's $10.00-25.00
FRED FLINTSTONE GAME, by Transogram, 1961..$10.00-30.00
FRED FLINTSTONE RIDING DINO WINDUP TOY, by LineMar, 1962, 8"............................$70.00-140.00
FRED FLINTSTONE VINYL SQUEAK TOY, 1960, 12"..$5.00-10.00
FROG WITH RED TOPHAT PULL TOY, by Fisher Price, 1956 ....$10.00-30.00
FRONTIERLAND, Walt Disney's Official Game, 1950's $20.00-45.00
FURY COLORING BOOK, 1960's.............$10.00-20.00
FUZZY THE DOG PULL TOY by Fisher Price, 1940..$30.00-60.00
GALLOPING HORSE AND WAGON PULL TOY, by Fisher Price, 1948 ....$35.00-65.00
GENE AUTRY BICYCLE HORN, 1950's ..$25.00-50.00
GENE AUTRY CAP PISTOL, by Kenton..$45.00-80.00
GENE AUTRY GUITAR, manufactured by Silvertone, 1950's $50.00-110.00
GENE AUTRY SIX SHOOTER CAP GUNS, pair, ivory handles, 9" long $45.00-90.00
GENE AUTRY TOY DRUM AND TRAP SET, 24" bass drum with Gene on horse $75.00-150.00
GENTLE BEN LUNCH BOX, 1960's $5.00-10.00
GILBERT ANCHOR BLOCKS SET, circa 1950, boxed $10.00-45.00
GILBERT CHEMISTRY SET, by Senior Laboratory $20.00-40.00
GILBERT ERECTOR SET, 1952, deluxe . $25.00-65.00
GILBERT MICROSCOPE SET, 1952 ....$20.00-40.00
GILBERT PUZZLES BOXED SET, wire puzzles, 1952...$10.00-25.00
GILBERT TOOL CHEST, ca. 1952 ....$20.00-35.00
GLORIA JEAN PAPER DOLLS, 1940, by Saalfield $25.00-50.00
GOLDEN GULCH EXPRESS PULL TOY, locomotive and tender, by Fisher Price, 1960's $10.00-20.00
GONE WITH THE WIND PAPER DOLLS, by Merrill, 1940..$75.00-150.00
GRACE KELLY COLORING BOOK, 1956.$20.00-40.00
GREEN HORNET JIGSAW PUZZLE, set of four, boxed $20.00-45.00
GREEN HORNET PLAYING CARDS, 1966, boxed $10.00-15.00
GROUCHO GOGGLES AND CIGAR SET ON CARD, by Eldon, 1950's.......................................$20.00-40.00

GROUCHO TELEVISION QUIZ GAME, based on television game 1954 ....$20.00-40.00

GUNSMOKE MARSHALL MATT DILLON HOLSTER SET, 1950's $20.00-50.00

GUNSMOKE MARSHALL MATT DILLON LUNCH BOX, 1959 ....$10.00-20.00

HAPPY HIPPO FISHER PRICE PULL TOY, 1960's $10.00-25.00

HERMAN MUNSTER TALKING PUPPET, by Mattel, 1964 ....$10.00-20.00

HIGHWAY PATROL OFFICIAL SQUAD CAR ROAD SET, by Schuco, 1958 ....$50.00-100.00

HOLGATE TAKE-APART SOLDIER, (coldstream guard) all wood, 1947, 17".............................$10.00-30.00

HOLGATE TASKET BASKET, 1950's, wood $5.00-10.00

HOPALONG CASSIDY COLORING OUTFIT, circa 1950..$50.00-70.00

HOPALONG CASSIDY COWGIRL SUIT, boxed set, 1950's $55.00-95.00

HOPALONG CASSIDY DART BOARD WITH METAL BOARD, GUN AND DARTS, boxed..$70.00-115.00

HOPALONG CASSIDY ON HIS HORSE, Marx, 1950's $25.00-65.00

HOPALONG CASSIDY PICTURE GUN AND THEATRE, 1950, Automagic.............................$75.00-135.00

HOPALONG CASSIDY POGO STICK, circa 1950, metal $45.00-85.00

HOPALONG CASSIDY TELEVISION PUZZLES, by Milton Bradley, 12" square $20.00-40.00

HOPPING RABBIT, by Marx, 4⅓" metal and plastic, 1950's-1960's $10.00-20.00

HOWDY DOODY BEAD GAME UNDER GLASS, 1950's $15.00-35.00

HOWDY DOODY BUBBLE PIPES............$25.00-60.00

HOWDY DOODY CLOCK-A-DOODLE, by Bengor Company $200.00-400.00

HOWDY DOODY DELIVERY LineMar Friction Toy, Clarabell on cart, 6"......................$200.00-400.00

HOWDY DOODY FOOTBALL, 1950's.......$10.00-30.00

HOWDY DOODY FUN BOOK by Whitman, 1951 ....$10.00-20.00

HOWDY DOODY MAGIC KIT, 1950's $20.00-40.00

HOWDY DOODY MAGIC PUZZLE BALL, by Kagran $20.00-55.00

HOWDY DOODY PHONO DOODLE RECORD PLAYER, 1950's....................................$75.00-125.00

HOWDY DOODY PLASTIC SAND TOYS SET, on original display card, 1954 ....$25.00-60.00

HOWDY DOODY STRING CLIMBING TOY, 1950's $20.00-40.00

HUCKLEBERRY HOUND CAMERA, Sun-Pix, 1964..$10.00-20.00

HUCKLEBERRY HOUND PLASTIC FIGURAL BANK, 10", 1960's $5.00-10.00

HUCKLEBERRY HOUND TELEVISION PLAYSET, by Marx, 1960's...$15.00-30.00

I DREAM OF JEANNIE BOARD GAME, 1965, by Milton Bradley $10.00-25.00

I DREAM OF JEANNIE DOLL, 19" Libby Majorette Doll Corporation, 1966......................$25.00-70.00

IDEAL BRITTLE PLASTIC RED TEA SET, 1950's $10.00-20.00

IDEAL MECHANICAL DISHWASHER, 1950's, all plastic, unique design, boxed $25.00-60.00

J. FRED MUGGS CHIMP HAND PUPPET, 1950's, Maytag ad premuim $10.00-20.00

J. FRED MUGGS CHIMP FROM NBC, PULL TOY, N. N. Brass Hill, 1950's, 9" $50.00-100.00

JACKIE GLEASON AND AWAY WE GO GAME, by Transogram, 1956...........................$25.00-55.00

JAMES BOND ACTION FIGURE, 1960's, scuba attire $20.00-45.00

JAMES BOND PLAY POOL TABLE, manufactured 1960's $10.00-20.00

JAMES BOND PUZZLE, 1960's $5.00-10.00

JANE POWELL PAPER DOLLS BOOK, published 1952..$15.00-30.00

JETSONS WINDUP FIGURE by Marx, 1960's, 4"..$50.00-90.00

JINGLE GIRAFFE PULL TOY, by Fisher Price, 1956..$10.00-30.00

JOE CARIOCA PARROT LAMP, Disney, 1940's..$100.00-200.00

JOE PALOOKA WOOD JOINTED FIGURE, 1940's, 4" tall...$40.00-80.00

JOHN TRAVOLTA DOLL, 1970's.............$10.00-20.00

JUDY GARLAND COLORING BOOK, published 1941..$30.00-50.00

JUNE ALLYSON COLORING BOOK, copyright 1952..$20.00-35.00

KENNER GIVE-A-SHOW PROJECTOR, 1960's, plastic $10.00-30.00

KEWTIE KIDS MISS AMERICA PULL TOY, by Gong Bell Toy, 1943 ....$10.00-35.00

KEYS OF LEARNING PLASTIC SHAPE KEY SORTER, 1950's $5.00-10.00

KITTEN WITH BALL AND BELL, by Fisher Price, pull toy, 1950's $10.00-35.00

KOO ZOO BLOCK SET, 1950's clear blocks with animals inside, set of six $5.00-10.00

LADY FROM LADY AND THE TRAMP PLASTIC PLATFORM PULL TOY, 1954 ....$25.00-65.00

LAMBCHOP, LAMB HAND PUPPET, made in the 1960's $20.00-45.00

LARRY, THREE STOOGES HAND PUPPET, 1950's $10.00-20.00

LASSIE PLASTIC TENITE FIGURE IN BOX, 1960's $30.00-50.00

LEAVE IT TO BEAVER MONEYMAKER BOARD GAME, 1950's $15.00-35.00

LEAVE IT TO BEAVER ROCKET TO THE MOON SPACE GAME, 1959 ....$15.00-30.00

LI'L ABNER CAN O'COINS metal, tin lithograph bank, 1953..$15.00-30.00

LINDSTROM SEWING MACHINE ca. 1940's, child's toy, 8" long, metal $10.00-25.00

LION AND DRUM PULL TOY "LEO" by Fisher Price, 1952..$25.00-50.00

LITTLE INDIAN AND DUCK WATERING CAN, by Ohio Art, tin lithograph, 1950's $10.00-20.00

LITTLE KING PLASTIC WALKING TOY by Marx, 1963, 3" $5.00-20.00

LITTLE KING WOOD COMPOSITION FIGURE, 3" tall, 1944..$30.00-65.00

LONE RANGER CARDBOARD DART TARGET by Marx, 1946..$25.00-60.00

LONE RANGER FILMSTRIP VIEWER ON CARD, 1955..$20.00-45.00

MODERN TOYS

LONE RANGER LUNCHBOX, 1950's $10.00-25.00
LONE RANGER PAINT BOOK, by Whitman, 1941 ....$10.00-25.00
LONE RANGER RING TOSS SET, boxed, 1950's $15.00-35.00
LOOKY CHUG CHUG LOCOMOTIVE PULL TOY, 1949, Fisher Price Toys $30.00-70.00
LOOKY FIRE TRUCK by Fisher Price, 1950's $15.00-30.00
LOST IN SPACE GAME, by Milton Bradley, 1965 ....$15.00-35.00
LOST IN SPACE LUNCHBOX, 1967 ....$10.00-20.00
LUCILLE BALL CHARACTER DOLL, 1950's, 27" tall $50.00-100.00
LUDWIG VON DRAKE BALL TOSS GAME, 1960's $10.00-25.00
LUDWIG VON DRAKE CERAMIC BANK, 1960's $10.00-30.00
LUDWIG VON DRAKE PLUSH DOLL, 1960's $35.00-60.00
LUDWIG VON DRAKE SQUEAK TOY, 1960's, Dell $5.00-10.00
LUDWIG VON DRAKE TALKING DOLL IN ORIGINAL BOX, 1960's $40.00-85.00
MAMMY YOKUM CHARACTER DOLL, vinyl, Barry Toys, 15" tall, 1950's $45.00-85.00
MAN FROM U.N.C.L.E. CARD GAME, circa 1960 ....$10.00-20.00
MAN FROM U.N.C.L.E. VIEWMASTER REEL SET, 1960's $5.00-10.00
MANDRAKE THE MAGICIAN MAGIC KIT, by Transogram, 1949 ....$30.00-50.00
MARIE OSMOND DOLL, 1970's $10.00-20.00
MARX JUNIOR TYPEWRITER, 1957, metal and tin $20.00-40.00
MARX LAZY DAYS FARM BARN, 1950's-1960's, metal $5.00-15.00
MARX MICKEY AND FRIENDS HOUSE, tin playhouse, 12" x 9", 1960's $10.00-35.00
MARX RIVER QUEEN PLASTIC RIVER STEAMER, boxed $25.00-40.00
MARX SKYVIEW PARKING PLAYSET, 1954, plastic cars, metal garage $40.00-75.00
MARX SPEEDBOAT, 1950's tin windup, actually floats, 8½" $10.00-20.00
MARY POPPINS CAROUSEL GAME, Walt Disney, 1960's, Parker Brothers $5.00-15.00
MARY POPPINS COLORING BOOK, Walt Disney, 1960's $5.00-10.00
MATTEL LIE DETECTOR GAME, 1960's $10.00-35.00
MATTEL TWIRL-A-TUNE, wood and metal, 1950's $10.00-30.00
MELODIE BELLS by Knickerbocker, ca. 1950's, hard plastic note bells $10.00-20.00
MERRY GO ROUND, Mattel, 1950's, 7", crank action $20.00-40.00
METAL MASTERS POPEYE XYLOPHONE PLAYER, ca. 1940's $50.00-100.00
MICKEY MOUSE DRUMMER, 1940 pull toy, modern Mickey version $30.00-75.00
MICKEY MOUSE EXPRESS by Marx, tin windup train and plane action $100.00-275.00
MICKEY MOUSE HAND PUPPET IN ORIGINAL BOX, by Gund, 1960's with squeaker.........$10.00-25.00

MICKEY MOUSE PUDDLE JUMPER CAR, 1953, by Fisher Price.................................$20.00-40.00
MICKEY MOUSE PULL TOY SEATED ON DRUM, 1940, polka dot bow tie on Mickey.$50.00-110.00
MICKEY MOUSE SAFETY PATROL, 1956.$25.00-50.00
MICKEY MOUSE ZILO, by Fisher Price, 1963, Mickey wears bandleader suit $10.00-30.00
MICKEY ROONEY PAINT BOOK, 1940 ..$20.00-40.00
MIGHTY MOUSE DOLL by Rushton, ca. 1950's, 16" $75.00-135.00
MINI-COPTER, by Fisher Price, 1970's $3.00-8.00
MISTER ED BOARD GAME by Parker Brothers, 1962 ....$10.00-20.00
MISTER MAGOO ADVERTISING DOLL, 12", 1960's, G. E. promotion $30.00-65.00
MISTER MAGOO CAR, by Hubley, 1961, 8" tall, metal $45.00-75.00
MISTER MAGOO DOLL WITH JOINTED LEGS, 16" tall $50.00-125.00
MISTER NOVAK TELEVISION GAME, by Transogram, 1963 ....$10.00-20.00
MISTER POTATOE HEAD SET, by Hasbro, 1950's, boxed $10.00-30.00
MISTER SPOCK STAR TREK KITE, 1970's $5.00-8.00
MO, THREE STOOGES PUPPET, 1950's.$10.00-20.00
MOLLY MOO-MOO COW, by Fisher Price, pull toy, 1956 ....$20.00-50.00
MONKEES LUNCHBOX, 1967 ....$10.00-20.00
MONKEES VIEWMASTER REEL SET, manufactured 1960's $5.00-10.00
MOO-OO COW, black spotted, by Fisher Price, 1958 ....$10.00-30.00
MUNSTERS CARD GAME, by Milton Bradley, 1966 ....$10.00-15.00
MUSIC BOX EGG, red, metal lithograph, 1953, plays "Here Comes Peter Cottontail" $5.00-10.00
MUSICAL CIRCUS HORSE by Marx, 10" long, metal drum rolls with chimes $20.00-45.00
MUSICAL ELEPHANT WITH CLOTH EARS, by Fisher Price, pull toy 1948 ....$30.00-75.00
MY FAVORITE MARTIAN GAME, 1963..$10.00-25.00
NAPOLEON SOLO MAN FROM U.N.C.L.E. GAME, Ideal, 1965 ....$10.00-20.00
NIFTY STATION WAGON, by Fisher Price, 1960 with four little people $10.00-25.00
NOSEY THE PUP, Fisher Price, 1956 .....$10.00-30.00
OCEAN LINER SIMPLE WOODEN RING BOAT, by Holgate, 1950's $5.00-15.00
ORPHAN ANNIE MINIATURE LEAD FIGURE, hand cast, 1940's, 2" $18.00-25.00
PAPPY YOKUM DOLL, Barry Toys, vinyl..$45.00-85.00
PARTRIDGE FAMILY LUNCHBOX, 1971 ....$3.00-7.00
PAT BOONE PAPER DOLL SET, 1959 ...$10.00-25.00
PATTY DUKE GAME, 1963 ....$5.00-10.00
PEANUTS LUNCHBOX SET, 1959 ....$20.00-35.00
PEANUTS GAME OF CHARLIE BROWN AND HIS PALS, 1959 board game $10.00-20.00
PEANUTS MAGNETIC BULLETIN BOARD, 1950..$20.00-40.00
PECKING CHICKEN ON WAGON, Ideal, 1950's, all plastic $5.00-15.00
PECOS BILL PLASTIC WINDUP COWBOY, by Marx, 1950's $25.00-60.00

PERRY MASON CASE OF THE MISSING SUSPECT GAME, 1950's $15.00-25.00

PETER BUNNY ENGINE, Fisher Price, pull toy, 1940 ....$30.00-70.00

PETER GUNN DETECTIVE GAME, 1960. $15.00-30.00

PETER PAN COLORING BOOK, by Whitman, 1950's $10.00-20.00

PHANTOM RAIDER BATTERY OPERATED SHIP, by Ideal, 34" $10.00-30.00

PHIL SILVERS SGT. BILKO "You'll Never Get Rich" game, 1950's..............................$15.00-40.00

PINKY PIG, Fisher Price, pull toy, 1956. $10.00-30.00

PINOCCHIO AND CLEO THE GOLDFISH PULL TOY, 1940, N. N. Hill Brass, Disney $75.00-150.00

PINOCCHIO AND FIGARO THE CAT PULL TOY, N. N. Hill Brass, 1940, Disney $75.00-150.00

PLASTICVILLE USA BARN, circa 1950, snap together $5.00-10.00

PLAY IRON, metal with plastic handle, circa 1950..............................$5.00-10.00

PLUTO ALARM CLOCK, by Bayard, French, circa 1960 ....$100.00-200.00

PLUTO BANK, ceramic, made by Leeds China, 1940's $20.00-40.00

PLUTO FIGURINE, made by American Pottery, 1940's $50.00-110.00

PLUTO SQUEAK TOY, circa 1940, Sun Rubber Company $15.00-25.00

PLUTO STRING PUPPET, boxed, 1950's. $20.00-40.00

POLLYANA PAPER DOLL BOOK, Walt Disney, 1960's $10.00-20.00

PONY CHIME PULL TOY, by Fisher Price, 1948..............................$30.00-70.00

POPEYE JOINTED CELLULOID FIGURE, 1940's, 6" $40.00-85.00

POPEYE LUNCHBOX, by Thermos, 1964 ..$5.00-15.00

POPEYE OIL PAINTING BY NUMBERS SET, 1950's $10.00-20.00

POPEYE PAINT SET BY PRESTO, 1961. $15.00-25.00

POPEYE PIPE, Lights up, 1950's $25.00-50.00

POPEYE SPINNING SPARKLER TOY, J. Chein, 1959, round $25.00-65.00

POPEYE TARGET, cardboard, S. S. Spinacher design $20.00-35.00

POPEYE WOOD STEPPING STOOL, 1957 . $15.00-40.00

PORKY PIG AND PETUNIA PIG PULL TOY, 1940's $65.00-130.00

PRICE IS RIGHT BOARD GAME, made in 1958, original $10.00-30.00

PUFFY TRAIN ENGINE PULL TOY, Fisher Price, 1950 ....$10.00-30.00

QUICK DRAW McGRAW STUFFED PLUSH TOY, 1960's $10.00-20.00

RAGGEDY ANN AND ANDY DRUMMERS PULL TOY, by Fisher Price, 1940 ....$100.00-300.00

RANCH PHONE, toy wall phone with cowboy lithography, by Gong Bell, 1950's $15.00-35.00

RAT PATROL, TELEVISION LUNCHBOX, circa 1960..............................$5.00-10.00

RED RANGER RID'EM COWBOY, tin windup, 1950's, Wyandotte, 6" $125.00-300.00

RED RYDER LUCKY TOYS, 1940's $8.00-12.00

RED RYDER PICTURE RECORD, 1948 . $15.00-25.00

RED SKELTON MASK SET, 1950's, three different character masks $30.00-55.00

RIDING HORSE ON FOUR WHEELS, by Gong Bell, 1950's $10.00-35.00

RIDING ZEBRA ON FOUR WHEELS, by Gong Bell, 1956 ....$15.00-30.00

RIFLEMAN, THE, BOARD GAME, dated, 1959 television version $10.00-25.00

RIN TIN TIN AT FORT APACHE, Marx playset, boxed $30.00-65.00

RIN TIN TIN COMPASS AND VIEWER, circa 1950 ....$35.00-70.00

RIN TIN TIN GAME, 1950 ....$20.00-30.00

ROAD RUNNER CHARACTER PUZZLES, set of two, boxed, 1969 ....$5.00-10.00

ROADSTER, made by Ideal, red hard plastic car, 1950's $10.00-25.00

ROBIN THE BOY WONDER MODEL KIT, 1966, Aurora $20.00-40.00

ROCKA-BYE BUNNY PUSHING CART, pull toy, Fisher Price, 1940 ....$50.00-120.00

ROOTIE KAZOOTIE HAND PUPPET.......$15.00-30.00

ROUTE 66 TRAVEL GAME, by Transogram, 1962 ....$15.00-30.00

ROY ROGERS AND TRIGGER METAL CATTLE TRUCK, by Marx, 15", 1950's..............$65.00-125.00

ROY ROGERS BOXED PAINT SET, 1950's, 10" x 14" $25.00-55.00

ROY ROGERS CAMERA, Herbert George Company, 1950's $20.00-40.00

ROY ROGERS CHUCK WAGON, 1950's $75.00-105.00

ROY ROGERS FIX-IT STAGECOACH, 1955, boxed, Ideal $35.00-70.00

ROY ROGERS HARMONICA..................$35.00-55.00

ROY ROGERS HORSESHOE GAME, by Ohio Art, 1950's $40.00-80.00

ROY ROGERS LUNCHBOX, 1950's $5.00-10.00

ROY ROGERS PLAYING CARDS, 1950's $15.00-25.00

ROY ROGERS RANCH LANTERN, Ohio Art Company, boxed $35.00-85.00

ROY ROGERS RIFLE by Marx, 1960's ... $25.00-75.00

ROY ROGERS RODEO BOXED PLAYSET, Marx, 1960's $25.00-75.00

ROY ROGERS TOY WAGON, 1950's, 16" x 27" child's wagon $50.00-125.00

ROY ROGERS TUCK-AWAY CAP GUN on original card $15.00-25.00

SCOOBY DOO RUBBER SQUEEZE TOY, 1970's $3.00-5.00

SCOOP LOADER, exceptionally bright red, blue, yellow plastics, brittle $10.00-20.00

SHAGGY ZILO BEAR DRUMMER PULL TOY, by Fisher Price, 1960 ....$10.00-20.00

SHARI LEWIS AND HER PUPPETS treasure board magic slate $5.00-15.00

SHOE WITH WOODEN TOKENS, "Old Woman and Shoe" printed on side, Holgate, 1940 $10.00-25.00

SKY KING TELEBLINKER, 1950's $40.00-80.00

SKYSCRAPER BUILDING SET, 1960's, Ideal, deluxe editon with helicopter $40.00-85.00

SLEEPING BEAUTY FRAME TRAY PUZZLE, 1959, Whitman $5.00-10.00

SLEEPING BEAUTY PAPER DOLLS BOOK, by Whitman, 1959..............................$10.00-25.00

SNOW WHITE SINK, by Wolverine, recent..$5.00-10.00

SNAP QUACK DUCK PULL TOY, Fisher Price, 1947...$30.00-70.00

SNORKEY FIRE ENGINE, Fisher Price, 1960, wood and plastic $10.00-20.00

SNOW WHITE REFRIGERATOR, by Wolverine, recent $5.00-10.00

SNOW WHITE STOVE, Wolverine, recent..$5.00-15.00

SOLDIER DONALD DUCK PULLED BY PLUTO, by Fisher Price, 1940 ....$100.00-250.00

SOLDIER TEN PINS by Artwood Manufacturing Company, 7½" soldiers, boxed $5.00-150.00

SPACE BLAZER SPACECRAFT TOY, by Fisher Price, 1950's $50.00-125.00

SPACE CRAWLER FOR MAJOR MATT MASON, 1960's space vehicle toy $15.00-40.00

SPECIAL DELIVERY SCOOTER, by Gong Bell, 1950's, wood and metal....................................$20.00-45.00

SPEEDBOAT by Ohio Art, 1950's, metal lithograph, windup crank on top $10.00-20.00

SPOTTED DOG IN FAST CAR PULL TOY, by Fisher Price, 1940 ....$30.00-65.00

SQUEAKY KITTY, molded vinyl, 1960's, 6" tall...$3.00-8.00

SQUEAKY TERRIER, vinyl dog, 1960.......$5.00-10.00

STACKING RINGS, wood, Holgate,1945 ..$10.00-30.00

STAR TREK ENTERPRISE LOGS, Western Publishing, 1977...$10.00-20.00

STAR TREK LUNCHBOX AND THERMOS, circa 1960 ....$10.00-20.00

STAR WARS ACTION FIGURES, 1978, 4" or less in height, first twelve editon.......... each $3.00-12.00

STAR WARS MOVIE VIEWER, made in 1978, with cartridge $5.00-15.00

STAR WARS X-WING FIGHTER (Luke's ship), late 1970's $20.00-40.00

STEVE CANYON SPACE HELMET, 1960's $10.00-25.00

SUNNY FISH PULL TOY, by Fisher Price, 1955...$10.00-40.00

SUPERMAN KIDDIE PADDLERS SWIM FINS, circa 1950 ....$50.00-85.00

SUPERMAN SPEED GAME made by Milton Bradley..$50.00-95.00

SUPERMAN OFFICIAL COSTUME BY BEN COOPER, circa 1950 ....$35.00-70.00

SUPERMAN WINDUP TANK TOY, by Marx, lifts tank, 1950's, tin lithograph $50.00-350.00

SYLVESTER HAND PUPPET, cat, 1950's...$10.00-20.00

TALE OF WELLS FARGO GAME, 1959..$15.00-30.00

TALKY PARROT FISHER PRICE TOY, circa 1960...$3.00-8.00

TEACH A TOT DAIRIES MILK BOTTLE SET IN CARTON (6), Holgate.................................$10.00-25.00

TEDDY BEAR IN STATION WAGON PULL TOY, Fisher Price, 1940 ....$30.00-60.00

TEDDY TOOTER BEAR RIDING BOX pull toy Fisher Price, 1940 ....$75.00-150.00

TEDDY TRUCKER PULL TOY, 1949, manufactured by Fisher Price..$20.00-40.00

TEDDY ZILO PULL TOY, manufactured by Fisher Price, 1940's $30.00-60.00

TELEPHONE, Fairline Plastics, 1950's $5.00-15.00

THE MUNSTERS CARD GAME, 1960's, Milton Bradley...$5.00-10.00

TIMMY TURTLE, Fisher Price, 1950's, hard plastic shelled pull toy.....................................$10.00-30.00

TINKLE ROLLER TODDLER'S PUSH TOY, metal, yellow and red, 1940's $10.00-20.00

TINY DING DONG ELEPHANT PULL TOY, Fisher Price, 1940 ....$60.00-120.00

TOE-JOE THE CLOWN ACROBATIC TOY, metal lithograph frame, 1950's, Ohio Art...........$30.00-60.00

TOM AND JERRY CAR, battery operated, 1950's, 12"..$100.00-225.00

TOM AND JERRY HAND PUPPETS, 1952 $15.00-30.00

TOP, SPINNING, TEN LITTLE INDIANS DESIGN, 1950's, Ohio Art.....................................$10.00-25.00

TOPO GIGIO MOUSE (from Ed Sullivan Show) 11" tall vinyl toy figure, 1960's $10.00-20.00

TOY WAGON, two ponies pulling toy cart, Fisher Price, 1940 ....$50.00-100.00

TUGBOAT SHOO-FLY ROCKER by Gong Bell Manufacturing, 1940's $20.00-45.00

TWEETIE PIE HAND PUPPET, 1950's $10.00-20.00

UNCLE FESTER'S MYSTERY LIGHT BULB FROM THE ADDAMS FAMILY, 1960's $10.00-25.00

UNCLE SCROOGE BANK, in bed, 1961 ...$10.00-20.00

UNTOUCHABLES MACHINE GUN, 1960's .$35.00-60.00

UNTOUCHABLES PLAYSET by Marx.....$50.00-120.00

VEGETABLES TRUCK, 1950's, hard plastic with transparent "vegetables" $5.00-12.00

VOICE PHONE, telephone toy by Gong Bell, 1952..$10.00-35.00

VOYAGE TO THE BOTTOM OF THE SEA lunchbox and thermos $10.00-20.00

WALT DISNEY'S DUMBO CIRCUS pull toy, Dumbo drives car...$100.00-250.00

WESTERN BOY PUSH ROLLER CHIME, by Gong Bell, 1950's, metal and wood $10.00-20.00

WHISTLING ENGINE PULL TOY, Fisher Price, 1957..$10.00-30.00

WINKY DINK AND YOU MAGIC TELEVISION KIT, 1940's $20.00-40.00

WINKY DINKS WINKO MAGIC SET, by Pressman Toys $30.00-60.00

WOLVERINE SULKY RACER HORSE, hard plastic, 1951, 9" long.....................................$15.00-30.00

WONDER WOMAN HAND MIRROR, 1970's ...$3.00-6.00

WOODY WOODPECKER ACTION WALL CLOCK, 1959, in original box $100.00-200.00

WOODY WOODPECKER LUNCHBOX, manufactured 1960's $5.00-10.00

WOOFY DOG PULL TOY, manufactured by Fisher Price, 1940 ....$40.00-70.00

WOOFY WAGGER DOGGY PULL TOY, by Fisher Price, 1947 ....$20.00-40.00

WYATT EARP TELEVISION BOARD GAME, made in 1958 ....$15.00-30.00

YOGI BEAR CARTOON GAME, made in circa 1950, boxed $5.00-15.00

ZORRO LUNCH, 1958, metal..................$10.00-20.00

ZORRO TARGET GAME, 1950's with dart gun, Knickerbocker Plastic $30.00-95.00

ZORRO WATER PISTOL by Knickerbocker Plastic Company $20.00-40.00

MOVIE AND PERSONALITY TOYS AND COLLECTIBLES

Hollywood has long been a source of fascination for the American public. From the big name, big star silver screen giants to the movie studio production lots themselves, Hollywood's command of the film industry has maintained an air of mystique and romance that is unmatched among the other entertainment media.

The stars of the movies and the movies themselves have inspired numerous toys and memorabilia over the years. Many of these items are paper dolls, books and paper items. One reason for the great "paper influence" upon Hollywood and movie subjects is that paper items could be quickly produced, published and moved to the masses to coincide exactly with the release of a top star's new film. In an industry where stars could be made or extinquished nearly overnight, paper items were a not-too-risky and easy way for publishers and toy producers to capitalize upon the popularity without losing too much on the bombs.

Generally, when a toy was produced in the likeness of a Hollywood star, that star was already a household word and a proven staple of the movies. The earliest film stars who were subjects of fine toys were Charlie Chaplin and Harold Lloyd. Both comic actors were transformed into wonderful windup toys in the 1920's. The Harold Lloyd windup walker of the 1920's is a hard-to-find variety of the popular "walker" toys of that decade. When he rocks back and forth, Harold's grinning teeth show and makes the toy quite comical. Early Charlie Chaplin toys were produced in abundant variety. The tin and pot metal wind-up version from the 1920's is probably the most attractive of all Charlie items with its polished metal and enamel appearance, but the tin and cloth covered windups by Schuco and others are by far more sculptural and a better likeness of the "Little Tramp." Also, because the felt-like fabric which covered these windups was easily a target of soil, age, water, soot and wear, it is tough to find examples of these in excellent or mint condition.

Movie stars of the 1930's also inspired some great toys. Milton Berle and Ed Wynn were the subjects of fine toys from this period, and a host of would-be big name stars appeared on the toy shelves in the form of paper items during the 1940's and 1950's.

When using this listing, first look for the star's name in order to identify character merchandise relating to that film actor or actress. Listings are also made here of a few film titles because the toys themselves were marketed by those names.

With the health of the film industry of today certain, it would be a good bet to stay on course in the field of Hollywood toys and memorabilia. Not only do these toys have a great popular-culture historical value, they are highly in demand among film buffs, movie star fans and general devotees of the cinema.

LOUIS ARMSTRONG PLASTIC AND TIN WINDUP TOY, Reynolds collection, $50.00-125.00.

ABBOT AND COSTELLO IN JACK AND THE BEAN-STALK, sheet music, 1952 ....$10.00-30.00
ANN SHERIDAN PAINT BOOK, large $10.00-20.00
AUDIE MURPHY POSTER, movie $20.00-45.00
AVA GARDNER CUT-OUT DOLLS, Whitman, 1949 ....$10.00-25.00
BEATLES BOOK, A HARD DAY'S NIGHT, 1964, paper back $10.00-20.00
BEATLES BUBBLE GUM CARDS, 1960's, set of hundred seventy-five $25.00-55.00
BEATLES CAR NODDERS in package of four, 1960's, rare $300.00-600.00
BEATLES CARD SET from "A Hard Days Night" $20.00-40.00
BEATLES COLORING BOOK, 1964 ....$10.00-30.00
BEATLES DOLL, Paul, by Remco $40.00-60.00
BEATLES GAME, FLIP YOUR WIG, early 1960's, unusual...$35.00-75.00
BEATLES HALLOWEEN COSTUME, John, boxed, 1960's $50.00-125.00
BEATLES INFLATABLE CARTOON DOLLS, set of all four $50.00-100.00
BEATLES MUSIC BOX, 1960's $10.00-20.00
BEATLES COIN PURSE, plastic, 1960's ..$20.00-40.00
BEATLES YELLOW SUBMARINE PAPERBACK, BOOK, 1960's $5.00-10.00
BEATLES YELLOW SUBMARINE THERMOS, 1960's $5.00-10.00
BETTE DAVIS PAPER DOLLS, made by Merrill, 1942 ....$20.00-40.00

BETTY BOOP AND BIMBO SINGLE BRIDGE TALLY CARDS, 1930's, unmarked.................$20.00-40.00
BETTY BOOP AND BIMBO WALL POCKET, 1930's, lusterware, 5½" $65.00-125.00
BETTY BOOP AND MICKEY MOUSE BOWL, 6", unmarked, 1930's $65.00-125.00
BETTY BOOP ASH TRAY, lusterware version, 1930's $60.00-100.00
BETTY BOOP BISQUE FIGURE, 1930's, 4" playing a horn $35.00-70.00
BETTY BOOP BISQUE FIGURE, playing a drum, 4" tall..$35.00-70.00
BETTY BOOP BOXED BRIDGE DECK AND SCORE PAD, 1930's, cover art on box $100.00-225.00
BETTY BOOP CANDY BAR BOX, 1920's, Fleischer Studios, 8" x 11½" $50.00-125.00
BETTY BOOP CELLULOID BELT BUCKLE, 1930's $30.00-65.00
BETTY BOOP CELLULOID MECHANICAL WINDUP, Japan, 1930's, 7" $350.00-650.00
BETTY BOOP HOLLOW CELLULOID FIGURE, 3", Japan, painted $40.00-85.00
BETTY BOOP JOINTED WOOD COMPOSITION DOLL, 1930's, large $300.00-600.00
BETTY BOOP POCKET WATCH, 1930's.$300.00-550.00
BETTY BOOP STRING HOLDER, plaster, 1930's $50.00-125.00
BETTY BOOP'S DOG BIMBO, wood jointed doll, Fleischer, 7" $200.00-400.00
BETTY GRABLE COLORING BOOK, dated 1951...$25.00-40.00
BING CROSBY COLORING BOOK, by Saalfield, 1954 ....$15.00-35.00
BING CROSBY RECORD DUSTER, 1950's.$10.00-20.00
BOB HOPE coloring book, Saalfield, 1954 $15.00-30.00
BOB HOPE HAND PUPPET, ca. 1950's ..$10.00-25.00
CARMEN MIRANDA DOLL, 8½" plastic, circa 1940...$45.00-85.00
CAROL LOMBARD with Charlie McCarthy on cover of Movie Life issue, 1930's $10.00-20.00
CHARLIE CHAN CARD GAME, by Whitman, 1939 ....$20.00-45.00
CHARLIE CHAN, THE GREAT CHARLIE CHAN DE-TECTIVE GAME, Milton Bradley, 1937.$50.00-100.00
CHARLIE CHAPLIN BUD VASE, ceramic, 2", 1930's $20.00-40.00
CHARLIE CHAPLIN CANDY CONTAINER, painted glass, 4" $65.00-120.00
CHARLIE CHAPLIN COMIC COLORING BOOK, 1917...$20.00-45.00
CHARLIE CHAPLIN COMPOSITION DOLL, dated 1915, 26" $400.00-800.00
CHARLIE CHAPLIN DOLL, composition, fabric, metal, 1930's, 11½" tall $300.00-650.00
CHARLIE CHAPLIN GERMAN WINDUP, 8½" tall, metal cast iron, painted $600.00-1,200.00
CHARLIE CHAPLIN GLOVE BOX, 1920's, leather, 10" tall..$40.00-85.00
CHARLIE CHAPLIN HAT TIPPER TOY, 7", plastic, Italy $50.00-110.00
CHARLIE CHAPLIN IN EASY STREET, Storm-Greg, 1932...$20.00-45.00
CHARLIE CHAPLIN IN THE GREAT DICTATOR COL-ORING BOOK, Saalfield, 1941 ....$25.00-55.00

CHARLIE CHAPLIN LEAD FIGURE, 1930's, 2½" tall, painted $15.00-35.00

CHARLIE CHAPLIN NOVELTY TOY, England, approximately 5", spring hat-tipper $40.00-75.00

CHARLIE CHAPLIN PAPIER MACHE DOLL, 8", 1920's or 1930's..$100.00-225.00

CHARLIE CHAPLIN PENCIL BOX, 1930's, tin lithograph...$20.00-40.00

CHARLIE CHAPLIN PENCIL SHARPENER, German, 1920's $75.00-110.00

CHARLIE CHAPLIN TOOTHPICK, HOLDER, probably 1930's $25.00-50.00

CHARLIE CHAPLIN "UP IN THE AIR," published by M. A. Donahue, 1917 ....$50.00-80.00

CHARLIE CHAPLIN WALK, sheet music, copyright 1915...$40.00-80.00

CHARLIE CHAPLIN WALKER, windup, 1920's, metal feet, composition body....................$400.00-800.00

CHARLIE CHAPLIN WHISTLE, tin lithograph, 1920's $40.00-80.00

CHARLIE CHAPLIN WINDUP CLOCKWORK TOY, c. 1915, 12" tall, composition $700.00-1,100.00

CHARLIE CHAPLIN WINDUP FIGURE, 1920's, metal and wood composition, 8", rare ..$500.00-1,000.00

CHARLIE CHAPLIN WINDUP, manufactured ca. 1960's, Spain $30.00-65.00

CHARLIE McCARTHY AND MORTIMER SNERD PRIVATE CAR, 1939, Marx car, 16" ..$300.00-650.00

CHARLIE McCARTHY BANK, composition, wears red beret, 6", 1930's $50.00-135.00

CHARLIE McCARTHY BOOK, "A Day with Charlie McCarthy, red cover $35.00-65.00

CHARLIE McCARTHY BOOK, "So Help Me Mister Bergen, 1930's $20.00-35.00

CHARLIE McCARTHY BOXED RUMMY CARD GAME, 1939..$25.00-50.00

CHARLIE McCARTHY CARNIVAL GIVE-AWAY CHALK FIGURE, 7½", 1930's $20.00-55.00

CHARLIE McCARTHY COMIC BOOK, 1948 $5.00-15.00

CHARLIE McCARTHY FIGURAL SOAP in box, 1930's, Kirk Guild..$25.00-60.00

CHARLIE McCARTHY FIGURAL SOAP, 1930's, Kirk Guild, in plastic container $35.00-75.00

CHARLIE McCARTHY GET WELL CARD, 1930's $10.00-25.00

CHARLIE McCARTHY JOINTED AND FOLDED CARDBOARD PUPPET, 18", 1930's $45.00-110.00

CHARLIE McCARTHY MEETS SNOW WHITE book by Whitman, 1930's...............................$20.00-45.00

CHARLIE McCARTHY PAINT BOOK, circa 1930..$15.00-30.00

CHARLIE McCARTHY PAINT BOOK, 1938, Whitman, 11" x 13½"..$35.00-60.00

CHARLIE McCARTHY PAPER MONEY PLAY SET, in original package $20.00-35.00

CHARLIE McCARTHY PUPPET, 12" tall, cloth and composition, 1930's $50.00-125.00

CHARLIE McCARTHY RADIO, manufactured by Majestic $300.00-550.00

CHARLIE McCARTHY SPOON, silverplate, circa 1930...$10.00-20.00

CHARLIE McCARTHY VENTRILOQUIST DOLL, by Effanbee, 17", 1930's $250.00-500.00

CHARLIE McCARTHY WINDUP CAR "BENZINE BUGGY," 1930's, Marx...................$275.00-550.00

CHARLIE McCARTHY WINDUP WALKER TOY by Marx, 1939, tin lithograph $200.00-450.00

CLAUDETTE COLBERT PAPER DOLL BOOK, by Saalfield 1943 ....$20.00-40.00

CREATURE FROM THE BLACK LAGOON 3-D glasses $20.00-40.00

CURLEY, THREE STOOGES, HAND PUPPET, 1950's $10.00-20.00

DAVID COPPERFIELD BIG LITTLE BOOK, 1930's, with Freddy Bartholomew...................$15.00-35.00

DEANNA DURBIN DOLL, 1939, Ideal toy and Novelty, 24" tall $150.00-350.00

DEBBIE REYNOLD'S COLORING BOOK, 1953..$15.00-30.00

DEBBIE REYNOLD'S DOLL WITH MAGIC STAY-ON CLOTHES, by Whitman, 1958 ....$15.00-30.00

DEBBY REYNOLD'S TWO PAPER DOLLS AND CLOTHES, by Whitman, 1957 ....$15.00-30.00

DORIS DAY COLORING BOOK copyright 1958..$10.00-20.00

ED WYNN PIPE FIRE CHIEF SIREN, 1930's, tin and paper...$15.00-35.00

ED WYNN JOINTED DOLL wood $30.00-65.00

EDDIE CANTOR JIGSAW PUZZLE, Einson-Freeman, 1933 ....$20.00-40.00

EDDIE CANTOR'S GAME, "Tell It to the Judge," $20.00-40.00

EDGAR BERGEN AND CHARLIE McCARTHY TIME MAGAZINE, cover issue...................$10.00-20.00

EDGAR BERGEN CARD, Arcade, 1940's .$10.00-20.00

EDGAR BERGEN'S CHARLIE McCARTHY DANCER, Marks Brothers, 1930's $65.00-135.00

EDGAR BERGEN'S CHARLIE McCARTHY MEETS SNOW WHITE BOOK, 1939............$20.00-40.00

EDGAR BERGEN'S, CHARLIE McCARTHY PICTURE PUZZLE, boxed set of two $35.00-65.00

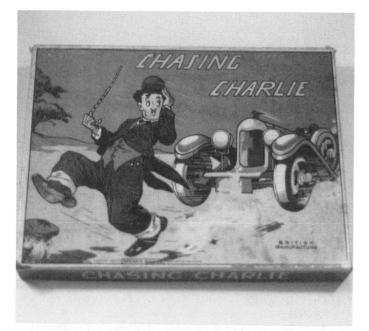

CHASING CHARLIE, CHAPLIN CHARACTER GAME BY SPEARS OF ENGLAND, early boxed, Furnish collection, $60.00-125.00.

CHARLIE CHAPLIN LITHOGRAPH AND PAINTED TIN WINDUP WITH HEAVY METAL FEET, walk action, Reynolds collection, $500.00-900.00.

EDGAR BERGEN'S CHARLIE McCARTHY PUT AND TAKE BINGO GAME, 1938 ....$35.00-75.00

EDGAR BERGEN'S MORTIMER SNERD PUPPET, rubber, boxed..$40.00-80.00

EDGAR BERGEN'S CHARLIE McCARTHY GAME OF TOPPER, boxed game, by Whitman ..$20.00-45.00

ELIZABETH TAYLOR COLORING BOOK, by Whitman, 1950..$15.00-30.00

ELIZABETH TAYLOR CUT-OUT DOLLS, by Whitman, 1949...$20.00-40.00

ELVIS PRESLEY BRACELET, 1960's, dog tag style $10.00-20.00

ELVIS PRESLEY HAT, 1950's, hat with original tag...$50.00-100.00

ELVIS PRESLEY GAME, "King of Rock" ...$5.00-15.00

ELVIS PRESLEY SOCKS, original packaging, 1956..$10.00-20.00

ESTER WILLIAMS COLORING BOOK, published in 1950..$10.00-30.00

EVE ARDEN COLORING BOOK, published in 1953..$10.00-30.00

FANNY BRICE BABY SNOOKS CHARACTER PREMIUM, cardboard doll, 15".................$30.00-65.00

FANNY BRICE BABY SNOOKS DOLL, 12" Ideal Toy and Novelty, 1930's $150.00-325.00

FREDDY BARTHOLOWMEW IN LITTLE LORD FAUNTLEROY, 1936 book, Saalfield.............$15.00-35.00

GLORIA JEAN PAPER DOLLS, by Saalfield, 1940, 11" x 13"...$25.00-50.00

GONE WITH THE WIND child's hanky, 1939, pictures Bonnie..$10.00-30.00

GONE WITH THE WIND PAINT BOOK, published by Merrill, 1940 ....$35.00-65.00

GONE WITH THE WIND PAPER DOLLS, Merrill, 1940...$75.00-150.00

GONE WITH THE WIND SCARLET O'HARA COIN PURSE, 1939..$20.00-45.00

GRACE KELLY COLORING BOOK, copyright 1956..$20.00-40.00

GROUCHO MARX WRIST WATCH, manufactured 1950's...$35.00-70.00

HAROLD LLOYD CELLULOID DOLL, Japan, 6½", 1930's, jointed arms.....................................$75.00-125.00

HAROLD LLOYD PAPER FACE MASK, 9", 1930's..$20.00-35.00

HAROLD LLOYD SMALL CELLULOID FIGURE, jointed arms, Japan, 2½" $50.00-125.00

HAROLD LLOYD SPARKLER TOY, push bottom type, tin lithograph, 5½"...........................$75.00-150.00

HAROLD LLOYD TIN WINDUP TOY, 11" rocks back and forth, grins, tin $200.00-450.00

JACKIE COOGAN CELLULOID FIGURE, pink and white, 5½" $50.00-110.00

JACKIE COOGAN PENCIL BOX, tin, with lithograph picture...$20.00-40.00

JACKIE COOPER CHARACTER DOLL, jointed arms, composition, 12", rare $200.00-400.00

JACKIE COOPER STAR OF SKIPPY, Big Little Book, 1933...$15.00-30.00

JAMES BOND ACTION FIGURE, 1960's, scuba attire $20.00-45.00

JAMES BOND PILLOWCASE, 1960's $10.00-20.00

JAMES BOND PLAY POOL TABLE, circa 1960...$10.00-20.00

JAMES BOND PUZZLE, 1960's $5.00-10.00

JANE POWELL PAPER DOLLS BOOK, 1952..$15.00-30.00

JANE WITHERS BOOK, HER LIFE STORY, Whitman Publishing, 1936...................................$20.00-40.00

JANE WITHERS DOLL, 15" composition, dressed in Scottish plaid, 1930's $150.00-300.00

JANE WYMAN movies pencil tablet.........$10.00-30.00

JOAN CARROLL COLORING BOOK, by Saalfield, 1942..$10.00-25.00

JOE E. BROWN bike club button...........$10.00-20.00

JOE PENNER AND HIS DUCK GOO-GOO, tin windup by Marx, 1930's.............................$250.00-500.00

JOE PENNER "WANNA BUY A DUCK" SQUEEZE TOY, cardboard, 7" tall $45.00-110.00

JOE PENNER'S DUCK GOO-GOO CANDY CONTAINER, pulp composition, yellow duck...........$40.00-85.00

JOHN TRAVOLTA DOLL, 1970's.............$10.00-20.00

JOHN WAYNE PICTURE PUZZLE, 1950's .$10.00-20.00

JUDY GARLAND AND THE WHOODOO COSTUME, book, hardcover, Whitman, 1945 ....$20.00-40.00

JUDY GARLAND COLORING BOOK, copyright 1941 ....$30.00-50.00

JUDY GARLAND DOLL, by Ideal Toy and Novelty, 1940, 18" composition, "Dorothy" ..$200.00-400.00

JUNE ALLYSON COLORING BOOK, copyright 1952 ....$20.00-35.00

LANA TURNER PAINT BOOK, by Whitman, 1947 ....$15.00-30.00

LARRY, THREE STOOGES, HAND PUPPET, circa 1950...$10.00-20.00

LAUREL AND HARDY CELLULOID push-up toy $50.00-100.00

LAUREL AND HARDY PLASTER FIGURES, early 1970's $10.00-25.00

LAUREL AND HARDY SALT AND PEPPER SHAKER glazed ceramic set, England..............$20.00-40.00

LITTLE RASCALS POSTER, reprint $10.00-20.00

LITTLE WOMEN FEATURING KATHYRN HEPBURN, Whitman Book, 1934 ....$20.00-40.00

LUCILLE BALL CHARACTER DOLL, 1950's, 27" $50.00-100.00

LUCILLE BALL PAPER DOLLS, by Saalfield, 1945 ....$20.00-40.00

MARGARET O'BRIEN COLORING BOOK, circa 1930 ....$10.00-25.00

MARGARET O'BRIEN PAINT BOOK, by Whitman, 1943 ....$15.00-35.00

MARGARET O'BRIEN WOOD COMPOSITION DOLL, 21", 1930's $300.00-475.00

MARIE OSMOND DOLL, 1970's $10.00-20.00

MARILYN MONROE DOLL, "Seven Year Itch," costume version $50.00-100.00

MARX BROTHERS AUTOGRAPHED PICTURE, 1930's $40.00-80.00

MARX PATHE MOVIE CAMERA, 6" tall, tin lithograph, 1930's $30.00-60.00

MARY MARTIN DOLLS AND COSTUMES, by Saalfield, 1942 ....$30.00-50.00

MICKEY ROONEY PAINT BOOK, 1940 ..$20.00-40.00

MICKEY ROONEY'S ONE MAN BAND, musical washboard toy, 1950's $15.00-35.00

MILTON BERLE FUNNY CAR by Marx, 6" tin lithograph crazy car windup $150.00-275.00

MO, THREE STOOGES PUPPET, 1950's .$10.00-20.00

MORTIMER SNERD CRAZY CAR, tin windup toy, by Marx, 1939 ....$250.00-475.00

MORTIMER SNERD HAND PUPPET, 1930's, composition and cloth, 10"............................$40.00-95.00

MORTIMER SNERD JACK IN THE BOX, composition....................................$50.00-100.00

MORTIMER SNERD JOINTED CARDBOARD PUPPET, 1930's, 18" $35.00-75.00

MORTIMER SNERD WINDUP WALKER TOY, by Marx, 1930's $150.00-300.00

MOVIE CAMERA marked "Pathe" by Marx, 6" tall, 1930's $30.00-60.00

MOVIE LIFE ISSUE FEATURING CHARLIE McCARTHY ON THE COVER, 1930's $10.00-20.00

MOVIELAND CUT UPS, Our Gang and Rin Tin Tin puzzles set, 1930, A. J. Saxe $50.00-95.00

MOVIELAND KEENO GAME, Wilder Manufacturing, 1929, movie stars on box $50.00-95.00

OUR GANG CHUBBY CHANEY BISQUE NODDER FIGURE, German $45.00-115.00

OUR GANG COLORING BOOK, published by Saalfield, 1938....................................$20.00-40.00

OUR GANG FARINA CHARACTER, bisque, made in Germany $35.00-90.00

OUR GANG FUN KIT, 1930's $30.00-60.00

OUR GANG IN RASCALS PHOTO PRINTER, 1930's, prints pictures from negatives $20.00-40.00

OUR GANG INK BLOTTER, Majestic electric radio....................................$15.00-35.00

OUR GANG MOVIE BOOK, 1929 ....$20.00-45.00

SHIRLEY TEMPLE FIVE BOOKS ABOUT ME, boxed set, by Saalfield, 1936, Reynolds collection, $100.00-200.00.

OUR GANG PENCIL BOX, ca. 1930's $20.00-35.00

OUR GANG PUZZLE SET, 1932, McKesson and Robbins $35.00-65.00

OUR GANG SCHOOL BOX, 1930's, blue and gold $15.00-35.00

OUR GANG TIPPLE TOPPLE GAME, 1930, copyright Hal Roach Studios..........................$40.00-85.00

OUR GANG WHEEZER CHARACTER BISQUE, German $35.00-90.00

OUR GANG, A STORY OF OUR GANG, storybook, Whitman, 1929 ....$25.00-40.00

PAT BOONE PAPER DOLLS SET, by Whitman, 1959....................................$10.00-25.00

PATHE MOVIE CAMERA, by Marx, 6" tall, 1930's $30.00-60.00

PIPER LAURIE COLORING BOOK, copyright 1953 ....$10.00-30.00

RED SKELTON MASK SET, 1950's, three different character masks $30.00-55.00

RHONDA FLEMING PAPER DOLLS, Saalfield, 1954 ....$20.00-40.00

RITA HAYWORTH IN CARMEN, paper dolls by Saalfield, 1948 ....$15.00-35.00

ROCK HUDSON CUT-OUTS, by Whitman, 1957 ....$10.00-25.00

ROCK HUDSON PAPER DOLLS BOOK, by Whitman, 1957 ....$15.00-30.00

RUDY VALEE VALENTINE, 1920's, "ABC," 6" tall $15.00-30.00

SHIRLEY TEMPLE ADVERTISING PAPER DOLL, 10" figure, 1930's $45.00-110.00

SHIRLEY TEMPLE AT PLAY BOOK, published by Saalfield, 1930's................................$20.00-35.00

SHIRLEY TEMPLE BARRETTE AND BOW SET, 1930's $25.00-50.00

SHIRLEY TEMPLE BOOK, "Now I Am Eight," Saalfield, 1937 ....$15.00-35.00

SHIRLEY TEMPLE BOOK, "Shirley Temple In Stowaway," Saalfield, 1937 ....$20.00-40.00

SHIRLEY TEMPLE BOOK, HEIDI, by Saalfield, 1937 ....$15.00-35.00

MOVIE RELATED TOYS

SHIRLEY TEMPLE BOOK, THE LITTLE COLONEL, with original dust jacket sleeve $20.00-45.00

SHIRLEY TEMPLE BOXED PAPER DOLL SET, 1930's $40.00-80.00

SHIRLEY TEMPLE BOXED STATIONERY, circa 1930 .... $30.00-65.00

SHIRLEY TEMPLE CEREAL BOWL, BLUE GLASS, some wear, 1930's $20.00-40.00

SHIRLEY TEMPLE CHILD'S COMPOSITION BOOK, 1930's $20.00-40.00

SHIRLEY TEMPLE PURSE, 1934 .... $50.00-110.00

SHIRLEY TEMPLE CHRISTMAS BOOK, #1770, by Saalfield, 1937 .... $20.00-40.00

SHIRLEY TEMPLE CHRISTMAS CARD, Hallmark, 1935 .... $15.00-30.00

SHIRLEY TEMPLE COLORING BOOK, crossing the country $15.00-25.00

SHIRLEY TEMPLE COLORING BOOK, by Saalfield, 1936 .... $25.00-50.00

SHIRLEY TEMPLE COLORING BOOK, 1935, by Saalfield 8" x 10" $45.00-85.00

SHIRLEY TEMPLE COLORING SET, manufactured by Saalfield, 1930's, boxed $50.00-100.00

SHIRLEY TEMPLE DIMPLES BOOK, published by Saalfield, 1936 .... $20.00-30.00

SHIRLEY TEMPLE DOLL BUGGY WITH ORIGINAL DECALS, 1930's, rare $400.00-750.00

SHIRLEY TEMPLE DOLL, 1935, 20" giant size, Ideal Toy and Novelty, jointed $500.00-900.00

SHIRLEY TEMPLE DOLLS AND DRESSES BOOK, published by Saalfield, 1934 .... $45.00-100.00

SHIRLEY TEMPLE DOLLS AND DRESSES cut-out dolls set, Saalfield, 1930's $50.00-95.00

SHIRLEY TEMPLE FIGURAL SOAP by Kirk Guild, 1930's, in original box $75.00-145.00

SHIRLEY TEMPLE IN LITTLE MISS BROADWAY BOOK, Saalfield, 1938 .... $20.00-45.00

SHIRLEY TEMPLE IN SUZANNA OF THE MOUNTIES BOOK, Saalfield, 1939 .... $20.00-50.00

SHIRLEY TEMPLE IN THE LITTLE COLONEL child's hanky $15.00-30.00

SHIRLEY TEMPLE IN THE LITTLE COLONEL, book, hardcover, ca. 1930's $20.00-40.00

SHIRLEY TEMPLE IN WEE WILLIE WINKLE BOOK, 1930's $15.00-35.00

SHIRLEY TEMPLE MILK PITCHER, 4", blue with white lettering, 1930's $25.00-50.00

SHIRLEY TEMPLE ON THE MOVIE LOT, paperback book, 1930's, Saalfield $20.00-40.00

SHIRLEY TEMPLE PLASTER FIGURE, 13", holding dress, 1930's $100.00-225.00

SHIRLEY TEMPLE PLAYING CARDS with original box, 1930's $30.00-65.00

SHIRLEY TEMPLE PLAYING CARDS, Shirley plays a drum, original box $30.00-65.00

SHIRLEY TEMPLE ROYAL CROWN COLA FAN, premium, 1930's $10.00-20.00

SHIRLEY TEMPLE SALT FIGURE, 4" tall, circa 1930 .... $30.00-65.00

SHIRLEY TEMPLE SALT FIGURE, 7" .. $75.00-135.00

SHIRLEY TEMPLE SCHOOL TABLET, 1930's, 6" x 9" $15.00-35.00

SHIRLEY TEMPLE SCRAPBOOK, 1935, by Saalfield, 12" x 13" $40.00-85.00

SHIRLEY TEMPLE SEWING CARDS, published by Saalfield, 1936 .... $50.00-90.00

SHIRLEY TEMPLE SONG ALBUM, published in the 1930's $20.00-30.00

SHIRLEY TEMPLE STARRING ROLES paperback book, Saalfield, 1930's $20.00-40.00

SHIRLEY TEMPLE STORE DISPLAY, Shirley plays pipe organ, 1930's $1,000.00-1,500.00

SHIRLEY TEMPLE TEA SET, 1930's, pink, boxed $100.00-200.00

SHIRLEY TEMPLE TRUNK WITH MOVIE DECALS, 1930's $75.00-150.00

SHIRLEY TEMPLE TWINKLETOES, paperback, book, Saalfield, 1930's $20.00-40.00

SHIRLEY TEMPLE WRITING TABLET, 1935, Western tablet $20.00-40.00

SHIRLEY TEMPLE'S FAVORITE POEMS BOOK, 1936 .... $15.00-30.00

SHIRLEY TEMPLE, THIS IS MY CRAYON BOOK, by Saalfield, 1935 .... $20.00-40.00

SHIRLEY'S FAVORITE PUZZLES, by Saalfield, 1937, boxed set of games $75.00-135.00

SONJA HENIE INK BLOTTER, "One in a Million" $10.00-20.00

SONJA HENIE CHARACTER DOLL, 1939, Madame Alexander Doll Company, 13" $200.00-350.00

THREE STOOGES, PILLSBURY'S FARINA MOVING PICTURE MACHINE, premium, 1937 $40.00-80.00

TIM McCOY POLICE CAR 17 ACTION STORYBOOK, Colombia, Whitman, 1930's $20.00-40.00

TOMMY KELLY GAME "Peck's Bad Boy with the Circus," 1939 Milton Bradley game $20.00-45.00

W. C. FIELDS ALUMINUM FIGURE (cast aluminum), 6½" $30.00-60.00

W. C. FIELDS CHARACTER DOLL by Effanbee, 18" tall, 1930's $200.00-375.00

W. C. FIELDS FILM, 16mm The Great Chase," boxed $15.00-30.00

WILL ROGERS THERMOMETER, metal . $25.00-50.00

WIZARD OF OZ PAINT BOOK, 1930's ... $20.00-40.00

WIZARD OF OZ SCARECROW PAPER MASK, 1939, by Einson-Freeman $15.00-30.00

WIZARD OF OZ SOAP FIGURES from 1930's film release, set of four, 4" tall $30.00-75.00

WIZARD OF OZ WIZARD'S MASK, 1939, paper, by Einson-Freeman $15.00-30.00

WIZARD OF OZ, DOROTHY CHARACTER FACE MASK, by Einson-Freeman, 1939 ...... $15.00-30.00

WIZARD OF OZ, DOROTHY SOAP FIGURE, 1930's, 4" tall $15.00-30.00

WIZARD OF OZ, LION SOAP FIGURE, 1930's, 4" $15.00-30.00

WIZARD OF OZ, SCARECROW SOAP FIGURE, 1930's, 4" $15.00-30.00

WIZARD OF OZ, THE STORY OF, Whitman, 1939, coloring book $15.00-35.00

WIZARD OF OZ, TIN MAN SOAP FIGURE, 4", 1930's $15.00-30.00

PLAYHOUSE TOYS

Even with the day of women's lib and the decline in the interest in being a "housewife" among most young women, today's little girls still like to play house. I know. My own young daughter adores her little tables, kitchen furniture, tea sets and rocking chairs. There's nothing wrong with being a "domestic engineer" in her eyes. Let's face it...little girls still like to play house regardless of how our society has changed the daily role and definition of Mom.

And playhouse toys were even more popular around the turn of the century. Along with the one or more dolls that each little girl owned went a nursery full of homemaker items to help care for the doll. Doll beds, blankets, dishes, tea sets, kitchen items, chairs, rockers and basically anything related to a little girl's playhouse or nursery are listed here.

Most differences in prices are related to the age of the item. One influential factor which keeps prices modest to expensive for most of these items is the interest in them by today's doll collectors. Doll dealers and collectors anxiously seek out playhouse related items because they are important display accessories for doll collection. Therefore, the toy collector must also compete with the doll collector in this area of the toy marketplace.

ALL METAL PRODUCTS REFRIGERATOR, 10", metal, with tray, opening door, compressor on top model, Furnish collection, $50.00-125.00.

CAST IRON STOVE, 8" WITH UTENSILS, marked "Favorite" on oven door, 1910's, Furnish collection, $100.00-200.00.

179

MARX TOY BATHROOM, tin, Furnish collection, $50.00-125.00.

MARX HONEYMOON SERIES, tin furnished bedroom, 3", Furnish collection, $50.00-100.00.

ABC PLATE, Drayton, Cambell Kids, 7" .$40.00-70.00
ALPHABET HIGH CHAIR, Victorian style, 1890's $200.00-500.00
ALUMINUM POTS AND PANS SET, "Domestic Science," 1919 ....$30.00-75.00
ALUMINUM TEA SET, manufactured 1922, thirty-one pieces $30.00-75.00
BABY BUNTING BABY DISH.................$20.00-40.00
BABY HIGH CHAIR with baby picture lithograph on chair back, 1890's $200.00-400.00
BABY PLATE AND MUG, Swedish enamel, 1930 ....$10.00-30.00
BAKE A CAKE SET, by Wolverine, No. 262, ten pieces $25.00-30.00
BAMBOO DOLL FURNITURE, 1900's, Japan, eight pieces $60.00-120.00
BARBIE DOLL SUITCASE, 1968 ....$10.00-20.00
BEDROOM SET, doll furniture, 1912, five pieces $100.00-350.00

BENTWOOD ARM CHAIR, 1930's $20.00-45.00
BETSY ROSS sewing machine $10.00-20.00
BINGOLA RECORD PLAYER WITH TWO RECORDS as originally boxed, 1920's, rare $100.00-200.00
BISSEL TOY FLOOR SWEEPER, 1914, metal and wood, works $35.00-80.00
BISSEL'S LITTLE HELPER CLEANING SET, 1920's, broom, sweeper, mop, etc. $25.00-75.00
BLUE BIRD GAS RANGE AND STOVE, 1920's, cast iron with utensils, 9" $40.00-100.00
BLUE ENAMELED TOY KITCHEN SET, 1912, twenty-one pieces, tin $50.00-95.00
BLUE WILLOW CREAMER, doll dish $5.00-10.00
BLUE WILLOW DOLL DISH SET, 1930's, twelve pieces in box $50.00-75.00
BOWL, Punch and Judy, English $40.00-70.00
BREAKFAST SET, Little Bo Peep, pink lusterware, German $50.00-120.00
BRIDESMAID MUG, child's, Germany, gold trim on brim $10.00-30.00
BUDDY TUCKER BEAR MUG $20.00-40.00
BUREAU WITH MIRROR, 1914, toy chest, 15", hardwood $50.00-100.00
CANE DOLL'S BED, wrapped cane with ornate design, 1890's $100.00-250.00
CANOPIED TOY BASSINET, 1914, metal with cloth trimmings $45.00-135.00
CASH REGISTER, play store type, 1930's, 5" x 5", metal construction $20.00-45.00
CAST IRON SEWING MACHINE, Hook Jr., original $50.00-100.00
CAST IRON STOVE, 1886, 4" $35.00-60.00
CAST IRON STOVE, circa 1880, 7" deluxe version $50.00-100.00
CAST IRON STOVE, 6", 1890's..............$40.00-80.00
CHILD'S CHAIR, bow back red chair, circa 1890 ....$50.00-120.00
CHILD'S LOVING CUP, two handles, 1900's, aluminum $30.00-60.00
CHILD'S SOUP BOWL, features bears, English maker $40.00-80.00
CHILD'S TABLE SET, aluminum, fancy design 1900's $20.00-45.00
CHILD'S TABLE, 1920's, red enameled with black stripe trim, 23" $20.00-45.00
CHINA CLOSET, toy, with glass doors, 32" tall...$65.00-140.00
CHINA TEA SET, child's, 1880's palm tree motif, twenty-three pieces $100.00-300.00
CHINA WASH SET WITH WASH BOWL AND PITCHER, 1889, decorated china $50.00-125.00
CLOTHES WRINGER, toy, has rubber rollers, 1903 ....$50.00-100.00
COLONIAL STYLE BRASS DOLL BED, 1912, 30" long $100.00-200.00
CRADLE, FOLDING WHITE ENAMELED, circa 1910 ....$40.00-95.00
CREAMER with ballerina on stage pictured, Japan, recent $3.00-8.00
CRYSTEEL ABC TABLE, 1920's $50.00-100.00
CRYSTEEL TABLE, 16" x 20" table, porcelain enameled, plain white $20.00-40.00
CUPBOARD, china with glass front, 1890's Victorian......................................$100.00-300.00

DECORATED TIN STOVE WITH HANGING KITCHEN UTENSILS, 1895.............................$100.00-300.00

DELUXE ELECTRIC RANGE FOR LITTLE GIRLS, 1920's, utensils, works, black..........$45.00-110.00

DIONNE QUINTUPLET SET OF FIGURAL SPOONS, five spoons.......................................$40.00-75.00

DOLL BED, brass, fancy, 1955 (or small child's bed).......................................$100.00-250.00

DOLL BED, SILVER QUEEN DOLL'S WIRE BED, 1890's.......................................$20.00-40.00

DOLL BED, SOLID BRASS, 1914........$100.00-200.00

DOLL BED, white enameled with brass trim, 1912.......................................$100.00-250.00

DOLL BEDROOM FURNITURE SET, eight pieces, 1890's, rare complete..................................$200.00-650.00

DOLL BEDSTEAD WITH CLOTH CANOPY, 1903.......................................$100.00-200.00

DOLL CRADLE, 1830, scalloped sides.$100.00-200.00

DOLL CRADLE, Victorian, 1894, wooden, adjustable sides.......................................$100.00-200.00

DOLL DRESSER WITH OVAL MIRROR, American Toy, 1917.......................................$100.00-150.00

DOLL HAMMOCK, 1890's, wood frame with cloth, 40" long.......................................$50.00-130.00

DOLL HOUSE, Built-Rite, Note 115, sedan, garage, shrubs, 1940's.......................................$75.00-95.00

DOLL HOUSE, cardboard, original box, George Borgfeldt.......................................$30.00-55.00

DOLL SWING, 1890's, wood, wire and cloth.......................................$30.00-85.00

DOLL TRUNK with inset box, 18" long, 1930's, papered inside lining.......................................$30.00-90.00

DOLL TRUNK, 16", 1919.......................$40.00-90.00

DOLLY CLOTHES LINE OUTFIT, 1912, rope, clothes-pins, etc.......................................$20.00-40.00

DOLL'S STROLLER, handle on back, single stick, 1920's wood and tin.......................................$40.00-85.00

DOLLY'S NURSING AND BATH SET, bisque doll, 1930's.......................................$15.00-25.00

DROP LEAF TABLE, child's, 1900's, oak, spindle legs.......................................$100.00-175.00

EASEL BLACKBOARD, Victorian, 1890's..$50.00-140.00

ELECTRIC MAGIC LANTERN, 1920's, with slides.......................................$50.00-120.00

ELECTRIC RANGE for little girls, 1930..$20.00-45.00

ELECTRIC TOY WAFFLE IRON, 1920's.$10.00-30.00

EMBOSSED RAISED PATTERN TIN TEA SET, seventeen pieces, 1912.......................$100.00-200.00

EMBROIDERY SET, little girl's, in original box, 1919.......................................$20.00-40.00

FEEDER DISH, Little Boy Blue, by Straffordshire.......................................$35.00-80.00

FIBER REED STROLLER, push or pull type, 1930.......................................$100.00-150.00

FOLDING BED, toy, 20" long, circa 1890, all wood.......................................$50.00-100.00

FOLDING CRADLE, metal with gilt finish, circa 1910.......................................$50.00-135.00

FOLDING WIRE MATTRESS BED, 1910, doll bed.......................................$40.00-75.00

GLASS DOLL NURSING BOTTLE with rubber nipple.......................................$50.00-100.00

HARDWOOD TABLE, child's, 1890's, 18" long.......................................$50.00-125.00

HAT SHOP, Miss America play set, No. 1800, Minerva Toy, three hats, misc.........................$20.00-30.00

ICE CHEST, toy, varnished wood, 1912.$100.00-150.00

IRON, Wolverine, Bakelite handle.............$5.00-12.00

IRONING BOARD, wood, 1910, folding...$30.00-60.00

IVORY COLORED VANITY SET, mirror, brush and comb for little girls, 1920's.................$10.00-35.00

KITCHEN AND WASH SET, boxed, kitchen utensils and washing items, 1894.................$50.00-150.00

KITCHEN CABINET, little girl's enameled, 1930, 26" tall.......................................$40.00-125.00

LEMONADE SET, imitaiton "cut glass" set with tray, pitcher and four glasses.................$50.00-125.00

LITTLE CHEF electric range...................$20.00-40.00

MARX BOX KITCHEN, tin, 3", "Honeymoon" Series, Furnish collection, $50.00-100.00.

NORTH WIND REFRIGERATOR BY MARX, 5" tall, all metal, Furnish collection, $40.00-80.00.

KEWPIE GERMAN THREE PIECE TEA SET, tin with bright color lithograph, Reynolds collection, $200.00-400.00.

GIRL IN BONNET BOXED TEA SET, tin lithograph, early, ten pieces, Furnish collection, $200.00-400.00.

THREE PIECE TIN TEA SET GROUPING, countryside garden and manor design teapot, 3" tall, 1890's, $100.00-225.00.

LITTLE HOSTESS, fifteen piece tea set, Japan blue with tan/pink roses $35.00-55.00

LITTLE LADY KITCHEN MINIATURE PLAY KITCHEN, metal and cardboard, 1930's $50.00-135.00

NICKEL PLATED TOY RANGE, fancy design, 1894 ....$50.00-125.00

NURSERY CLOCK, circa 1900, ornate design, wooden $100.00-300.00

PASTRY AND CANISTER SET, twenty-three pieces, 1940's, Ohio Art $20.00-30.00

PASTRY COOK, child's set of utensils, circa 1930..$20.00-45.00

PHONOGRAPH, TINY TOT, 1930 ....$40.00-80.00

PLUSH ROCKING HORSE, 24", 1914 .$300.00-400.00

PRACTICAL WASH SET with tub, bucket, stand, washboard, wringer, 1900 ....$100.00-250.00

PRINCESS DOLL PARLOR SET, 1912, two rockers, chair, table $100.00-250.00

REAL ELECTRIC TOY IRON 1930, metal ..$10.00-20.00

RED DINING SET FOR CHILDREN, 1920's, wood, enameled red, 17" tall.......................$30.00-60.00

RED ROCKING CHAIR, 1920's, child's ...$20.00-45.00

REED DOLL CARRIAGE made of reed material, 19" long, ornate $75.00-135.00

REFRIGERATOR, Marx, 1960, 7" x 14", lithograph box $10.00-25.00

REVERSIBLE DOLL BUGGY, 14" with 52" handle, 1914, chair buggy $100.00-225.00

REX TOY MOTOR AND FAN UNIT, child's size, 1900's, electric $25.00-80.00

ROBIN HOOD BOWL $5.00-10.00

ROCKER, square top and back, 1900's, wood red chair...$100.00-200.00

ROCKING CHAIR WITH WOVEN RUSH SEAT, 15" $50.00-100.00

ROCKING CHAIR, white enameled, 1923, bluebird stencil on back, 10" seat $25.00-65.00

ROLLTOP DESK, 1923, all wood construction, child's size $100.00-200.00

SAD IRON AND ORNATE STAND, child's, 1880's, cast iron $20.00-55.00

SARATOGA TRUNK, child's, 12" $100.00-200.00

SCALLOPED IRON BED, doll's, 16" tall, 1900's $50.00-120.00

SCHOENHUT TOY PIANO, 22 keys, 1930 .$40.00-80.00

SCHOENHUT TOY UPRIGHT PIANO, 1930, twenty-two keys...$50.00-110.00

SERVING SET, toy "Britannia," boxed place setting, 1894 ....$20.00-55.00

SEWING BASKET FOR LITTLE GIRLS, small size, 1920's, wooden $10.00-35.00

SEWING BASKET FOR LITTLE GIRLS, wicker, 1920's $10.00-35.00

SEWING MACHINE, by Wilcox and Gibbs $40.00-95.00

SEWING MACHINE, works, with child's carrying case, 1930's $50.00-75.00

SEWING SET, Princess Elizabeth, 1937 ..$30.00-60.00

SHELL CRAFTWARE BOX for trinkets, 1890's, good condition $40.00-85.00

SINGER SEWING MACHINE #20, 1926 ..$50.00-70.00

SINK, metal, Marx, 1950, 12" x 11" with doors and faucet with box $10.00-25.00

SNOW WHITE REFRIGERATOR, Disney, manufactured by Wolverine $5.00-15.00

SNOW WHITE SINK, Disney, manufactured by Wolverine, 1960's $5.00-15.00

SNOW WHITE STOVE, Disney, manufactured by Wolverine, 1960's $5.00-15.00

SODA FOUNTAIN BENT IRON CHAIR AND TABLE, child's size $75.00-150.00

SPELLING ROCKER CHAIR, words lithograph on chair back, 1890's $200.00-400.00

STAR STEEL SEWING MACHINE, 1914 $50.00-$125.00

STEEL BABY BUGGY, steel shell and frame, 1930's $35.00-70.00

STOVE, METAL, Marx, 1950, 10" x 12" tin lithograph, with box $10.00-25.00

STOVE, PASTTIME TOY HEATING STOVE, child's doll version, 1894 ....$100.00-200.00

STRAW DOLL'S HAT, 1890's, costume accessory, 3" $25.00-55.00

STROMBECKER DOLL FURNITURE SET, in original box $75.00-100.00

SUNNY MISS STROLLER, tin toy, Ohio Art $15.00-30.00

SUNNY SUZY GLASS BAKING SET, by Wolverine, original box $25.00-45.00

SUNNY SUZY WASHING MACHINE WITH WRINGER, metal and tin, 1934, Wyandotte $35.00-85.00

SWISS MUSIC BOX, 1900's, child's, wooden case $100.00-200.00

TEA CART, child's, pictures Dutch children, wood and tin, by Wolverine $40.00-85.00

TEA SET, circus scenes and animals with clowns, 1900's $100.00-300.00

TEA SET, German, 1920's, children and dogs, twelve pieces $75.00-145.00

TEA SET, German, with blue flowers, twenty-one pieces $100.00-200.00

TEA SET, turquoise blue colored enamel set, fifteen pieces, boxed, 1920's $40.00-80.00

TEAKETTLE, brass, child's $20.00-45.00

TEAPOT, with illustration of "This is the House that Jack," 6" $30.00-70.00

TEAPOT, "The House that Jack Built," 6" ..$20.00 55.00

TEAPOT, Doc and Snow White, Disney, 1930's, W.D. Enterprises, 1937 ....$20.00-50.00

TIN TEA SET, floral, made in Germany, decorated, boxed $40.00-95.00

TIN TEA SET, Ohio Art, boxed, with girls on top, 1930's $50.00-95.00

TOOTSIETOY DOLL HOUSE, ca. 1925, in carton $150.00-300.00

TOOTSIETOY DOLLHOUSE, KITCHEN SINK, two legged $15.00-30.00

TOOTSIETOY DOLLHOUSE ACCESSORY CANDLEBRA, five-light, 1925 ....$10.00-20.00

TOOTSIETOY DOLLHOUSE DINING ROOM SET, brown, ...$30.00-55.00

TOOTSIETOY DOLLHOUSE CHAIR, #113, 1925 ....$10.00-20.00

TOOTSIETOY DOLLHOUSE CONSOLE RADIO, brown $20.00-35.00

TOOTSIETOY DOLLHOUSE FURNITURE DESK, #4402,

TIN CHILD'S TEA SET TRAY BY AMSCO, 1900's, pictures settler boy and Indian girl, $60.00-125.00.

1925 ....$10.00-25.00

TOOTSIETOY DOLLHOUSE FURNITURE, 1925 floor lamp $5.00-15.00

TOOTSIETOY DOLLHOUSE grand piano with bench $20.00-45.00

TOOTSIETOY DOLLHOUSE green refrigerator with coil top $20.00-40.00

TOOTSIETOY DOLLHOUSE KITCHEN RANGE, #21, 1925 ....$10.00-20.00

TOOTSIETOY DOLLHOUSE LIBRARY TABLE, 1925 ....$10.00-20.00

TOOTSIETOY DOLLHOUSE ROCKING CHAIR, 1925, #114 ....$10.00-25.00

TOOTSIETOY DOLLHOUSE SLATTED CHAIRS, pair $6.00-12.00

TOOTSIETOY DOLLHOUSE VICTROLA, #105, 1925 ....$20.00-40.00

TOOTSIETOY DOLLHOUSE, white toilet with seat and brown lid $10.00-20.00

TOOTSIETOY DOLLHOUSE, five piece gold living room set $50.00-85.00

TOOTSIETOY FURNISHED MANSION, circa 1930 ....$200.00-400.00

TOOTSIETOY MANSION, book-board (cardboard) construction, 1930 ....$100.00-250.00

TOOTSIETOY TEA CART, miniature, 1925, doll house accessories $15.00-30.00

TOOTSIETOY UPRIGHT TELEPHONE, miniature, 1925 ....$20.00-40.00

TOY GROCERY STORE SHELF, CASS GROCERY SET, 1914 with toy food items $100.00-200.00

TOY LUNCHEON LINEN SET, 1920's, rabbit motif, cloth and four napkins $10.00-25.00

TOY PANTRY WITH TOY FOOD AND PAPER LITHOGRAPH ITEMS, 1914 ....$75.00-150.00

TOY REFRIGERATOR, metal, Lumar $15.00-35.00

TRUNK, canvas covered metal hinges and binding, 1903, child's size $100.00-200.00

TRUNK, child's size, wood with interior paper lining, 12" $50.00-125.00

VALORA CHILD'S PHONOGRAPH, 1930, crank phonograph $50.00-90.00

TIN CHILD'S TEA SET TRAY, 1900's, color lithograph, gold trim, $40.00-85.00.

TIN TEA TRAY, 1920's, children playing in snow, $25.00-60.00.

VICTORIAN BABY BUGGY, 40" $300.00-600.00
VICTORIAN DOLL BED, ornate, made of walnut, 1870's $200.00-475.00
VICTORIAN PIANO STOOL, child's, walnut, turned/ carved...$100.00-200.00
WAFFLE IRON FOR LITTLE GIRLS, circa 1920 ....$10.00-25.00
WHISTLING TEA KETTLE, child's version, 1930's, all

"VENUS," CAST IRON STOVE, 9" with additional accessories, Furnish collection, $125.00-200.00.

    aluminum, red handle........................$10.00-35.00
WHITE STONE CHINA TEAPOT, 1889 ...$10.00-25.00
WHITE STONE CHINA TOY CREAMER, circa 1890...$10.00-20.00
WHITE STONE CHINA TOY CUP AND SAUCER, 1889...$15.00-30.00
WHITE STONE CHINA TOY PLATE, 1889 .$5.00-15.00
WHITE STONE CHINA TOY SLOP BOWL, circa 1890...$15.00-25.00
WHITE STONE CHINA TOY SUGAR BOWL, circa 1890...$15.00-30.00
WICKER DOLL CRADLE, circa 1900, white enameled $100.00-200.00
WICKER STROLLER INCLUDING PARASOL, Victorian..$300.00-600.00
WILLOW CLOTHES BASKET, toy, 1910 .$30.00-60.00
WOOD BEAD STRINGING CRAFT SET, boxed, 1919...$20.00-50.00
WRISTWATCH FOR LITTLE GIRLS, tin and leather, 1920's, toy $10.00-30.00

PULL TOYS

The category of pull toys is based upon the general function of the toy and not its age. Pull toys have been around since long before the Victorian era, and they are still popular today. Usually, a string is attached to the front of a wooden, metal or plastic toy and then the child's own momentum as he walks along pulls the toy. Most versions of pull toys from all eras rely on the principle that the pulling action sets some other pleasing action of the toy into motion. The best pull toys usually do something other than just roll along behind the child. Characters play drums or musical instruments, flap their wings, rock back and forth, quack, click, pop, or perform some interesting action. The action mechanism is usually tied in directly to a wheel or axle of the toy so that when the child stops pulling the toy along, the action also stops.

The most famous American manufacturer of pull toys is without a doubt the Fisher Price Company (still quite healthy today). This company has been producing high quality pull toys (once *the* main staple of their line) for over fifty years. The toys are simple: a wood cutout figure on wheels is covered on both sides with a paper lithograph label. The toys from fifty years ago are still sturdy

and usually very functional, although the paper labels which give the toys their design and appeal are often found in various states of disrepair.

Other significant manufacturers of pull toys were Gong Bell (Victorian era cast iron bell toys. The company later branched into more general line toys) and N. N. Hill Brass which manufactured bell ringer and pull toys of the 1930's and 1940's. Because pull toys were intended to navigate kitchen floor and miles of sidewalks, their design and construction was usually sturdy and durable. Consequently, many fine examples of these toys survive today, and most work as well now as they did that first morning in the 1930's when they were discovered under the Christmas tree.

The color, ingenuity of design, and variety of style make these toys very popular among today's collectors, with at least some examples available in nearly every collector's price range.

As each collector can probably remember, there was most likely a favorite pull toy somewhere in the bottom of his own toy box just waiting for its next trip down the block. If mom didn't throw it out, it's probably still there waiting!

DONALD DUCK, long-billed pulling chick barrel, Fisher Price, 1930's, $75.00-200.00.

DOC AND DOPEY PULL TOY, by Fisher Price, 1938, 12" long, Walt Disney Enterprises, $100.00-200.00.

PULL TOYS

ALLIE GATOR PULL TOY, manufactured by Fisher Price, 1960 ....$10.00-20.00

AMERICAN FLAGSHIP AIRPLANE PULL TOY, 1940, by Fisher Price $50.00-150.00

ARABIAN HORSE ON CASTERS, circa 1890, gold color $200.00-400.00

BARKY PUPPY DOG, Fisher Price pull toy, 1931 ....$50.00-80.00

BEAR IN STEAMROLLER, red, pull toy, 1934 Fisher Price $50.00-100.00

BELL RINGER GIRL WITH DOG ON SLED, horse head sled, 1892 "Daisy" $1,500.00-3,000.00

BELL RINGER HORSE ON PEDESTAL TOY, Gong Bell, cast iron, 1892 ....$700.00-1,500.00

BELL RINGER HORSE WITH MONKEY ON SULKEY, 1892, cast iron $1,000.00-2,000.00

BELL RINGER PULL TOY, 1892, boy and girl on see-saw $700.00-1,450.00

BIG WOODEN GOOSE PULL TOY, 1921, 10" tall $100.00-200.00

BLACK BEAUTY HORSE PULL TOY, on platform with wheels, 1922, 16" $300.00-650.00

BLACKIE THE DRUMMER BEAR PULL TOY, Fisher Price, 1939 ....$55.00-110.00

BLUE HAY WAGON, cast iron, 16" long, 1910 ....$500.00-1,000.00

BOSTON TERRIER, wood and papier mache, on four wheels, 11" $100.00-250.00

BOUNCY RACE CAR, large plastic tires, 1960, Fisher Price $5.00-15.00

BOY PUSHING RED WAGON WITH BELL, 1940, Fisher Price, rare $200.00-400.00

BOY WITH DOG, tin, 7", four wheels, circa 1900 ....$200.00-400.00

BUCKY BURRO PULL TOY, by Fisher Price, 1955 ....$30.00-65.00

BUDDY BULLFROG, manufactured by Fisher Price, 1960's $5.00-15.00

BULL DOG, GROWLER, with glass eyes, circa 1900 ....$200.00-500.00

BUNNIES PULLING EGG CART, Fisher Price, 1950's $20.00-45.00

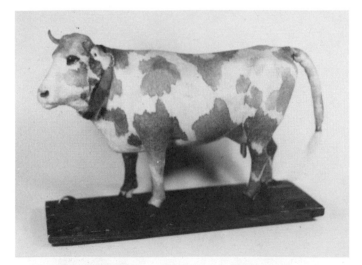

COMPOSITION COW ON WHEELS, 12" long, Furnish collection, $200.00-400.00.

BUNNIES PULLING EGG CART, pull toy, Fisher Price, 1937 ....$50.00-125.00

BUNNY ON SCOOTER, Fisher Price pull toy, 1931, floppy ears $50.00-100.00

BUNNY PULLING BERRY CONTAINER, 1930's, Fisher Price $30.00-70.00

BUNNY RACER PULL TOY, bunny in car, 1942 ....$35.00-65.00

BUZZY BEE, 1950's, manufactured by Fisher Price, pull toy $10.00-35.00

CACKLING HEN PULL TOY, made by Fisher Price, 1958 ....$10.00-30.00

CAMEL ON WHEELS PLATFORM TOY, 1914, tin, Germany $200.00-450.00

CAST IRON FIRE ENGINE #125, circa 1890, 19" $1,000.00-2,000.00

CAST IRON FIRE ENGINE PUMPER, 16" long, circa 1890 ....$800.00-1,700.00

CAST IRON HORSE CART #155, 1892, 10" $800.00-1,500.00

CAST IRON PONY CART, 4" long $100.00-250.00

CAST IRON SURREY WITH LADY DRIVER, 1914, 13" long $600.00-1,300.00

CAST IRON TALLY HO COACH, circa 1890, carpenter $2,000.00-3,200.00

CHATTER MONKEY PULL TOY, by Fisher Price, 1957 ....$10.00-35.00

CHIME PULL BELL TOY, 1886, cast iron and metal, 5½" long $300.00-600.00

CHOO-CHOO LOCAL DOG ON TRAIN ENGINE PULL TOY, 1936, Fisher Price, red $50.00-125.00

CHUBBY CHIEF THE ELEPHANT PULL TOY, Fisher Price, 1932, fireman design $100.00-200.00

CINDERELLA'S CHARIOT, Gong Bell Toy, cast iron bell ringer, 1893 ....$2,000.00-4,000.00

CLOTH HORSE ON ROLLING PLATFORM PULLING COAL WAGON, 16", 1912 ....$350.00-700.00

CLOTH HORSE ON ROLLING PLATFORM PULLING MOVING TRUCK, 1912, 16" $350.00-700.00

CLOTH HORSE ON ROLLING PLATFORM WITH MILK WAGON, 1912, 16" $300.00-700.00

CLOWN BELL TOY WITH TWO BELLS, cast iron bell pull toy, 1914, 7" $500.00-1,000.00

CRICKET PULL TOY, by Fisher Price, 1955 ....$10.00-30.00

DAIRY COW ON WHEELS, 6", 1895, platform type $100.00-250.00

DANDY ROPE JUMPER PULL TOY, wooden, 1929, skips rope, crude figure $20.00-40.00

DAPPLE GREY HORSE ON PLATFORM PULL TOY, 1921, 11" $200.00-400.00

DING DONG DUCKY PULL TOY, by Fisher Price, 1949 ....$20.00-55.00

DOBBIN THE PONY PULL TOY, Fisher Price, 1938 ....$50.00-120.00

DOC AND DOPEY PULL TOY, Fisher Price, 1938, Walt Disney Enterprises, 12" $100.00-200.00

DOC AND DOPEY PULLING SNOW WHITE AND SMALL CART, 1938, N. N. Hill Brass $100.00-250.00

DOG AND BALL PULL TOY, action when pulled, 1890's $100.00-200.00

DOG DRESSED IN PARADE OUTFIT, Fisher Price, 1934, pull toy $50.00-95.00

DOG FLOOR CHIME PULL TOY, circa 1912 ....$300.00-600.00

DOG LOCOMOTIVE, red base, blue engine, 1933, Fisher Price $50.00-100.00

DOG ON CASTERS, 1889, cotton flannel, wooden platform $100.00-300.00

DOG ON ICE CREAM WAGON PULL TOY, by Fisher Price, 1940 ....$50.00-100.00

DOG ON WHEELS, papier mache, circa 1910 ....$200.00-400.00

DOG WITH GLASS EYES, early 1900's, 12" $150.00-350.00

DOG, cotton flannel, on wheels, 1889 ...$200.00-400.00

DONALD AND DONNA DUCK PULL TOY, Donald wears Mexican hat, Fisher Price, 1937 ....$500.00-850.00

DONALD DUCK BEING PULLED BY PLUTO, red wagon, 1935, rare $300.00-650.00

DONALD DUCK CHOO-CHOO PULL TOY by Fisher Price, 1940, Walt Disney....................$45.00-75.00

DONALD DUCK DRUMMER, Disney, pull toy by Fisher Price, 1949 ....$40.00-85.00

DONALD DUCK ENGINEER PULL TOY, Fisher Price, 1940's $30.00-65.00

DONALD DUCK ON BLUE WAGON WEARING CHECKERED COAT/STRAW HAT, by Fisher Price, 1940 ....$100.00-200.00

DONALD DUCK PULL TOY WITH MECHANICAL, PLASTIC FEET, 1955, Fisher Price $30.00-65.00

DONALD DUCK PULL TOY, 1940's, Donald twirls red baton, by Fisher Price, red $35.00-75.00

DONALD DUCK PULL TOY, Donald pulls red cart, 1940's, Fisher Price $30.00-70.00

DONALD DUCK PULL TOY, Donald with baton pulls wagon, 1940's, Fisher Price $65.00-110.00

DONALD DUCK PULL TOY, by Fisher Price, 1930's, Donald with baton...........................$50.00-110.00

DONALD DUCK PULL TOY, Fisher Price, 1930's, long-billed, wings flap $125.00-200.00

DONALD DUCK PULL TOY, LONG-BILLED, 1930's, Fisher Price, wings hang.................$75.00-195.00

DONALD DUCK PULL TOY, XYLOPHONE PLAYER, by Fisher Price, 1938, 13" tall...........$100.00-200.00

DONALD DUCK RUNNING PULL TOY, N. N. Hill Brass, 1930's $75.00-150.00

DONALD DUCK, ANGRY LONG-BILLED PULLING CART, rare $400.00-850.00

DONALD DUCK, LONG-BILLED SMALL PULL TOY, four wheels, 1930's, Fisher Price $50.00-100.00

DONKEY ON PLATFORM WITH WHEELS, 1894, natural skin, 7" tall............................$150.00-300.00

DONKEY PULL TOY (kicks), manufactured by Fisher Price, 1937 ....$50.00-100.00

DONKEY, felt covered on platform with wheels, 1914, 6" $200.00-400.00

DOPEY THE DRUMMER PULL TOY, Fisher Price, 1939, Walt Disney $100.00-250.00

DR. DUCK, Fisher Price pull toy, 1931 ..$50.00-125.00

DRAY WITH DRIVER, cast iron toy, 10" long, 1889 ....$700.00-1,400.00

DRAY, CAST IRON, with horse and standing driver, 11½" long, 1892..........................$600.00-1,200.00

DRUMMER BEAR, Fisher Price pull toy, 1930's $30.00-75.00

CAST IRON ELEPHANT BELL RINGER PULL TOY, 1900's, 6" long, 5" tall, Furnish collection, $400.00-850.00.

DRUMMER BEAR, Fisher Price toys, wooden pull toy, 1931, red base, black hat $35.00-70.00

DUCK WITH FLAPPER FEET PULLING PURPLE CART, Fisher Price, 1937 ....$60.00-120.00

DUCK WITH FLAPPER FEET PULLING TWO DUCKLINGS IN CART, manufactured by Fisher Price, 1937 ....$100.00-160.00

DUMP CART, tin lithograph, 1886, with one horse, 12" long $200.00-450.00

EASTER BUNNY PULL TOY, by Fisher Price, 1936 ....$40.00-80.00

EASTER BUNNY PULLING CART, pull toy, Fisher Price, 1936 ....$50.00-100.00

EGG TRUCK DRIVEN BY FARMER DUCK, Fisher Price, 1947 pull toy $35.00-60.00

ELEPHANT ON PLATFORM WHEELS, 8" tall, 1890's $250.00-450.00

ELEPHANT ON PLATFORM, tin with wheels, 9", 1920's $150.00-300.00

ELEPHANT RIDING TRICYCLE WITH ROLLER WHEEL, by Fisher Price, 1950....................$20.00-45.00

ELEPHANT SEATED ON PLATFORM WITH WHEELS, 6", 1895 ....$200.00-400.00

ELEPHANT, composition with wood base, 1890's, 6" x 5" $75.00-150.00

ELEPHANT, straw stuffed, on iron wheels, 8" $100.00-200.00

ELMER THE ELEPHANT PULL TOY, N. N. Hill Brass, 1938, unusual $100.00-250.00

ELSIE'S DAIRY TRUCK, Elsie the Cow, Fisher Price, 1948 ....$65.00-135.00

FARM TRUCK WITH THE CAMPBELL'S SOUP KIDS, Fisher Price, 1954 ....$50.00-130.00

FELIX THE CAT PULL TOY, probably by Nifty, 1930's, tin lithograph $150.00-400.00

FERDINAND THE BULL AND THE MATADOR PULL TOY, N. N. Hill Brass, 1940 ....$100.00-250.00

FERDINAND THE BULL, Walt Disney, Fisher Price pull toy, 1939 ....$100.00-250.00

FIDO ZILO PULL TOY, manufactured by Fisher Price, 1955 ....$25.00-45.00

PULL TOYS

ELEPHANT ON WHEELS, STUFFED, 8" long, cast iron wheels, Furnish collection, $150.00-300.00.

PAINTED BLACK TIN HORSE ON TIN PLATFORM WITH CAST IRON WHEELS, 7", Furnish collection, $125.00-250.00.

FIRE ENGINE PUMPER WITH DRIVER AND TWO HORSES, cast iron, 1889 ....$600.00-1,300.00

FISHER PRICE BAND WAGON pulled by two horses, 1940 ....$50.00-125.00

FISHER PRICE CIRCUS WAGON PULL TOY, 1940, extremely colorful design $50.00-135.00

FISHER PRICE GENERAL HAULING HORSE AND WAGON PULL TOY, 1940 ....$40.00-80.00

FISHER PRICE GOLD STAR STAGECOACH PULL TOY, 1954, with two horses $30.00-65.00

FLOPPY EARED BUNNY ON PURPLE CART, Fisher Price, 1938 ....$35.00-70.00

FRAN-ZELL THE CUTE BOW-WOW (DOG) 1924, wooden, pull toy barks $100.00-200.00

FRED FLINTSTONE PULL TOY, Fisher Price, 1960's $20.00-65.00

FROG WITH RED TOP HAT PULL TOY, Fisher Price, 1956..$10.00-30.00

FUZZY THE DOG, manufactured by Fisher Price pull toy, 1940 ....$30.00-60.00

GABBY GOOSE WITH LONG-BILL PULL TOY, Fisher Price, 1935 ....$50.00-100.00

GALLOPING HORSE AND WAGON PULL TOY by Fisher Price, 1948 ....$35.00-65.00

GIBBS DERBY RIDER TOY, 1914, figures 8" tall, wood with paper litho $200.00-500.00

GIBBS ENGLISH PONY CART, 1914, 13", wood with paper litho $200.00-500.00

GIBBS GREY BEAUTY PACERS, double horses pull wagon, walking action, 1912.........$300.00-700.00

GIBBS HORSE WITH DUMPCART, 19", 1912 deluxe edtion $450.00-1,000.00

GIBBS JUMBO THE PERFORMING ELEPHANT PULL TOY with trick action, 1912 ....$150.00-350.00

GIBBS PACING BOB SINGLE HORSE AND CART, 1912 ....$175.00-350.00

GIBBS PERFORMING BOB THE TRICK PONY PULL TOY, 1912 ....$200.00-400.00

GIBBS PONY CIRCUS WAGON, 14" two horses, bright paper lithograph $1,000.00-2,000.00

GIBBS PONY PACER PULLING CART, 7" long, 1912 ....$200.00-400.00

GIBBS SINGLE HORSE GYPSY WAGON, 1912, two horses with covered wagon $500.00-1,000.00

GIBBS U.S. MAIL WAGON WITH HORSE, 1914, 12" long $150.00-375.00

GOAT, tin, early, 1910's, 9½" $100.00-300.00

GOLDEN GULCH EXPRESS, locomotive and tender, cowboys and Indians, manufactured by Fisher Price, 1960's $10.00-20.00

GRANNY DOODLE AND TWO DUCKLINGS PULL TOY, Fisher Price, 1933 ....$60.00-125.00

GRANNY DOODLE, Fisher Price pull toy, 1930's $40.00-100.00

GROCERY WAGON, covered, tin, 1894, excellent lithograph $200.00-400.00

HAPPY HIPPO FISHER PRICE PULL TOY, 1960's $10.00-25.00

HAY WAGON WITH SOLID WOOD HORSE, 1922, 18" pull toy $200.00-400.00

HORACE HORSECOLLAR PULL TOY, N. N. Hill Brass, 1935 ....$100.00-200.00

HORACE HORSECOLLAR PULLING MICKEY MOUSE, 1930's, chime pull toy, manufactured by N. N. Hill Brass $200.00-450.00

HORSE AND BELL CHIMES, 1921, pull toy, metal and cast iron $100.00-250.00

HORSE AND BUGGY, tin, 1900, 6" $100.00-300.00

HORSE AND CART, 1890's, plain, ...$200.00-450.00

HORSE AND RED WAGON PULL TOY, by Fisher Price, 1933 ....$100.00-200.00

HORSE ON PLATFORM WITH WHEELS, natural skin, 1894 with bridle $200.00-450.00

HORSE ON WHEELED PLATFORM papier mache construction, 1914, 7" tall...................$100.00-200.00

HORSE ON WHEELED PLATFORM, papier mache, 1914, 10" tall $200.00-400.00

HORSE ON WHEELS, tin 1886, Schwarz catalogue, 6" long $200.00-500.00

HORSE PULLING CHIME WHEELS, tin and cast iron, 1889 ....$300.00-800.00

HORSE WITH JOCKEY RIDING, tin, American, 1890, 14", rare.......................................$750.00-1,800.00

HORSE, GALLOPING, tin, circa 1920, painted, 7" long $100.00-200.00

HORSIE CHIME, gray iron horse pulls four-wheeled frame, 1924 ....$100.00-200.00

HOT DOG WAGON WITH CHEF DOG, Fisher Price pull toy, 1930's $40.00-85.00

JINGLE GIRAFFE PULL TOY, Fisher Price, 1956...$10.00-30.00

JOCKEY ON HORSE PLATFORM PULL TOY, Gong Bell Toy, 1914, 7" $700.00-1,200.00

JOCKEYS ON TALL HORSES WITH BELLS (2) connected, Fisher Price, 1937 ....$40.00-85.00

JOHNNY JUMBO THE ELEPHANT PULL TOY, Fisher Price, 1933 ....$45.00-120.00

JUMBO ELEPHANT XYLOPHONE PLAYER, Fisher Price, 1937 ....$100.00-145.00

KILTIE THE SCOTTY DOG PULL TOY, Fisher Price, 1935...$50.00-110.00

KITTEN WITH BALL AND BELL, Fisher Price pull toy, 1950's $10.00-35.00

KRAZY KAT PULL TOY, chases mice, on platform, tin lithograph, 1920's $300.00-750.00

LADY FROM LADY AND THE TRAMP PULL TOY, plastic, 1950's.....................................$25.00-65.00

LAMB PULL TOY, mounted on platform, 9" tall, 1890's $200.00-400.00

LAMB, PLUSH TOY ON WHEELS, 1895 $200.00-400.00

LION AND DRUM PULL TOY, Fisher Price, 1952, "Leo" $25.00-50.00

LITTLE COWBOY ON HORSE, 1938 Fisher Price toy, wooden $50.00-120.00

LITTLE DUCK ON PINK WAGON, Fisher Price, 1938...$30.00-70.00

LOOKY CHUG-CHUG LOCOMOTIVE PULL TOY, 1949, Fisher Price toys...................................$30.00-70.00

LOOKY FIRE TRUCK, manufactured by Fisher Price, 1950's $15.00-30.00

LUCKY MONEY, Fisher Price pull toy, 1932, orange base $40.00-80.00

MARY AND HER LITTLE LAMB, 1880's wood platform toy with wheels and figures $1,000.00-2,000.00

MARY'S LITTLE LAMB, Stevens and Brown, tin platform toy on wheels, 1870 ....$500.00-1,200.00

MERRY GO ROUND WITH CLOWN, tin lithograph, platfrom pull toy, 1929 ....$250.00-500.00

MERRY MUTT PULL TOY, by Fisher Price, 1939...$20.00-40.00

MICKEY MOUSE CAROUSEL CIRCUS WAGON, pull toy by Toy Kraft, 1930's $50.00-125.00

MICKEY MOUSE DOUBLE MICKEY'S PULL TOY, N. N. Hill Brass, 1930's $200.00-400.00

MICKEY MOUSE DRUMMER WITH CYMBALS, pie-eyed Mickey , 1937, Fisher Price ..$250.00-500.00

MICKEY MOUSE DRUMMER, 1940, modern version Mickey..$30.00-75.00

MICKEY MOUSE ICE SKATERS PULL TOY, N. N. Hill Brass, 1930's $175.00-375.00

MICKEY MOUSE PARADE DRUMMER, with brass drum and cymbals, 1938, Fisher Price ...$100.00-250.00

MICKEY MOUSE PUDDLE JUMPER CAR, Fisher Price, 1953...$20.00-40.00

MICKEY MOUSE PULL TOY SEATED ON DRUM, 1940, polka dot bow tie, Fisher Price.$50.00-110.00

MICKEY MOUSE PULL TOY, N. N. Hill Brass, double Mickeys pulled by Pluto, 1930's $100.00-200.00

MICKEY MOUSE PULL TOY, upright figure, N. N. Hill Brass, 1930's $75.00-125.00

MICKEY MOUSE PULLED BY HORACE HORSECOLLAR, celluloid pull toy, manufactured 1930's, rare $3,000.00-6,000.00

MICKEY MOUSE SAFETY PATROL, manufactured 1956...$25.00-50.00

MICKEY MOUSE SMALL WOODEN PULL WAGON, by Toy kraft, 1935...............................$75.00-125.00

MICKEY MOUSE TUMBLING CIRCUS PULL TOY, by Nifty, 1930's, 11" $500.00-950.00

MICKEY MOUSE WOODEN CAR WITH wOOD FIGURE PULL TOY, Borgfeldt, 1935, rare ..$200.00-450.00

MINI-COPTER, by Fisher Price, 1970's $3.00-8.00

MOLLY MOO-MOO COW PULL TOY, Fisher Price, 1956...$20.00-50.00

MONKEY CHIME CHARIOT TOY, cast iron and metal, chimes, 1886, 6" long $500.00-1,000.00

MONKEY ON TRICYCLE, by Fisher Price Toys, 1931...$40.00-80.00

MONEYMOBILE BELL TOY, 1903, cast iron toy $500.00-950.00

MOO-OO COW black spotted, by Fisher Price, 1958...$10.00-30.00

MUSICAL DUCK PULL TOY, by Fisher Price, 1952...$20.00-40.00

MUSICAL ELEPHANT WITH CLOTH EARS, Fisher Price pull toy, 1948 ....$30.00-75.00

MUSICAL MUTT, DOG PULL TOY, pulling red wheels/ bells, Fisher Price, 1935 ....$50.00-110.00

NIFTY STATION WAGON, by Fisher Price, 1960 with four little people $10.00-25.00

NODDING HEAD CALF ON WHEELED PLATFORM 1914, 6"...$150.00-300.00

NODDING HEAD DONKEY ON WHEELED PLATFORM, 6", 1914 ....$200.00-400.00

NOSEY THE PUP, Fisher Price pull toy, circa 1950...$10.00-30.00

PETER BUNNY ENGINE, Fisher Price pull toy, 1940...$30.00-70.00

PINKY PIG, Fisher Price pull toy, 1956..$10.00-30.00

PINOCCHIO AND CLEO THE GOLDFISH PULL TOY, N. N. Hill Brass, 1940, Disney $75.00-150.00

PINOCCHIO AND FIGARO THE CAT PULL TOY, N. N. Hill Brass, 1940 ....$75.00-150.00

PLUSH PUG DOG ON CASTERS, 1889, pull toy $200.00-350.00

PONY CHIME PULL TOY, by Fisher Price, circa 1940...$30.00-70.00

PONY CIRCUS WAGON, by Gibbs, 1912, bright lithograph, two horses $1,000.00-2,000.00

PONY, FELT COVERED ON PLATFORM WITH WHEELS, 1914, 6" $200.00-400.00

POPEYE RIDING CARTOON HORSE PULL TOY, by Fisher Price, 1937 ....$200.00-450.00

POPEYE THE SAILOR BEHIND SHIP'S WHEEL, PULL TOY, 1935, Fisher Price.................$150.00-300.00

PULL TOYS

POPEYE WITH MALLET AND BELL TOY, 1935, Fisher Price $100.00-225.00

POPEYE WITH SPINACH CAN DRUMMER PULL TOY, Fisher Price, 1939 ....$100.00-275.00

POPEYE, BOOM BOOM DRUMMER PULL TOY, by Fisher Price, 1937 ....$100.00-300.00

PRANCING HORSE, tin, 6", 1910 ....$200.00-300.00

PUFFY TRAIN ENGINE PULL TOY, by Fisher Price, 1950...$10.00-30.00

PUSHCART PETE THE BELLHOP PULL TOY, Fisher Price, 1936 ....$50.00-85.00

RACING PONIES PULL OR PUSH TOY, Fisher Price, 1935...$50.00-100.00

RACING PONY WITH MONKEY RIDER PULL TOY, Fisher Price, 1933 ....$50.00-125.00

RAGGEDY ANN AND ANDY DRUMMERS PULL TOY, Fisher Price, 1940 ....$100.00-300.00

REVOLVING BELL CHIME PULL TOY, manufactured 1889 ....$250.00-500.00

ROAMING TURTLE STRING PULL TOY, 1889, metal colorful popular design $100.00-220.00

ROCKA-BYE BUNNY PUSHING CART PULL TOY, Fisher Price, 1940 ....$50.00-120.00

ROOSTER PULLING CHICK CART, 1938, Fisher Price $40.00-80.00

ROOSTER, tin, 1920's, 3" with wheels ...$35.00-70.00

RUNNING MICKEY MOUSE, PULL TOY, small, 1930's, Fisher Price.....................................$50.00-135.00

SCOTTY DOG PULL TOY, Fisher Price, 1933...$40.00-85.00

SEATED DOGS ON WHEELED PLATFORM, 1914, 7" $200.00-400.00

SHAGGY ZILO BEAR DRUMMER PULL TOY, Fisher Price, 1960 ....$10.00-20.00

SHEEP FLOOR CHIME TOY, natural wool covered, 1912 ....$400.00-800.00

SHEEP, WITH WOOLY COAT, pull toy on wheels, 1900 ....$150.00-400.00

SKIPPER SAM LITTLE BLACK BOY IN BOAT PULL TOY, Fisher Price, 1934.................$100.00-200.00

SMALL ACTION BUNNY ON PINK CART PULL TOY, Fisher Price, 1937 ....$60.00-120.00

SNAP QUACK DUCK PULL TOY, 1947, Fisher Price $30.00-70.00

SNOOPY DOG (not Peanuts character) Fisher Price, 1938, spotted dog.............................$45.00-85.00

SNORKEY FIRE ENGINE, Fisher Price, 1960, wood and plastic $10.00-20.00

SNOW WHITE AND PRINCE ON HORSE PULL TOY, 1938, N. N. Hill Brass, rare $200.00-500.00

SNOW WHITE BEING PULLED BY ALL SEVEN DWARFS, N. N. Hill Brass, 1938 ..$150.00-300.00

SNOW WHITE PULLED BY DOC AND DOPEY PULL TOY, N. N. Hill Brass, 1938 ....$75.00-195.00

SOLDIER DONALD DUCK PULLED BY PLUTO, Fisher Price, 1940 ....$100.00-250.00

SPACE BLAZER SPACECRAFT PULL TOY, Fisher Price, 1950's, rare $50.00-125.00

SPOTTED DOG IN FAST CAR PULL TOY, Fisher Price, 1940 ....$30.00-65.00

SPOTTED HORSE ON WHEELS PULL TOY, Fisher Price, 1934 ....$50.00-125.00

STANDING BUNNY PUSHING CART PULL TOY, Fisher Price 1936 ....$50.00-110.00

STREAMLINED RACER WOODEN PULL TOY 1929...$25.00-50.00

SULKY WITH JOCKEY CAST IRON PULL TOY, 1889...$750.00-1,500.00

SUNNY FISH PULL TOY, manufactured by Fisher Price, 1955...$10.00-40.00

TABBY DING DONG CAT LOCOMOTIVE WITH BELL PULL TOY, by Fisher Price, 1939 .....$40.00-85.00

TALKY PARROT, by Fisher Price, 1963 .....$3.00-8.00

TANGLEFOOT (HORSE) PULLING MICKEY MOUSE, pull toy, N. N. Hill Brass, 1930's..$200.00-500.00

TEDDY BEAR IN STATION WAGON, 1940 pull toy, Fisher Price $30.00-60.00

TEDDY BEAR PARADE PULL TOY, two bears, Fisher Price, 1938.................................$100.00-200.00

TEDDY THE DRUMMER BEAR, standing, parade costume pull toy, Fisher Price $100.00-200.00

TEDDY TOOTER BEAR RIDING BOX PULL TOY, Fisher Price, 1940 ....$75.00-150.00

TEDDY TRUCKER PULL TOY, 1949, Fisher Price $20.00-40.00

TEDDY ZILO PULL TOY, manufactured by Fisher Price, 1940's $30.00-60.0

THUMPER THE RABBIT FROM BAMBI PULL TOY, 1930's or 1940's, Fisher Price $70.00-125.00

TINY DING DONG ELEPHANT PULL TOY, Fisher Price, 1940 ....$60.00-120.00

TOY WAGON two ponies pulling cart, Fisher Price, 1940 ....$50.00-100-00

TUMBLE BALLS, WOODEN PULL TOY, manufactured 1921 ....$30.00-60.00

WALT DISNEY'S DUMBO CIRCUS PULL TOY, 1940, Dumbo drives car, unusual $100.00-250.00

WHIRLING FIGURES PULL TOY, wood knobs, 1921...$40.00-80.00

WHIRLY TINKER PULL TOY, 1922, wooden knobs $30.00-70.00

WHISTLING ENGINE PULL TOY, locomotive theme, Fisher Price, 1957 ....$10.00-30.00

WHITE BUNNY WITH BELL ON BLUE WAGON PULL TOY, Fisher Price, late 1930's $40.00-85.00

WIGGLE DOGGIE PULL TOY, 1922 ....$30.00-50.00

WINKY BLINKY FIRE TRUCK, manufactured by Fisher Price $30.00-60.00

WOOD ELEPHANT, hand painted, 1924, 8" on platform with wheels $200.00-400.00

WOODEN MAMA DUCK PULLING THREE DUCKLINGS, solid wood, no paper, Fisher Price $25.00-60.00

WOOFY DOG PULL TOY, long yellow dog, Fisher Price 1940 ....$40-00-70.00

WOOFY WAGGER DOGGY PULL TOY, Fisher Price, 1947...$20.00-40.00

SPACE TOYS AND ROBOTS

The enormous popularity of the George Lucas' STAR WARS movie trilogy over the past ten years and the renewed popularity of Gene Roddenberry's STAR TREK stories have both ignited the public's imagination of the celestial unknown. Considering recent auction reports of the astronomical prices associated with relatively recent Japanese windup and battery operated robots, this interesting facet of toy collecting is at the point of ignition with all systems "Go" for blast-off!

Space toys have been around since the advent of the popular space comics heroes Flash Gordon, Buck Rogers, Tom Corbett and Superman, but this field of collecting has its greatest focus of energy and depth on the battery operated, friction and windup space toys produced in the U.S. and Japan during the 1950's and 1960's. This shouldn't come as a surprise that the greatest space toys and robots were produced when the U.S. was locked in a cold war space race with Russia.

The gallactic phenomenon currently taking place within the space toy collectibles scene is an interesting one. Some 1960's Japanese robots are outpricing valuable tin windups from the 1930's. How can this be? The answer is simple. It's still the old law of supply and demand that sets the pricing standard in the toy collecting marketplace. Even though the 1960's space robots may be thirty years newer than their tinplate ancestors of the 1930's, there are so many robot and space toy enthusiasts entering the market today that many scarcities have been created. Thus, even for toys less than thirty years old, the prices escalate.

Of course, the old space toys do occupy an important place in the universal fleet of space collectors. Flash Gordon items of the 1930's are some of the most colorful space toys ever made, and they are particularly valuable because they are cross-collected, that is, they are collected by both comic character and space toys enthusiasts alike.

CAPTAIN VIDEO BOXED ROCKET LAUNCHER SET, 8" x 10", Reynolds collection, $40.00-85.00.

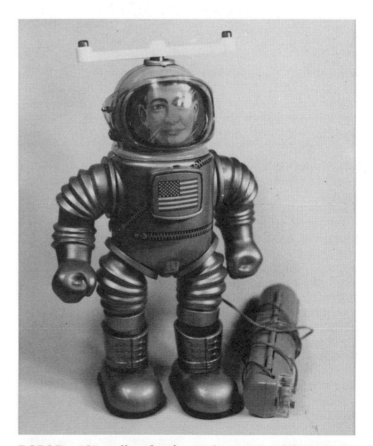

ROBOT, 12" tall, plastic and metal with battery operated box, Marx, 1967, Japan, Furnish collection, $100.00-225.00.

ATTACKING MARTIAN ROBOT, 9" battery operated, boxed, Reynolds collection, $50.00-125.00

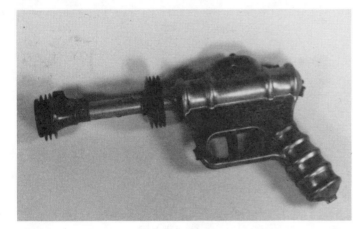

BUCK ROGERS ATOMIC DISINTEGRATOR GUN, 1930's, metal, Reynolds collection, $50.00-125.00.

ADVENTURES OF SUPERMAN GAME, Milton Bradley, 1950's, boxed board game $40.00-80.00

ALPHA-1 BALLISTIC MISSILE with remote launcher, USA, Scientific Toys, 10" $20.00-40.00

ANIMAL SATELLITE, Japan, 1950's, tin friction, 4" Sputnik type, dog inside $50.00-85.00

ANSWER GAME MACHINE ROBOT, Amico, Japan, 1950's, battery operated, 15" $150.00-300.00

APOLLO II LUNAR MODULE, Japan, Bump and Go, battery operated $70.00-150.00

APOLLO LUNAR MODULE KIT, Revell, unassembled, 1969 .... $40.00-65.00

ASTRONAUT ROBOT, battery operated, tin 12" tall, lights flash, antenna rotates $200.00-450.00

ASTRONAUT ROBOT, metal lithograph, panel on front $75.00-300.00

ASTRONAUT WITH A SPACE GUN RIFLE, windup $200.00-450.00

ATOM ROBOT, KO, made in Japan, crank action, 7" silver/blue $75.00-150.00

ATOM ROBOT, KO, Japan, tin windup with crank, 7" $100.00-300.00

ATOMIC DISENTEGRATOR GUN, Hubley cap gun, 1930's, cast metal, 6" $40.00-75.00

ATOMIC DISINTEGRATOR GUN, metal cap pistol with futuristic styling, 7" $35.00-80.00

ATOMIC GUN, tin lithograph, siren gun, ca. 1960's, Japan $10.00-35.00

ATTACKING MARTIAN ROBOT, battery operated, 9" $50.00-125.00

BUCK ROGERS "WILMA" CHARACTER MASK, paper, 11", 1930's $30.00-75.00

BUCK ROGERS 25TH CENTURY A.D. VS. THE FIEND OF SPACE, Better Little Book $10.00-30.00

BUCK ROGERS 25TH CENTURY ELECTRIC CASTER SET, Rapaport Brothers, 1930's $100.00-250.00

BUCK ROGERS 25TH CENTURY EQUIPMENT MERCHANDISE CATALOGUE, manufactured by Daisy, 1930's $25.00-70.00

BUCK ROGERS 25TH CENTURY HELMET, original box, rare, 1930's, Daisy $200.00-400.00

BUCK ROGERS 25TH CENTURY HOLSTER, 1934, Daisy $50.00-150.00

BUCK ROGERS 25TH CENTURY INTERPLANETARY SPACE FLEET, boxed construction set, 1934 .... $100.00-250.00

BUCK ROGERS 25TH CENTURY PENCIL BOX, red and blue, 1935 .... $40.00-80.00

BUCK ROGERS 25TH CENTURY SPACE PISTOL, XZ-31, 1934, boxed $100.00-200.00

BUCK ROGERS ALL-FAIR CARD GAME, ca. 1936 .... $75.00-125.00

BUCK ROGERS AND HIS COSMIC ROCKET WARS GAME BOARD, 1934, 16" x 16" $50.00-125.00

BUCK ROGERS AND HIS COSMIC ROCKET WARS, gameboard, 1934, 16" square $40.00-85.00

BUCK ROGERS AND WILMA PREMIUM PHOTO, by Cocomalt $70.00-125.00

BUCK ROGERS ATOMIC PISTOL HOLSTER SET, U-238, Daisy, 1930's, boxed $100.00-225.00

BUCK ROGERS ATTACK CRUISER, Tootsietoy, 1930's, 5" cast metal $50.00-135.00

BUCK ROGERS GAME OF THE 25TH CENTURY, A.D., 1930's, boxed board game $100.00-200.00

BUCK ROGERS HELMET AND ROCKET PISTOL, boxed set, manufactured by Einson-Freeman, paper, 1930's $100.00-200.00

BUCK ROGERS IN THE 25TH CENTURY POCKET WATCH AND BOX, 1930's $300.00-650.00

BUCK ROGERS IN THE 25TH CENTURY POP-UP BOOK published by Bluebird Press Books, 1935 .... $100.00-225.00

BUCK ROGERS KELLOG'S PREMIUM BOOLET, 1930's $50.00-100.00

BUCK ROGERS MAP OF THE SOLAR SYSTEM, 18" x 25", rare $300.00-450.00

BUCK ROGERS PUNCH-O-BAG, Official . $35.00-70.00

BUCK ROGERS PAINT BOOK, Whitman, 1935, 11" x 14" $30.00-75.00

BUCK ROGERS PAPER RUBBER BAND GUN, 1940, Onward School Supplies $50.00-100.00

BUCK ROGERS POCKET WATCH, manufactured 1930's $150.00-300.00

BUCK ROGERS ROCKET POLICE PATROL, windup, Marx, pilot head sticks out, 1930's $200.00-600.00

BUCK ROGERS ROCKET SHIP CONTROL BASE, 1937, paper, Warrem Paper Products $100.00-250.00

BUCK ROGERS ROCKET SHIP, Balsa wood die-cut, premium, 1930's, rare $75.00-200.00

BUCK ROGERS ROCKET SHIP, Marx, Buck and Wilma in window, 12" orange/green $100.00-300.00

BUCK ROGERS ROCKET SKATES, 1930's, metal roller skates with fins $50.00-135.00

BUCK ROGERS SEIGE OF GIGANTICA GAME BOARD, 1934 ....$100.00-200.00

BUCK ROGERS SOLAR SCOUTS Cream of Wheat premium manual, 1936...........................$30.00-75.00

BUCK ROGERS MANUAL, Solar Scouts...$50.00-125.00

BUCK ROGERS SONIC RAY GUN with plastic disks to fit over light bulb $50.00-125.00

BUCK ROGERS SONIC RAY GUN, plastic flashlight gun, original box, 7" $40.00-85.00

BUCK ROGERS SPACE GUN................$45.00-120.00

BUCK ROGERS SPACE RANGER KIT, Sylvania Premium, 1952, in original envelope $30.00-70.00

BUCK ROGERS SPACE SHIP, paper/cardboard premium, Morton Salt, in envelope $50.00-125.00

BUCK ROGERS SPACE SUIT, complete, circa 1930 ....$200.00-600.00

BUCK ROGERS STRATO-KITE, circa 1940 or 1950's $35.00-70.00

BUCK ROGERS TELESCOPE, 1930's $50.00-125.00

BUCK ROGERS TOOTSIETOY ROCKET SHIPS, boxed set of four with two figures, 1937 ..$300.00-600.00

BUCK ROGERS TRU-VUE SET, cards for 3-D viewer, 1953 ....$20.00-40.00

BUCK ROGERS VENUS DESTROYER, 5" cast metal, Tootsietoy, blue/white........................$50.00-135.00

BUCK ROGERS WAR WITH THE PLANET VENUS, Better Little Book, 1938.....................$10.00-25.00

BUCK ROGERS WATER PISTOL, 1930's, red and yellow $75.00-150.00

BUCK ROGERS WHISTLING ROCKET SHIP, paper and cardboard, 14", 1939 ....$100.00-175.00

BUMP 'N GO SPACE EXPLORER, KO, Japan, 1950's, crank action tank with bubble $70.00-140.00

BUZZ COREY'S SPACE PATROL WRIST WATCH, boxed, U.S. Time $125.00-250.00

CALLING SUPERMAN GAME, by Transogram, 1954 boxed board game $20.00-40.00

CAPE CANAVERAL MISSLE SET, by Marx, boxed $75.00-150.00

CAPTAIN MARVEL FLANNEL PATCH, Fawcett Publications $10.00-25.00

CAPTAIN MARVEL IRON-ONS SHEET, circa 1950..$15.00-35.00

CAPTAIN MARVEL MAGIC MEMBERSHIP CARD, 1940's..$10.00-25.00

CAPTAIN MARVEL MAGIC WHISTLE, manufactured 1948..$25.00-50.00

CAPTAIN MARVEL PAPER HORN, Fawcett Publications, yellow.......................................$20.00-40.00

CAPTAIN MARVEL PICTURE PUZZLE IN ENVELOPE, Reed and Associates $10.00-35.00

CAPTAIN MARVEL PICTURE PUZZLE, manufactured 1941 ....$25.00-50.00

CAPTAIN MARVEL TIN WINDUP CAR #1, green tin lithograph, 1947 ....$40.00-85.00

CAPTAIN MARVEL TIN WINDUP CAR #2, orange tin lithograph, 1947 ....$40.00-85.00

CAPTAIN MARVEL TIN WINDUP CAR #3, yellow tin lithograph, 1947 ....$40.00-85.00

CAPTAIN MARVEL TIN WINDUP CAR #4, blue tin lithograph, 1947 ....$40.00-85.00

FLASH GORDON ROCKET FIGHTER, MARX WIND-UP, 1930's, tin, Reynolds collection, $100.00-350.00.

TELEVISION ROBOT, JAPAN, TIN AND PLASTIC, battery operated, Reynolds collection, $70.00-150.00.

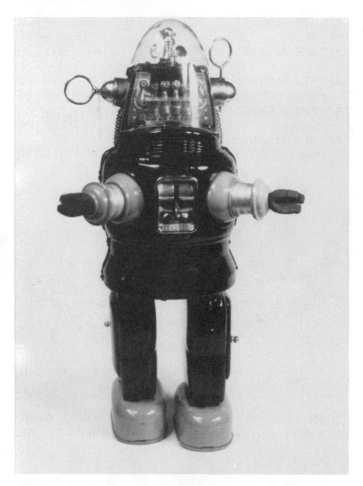

ROBOT, METAL AND PLASTIC, early design look, 13", Japan, Furnish collection, $100.00-200.00.

ROCKET FIGHTER SPACESHIP, by Marx, 1930's, 12" long, Furnish collection, $150.00-225.00.

CAPTAIN MARVEL TOSS BAG, felt $10.00-30.00

CAPTAIN MARVEL'S MAGIC DIME SAVER, dime register bank, 1948, by Fawcett Publications $10.00-85.00

CAPTAIN METEOR SPACE HOLSTER AND COSMIC RAY GUN, boxed $35.00-70.00

CAPTAIN SPACE SOLAR ACADEMY PLAYSET, Marx boxed, complete $100.00-300.00

CAPTAIN SPACE SOLAR SCOUT RIFLE, plastic rifle, by Marx $25.00-60.00

CAPTAIN VIDEO AND HIS VIDEO RANGERS rocket launcher, set, boxed, 8" x 10" $40.00-85.00

CAPTAIN VIDEO AND THE CAPTIVES OF SATURN RECORD, book, punch-out figures $20.00-45.00

CAPTAIN VIDEO BOXED BOARD GAME, 10" x 19" Milton Bradley $20.00-40.00

CAPTAIN VIDEO GALAXY CHILD'S TOY TO RIDE, rocket riding toy, rare $200.00-400.00

CAPTAIN VIDEO INLAID PUZZLE, 1950's, Milton Bradley $25.00-60.00

CAPTAIN VIDEO LEATHER BELT AND HOLSTER SET, by Carnell $40.00-85.00

COSMIC SCOUT plastic night light, 1950's $20.00-40.00

COSMIC VISION HELMET, in box, to assemble, one-way vision $30.00-60.00

EXCAVATOR ROBOT, SH, Japan, 1950's, 10" all plastic $50.00-90.00

FIGHTING ROBOT, battery operated, 11" tin, yellow light on head $175.00-250.00

FLASH GORDON AND THE ICE WORLD OF MONGO, Better Little Book, 1942 .... $10.00-25.00

FLASH GORDON AND THE MONSTERS OF MONGO Big Little Book, 1935 .... $10.00-30.00

FLASH GORDON AND THE POWER MEN OF MONGO, Better Little Book, 1943 .... $10.00-25.00

FLASH GORDON AND THE TOURNAMENTS OF MONGO, Big Little Books, 1935 .... $15.00-30.00

FLASH GORDON JIGSAW PUZZLES, Milton Bradley, 1951, set of three $20.00-40.00

FLASH GORDON ON THE PLANET MONGO, Feature Book # 25, 1940 .... $50.00-85.00

FLASH GORDON PAINT BOOK, Whitman, 1936, 11" x 14", large version $20.00-50.00

FLASH GORDON PENCIL BOX, Eagle Pencil Company, 1951 King Features $20.00-50.00

FLASH GORDON PICTURE RECORD, Record Guild of America, 1948 King Features $10.00-35.00

FLASH GORDON PIONEER BELTS STORE POINT OF SALE AD, 1940's, unusual $30.00-95.00

FLASH GORDON PLASTIC BELT, circa 1930, on card $45.00-85.00

FLASH GORDON RAY GUN, air pump type with Flash Gordon decal, 11" metal $100.00-200.00

FLASH GORDON ROCKET FIGHTER, Marx windup rocket ship, 1930's, tin $100.00-350.00

FLASH GORDON SIGNAL PISTOL, THE SCREAMING FLASHING SIGNAL GUN, in original box, 1935 .... $125.00-275.00

FLASH GORDON SOLAR COMMANDO SET, on original card, 1952 .... $75.00-195.00

FLASH GORDON SPACE COMPASS on original card, 1930's or 1940's $20.00-40.00

FLASH GORDON SPACE OUTFIT, 1952, boxed set, vest inside, colorful box $100.00-200.00

FLASH GORDON SPACE PHONES, on original card $65.00-150.00

FLASH GORDON'S RANGERS, 8" GUN with paper snapper inside $20.00-40.00

FLOATING SATELLITE TARGET GAME, Japan, battery operated, 9" x 7" target, boxed $25.00-050.00

FLYING SAUCER #8, Haji, Japan, 1950's, tin friction, 7" diameter $40.00-85.00

FLYING SPACE NOVELTY, Satellite Toy, Japan, tin and plastic, 1950's $10.00-20.00

FUTUREMAN SPACE WHISTLE, Lido Plastics, 1950's $10.00-20.00

G-MAN ROCKET SHIP, Pursuit rocket ...$30.00-65.00

GIANT ATTACK ROBOT, 16½" $400.00-700.00

GOLDEN ROBOT, SH, Japan, battery operated, tin body, rotates 360 degrees $85.00-270.00

HYSTERICAL ROBOT, battery operated, 13" laughs hysterically as face plate opens $100.00-250.00

INTERPLANETARY EXPLORER, Toytime, Japan, 1950's, 8" tin windup $300.00-600.00

INTERPLANETARY ROCKET, Y, Japan, battery operated, tin and plastic, stop and go, in original box $50.00-125.00

JOHN CARTER OF MARS, Edgar Rice Burroughs, Better Little Book, 1940 ....$10.00-35.00

JUPITER ROCKET, MS, Japan, 1950's, all tin, friction, 10" $20.00-45.00

KING FLYING SAUCER, KO, Japan, battery operated, 8" metallic blue and silver, tin and plastic $50.00-100.00

LIGHTED SPACE VEHICLE, Japan, with floating satellite, tank form $100.00-175.00

LOST IN SPACE ROBOT by Remco, original box, 16" plastic $120.00-375.00

LUNAR BUG FLYING MOON CRAFT, battery operated, 1965, remote controlled, plastic $15.00-30.00

MARS ROCKET, 3-Stage $20.00-45.00

MARTIANS, by Archer, 1950's, hard plastic figures, seven in set $20.00-45.00

MARY MARVEL BEAN TOSS BAG, 5" long $10.00-30.00

MECHANICAL JUMPING ROCKET ROBOT, Japan, tin windup, 6" robot in rocket $125.00-175.00

MECHANIZED ROBOT "ROBBIE," battery operated, 13" tall $1,300.00-2,000.00

MERCURY X-1 SPACE SAUCER, Japan, battery operated, 8" long, tin and plastic bump and go $50.00-100.00

MIGHTY ROBOT WITH APOLLO windup, 3" robot drags Apollo rocket, plastic $50.00-95.00

MIGHTY ROBOT, Japan, 6", tin windup, green $25.00-50.00

MIGHTY ROBOT, Sparkling chest, boxed, 6" tall, tin, green $70.00-135.00

MISSLE ROBOT, Japan, tin and plastic, battery operated, 10" fires missiles $40.00-65.00

MISTER HUSTLER ROBOT, 11", battery operated, astronaut's face in face shield, box $250.00-600.00

MISTER MERCURY ROBOT, Marx, Japan battery operated, remote controlled, 13" $275.00-500.00

MISTER ROBOT manufactured by Cragstan, Japan, tin $400.00-700.00

MISTER SANDMAN THE ROBOT, Wolverine, 11" tall $200.00-400.00

MISTER SANDMAN THE ROBOT by Wolverine, 1940, 12" robot sand toy $200.00-350.00

MOBILE SPACE TELEVISION UNIT with trailer $100.00-350.00

MONORAIL ROCKET SHIP, LineMar, 1950's, battery operated, 10" rocket, box $100.00-300.00

MOON CREATURE, MECHANICAL, by Marx, Japan, tin windup, 5½" $125.00-250.00

MOON GLOBE ORBITER, Mego, Japan, battery operated, plastic, orbits, 6" globe $25.00-70.00

ROBERT THE ROBOT BY IDEAL, 1950's, 14", crank remote operated, voice, Reynolds collection, $125.00-200.00.

SPACE TANK, TIN, MADE IN CHINA, battery operated, 10", Furnish collection, $60.00-140.00.

SOLAR X SPACE ROCKET, tin, battery operated, 16" long, Furnish collection, $45.00-135.00.

SNOOPY'S SPACE PATROL METAL AND PLASTIC SPACE SHIP, Reynolds collection, $35.00-75.00.

MOON HELICOPTER, Marx, Japan, battery operated, remote controlled, 7", NASA, boxed $30.00-55.00

MOON ORBITER, battery operated, boxed, 4" vehicle

on track $85.00-145.00

MOON PATROL HELICOPTER "Moon Scout," tin wind-up, Marx, NASA $30.00-85.00

MOON ROCKET, tin, 1950's, Japan $60.00-90.00

MORK AND MINDY EGGSHIP SPACE RADIO, 1970's, mint in box $12.00-18.00

NASA SPACECRAFT, Daiya, Japan, battery operated, 12", two sections $65.00-110.00

OCEANIC ROCKET SHIP $30.00-65.00

PISTON ROBOT, Japan, tin and plastic, battery operated, 11" pistons in chest move $25.00-50.00

PLANETARY SPACE FIGHTERS in box .$150.00-225.00

R-35 ROBOT, Japan, 8" tall battery operated tin, blue dot glass eyes $200.00-400.00

RADAR ROBOT, battery operated, remote, metal and plastice $100.00-400.00

RADAR ROBOT, TN, Japan, 8" battery operated, eyes light, battery operated is robot head shape $300.00-500.00

REX MARS PLANET PATROL FLASHLIGHT, made of plastic $10.00-35.00

REX MARS PLANET PATROL SPARKING PISTOL, plastic, boxed, 7".............................$30.00-60.00

REX MARS PLANET PATROL TANK, Marx, 1930's, 10" long, tin windup, boxed $150.00-270.00

ROBBIE THE ROBOT, 13" battery operated, rubber hands, tin, plastic dome $700.00-1,200.00

ROBERT THE ROBOT, Ideal, 1950's crank action with voice, 14", remote control $125.00-200.00

ROBO TANK, 2, SPACE TANK with robot driver..$300.00-700.00

ROBOT PHONE, 1980's, 10" silver, bullet shaped, actual telephone $25.00-55.00

ROBOT SAM, THE ANSWER MAN, made by Jaymar $20.00-50.00

ROBOT, GERMAN, 1950's, tin windup, spring antenna on head, walks, sparks $125.00-250.00

ROBOT, JUMPING MECHANICAL, Japan, 6", tin wind-up $125.00-175.00

ROBOT, LineMar, tin windup, 6", jointed arm, spring antenna $125.00-225.00

ROBOT, Marx, 1950's, plastic, battery operated, 15", black and red $30.00-55.00

ROBOT, MECHANICAL JUMPING, Japan, tin windup $125.00-175.00

ROBOT-7, Japan, tin wind-up, 4", bullet shape $10.00-20.00

ROCKET DART PISTOL, Daisy, 1930's, steel, 7" shoots wood darts $15.00-35.00

ROCKET FIGHTER SPACESHIP, Marx, 1930's, 12" long, celluloid wndow $100.00-225.00

ROCKET FIGHTER, Marx, tin, windup, 12" celluloid window $100.00-225.00

ROCKET LAUNCHER, Tootsietoy $15.00-30.00

ROCKET PENCIL CASE, Hasbro, 1950's, plastic, 5" $10.00-25.00

ROCKEY JONES OFFICIAL SPACE RANGER WINGS, 1950's $15.00-35.00

ROCKY JONES SPACE RANGER COLORING BOOK, by Whitman, 1951, 11" x 15" $10.00-20.00

ROCKY JONES SPACE RANGER WALLET with mechanical pencil inside $10.00-30.00

RUSHER ROBOT, friction powered, tin, with blue torso, original box $75.00-150.00

SATELLITE LAUNCHER, Ideal Toys, Mobile, plastic construction $40.00-75.00

SILVER RAY SECRET WEAPON SCOUT, Robot Spaceman, Japan, battery operated, 9" ..$150.00-275.00

SILVER ROBOT, Japan, battery operated, 12" red/yellow/black, boxed $40.00-95.00

SKY PATROL FLYING SAUCER, 1950's, battery operated $125.00-175.00

SOLAR X SPACE ROCKET, tin battery operated, 16" long, boxed $45.00-135.00

SONICON ROCKET, Japan, boxed, 1950's, tin and plastic, antenna, 14" $150.00-250.00

SPACE 1999 CARD SET, complete $5.00-10.00

SPACE BLAZER #150, Fisher Price $90.00-135.00

SPACE CADET BELT with original punch out card, 7" x 13" $20.00-45.00

SPACE CADET COLORING BOOK, Saalfield, 1953 ....$10.00-15.00

SPACE CAP BOMB TOY, 1950's $10.00-25.00

SPACE CAPSULE WITH FLOATING ASTRONAUT, MT, Japan, battery operated, 10", silver Apollo $50.00-100.00

SPACE DOG ROBOT, KO, Japan, tin friction, 6" $130.00-200.00

SPACE DOG, windup in box $150.00-225.00

SPACE EXPLORER SHIP, 1950's, 11" saucer, battery operated, bump and go $75.00-135.00

SPACE FRONTIER APOLLO 12 ROCKET, battery operated, 18", boxed $75.00-150.00

SPACE GHOST PUZZLES SET, based on 1967 Hanna Barbera cartoon series $10.00-15.00

SPACE GUN, Daiya, Japan, 1950's, tin windup, sparking, 7" $15.00-30.00

SPACE MAN ROBOT, Japan, tin windup gray with red feet $100.00-200.00

SPACE MODEL QX-2, WALKIE TALKIES, by Remco, 1950's, boxed....................................$20.00-45.00

SPACE NAVIGATOR SET, card containing space badge and compass, 1950's..........................$10.00-20.00

SPACE PATROL 2019 FLYING SAUCER, Japan, battery operated, made of tin and plastic, 8", boxed $50.00-100.00

SPACE PATROL ADVENTURES, by Decca record..$20.00-45.00

SPACE PATROL COMMANDER VINYL HAT, 1950's $20.00-45.00

SPACE PATROL DART GUN, 10", plastic, Buzz Corry item..$40.00-95.00

SPACE PATROL FRICTION ROBOT CAR, tin with gun on hood $100.00-175.00

SPACE PATROL INLAID PUZZLE, by Milton Bradley..$15.00-30.00

SPACE PATROL LUNAR FLEET BASE, punch-out premium set, very rare $300.00-600.00

SPACE PATROL PAPER PLATES in original package $10.00-25.00

SPACE PATROL PERISCOPE, Ralston, premium, rare $100.00-175.00

SPACE PATROL ROCKET GUN, in original packaging $55.00-100.00

SPACE PATROL SPACE GOGGLES, Hale Nass, 1953, 8" long on original card....................$15.00-35.00

SPACE PATROL SPACE-A-PHONES, Toys of Tomorrow, 1950's, boxed $30.00-80.00

SPACE PILOT SPACE PATROL HELMET, with original box....................................$100.00-200.00

SPACE PILOT TELESCOPE, 1950's, tin .$10.00-30.00

SPACE ROCKET #7 with robot, SY, Japan, tin friction, 6" $60.00-110.00

SPACE ROCKET PATROL CAR, Courtland, 1950's, 7" tin friction, sparks.............................$40.00-95.00

SPACE ROCKET PISTOL, tin, 1950's, battery operated, 9" long, dark blue, boxed $35.00-95.00

SPACE ROCKET WITH ROBOT RIDING, 1950's, 6" long, Japan, tin, boxed $200.00-450.00

SPACE ROCKET, Automatic Toy Company, 1950's, friction, 9"....................................$25.00-60.00

SPACE SCOUT BUBBLE GUM BANK, 1950's, plastic, with gum $20.00-55.00

SPACE SHIP ROCKET RACER, tin friction, 7" long, tin lithograph......................................$40.00-85.00

SPACE SHIP, TECHNOFIX, U.S. Zone Germany, 10" tin friction, tan and orange $20.00-50.00

SPACE SHIP, TECHNOFIX, U.S. Zone Germany, 10", red, white and blue..........................$20.00-50.00

SPACE SIREN GUN by Ideal, 1950's, 7" long, red plastic with silver trim......................$30.00-60.00

SPACE TANK M-41, MT, Japan, 1950's, battery operated, 8" $90.00-160.00

SPACE TANK WITH ROBOT, 10" battery operated $60.00-140.00

SPACE VEHICLES, five future cars on original card, Hong Kong, 1950's $10.00-20.00

SPACE WHALE, Japan, tin windup, 9" long, whale shaped space ship $140.00-280.00

TIN WINDUP SPACE RACER #3, tin lithograph, bullet shaped, Furnish collection, $70.00-140.00.

TOM CORBETT SPACE CADET 2, SPACESHIP, 1930's Marx, tin windup, 12" long, Furnish collection, $100.00-300.00.

SPACE TOYS

SPACE-O-PHONE, blue and yellow plastic, futuristic phone set, boxed $50.00-125.00

SPACECRAFT APOLLO by Alps, Japan, battery operated, 9" with three astronauts lithographed, box $65.00-120.00

SPACECRAFT JUPITER, K, Japan, tin windup, 5", saucer type with bubble $35.00-90.00

SPACECRAFT ROBOT, Japan, battery operated, 12" tall has astronauts face, double guns fire $50.00-125.00

SPACEMAN, manufactured by LineMar, Japan, 6" windup $85.00-300.00

SPACEMAN, television version, 7" tin windup, NASA on helmet, Alps, Japan $150.00-250.00

SPACEMAN, hard plastic, Lido, 4", bubble type helmet, set of four $30.00-60.00

SPARKING ROBOT, SY, Japan, 7" silver robot, square head and torso $75.00-165.00

SPARKING ROBOT, Japan, 1950's, 7" tin with plastic antenna $100.00-200.00

SPARKY ROBOT, Japan, tin windup, 6", two square gold robots on rocking horse $100.00-200.00

SPARKY ROBOT, KO, Japan, 8" tall, tin windup robot, silver with box $100.00-200.00

STAR TREK COMMUNICATORS in original packaging, 1970's $35.00-75.00

STAR TREK FILM VIEWER, red and black plastic, 1967 .... $10.00-20.00

STAR TREK USS ENTERPRISE ACTION PLAYSET, 1974, boxed set $95.00-150.00

STAR WARS ACTION FIGURES COLLECTORS CASE, 1979 .... $10.00-30.00

STAR WARS BEN KENOBI JOINTED PLASTIC DOLL, 12", Kenner, 1979 .... $25.00-65.00

STAR WARS BOBA FETT PLASTIC JOINTED FIGURE, 13", Kenner, 1979 .... $20.00-45.00

STAR WARS C3PO ROBOT DOLL, plastic, Kenner, 1970's $25.00-75.00

STAR WARS CHEWBACCA DOLL, 15" plastic, Kenner, 1978 .... $10.00-25.00

STAR WARS DARTH VADER BOP BAG, 1978, vinyl $12.00-20.00

STAR WARS DARTH VADAR DOLL, 15" molded plastic, jointed, Kenner, 1978 .... $35.00-65.00

STAR WARS DEATH STAR SPACE STATION PLAY SET, in original box $15.00-40.00

STAR WARS ESCAPE FROM DEATH STAR BOARD GAME, Kenner, 1978 .... $10.00-30.00

STAR WARS HAN SOLO ACTION FIGURE, 1978, Kenner $40.00-90.00

STAR WARS INFLATABLE LIGHT SABER, 35", Kenner $10.00-20.00

STAR WARS JIGSAW PUZZLE, boxed, 1978, Kenner $5.00-8.00

STAR WARS LAND SPEEDER, 1978 .... $20.00-40.00

STAR WARS LUKE SKYWALKER DOLL, 12", Kenner, 1970's, boxed $20.00-55.00

STAR WARS PRINCESS LEIA DOLL, boxed, Kenner, 1978 .... $25.00-60.00

STAR WARS R2D2 BOP BAG, 1978 ...... $10.00-20.00

STAR WARS RADIO CONTROLLED R2D2, 1978, Kenner $25.00-60.00

STAR WARS STORM TROOPER DOLL, Kenner, plastic, 12", jointed $35.00-85.00

STAR WARS TWIN ION ENGINE FIGHTER, (small enemy fighter) Kenner, 1978 .... $10.00-30.00

STAR WARS X-WING ACES TARGET GAME, electric, 1978 .... $30.00-65.00

STAR WARS X-WING FIGHTER SHIP, Kenner, 13½", 1978 version $20.00-40.00

STAR WARS, DIE-CAST X-WING FIGHTER, 5", 1978 .... $10.00-22.00

STAR WARS, LAND SPEEDER, die-cast metal, 1978 .... $10.00-20.00

STAR WARS, LASER PISTOL, replica of Han Solo's gun, 1978 .... $10.00-30.00

STEVE SCOTT SPACE SCOUT GAME, by Transogram, 1952 .... $15.00-25.00

SUPER ASTRONAUT, tin and plastic, battery operated, boxed, fires guns $40.00-100.00

SUPER ROBOT, Hong Kong, battery operated, plastic, converts to twelve figures $15.00-30.00

SUPER SPACE CAPSULE, Japan, battery operated, 10" tin and plastic $45.00-95.00

SUPERBOY GAME, 1965, 8½" x 16", in original box $5.00-12.00

SUPERIOR SPACE PORT AND SPACE DROME, by Cohn, 1950's, tin and plastic $200.00-450.00

SUPERMAN ACTION GAME, manufactured by American Toy works, 1940 dart game $100.00-225.00

SUPERMAN ADVENTURE BOOK, Atlas Publishing, England, 1957 .... $20.00-40.00

SUPERMAN BILLFOLD, 1947 .... $10.00-20.00

SUPERMAN CARDS, boxed set, 1966, black and white cards $55.00-120.00

SUPERMAN CHALK FIGURE, from carnival 16" $20.00-45.00

SUPERMAN CHILD'S NECKTIE, 1940's .. $10.00-25.00

SUPERMAN COLORING BOOK, Saalfield, 1940, 11" x 15" $40.00-85.00

SUPERMAN COMIC NUMBER 11, 1941, early book $30.00-90.00

SUPERMAN DAISY CINEMATIC PICTURE PISTOL, 4" x 6" box $60.00-135.00

SUPERMAN DIME REGISTER BANK, tin lithograph $25.00-60.00

SUPERMAN GOLDEN MUSCLE BUILDING SET, 1950's, boxed set of muscle equipment $100.00-200.00

SUPERMAN HAND PUPPET, 1960's $10.00-20.00

SUPERMAN KRYPTON RAYGUN, Daisy, 7" long gun in bright box, 16mm films $100.00-250.00

SUPERMAN KRYPTON ROCKET, 1956, original box $65.00-140.00

SUPERMAN MEMBERSHIP CARD, 1948 ... $10.00-20.00

SUPERMAN MOVIE VIEWER, 1960's $5.00-10.00

SUPERMAN PUZZLES, three (set), 1966 . $10.00-20.00

SUPERMAN RECORD SET, "The Magic Ring," 1947 two records $20.00-40.00

SUPERMAN SPOON, 1966 .... $10.00-20.00

SUPERMAN TIME CAPSULE, 1955 premium comic $10.00-25.00

SUPERMAN VALENTINE, 1940's $5.00-12.00

SUPERSONIC ACES ROCKETS with spacemen, 1950's $20.00-45.00

SUPERSONIC SPEEDSTER ROCKET, MT, Japan, 1950's, tin friction rocket/car $80.00-175.00

SWINGING BABY ROBOT, Japan, tin windup, 6" yellow, with box $165.00-300.00

TEARDROP SPACESHIP, USA, 1930's, blue/yellow, "Oceanic Rocket Ship" $30.00-65.00

TEARDROP SPACESHIP, USA, 1930's, orange/blue "G-Man Pursuit Rocket Ship," $30.00-65.00

TIC-TAC EXPRESS, futuristic cars move about, space lithograph on sides, tin, windup $40.00-80.00

TOM CORBETT SPACE CADET COLORING BOOK, Saalfield, 1953 ....$20.00-45.00

TOM CORBETT A TRIP TO THE MOON, Wonder Book, 1958 ....$10.00-20.00

TOM CORBETT OFFICIAL SPACE GUN, Marx, 21" sparking gun $85.00-195.00

TOM CORBETT PICTURE PUZZLES, 1952, boxed $60.00-125.00

TOM CORBETT SPACE CADET ATOMIC RIFLE, Marx, 24" long $35.00-65.00

TOM CORBETT SPACE CADET BLUE LUNCHBOX, 1952......................................$20.00-35.00

TOM CORBETT SPACE CADET BOOK BAG, plastic, 1950's $20.00-40.00

TOM CORBETT SPACE CADET UNIFORM, child's..$30.00-75.00

TOM CORBETT SPACE CADET COLORING BOOK, 1942......................................$20.00-40.00

TOM CORBETT SPACE CADET PIN ON ROCKET LITE STORE DISPLAY, six lites .$100.00-225.00

TOM CORBETT SPACE CADET SUPER BEAM SIGNAL RAY, 8" flashlight $20.00-40.00

TOM CORBETT SPACE CADET THERMOS, Rockhill Radio, 1952 ....$10.00-20.00

TOM CORBETT SPACE CADET VIEW MASTER REELS SET, three, ca. 1954..........................$10.00-35.00

TOM CORBETT SPACE CADET VIEWMASTER SLIDES, complete set, three reels, package $15.00-30.00

TOM CORBETT SPACE CODE DECODER, cardboard wheel...$20.00-40.00

TOM CORBETT THE MYSTERY OF THE ASTEROIDS view master set $5.00-10.00

TOM CORBETT'S WONDER BOOK OF SPACE, Wonderbooks, 1953 ....$10.00-20.00

TOOTSIETOY FLASH BLAST ATTACK SHIP, Buck Rogers, 1930's cast metal, boxed $95.00-165.00

TELEVISION SPACE PATROL CAR, Japan, tin, friction, 8", cadillac style body $75.00-140.00

TELEVISION SPACE ROBOT, battery operated, 11", tin, television in chest, tall antenna on head $200.00-475.00

TWO STAGE EARTH SATELLITE, LineMar, Japan, 1950's, 8"...$70.00-150.00

TWO STAGE ROCKET LAUNCHER, Japan, battery operated, 1950's, boxed $150.00-275.00

UFO X05, MT, 7" diameter saucer, tin and plastic, boxed $30.00-75.00

USA NASA GEMINI, Japan, battery operated, all tin, 9", silver/red/blue, with box............$90.00-180.00

VIDEO ROBOT, Japan, battery operated, 10" tin and plastic, television screen in chest $50.00-100.00

WALKING ROBOT, ST JAPAN, 7" windup, all plastic (recent) $10.00-20.00

WALT DISNEY'S SATELLITE LAUNCHER, Strombecker kit, 1950's...$20.00-35.00

WONDER L ROCKET, Japan, battery operated, 14" plastic rocket spreads wings, boxed ..$30.00-65.00

X-7 SPACE EXPLORER, MT, Japan, 1950's, battery operated, 8" tin saucer $70.00-110.00

X-70 ROBOT, Japan, battery operated, 12½" tin body, plastic arms, silver and purple $200.00-400.00

X-70 ROBOT, Japan, battery operated, 12", tin body with plastic arms..........................$400.00-800.00

ZOOMER ROBOT, TN, Japan, 1950's, 8" tall, metallic blue, George Wagner $200.00-350.00

ZOOMER THE ROBOT, metal $150.00-400.00

SATELLITE BY CRAGSTAN, 9" diameter, battery operated, Furnish collection, $40.00-85.00.

SPACE CAPSULE #7, battery operated, Japan, with space-walking astronaut, TM Company, 10", Furnish collection, $50.00-100.00.

TELEVISION AND RADIO CHARACTER TOYS

Television and radio have both played a most important part in American popular culture. Both mass media have served to entertain, inform and even change our way of thinking. With the fantastic popularity of radio in the 1920's and 1930's, American audiences were primed and ready to be virtually mesmerized by television. As both electronic media brought entertainment daily into our homes, these media greatly influenced the toy industry.

The most popular radio character of all time had to be none other than Little Orphan Annie. Based on the Harold Gray comic strip which had already gained popularity in national newspapers, the radio show made a few departures from the limits of the original comic strip. First, in the original comic strip form, Gray allowed Annie to often become a little political spokesperson, commenting from time to time about the great needs for social change. On radio the little gal became more of an adventurous little heroine who utilized the premium marketing gimmicks of the day-secret decoders, secret clubs and messages and, of course, Ovaltine premiums. Captain Midnight, Tom Mix and a host of other radio programs promoted their sponsors and their program by the use of premiums which are prized among collectors today.

Because television was a relatively new invention in the 1940's, it is difficult to find examples of the earliest television toy memorabilia. For one thing, there just weren't that many shows on the air when television networks first began regular programming. It is not until the very early 1950's that television began to exert its strong influence upon the toy industry. Not only were television characters such as Howdy Doody, the Mickey Mouse Club cast and early game shows popular among the toy buying public, but also the sponsors of early children's programming made big names for themselves during the 1950's. Mattel, Remco, Hasbro and Kenner all were made popular by smartly placed toy ads in children's programming time slots.

Collectors new to the field of toy collecting would be very surprised at the popularity of relatively recent television characters among those who specialize in television memorabilia. Leave it to Beaver, I Love Lucy, The Munsters and Star Trek are only a few of the popular shows of the 1950's and 1960's which inspired toys of great popularity among today's collectors.

One important point that must be made is that these toys are not yet rare. As a result, neighborhood yard sales and flea markets abound with these items. The fact that these toys are both relatively new and abundant keeps their prices down. Collectors should realize that scarcity of these items is not a problem, so patience could help the collector locate the items eventually at a reasonable price.

Television continues to be an important force in shaping American culture. Our tastes, our values and even our political viewpoints continue to be shaped by the electronic media. There is no doubt among today's toy collectors that television-related toys will increase in value in the coming years. The determining factor of how much they will increase will depend, in major part, upon how many new, interested collectors enter the field.

77 SUNSET STRIP BOARD GAME, 1960, c. Warner Brothers $15.00-35.00

ADAM 12 LUNCHBOX, 1972 television series, tie-in $5.00-10.00

ADDAMS FAMILY "The Thing," battery operated bank, 1960's $20.00-45.00

ADDAMS FAMILY LUNCHBOX, 1960's $5.00-10.00

ALFRED HITCHCOCK PRESENTS GAME, Milton Bradley, 1958 ....$15.00-30.00

AMOS AN' ANDY ASH TRAY, chalkware, 1940, 8" tall figures $50.00-135.00

AMOS AN' ANDY, "AMOS" CHARACTER TIN WIND-UP FIGURE, 1930's $250.00-500.00

AMOS AN' ANDY "ANDY" CHARACTER TIN WINDUP FIGURE, 12", 1930's $250.00-500.00

AMOS AN' ANDY CARD PARTY SET, 1930's, boxed $20.00-45.00

AMOS AN' ANDY FRESH AIR TAXI CAB TIN WIND-UP, Marx, 1930's $300.00-700.00

AMOS AN' ANDY JIGSAW PUZZLE, 1932, Pepsodent premium $20.00-45.00

ARTHUR GODFREY UKELELE with song book $20.00-45.00

BABA LOOEY CERAMIC FIGURE, 5½", 1960's, Hanna Barbera $5.00-10.00

BARNEY RUBBLE RIDING DINO TIN WINDUP TOY, by Marx, 1960's, 8" $70.00-140.00

BARNEY RUBBLE VINYL SQUEAK TOY, 1960 ....$5.00-10.00

BAT MASTERSON HOLSTER, CANE AND VEST SET (television), made by Carnell Manufacturing Company $20.00-45.00

BATMAN AND ROBIN GAME, 1965 ....$20.00-30.00

BATMAN AND ROBIN TALKING CLOCK, circa 1970 ....$20.00-40.00

BATMAN BATBRUSH ON ORIGINAL CARD, 1960's $12.00-18.00

BATMAN BOARD GAME, 1966 ....$15.00-25.00

BATMAN MILK GLASS, 1966 ....$5.00-10.00

BATMAN TELEVISION VERSION LUNCHBOX, 1960's $5.00-20.00

BEN CASEY M.D. GAME, manufactured by Transogram, 1961 ....$10.00-20.00

BEN CASEY NOTEBOOK, 1962 ....$10.00-20.00

BEN CASEY OVERNIGHT CASE, vinyl, manufactured 1962 ....$20.00-30.00

BEVERLY HILLBILLIES CARD GAME, 1960's, Milton Bradley $5.00-10.00

BEVERLY HILLBILLIES FRAME TRAY PUZZLE, Jaymar, 1963 ....$5.00-10.00

BEVERLY HILLBILLIES JIGSAW PUZZLE, boxed, 1960's $5.00-10.00

BONANZA LUNCH KIT WITH THERMOS, circa 1960 ....$5.00-15.00

BONANZA LUNCHBOX SET, 1960's $10.00-20.00

BONANZA TIN MUG, 1960's $10.00-20.00

BOZO THE CLOWN NODDER made by Bayard, 1950's $40.00-85.00

BOZO THE CLOWN RADIO, in original box, 1960's $20.00-35.00

BUGS BUNNY CAST METAL PLANTER, 1940's, 6" tall $50.00-100.00

CAPTAIN GALLANT ADVENTURE GAME, by Transogram, 1955 ....$15.00-30.00

BATMAN AND ROBIN PLASTER BOOKENDS, 1960's Reynolds collection, (pair) $25.00-65.00.

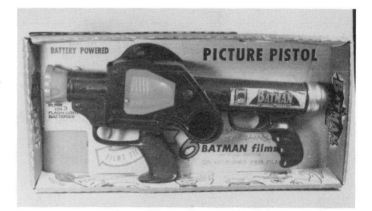

BATMAN PICTURE PISTOL, 1960's, battery operated, boxed, Reynolds collection, $15.00-40.00.

BONANZA PONDEROSA RANCH TIN CUP, 1960's, Reynolds collection, $5.00-15.00.

BUGS BUNNY ALARM CLOCK BY INGRAHAM, square, 1940's, $200.00-400.00, Reynolds collection.

ELSIE THE COW CERAMIC CHARACTER LAMP, BORDEN AD CHARACTER, Reynolds collection, $30.00-65.00.

CAPTAIN GALLANT DESERT FORT GAME, 1956, pictures Buster Crabbe $20.00-45.00
CAPTAIN GALLANT FOREIGN LEGION HOLSTER SET, based upon 1950's television show $25.00-60.00

CAPTAIN KANGAROO'S FINGERPAINT SET, 1956 ....$15.00-30.00
CAPTAIN KANGAROO'S SCHOOL TABLET, circa 1950 ....$5.00-10.00
CAPTAIN MIDNIGHT COMIC BOOK, #23 ... $5.00-10.00
CAPTAIN MIDNIGHT CUP, Ovaltine Premium, 1930's-1940's, plastic with decal $15.00-35.00
CAPTAIN MIDNIGHT'S SECRET SOCIETY DECODER PIN, 1949 .... $15.00-35.00
CASPER THE FRIENDLY GHOST DOLL, 1960's, pull string, he talks, Mattel $15.00-35.00
CASPER THE FRIENDLY GHOST JACK IN THE BOX, Mattel, 1960's $10.00-20.00
CASPER THE GHOST GUITAR, crank with music box, 1959, Mattel $10.00-20.00
CASPER THE GHOST LITTLE GOLDEN RECORD, 1962 ....$3.00-6.00
CHARLIE McCARTHY AND MORTIMER SNERD PRIVATE CAR, 1939 Marx windup $300.00-650.00
CHARLIE McCARTHY BANK, composition, wears red beret, 6", 1930's $50.00-135.00
CHARLIE McCARTHY BOOK, A DAY WITH CHARLIE McCARTHY, red cover $35.00-65.00
CHARLIE McCARTHY BOOK, "Charlie McCarthy Meets Snow White," Whitman, 1930's $20.00-45.00
CHARLIE McCARTHY BOOK, SO HELP ME MISTER BERGEN, 1930's $20.00-35.00
CHARLIE McCARTHY BOXED RUMMY GAME, card set, 1939 .... $25.00-50.00
CHARLIE McCARTHY CARNIVAL GIVE-AWAY CHALK FIGURE, 1930's, 7½" $20.00-55.00
CHARLIE McCARTHY CHARACTER SALT AND PEPPER SHAKERS, ceramic, 1930's $15.00-40.00
CHARLIE McCARTHY COMIC BOOK, 1948 . $5.00-15.00
CHARLIE McCARTHY FIGURAL SOAP IN BOX, 1930's, Kerk Guild $25.00-60.00
CHARLIE McCARTHY FIGURAL SOAP, 1930's, in plastic cylinder container $35.00-75.00
CHARLIE McCARTHY GAME, RADIO PARTY, Chase and Sanborn premium, 1938 .... $30.00-60.00
CHARLIE McCARTHY GET WELL CARD, circa 1930 .... $10.00-25.00
CHARLIE McCARTHY JOINTED CARDBOARD PUPPET, premium, 1930's, 18" $45.00-110.00
CHARLIE McCARTHY PAINT BOOK, published 1930's $15.00-30.00
CHARLIE McCARTHY PAINT BOOK, by Whitman, 11" x 13½", 1938 .... $35.00-60.0
CHARLIE McCARTHY PLAY MONEY SET, original package $20.00-35.00
CHARLIE McCARTHY PUPPET, 12" tall, cloth and composition, 1930's $50.00-125.00
CHARLIE McCARTHY PUT AND TAKE BINGO GAME, Whitman, 1938, 9" x 15" $40.00-85.00
CHARLIE McCARTHY RADIO manufactured by Majestic, 1930's $300.00-550.00
CHARLIE McCARTHY SPOON, silverplate, circa 1930 .... $10.00-20.00
CHARLIE McCARTHY TIN WINDUP CAR "BENZINE BUGGY," 1930's, Marx $275.00-550.00
CHARLIE McCARTHY VENTRILOQUIST'S DOLL, by Effanbee, 17", 1930's $250.00-500.00

CHARLIE McCARTHY WINDUP WALKER TOY by Marx, 1939, tin lithograph $200.00-450.00

CHARLIE TUNA LAMP, plaster with original shade, 1960's $25.00-45.00

CHARLIE TUNA WRIST WATCH, 1960's $20.00-45.00

CLARABELL THE CLOWN (HOWDY DOODY) PUPPET, by Kohner, 1950's $15.00-40.00

CONCENTRATION NBC TELEVISION GAME, circa 1960..$5.00-15.00

DADDY WARBUCKS BISQUE FIGURE, 1930's, 3½", from set $30.00-60.00

DADDY WARBUCKS NODDER, Orphan Annie comic strip, 1930's, bisque, 3½" tall $45.00-75.00

DALE EVANS AND BUTTERMILK, by Whitman, 1956..$5.00-10.00

DALE EVANS BOXED HAT AND OUTFIT, 1950's set $45.00-90.00

DALE EVANS CHARACTER FIGURE, manufactured by Hartland plastic $60.00-100.00

DALE EVANS CHARACTER NECKLACE, on card, lucky horseshoe, 1950's $10.00-22.00

DALE EVANS HAT, 1950's, felt..............$10.00-20.00

DALE EVANS WRIST WATCH, made by U.S. Time $75.00-135.00

DANIEL BOONE COONSKIN CAP, 1950's, television version $15.00-25.00

DANIEL BOONE RIFLE, cap-shooting model, flintlock type $20.00-45.00

DARK SHADOWS GAME, 1960's, based on television series..$10.00-25.00

DENNIS THE MENACE BASEBALL GAME, 1960, lithograph, tin...$10.00-30.00

DENNIS THE MENACE FRAME TRAY PUZZLE, 1960, by Whitman $5.00-10.00

DENNIS THE MENACE FRAME TRAY PUZZLE, by Whitman, 1960 ....$5.00-10.00

DICK CLARK AMERICAN BANDSTAND PIN, 1950's $10.00-20.00

DING DONG SCHOOL SHAKE-UP MUG, Ovaltine premium, 1950's.......................................$15.00-30.00

DINO THE DINOSAUR CERAMIC BANK, circa 1960..$15.00-35.00

DINO THE DINOSAUR VINYL SQUEAK TOY, 1960, 12" $5.00-10.00

DOROTHY HAMILL DOLL, Ideal, 1977 ...$20.00-40.00

DR. KILDARE GAME, 1967 ....$15.00-30.00

DR. KILDARE MEDICAL GAME FOR THE YOUNG, 1962 board game by Ideal................$10.00-20.00

DR. KILDARE NOTEBOOK, 1962 ....$10.00-20.00

DRAGNET ADVENTURE BOOK, 1958......$5.00-10.00

DRAGNET CRIME LAB, complete boxed set, 1950's $20.00-45.00

DRAGNET GAME, 1967 ....$15.00-30.00

DRAGNET OFFICIAL TARGET, 1955......$15.00-40.00

DRAGNET PLASTIC DART GUN, 1955...$10.00-20.00

DRAGNET POLICE HOLSTER SET, 1955, box pictures Jack Webb $20.00-60.00

DRAGNET RADAR ACTION GAME, manufactured 1950's $15.00-35.00

DRAGNET TALKING POLICE CAR, manufactured 1950's $40.00-75.00

DRAGNET TRIPLE FIRE TARGET GAME, circa 1955..$25.00-60.00

ELMER FUDD cast metal planter, 1940's, 5".$50.00-85.00

ELSIE THE COW CREAM PITCHER, 1950's or 1960's $15.00-30.00

ELSIE THE COW FUNBOOK, 1950' $10.00-20.00

ELSIE THE COW SOAP FIGURE, boxed $25.00-50.00

ELSIE THE COW, COOKIE JAR Borden ad character $20.00-45.00

EMERGENCY TELEVISION SERIES LUNCH-BOX, television version $5.00-10.00

FAT ALBERT LUNCHBOX, 1970's $3.00-8.00

FAT ALBERT VINYL DOLL, 1970's $4.00-10.00

FIREBALL XL5 LUNCHBOX, 1960's $10.00-20.00

FLINTSTONES STONE AGE TIDDLEY WINKS GAME, 1961......................................$15.00-30.00

FLINTSTONES AND DINO LUNCHBOX, television version, 1962......................................$10.00-15.00

FLIP WILSON, GERALDINE DOLL, television character, 1970's $15.00-30.00

FLIPPER LUNCHBOX KIT, 1960's $5.00-10.00

FLUB-A-DUB PLASTIC HOWDY DOODY CHARACTER, boxed, 3½" tall.....................................$30.00-60.00

FRED FLINTSTONE RIDING DINO WINDUP TOY, Line-Mar, 1962, 8"......................................$70.00-140.00

FRED FLINTSTONE AND DINO BATTERY OPERATED TOY, LineMar, 22" long $100.00-275.00

FRED FLINTSTONE GAME, STONE AGE, Transogram, 1960's $10.00-25.00

FRED FLINTSTONE VINYL SQUEAK TOY, 1960, 12" $5.00-10.00

FURY COLORING BOOK, published by Whitman, 1958 ....$10.00-20.00

GENTLE BEN LUNCHBOX, 1960's $5.00-10.00

GREEN HORNET JIGSAW PUZZLE, boxed set of four $20.00-45.00

GREEN HORNET MILK GLASS MUG, manufactured 1966 ....$5.00-10.00

GREEN HORNET PLAYING CARDS, copyright 1966, boxed $10.00-15.00

GREEN HORNET SOCIETY BUTTON, 1950's or 1960's $5.00-10.00

GREEN HORNET VIEWMASTER REELS PACKAGE, 1960's $5.00-10.00

GROUCHO GOGGLES AND CIGAR SET ON CARD, by Eldon, 1950's...$20.00-40.00

GROUCHO MARX NECKTIE, 1950's $15.00-30.00

GROUCHO TELEVISION QUIZ GAME, television version,1954 ....$20.00-40.00

GUNSMOKE MARSHALL MATT DILLON HOSTER SET, 1950's $20.00-50.00

GUNSMOKE MARSHALL MATT DILLON LUNCHBOX, 1959..$10.00-20.00

GUNSMOKE, TELEVISION'S FAMOUS MARSHALL IN NEW ADVENTURES, book, 1966 ....$10.00-20.00

H. R. PUFNSTUF LUNCHBOX SET by Alladin, 1970's $3.00-8.00

HANNA BARBERA CHRISTMAS ALBUM, circa 1965 ....$3.00-5.0

HAVE GUN WILL TRAVEL PALLADIN LUNCHBOX, 1950's $15.00-30.00

HERMAN MUNSTER TALKING PUPPET, Mattel, 1964..$10.00-20.00

HIGHWAY PATROL DAN MATHEWS HOLSTER AND REVOLVER SET, Official, 1950's $20.00-40.00

FIBBER McGEE AND MOLLY GAME, Milton Bradley, Reynolds collection, $20.00-40.00.

HIGHWAY PATROL OFFICIAL SQUAD CAR ROAD SET, by Schuco, 1958 ....$50.00-100.00

HOWDY DOODY AND CLARABELL SLIPPER SOCK CRAFT KIT, 1950's, boxed $20.00-40.00

HOWDY DOODY BANK, plastic, flocked, National Broadcasting Company, 1960's $15.00-35.00

HOWDY DOODY BEAD GAME UNDER GLASS, 1950's $15.00-35.00

HOWDY DOODY BUBBLE BATH SET, circa 1950...$20.00-40.00

HOWDY DOODY BUBBLE PIPES, boxed set with two pipes $25.00-60.0

HOWDY DOODY CERAMIC CUP, manufactured 1950's $10.00-20.00

HOWDY DOODY CHARACTER BLOW UP WATER RING, 1950's, vinyl $10.00-30.00

HOWDY DOODY CHARACTER CLARABELL THE CLOWN MARIONETTE, 15", boxed ...$65.00-140.00

HOWDY DOODY CHARACTER DOLL, cloth body, composition head, 16", cowboy $100.00-200.00

HOWDY DOODY CHARACTER FLUB-A-DUB HAND PUPPET, Peter Puppet Playthings $25.00-50.00

HOWDY DOODY CHARACTER FLUB-A-DUB MARIONETTE, boxed, 1950's, rare $100.00-200.00

HOWDY DOODY CHARACTER GLASS LAMPSHADE, 1950's for overhead light $10.00-35.00

HOWDY DOODY CHARACTER UMBRELLA, 1950's, plastic handle $20.00-40.00

HOWDY DOODY CHILD'S FOOTBALL, circa 1950...$10.00-30.00

HOWDY DOODY CHILD'S THREE PIECE CERAMIC DINNER SETTING, 1950's $40.00-80.00

HOWDY DOODY CHRISTMAS CARD, 1950's, Kagran $5.00-10.00

HOWDY DOODY CHRISTMAS LIGHT, wall version with Santa, Royalite $20.00-45.00

HOWDY DOODY CLARABELL PUPPET MITTEN CRAFT KIT, 1950's.............................$20.00-40.00

HOWDY DOODY CLOCK-A-DOODLE, Bengor Company, mint in box $200.00-400.00

HOWDY DOODY COLOR TELEVISION TIME PICTURE SET, Donald Art Company, 1950's $30.00-60.00

HOWDY DOODY COLORING BOOK, Whitman, 1950's $5.00-15.00

HOWDY DOODY DELIVERY, LineMar friction toy, Clarabell steers cart, 6" $200.00-400.00

HOWDY DOODY EARMUFFS, vinyl Howdy head on each ear, 1950's $15.00-40.00

HOWDY DOODY ELECTRIC CARNIVAL GAME, by Wiry Dan Electric Games, 1950's $20.00-45.00

HOWDY DOODY FOLLOW THE DOTS BOOK, 1950's, Whitman $5.00-15.00

HOWDY DOODY FUDGE BAR WRAPPER, circa 1950...$20.00-30.00

HOWDY DOODY FUN BOOK, published by Whitman, 1951 ....$10.00-20.00

HOWDY DOODY IN THE WILD WEST BOOK, Simon and Schuster, 1952......................$10.00-20.00

HOWDY DOODY JIGSAW PUZZLE, 1950's, with Polly Parrot ad $35.00-50.00

HOWDY DOODY MAGIC KIT, 1950's $20.00-40.00

HOWDY DOODY MAGIC PUZZLE BALL, on original card, Kagran $20.00-55.00

HOWDY DOODY MAKE IT YOURSELF BEE-NEE KIT, 1950's, boxed $25.00-50.00

HOWDY DOODY MAKE YOUR HOWDY DOODY PUPPET SHOW, punch-out book, by Whitman, 1952...$20.00-40.00

HOWDY DOODY MARIONETTE, boxed, circa 1950, 16" $40.00-95.00

HOWDY DOODY FIGURE, by Mars Candy, premium..$10.00-20.00

HOWDY DOODY MISTER BLUSTER MARIONETTE, boxed, 15"...$50.00-125.00

HOWDY DOODY MUSICAL ROCKING CHAIR, 1950's $50.00-100.00

HOWDY DOODY NITE LIGHT, 1950's, 7" seated, Nor'East Nauticals $25.00-60.00

HOWDY DOODY OVALTINE PREMIUM PLASTIC CUP with decal, 3" $15.00-35.00

HOWDY DOODY PAINT SET, boxed, manufactured 1950's $15.00-35.00

HOWDY DOODY PALMOLIVE SOAP AD FIGURE, 7" tall, 1950's $15.00-30.00

HOWDY DOODY PHONO DOODLE, record player, 1950's $75.00-125.00

HOWDY DOODY PLASTIC CAKE DECORATIONS, 1950's $10.00-20.00

HOWDY DOODY PLASTIC DOLL FIGURE, movable mouth, 6", 1950's...........................$35.00-60.00

HOWDY DOODY PRINCESS SUMMER, FALL, WINTER, SPRING MARIONETTE, boxed, 14" $50.00-125.00

HOWDY DOODY PUPPET SHOW FIGURES ON ORIGINAL CARD, 1950's $30.00-75.00

HOWDY DOODY PUSH-PUPPET by Kohner, 1950's, 5" $20.00-50.00

HOWDY DOODY PUZZLE TOY KEY CHAIN, 1950's, 2" on original card $10.00-20.00

HOWDY DOODY RUBBER BALL, 1950's, 4½" diameter $15.00-30.0

HOWDY DOODY SAND SET, on original card, 1954, plastic $25.00-60.00

HOWDY DOODY SHOE POLISH by Kunkel, 1950's, boxed $10.00-18.00

HOWDY DOODY SODA STRAW HOLDER, 1950's, in original box.....................................$20.00-30.00

HOWDY DOODY STRING CLIMBING TOY, 1950's $20.00-40.00

HOWDY DOODY TRAPEZE TOY made in Western Germany, Toy Novelty Associates $75.00-140.00

HOWDY DOODY UKE by Emenee, 1950's, 17", boxed $35.00-75.00

HOWDY DOODY WINDUP PIANO AND DANCER, Unique Art, 8½" $250.00-475.00

HOWDY DOODY WOOD JOINTED DOLL, 13", original decal on stomach $75.00-195.00

HOWDY DOODY WRIST WATCH, 1950's, Ideal watch, original display case $50.00-125.00

HOWDY DOODY'S AIR DOODLE CIRCUS TRAIN by Kagran, 1950's, plastic, 16" $50.00-100.00

HOWDY DOODY'S CHILD'S PLATE, 1950's, large size, ceramic $20.00-30.00

HOWDY DOODY'S CHINA CEREAL BOWL, 1950's $10.00-25.00

HOWDY DOODY'S OFFICIAL OUTDOORS SPORTS BOX, tin, 1950's $20.00-35.00

HOWDY DOODY'S OWN GAME, ball roller game with targets, by Parker Brothers...............$20.00-50.00

HOWDY DOODY'S THREE RING CIRCUS, Wiry Dan Electric, 1950's, battery operated $25.00-65.00

HOWDY DOODY, SURPRISE FOR HOWDY DOODY, Tell a Tale Books, 1950......................$5.00-10.00

HUCKLEBERRY HOUND CAMERA by Sun-Pix, 1964..$10.00-20.00

HUCKLEBERRY HOUND CHARM BRACELET, 1959 ....$10.00-20.00

HUCLEBERRY HOUND CLUB OFFICIAL CLUB PICTURE, 1960's $5.00-10.00

HUCKLEBERRY HOUND CUFF LINKS AND TIE CLIP SET, 1959 ....$5.00-15.00

I DREAM OF JEANNIE BOARD GAME, 1965, by Milton Bradley $10.00-25.00

I DREAM OF JEANNIE DOLL, 19", Libby Majorette Doll Corporation, 1966, boxed $25.00-70.00

IT'S ABOUT TIME LUNCHBOX by Alladin, circa 1960 ....$4.00-8.0

J. FRED MUGGS (NBC CHIMP) PULL TOY by N. N. Hill Brass, 1950's, 9" $50.00-100.00

J. FRED MUGGS CHIMP FROM NBC HAND PUPPET, 1954..$20.00-40.00

J. FRED MUGGS HAND PUPPET, 1950's, Maytag ad piece...$10.00-20.00

JACK WEBB'S SAFETY SQUAD COLORING BOOK, 1955...$10.00-20.00

JACKIE GLEASON AND AWAY WE GO GAME, by Transogram, 1956, 10" x 19" $25.00-55.00

JACKIE GLEASON AND HIS TELEVISION TROUPE GAME, 1955 VIP Corporation $60.00-95.00

JACKIE GLEASON BUS DRIVER'S OUTFIT, Empire Plastics, boxed, 1956 ....$50.00-90.00

JACKIE GLEASON COLORING BOOK, published 1956...$5.00-15.00

JACKIE GLEASON FUNNY BOOK FOR BOYS AND GIRLS, Lowe, 1956 ....$10.00-20.00

JAN MURRAY'S TREASURE HUNT BOARD GAME...$10.00-20.00

JERRY MAHONEY AND PAUL WINCHELL TELEVISON CLUB RECORD by Decca $10.00-20.00

JIM HENSON'S MUPPET SHOW THERMOS, 1970's $5.00-7.00

JOE PENNER AND GOO-GOO MARX WINDUP, 1930's $250.00-500.00

KUKLA AND OLLIE A GAME BASED ON THE NBC TELEVISION PROGRAM, circa 1962, Parker Brothers $10.00-25.00

KUKLA SILVERPLATED CHILD'S SPOON, 1960's $5.00-12.00

LASSIE COLORING BOOK SET by Whitman, dozen in box $10.00-30.00

LASSIE PLASTIC FIGURE "TENITE" in original box, 1960's $30.00-50.00

LAWRENCE WELK AND THE LENNON SISTERS SNACK TRAY, tin, 1960's $15.00-30.00

LEAVE IT TO BEAVER BOOK by Whitman, 1962..5.00-10.00

LEAVE IT TO BEAVER MONEY MAKER BOARD GAME, Gomalco Productions, 1950's $15.00-35.00

LEAVE IT TO BEAVER ROCKET TO THE MOON SPACE GAME, 1959 ....$15.00-30.00

LEAVE IT TO BEAVER, A COLORING BOOK, Saalfield Publishing, 1958............................$10.00-20.00

LEAVE IT TO BEAVER, BEAVER AND WALLY MAGIC SLATE, 1950's $5.00-20.00

LITTLE ORPHAN ANNIE $1,000,000, Big Little Book, 1930's $15.00-30.00

LITTLE ORPHAN ANNIE A WILLING HELPER, book, Cupples and Leon, 1932 ....$20.00-45.00

HOWDY DOODY TRAPEZE TOY, tin and composition, Reynolds collection, $75.00-135.00.

205

TELEVISION AND RADIO TOYS

LITTLE ORPHAN ANNIE AND CHIZZLER, Big Little Book 1930's $15.00-30.00

LITTLE ORPHAN ANNIE AND DADDY WARBUCKS, Little Library, 1930's $10.00-20.00

LITTLE ORPHAN ANNIE AND HER DOG SANDY, book, Little Library, 1930's $10.00-20.00

LITTLE ORPHAN ANNIE AND SANDY TOOTHBRUSH HOLDER, seated on couch, 1930's .$70.00-140.00

LITTLE ORPHAN ANNIE AND SANDY BISQUE TOOTHBRUSH HOLDER, 5", 1930's $75.00-150.00

LITTLE ORPHAN ANNIE AND SANDY LUSTERWARE ASH TRAY, 1930's, glazed, 3".........$45.00-100.00

LITTLE ORPHAN ANNIE AND THE CIRCUS, Big Little Book, 1930's $15.00-30.00

LITTLE ORPHAN ANNIE AND THE GHOST GANG, Big Little Book, 1930's $15.00-30.00

LITTLE ORPHAN ANNIE AND THE GOONEYVILLE MYSTERY, Better Little Books $12.00-25.00

LITTLE ORPHAN ANNIE AND THE HAUNTED HOUSE, book, Cupples and Leon, 1928.........$20.00-45.00

LITTLE ORPHAN ANNIE AND THE LUCKY KNIFE, book, Little Library, 1930's $10.00-20.00

LITTLE ORPHAN ANNIE AND THE MYSTERIOUS SPICE MAKER, Big Little Books $15.00-30.00

LITTLE ORPHAN ANNIE AND UNCLE DAN, Cupples and Leon, book, 1930's......................$20.00-45.00

LITTLE ORPHAN ANNIE AT HAPPY HOME, book, Little Library, 1930's $10.00-20.00

LITTLE ORPHAN ANNIE BEAD GAME "Light up the Candles," 1930's, under glass............$30.00-65.00

LITTLE ORPHAN ANNIE BEAD GAME TOY, 1930's, 3½" x 5", glass cover $50.00-95.00

LITTLE ORPHAN ANNIE BIG PAINT AND CRAYON BOOK 1930's, Brunette Annie $20.00-40.00

LITTLE ORPHAN ANNIE BOARD GAME, Milton Bradley, 1927 ....$30.00-65.00

LITTLE ORPHAN ANNIE BOOK, Cupples and Leon, 1925, early, she carries doll $30.00-50.00

LITTLE ORPHAN ANNIE BOXED BISQUE SET, 1930's, Sandy, Annie, Daddy, radio $125.00-250.00

LITTLE ORPHAN ANNIE BUBBLE SET, beautiful box lid with bubbles, 1930's..................$65.00-125.00

LITTLE ORPHAN ANNIE BUCKING THE WORLD, book, Cupples and Leon, 1929 ....$20.00-45.00

LITTLE ORPHAN ANNIE CELLULOID DOLL, 1930's, Japan 7½" tall, rare $150.00-400.00

LITTLE ORPHAN ANNIE CHARACTER DECORATED TABLECLOTH, 1930's, paper.............$40.00-80.00

LITTLE ORPHAN ANNIE CHINA TEA SET, fifteen pieces, colorful design, 1930's $100.00-200.00

LITTLE ORPHAN ANNIE CLOTHES PINS on original card, 1930's $35.00-65.00

LITTLE ORPHAN ANNIE COLOR BOOK, 1930's, McLoughlin, Annie paints sign...........$20.00-45.00

LITTLE ORPHAN ANNIE COLORING BOOK, 1943, Saalfield, large format $25.00-50.00

LITTLE ORPHAN ANNIE COMPOSITION DOLL, 1930's, original box, 10" tall $125.00-275.00

LITTLE ORPHAN ANNIE CRAYON AND COLORING BOOK, McLoughlin, 1933 ....$30.00-60.00

LITTLE ORPHAN ANNIE CRAYON SET, 1930's, Milton Bradley, 10" x 14" box $60.00-110.00

LITTLE ORPHAN ANNIE CRAYONS, boxed set, 4" x 8",

colorful, Milton Bradley $35.00-75.00

LITTLE ORPHAN ANNIE ELECTRIC STOVE, metal, 1930's, green and beige, works $25.00-65.00

LITTLE ORPHAN ANNIE ELECTRIC STOVE, red, works when plugged in, 8" tall $25.00-50.00

LITTLE ORPHAN ANNIE EMBROIDERY SPOOL, 1930's, from set, Annie figure $20.00-35.00

LITTLE ORPHAN ANNIE EMBROIDERY SET, 1930's, J. Pressman, Circus Animals $100.00-200.00

LITTLE ORPHAN ANNIE FAMOUS COMICS JIGSAW PUZZLE, Stephens and Kindred $35.00-70.00

LITTLE ORPHAN ANNIE FINDS MICKEY, book, Little Library, 1930's..................................$10.00-20.00

LITTLE ORPHAN ANNIE HANKY HOLDER PURSE IN BOX, 1930's $35.00-75.00

LITTLE ORPHAN ANNIE HINGEES, paper figures set, 1944...$10.00-25.00

LITTLE ORPHAN ANNIE IN COSMIC CITY, Cupples and Leon, book, 1940's.......................$20.00-45.00

LITTLE ORPHAN ANNIE IN THE CIRCUS, Cupples and Leon, book, 1930's.......................$20.00-45.00

LITTLE ORPHAN ANNIE JACKS SET on original 1930's card $25.00-65.00

LITTLE ORPHAN ANNIE KNITTING OUTFIT, 1930's, J. Pressman, boxed $50.00-100.00

LITTLE ORPHAN ANNIE KNITTING OUTFIT, J. Pressman, 1930's, colorful box $50.00-100.00

LITTLE ORPHAN ANNIE MINIATURE BOOKS, Little Library, complete set of six $65.00-125.00

LITTLE ORPHAN ANNIE LUSTERWARE TEA SET, 1930's, five pieces $40.00-80.00

LITTLE ORPHAN ANNIE MOCCASINS, box only, 1930's, colorful art $35.00-70.00

LITTLE ORPHAN ANNIE MUG, 1930's, ceramic, Ovaltine premium, 3"......................................$20.00-45.00

LITTLE ORPHAN ANNIE NAPKIN RING, tin, enameled, bright colors, 1930's.........................$35.00-65.00

LITTLE ORPHAN ANNIE, "NEVER SAY DIE," Cupples and Leon, book, 1930's.......................$20.00-45.00

LITTLE ORPHAN ANNIE OILCLOTH DOLL, 1930's, red dress, 13".......................................$100.00-200.00

LITTLE ORPHAN ANNIE OILCLOTH DOLL, blue polka-dot dress, 1930's, 15" $75.00-150.00

LITTLE ORPHAN ANNIE OILCLOTH DOLL, bright red dress, marked Harold Gray, 10" $100.00-175.00

LITTLE ORPHAN ANNIE PAINT SET, Milton Bradley, 1930's, large set $40.00-80.00

LITTLE ORPHAN ANNIE PAPER COSTUME SET, television company premium, 1940's $20.00-40.00

LITTLE ORPHAN ANNIE PLASTIC "BEETLEWARE CUP," Ovaltine premium, 3" $15.00-30.00

LITTLE ORPHAN ANNIE PLASTIC OVALTINE PREMIUM CUP, green, 4" $20.00-40.00

LITTLE ORPHAN ANNIE POP-UP BOOK, by Pleasure Books, 1935 ....$100.00-200.00

LITTLE ORPHAN ANNIE PULL TOY, Annie pulled by Sandy, 8", yellow Sandy....................$45.00-85.00

LITTLE ORPHAN ANNIE RUMMY CARDS, Whitman, 1935 ....$20.00-40.00

LITTLE ORPHAN ANNIE RUMMY CARDS, Whitman, 1937, blue box $25.00-55.00

LITTLE ORPHAN ANNIE SHEET MUSIC, 1925, color cover $50.00-95.00

LITTLE ORPHAN ANNIE BOOK, "SHIPWRECKED," Cupples and Leon, 1931 ....$20.00-45.00

LITTLE ORPHAN ANNIE STOVE, two-tone blue version, 1930's, non-electric $20.00-45.00

LITTLE ORPHAN ANNIE TIN WINDUP ROPE JUMPER, Marx, 1930's $200.00-400.00

LITTLE ORPHAN ANNIE TRAVEL GAME, Milton Bradley, 1930's, 7" x 13" $50.00-100.00

LITTLE ORPHAN ANNIE WALL POCKET, lusterware, 1930's $35.00-75.00

LITTLE ORPHAN ANNIE WOOD JOINTED FIGURE, 1930's, 5" tall $60.00-125.00

LITTLE ORPHAN ANNIE WOODEN PULL TOY, by Trixitoy, 1930's, 13" $40.00-85.00

LITTLE ORPHAN ANNIE'S COLORING BOOK, 1943, 11" x 15" $30.00-60.00

LITTLE ORPHAN ANNIE'S RADIO SECRET SOCIETY MANUAL, 1936 ....$30.00-60.00

LITTLE ORPHAN ANNIE'S TREASURE HUNT BOARD GAME, Wander Company, 11" x 17" ...$35.00-75.00

LITTLE ORPHAN ANNIE, Big Crayon Book, McLoughlin Brothers, 1935 ....$20.00-45.00

LITTLE ORPHAN ANNIE BOOK, The Story of, Big Big Book by Whitman, 1934 ....$50.00-80.00

LONE RANGER LUNCHBOX, 1950's $10.00-25.00

LOST IN SPACE GAME, by Milton Bradley, 1965 ....$15.00-35.00

LOST IN SPACE LUNCHBOX, 1967........$10.00-15.00

LUCILLE BALL AND DESI ARNAZ COLORING BOOK, fifty pages, 1950's $15.00-30.00

LUCY, DESI, LITTLE RICKY COLORING BOOK, by Dell, copyright 1955 ....$10.00-20.00

MAN FROM U.N.C.L.E. ILLYA KURYAKIN CARD GAME, 1960's $10.00-20.00

MAN FROM U.N.C.L.E. VIEWMASTER REEL SET, 1960's television show.................$5.00-10.00

MARSHALL MATT DILLON GUNSMOKE HOLSTER SET, 1960's $20.00-50.00

MISTER MAGOO DOLL WITH JOINTED LEGS, 16" tall.............................$50.00-125.00

MISTER MAGOO GLASS TUMBLER, dated 1963 ....$5.00-10.00

MISTER SPOCK KITE in original wrapper, 1970's $5.00-8.00

MONKEES BOOK, "WHO'S GOT THE BUTTON," 1968 ....$5.00-8.00

MONKEES VIEWMASTER THREE REEL SET, 1960's, television show $5.00-10.00

MONKEES, THE LUNCHBOX, with thermos, 1967 ....$10.00-20.00

MORTIMER SNERD CRAZY CAR tin windup toy, by Marx, 1939 ....$250.00-475.00

MORTIMER SNERD JACK-IN-THE-BOX, composition....................................$50.00-100.00

MORTIMER SNERD JOINTED CARDBOARD PUPPET, 1930's, 18" $35.00-75.00

MORTIMER SNERD WINDUP WALKER TOY, by Marx, 1930's $150.00-300.00

MR. ED BOARD GAME by Parker Brothers, 1962 ....$10.00-20.00

MR. NOVAK GAME, Transogram, 1963 ..$10.00-20.00

MUNSTERS CARD GAME, by Milton Bradley, 1966 ....$10.00-15.00

MUNSTERS PAPER DOLLS by Whitman, 1966 ....$5.00-15.00

MUNSTERS THEATRE GUM BOX AND WRAPPERS SET, Leaf, 1964 ....$15.00-25.00

MY FAVORITE MARTIAN GAME, 1963 ..$10.00-25.00

NAPOLEON SOLO, MAN FROM UNCLE GAME, Ideal, 1965 ....$10.00-20.00

OLLIE BAKES A CAKE, Wonder Book, 1964 from Kukla, Fran and Ollie show $5.00-10.00

ORPHAN ANNIE BISQUE FIGURE, 1930's, 1½" tall miniature $20.00-45.00

ORPHAN ANNIE BISQUE NODDER, 2½" tall, 1930's $45.00-75.00

ORPHAN ANNIE BISQUE FIGURE, 3½" tall, red dress, from 1930's set $30.00-60.00

ORPHAN ANNIE BISQUE FIGURE, 1930's, 3", red dress $30.00-60.00

ORPHAN ANNIE WATCH, 1930's, Annie and Sandy on box lid, New Haven Clock.......$125.00-275.00

PALADIN WESTERN TELEVISION CHARACTER GUN AND HOLSTER SET, 9" guns $20.00-45.00

PARTRIDGE FAMILY LUNCHBOX, 1971 ....$3.00-7.00

PATTY DUKE GAME, 1963 ....$5.00-10.00

PEANUTS THE GAME OF CHARLIE BROWN AND HIS PALS, 1959 board game $10.00-20.00

PERRY MASON CASE OF THE MISSING SUSPECT GAME, 1950's $15.00-25.00

PETER GUNN DETECTIVE GAME, 1960 ...$15.00-30.00

PHIL SILVERS, SGT. BILKO, "YOU'LL NEVER GET RICH" GAME, 1950's $15.00-40.00

PORKY PIG BANK, BISQUE, 5".............$30.00-65.00

PORKY PIG CAST METAL PLANTER, 1940's, 5" $50.00-85.00

PORKY PIG CHALK FIGURE, a carnival give-away toy $10.00-30.00

PORKY PIG PENCIL HOLDER, cast metal construction $20.00-40.00

PORKY PIG WRIST WATCH, Warner Brothers Cartoons, 1949, Ingraham $100.00-200.00

QUICK DRAW McGRAW STUFFED PLUSH TOY, 1960's $10.00-20.00

RADIO ORPHAN ANNIE SECRET DECODER PIN, 1936 ....$20.00-40.00

RADIO ORPHAN ANNIE SECRET DECODER PIN, 1937 ....$20.00-40.00

RADIO ORPHAN ANNIE SECRET DECODER PIN, 1938 ....$20.00-40.00

RADIO ORPHAN ANNIE SECRET SOCIETY MEMBERSHIP CERTIFICATE, 1937, roll call .$20.00-40.00

RADIO ORPHAN ANNIE'S SECRET SOCIETY MANUAL, 1937 ....$25.00-50.00

RADIO ORPHAN ANNIE'S SECRET SOCIETY MANUAL, 1938, colorful cover $20.00-45.00

RALPH EDWARDS THIS IS YOUR LIFE GAME, 1950's-1960's $10.00-20.00

RAT PATROL LUNCHBOX, 1960's $5.00-10.00

RIFLEMAN, THE, BOARD GAME, dated 1959 television version $10.00-25.00

RIN TIN TIN AT FORT APACHE PLAYSET by Marx, boxed $30.00-65.00

RIN TIN TIN COMPASS AND VIEWER, circa 1950..................................$35.00-70.00

RIN RIN TIN COMPASS, television version toy $35.00-60.00

RIN TIN TIN FIGURAL PLASTER LAMP, 14" tall, rare $100.00-200.00

RIN TIN TIN GAME, 1950 ....$20.00-30.00

RIN TIN TIN RIFLE PEN, 1950's, in original package $35.00-65.00

RIN TIN TIN STICKERS SET, package of six, 1950's $10.00-20.00

RIN TIN TIN WONDA SCOPE, 1950's, television series...$20.00-40.00

RIN TIN TIN RUSTY CHARACTER CAVALRY MASK, Nabisco premium.................................$10.00-25.00

ROBIN THE BOY WONDER MODEL KIT by Aurora, 1966 ....$20.00-40.00

ROOTIE KAZOOTIE hand puppet $15.00-30.00

ROOTIE KAZOOTIE DRUM, 8" diameter $10.00-20.00

ROOTIE KAZOOTIE TELEVISION PUPPET SHOW SET WITH THREE PUPPETS, 1940's $30.00-50.00

ROOTY KAZOOTY RECORD, Little Golden.$5.00-10.00

ROUTE 66 TRAVEL GAME, Travel with Todd and Buzz, transogram, 1962 ....$15.00-30.00

ROY ROGERS AND DALE EVANS COLORING BOOK, 1951, Whitman $15.00-25.00

ROY ROGERS AND DALE EVANS CUT-OUT PAPER DOLLS BOOK, Whitman, 1954..........$25.00-50.00

ROY ROGERS AND DALE EVANS PAPER DOLL BOOK, 1950's, Whitman $15.00-35.00

ROY ROGERS AND DALE EVANS RECORD, 78 rpm. original sleeve, 1950's $5.00-10.00

ROY ROGERS AND DALE EVANS THERMOS AND LUNCHBOX KIT, 1960's $15.00-35.00

ROY ROGERS AND TRIGGER METAL CATTLE TRUCK, by Marx, 15", 1950's........................$65.00-125.00

ROY ROGERS AND TRIGGER POST CARD, fan club, 1955..$10.00-30.00

ROY ROGERS AND TRIGGER BANDANA, 1950's...$10.00-20.00

ROY ROGERS ARCADE CARD, 1950's.....$7.00-20.00

ROY ROGERS BOLO TIE on the original card..$10.00-15.00

ROY ROGERS BOOK, ROY ROGERS AND THE MOUNTAIN LION, 1955 ....$5.00-10.00

ROY ROGERS BOXED PAINT SET, 1950's, 10" x 14"...$25.00-55.00

ROY ROGERS CAMERA, Herbert George Company, 1950's $20.00-40.00

ROY ROGERS CHUCK WAGON, 1950's $75.00-105.00

ROY ROGERS CLOCK, Roy figure moves (animated) by Ingraham...$50.00-100.00

ROY ROGERS COLORING BOOK, 1951 .$15.00-25.00

ROY ROGERS COWBOY OUTFIT WITH SPURS, GLOVES, ETC. original box, 1950's ..$80.00-140.00

ROY ROGERS DEPUTY BADGE on original card, tin, 1950's $10.00-22.00

ROY ROGERS DISPLAY PLATE, 1950's .$20.00-45.00

ROY ROGERS FIGURAL PLASTIC MUG, 4" tall, painted $15.00-35.00

ROY ROGERS FIX-IT STAGECOACH, in original box $35.00-65.00

ROY ROGERS GUITAR, 28", pictures Roy and Trigger on front $40.00-80.00

ROY ROGERS GUN AND HOLSTER, red holster, gun 5" long, small version $20.00-50.00

ROY ROGERS HAPPY TRAILS BUTTON, pinback $5.00-10.00

ROY ROGERS HARMONICA on original display card $35.00-55.00

ROY ROGERS HORSESHOE GAME by Ohio Art, 1950's in original package $40.00-80.00

ROY ROGERS LAMP, 24" tall, plaster-cast, 1950's $75.00-135.00

ROY ROGERS LARIAT FLASHLIGHT on original card, 1950's $40.00-70.00

ROY ROGERS LUNCHBOX, 1950's $5.00-10.00

ROY ROGERS MINI-GUN on original card, 1950's $10.00-30.00

ROY ROGERS NECKERCHIEF SLIDE, gun shape, 1950's $20.00-30.00

ROY ROGERS NELLYBELLE JEEP with figures $25.00-50.00

ROY ROGERS PAINT BY NUMBER SET, circa 1950 ....$25.00-60.00

ROY ROGERS PLASTIC FIGURE, Hartland, Roy on Trigger, horse rearing up $80.00-135.00

ROY ROGERS PLAYING CARDS, 1950's.$15.00-25.00

ROY ROGERS RANCH CALENDAR, dated 1959 ....$50.00-100.00

ROY ROGERS RANCH LANTERN, Ohio Art Company, original box $35.00-85.00

ROY ROGERS RIFLE by Marx, 1950's, 26" long $25.00-65.00

ROY ROGERS RODEO BOXED PLAYSET by Marx, 1960's, plastic figures $25.00-75.00

ROY ROGERS RODEO GAME, manufactured 1950's, boxed $35.00-75.00

ROY ROGERS SPURS pair with jewels...$10.00-25.00

ROY ROGERS STAGECOACH PLAYSET, with original box, 1950's $40.00-80.00

ROY ROGERS STRAIGHT SHOOTER GUN PUZZLE, 1950's, plastic on card $25.00-50.00

ROY ROGERS TENT (in original the box) 1950's $60.00-95.00

ROY ROGERS TOY WAGON, 1950's, 16" x 27", child's wagon $50.00-125.00

ROY ROGERS TUCK AWAY CAP GUN on original card $15.00-25.00

ROY ROGERS VINYL WALLET, 1950's $5.00-10.00

ROY ROGERS WITH TRIGGER BELT BUCKLE, 1950's $35.00-60.00

SANDY (ORPHAN ANNIE) character bisque figure, 1930's, 1" $20.00-40.00

SANDY (ORPHAN ANNIE) BISQUE, 1930's, 2" tall..$20.00-45.00

SANDY (ORPHAN ANNIE) BISQUE, 2½" tall, 1930's, German $30.00-60.00

SANDY (ORPHAN ANNIE) OILCLOTH DOLL, 1930's, 8" tall..$50.00-125.00

SANDY JOINTED WOOD FIGURE, 1930's, 3½" tall..$45.00-85.00

SANDY JOINTED WOOD FIGURE, 4" tall..$50.00-100.00

SANDY TIN CAT AND BALL TOY, lever action windup tail, 8" long, 1930's $100.00-200.00

SANDY TIN WINDUP DOG (ORPHAN ANNIE), Marx, 1930's $100.00-250.00

SCOOBY DOO RUBBER SQUEEZE TOY, 1970's $3.00-5.00

SHARI LEWIS AND HER PUPPETS COLORING BOOK by Saalfield, 1960's $5.00-10.00

SHARI LEWIS AND HER PUPPETS TREASURE BOARD MAGIC SLATE, Saalfield $5.00-15.00

SHARI LEWIS' LAMB CHOP PUPPET DOLL, 1960's, 11" tall $10.00-25.00

SKIPPY CHARACTER BISQUE, 5", extremely colorful, one jointed arm, 1930's $50.00-125.00

SKIPPY CHARACTER MUG, silverplate with whistle on cup handle, 3" $25.00-60.00

SKIPPY DOLL, by Effanbee, dressed as little sailor, 1930's or 1940's $75.00-135.00

SKIPPY IN JIGSAW CHARACTER PUZZLE SET, 1930's, Percy Crosby $30.00-65.00

SKIPPY JIGSAW PUZZLE, 1933, manufactured by Skippy Incorporated $10.00-30.00

SKIPPY RADIO CHARACTER SHEET MUSIC, Percy Crosby, 1930's $10.00-25.00

SKIPPY SILVERWARE SET, International Silver Company, character decorate, 1930's $50.00-125.00

SKY KING BRASS DETECTO WRITER, circa 1960 ....$35.00-60.00

SKY KING DETECTO WRITER, 1950's ..$20.00-40.00

SKY KING SECRET SIGNALSCOPE, manufactured 1960's $20.00-40.00

SKY KING TELEBLINKER, 1950's $40.00-80.00

SOUPY SALES BOOK by Wonder Books, circa 1965..$3.00-6.00

STAR TREK, ENTERPRISE LOGS, Western Publishing, 1977 ....$10.00-20.00

STAR TREK LUNCHBOX AND THERMOS, manufactured 1960's $10.00-20.00

STAR TREK RAPID FIRE TRACER GUN, 1967 in original package $15.00-40.00

TALE OF WELLS FARGO GAME, 1959, boxed board game $15.00-30.00

THE FLYING NUN GAME, by Milton Bradley, 1968...$5.00-10.00

THE MAN FROM U.N.C.L.E. ACTION FIGURE ACCESSORIES, Gilbert, 1965 ....$15.00-30.00

THE MAN FROM U.N.C.L.E. PLAYING CARDS, 1965...$5.00-10.00

THE MAN FROM U.N.C.L.E. soft cover book by Wonder Books, 1960's $3.00-7.00

THE MAN FROM U.N.C.L.E. TOY CAR, by Corgi, 1960's $15.00-25.00

THE MAN FROM U.N.C.L.E. TELEVISION ACTION FIGURE APPAREL, Gilbert, 1960's ...$20.00-40.00

THE MUNSTERS CARD GAME, 1960's, by Milton Bradley...$5.00-10.00

THE PRICE IS RIGHT BOARD GAME, 1958, original $10.00-30.00

THE UNTOUCHABLES PLAYSET manufactured by Marx $50.00-120.00

TOPO GIGIO MOUSE (ED SULLIVAN) 11" tall vinyl toy figure, 1960's $10.00-20.00

UNCLE FESTER'S MYSTERY LIGHT BULB from the Adams Family, 1960's $10.00-25.00

UNTOUCHABLES MACHINE GUN, battery operated, Desilu Productions 1960's $35.00-60.00

VIDEO VILLAGE TELEVISION GAME based on television show, 1960, Milton Bradley $10.00-25.00

VOYAGE TO THE BOTTOM OF THE SEA LUNCHBOX AND THERMOS, 1960's $10.00-20.00

WAGON TRAIN WESTERN TELEVISION SERIES LUNCHBOX, 1950's $5.00-20.00

WALT DISNEY'S WONDERFUL WORLD OF COLOR TELEVISION TRAY, metal, 1960's $10.00-20.00

WINKY DINK AND YOU MAGIC TELEVISION KIT, 1950's $20.00-40.00

WINKY DINK LITTLE GOLDEN BOOK, 1956..$10.00-15.00

WINKY DINK WINKO MAGIC SET, by Pressman Toys, CBS television $30.00-60.00

WONDER WOMAN HAND MIRROR, 1970's ..$3.00-6.00

WOODY WOODPECKER LUNCHBOX, manufactured 1960's $5.00-10.00

WYATT EARP TELEVISON BOARD GAME, dated 1958, boxed $15.00-30.00

WYATT EARP COLORING BOOK, 1950's$10.00-20.00

WYATT EARP GUN AND HOLSTER SET, no box $25.00-65.00

WYATT EARP GUN by Hubley, 1959, original package $20.00-45.00

WYATT EARP HARTLAND FIGURE, on horseback, 1950's $50.00-110.00

WYATT EARP MILK GLASS MUG, 1950's ..$5.00-10.00

WYATT EARP TWO GUN AND HOLSTER SET, by Hubley, box picture Hugh O'Brian $45.00-90.00

YOGI BEAR CARTOON GAME, 1950's, boxed board game $5.00-15.00

YOGI BEAR CHARACTER CERAMIC COOKIE JAR, 1960's $15.00-35.00

YOGI BEAR CHARACTER POSTCARD, multi-colored, 1963..$4.00-8.00

ZORRO BOOK by Whitman, 1958 ....$5.00-15.00

ZORRO CHARM BRACELET with various Zorro emblems, 1950's $10.00-20.00

ZORRO CHARM BRACELET, 1960's, ...$20.00-35.00

ZORRO COSTUME, not Halloween $20.00-35.00

ZORRO HAND PUPPET, 1950's, probably by Gund, Disney $10.00-20.00

ZORRO HAND PUPPET, cloth and vinyl, 1960's $8.00-15.00

ZORRO HAT WITH MASK ATTACHED, by Bailey Company, Walt Disney, 1950's $35.00-70.00

ZORRO LUNCHBOX, 1958, metal $10.00-20.00

ZORRO OFFICIAL SHOOTING OUTFIT, Daisy gun, rifle, cuffs, belt, boxed $65.00-125.00

ZORRO PENCIL HOLDER AND PENCIL SHARPENER, ceramic, 6", Disney Productions $35.00-65.00

ZORRO SECRET SCARF MASK, 1950's, on original card $25.00-55.00

ZORRO SECRET SIGHT MASK on card, 1950's $10.00-20.00

ZORRO TARGET GAME, 1950's with dart gun, Knickerbocker Plastic Company $30.00-95.00

ZORRO WATER PISTOL by Knickerbocker Plastic Company $20.00-40.00

ZORRO WHIP SET by Shimmel Sons, 1950's, whip, mask on display card $30.00-70.00

VICTORIAN AND EARLY TOYS, 1800'S TO 1919

Victorian toys, like the Victorian period in English history, generally begins with the latter half of the 19th Century and continues on through the first decade or so of this century. For the sake of the organization of this chapter, this listing will include toys manufactured through 1919.

Victorian and early 20th century toys closely follow and mirror the development of the Industrial Revolution in America and abroad. During the first half of the 19th Century, most European and American toys were handmade by craftsmen and artisans and such a limited number of these folk-art pieces were made that they are not readily available to today's collectors. So, the collectors of today usually begin their collections chronologically with toys produced since the Industrial Revolution.

This revolution was important to toy production since it allowed for machining of toy designs rather than hand carving or hand production. As the American auto industry developed mass production at the initiation of Henry Ford, toys became less the property of only the elite or rich and more the property of the middle class who could now afford them. Mass production was to children and toys what the invention of the printing press had been to Europe many centuries earlier. It gave the middle class a chance to share in the quality of life; this time with toys.

The early Victorian toys consist of very fine clockwork windup mechanisms with precision movement, articulation and animated movement, cast iron horse drawn vehicles in a vast array of shapes and styles, very early comic character toys, superbly lithographed puzzles and games by McLoughlin Brothers and Parker Brothers, and bright wood and paper lithographed pull toys and doll houses by the Bliss Company and Gibbs.

Even the simplest toys from this era can command high prices. As the years advance, most toys from this time period are already or are approaching 100 years old. Since they are a century old, they are desired not just because of their unique design, but also because they are true objects of antiquity.

The toys of the Victorian era have a certain "romance" about them known by no others. Their functional designs may be simple, but their style is usually very ornate and attractive. These old doll houses, cast iron horse drawn fire engines, pull toys, clockwork figures and lithographed paper toys are a part of the nostalgic America collectors constantly dream about when they "open" that imaginary trunk in Grandma's attic. Usually, old newspapers or moth-eaten clothes are all that's discovered when such trunks are actually found, but occasionally, a treasure trove of Victorian toys can make a lifelong hunt worth the wait.

The toys in this listing are the toys of our grandparents and great grandparents, and because they come from a simpler time and place when Main Street America seemed to exemplify the very best in our past, they hold a special place in the hearts of toy collectors.

Conditon is certainly a primary concern when it comes to evaluating and selecting Victorian toys. Because these toys are older than those in most sections of this book their condition may not always be impeccable. Generally, if a vintage Victorian toy shows some minor aging or wear, that can be expected and does not devalue the toy greatly. However, toys with significant rust are to be avoided altogether unless they are being purchased for spare parts only.

Victorian toys are permanent reminders to us that the gaslight days of America when horses were more common than auto engines and cobblestone streets did actually exist. From the cast iron horse drawn toys of yesteryear to the fancy boxed parlor games from the turn of the century, charming toys of the past take us back to the simpler days when our grandparents were children.

ANGORA GOAT PULL TOY ON WHEELED PLATFORM, wood and cast iron, 11", Furnish collection, $100.00-350.00.

BAKER'S APPRENTICE AND CHIMNEY SWEEP PAINTED TIN MECHANICAL PULL TOY, 5" wide x 8" tall, Furnish collection, $400.00-900.00.

A NEW DISSECTED MAP OF THE UNITED STATES, 1892, boxed $100.00-225.00

A NEW DISSECTED MAP OF THE WORLD, McLoughlin Brothers, 1892, boxed $100.00-250.00

A PEEP AT THE CIRCUS PICTURE PUZZLE, 1887, McLoughlin Brothers......................$100.00-250.00

ACROSS THE CONTINENT A GAME OF TRAVELS, Parker Brothers, 1892 ....$100.00-300.00

ACROSS THE SEA BOXED CARDBOARD GAME, 1914, 15" x 16" box $100.00-250.00

ALPHABET SPELLING BLOCKS, 1899 ..$100.00-250.00

ALPHABETICAL BLOCKS, letters, figures, six pictures, 1889 ....$100.00-275.00

AMUSING GAME OF INNOCENTS ABROAD, boxed board game, 1892 ....$150.00-325.00

AMUSING GAME OF THE CORNER GROCERY, 1890's, boxed board game $100.00-200.00

ANCHOR STONE BUILDING BLOCKS, 1888, F.A.C. Richter and Company, three color.$100.00-200.00

ANIMALS OF THE ARK, an assorted set, 1912..$100.00-225.00

APPLE MAN REVERSE RUNNING MAN AND CART, tin windup, unusual, ca. 1912 ......$400.00-800.00

ARTILLERY, cast iron, 34" long with four horses and single cannon wagon $1,000.00-2,200.00

ARTISTIC CUBES PUZZLE, ca. 1892..$100.00-225.00

AUTHOR'S GAME, 1890's, early, unusual boxed card game $100.00-200.00

AUTO TRUCK by Bing, 1910, pickup.$800.0-1,400.00

AUTOMATIC CART WAGON, 1889, tin $400.00-900.00

BABY CARRIAGE, circa 1870, child's toy $500.00-775.00

BAGATELLE BOARD, 16" long, 1889, paper, wood, spring action $50.00-125.00

BALANCING TOY, GIRL ON WHEELS, Stevens and Brown, 1879 ....$600.00-1,300.00

BANJO, toy, ca. 1899 ....$100.00-200.00

BANK, PAVILION CAST IRON ORNAMENTAL, 3½" tall, 1886 ....$150.00-300.00

BAROUCHE COACH WITH DRIVER AND TWO HORSES, cast iron, 1889 ....$800.00-1,600.00

BATTLE GAME, THE, Parker Brothers, 1890's, with soldiers $200.00-400.00

BATTLESHIP, toy, lithograph, cardboard on wheels, 21", 1914 ....$300.00-650.00

BEAR (SEATED) ON PLATFORM WITH ROLLERS, 1895..$200.00-500.00

BEAR ON BELL GONG TOY, 1914, cast iron and metal $600.00-1,000.00

BEAR ON WHEELS, BROWN PLUSH WITH CHAIN LEASH, 1914, 8" long $1,000.00-1,500.00

BEAR WALKING by Bing, ca. 1910 ....$200.00-500.00

BELL REVOTINA, music box crank mechanism, 1912 ....$100.00-200.00

BELL RINGER GIRL WITH DOLL ON SLED, horse head sled, 1892, "Daisy" cast iron ...$1,500.00-3,000.00

BELL RINGER HORSE ON PEDESTAL TOY, Gong Bell, 1892, cast iron $700.00-1,500.00

BELL RINGER HORSE WITH MONKEY ON SULKEY, 1892, cast iron $1,000.00-2,000.00

BELL RINGER PULL TOY, 1892, boy and girl on seesaw $700.00-1,450.00

BICYCLE RACE BOXED CARDBOARD GAME, 1910..$100.00-200.00

BIG CHIEF BOW AND ARROW, 1889, child's toy $65.00-125.00

BILLY BUMPS VISIT TO BOSTON GAME, 1890's, reading game $100.00-200.00

BING AUTO GARAGE WITH CAR, manufactured ca. 1912..$400.00-900.00

BING BATTLESHIP, ca. 1910, clockwise mechanism $750.00-1,500.00

BING DOUBLE AUTO GARAGE WITH TWO CARS, ca. 1912............................$600.00-1,200.00

BING AUTO MECHANICAL RACING BOAT, 9", ca. 1912............................$300.00-600.00

BING AUTO MECHANICAL STREET CAR track, clockwise, set, 1912 ....$400.00-900.00

BING MOTOR LAUNCH with clockwork mechanism, ca. 1910............................$500.00-1,100.00

BING OCEAN LINER, ca. 1910 ......$1,000.00-2000.00

BING OCEAN STEAMER, 13" long, 1912, four smoke stacks............................$800.00-1,600.00

BING OCEAN STEAMER four smoke stacks, 10" long 1912 ....$500.00-1,000.00

BING OCEAN STEAMER two smoke stacks, 8" long, 1912 ....$300.00-600.00

BING RIVER BOAT WITH SIDEWHEELS, clockwork mechanism, 1910 ....$750.00-1,400.00

BING RUNABOUT CAR, 1912, strong clockwork mechanism $600.00-1,200.00

BING SUBMARINE, ca. 1910, clockwork, actually dives and surfaces $1,000.00-1,800.00

BING TORPEDO BOAT, manufactured 1910, clockwork $500.00-1,250.00

BING U.S. FIRE BOAT, 1910............................$400.00-950.00

BING'S ALL METAL WATER WAGON, ca. 1912, 11" long............................$200.00-400.00

BIPLANE AND AIRSHIP CLOCKWORK TOY, European, ca. 1912 ....$1,200.00-2,500.0

BLISS CARRIAGE BARN, ca. 1900, paper lithograph wood barn............................$800.00-1,600.00

BLISS DOLL HOUSE, 1900, two story with front gable, paper and wood............................$700.00-1,800.00

BLISS DOLLHOUSE, 2½" story, front gable, two front doors, two steps sets $1000.00-2000.00

BLISS STONE AND STUCCO STYLE DOLLHOUSE, ca. 1910, 24" tall $1,000.00-2,200.00

BLISS WOOD PAPER LITHOGRAPH DOLLHOUSE, 1905, three story house, Victorian trim, fancy $1,500.00-2,400.00

BLOCKS, PICTURE AND ALPHABET, ca. 1890, set of twelve oblong blocks............................$100.00-225.00

BLOW FOOTBALL GAME, ca. 1912 table top game, boxed $50.00-100.00

BOAR MENAGERIE COPPERED IRON TOY, 1½", 1886............................$25.00-60.00

BOAT, STEAM PROPELLER, brass finish, 1892 ....$100.00-300.00

BOY ON SLED, friction, manufactured by Dayton, 1912 ....$250.00-500.00

BOY ON SLED, manufactured by Hess, ca. 1912, tin windup $300.00-750.00

BOY SCOUT WHISTLE, official, 1912, metal $50.00-125.00

BOY'S HAND PROPELLER WAGON, wood construction, 1870 ....$500.00-1,200.00

BRADLEY'S CROQUET SET, 1875......$100.00-175.00

BRITANNIA TOY PLACE SERVICE, knife, fork, spoon, boxed, 1889 ....$50.00-100.00

BROWNIE CHARACTER LADDER, animated, 32", 1894 ....$250.00-500.00

BROWNIE CHARACTER TEN PINS GAME, 1890's $200.00-450.00

BROWNIE FIGURES, uncut sheet, ca. 1890's, Palmer Cox............................$200.00-400.00

BUFFALLO BILL WOODEN STATUE FIGURE, 1894............................$100.00-250.00

BUFFALO HUNT BOXED CARDBOARD GAME, 1914............................$100.00-250.00

BUFFALO MENAGERIE COPPERED IRON TOY, 1886, 2"............................$25.00-60.00

BULL TERRIER, WHITE, WALKING DOG, by Bing, ca. 1910............................$200.00-500.00

BULLDOG FIGURE, rubber, ca. 1892 .....$20.00-45.00

BUTTERFLY PUSH TOY, ca. 1910, 9" wingspan, with long push handle $100.00-250.00

BUTTERFLY AUTOMATIC, wings move when flown, 1889............................$100.00-350.00

BUYING AND SELLING GAME, 1903......$35.00-70.00

CABIN BOY BOXED CARDBOARD GAME, ca. 1910, 11" x 11"............................$100.00-225.00

CALLIOPE WHISTLE, child's, 1889 ....$50.00-100.00

CAMEL MENAGERIE COPPERED IRON TOY, 1886, 2"............................$25.00-60.00

CAMEL ON WHEELS, platform style, 1914, tin, Germany $200.00-450.00

CAMERA, BROWNIE CHARACTER, 1903, box style camera $45.00-110.00

CANARY WHISTLE, ca. 1903, all metal, pipe style with bird on top $50.00-120.00

CANNON, CHILD'S TOY, COLUMBUS KRUPP, wooden $100.00-250.00

CANNON, TOY, wood construction, spring action, with nine pins target, 1875 ....$50.00-125.00

CAST IRON, 16", BLUE HAY WAGON, child's toy, ca. 1910............................$500.00-1,000.00

CAST IRON COACH, TALLY HO, ca. 1890's, carpenter, seven riders, four horses..........$2,000.00-3,200.00

CAST IRON ENGINE HOUSE FIVE, canvas roof, cast iron frame, 26", 1892 ....$700.00-1,000.00

CAST IRON FIRE ENGINE NUMBER 125, 1892, 19"............................$1,000.00-2,000.00

CAST IRON FIRE ENGINE PUMPER, 16" long, 1892 ....$800.00-1,700.00

CAST IRON HOSE CART NUMBER 155, 1892, 10" $800.00-1,500.00

CAST IRON PONY CART, 4" long.......$100.00-250.00

CAST IRON SURREY WITH LADY DRIVER, ca. 1914, 13" long $600.00-1,300.00

CAT MENAGERIE COPPERED IRON TOY, 2", 1886............................$25.00-60.00

CAT, rubber, 1892 ....$20.00-45.00

CAT, stuffed, woolly, 1889 ....$50.00-150.00

CATS AND MICE AND TOUSEL, McLoughlin Brothers Game, 1890's $100.00-225.00

CAXTON TOY PRINTING PRESS, self-linking, 1875............................$200.00-350.00

CHAIR ROCKER with double horse heads, ca. 1870, child's............................$200.00-400.00

CHICKEN MENAGERIE COPPERED IRON TOY, 1886, 2" tall............................$25.00-60.00

CHIME PULL BELL TOY, 1886, cast iron and metal, 5½" long............................$300.00-600.00

CHINA TEA SET, child's, twenty-three pieces, 1888, German $100.00-275.00

CHINA TOY TOILET SET, decorated china with wash bowl, pitcher, etc. $100.00-200.00

CHIVALRIE LAWN GAME, 1875, similiar to croquet $100.00-200.00

CHORAL MUSICAL TOP, French, hums when spinning, 1889, 5" tall, metal...............$100.00-250.00

CINDERELLA BOXED CARD GAME, manufactured 1914 ....$25.00-50.00

CINDERELLA'S CHARIOT, Gong Bell Toy manufacturing, 1893, bell ringer, rare.......$2,000.00-4,000.00

CIRCUS, BOXED CARDBOARD GAME, 1914 ....$125.00-250.00

CLOTH HORSE ON ROLLING PLATFORM PULLING COAL WAGON, 16", 1912 ....$350.00-700.00

CLOTH HORSE ON ROLLING PLATFORM PULLING LOADED TRUCK, 16", 1912 ....$300.00-600.00

CLOTH HORSE ON ROLLING PLATFORM PULLING MOVING TRUCK, 16", 1912 ....$350.00-700.00

CLOTH HORSE ON ROLLING PLATFORM PULLING MOVING VAN, 1912, 16" $400.00-800.00

CLOTH HORSE ON ROLLING PLATFORM WITH MILK WAGON, 1912, 16" $300.00-700.00

CLOWN BELL TOY WITH NO BELLS, cast iron 1914 bell toy, 7" long...........................$500.00-1,000.00

CLOWN ON STICK ANIMATED TOY, single stick with push lever action, 1890 ....$100.00-300.00

CLOWN TENPINS GAME, 1912, boxed with ball $100.00-165.00

COAL HOD AND SHOVEL, tin, 1914 .....$20.00-35.00

COCK-A-DOODLE-DOO BOXED CARDBOARD GAME, 1914 ....$100.00-200.00

COLDWELL'S PATENT BABY JUMPER, 1870, oak construction..$100.00-300.00

COLUMBIA SHIP, 36", lithographed details, 1894 ....$300.00-700.00

CONFECTIONARY BANK, mechanical, 1886, cast iron, lady in shop $600.00-1,250.00

CONTRACTOR'S WAGON CAST IRON TOY, black horses, 1892, red wagon $700.00-1,250.00

CORN COB PIPE WITH APPEARING DONKEY HEAD, ca. 1914 ....$50.00-125.00

CORNET, TOY, ca. 1899, nickel-plated metal, eight keys..$50.00-125.00

COTTAGE, WEATHERBOARD PLAYHOUSE, 18" tall, 1914 ....$100.00-300.00

COUNTY FAIR GAME, Parker Brothers, boxed board game $75.00-150.00

COUNTY FAIR TOWER, 16", ca. 1914, airplanes and cars circle $200.00-500.00

COVERED PICTURE WAGON, lithograph sides, tin construction, two horses, 1894 ......$200.00-500.00

COW FIGURE, rubber, 1892 ....$20.00-45.00

COW PULL TOY, natural skin, 1890's, mounted on platform with wheels $200.00-400.00

COWBOY DOLL, 8" tall, papier mache construction, 1889 ....$100.00-240.00

COWBOY ON HORSE, tin, from Europe, ca. 1910...$200.00-500.00

CRANDALL'S BUILDING BLOCK ACROBATS, ca. 1867, boxed, four figures $200.00-500.00

CRANDALL'S BUILDING BLOCKS, 1889, dove-tailed blocks set......................................$150.00-300.00

CRAZY TRAVELER GAME, ca. 1892, board game $100.00-200.00

CROKINOLE BOXED CARDBOARD GAME, 1914, 15" x 16" box $100.00-150.00

CROOKED MAN GAME, 1914, boxed cardboard game, 8" x 14"...$75.00-160.00

CAST IRON TROLLEY, 1900's, 8" long, Furnish collection, $125.00-200.00.

CHILDS PAPER LITHOGRAPH WOOD BLOCKS, ca. 1890's, value each: $50.00-100.00.

COMPOSITION KEYSTONE COP AND BILLIKEN CLOWN ROLY-POLYS, Furnish collection, each $50.00-100.00.

CROQUET SET, Bradley's Patent, circa 1875 ....$100.00-175.00

CRUISER SHIP "New York," 1890's, 29" long $600.00-1,250.00

CRUISER SHIP BOSTON, 19" long boat, 1895 ....$500.00-1,000.00

CLOWN PLAYING BASS DRUM PAINTED TIN WIND-UP, early toy, Furnish collection, $300.00-700.00.

CRUISER SHIP MINNEAPOLIS, 1890's, 38" long, ...$750.00-1,500.00

CURLY LOCKS CARDBOARD GAME, manufactured ca. 1910..$100.00-200.00

CYLINDRICAL ALPHABET BLOCKS, Bliss Manufacturing, 1889, set of twelve $200.00-400.00

CYMBAL CLAPPING CLOWN TOY WITH DOUBLE FACE (reverse), 1889 ....$100.00-225.00

CYMBAL CLAPPING CLOWN TOY, 1899, action toy $100.00-200.00

DAIRY COW ON WHEELS, 6", 1895, platform, painted, pressed paper $100.00-250.00

DECK RING TOSS GAME, circa 1910, boxed set $50.00-120.00

DIAMOND C STATIONARY STEAM ENGINE, 1889, toy $200.00-500.00

DING DONG BELL, figures with well on platform, 1902, by Gong Bell Manufacturing $1,000.00-2,000.00

DINNER BELL TOY, brass with wood handle, 1890's $30.00-75.00

DOCTOR BUSBY BOXED CARD GAME, circa 1910..$25.00-60.00

DOG AND BALL PULL TOY, action when pulled, 1890's $100.00-200.00

DOG CART CAST IRON TOY WITH DRIVER, 12", 1889..$750.00-1,500.00

DOG FIGURE, rubber, 1892 ....$20.00-45.00

DOG FLOOR CHIME PULL TOY, manufactured ca. 1912..$30.00-600.00

DOG ON WHEELED PLATFORM, red wood, 1914, 5" $100.00-400.00

DOG, COTTON FLANNEL construction, on wheels, 1889 ....$200.00-400.00

DOG, SHORT-HAIRED WITH COLLAR, 1892, rubber $20.00-45.00

DOG, WHITE WOOLY, stuffed, 1889 ...$100.00-200.00

DOLL BUGGY, WILLOW, 1890's $100.00-300.00

DOLL CARRIAGE, WILLOW, 1895 ......$100.00-400.00

DOLL CARRIAGE, wood with wicker canopy, large size, ca. 1870.............................$200.00-400.00

DOLL CRADLE, VICTORIAN, 16" long, ornate, wood construction $100.00-200.00

DONKEY AT THE PUMP MECHANICAL TOY, metal, 1903 ....$500.00-750.00

DONKEY ON PLATFORM WITH WHEELS, 1894, natural skin, 7" tall.............................$150.00-300.00

DONKEY, felt covered on platform with wheels, 1914, 6" $200.00-400.00

DONKEY, SHAKING HEAD, circa 1895, on wheels $200.00-350.00

DOUBLE FERRIS SWING WINDUP, metal, 1914, 14" long $100.00-300.00

DOUBLE TRUCK WITH DRIVER AND TWO HORSES CAST IRON TOY, 1889 ....$1,000.00-1,700.00

DOVE TOY FIGURE, RUBBER, circa 1890, scarce $50.00-100.00

DOWN ON THE FARM PICTURE PUZZLE BLOCKS, 1903, boxed $100.00-200.00

DRAY WITH DRIVER, cast iron toy, 10" long, 1889 ....$700.00-1,400.00

DRAY, CAST IRON, with horse and standing driver, 11½" long, 1892.........................$600.00-1,200.00

DREAMLAND WONDER RESORT GAME, 1914, 14" x 23" box $150.00-300.00

DRUM, TOY, brass body with cord and sticks, 1889, 7" in diameter $100.00-200.00

DRUMMER BOY BOXED CARDBOARD GAME, 1914, 10" x 20" box $100.00-225.00

DUCK FAMILY, tin, on platform rolling toy, 1895 ....$200.00-400.00

DUMP CART, toy, tin, 1887, 12" long with one horse $200.00-450.00

DUST PAN, tin, 1886.............................$10.00-30.00

DUST PAN, toy, tin lithograph, with kitten design, 1914......................................$15.00-40.00

DYNAMO ELECTRIC TOY, manufactured ca. 1892, battery...$100.00-200.00

ECHO MUSICAL CRANK TOY "REVOTINA," eight musical notes (full octave) 1895 ......$50.00-125.00

ECHO REVOTINA MUSICAL CRANK TOY, 1895, largest version, eighteen notes $100.00-200.00

ECHO REVOTINA, musical crank toy, tin, 1895, six notes $40.00-95.00

ELECTRIC MERRY GO ROUND, 1892, motor and battery, rare $700.00-1,500.00

ELECTRIC TROLLEY CAR, 16" long, model, 1903 ....$300.00-750.00

ELEPHANT (SEATED) ON PLATFORM WITH WHEELS, 6", 1895 ....$200.00-400.00

ELEPHANT MENAGERIE COPPER IRON TOY, 1886, 2" $25.00-60.00

ELEPHANT ON PLATFORM WITH WHEELS, 8" tall, 1890's $250.00-450.00

ELEPHANT STUFFED ANIMAL, white, woolly, with blanket, 1889..............................$200.00-400.00

ELITE BOY'S TOOL CHEST, 1912, 17" long, complete $100.00-300.00

ENCHANTED FOREST BOXED CARDBOARD GAME, 1914, 11" x 11" box $200.00-400.00

EXPRESS WAGON CAST IRON TOY, ca. 1890's, 17½" long, two horses $700.00-1,400.00

EXPRESS WAGON, tin, 1886, with one horse, 13" long $200.00-600.00

EXPRESSMAN WINDUP PORTER TOY by Bing, 1912 ....$400.00-800.00

FARM TABLE SET, 1912, boxed with barn stable and assorted animals $100.00-200.00

FARM YARD ANIMALS, papier mache, set of six, boxed, 1914 ....$250.00-500.00

FAST MAIL CARDBOARD GAME, 1910, 10" x 20" box $100.00-175.00

FIRE CAPTAIN'S WAGON CAST IRON TOY, 1892, 12½" long $700.00-1,250.00

FIRE CHIEF'S WAGON, cast iron construction, 1892 ....$750.00-1200.00

FIRE COMPANY HOOK AND LADDER TRUCK, 1889, cast iron, 24" $1,000.00-2,000.00

FIRE ENGINE HOSE CART, cast iron, 1889, with driver, rider, two horses $800.00-1,600.00

FIRE ENGINE PUMPER WITH DRIVER AND TWO HORSES, cast iron, 1889 ....$600.00-1,300.00

FIRE ENGINE, friction, manufactured by Dayton, 1912 ....$300.00-650.00

FIRE FIGHTERS BOXED CARDBOARD GAME, 1914, 7" x 16" box $200.00-350.00

FIRE PATROL CAST IRON WAGON WITH DRIVER, TWO HORSES AND THREE FIREMAN, 18" long $1,200.00-2200.00

FIREHOUSE, MECHANICAL, by Ives, ca. 1890's, rare $2,000.00-4,000.00

FISHERMAN, tin windup, ca. 1912 .....$300.00-600.00

FLOOR CROQUET GAME, manufactured 1912, with box $100.00-225.00

FLYING ARTILLERY, cast iron, 1892, 24" long, two horses, two soldiers, cannon $1,000.00-1,800.00

FOLDING BABY CARRIAGE, ca. 1870, umbrella canopy, Schwarz catalogue $200.00-550.00

FOOT RACE BOXED CARDBOARD GAME, 1914 ....$100.00-150.00

FORT, THE, home game, boxed, 1889 .$50.00-125.00

FORTUNE TELLER GAME, boxed cardboard game, ca. 1910, 14" x 21" $100.00-200.00

FORTUNE TELLING AND BASEBALL GAME, 1889, combination set, boxed.....................$50.00-140.00

FOX AND HOUNDS BOXED BOARD GAME, ca. 1912 ....$100.00-200.00

FOXY GRANDPA CARD GAME, manufactured 1903, boxed $50.00-125.00

FROG MENAGERIE COPPERED IRON TOY, 1886, 1" $25.00-60.00

FROG SCHOOL BOXED CARDBOARD GAME, 1914, 11" x 11" box $75.00-150.00

FROG WHO WOULD A WOOING GO, boxed cardboard game, 10" x 18", 1914 ....$100.00-250.00

FROLICKING CLOWNS, THREE CLOWNS, operate seesaw, musical, windup, 1914 ....$400.00-1,000.00

GALLOPING PONY PUSH TOY ON STICK, 20" handle, wood and paper lithograph pony ...$200.00-400.00

GAME OF ABC BOXED GAME, 1914 .$100.00-200.00

GAME OF AMERICAN HISTORY, by Parker Brothers, 1892 board game $100.00-200.00

DIE-CUT CHRISTMAS CARD OF GIRL ON TOY HORSE, ca. 1880's, probably a trade card, $20.00-40.00.

DOG ON CAST IRON WHEELS, 11" LONG, STUFFED PULL TOY, Furnish collection, $150.00-300.00.

GAME OF BEAUTY AND THE BEAST, boxed cardboard game, 1914, 9" x 9" box $125.00-250.00

GAME OF FISHPOND, circa 1890, by Westcott, boxed $100.00-200.00

GAME OF FOOTBALL, Parker Brothers, 1890's, boxed game $100.00-250.00

GAME OF LETTERS, made by Parker Brothers, 1890's $50.00-90.00

DOLL HOUSE, QUEEN ANNE STYLE, probably by Bliss, 1900's, Furnish collection, $600.00-1,200.00.

EMBOSSED AND LITHOGRAPHED TIN SAND PAIL, seashore scene, 6", 1900's, Furnish collection, $70.00-150.00.

GAME OF LOUISA, manufactured ca. 1890's, box 9" x 16" $125.00-225.00

GAME OF LUCK, Parker Brothers, 1892, boxed game $100.00-200.00

GAME OF MONETA "Money Makes Money" game, 1889, F. A. Wright Publishers $150.00-275.00

GAME OF MOTHER GOOSE, 1914, cardboard game, box, 10" x 20" $125.00-275.00

GAME OF PITCH, 1914, boxed skill game, 11" x 11" box $100.00-200.00

GAME OF ROBIN HOOD, boxed board game, 1895 ....$100.00-275.00

GAME OF STEEPLE CHASE BOXED CARDBOARD GAME, 1914, 7" x 16" $100.00-200.00

GAME OF TRAVEL BOARD GAME, manufactured 1890's $100.00-200.00

GATHMANN TORPEDO GUN, ca. 1892, 11" cannon $200.00-400.00

GIBBS DERBY RIDER PUSH TOY, 1914, 8" figures with 24" handle $200.00-400.00

GIBBS ENGLISH PONY CART, ca. 1914, 13" long $200.00-500.00

GIBBS GREY BEAUTY PACERS double horses pull wagon, walking action, 1912..........$300.00-700.00

GIBBS HOBBY HORSE, miniature model, 6", 1912, wood and paper lithograph $100.00-250.00

GIBBS HORSE PULLING CART THAT DUMPS, unusual, 1912, 19", deluxe version .$450.00-1000.00

GIBBS JUMBO THE PERFORMING ELEPHANT rolling toy with trick action 1912 ....$150.00-350.00

GIBBS PACING BOB single horse pulling two-wheeled cart, 1912 ....$175.00-350.00

GIBBS PERFORMING BOB THE TRICK PONY, ca. 1912...$200.00-400.00

GIBBS PONY CIRCUS WAGON, 14" long, double horses, bright lithograph $1,000.00-2,000.00

GIBBS PONY PACER PULLING CART, 7" long, ca. 1912...$200.00-400.00

GIBBS SINGLE HORSE GYPSY WAGON, covered wagon, ca. 1912, 14" long.........................$200.00-500.00

GIBBS TEETER TOTTER turnabout toy, boy and girl see-saw, 1912 ....$300.00-700.00

GIBBS TWO HORSE GYPSY WAGON, ca. 1912, two horses with covered wagon $500.00-1,000.00

GIBBS U.S. MAIL WAGON WITH HORSE, ca. 1914, 12" long..$150.00-375.00

GILT EDGE BUILDING BLOCKS, 1889, boxed set, fancy $150.00-300.00

GIRAFFE, MENAGERIE COPPERED IRON TOY, 1886, 3" $25.00-60.00

GOAT FIGURE, rubber, 1892 ....$20.00-45.00

GOAT MENAGERIE COPPERED IRON TOY, 2", 1886 ....$25.00-60.00

GOING TO THE FIRE, BOXED CARDBOARD GAME, 1914 ....$150.00-300.00

GOOD OLD GAME OF PROVERBS, Parker Brothers, 1890's, boxed $75.00-150.00

GREAT BATTLEFIELDS GAME, ca. 1890's, board game $100.00-200.00

GROCERY WAGON, covered, tin, 1894, lithograph details $200.00-400.00

GYROSCOPE TOP, metal and cast iron, 1889, with stand $30.00-75.00

HANSOM RIG WITH DRIVER AND SINGLE BLACK HORSE, 1890's, cast iron $600.00-1,250.00

HARDWOOD TEN PINS WOODEN BOXED GAME, 1889 .... $100.00-200.00

HATCHET, TOY, 1886, japanned, polished metal, 8" long $30.00-60.00

HESS COLUMBIA BATTLESHIP, manufactured ca. 1912 .... $600.00-1,200.00

HESS FRICTION BATTLESHIP, 9" long, ca. 1912 .... $300.00-600.00

HESSMOBILE RACER, ca. 1911, friction powered, with driver $400.00-700.00

HESSMOBILE with friction motor, 1912 roadster with driver $500.00-1,200.00

HILL CLIMBER CIRCUS MENAGERIE WAGON, ca. 1903, friction powered $400.00-800.00

HILL CLIMBER HOOK AND LADDER TRUCK, friction toy, 1903, 19" $200.00-500.00

HILL'S ALPHABET BLOCKS, 1875 ..... $100.00-200.00

HOME MAGIC LANTERN, circa 1900, twelve slides $100.00-200.00

HORSE AND CART, tin, 1890's, plain .. $200.00-450.00

HORSE AND PIE WAGON, Bergmann, 1870's, tin, painted features $500.00-1,400.00

HORSE FIGURE, rubber, 1892 .... $20.00-45.00

HORSE ON PLATFORM WITH WHEELS, natural skin, 1894, with bridle $200.00-450.00

HORSE ON PLATFORM, tin, with wheels, 4", 1895 .... $100.00-200.00

HORSE ON WHEELED PLATFORM 1914, papier mache construction, 7" tall $100.00-200.00

HORSE ON WHEELED PLATFORM, papier mache horse, 1914, 10" tall $200.00-400.00

HORSE ON WHEELS, tin, 1886, Schwarz catalogue, 6" long $200.00-500.00

HORSE PULLED TROLLEY CAR, Wilkins, ca. 1890's $600.00-1,200.00

HORSE PULLING CHIME WHEELS, tin and cast iron toy, 1889 .... $300.00-800.00

HORSE, ARABIAN, on casters, stuffed, circa 1890 .... $300.00-750.00

HORSE, PRESSED PAPER on platform with wheels, 1890's $100.00 250.00

HORSES IN STABLE, pressed paper horses in wooden stable (two) $100.00-350.00

HORSES PULLING ICE WAGON, 1912, 17" light steel construction wagon $200.00-450.00

HOSE WAGON WITH SINGLE DRIVER AND HORSE, cast iron, Ives, 1890's $800.00-1,750.00

HUBLEY CAST IRON NODDER, "The Nodder," 1910 .... $750.00-1,800.00

IDEAL GUN AND PISTOL SET with target, boxed, 1912 .... $100.00-250.00

IDEAL MACHINE RIFLE, 1912 .... $100.00-200.00

IDEAL SHOOTING GALLERY, ca. 1912, boxed set $100.00-200.00

IDEAL TOY MACHINE FIRE GUN, circa 1910 .... $50.00-150.00

IMPROVED GAME OF FISH POND, 1890's, long box version $100.00-250.00

IMPROVED GEOGRAPHICAL CARDS, 1890's, boxed $100.00-150.00

IRISH JIG, mechanical attachment for steam engine, 1892 .... $300.00-600.00

FIRE DEPARTMENT HOOK AND LADDER TRUCK, 13" long, wood with cast iron wheels, Furnish collection $200.00-400.00.

GERMAN FABRIC COVERED COMPOSITION DOG, 4" on metal wheels, $50.00-110.00.

GIBBS PONY CART TIN LITHOGRAPH PAPER ON WOOD, WOOD CART, CAST IRON WHEELS, 12" long, 1910's, $100.00-250.00.

IRON STOVE, 4", 1886 .... $100.00-250.00

IVES CLOCKWORK DANCERS ON WOODEN PEDESTAL, ca. 1880's, clockwork $1,000.00-2000.00

JACK AND JILL BOXED CARD GAME, 1914 .... $25.00-50.00

JACK AND JILL GAME, boxed cardboard game, 1914, 7" x 16" $100.00-225.00

JACK IN THE BOX, 1890's, paper lithograph box, scenic $100.00-200.00

VICTORIAN TOYS

JACK IN THE BOX, 1903 version where clown's entire body springs out $100.00-300.00

JACK SPRATT BOXED CARDBOARD GAME, 1914, 8" x 14" $75.00-150.00

JACKSTRAWS IMPROVED, 1890's game by Parker Brothers $50.00-125.00

JENNY LYND ROCKER, child's rocker, 1878, shape of winged horses $300.00-700.00

JOCKEY ON HORSE PLATFORM GONG BELL TOY, ca. 1914, 7" long.........................$700.00-1,200.00

JOCKEY ON HORSE PUSH TOY WITH ROD, ca. 1900's, Wilkins, cast iron $500.00-1,250.00

JOHNNY'S HISTORICAL GAME, Parker Brothers, 1890's boxed game......................................$100.00-225.00

JUMPING DOG IN HOUSE, tin and fur, 1912...$200.00-400.00

JUMPING GRASSHOPPER, tin windup, ca. 1912...$300.00-650.00

JUMPING RABBIT, MECHANICAL, natural skin, 1894 ....$100.00-300.00

JUMPING ROPE, 1912, fancy handles $40.00-80.00

KALEIDOSCOPE, Aniline colors, 8" long, 1886 ....$100.00-200.00

KITCHEN AND WASH SET, little girl's, 1899, boxed with twenty-two wooden pieces $100.00-250.00

KITE, DRAGON DESIGN, 1875, paper, oriental design..$30.00-75.00

KNITTER TOY, 1886 ....$40.00-85.00

KNUCKLE BILLIARDS, 1892, Parker Brothers, boxed...$100.00-250.00

LAMB PULL TOY, mounted on platform, 9" tall, 1890's $200.00-400.00

LAMB, PLUSH ON WHEELS, 1895 .....$200.00-400.00

LANDAU COACH, CAST IRON, 1892, 16½" long, deluxe toy, two horses $1,500.00-3,000.00

LASSO THE JUMPING RING, A NOVEL GAME, 1912 boxed ring game, clown box $100.00-250.00

LAWN MOWER, toy, push type, 20" handle, ca. 1914..$50.00-100.00

LEHMANN ADAMS EXPRESSMAN, 1914, 8" figure pushes hand truck $400.00-950.00

LEHMANN BALKING MULE, 1912 ......$250.00-800.00

LEHMANN CRAWLING BEETLE, 5" long, ca. 1912, tin wind-up $400.00-800.00

LEHMANN DANCING SAILOR WIND-UP, ca. 1910, tin and cloth $500.00-1,200.00

LEHMANN MAN ON MOTORCYCLE (three-wheeled) 1912, tin windup.........................$700.00-1,250.00

LEHMANN NAUGHTY BOY AUTO, 1912, tin windup $700.00-1,300.00

LEHMANN VINETA MONORAIL CAR, 10" long, ca. 1914..$300.00-600.00

LEHMANN WALKING BOY WITH CART, 1912 ....$600.00-1,200.00

LEHMANN'S ZIG-ZAG, ca. 1912, two wheeled comical action toy with riders $600.00-1,350.00

LIBERTY CHIME PULL TOY, 7½" long cast iron, 1886, Liberty with flag $1,000.00-1,650.00

LION MENAGERIE COPPERED IRON TOY, 1886, 2" $25.00-60.00

LITERARY GAME OF QUOTATIONS, Parker Brothers, 1892..$100.00-200.00

LITTLE BO-PEEP BOXED CARDBOARD GAME, 1914, 8" x 14" $100.00-200.00

LITTLE FARMER BLOCKS SET, 1899 $100.00-200.00

LITTLE FOLKS CUBES BABES IN THE WOOD, blocks, 1892, ornate box $500.00-900.00

LITTLE GOLDENLOCKS AND THE THREE BEARS, McLoughlin Brothers Game, 1892 .$250.00-500.00

LITTLE JACK HORNER BOXED CARDBOARD GAME, 1924, 7" x 14"..................................$75.00-175.00

LITTLE NEMO GAME, BOXED CARDBOARD GAME, 9" x 9", 1914................................$100.00-300.00

LITTLE RED RIDING HOOD BOXED CARDBOARD GAME, 1914, 10" x 20" box $150.00-300.00

LITTLE SOLDIER BOXED CARDBOARD GAME, 1914 ....$100.00-225.00

LOADED DRAY CAST IRON WAGON AND TWO HORSES, 23" long....................$1,000.00-1,900.00

LOCOMOTIVE PICTURE PUZZLES, 1892, 18" x 24", boxed...$100.00-300.00

LOCOMOTIVE SAVINGS BANK, puzzle type, will not open until full, 1889 ....$350.00-800.00

LOG CABIN building block set, 1903..$100.00-250.00

LOGOMACHY OR WAR OF WORDS GAME, 1903...$40.00-80.00

MADCAP, THE NEW GAME OF, box 11" x 11" 1914...$75.00-185.00

MAGIC LANTERN SLIDES, 1899.. each $10.00-20.00

MAGIC LANTERN, 1889, twelve slides.$100.00-250.00

MAGNETIC FISH POND GAME, circa 1910, boxed...$100.00-200.00

MAGNETIC FLOATING TOYS SET, ca. 1903, boxed $50.00-120.00

MAN IN THE MOON RETURN TOY BALL, 10", papier mache, very rare $250.00-600.00

MAN O' WAR TOY BOAT, 17", ca. 1914, mechanical boat $500.00-1,000.00

MARBLE GAME WITH WIRE SPIRAL, 1890's, by Bliss, beautiful gypsy girl........................$200.00-450.00

MARBLES, twenty-five in original sack, 1895, assorted...$50.00-125.00

MARY AND HER LITTLE LAMB, ca. 1880's, wood platform on wheels/figures.............$1,000.00-2,000.00

MARY'S LITTLE LAMB, Stevens and Brown, tin platform toy on wheels, 1870 ....$500.00-1,200.00

MATCH SAFE, calender, nickel, 1886.. $40.00-100.00

MECHANICAL ACROBATS, performing on bar, 1892, clockwork toy $700.00-1,500.00

MECHANICAL BEAR, clockwork toy, manufactured 1892 ....$1,000.00-2,000.00

MECHANICAL BLACK NURSE WITH CHILD, 1892 ....$1,000.00-2,000.00

MECHANICAL BUTTERFLY, ca. 1912, tin windup, flaps wings, rolls $400.00-700.00

MECHANICAL CAKE WALK, two black dancers, clockwork toy, 1892 ....$1,500.00-2,500.00

MECHANICAL CAST IRON FIRE ENGINE with driver, rider two horses, 1892, 19" $1,200.00-2,400.00

MECHANICAL CLOWN RIDER, clockwork toy, 1892, clown on horse $1,500.00-3,000.00

MECHANICAL DOVE, windup on wheels, tin, 8" long, ca. 1912..$300.00-500.00

MECHANICAL DUDE WINDUP TOY, walking well-dressed man, 1912, tin windup...$200.00-500.00

MECHANICAL FIRE ENGINE HOUSE WITH FIRE ENGINE, 1892.................................$700.00-1,600.00

MECHANICAL HEN, 1903, metal $100.00-200.00

MECHANICAL HORSE RACE, circular track, lever action, four horses/riders, 1903 .... $300.00-750.00

MECHANICAL MONKEY, circa 1890, clockwork toy $1,000.00-2,400.00

MECHANICAL MOWER, windup, 7" tall man with scythe, 1903 .... $300.00-550.00

MECHANICAL MULE CLOWNS, clockwork toy, 1892 .... $1,200.00-2,400.00

MENAGERIE GAME, 1895, boxed board game $200.00-400.00

MERRY GAME OF THE COUNTRY AUCTION, 1890's, boxed $100.00-200.00

MERRY GO ROUND BOXED CARD GAME, 1914 .... $25.00-60.00

MERRY WHIRL TOY, boy and girl, twist down pole, tin and metal, 1914 .... $100.00-225.00

MESSENGER BOY GAME, cardboard, 10" x 20" box, 1910 .... $75.00-145.00

METALLOPHONE (xylophone toy) 1886, twelve notes with mallet $100.00-200.00

METALLOPHONE (xylophone toy) twenty-four notes with mallets $150.00-225.00

MILK WAGON PULLED BY HORSE, ca. 1912, wood frame, horse on rollers $200.00-450.00

MILK WAGON, tin, one horse with gong, 1886, 12" long $300.00-600.00

MISS MUFFET BOXED BOARD GAME, 1914, 7" x 16" $100.00-200.00

MISTRESS MARY BOXED CARDBOARD GAME, 1914 .... $100.00-225.00

MODEL HOSE CART, cast iron, 1892, 15" with rubber hose $1,000.00-2,000.00

MODEL STEAM FIRE ENGINE, scale model works, cast iron and metal, 1889 .... $500.00-1,200.00

MONKEY CHIME CHARIOT TOY, cast iron and metal chimes, 1886, 6" long $500.00-1,000.00

MONKEY ON ORGAN CAST IRON MECHANICAL BANK, 1889, rare $800.00-1,300.00

MONKEY ON THE BAR, string pull action, ca. 1912 .... $200.00-400.00

MONKEY ON TRICYCLE BELL TOY, J. E. Stevens Company, ca. 1880's $700.00-1,500.00

MONKEY, SEATED, MENAGERIE COPPERED IRON TOY, 1886, 2" $25.00-60.00

MONKEYMOBILE BELL TOY, 1903, cast iron and metal $500.00-950.00

MOTHER GOOSE GAME, BOXED, CARDBOARD, 7" x 7" box, 1914 .... $100.00-170.00

MOTHER HUBBARD BOXED BOARD GAME, 1914 .... $100.00-225.00

MOTOR BANK TROLLEY CAR MOTION BANK, 1889 .... $400.00-1,000.00

MOTOR HOOK AND LADDER CAR, clockwise, ca. 1910 .... $600.00-1,300.00

MOTOR PATROL WAGON, ca. 1910, clockwork signal bell $600.00-1,250.00

MOUSE TOY, rubber, 1889 .... $50.00-90.00

MOVING DUCK, tin windup by Hess, Germany, ca. 1912, 4" long $100.00-350.00

MUG, CHILD'S, 1914, tin lithograph mug, seashore pictures on front $20.00-45.00

MUSICAL CLOWN, 1914, platform windup toy, bisque and cloth, 15" $500.00-1,000.00

CAST IRON GOAT PULLING WAGON, Furnish collection, $65.00-130.00.

PAINTED TIN GOAT PLATFORM TOY, 5" long, early, Furnish collection, $100.00-250.00.

PAPER LITHOGRAPH OVER CARDBOARD BLOCKS picturing animals dressed as soldiers, ca. 1890's, value each: $10.00-30.00.

219

PAPER COVER EARLY CHILD'S BOOK BY McLOUGH-LIN BROTHERS, ca. 1880's, (1884), $40.00-85.00.

NATIONAL EXPRESS BUILDING BLOCKS IN WAGON, 1899 ....$150.00-300.00

NEW AND IMPROVED FISH POND GAME, McLoughlin Brothers, 1890's $125.00-250.00

NOAH'S ARK WITH ANIMALS, detailed wood with paper lithograph, lift-off roof $300.00-750.00

NOAH'S ARK WOODEN BOAT AND ANIMALS SET, ca. 1889, ark roof open $200.00-600.00

NODDING DONKEY WITH KEYSTONE COP RIDER, 9" x 12", ca. 1914 ....$250.00-500.00

NODDING HEAD CALF ON WHEELED PLATFORM, 1914, 6" $150.00-300.00

NODDING HEAD DONKEY ON WHEELED PLATFORM, 6", 1914 ....$200.00-400.00

NORTH POLE GAME, 1914, boxed cardboard game $75.00-175.00

NOVELTY BABY CARRIAGE WITH SUSPENDED UM-BRELLA, ca. 1870, child's $1,000.00-1,700.00

OFFICE BOY BOARD GAME, 1892 .....$50.00-150.00

OLD MAID CARD GAME, ca. 1889 ....$30.00-65.00

OLD MILL, mechanical attachment for steam engine, 1892 ....$300.00-600.00

OLD WOMAN JACK IN THE BOX, composition and wood, ca. 1890's $200.00-400.00

ONE THOUSAND JOLLY CATS AND DOGS, nine cube blocks, animals on box, 1892 ....$150.00-375.00

ORCHESTRA TOY PIPE ORGAN, crank activated, or-nate, ca. 1912 ....$100.00-250.00

ORGAN GRINDER, mechanical attachment for steam engine, 1892 ....$300.00-600.00

P. T. BARNUM'S CIRCUS AND MENAGERIE, picture book, 1888 ....$50.00-100.00

PANAMA DIRT CART, cast iron wagon with driver and horses, 20", 1914 ....$1,000.00-1,600.00

PANAMA DRIVER TOOL TOY, digging rig, ca. 1914, 17" steel $100.00-200.00

PAPER SOLDIERS WITH TENTS AND STANDS TO CUT OUT, 1892, boxed.................$200.00-450.00

PARASOL, fancy handle, ca. 1912, with tassels and decorations $100.00-200.00

PARLOR AIR PISTOL, 1875, shoots darts, 6" long $100.00-200.00

PASTRY SET, with wooden kitchen tools, 1895 ....$20.00-55.00

PECULIAR GAME OF MY WIFE AND I, 1890's, "Going to Town," boxed $125.00-200.00

PETER CODDLE BOXED CARD GAME, circa 1910 ....$25.00-50.00

PETER CODDLE BOXED CARD GAME, story game, 1889 ....$70.00-150.00

PETER PETER PUMPKIN EATER BOXED CARDBOARD GAME, 1914, 8" x 14" $100.00-200.00

PEWTER DOLL FURNITURE, four pieces parlor suite, 1895 ....$100.00-250.00

PIANO STOOL, child's, 1899 ....$25.00-70.00

PIANO, SCHOENHUT "CHAMPION" SQUARE PIANO, 1895 ....$100.00-250.00

PIANO, SCHOENHUT, K1895, "HOFFMAN" UPRIGHT TOY PIANO $150.00-250.00

PIANO, TOY 11", fifteen keys, ornate, 1889, wood case $35.00-80.00

PIANO, TOY, by Schoenhut, 1895, "Rubenstein" ver-sion square piano $100.00-300.00

PLEASURE YACHT METAL TOY BOAT, 1914, 10" long $200.00-500.00

POLICE LANTERN, toy, 1889 ....$50.00-125.00

PONY CIRCUS WAGON, by Gibbs, 1912, bright lig-hograph, 14" long, two horses .$1,000.00-2,000.00

PONY PHAETON CAST IRON RIG, 1892, with single lady driver $1,000.00-1,800.00

PONY, felt covered figure on platform with wheels, 1914, 6" $200.00-400.00

POP GUN, double type, 1889 ....$30.00-65.00

PREAMBULATOR, DOLL CARRIAGE, circa 1880 ....$1,000.00-1,500.00

PRESIDENTIAL ELECTION GAME, 1892, board game, boxed $200.00-400.00

PRINCESS IN THE TOWER, boxed board game, by Parker Brothers, 1890's $150.00-300.00

PROGRESSIVE QUERIES GAME, circa 1900, boxed $35.00-70.00

PUG DOG ON CASTERS, circa 1890, plush, stuffed $200.00-400.00

PUNCH THE TUMBLING CLOWN, ca. 1912, windup toy $100.00-350.00

PUSS-IN-BOOTS BOXED CARD GAME, circa 1910 ....$25.00-50.00

RABBIT, TOY, natural skin, 1890's $50.00-125.00

RACE FOR THE CUP BOXED CARDBOARD GAME, 1914 ....$100.00-200.00

RAILROAD MENAGERIE BLOCKS, 1892, six in pack-age, boxed $200.00-400.00

RAILROAD TRAIN, circa 1890, tin, four piece $200.00-400.00

RAM FIGURE, rubber, 1892 ....$20.00-45.00
RATTLE, CELLULOID DOLLY FACE, 12" with bells, 1912 ....$50.00-120.00
RATTLE, fancy shape, scrolled, tin, circa 1890 ....$50.00-100.00
RATTLE, tin, ca. 1890's $30.00-75.00
REED'S CIRCUS AND MOMMOTH HIPPODROME, W. S. Reed Co., 1880's, 26" wide ...$2000.00-3000.00
REVOLVING BELL CHIME, rolls, 1889 $250.00-500.00
REX AND THE KILKENNY CATS, Parker Brothers board game, 1892 ....$75.00-150.00
RICH MRS. DUCK BLOCKS, 1892, boxed set $100.00-250.00
RIFLE AIR PISTOL, 1875, metal parts, silver plated $100.00-250.00
RING MY NOSE GAME, ca. 1912, boxed ring game $100.00-150.00
RINK CLUB SKATES, 1886, unusual $20.00-50.00
ROAMING TURTLE STRING PULL TOY, 1889, metal, colorful, popular design $100.00-220.00
ROBINSON CRUSOE GAME, ca. 1914, 7" x 16" box, cardboard $200.00-400.00
ROCKING HORSE, 6" x 6" carved legs, stirrups, saddle, 1878 ....$500.00-1,400.00
ROCKING PONY WITH CLOWN RIDER, 9" tall, wood and cloth, 1914 ....$300.00-500.00
ROLLER SKATING BEAR by Bing, ca. 1912, key wound $750.00-2,000.00
ROLY POLY GAME, circa 1910, box 13" x 10" $50.00-150.00
ROMEO AND JULIET, mechanical attachment for steam engine, 1892 ....$300.00-600.00
ROOSTER MENAGERIE COPPERED IRON TOY, 1886, 2" $25.00-60.00
ROTARY WASHING MACHINE TOY ca. 1912, with real wringer $100.00-200.00
ROUND THE WORLD BOXED CARDBOARD GAME, 7" x 7", ca. 1914 ....$100.00-200.00
ROW BOAT, tin toy, 12" long, 1886 ...$300.00-600.00
ROWING SCULL TOY, on wheels, 1898, U. S. Hardware Company $600.00-1,400.00
RUBBER BALL SHOOTING GALLERY, 1903, 18" wide...$100.00 300.00
RUBBER BALL, painted, 1912, with scene, 4" $50.00-125.00
RUBBER BOY DRESSED AS CLOWN, 1899, 10½" tall...$150.00-300.00
RUBBER BOY RIDING ELEPHANT FIGURE, 1889 ....$100.00-200.00
RUBBER HORSE AND RIDER, circa 1890, 6" x 7" $100.00-200.00
RUBBER YOUNG CHICK, 1899 ....$40.00-75.00
SAD IRON AND STAND, 1886, cast iron, child's...$20.00-40.00
SAILOR BOY BOXED CARDBOARD GAME, circa 1910 ....$100.00-200.00
SANTA CLAUS CAST IRON BANK, 1889, mechanical toy $600.00-1,300.00
SANTA CLAUS CUBE PUZZLES, circa 1890, boxed..$100.00-250.00
SANTA CLAUS PICTURE PUZZLES, 1892, Victorian scroll puzzle, boxed $300.00-500.00
SCHOENHUT ACROBAT FIGURE, ca. 1905, woman, jointed $200.00-350.00

SCHOENHUT ACROBAT FIGURE, wood jointed, man, ca. 1905..$100.00-300.00
SCHOENHUT CIRCUS CLOWN, ca. 1905, posable, with original hat $100.00-300.00
SCHOENHUT CIRCUS LION, wood jointed figure, ca. 1900...$200.00-350.00
SCHOENHUT LEOPARD, ca. 1900, wood jointed figure $100.00-300.00
SCHOENHUT TOY PIANO, six key, circa 1890 ....$50.00-150.00
SCHOENHUT TOY PIANO, eight key full octave, 1895 ....$100.00-200.00
SCHOENHUT UPRIGHT TOY PIANO, 1895, eight key full octave $100.00-200.00
SCHOENHUT WOODEN JOINTED PIG, ca. 1905 ....$100.00-250.00
SCRIPTURE CARDS, IMPROVED, 1888 McLoughlin cards set, each 6" x 9" $75.00-145.00
SEATED DOG ON WHEELED PLATFORM, ca. 1914, 7" $200.00-450.00
SHARP SHOOTERS, lithograph soldiers set on wood bases, boxed, 1914 ....$200.00-400.00
SHEEP FLOOR CHIME TOY, natural wool covered, 1912 ....$400.00-800.00
SHOO FLY ROCKING HORSE, 1890's, dapple horse version, upholstered chair $300.00-600.00
SINGLE TRUCK CAST IRON PULL TOY with driver and merchandise, 1889 ....$800.00-1,700.00
SINGLE TRUCK CAST IRON TOY with galloping horse figure, 15", 1889 ....$400.00-1,000.00
SLED, BENT HEAD, child's sleigh, Bodine decal $600.00-1,250.00
SLED, BENT KNEE SWAN HEAD VERSION, 1878 ....$300.00-675.00
SLICED ANIMALS DISSECTED PICTURE PUZZLES, 1903 ....$65.00-140.00
SMOKER, mechanical attachment for steam engine, 1892 ....$300.00-600.00
SNAKE, wood jointed, circa 1890, 16" long, novelty...$40.00-100.00

WINDUP DUCK, PAINTED TIN cast iron or metal wheels, early, 6", Furnish collection, $100.00-275.00.

VICTORIAN TOYS

SOAP BUBBLE OUTFIT, 1912 .... $50.00-90.00

SOLDIER BELL TOY, Watrous Company, ca. 1910, two soldiers, three bells $700.00-1,200.00

SOLDIER BOY BOXED CARDBOARD GAME, 1914 14" x 21" $100.00-175.00

SPELLING BOARD, 14" long, 1889, learning game $50.00-125.00

SPRING HORSE RIDING TOY, 1870. $1,200.00-1,800.00

SPRING SKATE, ice skates, "Florence" style, 1875, forged steel blades $100.00-200.00

SPY GLASS, VICTORIAN CHILD'S TELESCOPE, pocket version, 1875 .... $100.00-200.00

SQUIRREL MENAGERIE COPPERED IRON TOY, 1886, 3" $25.00-60.00

ST. NICHOLAS A B C PICTURE BLOCKS, 1892, twenty-four in set, ornate box $500.00-1,000.00

STEAM DREDGE AND CONVEYOR, 1892, brass trimmed $200.00-400.00

STEAM ENGINE, HORIZONTAL, toy, 1875, fires at 1,000 rpm $100.00-200.00

STEAM ENGINE, toy, model, "The Ajax," F.A.O. Schwarz catalogue, 1886 .... $100.00-300.00

STEAM FOUNTAIN WITH BRASS FINISHED ENGINE, 1892 .... $100.00-300.00

STEAM SWITCH LOCOMOTIVE WITH TENDER CAR, brass boiler, 1892 .... $300.00-500.00

STEAM SWITCH LOCOMOTIVE, 1892, brass boiler $200.00-400.00

STEAM TOY FORGE WITH STEAM ENGINE, brass finish, 1892 .... $200.00-400.00

STEAMBOAT, ALCOHOL FUELED, ca. 1905, tin and metal $300.00-500.00

STEAMBOAT, tin, 1886, 20½" long, Jumbo on side wheeler $600.00-1,200.00

STEAMBOAT, tin, patented, 17" long, 1886 .... $400.00-950.00

STEEPLE CHASE, THE IMPROVED GAME, McLoughlin Brothers, 1892 .... $200.00-400.00

STEREOSCOPE, TOY, 1903 .... $100.00-175.00

STOCK FARM WOOD LITHOGRAPH, FARM SET, 1903, extremely rare $1,000.00-2000.00

STRANGE GAME OF FORBIDDEN FRUIT, 1890's, boxed $50.00-125.00

STREET ROLLER, mechanical, ca. 1910, 9" long, clockwork $500.00-1,000.00

SULKEY CAST IRON TOY, 9" long, ca. 1892, with jockey driver $650.00-1,200.00

SULKEY WITH JOCKEY CAST IRON PULL TOY, 1889 .... $750.00-1,500.00

SUNNYSIDE STOCK FARM, 1912, animals, buildings, etc., boxed set $100.00-300.00

SUNSHINE TOY COOK STOVE, 1889, cast iron $100.00-230.00

SURREY, CAST IRON, 1892, with driver in tall hat and single horse, 15" $1,000.00-1,700.00

SWINGING HOBBY HORSE, glass eye, 1912, 33" from nose to hoof $600.00-1,500.00

SWISS BUILDING BLOCKS IN WOODEN BOX WITH SLIDING COVER, 1889 .... $100.00-250.00

TABLE CROQUET GAME, 1912 .... $100.00-200.00

TABLE CROQUET SET, 1889 .... $50.00-100.00

TABLE WARE, CHILD'S ALUMINUM PLACE SETTING, 1903 .... $20.00-45.00

TALLY-HO STAGECOACH WAGON, cast iron, 1892, four galloping horses, 18" $1,000.00-2,000.00

TEDDY "R" TOY PISTOL BELT, circa 1912 .... $50.00-100.00

TEDDY BEAR MUFF, hand warmer, circa 1910 .... $100.00-300.00

TELEPHONE, wall type with crank, ca. 1912, toy $100.00-200.00

TELESCOPE, POCKET VERSION, collapses, 1875, spy glass $100.00-200.00

THE IMPROVED GEOGRAPHICAL GAME, 1890's, Parker Brothers $100.00-200.00

THE PRETTY VILLAGE by McLoughlin Brothers, 1892, boxed, ten buildings $150.00-300.00

THE WHITE SQUADRON PICTURE PUZZLES, nautical theme, 1892, McLoughlin $100.00-200.00

THE WORLD'S COLUMBIAN EXPOSITION PICTURE PUZZLE BLOCKS, thirty-two puzzles in set, 1892 .... $200.00-400.00

THE WORLD'S FAIR BUILDING BLOCKS, 1892, boxed, twelve blocks $200.00-400.00

THREE LITTLE KITTENS, BOXED CARDBOARD GAME, ca. 1910 .... $100.00-225.00

TIVOLI GAME OF MARBLES, 1886, cup with target $100.00-150.00

TOMMY SNOOKS PICTURE BLOCKS, 1892, boxed set, twenty-four block set, 7" x 12" $200.00-375.00

TOOL CHEST, "The Companion," deluxe boy's tool chest, 1886 with tools $150.00-300.00

TOOL CHEST, boy's "Little Buttercup," 9½" long, 1889 .... $100.00-220.00

TOOL CHEST, boy's "The Daisy," 10" long, 1886 .... $125.00-250.00

TOP, hardwood, peg spinner, ca. 1889 ... $25.00-65.00

TOY BED, ENAMELED AND GILT, 1914 doll bed $50.00-125.00

TOY BEDROOM SET with furniture and room, 1889, miniature scale $100.00-250.00

TOY DOLL IN SWING, 10½" tall, wood, momentum/gravity action, 1875 .... $100.00-300.00

TOY HORSE REINS, 1899 .... $25.00-80.00

TOY MACHINERY, circular saw and table, 1886 .... $100.00-225.00

TOY MACHINERY, cone pulley for lathe attachment $50.00-100.00

TOY MACHINERY, grindstone, 1886 .... $100.0200.00

TOY MACHINERY, pulleys set, 1886 .... $25.00-100.00

TOY MACHINERY, TURNING LATHE, circa 1880 .... $100.00-225.00

TOY PARLOR SET with room and furniture, miniature, 1889 .... $100.00-250.00

TOY PISTOL, ECHO, 1894, shoots peas or beans $50.00-100.00

TOY SCALES, scoop style, 1886 marked, "Gem" toy scales $100.00-200.00

TOY SOLDIER, COPPERED IRON, circa 1890, 2" $50.00-95.00

TOY STEAM ENGINEER, 1886, "The Hero" brass boiler $200.00-375.00

TOY SWORD, 1889, with sheath, Montgomery Ward catalogue $100.00-220.00

TOY TOWN TELEGRAPH OFFICE, boxed playset, 1914 .... $100.00-275.00

TRAIN IRON "HERO" TRAIN, 1889, engine, tender and two passenger cars $300.00-750.00

TRANSFER WAGON, cast iron, 18" with driver and double horses $700.00-1,500.00

TRICKY DUCK FRICTION TOY, ca. 1914, 9" tall, bright colors, circles $200.00-400.00

TROLLEY CAME OFF, boxed game by Parker Brothers, 1914 .... $100.00-175.00

TRUMPET, TOY, tin 1886, 14" $100.00-200.00

TRUMPET, TOY, tin, 1886, 4" $35.00-70.00

TRUNK BOX LOTTO GAME, 1890's, McLoughlin Brothers $40.00-85.00

TUGBOAT AND BARGE, circa 1890, 25" long $400.00-800.00

TUMBLING FROG, multi-colored, ca. 1914, wind arms $100.00-150.00

TUMBLING INDIAN, circa 1910, wind arms $100.00-225.00

U.S. MAIL WAGON, child's version, 1878, 14" x 28", painted, striped $500.00-1,200.00

U.S. POSTMAN GAME, ca. 1914, 10" x 20" box $100.00-200.00

UNCLE SAM'S MAIL GAME, 1914, 15" x 16" cardboard game $200.00-500.00

UNITED STATES SPELLING PUZZLE, boxed, 1889 .... $50.00-130.00

VELOCIPEDE, boy's, ca. 1870 .... $300.00-675.00

VELOCIPEDE, child's tricycle, 1878, 24" and 28" wheels, iron frame $300.00-650.00

VICTOR, THE, BOXED CARDBOARD GAME, 1914 .... $75.00-150.00

VILLAGE PUMP, mechanical attachment for steam engine, 1892 .... $300.00-600.00

VIOLIN TOY, in original case, circa 1890, 16" long $200.00-500.00

WAGON, boy's, ca. 1870, wood frame, sides and wheels, T-tongue $700.00-1,250.00

WAGON, boy's, Taylor of Chicago, 1878, wood frame, T-tongue $400.00-800.00

WALKING BEAM STEAM ENGINE, circa 1890, toy $200.00-450.00

WALKING TEDDY BEAR, by Bing, ca. 1912, pull-type toy $700.00-1,500.00

WAR SHIP PICTURE BLOCKS, 1890's . $100.00-200.00

WARSHIP SQUADRON seven assorted small boats, boxed, ca. 1914 .... $200.00-400.00

WASH SET, "Unique" wash basin, board, wringer, etc. 1890's $100.00-200.00

WASHBOARD, TOY, 1914, wood/tin $20.00-40.00

WASHTUB, TOY, 1914, tin $20.00-35.00

WATCH, TOY, 1890's, tin, gilt chain $25.00-50.00

WATERING CAN, tin, lithograph with ornate children's design, 1914 .... $40.00-100.00

WATERLOO A BATTLE GAME, 1895, boxed board game $100.00-300.00

WAX DOLL, 12", 1875 .... $300.00-500.00

WESTCOTT'S COMBINATION BUILDING AND SPELLING BLOCKS, 1899 .... $200.00-400.00

WESTCOTT'S SPELLING BLOCKS, 1899, wooden box with paper lithograph label $100.00-250.00

WHEELBARROW, CHILD'S, 30", 1895 . $100.00-300.00

WHITE STONE CHINA TEA SET, 1889 $65.00-140.00

WILD FLOWER GAME, Parker Brothers, 1892 .... $100.00-300.00

WILD WEST BOXED CARDBOARD GAME, 1914 9 x 9" box $150.00-275.00

WOODEN FORT SET, 1889, cannons, sentinels, blocks, etc. set $100.00-300.00

WOODEN SOLDIERS, lithograph paper over wood, boxed set, 1889 .... $200.00-500.00

WORLD'S COLUMBIAN EXPOSITION PICTURE PUZZLES, McLoughlin, 1892, six... $200.00-475.00

WORLD'S EDUCATOR GAME, 1889 ...... $75.00-150.00

WORLD'S FAIR GAME, Parker Brothers, 1890's boxed board game $200.00-400.00

WORLD'S TOWER PICTURE BUILDING BLOCKS, ca. 1895 .... $300.00-650.00

YANKEE DOODLE A GAME OF AMERICA, 1895 boxed board game $250.00-500.00

YOUNG PEOPLE'S GEOGRAPHICAL GAME, 1890's, Parker Brothers $100.00-250.00

ZITHER, autoharp toy, 1899, American .. $30.00-70.00

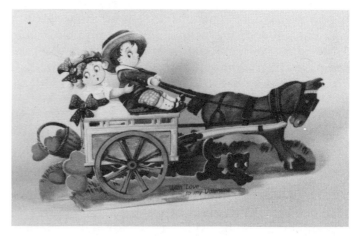

VALENTINE, EARLY, PONY PULLING CHILDREN IN CART, 10" long, German, Furnish collection, $30.00-65.00.

WINDUP TOYS

Windup toys are functionally grouped in this classification. The toys listed in this category are all operated by the winding of some mechanism. Some toys are key wound with a removable key such as those found in most of the Marx toys of the 1920's through the 1950's. Others are lever action with an attached spring-type lever which when pulled or pushed tightens the mainspring and releases the toy's action. Regardless of the external setup, all windup toys have some sort of internal tension spring which stores the inertia of the winding and gradually releases the energy (tension) to make the action of the toy work.

The two most popular materials for windup toys were tin and celluloid. Tin windup toys make up the vast majority of all windup toys. Tin was perfectly suited for the design of windups because it was both relatively inexpensive and sturdy. It could also be lithographed colorfully and brightly, and finished with an attractive shining lustre.

Another medium for windup toy production was celluloid. Now, this material was a strange "marriage" for the toy production industry. Celluloid was a lightweight, inexpensive ancestor of today's modern plastics, but it had some drawbacks: it was extremely brittle, fragile and highly flammable. Toys made of celluloid are very lightweight and seem to weigh almost nothing at all. This lightweight characteristic allowed toys with spinning whirligigs of umbrellas as canopies to appear to be on the verge of liftoff when their spinners start spinning. The toys seem to float through their action on the tabletop.

This lightweight quality was also the greatest threat to the toy's longevity, for because the toys were extremely fragile, a couple of excursions off the tabletop could reduce their wonderful designs to little chunks of brittle plastic. Another fascinating paradox here is the relative power of a windup concealed within the fragile celluloid exterior. It seems that some of the most dainty of these toys were destined for self-destruction from the day they were produced.

Because of the fragile nature of celluloid, these toys are relatively difficult to find today in mint condition. The novice collector should be careful to check thoroughly the celluloid toy before purchasing it. Often toys may have serious splits, cracks or even holes in them that are not visible from a shelftop inspection. Minor splits can be easily mended with glue, but major splits and defects should signal avoidance of the toy altogether.

Another word of advice to the new collector: absolutely avoid celluloid windup toys with non-working windup mechanisms. This author knows of several fine toy fix-it men who can avidly take apart a precious Marx windup and restore it like new. They can do it even without breaking off the little connecting tabs which hold together most of the best 1920's and 1930's windups. But they shun a broken celluloid windup like the plague. Why? To get nto the windup mechanism of most celluloid toys requires nothing short of major surgery and the splitting apart of the entire glue or molded seam of the toy. Even if the windup mechanism could be repaired, the resulting glue seams on the toy would so seriously devalue it that it would simply not be worth all the trouble.

So the advice here is, demand near mint to mint condition for all your toys, especially celluloid windups. You and your collection will be better off in the long run.

The mass appeal of windup toys is their clever actions. Windup toys dance, waddle, jiggle, eat, twirl, drive, circle, ride, peddle, scoot, walk, skate and do nearly every action possible to a human or animal. They are also desirable for their excellent lithography such as the 1930's toys of Louis Marx and Unique Art. Seeing windup toys is only a part of the pleasure, they must be wound to be completely enjoyed.

Windup toys today, particularly personality and comic character examples, are extremely popular among collectors and are greatly in demand. Disney and comic character windups, particularly Marx and LineMar, can now match the selling prices once only reserved for pristine condition, cast iron toys and the windups are fifty years newer! Even though windup toys of the 1930's, 1940's and 1950's may be half a century newer than valuable turn of the century cast iron toys, they are equally matched in today's collecting marketplace and they are worthy investment items.

A GROUPING OF TIN WINDUPS, 1920's-1940's, G.I. Joe, $65.00-125.00, HAPPY HOOLIGAN, $175.00-250.00, JOE PENNER, $250.00-500.00, Reynolds collection.

BOMBO CHIMP WINDUP BY UNIQUE ART, tin windup, 12" tall, 1930's, Reynolds collection, $60.00-100.00.

ACROBATIC MARVEL, rocking monkey windup, good colors, 1930's, Marx $60.00-90.00

ACROBATIC MONKEY, all celluloid, Japan, 5" red tux, circles on hands $35.00-65.00

ACROBATIC MONKEY, Marx, 1930's, tin windup, balances on two chairs $60.00-95.00

ACTION CLOWNS, Expert Toys, tin, clowns turn $35.00-60.00

ANDY "ANDREW BROWN" OF AMOS 'N ANDY, tin windup, Marx, 1930, 12" $250.00-550.00

ARTIE THE CLOWN, Unique Art, tin windup, 7" clown with tall hat drives $150.00-300.00

BABY CYCLE, Occupied Japan, little boy on trike, tin windup, celluloid, 3".........................$30.00-50.00

BALANCING CLOWN, manufactured by Chein, 1930's, 5" tall $20.00-65.00

BALANCING CLOWN, U. S. Zone Germany, clown balances on hands, 5" tin $50.00-100.00

BALLERINA, Marx, 1930's, toothed pull rod activated $50.00-95.00

BALOON SANTA WINDUP, Alps Manufacturing, 1950's $50.00-100.00

BALOON SANTA, Alps, Japan, 1950's, 7" windup, bell ringer $35.00-80.00

BARBER RABBIT, simulates cutting hair, 1940's all tin lithograph..$25.00-45.00

BARNACLE BILL, Chein, 1940, salty sailor, Popeye look-a-like, waddles $80.00-195.00

BARNEY GOOGLE AND SPARK PLUG, tin windup, German, Nifty, 7" tall, boxed $900.00-1,350.00

BASEBALL CATCHER, celluloid windup, Occupied Japan, 5", NY emblem on sleeve $40.00-85.00

BAVARIAN BOY HOLDING GIRL, by Schuco, pre-war Germany, 5" tin and cloth $65.00-155.00

BE-BOP JIGGER, plastic and tin, manufactued by Marx $75.00-200.00

BEAR GOLFER, TPS, Japan, tin windup, 7" tall $70.00-110.00

BEAR ROWING BOAT, S & E, Japan, tin windup, 10" $75.00-140.00

BEAR WADDLER, tin, Marx, 4", 1960's..$10.00-20.00

BEAR, hands in pockets, by Chein, 1940's, common toy $15.00-35.00

BETTY BOOP, all celluloid windup, 7", Fleischer Studios with box...$650.00-1,300.00

BIG LEAGUE HOCKEY PLAYER, Ahi, Japan, 1950's, 6" tin windup $100.00-200.0

BLEATING PIG, celluloid windup $20.00-40.00

BLONDIE'S JALOPY WINDUP CAR, Louis Marx, 1945 K.F.S. tin lithograph $675.00-1,250.00

BLUE RABBIT WITH GUITAR, Occupied Japan $65.00-80.00

BLUTO DIPPY DUMPER TIN WINDUP TRUCK, Marx, 1930's, celluloid figure $275.00-600.00

BOBBY THE POLICEMAN, English, tin windup, 5" boxed $40.00-85.00

BOOB McNUTT, Strauss, 1925, tin windup, 9" $350.00-700.00

BOXING CLOWN, made by Chein, 8" tin windup $200.00-500.00

BOXING KIDS, Occupied Japan, 6" celluloid and tin windup $60.00-120.00

BOY ON BIKE, Japan, 4" celluloid windup, circle action $20.00-40.00

BOY ON TRICYCLE, Unique Art, 8" ...$150.00-395.00

BOY PLAYING DRUM AND CYMBAL, Japan, 8", tin lithograph base $150.00-300.00

BOY SKIING, probably Chein, 1940's, very bright colors, all tin $45.00-80.00

BOY WITH HOOP, German windup, hand painted, 1900 ....$500.00-1,000.00

WINDUP TOYS

CELLULOID PUPPY AND SHOE WINDUP, Japan, tin shoe, 8" long, Furnish collection, $100.00-250.00.

CELLULOID DANCING COUPLE, Japan, 4", $125.00-175.00.

BRITISH MILITARY BAND CYMBAL PLAYER, Japan, windup, 11" composition, cloth..........$40.00-75.00
BRUNO THE SPECTACLE BEAR, Japan, windup, 7" tin and plush $35.00-65.00
BUCKING BRONCO, Lehmann, early German, tin windup, 1881, 7½" $300.00-600.00
BUCKING BRONCO, MT, Japan, 1950's, 4" all celluloid windup horse and cowboy $35.00-60.00
BULLY, U.S. Zone Germany, tin windup bullfrog, boxed, 8" $110.00-250.00
BUMPER CAR WINDUP, 6½" $50.00-100.00
BUNNY CARRIAGE, Japan, windup, all celluloid, 5" $35.00-75.00

BUNNY THE HAPPY DRUMMER, Alps, Japan, 6" $25.00-55.00
BUNNY, by Chein, 1940's, bright colors tin lithograph $20.00-40.00
BUTTER AND EGGMAN, by Marx, windup similar to Joe Penner, boxed $900.00-1,700.00
BUTTERCUP CRAWLING BABY windup, 8" long, German $500.00-1,000.00
CAMEL BOY, Occupied Japan, 5" windup, tin and plush, boxed $25.00-45.00
CAT AND BALL, (on back) all celluloid windup, Occupied Japan, 4" boxed $35.00-75.00
CAT PUSHING BALL, Marx, 1938, all tin, wood ball, windup push tail $45.00-85.00
CHARLIE CHAPLIN BOXER, CHAMPION, tin, metal, cloth, ...$1,000.00-2,000.00
CHARLIE McCARTHY BASS DRUMMER WINDUP TOY, Marx, 1939 ....$450.00-865.00
CHEERY COOK with box, celluloid $35.00-55.00
CHICK MERRY-GO-ROUND, Japan, celluloid windup, 7" boxed...$15.00-35.00
CHICKEN, Germany, 1920's, tin windup, 7", good details on lithograph $90.00-225.00
CIRCUS CYCLIST, Hi-wheel, TPS, Japan, tin windup, 7" $90.00-150.00
CIRCUS ELEPHANT, KA, Japan, windup, 7" tin, pushes ball, with umbrella $45.00-90.00
CIRCUS ELEPHANT, TPS, Japan, tin windup, 11" pulls three clowns $60.00-95.00
CIRCUS MONKEY ON HORSEBACK, Haji, Japan, 1950's, tin windup $35.00-55.00
CIRCUS SEAL, MT, Japan, plush tin windup, 5" walks on flippers, ball spins $30.00-65.00
CLIMBING FIREMAN, Marx, 1950's $40.00-85.00
CLOWN IN BARREL, Chein, 1930's, 8" tin windup, waddles $125.00-250.00
CLOWN MAKING THE LION JUMP THROUGH THE FLAMING HOOP, TPS, made in Japan, 1950's $100.00-175.00
CLOWN ON DONKEY, pre-war Germany, tin windup, 6" $50.00-125.00
CLOWN ON DONKEY, U.S. Germany, Bloomer and Schuler tin windup, 6" $100.00-150.00
CLOWN ON ROLLER SKATES, TPS, Japan, tin windup, 6" $125.00-200.00
CLOWN PLAYING FLUTE AND DRUM, 9" windup $80.00-160.00
CLOWN VIOLINIST, Schuco, tin windup, cloth covered body, 4½" $95.00-145.00
CLOWN WITH PARASOL, Chein, 1920's, 8" windup springs parasol on nose $100.00-175.00
COMMANDO JOE, Ohio Art, 8" tin windup crawling soldier with rifle $65.00-140.00
COOLIE PUSHING CART, possibly Girard, 1930, tin windup, 6" $80.00-125.00
COWBOY ON DONKEY, all celluloid windup, Japan 5" $30.00-60.00
COWBOY ON HORSE, Marx, 1925, 6" tin windup $80.00-140.00
COWBOY ON HORSE, Marx, tin $125.00-175.00
COWBOY ON HORSE, Occupied Japan, celluloid windup, 7" horse galloping.............................$30.00-65.00
COWBOY RIDER, black horse version, Marx, 1930's, tin, 7"...............................$140.00-250.00

CRAWLING SOLDIER, celluloid windup, Occupied Japan $25.00-70.00

CRAZY CLOWN, Yone, Japan, tin windup, plastic wheels, 4½" long $20.00-40.00

DAGWOOD THE DRIVER, Marx, crazy car action, all tin lithograph $400.00-900.00

DAGWOOD'S SOLO FLIGHT WINDUP AIRPLANE, Marx, 9", 1935 ....$200.00-425.00

DANCE HAWAIIAN, Occupied Japan, 6" celluloid windup hula dancer, box $75.00-140.00

DANCING COUPLE, Occupied Japan, all celluloid windup, 4" boy in sailor suit $35.00-60.00

DANCING DOLL, Japan, 1950's, 6" tall, windup, vinyl head, boxed $20.00-35.00

DANCING LASSIE, Lindstrom, USA, 1930's, 8" tin windup $65.00-135.00

DANDY, Mikuni, Japan, 1950's, tin $60.00-85.00

DAPPER DAN, Marx, USA, 1920, a Jigger Bank $600.00-900.00

DISNEYLAND EXPRESS CASEY JR., tin windup train, Marx, 12" with box $65.00-95.00

DISNEYLAND FERRIS WHEEL, manufactured by Chein, 1940's $100.00-250.00

DODGE 'M CAR, English, 1950's tin windup, clown in car...$40.00-80.00

DONALD DUCK ACROBAT, LineMar, Japan, 1950's, Walt Disney Productions, boxed.....$150.00-350.00

DONALD DUCK CELLULOID WINDUP NODDER, 1930's, long-billed Donald $200.00-425.00

DONALD DUCK DIPSY CAR, manufactured by LineMar $200.00-450.00

DONALD DUCK DIPSY CAR, Marx, windup, tin, plastic Donald figure, 6" $200.00-400.00

DONALD DUCK DRUMMER, 6" windup, by LineMar, in original box $200.00-450.00

DONALD DUCK DUET, Walt Disney by Marx, 1946, Donald and Goofy...........................$225.00-500.00

DONALD DUCK DUET, Marx, 1946, tin windup, 10", two figures, boxed $400.00-850.00

DONALD DUCK PLASTIC WINDUP TOY, Donald dressed in Mexican garb, 1950's.....................$50.00-85.00

DONALD DUCK THE SKIER, large plastic windup by Marx, 1950's, boxed $100.00-175.00

DONALD DUCK WINDUP by Schuco, Germany, 1960's version with plastic $75.00-135.00

DONALD DUCK WINDUP by Schuco, long-billed, cloth and tin, 1930's, boxed $500.00-1,000.00

DONKEY, The Obstinate, Japan, pre-war, 7", all celluloid, with circus box................................$50.00-110.00

DOPEY THE DWARF, Disney, windup by Chad Valley, England, 1930's $100.00-200.00

DOPEY TIN WINDUP TOY by Marx, 1938, waddles or walks, 10" $125.00-200.00

DORA DIPSY CAR, Marx, 1950's, tin windup, 6" $125.00-175.00

DOUGHBOY, by Chein, tin winup, 6" tin lithograph, WWI soldier with rifle.....................$120.00-240.00

DRINKING BEAR, 8" plush windup, boxed, Japan $30.00-60.00

DRINKING DAN, tin windup, 7" cloth, tin, vinyl face $30.00-65.00

DRUM MAJOR, Wolverine, 1930's, 14" red jacket $60.00-120.00

DRUMMER MONKEY, SK, Japan, plush windup, 7" plays drum $20.00-35.00

DRUMMING SOLDIER, LineMar, Japan, 5" in box $45.00-85.00

DUCK, 1930's, 9" long, tin windup, lithograph, zig-zag action $20.00-45.00

DUCK, by Chein $15.00-40.00

DUMBO, Marx, Walt Disney Productions, 1941, tin windup, 4" flips $100.00-240.00

EASTER RABBIT, tin windup, Marx, 5" holds lithograph Easter basket.....................................$35.00-70.00

FANTASYLAND WAGON, TPS, Japan, 11" windup beetle with squirrels, box $75.00-135.00

FELIX THE CAT ON A SCOOTER, tin lithograph, toy, Nifty, German, 1924 ....$385.00-600.00

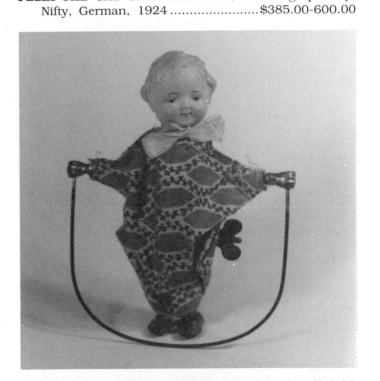

CLOWN BOY JUMPING ROPE, metal and celluloid, 6", Reynolds collection, $75.00-180.00.

CHEIN DUCK, TIN WINDUP, 3", 1940's, Reynolds collection, $15.00-40.00.

CELLULOID WINDUP, LITTLE BLACK BOY AND DOG, 6", colorful, excellent detail, Furnish collection, $200.00-400.00.

SELECTION OF DONALD DUCK by Marx and LineMar Toys of the 1940's-1950's, Reynolds collection, values $200.00-450.00.

FERDINAND THE BULL WINDUP TOY, Marx, Disney Enterprises, 1930's, tail moves, tin ...$65.00-125.00

FERDINAND THE BULL, manufactured by LineMar, Japan $150.00-350.00

FIGHTING COCKS, Nifty, 1920 ....$200.00-500.00

FIREMAN JOE, Marx, tin windup, 8" Joe climbs ladder $125.00-200.00

FIRING CYCLE #2, windup, tin, made in Japan, 1930's $200.00-450.00

FLINTSTONES WINDUP FLIP-OVER TANK, LineMar, 1960's $75.00-125.00

FLIP OVER AIRPLANE by Marx $150.00-350.00

FLYING BIRD, Lehmann, 1895, 7" "flies" suspended from wing cords....................$800.00-1,250.00

FREIGHT WAGON, 1940's, porter and lithograph crates, tin $45.00-85.00

G.I. JOE WINDUP CRAZY CAR, tin ...$125.00-225.00

G.I. JOE, JUMPING JEEP, Unique Art, tin windup, 6½" crazy car...................................$70.00-225.00

G.I. JOE K9 PUPS, Unique Art, tin windup, 9" $65.00-125.00

GALLOPING COWBOY, Daiya, Japan, 1950's, tin and celluloid, boxed $40.00-95.00

GAY NINETIES CYCLIST, TPS, Japan, 7" windup $65.00-110.00

GEORGE THE DRUMMER BOY, tin drum major with drum, bright colors $40.00-70.00

GERTIE THE GALLOPING GOOSE, tin windup, Unique Art, 9" long, hops......................$75.00-125.00

GIRARD HANDCAR, 1930's, tin lithograph, two men pump handcar, 6" long $80.00-175.00

GONDOLA RIDE, 10", four gondolas with lithographed children riders, music $100.00-200.00

GOOFY PLASTIC WINDUP TOY, Marx, 1950's, tail spins, 9" $50.00-75.00

GOOFY WINDUP, tin, manufactured by LineMar, 1950's $100.00-220.00

GOOSE, by Unique Art, 1930's, neck bobbing action, tin lithograph $40.00-70.00

GRANDPA'S NEW CAR, Japan, tin, 5½"$85.00-150.00

GYMNAST, Kikaitaiso, Japan, pre-war, 7" celluloid girl on trapeze $45.00-70.00

HAPPI TIME, Alps, Japan, 1950's, windup, 4" celluloid girl on beach with umbrella $125.00-175.00

HAPPY GRANDPA, Yone, Japan, tin windup, 4", Grandpa and house, boxed $25.00-40.00

HAPPY HOOLIGAN WINDUP TOY, tin lithograph, Chein, 1932, 6" $175.00-250.00

HAPPY JACK, tin lever action, German, 1920's, 7" black man dancer.........................$150.00-350.00

HAPPY THE TROMBONE PLAYER, TPS, Japan, 10", cloth clothes, clown figure $90.00-150.00

HAROLD LLOYD TIN WINDUP, Marx, 1930's, 11" $175.00-400.00

HAWAIIAN DANCER, large version, Japan, 9" all celluloid..$35.00-75.00

HENRY AND HIS BROTHER CELLULOID WINDUP TOY, 1934 ....$1,200.00-2,300.00

HENRY AND THE SWAN CELLULOID WINDUP, 4" x 9", Japan $275.00-595.00

HENRY RIDING ON THE ELEPHANT, celluloid windup, 1930's...$975.00-2,400.00

HENRY THE ACROBAT TRAPEZE WINDUP TOY, 1930's, celluloid figure $465.00-675.00

HEY HEY THE CHICKEN SNATCHER, Marx, black man with dog hanging behind $600.00-1,200.00

HI-WAY HENRY COMIC CHARACTER WINDUP TOY, 1920's, tin lithograph car.........$2,500.00-3,900.00

HI-WHEEL CLOWN CYCLIST, TPS, Japan, 6½" tin windup $100.00-200.00

HOKEY POKEY ICE CREAM PUSH CART VENDOR, 1910, German $1,500.00-2,500.00

HONEYMOON EXPRESS train $75.00-135.00

HOPPO THE MONKEY, tin windup, Marx, 1925, 8", plays cymbals $65.00-120.00

HORSE AND INDIAN WINDUP, U.S. Zone Germany, tin 4" hors, Elaston-like $50.00-100.00

HORSE AND JOCKEY, German, tin windup, 5" $60.00-90.00

HORSE CART WITH DRIVER, tin windup, 10", Marx, wood grain, lithograph on cart $30.00-65.00

HUMPHREY MOBILE, Wyandotte, tin, 9", Humphrey pulls shack on wheels $250.00-500.00

ICE CREAM CART, by Cortland, tin lithograph with large bell, 1940's $60.00-95.00

INDIAN IN CANOE, rows, tin, 8½" $300.00-600.00

INDIAN, hopping stand-up version, 5" tall, ca. 1930's $30.00-60.00

INJUN CHIEF, tin windup, Ohio Art, 8" long, crawling Indian, boxed $50.00-100.00

JAZZBO JIM, Marx, 1920's, tin windup, 9", jigger dances on roof................................$300.00-500.00

JENNY THE BALANCING MULE, Strauss, 1920's, tin windup, 9" boxed $250.00-525.00

JET ROLLER COASTER, Wolverine, tin, ramp toy with tunnel, box $55.00-120.00

JIGGER, tin windup, Lindstrom, 8", 1930's dancer $150.00-275.00

JIMINY CRICKET WINDUP FIGURE, LineMar, 1950's with umbrella $200.00-400.00

JOCK-O-STICK, Monkey riding toy horse, Japan, tin and cloth, 7", boxed..........................$20.00-45.00

JOLLY DRUMMER WINDUP, Japan, plastic with composition figure beats drum $35.00-75.00

JOLLY JOCKO, pre-war, Japan, 5" plush monkey combs his hair windup..................................$30.00-60.00

JOY RIDERS, manufactured by Marx, 1925, 7" long, crazy car $150.00-375.00

JUMPIN' JEEP, by Marx, tin, boxed ...$100.00-185.00

JUMPING DOG, 1950's, windup, 5" hops, jumps, Japan $10.00-25.00

JUMPING DOG, by Marx, 1940, legs outstretched, tin lithograph...$40.00-65.00

JUNGLE PETE, THE ALLIGATOR, Automatic Toy, USA, 15" long, tin windup $40.00-65.00

KIDDY AMUSEMENT PARK, toy $200.00-400.00

KNITTING CAT, TN, Japan, windup, 6" plush cat in tin chair..$30.00-50.00

KNOCKOUT CHAMPS, manufactued by Marx, 1930's, boxing ring......................................$200.00-400.00

KO-KO THE SANDWICH MAN, TN, Japan, 7" windup, cloth and vinyl, boxed.....................$70.00-130.00

LADY BUG FAMILY, TPS, Japan, 12" tin windup family of ladybugs $10.00-22.00

LEHMANN ALABAMA COON JIGGER, windup toy $500.00-950.00

LEHMANN BUCKING BRONCO, early German, tin windup, 1881, 7½" $300.00-600.00

LEHMANN CLIMBING MONKEY, boxed .$200.00-450.00

LEHMANN CLOWN ON DONKEY, tin windup, 1911 ....$250.00-500.00

LEHMANN KADI, two chinamen $800.00-1,100.00

LEHMANN LILA MOTORCAR, German windup toy $1,250.00-1,900.00

LEHMANN MANDARIN, three figures, tin windup, German $875.00-1,500.00

LEHMANN NAUGHTY BOY, tin lithograph windup $900.00-1,200.00

LEHMANN STUBBORN MONKEY, toy ..$400.00-850.00

DUCK TIN WINDUP, PAINTED TIN, 6" long, permanent windup key, Furnish collection, $150.00-350.00.

HAM AND SAM MINSTRELS, STRAUSS, 1921 WINDUP, all tin, Reynolds collection, $700.00-1,200.00.

LET THE DRUMMER BOY PLAY, Marx, 1930's, tin windup walking drummer, bass.......$80.00-150.00

LI'L ABNER DOGPATCH BAND, tin lithograph, by Unique Art $300.00-500.00

LINCOLN TUNNEL, Unique Art...........$100.00-175.00

LITTLE PIG, Walt Disney Productions, LineMar, Japan, 4" hops, plays flute $50.00-120.00

LONG NECKED clown car $900.00-1,500.00

LOOPING PLANE, Marx, 1940, tin windup, 7" wingspan $50.00-75.00

KIDDY CYCLIST BY UNIQUE ART, 8½" tall, Reynolds collection, $100.00-250.00.

KNOCK-OUT PRIZE FIGHTERS, Strauss windup, 6", Reynolds collection, $150.00-350.00.

LOUIS ARMSTRONG TIN WINDUP with vinyl head and hands, 10" cloth costume $125.00-200.00

MAGGIE AND JIGGS WINDUP, c. George McManus, 7" tin toy $650.00-1,100.00

MAIN STREET by Marx, street scene with little cars, windup, original box $200.00-300.00

MAN WITH DRUM, Germany, pre-war, tin windup, 5", man in checkered coat $75.00-110.00

MARINE, in uniform, tin lithograph, windup, hopping version, 1930's $30.00-60.00

MARX AIRPLANE, Flip-Over $150.00-350.00

MECHANICAL DRUMMER, Chein, 1930's, 9" common, boxed $75.00-125.00

MECHANICAL TRACTOR, windup, Marx, with earth grader, boxed $55.00-125.00

MEGO MAN, similar to Mr. Machine, Japan, tin windup, 7" $125.00-400.00

MERRY BALL BLOWER CIRCUS TRUCK, Japan, 5" windup, with lithograph, clowns $50.00-95.00

MERRY CHRISTMAS SANTA, TN, Japan, 1950's, 7" windup, tin body, celluloid head $35.00-170.00

MERRY DUCK, Japan, plush/tin/vinyl 6" plays cymbals, walks, boxed $20.00-30.00

MERRY GONDOLA tin windup with four rocket shaped gondolas, 5" base $100.00-200.00

MICKEY MOUSE, LineMar, Japan 5½" whirling tail, in box $200.00-600.00

MILK DRINKING BEAR, Japan, windup, 6" Panda Bear, pours and drinks......................$20.00-40.00

MISTER DAN THE HOTDOG EATING MAN, TN, Japan, windup, 7", box $25.00-55.00

MONKEY BANJO PLAYER, Japan, windup, plush, dressed as cowboy, boxed $50.00-95.00

MONKEY BARTENDER Japan, 8", windup, shakes drinks..$30.00-45.00

MONKEY BATTER, AAA, Japan, 1950's, tin windup, 8" boxed...$125.00-225.00

MONKEY CYCLE, Occupied, Japan, celluloid and tin windup, 3" boxed $35.00-65.00

MONKEY PLAYING BANJO, Occupied Japan, celluloid windup, 7½" $65.00-120.00

MONKEY RIDING A CANDY CART, ca. 1950's, all tin lithograph $40.00-70.00

MONKEY WITH CAMERA, tin windup, fabric clothes..$20.00-40.00

MONKEY WITH FIELD GLASSES, Japan, 1950's, 6" tin windup, glasses raise $20.00-45.00

MOON MULLINS AND KAYO WINDUP CAR, 6" long tin lithograph $375.00-525.00

MORTIMER SNERD BASS DRUMMER TIN WINDUP, Marx, 1939 ....$450.00-865.00

MORTIMER SNERD CRAZY CAR, windup, Louis Marx, 1930's $200.00-425.00

MOTHER GOOSE WITH CAT, tin windup, 1920's, 9" $200.00-400.00

MOTORCYCLE WITH SIDECAR, Tippco, U.S. Zone Germany, 8" $175.00-350.00

MOTORCYCLE, Occupied Japan, tin windup, 5" $90.00-185.00

MUSICAL ELEPHANT, Japan, windup, 6" plush, tin ears, plays drums and cymbals........$35.00-65.00

MYSTERY ALPINE EXPRESS, 1950's, automatic toy, tin windup $65.00-135.00

MYSTERY POLICE CYCLE, Marx, 1930's, tin windup, 4½", yellow motorcycle......................$45.00-75.00

NATIVE ON TURTLE, ca. 1930's, tin lithograph..$45.00-90.00

NAZI ON HORSEBACK, tin windup, Bloomer Schuler, ca. 1936, 5" $275.00-520.00

NEWSBOY, lithograph, tin holding a newspaper, 1930's $35.00-60.00
OVER THE HILL RACE CAR AND TRACK, boxed, tin windup, Alps, Japan $65.00-135.00
OWL, plush, tin windup, 8" walks, eyes open and close $30.00-50.00

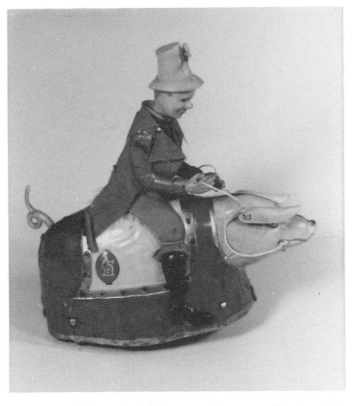

MARX STUNT PLANE WINDUP, 6" long, tin, Reynolds collection, $65.00-135.00.

LEHMANN MAN ON PIG TIN WINDUP 6", Furnish collection, $400.00-850.00.

LINDSTROM MAMMY, 8" TIN LITHOGRAPH WINDUP, Reynolds collection, $75.00-175.00.

MAID TIN WINDUP BY LINDSTROM, 8", arm action with broom, Reynolds collection, $100.00-200.00.

MONKEY ON TRICYCLE TIN WINDUP, 5½" tall, tin with fiber board arms, Reynolds collection, $50.00-125.00.

RED CAP PORTER, TIN WINDUP, 8" tall, Reynolds collection, $100.00-275.00.

PANGEE THE FUNNY DANCER, white jigger toy, tin windup $100.00-200.00

PARTY ANIMALS, Yone, Japan, tine windup, 6", monkey and dog sit at table $40.00-90.00

PAT AND PATACHON JOURNEY CAR, tin lithograph, windup $400.00-900.00

PECOS BILL PLASTIC WINDUP TOY by Marx, 1950's $25.00-60.00

PELICAN, made in pre-war Japan, 4" tin windup, waddles $30.00-75.00

PENGUIN, small tin lithograph windup by Chein, 1940's $25.00-50.00

PINOCCHIO THE ACROBAT, Marx, 1939, W. D. P., rocking windup $150.00-300.00

PINOCCHIO THE ACROBAT, Walt Disney Enterprises, 1939, tin, 17" $85.00-350.00

PINOCCHIO TIN WINDUP WALKER TOY, by Marx, 1939, 10" $125.00-200.00

PINOCCHIO, by Marx, 1930's, walker, stationary eyes $75.00-185.00

PINOCCHIO, by Marx, walker, animated eyes, 1939 ....$125.00-250.00

PLAY GOLF, Strauss, 1920's, golfer on green, tin windup, 5" figure $300.00-575.00

PLAYFUL PLUTO, manufactured by LineMar, Japan, 6", boxed $200.00-400.00

PLAYFUL PUPPY, Alps, Japan, plastic windup, 6", tail spins, head moves $20.00-30.00

PLAYING DOG WITH SHOE, Occupied Japan, windup celluloid dog shakes tin shoe $40.00-100.00

PLAYLAND SCOOTER, TPS, Japan, windup, 2" car, 9" x 6" base, lithograph carnival $35.00-60.00

PLUTO WATCH ME ROLL OVER WINDUP TOY, Marx, 1930's, Walt Disney Enterprises $50.00-125.00

PLUTO WINDUP TOY, plastic, Marx, 1950's, large version, Pluto in hat $100.00-175.00

POLAR BEAR, mechanical, plush, 1950's, 5" mother with baby..$35.00-65.00

POLICE CAR CHASE, TPS, Japan, all tin windup, 2½" car on 9" x 6" base $30.00-60.00

POLICE CAR, unmarked, tin, 1930's $15.00-30.00

POPEYE AND BLUTO WINDUP BOXING TOY, LineMar, 4" tall tin and celluloid..................$125.00-350.00

POPEYE AND OLIVE OYL ON THE ROOF TIN WINDUP, 1930's $400.00-950.00

POPEYE DIPPY DUMPER TIN WINDUP TRUCK, Marx, Popeye figure is celluloid...............$275.00-600.00

POPEYE EXPRESS Popeye pushes wheelbarrow with parrot on top, Marx $400.00-750.00

POPEYE ON ROLLER SKATES, tin lithograph, by LineMar $375.00-625.00

POPEYE ON TRICYCLE TIN WINDUP, tin and cloth, LineMar $700.00-1,200.00

POPEYE ROW BOAT, tin lithograph windup, LineMar, Japan $1,400.00-2,500.00

POPEYE TANK TOY, tin windup, LineMar, King Features $75.00-225.00

POPEYE THE CHAMP BIG FIGHT WINDUP TOY, Marx, 1930's, tin/celluloid $1,000.00-2,000.00

POPEYE THE FLYER AIRPLANE AND TIN LITHOGRAPH TOWER, Marx........$375.00-545.00

POPEYE THE HEAVY HITTER, bell and mallet, Chein windup $895.00-1,300.00

POPEYE WITH OLIVE OYL IN CHAIR WINDUP, LineMar, Japan, with Olive Oyl .. $500.00-1,000.00

PORKY PIG, Marx, 1939, tin windup, 8" twirls umbrella $125.00-225.00

PROUD PEACOCK, Alps, Japan, 6½", tin windup, boxed $85.00-140.00

PUZZLE CAT, Japan, 6" tin winup, pushes ball, boxed $20.00-40.00

QUACK QUACK, Lehmann, 1903, 7", windup, mother duck and three ducklings $150.00-450.00

RABBIT AND BEAR PLAYING BALL, TPS, Japan, tin windup, boxed $80.00-125.00

RABBIT EATING CARROT, Japan, plastic windup, 6" $25.00-55.00

RACER #39, Lupor, USA, 1950's, Indy Style racer, tin, boxed $85.00-150.00

RANCHER, all celluloid, boxed, made in Occupied Japan $50.00-95.00

RAP AND TAP IN A FAMILY SCRAP, Unique Art, tin windup, 1925.............................$250.00-550.00

RED RANGER RID'EM COWBOY, tin windup, 1930's, Wyandotte, 6" $125.00-300.00

REX THE RECKONING DOG, W. German, celluloid windup dog on tin base, boxed $30.00-50.00

ROARING LION, Alps, Japan, plush windup, boxed, 5" $30.00-50.00

RODEO JOE, Unique Art $75.00-195.00

ROLLERSKATING HOBO CLOWN, tin windup, TPS, Japan, 6" $85.00-195.00

ROLLOVER AIRPLANE, Marx, 1920's $90.00-140.00

ROLLOVER CAT, Marx, 1930's black cat holds ball, boxed $35.00-95.00

ROOKIE PILOT, Marx, 1930's, tin lithograph, 7" plane, crazy car action $150.00-325.00

ROUND UP TEX THE WHIRLING COWBOY, Irwin, 1950's, plastic, 10"..............................$15.00-40.00

RUDY, comic character, Nifty $1,200.00-1,600.00

SAM THE CITY GARDENER, plastic and tin windup, Marx, 1950's, boxed $75.00-150.00

SAMBO, Alps, Japan, windup, 10" composition head, cloth/tin, Monkey with quitar $55.00-120.00

SANTA AND REINDEER, Occupied Japan, windup, 8" celluloid, Santa and sled with reindeer $50.00-90.00

SANTA CLAUS ON SLED, Occupied Japan, 8" windup, all celluloid, boxcd $60.00-95.00

SANTA CLAUS, TN, Japan, 6" all tin windup, boxed $90.00-170.00

SANTA PUSHING CARRIAGE WITH UMBRELLA, Japan, 1950's, celluloid and tin, 5" $60.00-125.00

SANTA WALKER, tin windup, English, 5" with key $60.00-140.00

SANTA'S ELF, Chein, 1925, boxed, looks like a short Santa.................................$200.00-500.00

SCHUCO MONKEY, 3½" $55.00-125.00

SEAL, TPS, Japan, 1950's, tin windup, 7" spins umbrella $35.00-50.00

SEESAW MONKEYS, Distler, German, 1920, tin windup, 10" $175.00-400.00

SHERIFF SAM WHOPEE CAR, boxed, 6", windup toy $95.00-150.00

SHIP AHOY, 1925, tin windup, similar to Marx Honeymoon Express, lighthouse ..$600.00-1,200.00

SINGING BIRD IN CAGE, Japan, 1950's, 6" windup, 2" celluloid bird in cage $20.00-45.00

SITTING RABBIT, spinning umbrella $25.00-55.00

SKATING COUPLE, all celluloid windup, Occupied Japan, 5½" tall $75.00-150.00

LEHMANN TIN WINDUP CAR, 5" tall, Furnish collection, $400.00-800.00.

LADY WITH FRUIT CART, composition and tin windup, 6" long, Furnish collection, $200.00-400.00.

MARX MERRY MAKERS BAND, 1920's, tin windup mouse band, Reynolds collection, $300.00-650.00.

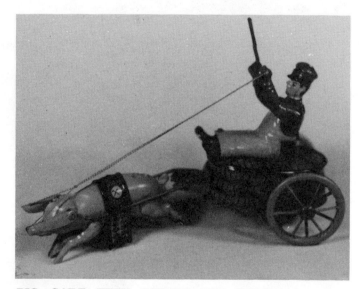

PIG CART WITH DRIVER TIN WINDUP, German marked "Marke Stock," 8" long, Furnish collection, $300.00-700.00.

SKI BOY, Chein, 1930's, boxed, 6" tin windup toy $100.00-200.00
SKIDOODLE CAR, tin windup $750.00-1,500.00
SKIP ROPE ANIMALS, TPS, Japan, 8", tin windup, squirrel and bear, boxed $60.00-125.00
SKIP ROPE ANIMALS, TPS, Japan, tin windup, 9" long, bears and squirrels $60.00-100.00
SKIPPY THE TRICKY CYCLIST, CLOWN, TPS, Japan, tin windup, boxed $125.00-200.00
SKY RANGERS, by Unique Art, 1930's, tin plane and blimp $150.00-275.00
SMILING SAM THE CARNIVAL MAN, tin windup, Alps, Japan, 9", boxed $100.00-195.00

SMITTY RIDING A SCOOTER WINDUP, Marx, 8" tall, 1930's $550.00-875.00
SMOKEY SAM THE WORLD FIREMAN, windup, 1950's, Marx, 7" boxed $120.00-180.00
SOLDIER, WWI, Marx, prone position with rifle $65.00-105.00
SOLDIER, WWI, prone with rifle, tin windup, 7" long $80.00-125.00
STAGECOACH WITH HORSES WINDUP TOY, 9" $50.00-125.00
SUBWAY EXPRESS, Marx, 1950's, tin windup, 9" diameter base, with box $65.00-145.00
SURPRISE SANTA CLAUS, 8", 1950's, windup, cloth and vinyl..$50.00-85.00
SWAN, Occupied Japan, celluloid windup, 3" long, pink, boxed $20.00-45.00
SWINGING WINKY BUNNY, plush and tin windup with box $10.00-25.00
TAP TAP, Lehmann, Germany, 1905, 6" with original box $400.00-950.00
TIGER, Marx, plush windup with vinyl head, walks and growls, boxed $45.00-70.00
TIMMY, TWO CATS ROCK, canopy, spins, 10", Japan $110.00-250.00
TIP TOP PORTER, Strauss, tin windup, 6" pushes cart..$175.00-375.00
TODDLING BABE, windup, celluloid, Occupied Japan, 4" boxed $35.00-65.00
TOM TOM JUNGLE BOY, Marx, Japan, 7", windup, tin, boxed $45.00-85.00
TONY THE TIGER WINDUP, Marx $50.00-155.00
TOONERVILLE TROLLEY TIN LITHOGRAPH WINDUP, 1920's, with driver and stovepipe ..$450.00-800.00
TOYLAND SEESAW, lithograph of carnival rides, tin windup, 7", Japan $110.00-195.00
TRAIN SET, Brim-Toy, Wells, England, tin windup, 16" long, three cars $75.00-140.00
TRAVELING BOY, Occupied Japan, celluloid windup, 4½" $40.00-75.00
TRICKY TAXI WINDUP, Marx, 1930's, red/white, 4½" $20.00-40.00
TRICYCLE WITH TRAILER, Kanto, Japan, celluloid and tin with vinyl head, 7 ....$20.00-40.00
TURKEY, U.S. Zone Germany, tin windup, 5½" walks, spreads feathers............................$110.00-200.00
TURTLE WINDUP, Gunthermann, tin windup, 5" $20.00-40.00
TWIST DANCER, 1960's, S & E, Japan, tin and cloth, 7" boxed..$35.00-60.00
TYPEWRITER DOG, Japan, 1950's, 5" plush poodle windup, "types" at desk $30.00-75.00
UNCLE WIGGLY CRAZY CAR, rabbit driving, Marx, 1935, tin windup, 7" $300.00-650.00
UNIQUE ART LINCOLN TUNNEL $100.00-175.00
VAGABUNDO, Spain, Charlie Chaplin figure plastic windup, 6" boxed $40.00-95.00
WHAT'S WRONG CAR, tin lithograph windup toy $350.00-800.00
WILD WEST BUCKING BRONCO, by Lehmann, 1910 ....$275.00-600.00
XYLOPHONE PLAYER, Occupied Japan, celluloid windup, 7½" $65.00-120.00

TURKEY TIN WINDUP, U.S. Zone Germany, GES. Geschutzt, 6" tall, Furnish collection, $75.00-175.00.

CELLULOID WINDUP TOY, BOY AND GIRL ON SWING, Japan, 8", Furnish collection, $125.00-275.00.

SELECTION OF POPEYE TIN TOYS, 1930's-1940's, Reynolds collection, values: $200.00-950.00.

SQUIRREL BARBER, TPS, Japan, tin windup, 5", Reynolds collection, $25.00-45.00.

TIN WINDUP BOY ON SLED, feet move, 6" long, Furnish collection, $150.00-350.00.

235

CONCLUSION

"THE FUTURE OF TOY COLLECTING, OR, WHERE DO WE GO FROM HERE?"

Being a toy collector for over a decade now has allowed me many opportunities to debate, discuss and dream a little with antique toy dealers and fellow collectors. One question that often comes up in discussions is "what are the ten most wanted toys." I've found that answers to this question depend greatly upon the toy collector's own knowledge of the overall toy collecting field and his own particular interests and specialties. This author will not answer such an open and debatable question here, but I will address an issue closely related to that one.

What I will answer is the second most often asked question and debated answer-what all of us call the "time capsule" question. A toy contributor to this book built a new home several years ago and as the house was being built, he placed several gift sets of uncirculated U.S. mint coins in plastic containers inside the walls of the new construction. They were then sealed up. He knew he would probably never see the coins again in his own lifetime, yet he appreciated the importance of leaving behind a legacy. He enjoyed the speculation and anticipation of the thrill a later owner of the house might have when the coins are discovered in a hundred years or so. It takes foresight and a belief in the far distant future to perform such a kind act.

In the same vein, collectors often wonder what items, which can be acquired cheaply today, will increase in value greatly in the years to come. What items should go into a toy "time capsule" and remain undisturbed for several generations? Such a capsule is a simple legacy to leave behind to our great grandchildren. '

Consider first a little collector's mathematics. In a turn of the century Montgomery Ward's catalogue, a *dozen* Lehmann "OHO" cars could be purchased for ninety-five cents intended to retail at twenty cents a piece. Had my Great-Grandpa Longest, for some odd reason, managed to purchase a gross of these (144) he would have paid just under $10.00. Now, granted, $10.00 would have been at least half a week's wages in those days, but let's suppose he had a little disposable income and wanted to put something away for posterity.

The Lehman OHO is worth between $300.00 to $650.00 at today's prices. Had Granpa packed away a gross of them in a trunk in 1944, (all boxed and in mint condition, they would be worth a little higher value since the box adds value), each one would fetch about $700.00 on today's toy market. Take $700.00 times 144 and the figure is an astounding-$100,800.00. Not a bad legacy for a grandpa to leave behind. That would pay off most

of our mortgages today. Needless to say, the $10.00 wouldn't have done that well in a bank account considering it might all have been lost in the depression.

So, toys can even be a good long-term investment if the right ones are selected and they're kept dry, clean and safe. Now, what would this author put away in the time capsule that could be acquired relatively cheaply today which will likely increase in great value in the future? For what it's worth, here's my list.

1. MOVIE RELATED TOYS: The movies are here to stay, so toys related to the "Wizard of Oz," Charlie Chaplin, Shirley Temple and other Hollywood properties will increase in value as Americans continue their love affair with the movies. Even items such as currently abundant "Star Wars" toys will be anxiously sought in the future.

2. COMIC CHARACTER TOYS OF THE PRESENT: We all know how comic character toys from the past have soared in value, well, there's no reason to believe that this phenomenom will not last. Garfield, Snoopy and Peanuts, Yogi Bear and yes, even the Smurfs, will be recognized collectibles when current toddlers grow up and want to get them all back. Remember-*save all the original boxes.* Not only will these help protect the toy, a good box can add as much as another 50% in future value to a toy.

3. HARD PLASTIC TOYS OF THE 1950's: No vinyls here! It's amazing to me that most toy collectors still snub toys made of this material. Sometime in the late 1940's when celluloid was being phased out and hard, brittle, shiny plastics were being phased in, a silent transition took place that put toys into the "PLASTICS ERA." Now, it is true that plastic toys in general are not worth as much as earlier tin toys, but a collector doesn't have to pay as much for them today, either. Just as celluloid is a toy production medium dearly loved by some collectors today, *hard plastics* will someday be prized as the *Grandaddy of the plastics era.* In fact only about fifteen years of hard plastic production took place and then toymakers switched over to softer, safer, more flexible vinyls. Snatch these toys up!

4. LINEMAR DISNEY TOYS: Some caution must be used here. These toys are currently sending prices through the roof at auction houses on both coasts, partly because of their relative rarity and partly because they are currently a very "trendy" fad. Fortunately for the collector, these windups are recent enough that with great perserverance, they can still be picked up at yard sales and flea markets quite reasonably since many are less than

236

thirty years old. Don't pay hundreds of dollars for one of these simply as an investment. But if you can acquire and example for under $100.00 today, grab it! In the next decade or two, their prices will continue to soar.

5. MODERN SPACE TOYS AND COLLECTIBLES: "Star Wars" and "Star Trek" items will be prime collectibles in fifty years. Pure nostalgia as little kids of today laugh at the way we thought the future would be. Get them now while the going is cheap and put some away.

6. TELEVISION COLLECTIBLES FROM THE 1940's-1960's. Many items in this realm are still relatively bargain priced and they have both popular and historical value.

7. VICTORIAN ERA BOOKS AND GENERAL-LINE TOYS FROM THE TURN OF THE CENTURY: Believe it or not, some of these toys are a hundred years old and they sell for less than a hundred dollars at antique shows. The older they get, the less there are around. Think of it this way, in another hundred years, they will be respectively as old as toys from the 1790's are today. Now that's old and rare! If you can acquire these reasonably, do so.

8. REPRESENTATIVE TOY AUTOMOBILES FROM EACH DECADE WE PASS THROUGH: Purchase die cast metal cars in larger scales if possible and tin autos representing cars from the present or the recent past. Toy cars always make a good hedge of future values as long as they are in mint condition and a quality item.

Well, that's my list. If a copy of this book still exists in 2090 (one hundred years) it would be interesting to see how my predictions did. Certainly I won't be around to know the results, but it would be good shop talk for toy collectors one hundred years into the future.

In addition to the predictions above, I have decided to include some helpful general information that might be of benefit to all toy collectors, especially new ones. I have included this information in what I call the Collectors Resource Guide.

COLLECTORS RESOURCE GUIDE

Listed are toy dealers and collectors who encourage dealing by mail and/or who invite correspondence (listed with specialties, if any).

Allan Kessler
c/o Gullivers
2727 W. Howard St.
Chicago, IL 60645
(312) 465-2060
Specialty areas: buying early Disney, comic characters, tin windups, celluloid toys.

Saturday Matinee
P.O. Box 7047
Panama City Beach, Florida 32413
Contact: Ron Donnelly, (buying and selling) Specializing in shows and mail order sale of western heroes, Big Little Books and comic character items.

Doug Moore (buying and selling)
57 Hickory Ridge Circle
Cicero, Indiana 46034
(317) 877-1741
Specialty areas: tin windups, Buddy L toys, character toys and cast iron toys.

Pin-on
Helen and Foster Pollack (buying and selling)
120 Bennetts Farm Road
Ridgefield, Connecticut 06877
Specialty areas: comic character toys, pin-back buttons and popular memorabilia.

Joe and Juanita Reese (buying and selling)
511 Dair Avenue
Harrison, Ohio 45030
Specialty areas: character collectibles, western items, Madame Alexander dolls and pocket knives.

Elmer and Viola Reynolds (buying and selling)
P.O. Box 2183
Clarksville, Indiana, 47131
Specialty areas: pre-1950's comic character items, Kewpie items, Disneyana, Mickey Mouse, Snow White, and more.

O.E. and Julia Gernand (buying and selling)
Rural Route 2
Yorktown, Indiana 47396

Terry and Jeannie Quadnau (buying and selling)
434 Hillside Ave. #28
Cincinnati, Ohio 45215
Specialty areas: Howdy Doody, Hopalong Cassidy, character paper dolls, coloring books, board games and character items.

Ken Schmitz (buying and selling)
2405 West Carrington
Oak Creek, Wisconsin 53154
Specialty areas: space character toys, western toys, comic characters, figures, books and games.

P. David and Cynthia Vaughan Welch (buying and selling)
Rural Route 2, Box 233
Murphysboro, Illinois 62966
Specialty areas: cartoon, comic and television characters, movie character items, 1900-1980.

The Hoosier Peddler
Dave Harris (buying and selling)
5400 S. Webster Street
Kokomo, Indiana 46902
Specialty areas: rare comic character toys and tin windups. antique advertising and Disneyana.

MAGAZINES DEVOTED TO TOY COLLECTING

Antique Toy World
4419 Irving Park
Chicago, Illinois 60641
Publisher, Dale Kelley. A monthly, black, white and color magazine devoted strictly to collecting antique toys.

Collectors' Showcase
P.O. Box 271369
Escondido, California 92027-9962
Publisher, D. Keith Kaonis, creative director. Monthly and bi-monthly full color magazine devoted to toy and antique advertising collecting. Beautiful photography, full color.

Toy Shop
700 East State Street
Iola, Wisconsin 54990
Publisher: Krause Publications. Monthly classified ad tabloid filled with for sale and want ads by toy dealers and collectors.

The Mouse Club Newsletter
2056 Cirone Way
San Jose, California 95124
Publishers: Kim and Julie McKuen. Bi-monthly newsletter devoted to articles about Disneyana collecting. Subscription with membership.

National Fantasy Fan Club for Disneyana Collectors
P.O. Box 19212
Irvine, California, 92713
Regular newsletters devoted to Disneyana collecting and collectibles.

Storyboard Magazine for Disneyana Collectors
2512 Artesia Boulevard
Redondo Beach, California, 90278-9984
Publisher: Jay Garbutt. Bi-monthly full color publication for Disneyana collectors.

Toy Soldier Review Magazine
Vintage Castings, Inc.
127-74th Street
North Bergen, New Jersey, 07047
Published four times annually.

The Toy Farmer
Rural Route 2, Box 5
LaMoure, North Dakota, 58458
Published monthly, devoted to farm toys early and modern.

AUCTION COMPANIES DEVOTED TO ANTIQUE TOYS AND COLLECTIBLES

Smith House Toy Sales
P.O. Box 336
Eliot, Maine 03903
(207) 439-4614
Specialties: four mail auctions with catalogue annually, specializing in transportation toys, windups, Disneyana, space toys and battery operated toys. An excellent general-line auction company, Herb and Barb Smith have created one of the newer mail order auction companies that is right on track. Prices realized from present and past sales were used widely throughout the preparation of this Collector's Antique Toy Price Guide.

Christie's East
219 East 67th Street
New York, New York 10021
(718) 784-1480
Specialties: rare toys of all kinds. Contact above address for further dates and details on frequency.

Lloyd Ralston Toy Auctions
447 Stratfield Road
Fairfield, Connecticut 06432
(203) 366-3399
Specialties: toys of all kinds, cast iron, windups, character toys, rarities. Ralston is recognized as an expert in his field.

Hake's Americana and Collectibles
P.O. Box 1444
York, Pennsylvania 17405
Specialties: Ted Hake and his staff are recognized as leaders in the character toy mail auction field. Publishes at least four large toy auction catalogues annually. Well established business and clients, Hake's has been in business for over twenty years.

Historicana
1632 Robert Road
Lancaster, Pennsylvania
Specialties: Mail auctions in political memorabilia, character items, Disneyana and paper ephemera. Publishes several tabloids annually.

Contact: Bob Coup
P.O. Box 84
171 East 84th Street
New York, New York 10021
Specialties: Antique toys (division of Sotheby's) rare antique toy items.

BIBLIOGRAPHY

Ayres, William S., "The Main Street Pocket Guide to Toys," The Main Street Press, Pittstown, New York, 1984.

Baker, Linda, "Modern Toys," Collector Books, Paducah, Kentucky, 1985, 1988.

Coup, Robert, "Historicana," Lancaster, Pennsylvania, various auction catalogues, 1980's.

Cranmer, Don, "Collectors Encyclopedia of Toys and Banks, L-W Books, Marion, Indiana, 1986.

Hake, Ted, "Hake's Americana and Collectibles," York, Pennsylvania, various mail auction catalogues, 1980's.

Harman, Kenny, "Comic Strip Toys," Wallace Homestead, Des Moines, Iowa, 1975.

Heide, Robert, and Gilman, John, "Cartoon Collectibles," Doubleday and Company, Garden City, New York, 1983.

Huxford, Sharon and Bob, editors, "Schroeder's Antiques Price Guide," Collector Books, Paducah, Kentucky, Fourth through Seventh Editions, 1986 through 1989.

Kaonis, Keith, creative director, "Collectors' Showcase Magazine," Magazines of America, Tulsa, Oklahoma, various issues, 1982-1989.

Kelley Dale, publisher, "Antique Toy World Magazine," Antique Toy World Publications, Chicago, Illinois, various issues and volumes, 1985-1989.

Kimbell, Ward, "Toys, Delights from the Past," Applied Arts Books, Lebanon, Pennsylvania, 1976.

King, Constance Eileen, "The Encyclopedia of Toys," Chartwell Books, Secaucus, New Jersey, 1978, 1986.

Lesser, Robert, "A Celebration of Comic Art and Memorabilia," Hawthorn Books, New York, 1981.

Longest, David, "Character Toys and Collectibles," Volumes I and II, update of Volume I, Collector Books, Paducah, Kentucky, 1984-1988.

Munsey, Cecil, "Disneyana: Walt Disney Collectibles," Hawthorn Books, New York, 1974.

Murray, John, J. and Fox, Bruce, R. "A Historical, Rarity and Value Guide, Fisher Price, 1931-1963," Books Americana, Florence, Alabama, 1987.

O'Brien, Richard, "Collecting Toys, 4th Edition," Books Americana, Florence, Alabama, 1985.

O'Neill, editor, "The Collector's Encyclopedia of Metal Toys," Crescent Books, New York, 1988.

Schorr, Martyn L., "The Guide to Mechanical Toy Collecting," Performance Media, Haworth, New Jersey, 1979.

Schroeder, Joseph J. Jr., "The Wonderful World of Toys, Games and Dolls," DBI Books, Northfield, Illinois, 1971.

Smith, Herb and Barb, "Smith House Toy Sales," Elliot, Maine, various mail auction catalogues, 1987-1989.

Stern, Michael, "Stern's Price Guide to Disney Collectibles," Collector Books, Paducah, Kentucky, 1989.

Tumbusch, Tom, "Tomart's Illustrated Disneyana Catalogue and Price Guide, Volume 4, Supplement Edition," Tomart Publications, Dayton, Ohio, 1987.

Tumbusch, Tom, "Tomart's Illustrated Disneyana Catalogue and Price Guides, Volumes I-III," Tomart Publications, Dayton, Ohio, 1985.

Whitton, Blair, "The Knopf Collectors Guide to American Antique Toys," Alfred A. Knopf, Publishers, New York, New York, 1984.

Schroeder's Antiques Price Guide

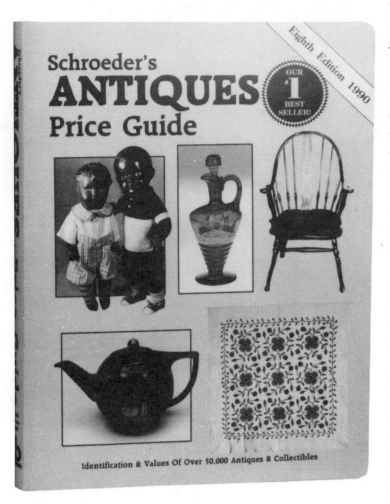

Schroeder's Antiques Price Guide has climbed its way to the top in a field already supplied with several well-established publications! The word is out, *Schroeder's Price Guide* is the best buy at any price. Over 500 categories are covered, with more than 50,000 listings. But it's not volume alone that makes Schroeder's the unique guide it is recognized to be. From ABC Plates to Zsolnay, if it merits the interest of today's collector, you'll find it in Schroeder's. Each subject is represented with histories and background information. In addition, hundreds of sharp original photos are used each year to illustrate not only the rare and the unusual, but the everyday "fun-type" collectibles as well -- not postage stamp pictures, but large close-up shots that show important details clearly.

Each edition is completely re-typeset from all new sources. We have not and will not simply change prices in each new edition. All new copy and all new illustrations make Schroeder's THE price guide on antiques and collectibles.

The writing and researching team behind this giant is proportionately large. It is backed by a staff of more than seventy of Collector Books' finest authors, as well as a board of advisors made up of well-known antique authorities and the country's top dealers, all specialists in their fields. Accuracy is their primary aim. Prices are gathered over the entire year previous to publication, from ads and personal contacts. Then each category is thoroughly checked to spot inconsistencies, listings that may not be entirely reflective of actual market dealings, and lines too vague to be of merit.

Only the best of the lot remains for publication. You'll find *Schroeder's Antiques Price Guide* the one to buy for factual information and quality.

No dealer, collector or investor can afford not to own this book. It is available from your favorite bookseller or antiques dealer at the low price of $12.95. If you are unable to find this price guide in your area, it's available from Collector Books, P. O. Box 3009, Paducah, KY 42001 at $12.95 plus $2.00 for postage and handling.

8½ x 11, 608 Pages $12.95

COLLECTOR BOOKS

A Division of Schroeder Publishing Co., Inc.